Biomedical Ethics
and the Law

Biomedical Ethics and the Law

SECOND EDITION

Edited by

James M. Humber and
Robert F. Almeder

Georgia State University, Atlanta

PLENUM PRESS • NEW YORK AND LONDON

W
50
B6155
1979
2d. ed.

Library of Congress Cataloging in Publication Data

Main entry under title:

Biomedical ethics and the law.

  Includes bibliographies and index.
  1. Medical laws and legislation—Addresses, essays, lectures. 2. Medical ethics—
Addresses, essays, lectures. I. Humber, James M. II. Almeder, Robert F.
K3601.Z9B56 1979   344.4   79-17758
ISBN 0-306-40239-4

© 1976, 1979 Plenum Press, New York
A Division of Plenum Publishing Corporation
227 West 17th Street, New York, N.Y. 10011

Printed in the United States of America

CONTRIBUTORS X

Robert F. Almeder, Department of Philosophy, Georgia State University, University Plaza, Atlanta, Georgia 30303

David L. Bazelon, Chief Judge, United States Court of Appeals, Washington, D.C. 20001

Thomas L. Beauchamp, Department of Philosophy, Georgetown University, Washington, D.C. 20057

Henry K. Beecher, late of the Harvard Medical School, 10 Shattuck Street, Boston, Massachusetts 02115

Baruch A. Brody, Department of Philosophy, Rice University, Houston, Texas 77001

Alexander M. Capron, University of Pennsylvania, 3400 Chestnut Street, Philadelphia, Pennsylvania 19174

C. J. Ducasse, late of the Department of Philosophy, Brown University, Providence, Rhode Island 02912

Antony Duff, Department of Philosophy, University of Stirling, Stirling, FK9 4LA, Scotland

Leon Eisenberg, Harvard Medical School, Department of Psychiatry, Children's Hospital Medical Center, 300 Longwood Avenue, Boston, Massachusetts 02115

John Hart Ely, The Wilson Center, Smithsonian Institute Building, Washington, D.C. 20560

Arthur Falek, Human and Behavioral Genetics Research Laboratory, Georgia Mental Health Institute, 1256 Briarcliff Road, Atlanta, Georgia 30306

John Fletcher, Inter/Met Theological Education, 1419 V. Street, N.W., Washington, D.C. 20009

Kurt Hirschhorn, Mt. Sinai School of Medicine, The City University of New York, Fifth Avenue at 100 Street, New York, N.Y. 10029

James M. Humber, Department of Philosophy, Georgia State University, University Plaza, Atlanta, Georgia 30303

Franz J. Ingelfinger, New England Journal of Medicine, 10 Shattuck Street, Boston, Massachusetts 02115

Hans Jonas, Department of Philosophy, New School for Social Research, 66 West 12 Street, New York, N.Y. 10011

Leon R. Kass, The Kennedy Center for Bioethics, Georgetown University, Washington, D.C. 20007

Herbert A. Lubs, Department of Pediatrics, University of Colorado Medical Center, 4200 East Ninth Avenue, Denver, Colorado 80220

Ruth Macklin, Hastings Center, 360 Broadway, Hastings-on-Hudson, New York 10706

John J. Madden, Human and Behavioral Genetics Research Laboratory, Georgia Mental Health Institute, 1256 Briarcliff Road, Atlanta, Georgia 30306

Richard A. McCormick, The Kennedy Center for Bioethics, Georgetown University, Washington, D.C. 20007

Raymond Moody, University of Virginia Medical School, Charlottesville, Virginia 22903

Robert S. Morison, Box 277, Peterborough, New Hampshire 03458

James Rachels, Department of Philosophy, University of Alabama at Birmingham, Birmingham, Alabama 35233

Nicholas Rescher, Department of Philosophy, University of Pittsburgh, Pittsburgh, Pennsylvania 15213

Jonas Robitscher, School of Law, Emory University, Atlanta, Georgia 30322

Michael B. Shimkin, Department of Community Medicine, School of Medicine, University of California at San Diego, La Jolla, California 92037

Michael A. Slote, Department of Philosophy, Trinity College, Dublin, Ireland

Tracy M. Sonneborn, Department of Zoology, Jordan Hall 224, Indiana University, Bloomington, Indiana 47401

Stephen P. Stich, Department of Philosophy and the Committee on the History and Philosophy of Science, University of Maryland, College Park, Maryland 20742

Thomas Szasz, Department of Psychiatry, Upstate Medical Center, 750 East Adams Street, Syracuse, New York 13210

Judith Jarvis Thomson, Department of Philosophy, Massachusetts Institute of Technology, Cambridge, Massachusetts 02139

Lawrence P. Ulrich, Philosophy Department, University of Dayton, Dayton, Ohio 45469

Robert M. Veatch, Institute of Society, Ethics, and Life Sciences, The Hastings Center, 360 Broadway, Hastings-on-Hudson, New York 10706

Richard Wasserstrom, School of Law and Department of Philosophy, University of California, Los Angeles, California 90024

PREFACE

In the past few years, an increasing number of colleges and universities have added courses in biomedical ethics to their curricula. To some extent, these additions serve to satisfy student demands for "relevance." But it is also true that such changes reflect a deepening desire on the part of the academic community to deal effectively with a host of problems which must be solved if we are to have a health-care delivery system which is efficient, humane, and just. To a large degree, these problems are the unique result of both rapidly changing moral values and dramatic advances in biomedical technology.

The past decade has witnessed sudden and conspicuous controversy over the morality and legality of new practices relating to abortion, therapy for the mentally ill, experimentation using human subjects, forms of genetic intervention, and euthanasia. Malpractice suits abound, and astronomical fees for malpractice insurance threaten the very possibility of medical and health-care practice. Without the backing of a clear moral consensus, the law is frequently forced into resolving these conflicts only to see the moral issues involved still hotly debated and the validity of the existing law further questioned. Take abortion, for example. Rather than settling the legal issue, the Supreme Court's original abortion decision in *Roe* v. *Wade* (1973), seems only to have spurred further legal debate. And of course, whether or not abortion is a morally acceptable procedure is still the subject of heated dispute. To take another example, the recent birth of a "test tube" baby in England has prompted the National Institutes of Health to reconsider its stand on fetal experimentation. Should such experimentation go forward in an attempt to assure that future test-tube babies are free from mental and/or physical deformity? Or should such nontherapeutic research be proscribed? The issue is not one which is easily decided; and equally difficult questions arise in the areas of genetic intervention, therapy for the mentally ill, and practices relating to euthanasia.

As profound as the social and moral changes in this country have been in the recent past, they are outstripped by recent scientific and technological advances in the biomedical field. Deformed and mentally disabled children, who once would have died at birth, can now be kept alive. Should such beings be allowed to live? Like problems also arise at the other end of the life cycle. Should a person be kept alive even if he wishes a peaceful and "dignified" death? And when *is* a person dead? With the development of the heart-lung machine and intravenous feeding, a person's body can be kept functioning indefinitely, long after his brain has ceased showing any activity. Does one die when one's brain dies? If not, when does one die? If so, how does one determine when the brain is dead? And then there are the moral and legal problems arising from recent advances in genetics. For instance, consider the dispute over recombinant DNA research. Should such experimentation be permitted? The potential benefits are great—it was through the use of this procedure, for example, that human insulin was able to be synthesized. At the same time, however, the dangers inherent in recombinant DNA research are not able to be assessed fully. In theory, at least, experimentation of this sort can be quite hazardous. What then should be done? The answer is far from clear; and in a milieu of shifting moral values, the conceptual, moral, and legal problems generated by advances in scientific and medical technology are all the more perplexing and worthy of urgent attention.

The problems faced by medical practitioners, researchers, and geneticists raise questions having social, moral, legal, philosophical, and theological implications. In a very real sense, then, the field of biomedical ethics is essentially interdisciplinary; and in constructing this anthology we have done our best to represent the interdisciplinary character of these problems.

The book begins with a brief introduction to ethical theory. The text itself is divided into five parts, each part being prefaced by an introduction in which the theses of the various authors are briefly stated. Our division of the subject matter is not hard and fast, and the student will no doubt perceive that the problems dealt with in each part are interrelated.

It is impossible to put together an anthology of this sort without the aid and assistance of many. However, we are especially indebted to our graduate students Dexter Christian and Mircea Manoliu, for compiling the bibliographies at the end of each chapter, and to Thomas Lanigan, formerly of Plenum Press, for his insightful suggestions and encouragement. Special thanks also go to Lynn Humber and Virginia Almeder, whose patience and understanding make our work considerably easier than it might otherwise be.

JAMES M. HUMBER
ROBERT F. ALMEDER

Georgia State University

CONTENTS

INTRODUCTION TO ETHICAL THEORY

Consider the following case. A doctor has just examined his patient, Mr. P. Both the doctor and Mr. P know that P has a very bad heart and that he must avoid overexcitement for fear of precipitating a heart attack. In the course of his examination of Mr. P, the doctor discovers that P has cancer of the liver and will die in approximately six months. Naturally, P asks the doctor for the results of his latest physical examination. Sould the doctor tell P the truth, and so chance causing him to suffer a fatal heart attack? Or should he lie and tell P that all is well? The issue is not an easy one to resolve because we feel pulled in two directions at once. But let us assume that the doctor does decide the issue, and that he opts to tell P the truth. How could the doctor argue for the rightness of his action as against one who disagreed with his decision?[1] One possibility is as follows:

DOCTOR: I told P the truth because it is always wrong to lie. That, after all, is the moral rule: it is wrong to lie.

CRITIC: Well, I don't like your moral rule; following it in all cases can lead to harm. Why should I accept your rule anyway?

DOCTOR: My rule must be accepted because it is what God wills. God wants us to tell the truth; and it is always right to do what God wants. God is the moral lawgiver, and His injuctions apply to all men whether you like it or not.

Whether or not the doctor's argument "works," and whether or not his decision to tell the truth is correct is, for our purposes, unimportant. What is noteworthy is that the above exchange illustrates how one usually goes about justifying his or her moral judgments. Ordinarily, what one judges are actions—in the case at hand, for example, the doctor's telling the truth to P. And in judg-

---

[1] Some would say that the doctor's action cannot be shown to be right or wrong because there *are* no morally right or wrong acts. Others would say that the action cannot be shown to be right or wrong because it is impossible *to know* which acts are right and which wrong. Advocates of the first view are ethical nihilists, and those who accept the second view are ethical skeptics. A reader who accepts either of these positions need go no further. Indeed, he has erred in buying this text.

1

ing actions, one may appeal to a moral rule.[2] But moral rules can differ; and if a judgment concerning the rightness or wrongness of an action is to be fully defended, the rule to which an appeal has been made must itself be justified. For this purpose, then, one usually refers to an ultimate moral principle or standard.[3] (In the above example, for instance, the standard to which the doctor is appealing is this: A rule (or act) is morally right if, and only if, it is in accord with what God wills.)

For the present, let us call a set of moral rules, justified by an appeal to an ultimate moral principle, an *ethical theory*. If there were only one ethical theory to which appeal could be made in making moral judgments, all ethical disputes would be, in principle at least, resolvable. Of course, things are not that simple in real life, and what we find as we go about the process of living is that we have to choose among many competing ethical theories. These theories can and do differ, sometimes quite radically. Despite individual differences, however, most ethical theories may be classified under one or the other of the following headings: (1) teleological ethical theories, (2) deontological ethical theories. Teleological theories assert that the rightness or wrongness of an act is ultimately to be determined by the action's *consequences*, i.e., an action is said to be morally right if it produces good consequences, wrong if it produces bad consequences. Deontologists reject this view and hold that an act ultimately is right or wrong because of its character, form, or nature. In addition, many deontologists insist that an act cannot be morally right unless the person doing the act does it for the right reason. In order to clarify the teleology/deontology distinction and at the same time introduce the reader to some of the elementary problems encountered by ethical theories within each class, we will summarize and criticize two theories within each ethical tradition.

Teleology: Act Utilitarianism and Rule Utilitarianism

What all utilitarians have in common is acceptance of the principle of utility as the *ultimate* test of the rightness or wrongness of human action. The principle of utility asserts that an act is morally right if, an only if, it tends, more than any alternative available to the agent at the time, to produce the greatest good for

[2] Sometimes there is an appeal to a moral rule, but not always; for there are ethical theories in which moral rules play no part.

[3] Again, it is notoriously difficult to generalize when discussing ethical theory; and it is possible not to appeal to an ultimate moral principle to justify moral rules. An ethical intuitionist, for example, could claim that he has a special moral faculty and that this just allows him to "see" or intuit the truth of certain moral rules. Also, the ethical intuitionist could omit all reference to moral rules and claim that he "sees" that certain individual acts are right and others wrong. For a discussion of ethical intuitionism, see pp. 6–7.

the greatest number of all those affected by the act. This sounds simple enough, but unfortunately utilitarians are not all in agreement as to the meaning of "good." Some, like Jeremy Bentham, the founder of utilitarianism, take "good" to mean "pleasure." Others indentify "good" with "happiness"; and still others claim that "good" cannot be defined but is an indefinable "nonnatural" property of things.[4] To simplify matters, we shall limit our discussion to hedonistic utilitarianism and assume that "good" = df. "pleasure," where "pleasure" refers to any kind of pleasure.[5]

Utilitarianism is a teleological position because it asserts that the rightness or wrongness of an action ultimately depends upon the achievement of certain consequences. What makes a utilitarian an *act utilitarian* is acceptance of the view that the principle of utility is to be applied directly to *particular actions* (e.g., X lying to Y at time T) to judge their moral worth. Given this view, then, what we have is an ethical theory in which moral rules play no part.[6] It is at this point that the *rule utilitarian* disagrees with the *act utilitarian*. What the *rule utilitarian* tells us is that we should use the principle of utility to justify certain *rules of conduct* and then use those rules to determine the rightness or wrongness of particular actions. For example, a rule utilitarian might hold that "do not kill innocent human beings" and "tell the truth" are proper rules of human conduct, because if these rules were followed by everybody, greater overall pleasure and less pain would result for everyone. And then, using these rules, the rule utilitarian would conclude that an action such as X lying to Y at time T was wrong because it violated the rule, "tell the truth."

An individual being introduced to utilitarianism for the first time might well wonder why the distinction between act and rule utilitarianism ever arose. Historically, rule utilitarianism evolved because of certain criticisms which were brought against act utilitarianism. Consider, for example, the following paradigm. Let us say that M is a totally amoral person, a man who will feel absolutely no pangs of guilt or conscience upon doing an evil act. M is alone with his mother

[4]The first position is known as hedonistic utilitarianism, the second as eudaemonistic utilitarianism, and the third as agathistic utilitarianism.

[5]For instance, we will not distinguish between sensual pleasure (e.g., eating, sex) and intellectual pleasure (e.g., reading Plato's *Dialogues*). It should be noted, however, that some utilitarians insist upon making this distinction, and argue that intellectual pleasure is intrinsically more valuable than sensual pleasure.

[6]This needs qualification, for some act utilitarians do allow that moral rules have a use in everyday life. For example, an act utilitarian might admit that there are situations when he will not have time to determine which act will produce the greatest amount of pleasure for the greatest number of people. In this case, then, he might say that the rational thing to do is to follow the moral rules accepted in his society. The important point, however, is that following the rule will *not* make the act utilitarian's action right. For the act utilitarian, our moral duty is *always* to obey the utilitarian moral maxim; and an act is right if, and only if, it does what this principle specifies. As a practical affair, we may have to refer to moral rules; but when we do so, we simply "take a chance" that we are acting rightly.

as she lies dying. M's mother tells him that she has $100,000 hidden in her attic, and just before she dies, she gets M to promise faithfully that he will find the money and split it equally with her daughter, M's sister. After his mother dies, M finds the money and keeps it for himself and his wife. M's deceit goes undetected, and both he and his wife live happily ever after. Now, let us further suppose that had M's sister been given her share of the $100,000, she would have derived very little enjoyment from it. Like her mother before her, she simply would have put it in the attic and forgotten about it until she died. Both M and his wife, on the other hand, know how to enjoy their money. The question then is this: Did M do anything wrong when he refused to share the $100,000 with his sister? An act utilitarian would have to say no. Indeed, he would have to insist that M did the right thing, for he maximized pleasure. But this moral judgment violates our ordinary moral intuitions. We want to say that M should have kept his promise to his dying mother, that his failure to do so constitutes immoral behavior, and that any ethical theory which tells us the contrary is a theory which must be rejected.

Although a criticism of the above sort is telling as against act utilitarianism, it has no force whatsoever when directed against rule utilitarianism, because rule utilitarianism need not allow that M's action was morally right. It is easy enough to see why this is so. In reply to the above criticism, for example, a rule utilitarian need only say that "keep your promises" is a moral rule validated by the principle of utility, and that M's action is wrong because it violates that rule. Furthermore, since rule utilitarianism validates our ordinary moral intuitions in cases where act utilitarianism does not, the rule utilitarian would insist that his moral theory constitutes an advance over act utilitarianism.

Although rule utilitarianism is able to avoid many of the criticisms levelled against act utilitarianism, rule utilitarianism is not without its detractors. The common criticism of this position is that it fails to provide a sufficient ground for ethics because it may justify unfair or unjust treatment of some individuals for the sake of others. Consider this case. Let us say that you live in a society in which 95% of the population have red hair and 5% have blond hair. After some computation, the majority discovers that the greatest overall pleasure and least overall pain will result if the redheads enslave blonds and force them to do their bidding. If we assume that the redheads' computations are correct, it seems that rule utilitarianism must endorse a rule stating that it is morally right for redheads in this society to enslave blonds. But this is unjust or unfair, i.e., it is morally wrong for reasons which (apparently) have nothing to do with the principle of utility. Hence, it is said, the principle of utility alone is insufficient to provide an adequate foundation for ethics. Somehow, the demands of the principle of justice must also be met. But is this possible? At first glance, at least, the principle of utility and the principle of justice seem to be in opposition. On the one hand, the principle of justice tells us that no person should serve as a mere instrument or means for the achievement of someone else's pleasure. But the principle of utility actually seems to require the opposite, viz., that a person be "used" when such usage serves the greatest good for the greatest number.

Whether the principles of justice and utility can be reconciled in an ethical theory which ultimately is utilitarian is the subject of some dispute. Many utilitarians insist that although the two principles do yield inconsistent results in "idealized" examples, such as that of our red and blond-haired society, in actual practice the two principles are compatible. An argument in favor of this view might go as follows: First, it could be said, a society in which redheads enslaved blonds would be a culture in which the redheads would have to worry continually about slave revolt and dissident action. Furthermore, some of the red-haired individuals no doubt would feel guilty about enslaving their blond counterparts. As a result, freedom of speech would have to be restricted so that these "soft-hearted" individuals would be unable to upset the status quo. In addition, each redhead would begin to realize that he or she might be part of a minority able to be drawn on grounds other than hair color (e.g., by blood type or height), and that it might someday become useful for society to "sacrifice" the minority in which one found himself or herself as a member. (For example, our mythical society might find it to be in the best interest of the majority to perform risk-bearing experiments upon all persons who have a very rare blood type. And *this* minority might include only redheads.) The point is this: a society which follows the principle of utility blindly without regard to the principle of justice puts everyone "under the gun," at least potentially. Realizing this, all members of an unjust society will worry, and this worry no doubt will prompt ever greater demands for justice and fairness. If the controlling group within the unjust society were to react to these demands negatively, it would be forced to use repressive measures and place restrictions upon individual freedom. But such action as this is not obviously productive of the greatest pleasure for the greatest number. Thus, because human nature is as it is, the principle of utility requires that any actually existing society recognize the principle of justice and not treat some of its citizens as mere "means" for the achievement of someone else's pleasure or happiness.

Whether or not utilitarianism is successful in attempting to show that there is no actual opposition between the principle of utility and the principle of justice is debatable. The issue is one which we cannot hope to resolve here, and we must pass on to discuss an even broader challenge to utilitarianism.

Some moral philosophers reject utilitarianism simply because it is a species of teleology. For these individuals, it is a mistake to try to determine the rightness or wrongness of an action merely by referring to that action's consequences. Philosophers of this sort are deontologists; and their claim is that the rightness of wrongness of an act is properly determined, not by considering that action's consequences, but rather by considering that action's form or character. Furthermore, some deontologists argue that teleologists err by not paying sufficient attention to the motives an agent has when he performs a certain act. In what follows, we shall consider two examples of deontological ethical theories, and briefly examine some of the problems faced by advocates of those theories.

Deontology: Intuitionism and Theologism

An ethical intuitionist may be either an act intuitionist or a rule intuitionist. Act intuitionists hold that we have a special moral faculty which allows us to "see" or intuit the rightness and wrongness of specific, individual actions. Rule intuitionists, on the other hand, claim to have the ability to see intuitively that certain positive rules of conduct specify right action, whereas certain negative rules specify wrong action. Of course, once a rule intuitionist has a set of moral rules, he appeals to those rules in order to determine the moral quality of particular actions.

The objection most often brought against both forms of intuitionism is that this position does not allow us to resolve moral differences at the most basic level. For example, let us say that person P can save the lives of ten innocent people if and only if he kills another innocent human being. One act intuitionist might claim that his moral intuitions tell him that it would be wrong for P to kill the innocent person, but another act intuitionist could say that his moral intuitions tell him just the opposite. And, with this difference of opinion, discussion would come to an end. Furthermore, two rule intuitionists could find themselves in exactly the same position even if they accepted the same set of moral rules (which clearly need not be the case). For example, let us say that we have two rule intuitionists who accept a set of moral rules which includes the following: (1) It is morally right to help one's fellow man, and (2) It is morally wrong to harm one's fellow man. In this case, then, killing one person to save ten is wrong by Rule 2 but right by Rule 1. Not to kill, on the other hand, violates Rule 1 but not Rule 2. What, then, ought to be done? The only way a rule intuitionist could answer this question is by ranking moral rules in terms of their relative strength. If the duty specified by Rule 1 were taken to be stronger than that specified by Rule 2, it would be right to kill one person to save ten. If, on the other hand, Rule 2 were held to be more important than Rule 1, the opposite conclusion would follow. But how are the relative strengths of moral rules to be determined? By intuition? This, apparently, would be the rule intuitionists' reply; but appeal to intuition at this level could lead to differences in ranking and also to differences in individual moral judgment. In the end, then, rule intuitionism, like act intuitionism, seems subject to the criticism that it is unable, ultimately, to resolve moral disagreements.

No true intuitionist need give up his moral theory in the face of the above criticism. What the objection presupposes, he could say, is that the adequacy of a moral theory is to be determined by its ability to resolve ethical disputes. But this is not the proper way to assess the merits of any ethical system. Rather, the intuitionist could insist, an ethical theory is to be evaluated in terms of whether or not it is true to, or captures, the facts of our ordinary ethical experience. And, the intuitionist could urge, the most conspicuous fact of our ethical experience is that, although we may agree from time to time that certain acts are right or wrong, we generally are incapable of agreeing on some very basic moral matters. Furthermore, where such differences exist, it should not be viewed as the result of differences in our understanding of the facts involved but rather as being due to unarguable differences at the intuitive level.[7] And because this is so, intuitionists could say that their ethical theory ought to be accepted as true even though it is unable to provide us with a method for resolving all moral conflicts.

Whether or not intuitionists would be correct when insisting that their moral theory captures the facts of everyday moral experience is debatable. Certainly it must be admitted that the claims of intuitionism may be true; and because this is so, there is an obvious need to inquire more deeply into the role of intuition in ethics and philosophy in general. The importance of reflecting on intuitionism in general is manifested in Aristotle's argument to the effect that there must be in every area of human inquiry some things we know without evidence, things we know but cannot say how we know.[8] The more we reflect on this thesis, the more we may be affected by the profoundly mysterious nature of human knowledge and its role in the acquisition of moral understanding and human happiness. Let us turn to our last major deontological position before offering a few closing remarks.

Theologism asserts that an act is right, if, and only if, more than any alternative open to the agent at the time, it is the one which is most consistent with what God wills, either directly or indirectly. Usually, theologism provides us with a set of rules (e.g., the Ten Commandments) which are taken to be expressive of God's will. Whether or not an act is right or wrong, then, is determined *in part* by reference to these rules. We say that the rightness or wrongness of an action is *partially* to be determined by reference to moral rules, because most theologians hold that an act may conform to the requirements specified by a legitimate rule of conduct and still be morally proper. For example, let us say that person P accepts the Ten Commandments as specifying God's will, and that P refuses to steal when he has an opportunity to do so. In this case, then, P has

---

[7]For example, Professor Elizabeth Anscombe is of the opinion that *nothing* ever can justify killing an innocent baby (see "Modern Moral Philosophy," *Philosophy*, Vol. 33, (1958), pp. 1–19). Of course, act utilitarians must disagree, and it is difficult to see how this difference of opinion could be due to different interpretations of the facts by Professor Anscombe and the act utilitarian.

[8]Aristotle, *Posterior Analytics*, Book I, Chapters 1–5, in the *Oxford Translation of Aristotle*, Clarendon Press, Oxford (1947).

followed one of God's commands. But if P refuses to steal because he was afraid of being caught, or because he only wanted to be rewarded in heaven for his good behavior, his action would not be truly right. The reason this is so is that P's motives for action would be "impure," and this impurity would affect (perhaps "infect" is a better word) the moral character of his action. For P's action to be truly right, P must follow God's rule for the right reason, viz., he must refuse to steal, not out of concern for himself, but rather out of love for God and fellow man. Given this motive, then, P's action would be right, and he truly would be deserving of reward in heaven. In short, most versions of theologism hold that God not only wants us to act in certain ways but also to act in those ways for the right reasons.

Theologism admits of a number of difficulties. For one thing, the theory cannot be taken seriously be anyone who does not believe in the existence of a Divine Moral Lawgiver. Thus, the theory lacks universal appeal. For another thing, theologism, like rule intuitionism, fails to provide a criterion for determining right action when moral rules conflict, i.e., when different moral rules appear to specify different courses of action as morally right. (Remember the example of Rules 1 and 2 above.) Finally, and perhaps most importantly, there is a troublesome question concerning whether what is right is so independently of God's command. Bertrand Russell states the problem in the following way:

> The point I am concerned with is that, if you are quite sure there is a difference between right and wrong, you are then in this situation: Is that difference due to God's fiat or is it not? If it is due to God's fiat, then for God Himself there is no difference between right and wrong, and it is no longer a significant statement to say that God is good. If you are going to say, as theologians do, that God is good, you must then say that right and wrong have some meaning which is independent of God's fiat, because God's fiats are good and not bad independently of the mere fact that he makes them. If you are going to say that, you will then have to say that it is not only through God that right and wrong come into being, but that they are in their essence logically anterior to God.[9]

The problem can be formulated in a slightly different way. If what is right is so independently of what God wills, then God is *not* a Moral Lawgiver, for the moral laws exist independently of Him and outside His sphere of influence. If, on the other hand, anything is right or wrong just so long as God wills it, then, if God were to command murder, theft, or cruelty, these things would be right and obligatory. But few people—theologians included—are willing to admit that it ever could be the case that actions of this sort could be morally right.

If a consideration of ethical intuitionism leads one to inquire into the role of intuition in ethics and philosophy in general, consideration of theologism points to the need for a closer examination of the importance of motives in

---

[9] B. Russell, "Why I am not a Christian," in *Philosophy and Contemporary Issues*, 2nd ed., Burr, J. R. and Goldinger, M., editors, Macmillan, New York (1976), p. 119.

assessing the moral worth of actions. The importance of this factor in assessing the morality of human acts perhaps may be seen by reconsidering our earlier example of M, the man who broke his deathbed promise to his mother. What if M, instead of keeping the $100,000 for himself and his wife, used that money to save the life of a young orphan child who needed a very expensive operation? In this case M would have broken the rule, "Keep your promises," but he would have done so for reasons that essentially were laudable. In this case, then, would we still want to say that what M had done wrong? The question is not easy to answer, and, luckily, we need not resolve the issue here. What the question does indicate, however, is that consideration of a person's motives for action ordinarily plays some role in our moral judgments. What that role is needs to be specified with greater exactness. Any ethical theory which fails to do this falls short of perfection. But then, ethics is not an exact science, and perhaps we must rest content with something less than perfection.

Concluding Remarks

The reader must be warned that we have only scratched the surface so far as our investigation into ethical theory is concerned.[10] Not only have our analyses of utilitarianism, intuitionism, etc., been synoptic and superficial, there also are numerous ethical theories which we have not discussed.[11] Throughout, however, our intention was only to introduce the reader to some of the complexities involved in ethical theorizing, and for the achievement of this limited purpose, the above discussion is, hopefully, sufficient. Before closing, however, it might be useful to draw the reader's attention to one or two further distinctions of importance.

First, when a person engages in a discussion of ethical theories in the manner pursued above, he or she is not doing ethics but *metaethics*. Metaethics usually is not conceived of as a *normative* venture, but rather as a *descriptive* one.[12] The task of metaethics is to clarify and define certain key ethical terms (e.g., "good," "right," "duty," etc.), and to analyze, evaluate, and criticize different ethical theories. *Ethics*, on the other hand, is a normative discipline, usually divided into two broad fields. First, there is *general normative ethics*. Here an

---

[10] Those interested in more complete introductions to ethical theory should see, William Frankena, *Ethics*, 2nd ed., Prentice Hall (1973), and Paul Taylor, *Principles of Ethics: An Introduction*, Dickenson Publishing Company (1975).

[11] For example, ethical theories not discussed include the following: egoistic eudaemonism, Kantianism, ethical relativism, egoistic hedonism, and self-realizationism.

[12] A normative discipline is one which attempts to lay down *prescriptive* norms or rules for proper behavior. That is to say, it seeks to tell us what we *ought* (morally) to do. A descriptive discipline, on the other hand, *describes* what conceptually or factually *is* the case and does not seek to determine what morally ought to be the case.

ethicist will seek to develop and defend an ethical theory which he feels will be valid for everyone, e.g., Bentham's developing act utilitarianism. In addition to general normative ethics there is also *applied normative ethics.* A person engaged in applied normative ethics attempts to resolve specific moral problems, e.g., an ethicist may seek to determine whether or not abortion is a morally acceptable procedure.

Many of those introduced to the ethics/metaethics distinction for the first time may wonder why philosophers bother with the latter discipline. There are a variety of reasons, but one of the most important is that ethical disputes often occur because participants in an argument accept different basic moral assumptions. As such, a thorough knowledge of metaethics sometimes can help to resolve moral disputes. For instance, assume that a seventeen-year-old girl comes to her father and says she wants to live with her boyfriend without benefit of marriage. The discussion might go something like this:

DAUGHTER: Dad, I'd like to live with John for a year or two in order to find out whether I want to marry him.

FATHER: That's awful! How can you even think of doing such a thing!

DAUGHTER: What do you mean it's awful? Is it better to get married, have children, and then find out I can't really live with John and be happy? Separation, divorce, I want to avoid all that. Don't worry, we'll take precautions. There'll be no illegitimate children or anything like that. Surely you see that it's wiser to live together to see if we're really in love than to marry and then find out we've made a mistake.

FATHER: Bah! I don't care what you say; you're just looking for excuses for living in sin. My own daughter is a tramp. Where did I make my mistake in raising you?

DAUGHTER: Your're close-minded. You didn't hear a word I said, did you? I don't know why I even talk to you.

If the father and daughter in the above example know nothing of metaethical distinctions, there is no hope that their argument will be resolved by rational discussion. The father will continue to think his daughter " a tramp," and the daughter no doubt will persist in believing that her father is irrational and close-minded. For one knowledgeable in metaethics, however, the true character of the dispute becomes clear. Most likely the daughter is a teleologist; for she is pointing to the consequences of her action and claiming that they make her act right. The father, on the other hand, is probably a deontologist. He does not "listen to his daughter's reasons," because for him they are unimportant in determining the moral quality of any action. Furthermore, the action his daughter is contemplating is one of a kind which his moral theory condemns. Thus, father and daughter disagree. But this does not mean that the argument must end; for once the real source of disagreement is uncovered, the discussion can continue on a "higher level" with father and daughter arguing the relative merits of teleology and deontology. Of course, it may well be that neither the father nor the daughter will be able to convince the other on this level of discussion either. But the discussion is now enlightened, and there is at least *hope* for agreement. Surely this is a better position to be in than the preceding one, where both father and daughter were condemned by their ignorance to name-calling.

PART I: ABORTION

INTRODUCTION

Our discussion of abortion is divided into two sections: Legal Issues and Moral Issues. The first selection under the heading of "Legal Issues" is the U.S. Supreme Court's decision in *Roe* v. *Wade*. In this case a pregnant single woman adopted the fictitious name Jane Roe and brought a class action in federal court challenging the constitutionality of the Texas criminal abortion laws. Under the Texas statutes, abortions were prohibited except for the purpose of saving the mother's life. Roe claimed that she could not procure a safe abortion (i.e., and abortion performed by a licensed physician under clinical conditions) in Texas, because her life was not put in jeopardy by her pregnancy. She also claimed that she could not afford to travel to a state where safe abortions for persons such as herself were legal. Accordingly, she asked the court to declare the Texas criminal abortion statutes unconstitutional and to enjoin the state from enforcing these laws.

In its decision, the Supreme Court refuses to rule on the difficult question as to when human life begins. Instead, the Court declares the Texas statutes unconstitutional because it holds that these laws violate the right to privacy guaranteed to all persons in the Fourteenth Amendment. But the right to privacy is not held to be an absolute or unqualified right. At some point, the Court says, the state's interest in health, medical standards, and prenatal life may supersede the mother's right to privacy. And at this "compelling" point, the state may choose to regulate abortion. Hence the Court concludes:

(a) For the stage prior to approximately the end of the first trimester, the abortion decision and its effectuation must be left to the medical judgment of the pregnant woman's attending physician.

(b) For the stage subsequent to approximately the end of the first trimester, the State, in promoting its interest in the health of the mother, may, if it chooses, regulate the abortion procedure in ways that are reasonably related to maternal health.

(c) For the stage subsequent to viability, the State, in promoting its interest in the potentiality of human life may, if it chooses, regulate, and even proscribe, abortion except where necessary, in appropriate medical judgment, for the preservation of the life or health of the mother.

Roe v. *Wade* is immediately followed by the dissenting opinion of Mr. Justice White. White contends that the Court's decision in *Roe* "simply fashions and announces a new constitutional right for pregnant mothers and, with scarcely any reason or authority for its action, invests that right with sufficient substance to override most existing State abortion statutes." John Hart Ely argues for essentially the same position, although in far greater detail. His criticisms bear special notice, because Ely is himself in favor of abortion.

The final selection under the heading of "Legal Issues" is the U.S. Supreme Court's decision in *Maher* v. *Roe* together with the dissenting opinion of Mr. Justice Brennan. The issue being debated here is whether or not the Constitution or the Supreme Court's ruling in *Roe* v. *Wade* requires a state participating in the joint federal-state Medicaid program to pay for nontherapeutic abortions when it pays for childbirth. The Court holds that a participating state is not required to pay for nontherapeutic abortion when it pays for childbirth; but the contrasting opinions of Mr. Justice Powell (who delivered the opinion of the Court) and Mr. Justice Brennan make it clear that there is great disagreement among the Justices of the Supreme Court as to what exactly was held by the Court in *Roe* v. *Wade*.

The section entitled "Moral Issues" begins with an essay by Baruch Brody. Given the Supreme Court's refusal in *Roe* v. *Wade* to decide the question of when human life begins, Brody's argument may be interpreted as a challenge to that ruling. Brody asks if it is possible to consistently maintain (1) that abortion is morally wrong because it is the taking of an innocent human life, and (2) that it is wrong (or at least inappropriate) for the state to have laws prohibiting abortion. He considers many of the arguments commonly offered in defense of the legalization of abortion, including the argument accepted by the Supreme Court (viz., the view that laws prohibiting abortion interfere with a woman's right to privacy by limiting her right to do what she wants with her own body). In the end Brody concludes that there is no possibility of arguing for the legalization of abortion if (1) is true, and that, as a consequence, the legal problem about abortion cannot be resolved independently of the status of the fetus problem.

If Brody is correct, one cannot argue for the legalization of abortion and consistently maintain that abortion is morally wrong because it is the killing of an innocent human being. But even if this fact is true, it does not follow that the Supreme Court was in error in not deciding the question of when human life begins. For example, Judith J. Thomson admits that abortion constitutes the destruction of human life, yet she claims that it is not morally wrong to perform such an act. In support of her position, Thomson argues that having a right to life does not guarantee either a right to be given use of, or a right to be allowed continued use of, another person's body. And this holds true, she says, even if one needs the body of another in order to support life itself.

The section on "Moral Issues" ends with an essay by James Humber. Humber claims that it is contradictory to deny that human life begins at conception. He criticizes the argument of Thomson as well as the arguments of other pro-abortionists, and contends that the decision of *Roe* v. *Wade* gives legal sanction to immoral conduct. Still, he recognizes the emotive force of the pro-abortionist's stance, and sees present anti-abortionists' attempts to change the law as futile. As an alternative to this course of action, then, Humber proposes a new program for anti-abortion action—a program which he holds would, if successful, dissolve the problem of abortion by making such killings unnecessary.

ROE v. WADE

410 U.S. 113, 93 S.CT. 705 (1973)

What follows are portions of the majority opinion by Justice Blackmun, together with the dissenting opinion of Justice White. The concurring opinions of Justices Douglas and Stewart have been omitted. Some footnotes have been dropped, with those remaining having been renumbered.

MR. JUSTICE BLACKMUN delivered the opinion of the Court.

The principal thrust of appellant's attack on the Texas statutes is that they improperly invade a right, said to be possessed by the pregnant woman, to choose to terminate her pregnancy. Appellant would discover this right in the concept of personal "liberty" embodied in the Fourteenth Amendment's Due Process Clause; or in personal, marital, familial, and sexual privacy said to be protected by the Bill of Rights or its penumbras . . . or among those rights reserved to the people by the Ninth Amendment. . . .

Three reasons have been advanced to explain historically the enactment of criminal abortion laws in the 19th century and to justify their continued existence.

It has been argued occasionally that these laws were the product of a Victorian social concern to discourage illicit sexual conduct. Texas, however, does not advance this justification in the present case, and it appears that no court or commentator has taken the argument seriously. The appellants and *amici* contend, moreover, that this is not a proper state purpose at all and suggest that, if it were, the Texas statutes are overbroad in protecting it since the law fails to distinguish between married and unwed mothers.

A second reason is concerned with abortion as a medical procedure. When most criminal abortion laws were first enacted, the procedure was a hazardous one for the woman.[1] This was particularly true prior to the development of antisepsis. Antiseptic techniques, of course, were based on discoveries by Lister, Pasteur, and others first announced in 1867, but were not generally accepted and employed until about the turn of the century. Abortion mortality was high. Even after 1900, and perhaps until as late as the development of antibiotics in the 1940s, standard modern techniques such as dilation and curettage were not nearly so safe as they are today. Thus, it has been argued that a State's real concern in enacting a criminal abortion law was to protect the pregnant woman, that is, to restrain her from submitting to a procedure that placed her life in serious jeopardy.

---

[1] See C. Haagensen & W. Lloyd, A Hundred Years of Medicine 19 (1943).

Modern medical techniques have altered this situation. Appellants and various *amici* refer to medical data indicating that abortion in early pregnancy, that is, prior to the end of the first trimester, although not without its risk, is now relatively safe. Mortality rates for women undergoing early abortions, where the procedure is legal, appear to be as low as or lower than the rates for normal childbirth.[2] Consequently, any interest of the State in protecting the woman from an inherently hazardous procedure, except when it would be equally dangerous for her to forgo it, has largely disappeared. Of course, important state interests in the areas of health and medical standards do remain. The State has a legitimate interest in seeing to it that abortion, like any other medical procedure, is performed under circumstances that insure maximum safety for the patient. This interest obviously extends at least to the performing physician and his staff, to the facilities involved, to the availability of after-care, and to adequate provision for any complication or emergency that might arise. The prevalence of high mortality rates at illegal "abortion mills" strengthens, rather than weakens, the State's interest in regulating the conditions under which abortions are performed. Moreover, the risk to the woman increases as her pregnancy continues. Thus, the State retains a definite interest in protecting the woman's own health and safety when an abortion is proposed at a late stage of pregnancy.

The third reason is the State's interest—some phrase it in terms of duty—in protecting prenatal life. Some of the argument for this justification rests on the theory that a new human life is present from the moment of conception.[3] The State's interest and general obligation to protect life then extends, it is argued, to prenatal life. Only when the life of the pregnant mother herself is at stake, balanced against the life she carries within her, should the interest of the embryo or fetus not prevail. Logically, of course, a legitimate state interest in this area need not stand or fall on acceptance of the belief that life begins at conception or at some other point prior to live birth. In assessing the State's interest, recognition may be given to the less rigid claim that as long as at least *potential* life is involved, the State may assert interests beyond the protection of the pregnant woman alone.

---

[2] Potts, Postconceptive Control of Fertility, 8 Int'l J. of G. & O. 957, 967 (1970) (England and Wales); Abortion Mortality, 20 Morbidity and Mortality 208, 209 (June 12, 1971) (U. S. Dept. of HEW, Public Health Service) (New York City); Tietze, United States: Therapeutic Abortions, 1963–1968, 59 Studies in Family Planning 5, 7 (1970); Tietze, Mortality with Contraception and Induced Abortion, 45 Studies in Family Planning 6 (1969) (Japan, Czechoslovakia, Hungary); Tietze & Lehfeldt, Legal Abortion in Eastern Europe, 175 J. A. M. A. 1149, 1152 (April 1961). Other sources are discussed in Lader 17–23.

[3] See Brief of *Amicus* National Right to Life Committee; R. Drinan, The Inviolability of the Right to Be Born, in Abortion and the Law 107 (D. Smith ed. 1967); Louisell, Abortion, The Practice of Medicine and the Due Process of Law, 16 U. C. L. A. L. Rev. 233 (1969); Noonan 1.

Parties challenging state abortion laws have sharply disputed in some courts the contention that a purpose of these laws, when enacted, was to protect prenatal life. Pointing to the absence of legislative history to support the contention, they claim that most state laws were designed solely to protect the woman. Because medical advances have lessened this concern, at least with respect to abortion in early pregnancy, they argue that with respect to such abortions the laws can no longer be justified by any state interest. There is some scholarly support for this view of original purpose. The few state courts called upon to interpret their laws in the late 19th and early 20th centuries did focus on the State's interest in protecting the woman's health rather than in preserving the embryo and fetus. Proponents of this view point out that in many States, including Texas, by statute or judicial interpretation, the pregnant woman herself could not be prosecuted for self-abortion or for cooperating in an abortion performed upon her by another. They claim that adoption of the "quickening" distinction through received common law and state statutes tacitly recognizes the greater health hazards inherent in late abortion and impliedly repudiates the theory that life begins at conception.

It is with these interests, and the weight to be attached to them, that this case is concerned.

The Constitution does not explicitly mention any right of privacy. In a line of decisions, however, going back perhaps as far as *Union Pacific R. Co.* v. *Botsford,* 141 U.S. 250,251 (1891), the Court has recognized that a right of personal privacy, does exist under the Constitution. In varying contexts, the Court or individual Justices have, indeed, found at least the roots of that right in the First Amendment . . . in the Fourth and Fifth Amendments . . . in the penumbras of the Bill of Rights . . . in the Ninth Amendment . . . or in the concept of liberty guaranteed by the first section of the Fourteenth Amendment. . . . These decisions make it clear that only personal rights that can be deemed "fundamental" or "implicit in the concept of ordered liberty," . . . are included in this guarantee of personal privacy. They also make it clear that the right has some extension to activities relating to marriage . . . procreation . . . contraception . . . family relationships . . . and child rearing and education. . . .

This right of privacy, whether it be founded in the Fourteenth Amendment's concept of personal liberty and restrictions upon state action, as we feel it is, or, as the District Court determined, in the Ninth Amendment's reservation of rights to the people, is broad enough to encompass a woman's decision whether or not to terminate her pregnancy. The detriment that the State would impose upon the pregnant woman by denying this choice altogether is apparent. Specific and direct harm medically diagnosable even in early pregnancy may be involved. Maternity, or additional offspring, may force upon the woman a distressful life and future. Psychological harm may be imminent. Mental and physical health may be taxed by child care. There is also the distress, for all concerned, associated with the unwanted child, and there is the problem of bringing a child into a family already unable, psychologically and otherwise, to care for it. In other cases, as in this one, the additional difficulties and continuing stigma of unwed motherhood may be involved. All these are factors the woman and her responsible physician necessarily will consider in consultation.

On the basis of elements such as these, appellant and some *amici* argue that the woman's right is absolute and that she is entitled to terminate her pregnancy at whatever time, in whatever way, and for whatever reason she alone chooses. With this we do not agree. Appellant's arguments that Texas either has no valid interest at all in regulating the abortion decision, or no interest strong enough to support any limitation upon the woman's sole determination, are unpersuasive. The Court's decisions recognizing a right of privacy also acknowledge that some state regulation in areas protected by that right is appropriate. As noted above, a State may properly assert important interests in safeguarding health, in maintaining medical standards, and in protecting potential life. At some point in pregnancy, these respective interests become sufficiently compelling to sustain regulation of the factors that govern the abortion decision. The privacy right involved, therefore, cannot be said to be absolute. In fact, it is not clear to us that the claim asserted by some *amici* that one has an unlimited right to do with one's body as one pleases bears a close relationship to the right of privacy previously articulated in the Court's decisions. The Court has refused to recognize an unlimited right of this kind in the past. *Jacobson* v. *Massachusetts*, 197 U.S. 11 (1905) (vaccination); *Buck* v. *Bell*, 274 U.S. 200 (1927) (sterilization).

We, therefore, conclude that the right of personal privacy includes the abortion decision, but that this right is not unqualified and must be considered against important state interests in regulation.

We note that those federal and state courts that have recently considered abortion law challenges have reached the same conclusion. A majority, in addition to the District Court in the present case, have held state laws unconstitutional, at least in part, because of vagueness or because of overbreadth and abridgment of rights. . . .

Although the results are divided, most of these courts have agreed that the right of privacy, however based, is broad enough to cover the abortion decision; that the right, nonetheless, is not absolute and is subject to some limitations; and that at some point the state interests as to protection of health, medical standards, and prenatal life, become dominant. We agree with this approach.

Where certain "fundamental rights" are involved, the Court has held that regulation limiting these rights may be justified only by a "compelling state interest," . . . and that legislative enactments must be narrowly drawn to express only the legitimate state interests at stake.

In the recent abortion cases ... courts have recognized these principles. Those striking down state laws have generally scrutinized the State's interests in protecting health and potential life, and have concluded that neither interest justified broad limitations on the reasons for which a physician and his pregnant patient might decide that she should have an abortion in the early stages of pregnancy. Courts sustaining state laws have held that the State's determinations to protect health or prenatal life are dominant and constitutionally justifiable.

The District Court held that the appellee failed to meet his burden of demonstrating that the Texas statute's infringement upon Roe's rights was necessary to support a compelling state interest, and that, although the appellee presented "several compelling justifications for state presence in the area of abortions," the statutes outstripped these justifications and swept "far beyond any areas of compelling state interest." . . . Appellant and appellee both contest that holding. Appellant, as has been indicated, claims an absolute right that bars any state imposition of criminal penalties in the area. Appellee argues that the State's determination to recognize and protect prenatal life from and after conception constitutes a compelling state interest. As noted above, we do not agree fully with either formulation.

A. The appellee and certain *amici* argue that the fetus is a "person" within the language and meaning of the Fourteenth Amendment. In support of this, they outline at length and in detail the well-known facts of fetal development. If this suggestion of personhood is established, the appellant's case, of course, collapses, for the fetus' right to life would then be guaranteed specifically by the Amendment. The appellant conceded as much on reargument. On the other hand, the appellee conceded on reargument that no case could be cited that holds that a fetus is a person within the meaning of the Fourteenth Amendment.

The Constitution does not define "person" in so many words. Section 1 of the Fourteenth Amendment contains three references to "person." The first, in defining "citizens," speaks of "persons born or naturalized in the United States." The word also appears both in the Due Process Clause and in the Equal Protection Clause. "Person" is used in other places in the Constitution: in the listing of qualifications for Representatives and Senators, Art. I, §2, cl. 2, and §3, cl. 3; in the Apportionment Clause, Art. I, §2, cl. 3;[4] in the Migration and Importation provision, Art. I, §9, cl. 1; in the Emolument Clause, Art. II, §9, cl. 8; in the Electors provisions, Art. II, §1, cl. 2, and the superseded cl. 3; in the provision outlining qualifications for the office of President, Art. II, §1, cl. 5; in the Extradition provisions, Art. IV, §2, cl. 2, and the superseded Fugitive Slave Clause 3; and in the Fifth, Twelfth, and Twenty-second Amendments, as well as

[4] We are not aware that in the taking of any census under this clause, a fetus has ever been counted.

in §§2 and 3 of the Fourteenth Amendment. But in nearly all these instances, the use of the word is such that it has application only postnatally. None indicates, with any assurance, that it has any possible pre-natal application.[5]

All this, together with our observation, *supra,* that throughout the major portion of the 19th century prevailing legal abortion practices were far freer than they are today, persuades us that the word "person," as used in the Fourteenth Amendment, does not include the unborn.[6] This is in accord with the results reached in those few cases where the issue has been squarely presented. . . . Indeed, our decision in *United States* v. *Vuitch,* 402 U.S. 62, 91 S.Ct. 1294, 28 L.Ed.2d 601 (1971), inferentially is to the same effect, for we there would not have indulged in statutory interpretation favorable to abortion in specified circumstances if the necessary consequence was the termination of life entitled to Fourteenth Amendment protection.

This conclusion, however, does not of itself fully answer the contentions raised by Texas, and we pass on to other considerations.

B. The pregnant woman cannot be isolated in her privacy. She carries an embryo and, later, a fetus, if one accepts the medical definitions of the developing young in the human uterus. See Dorland's Illustrated Medical Dictionary 478–479, 547 (24th ed. 1965). The situation therefore is inherently different from marital intimacy, or bedroom possession of obscene material, or marriage, or procreation, or education, with which *Eisenstadt* and *Griswold, Stanley, Loving, Skinner,* and *Pierce* and *Meyer* were respectively concerned. As we have intimated above, it is reasonable and appropriate for a State to decide that at some point in time another interest, that of health of the mother or that

---

[5] When Texas urges that a fetus is entitled to Fourteenth Amendment protection as a person, it faces a dilemma. Neither in Texas nor in any other State are all abortions prohibited. Despite broad proscription, an exception always exists. The exception contained in art. 1196, for an abortion procured or attempted by medical advice for the purpose of saving the life of the mother, is typical. But if the fetus is a person who is not to be deprived of life without due process of law, and if the mother's condition is the sole determinant, does not the Texas exception appear to be out of line with the Amendment's command?

There are other inconsistencies between Fourteenth Amendment status and the typical abortion statute. It has already been pointed out . . . that in Texas the woman is not a principal or an accomplice with respect to an abortion upon her. If the fetus is a person, why is the woman not a principal or an accomplice? Further, the penalty for criminal abortion specified by Art. 1195 is significantly less than the maximum penalty for murder prescribed by Art. 1257 of the Texas Penal Code. If the fetus is a person, may the penalties by different?

[6] Cf. the Wisconsin abortion statute, defining "unborn child" to mean "a human being from the time of conception until it is born alive," Wis. Stat. §940.04(6) (1969), and the new Connecticut statute, Public Act No. 1, May 1972 Special Session, declaring it to be the public policy of the State and the legislative intent "to protect and preserve human life from the moment of conception."

of potential human life, becomes significantly involved. The woman's privacy is no longer sole and any right of privacy she possesses must be measured accordingly.

Texas urges that, apart from the Fourteenth Amendment, life begins at conception and is present throughout pregnancy, and that, therefore, the State has a compelling interest in protecting that life from and after conception. We need not resolve the difficult question of when life begins. When those trained in the respective disciplines of medicine, philosophy, and theology are unable to arrive at any consensus, the judiciary, at this point in the development of man's knowledge, is not in a position to speculate as to the answer.

It should be sufficient to note briefly the wide divergence of thinking on this most sensitive and difficult question. There has always been strong support for the view that life does not begin until live birth. This was the belief of the Stoics. It appears to be the predominant, though not the unanimous, attitude of the Jewish faith.[7] It may be taken to represent also the position of a large segment of the Protestant community, insofar as that can be ascertained; organized groups that have taken a formal position on the abortion issue have generally regarded abortion as a matter for the conscience of the individual and her family. As we have noted, the common law found greater significance in quickening. Physicians and their scientific colleagues have regarded that event with less interest and have tended to focus either upon conception, upon live birth, or upon the interim point at which the fetus becomes "viable," that is, potentially able to live outside the mother's womb, albeit with artificial aid.[8] Viability is usually placed at about seven months (28 weeks) but may occur earlier, even at 24 weeks.[9] The Aristotelian theory of "mediate animation," that held sway throughout the Middle Ages and the Renaissance in Europe, continued to be official Roman Catholic dogma until the 19th century, despite opposition to this "ensoulment" theory from those in the Church who would recognize the existence of life from the moment of conception.[10] The latter is now, of course, the official belief of the Catholic Church. As one brief *amicus* discloses, this is a view strongly held by many non-Catholics as well, and by many physicians. Substantial problems for precise definition of this view are posed, however, by new embryological data that purport to indicate that conception is a "process" over time, rather than an event, and by new medical

---

[7] Lader 97–99; D. Feldman, Birth Control in Jewish Law 251–294 (1968). For a stricter view, see I. Jakobovits, Jewish Views on Abortion, in Abortion and the Law 124 (D. Smith ed. 1967).

[8] L. Hellman & J. Pritchard, Williams Obstetrics 493 (14th ed. 1971); Dorland's Illustrated Medical Dictionary 1689 (24th ed. 1965).

[9] Hellman & Pritchard, *supra*, n. 59, at 493.

[10] For discussions of the development of the Roman Catholic position, see D. Callahan, Abortion: Law, Choice, and Morality 409–447 (1970); Noonan 1.

techniques such as menstrual extraction, the "morning-after" pill, implantation of embryos, artificial insemination, and even artifical wombs.[11]

In areas other than criminal abortion, the law has been reluctant to endorse any theory that life, as we recognize it, begins before live birth or to accord legal rights to the unborn except in narrowly defined situations and except when the rights are contingent upon live birth. For example, the traditional rule of tort law denied recovery for prenatal injuries even though the child was born alive.[12] That rule has been changed in almost every jurisdiction. In most States, recovery is said to be permitted only if the fetus was viable, or at least quick, when the injuries were sustained, though few courts have squarely so held. In a recent development, generally opposed by the commentators, some States permit the parents of a stillborn child to maintain an action for wrongful death because of prenatal injuries. Such an action, however, would appear to be one to vindicate the parents' interest and is thus consistent with the view that the fetus, at most, represents only the potentiality of life. Similarly, unborn children have been recognized as acquiring rights or interests by way of inheritance or other devolution of property, and have been represented by guardians *ad litem.* [13] Perfection of the interests involved, again, has generally been contingent upon live birth. In short, the unborn have never been recognized in the law as persons in the whole sense.

In view of all this, we do not agree that, by adopting one theory of life, Texas may override the rights of the pregnant woman that are at stake. We repeat, however, that the State does have an important and legitimate interest in preserving and protecting the health of the pregnant woman, whether she be a resident of the State or a nonresident who seeks medical consultation and treatment there, and that it has still *another* important and legitimate interest in protecting the potentiality of human life. These interests are separate and distinct. Each grows in substantiality as the woman approaches term and, at a point during pregnancy, each becomes "compelling."

With respect to the State's important and legitimate interest in the health of the mother, the "compelling" point, in the light of present medical knowledge,

---

[11] See Brodie, The New Biology and the Prenatal Child, 9 J. Family L. 391,397 (1970); Gorney, The New Biology and the Future of Man, 15 U. C. L. A. L. Rev. 273 (1968); Note, Criminal Law—Abortion—The "Morning-After Pill" and Other Pre-Implantation Birth-Control Methods and the Law, 46 Ore. L. Rev. 211 (1967); G. Taylor, The Biological Time Bomb 32 (1968); A. Rosenfeld, The Second Genesis 138–139 (1969); Smith, Through a Test Tube Darkly: Artificial Insemination and the Law, 67 Mich. L. Rev. 127 (1968); Note, Artificial Insemination and the Law, 1968 U. Ill. L. F. 203.

[12] W. Prosser, The Law of Torts 335–338 (4th ed. 1971); 2 F. Harper & F. James, The Law of Torts 1028–1031 (1956); Note, 63 Harv. L. Rev. 173 (1949).

[13] Louisell, Abortion, The Practice of Medicine and the Due Process of Law, 16 U. C. L. A. L. Rev. 233, 235–238 (1969); Note, 56 Iowa L. Rev. 994, 999–1000 (1971); Note, The Law and the Unborn Child, 46 Notre Dame Law. 349, 351–354 (1971).

is at approximately the end of the first trimester. This is so because of the now-established medical fact, referred to above . . . that until the end of the first trimester mortality in abortion may be less than mortality in normal childbirth. It follows that, from and after this point, a State may regulate the abortion procedure to the extent that the regulation reasonably relates to the preservation and protection of maternal health. Examples of permissible state regulation in this area are requirements as to the qualifications of the person who is to perform the abortion; as to the licensure of that person; as to the facility in which the procedure is to be performed, that is, whether it must be a hospital or may be a clinic or some other place of less-than-hospital status; as to the licensing of the facility; and the like.

This means, on the other hand, that, for the period of pregnancy prior to this "compelling" point, the attending physician, in consultation with his patient, is free to determine, without regulation by the State, that, in his medical judgment, the patient's pregnancy should be terminated. If that decision is reached, the judgment may be effectuated by an abortion free of interference by the State.

With respect to the State's important and legitimate interest in potential life, the "compelling" point is at viability. This is so because the fetus then presumably has the capability of meaningful life outside the mother's womb. State regulation protective of fetal life after viability thus has both logical and biological justifications. If the State is interested in protecting fetal life after viability, it may go so far as to proscribe abortion during that period, except when it is necessary to preserve the life or health of the mother.

Measured against these standards, Art. 1196 of the Texas Penal Code, in restricting legal abortions to those "procured or attempted by medical advice for the purpose of saving the life of the mother," sweeps too broadly. The statute makes no distinction between abortions performed early in pregnancy and those performed later, and it limits to a single reason, "saving" the mother's life, the legal justification for the procedure. The statute, therefore, cannot survive the constitutional attack made upon it here.

This conclusion makes it unnecessary for us to consider the additional challenge to the Texas statute asserted on grounds of vagueness. . . .

MR. JUSTICE WHITE, with whom MR. JUSTICE REHNQUIST joins, dissenting.

At the heart of the controversy in these cases are those recurring pregnancies that pose no danger whatsoever to the life or health of the mother but are, nevertheless, unwanted for any one or more of a variety of reasons—convenience, family planning, economics, dislike of children, the embarrassment of illegitimacy, etc. The common claim before us is that for any one of such reasons, or for no reason at all, and without asserting or claiming any threat to life or health, any woman is entitled to an abortion at her request if she is able to find a medical advisor willing to undertake the procedure.

The Court for the most part sustains this position: During the period prior to the time the fetus becomes viable, the Constitution of the United States values the convenience, whim, or caprice of the putative mother more than the life or potential life of the fetus; the Constitution, therefore, guarantees the right to an abortion as against any state law or policy seeking to protect the fetus from an abortion not prompted by more compelling reasons of the mother.

With all due respect, I dissent. I find nothing in the language or history of the Constitution to support the Court's judgment. The Court simply fashions and announces a new constitutional right for pregnant mothers and, with scarcely any reason or authority for its action, invests that right with sufficient substance to override most existing state abortion statutes. The upshot is that the people and the legislatures of the 50 states are constitutionally disentitled to weigh the relative importance of the continued existence and development of the fetus, on the one hand, against a spectrum of possible impacts on the mother, on the other hand. As an exercise of raw judicial power, the Court perhaps has authority to do what it does today; but in my view its judgment is an improvident and extravagent exercise of the power of judicial review that the Constitution extends to this Court.

The Court apparently values the convenience of the pregnant mother more than the continued existence and development of the life or potential life that she carries. Whether or not I might agree with that marshaling of values, I can in no event join the Court's judgment because I find no constitutional warrant for imposing such an order of priorities on the people and legislatures of the States. In a sensitive area such as this, involving as it does issues over which reasonable men may easily and heatedly differ, I cannot accept the Court's exercise of its clear power of choice by interposing a constitutional barrier to state efforts to protect human life and by investing mothers and doctors with the constitutionally protected right to exterminate it. This issue, for the most part, should be left with the people and to the political processes the people have devised to govern their affairs.

It is my view, therefore, that the Texas statute is not constitutionally infirm because it denies abortions to those who seek to serve only their convenience rather than to protect their life or health. Nor is this plaintiff, who claims no threat to her mental or physical health, entitled to assert the possible rights of those women whose pregnancy assertedly implicated their health. This, together with *United States* v. *Vuitch,* 402 U.S. 62 (1971), dictates reversal of the judgment of the District Court. . . .

THE WAGES OF CRYING WOLF

A COMMENT ON ROE v. WADE

JOHN HART ELY

Let us not underestimate what is at stake: Having an unwanted child can go a long way toward ruining a woman's life. And at bottom *Roe* signals the Court's judgment that this result cannot be justified by any good that anti-abortion legislation accomplishes. This surely is an understandable conclusion—indeed it is one with which I agree—but ordinarily the Court claims no mandate to second-guess legislative balances, at least not when the Constitution has designated neither of the values in conflict as entitled to special protection. But even assuming it would be a good idea for the Court to assume this function, *Roe* seems a curious place to have begun. Laws prohibiting the use of "soft" drugs or, even more obviously, homosexual acts between consenting adults can stunt "the preferred life styles"[1] of those against whom enforcement is threatened in very serious ways. It is clear such acts harm no one besides the participants, and indeed the case that the participants are harmed is a rather shaky one. Yet such laws survive,[2] on the theory that there exists a societal consensus that the behavior involved is revolting or at any rate immoral.[3] Of course the consensus is not universal but it is sufficient, and this is what is counted crucial, to get the laws passed and keep them on the books. Whether anti-abortion legislation cramps the life style of an unwilling mother more significantly than anti-homosexuality legislation cramps the life style of a homosexual is a close question. But even granting that it does, the *other* side of the balance looks very different. For there is more than simple societal revulsion to support

---

[1] 93 S. Ct. at 759 (Douglas, J., concurring).

[2] Cf. *Poe v. Ullman*, 367 U.S. 497, 551–53 (1961), (Harlan, J., dissenting), *quoted* in part in *Griswold* v. *Connecticut*, 381 U.S. 479, 499 (1965) (Goldberg, J., concurring), distinguishing laws proscribing homosexual acts even those performed in the home) as not involving the "right" at stake in those cases.

[3] See, e.g., *Poe* v. *Ullman*, 367 U.S. 497, 545–46 (Harlan, J., dissenting).

---

legislation restricting abortion:[4] Abortion ends (or if it makes a difference, prevents) the life of a human being other than the one making the choice.

The Court's response here is simply not adequate. It agrees, indeed it holds, that after the point of viability (a concept it fails to note will become even less clear than it is now as the technology of birth continues to develop[5]) the interest in protecting the fetus is compelling.[6] Exactly why that is the magic moment is not made clear: viability, as the Court defines it, is achieved some six to twelve weeks after quickening.[7] (Quickening is the point at which the fetus begins discernibly to move independently of the mother[8] and the point that has historically been deemed crucial—to the extent *any* point between conception and birth has been focused on.[9]) But no, it is *viability* that is constitutionally critical: The Court's defense seems to mistake a definition for a syllogism.

> With respect to the State's important and legitimate interest in potential life, the "compelling" point is at viability. This is so because the fetus then presumably has the capacity of meaningful life outside the mother's womb.[10]

With regard to why the state cannot consider this "important and legitimate interest" prior to viability, the opinion is even less satisfactory. The discussion begins sensibly enough: The interest asserted is not necessarily tied to the question whether the fetus is "alive" for whether or not one calls it a living being, it is an entity with the potential for (and indeed the likelihood of) life. But all of arguable relevance that follows[11] are arguments that fetuses (a) are not recog-

---

[4] Nor is the Court's conclusion that early abortion does not present serious physical risk to the woman involved shared by all doctors.

[5] It defines viability so as not to exclude the possibility of artificial support, 93 S. Ct. at 730, and later indicates its awareness of the continuing development of artificial wombs. Id. at 731. It gives no sign of having considered the implications of that combination for the trimester program the Constitution is held to mandate, however.

[6] Albeit not so compelling that a state is permitted to honor it at the expense of the mother's health.

[7] See 93 S. Ct. at 716.

[8] Id.

[9] Id. at 716–20.

[10] Id. at 732. See also id. at 730.

[11] The opinion does contain a lengthy survey of "historical attitudes" toward abortion, culminating in a discussion of the positions of the American Medical Association, the American Public Health Association, and the American Bar Association. Id. at 715–24. (The discussion's high point is probably reached where the Court explains away the Hippocratic Oath's prohibition of abortion on the grounds that Hippocrates was a Pythagorean, and Pythagoreans were a minority. Id. at 715–16.) The Court does not seem entirely clear as to what this discussion has to do with the legal argument, id. at 709, 715, and the reader is left in much the same quandary. It surely does not seem to support the Court's position, unless a record of serious historical and contemporary dispute is somehow thought to generate a constitutional mandate.

nized as "persons in the whole sense" by legal doctrine generally and (b) are not "persons" protected by the Fourteenth Amendment.

To the extent they are not entirely inconclusive, the bodies of doctrine to which the Court adverts respecting the protection of fetuses under general legal doctrine tend to undercut rather than support its conclusion. And the argument that fetuses (unlike, say, corporations) are not "persons" under the Fourteenth Amendment fares little better. The Court notes that most constitutional clauses using the word "persons"—such as the one outlining the qualifications for the Presidency—appear to have been drafted with postnatal beings in mind. (It might have added that most of them were plainly drafted with *adults* in mind, but I suppose that wouldn't have helped.) In addition, "the appellee conceded on reargument that no case can be cited that holds that a fetus is a person within the meaning of the Fourteenth Amendment."[12]   (The other legal contexts in which the question could have arisen are not enumerated.)

The canons of construction employed here are perhaps most intriguing when they are contrasted with those invoked to derive the constitutional right to an abortion. But in any event, the argument that fetuses lack constitutional rights is simply irrelevant. For it has never been held or even asserted that the state interest needed to justify forcing a person to refrain from an activity, *whether or not that activity is constitutionally protected*, must implicate either the life or the constitutional rights of another person. Dogs are not "persons in the whole sense" nor have they constitutional rights, but that does not mean the state cannot prohibit killing them; it does not even mean the state cannot prohibit killing them in the exercise of the First Amendment right of political protest. Come to think of it, draft cards aren't persons either.

Thus, even assuming the Court ought generally to get into the business of second-guessing legislative balances, it has picked a strange case with which to begin. Its purported evaluation of the balance that produced anti-abortion legislation simply does not meet the issue: that the life plans of the mother must, not simply may, prevail over the state's desire to protect the fetus simply does not follow from the judgment that the fetus is not a person. Beyond all that, however, the Court has no business getting into that business.

Were I a legislator, I would vote for a statute very much like the one the Court ends up drafting.[13]   I hope this reaction reflects more than the psychological phenomenon that keeps bombardiers sane—the fact that it is somehow easier to "terminate" those you cannot see—and am inclined to think it does; that the mother, unlike the unborn child, has begun to imagine a future for herself

---

[12]Id. at 728-29 (footnote omitted).

[13]I would, however, omit the serious restrictions the Court puts on state health regulation of the conditions under which an abortion can be performed, and give serious thought—though the practical difference here is not likely to be great—to placing the critical line at quickening rather than viability.

strikes me as morally quite significant. But God knows I'm not *happy* with that resolution. Abortion is too much life infanticide on the one hand, and too much like contraception on the other, to leave one comfortable with any answer; and the moral issue it poses is as fiendish as any philosopher's hypothetical.

Of course, the Court often resolves difficult moral questions, and difficult questions yield controversial answers. I doubt, for example, that most people would agree that letting a drug peddler go unapprehended is morally preferable to letting the police kick down his door without probable cause. The difference, of course, is that the Constitution, which legitimates and theoretically controls judicial intervention, has some rather pointed things to say about this choice. There will of course be difficult questions about the applicability of its language to specific facts, but at least the document's special concern with one of the values in conflict is manifest. It simply says nothing, clear or fuzzy, about abortion.

The matter cannot end there, however. The Burger Court, like the Warren Court before it, has been especially solicitous of the right to travel from state to state, demanding a compelling state interest if it is to be inhibited.[14] Yet nowhere in the Constitution is such a right mentioned. It is, however, as clear as such things can be that this right was one the framers intended to protect, most specifically[15] by the Privileges and Immunities Clause of Article IV.[16] The right is, moreover, plausibly inferable from the system of government, and the citizen's role therein, contemplated by the Constitution.[17] The Court in *Roe* suggests an inference of neither sort—from the intent of the framers, or from the governmental system contemplated by the Constitution—in support of the constitutional right to an abortion.

What the Court does assert is that there is a general right of privacy granted special protection—that is, protection above and beyond the baseline requirement of "rationality"—by the Fourteenth Amendment, and that that right "is broad enough to encompass" the right to an abortion. The general right of pri-

---

[14] See, e.g., *Dunn* v. *Blumstein*, 405 U.S. 330 (1972); *Shapiro* v. *Thompson*, 394 U.S. 618 (1969).

[15] See also *Edwards* v. *California*, 314 U. S. 160 (1941).

[16] See *United States* v. *Wheeler*, 254 U. S. 281, 294 (1920); *Slaughterhouse Cases*, 83 U.S. (16 Wall.) 36, 75 (1872); *U.S. Arts. Confed.* art. IV; 3 M. Farrand, *The Records of the Federal Convention of 1787*, at 112 (1911); cf. *The Federalist*, No. 42, at 307 (Wright ed. 1961).

[17] See *Crandall* v. *Nevada*, 73 U.S. (6 Wall.) 35 (1867); C. Black, *Structure and Relationship in Constitutional Law* (1969). The Court seems to regard the opportunity to travel *outside* the United States as merely an aspect of the "liberty" that under the Fifth and Fourteenth Amendments cannot be denied without due process. Seè *Zemel* v. *Rusk*, 381 U.S. 1, 14 (1965).

vacy is inferred, as it was in *Griswold* v. *Connecticut*,[18] from various provisions of the Bill of Rights manifesting a concern with privacy, notably the Fourth Amendment's guarantee against unreasonable searches, the Fifth Amendment's privilege against self-incrimination, and the right, inferred from the First Amendment, to keep one's political associations secret.

One possible response is that all this proves is that the things explicitly mentioned are forbidden, if indeed it does not actually demonstrate a disposition *not* to enshrine anything that might be called a general right of privacy. In fact the Court takes this view when it suits its purposes. (On the *same day* it decided *Roe*, the Court held that a showing of reasonableness was not needed to force someone to provide a grand jury with a voice exemplar, reasoning that the Fifth Amendment was not implicated because the evidence was not "testimonial" and that the Fourth Amendment did not apply because there was no "seizure."[19]) But this approach is unduly crabbed. Surely the Court is entitled, indeed I think it is obligated, to seek out the sorts of evils the framers meant to combat and to move against their twentieth century counterparts.

Thus it seems to me entirely proper to infer a general right of privacy, *so long as some care is taken in defining the sort of right the inference will support*. Those aspects of the First, Fourth and Fifth Amendments to which the Court refers all limit the ways in which, and the circumstances under which, the government can go about gathering information about a person he would rather it did not have. *Katz* v. *United States*,[20] limiting governmental tapping of telephones, may not involve what the framers would have called a "search," but it plainly involves this general concern with privacy. *Griswold* is a long step, even a leap, beyond this, but at least the connection is discernible. Had it been a case that purported to discover in the Constitution a "right to contraception," it would have been *Roe*'s strongest precedent. But the Court in *Roe* gives no evidence of so regarding it, and rightly not. Commentators tend to forget, though the Court plainly has not,[21] that the Court in *Griswold* stressed that it was invalidating only that portion of the Connecticut law that proscribed the *use*, as opposed to the manufacture, sale, or other distribution of contraceptives. That distinction (which would be silly were the right to contraception being constitutionally enshrined) makes sense if the case is rationalized on the ground that the section of the law whose constitutionality was in issue was such that *its enforcement*

[18] 381 U.S. 479 (1965).
[19] *United States* v. *Dionisio*, 93 S. Ct. 764 (1973). See also *United States* v. *Mara*, 93 S. Ct. 774 (1973) (handwriting exemplars), also decided the same day as *Roe*, and *Couch* v. *United States*, 93 S. Ct. 611 (1973) (finding no privacy interest in records a taxpayer had turned over to her accountant) decided thirteen days earlier.
[20] 389 U.S. 347 (1967).
[21] See *Eisenstadt* v. *Baird*, 405 U.S. 438, 443 (1972).

would have been virtually impossible without the most outrageous sort of governmental prying into the privacy of the home.[22]   And this, indeed, is the theory on which the Court appeared rather explicitly to settle:

> The present case, then, concerns a relationship lying within the zone of privacy created by several fundamental constitutional guarantees. And it concerns a law which, in forbidding the *use* of contraceptives rather than regulating their manufacture or sale, seeks to achieve its goals by means having a maximum destructive impact upon that relationship. Such a law cannot stand in light of the familiar principle, so often applied by this Court, that "a governmental purpose to control or prevent activities constitutionally subject to state regulation may not be achieved by means which sweep unnecessarily broadly and thereby invade the area of protected freedoms." *NAACP* v. *Alabama*, 377 U.S. 288, 307. Would we allow the police to search the sacred precincts of marital bedrooms for telltale signs of the use of contraceptives? The very idea is repulsive to the notions of privacy surrounding the marriage relationship.[23]

Thus even assuming (as the Court surely seemed to) that a state can constitutionally seek to minimize or eliminate the circulation and use of contraceptives, Connecticut had acted unconstitutionally by selecting a means, that is a direct ban on use, that would generate intolerably intrusive modes of data-gathering. No such rationalization is attempted by the Court in *Roe*—and understandably not, for whatever else may be involved, it is not a case about governmental snooping.

The Court reports that some *amici curiae* argued for an unlimited right to do as one wishes with one's body. This theory holds, for me at any rate, much appeal. However, there would have been serious problems with its invocation in this case. In the first place, more than the mother's own body is involved in a decision to have an abortion; a fetus may not be a "person in the whole sense," but it is certainly not nothing. Second, it is difficult to find a basis for thinking that the theory was meant to be given constitutional sanction: surely it is no part of the "privacy" interest the Bill of Rights suggests.

> [I]t is not clear to us that the claim . . . that one has an unlimited right to do with one's body as one pleases bears a close relationship to the right of privacy. . . .[24]

Unfortunately, having thus rejected the amici's attempt to define the bounds of the general constitutional right of which the right to an abortion is a part, on the theory that the general right described has little to do with privacy, the Court provides neither an alternative definition nor an account of why *it* thinks privacy is involved. It simply announces that the right to privacy "is broad

---

[22]*Stanley* v. *Georgia*, 394 U.S. 557 (1969), cited by the Court in *Roe*, might also be rationalized on such a theory, cf. id. at 565, though it reads more like a "pure" First Amendment case concerned with governmental attempts at thought control.

[23]381 U.S. at 485-86 (emphasis in original).

[24]93 S. Ct. at 727.

enough to encompass a woman's decision whether or not to terminate her pregnancy." Apparently this conclusion is thought to derive from the passage that immediately follows it:

> The detriment that the State would impose upon the pregnant woman by denying this choice altogether is apparent. Specific and direct harm medically diagnosable even in early pregnancy may be involved. Maternity, or additional offspring, may force upon the woman a distressful life and future. Psychological harm may be imminent. Mental and physical health may be taxed by child care. There is also the distress, for all concerned, associated with the unwanted child, and there is the problem of bringing a child into a family already unable, psychologically and otherwise, to care for it. In other cases, as in this one, the additional difficulties and continuing stigma of unwed motherhood may be involved.[25]

All of this is true and ought to be taken very seriously. But it has nothing to do with privacy in the Bill of Rights sense or any other the Constitution suggests.[26] I suppose there is nothing to prevent one from using the word "privacy" to mean the freedom to live one's life without governmental interference. But the Court obviously does not so use the term.[27] Nor could it, for such a right is at stake in *every* case. Our life styles are constantly limited, often seriously, by governmental regulation; and while many of us would prefer less direction, granting that desire the status of a preferred constitutional right would yield a system of "government" virtually unrecognizable to us and only slightly more recognizable to our forefathers.[28] The Court's observations concerning the serious, life-shaping costs of having a child prove what might to the thoughtless have seemed unprovable: that even though a human life, or a potential human life, hangs in the balance, the moral dilemma abortion poses is so difficult as to be heartbreaking. What they fail to do is even begin to resolve that dilemma so far as our governmental system is concerned by associating either side of the balance with a value inferable from the Constitution.

But perhaps the inquiry should not end even there. In his famous *Carolene Products* footnote, Justice Stone suggested that the interests to which the Court can responsibly give extraordinary constitutional protection include not only those expressed in the Constitution but also those that are unlikely to receive adequate consideration in the political process, specifically the interests of "dis-

---

[25] 93 S. Ct. at 727. See also id. at 757 (Douglas, J., concurring).

[26] It might be noted that most of the factors enumerated also apply to the inconvenience of having an unwanted two-year-old, or a senile parent, around. Would the Court find the constitutional right of privacy invaded in those situations too? I find it hard to believe it would; even if it did, of course, it would not find a constitutional right to "terminate" the annoyance—presumably because "real" persons are now involved. But what about ways of removing the annoyance that do not involve "termination"? Can they really be matters of constitutional entitlement?

[27] *But* cf. 93 S. Ct at 758–59 (Douglas, J., concurring).

[28] Cf. *Katz* v. *United States*, 389 U.S. 347, 350–51 (1967).

crete and insular minorities" unable to form effective political alliances.[29]
There can be little doubt that such considerations have influenced the direction,
if only occasionally the rhetoric, of the recent Courts. My repeated efforts to
convince my students that sex should be treated as a "suspect classification"
have convinced me it is no easy matter to state such considerations in a "principled" way. But passing that problem, *Roe* is not an appropriate case for their
invocation.

Compared with men, very few women sit in our legislatures, a fact I believe
should bear some relevance—even without an Equal Rights Amendment—to the
appropriate standard of review for legislation that favors men over women. But
no fetuses sit in our legislatures. Of course they have their champions, but so
have women. The two interests have clashed repeatedly in the political arena,
and had continued to do so up to the date of the opinion, generating quite a
wide variety of accommodations. By the Court's lights virtually all of the legislative accommodations had unduly favored fetuses; by its definition of victory,
women had lost. Yet in every legislative balance one of the competing interests
loses to some extent; indeed usually, as here, they both do. On some occasions
the Constitution throws its weight on the side of one of them, indicating the
balance must be restruck. And on others—and this is Justice Stone's suggestion—
it is at least arguable that, constitutional directive or not, the Court should
throw *its* weight on the side of a minority demanding in court more than it was
able to achieve politically. But even assuming this suggestion can be given principled content, it was clearly intended and should be reserved for those interests
which, *as compared with the interests to which they have been subordinated*,
constitute minorities unusually incapable of protecting themselves.[30] Compared
with men, women they constitute such a "minority"; compared with the unborn,
they do not. I'm not sure I'd know a discrete and insular minority if I saw one,
but confronted with a multiple choice question requiring me to designate (a)
women or (b) fetuses as one, I'd expect no credit for the former answer.

Of course a woman's freedom to choose an abortion is part of the "liberty"
the Fourteenth Amendment says shall not be denied without the process of
law, as indeed is anyone's freedom to do what he wants. But "due process"
generally guarantees only that the inhibition be procedurally fair and that it
have some "rational" connection—though plausible is probably a better word—
with a permissible governmental goal.[31] What is unusual about *Roe* is that the
liberty involved is accorded a far more stringent protection, so stringent that a

---

[29] *United States* v. *Carolene Products Co.*, 304 U.S. 144, 152 n.4 (1938).

[30] If the mere fact that the classification in issue disadvantages a minority whose viewpoint
was not appreciated by a majority of the legislature that enacted it were sufficient to
render, it suspect, *all* classifications would be suspect.

[31] Even this statement of the demands of "substantive due process" is too strong for many
Justices and commentators, who deny that any such doctrine should exist.

desire to preserve the fetus's existence is unable to overcome it—a protection more stringent, I think it fair to say, than that the present Court accords the freedom of the press explicitly guaranteed by the First Amendment.[32] What is frightening about *Roe* is that this super-protected right is not inferable from the language of the Constitution, the framers' thinking respecting the specific problem in issue, any general value derivable from the provisions they included, or the nations' governmental structure. Nor is it explainable in terms of the unusual political impotence of the group judicially protected vis-à-vis the interest that legislatively prevailed over it. And that, I believe—the predictable early reaction to *Roe* not withstanding ("more of the same Warren-type activism"[33])— is a charge that can responsibly be leveled at no other decision of the past twenty years. At times the inferences the Court has drawn from the values the Constitution marks for special protection have been controversial, even shaky, but never before has its sense of an obligation to draw one been so obviously lacking.

[32] See *Branzburg* v. *Hayes*, 408 U.S. 665 (1972).
[33] See, e.g., "Abortion," *The New Republic*, Feb. 10, 1973, at 9.

MAHER v. ROE

432 US 464, 53 L Ed 2d 484, 97 S Ct 2376

What follows are portions of the majority opinion by Justice Powell, together with the dissenting opinion of Justice Brennan. Some footnotes have been dropped, with those remaining having been renumbered.

Mr. Justice Powell delivered the opinion of the Court.

I

A regulation of the Connecticut Welfare Department limits state Medicaid benefits for first trimester abortions[1] to those that are "medically necessary," a term defined to include psychiatric necessity.[2] Connecticut enforces this limitation through a system of prior authorization from its Department of Social Services. In order to obtain authorization for a first trimester abortion, the hospital or clinic where the abortion is to be performed must submit, among other things, a certificate from the patient's attending physician stating that the abortion is medically necessary.

This attack on the validity of the Connecticut regulation was brought against appellant Maher, the Commissioner of Social Services, by appellees Poe and Roe, two indigent women who were unable to obtain a physician's certificate of medical necessity.[3] In a complaint filed in the United States

[1] The procedures governing abortions beyond the first trimester are not challenged here.

[2] Section 275 provides in relevant part: "The Department makes payment for abortion services under the Medical Assistance (Title XIX) Program when the following conditions are met:

    1. In the opinion of the attending physician the abortion is medically necessary. The term "Medically Necessary" includes psychiatric necessity.
    2. The abortion is to be performed in an accredited hospital or licensed clinic when the patient is in the first trimester of pregnancy. . . .
    3 The written request for the abortion is submitted by the patient, and in the case of a minor, from the parent or guardian.

    .   .   .   .

    4. Prior authorization for the abortion is secured from the Chief of Medical Services, Division of Health Services, Department of Social Services."

[3] At the time this action was filed, Mary Poe, a 16-year-old high school junior, had already obtained an abortion at a Connecticut hospital. Apparently because of Poe's inability to obtain a certificate of medical necessity, the hospital was denied reimbursement by the Department of Social Services. As a result Poe was being pressed to pay the hospital bill of $244. Susan Roe, an unwed mother of three children, was unable to obtain an abortion

37

District Court for the District of Connecticut, they challenged the regulation both as inconsistent with the requirements of Title XIX of the Social Security Act, and as violative of their constitutional rights, including the Fourteenth Amendment's guarantees of due process and equal protection. . . .

Although it found no independent constitutional right to a state-financed abortion, the District Court held that the Equal Protection Clause forbids the exclusion of nontherapeutic abortions from a state welfare program that generally subsidizes the medical expenses incident to pregnancy and childbirth. The court found implicit in *Roe* v. *Wade*, the view that "abortion and childbirth, when stripped of the sensitive moral arguments surrounding the abortion controversy, are simply two alternative medical methods of dealing with pregnancy. . . ." Relying also on *Shapiro* v. *Thompson*, 394 US 618. . . , the court held that the Connecticut program "weights the choice of the pregnant mother against choosing to exercise her constitutionally protected right" to a nontherapeutic abortion and "thus infringes upon a fundamental interest."

The court found no state interest to justify this infringement. The State's fiscal interest was held to be "wholly chimerical because abortion is the least expensive medical response to a pregnancy." And any moral objection to abortion was deemed constitutionally irrelevant:

> The state may not justify its refusal to pay for one type of expense arising from pregnancy on the basis that it morally opposes such an expenditure of money. To sanction such a justification would be to permit discrimination against those seeking to exercise a constitutional right on the basis that the state simply does not approve of the exercise of that right. Ibid.

The District Court enjoined the State from requiring the certificate of medical necessity for Medicaid-funded abortions. The court also struck down the related requirements of prior written request by the pregnant woman and prior authorization by the Department of Social Services, holding that the State could not impose any requirements on Medicaid payments for abortions that are not "equally applicable to medicaid payments for childbirth, if such conditions or requirements tend to discourage a woman from choosing an abortion or to delay the occurrence of an abortion that she has asked her physician to perform." . . .

II

The Constitution imposes no obligation on the States to pay the pregnancy-related medical expenses of indigent women, or indeed to pay any of the medical

---

because of her physician's refusal to certify that the procedure was medically necessary. By consent, a temporary restraining order was entered by the District Court enjoining the Connecticut officials from refusing to pay for Roe's abortion. After the remand from the Court of Appeals, the District Court issued temporary restraining orders covering three additional women. *Roe* v. *Norton*, 408 F Supp 660, 663 (1975).

expenses of indigents. But when a State decides to alleviate some of the hardships of poverty by providing medical care, the manner in which it dispenses benefits is subject to constitutional limitations. Appellees' claim is that Connecticut must accord equal treatment to both abortion and childbirth, and may not evidence a policy preference by funding only the medical expenses incident to childbirth. This challenge to the classifications established by the Connecticut regulation presents a question arising under the Equal Protection Clause of the Fourteenth Amendment. The basic framework of analysis of such a claim is well settled:

> "We must decide, first, whether [state legislation] operates to the disadvantage of some suspect class or impinges upon a fundamental right explicitly or implicitly protected by the Constitution, thereby requiring strict judicial scrutiny. . . . If not, the [legislative] scheme must still be examined to determine whether it rationally furthers some legitimate, articulated state purpose and therefore does not constitute an invidious discrimination . . . *San Antonio School Dist.* v. *Rodriguez*, 411 US 1, 17, 36 L Ed 2d 16, 93 S Ct 1278 (1973).

Applying this analysis here, we think the District Court erred in holding that the Connecticut regulation violated the Equal Protection Clause of the Fourteenth Amendment.

A

This case involves no discrimination against a suspect class. An indigent woman desiring an abortion does not come within the limited category of disadvantaged classes so recognized by our cases. Nor does the fact that the impact of the regulation falls upon those who cannot pay lead to a different conclusion. In a sense, every denial of welfare to an indigent creates a wealth classification as compared to nonindigents who are able to pay for the desired goods or services. But this Court has never held that financial need alone identifies a suspect class for purposes of equal protection analysis. Accordingly, the central question in this case is whether the regulation "impinges upon a fundamental right explicitly or implicitly protected by the Constitution." The District Court read our decisions in *Roe* v. *Wade*, and the subsequent cases applying it, as establishing a fundamental right to abortion and therefore concluded that nothing less than a compelling state interest would justify Connecticut's different treatment of abortion and childbirth. We think the District Court misconceived the nature and scope of the fundamental right recognized in Roe.

B

At issue in Roe was the constitutionality of a Texas law making it a crime to procure or attempt to procure an abortion, except on medical advice for the purpose of saving the life of the mother. Drawing on a group of disparate cases restricting governmental intrusion, physical coercion, and criminal prohibition of certain activities, we concluded that the Fourteenth Amendment's concept of personal liberty affords constitutional protection against state interference with certain aspects of an individual's personal "privacy," including a woman's decision to terminate her pregnancy.

The Texas statute imposed severe criminal sanctions on the physicians and other medical personnel who performed abortions, thus drastically limiting the availability and safety of the desired service. As Mr Justice Stewart observed, "it is difficult to imagine a more complete abridgment of a constitutional freedom. . . ." We held that only a compelling state interest would justify such a sweeping restriction on a constitutionally protected interest, and we found no such state interest during the first trimester. Even when judged against this demanding standard, however, the State's dual interest in the health of the pregnant woman and the potential life of the fetus were deemed sufficient to justify substantial regulation of abortions in the second and third trimesters.

C

The right in *Roe* v. *Wade* can be understood only by considering both the woman's interest and the nature of the State's interference with it. Roe did not declare an unqualified "constitutional right to an abortion," as the District Court seemed to think. Rather, the right protects the woman from unduly burdensome interference with her freedom to decide whether to terminate her pregnancy. It implies no limitation on the authority of a State to make a value judgment favoring childbirth over abortion, and to implement that judgment by the allocation of public funds.

The Connecticut regulation before us is different in kind from the laws invalidated in our previous abortion decisions. The Connecticut regulation places no obstacles—absolute or otherwise—in the pregnant woman's path to an abortion. An indigent woman who desires an abortion suffers no disadvantage as a consequence of Connecticut's decision to fund childbirth; she continues as before to be dependent on private sources for the service she desires. The State may have made childbirth a more attractive alternative, thereby influencing the woman's decision, but it has imposed no restriction on access to abortions that was not already there. The indigency that may make it difficult—and in some cases, perhaps, impossible—for some women to have abortions is neither created nor in any way affected by the Connecticut regulation. We conclude that the Connecticut regulation does not impinge upon the fundamental right recognized in Roe. . . .

D

The question remains whether Connecticut's regulation can be sustained under the less demanding test of rationality that applies in the absence of a suspect classification or the impingement of a fundamental right. This test requires that the distinction drawn between childbirth and nontherapeutic abortion by the regulation be "rationally related" to a "constitutionally permissible" purpose. We hold that the Connecticut funding scheme satisfies this standard.

Roe itself explicitly acknowledged the State's strong interest in protecting the potential life of the fetus. That interest exists throughout the pregnancy, "grow[ing] in substantiality as the woman approaches term." Because the pregnant woman carries a potential human being, she "cannot be isolated in her privacy.... [Her] privacy is no longer sole and any right of privacy she possesses must be measured accordingly." The State unquestionably has a "strong and legitimate interest in encouraging normal childbirth," an interest honored over the centuries.[4] Nor can there be any question that the Connecticut regulation rationally furthers that interest. The medical costs associated with childbirth are substantial, and have increased significantly in recent years. As recognized by the District Court in this case, such costs are significantly greater than those normally associated with elective abortions during the first trimester. The subsidizing of costs incident to childbirth is a rational means of encouraging childbirth.

In conclusion, we emphasize that our decision today does not proscribe government funding of nontherapeutic abortions. It is open to Congress to require provision of Medicaid benefits for such abortions as a condition of state participation in the Medicaid program. Also, under Title XIX as construed in *Beal* v. *Doe.* Connecticut is free—through normal democratic processes—to decide that such benefits should be provided. We hold only that the Constitution does not require a judicially imposed resolution of these difficult issues.

III

The District Court also invalidated Connecticut's requirements of prior written request by the pregnant woman and prior authorization by the Department of Social Services. Our analysis above rejects the basic premise that prompted invalidation of these procedural requirements. It is not unreasonable for a State to

---

[4] In addition to the direct interest in protecting the fetus, a State may have legitimate demographic concerns about its rate of population growth. Such concerns are basic to the future of the State and in some circumstances could constitute a substantial reason for departure from a position of neutrality between abortion and childbirth.

insist upon a prior showing of medical necessity to insure that its money is
being spent only for authorized purposes. The simple answer to the argument
that similar requirements are not imposed for other medical procedures is that
such procedures do not involve the termination of a potential human life. In
Planned Parenthood of Central *Missouri* v. *Danforth*, we held that the woman's
written consent to an abortion was not an impermissible burden under Roe.
We think that decision is controlling on the similar issue here.

The judgment of the District Court is reversed, and the case is remanded for
further proceedings consistent with this opinion.

It is so ordered.

Mr. Justice Brennan, with whom Mr. Justice Marshall and Mr. Justice Blackmun
join, dissenting.

This Court reverses on the ground that "the District Court Misconceived the
nature and scope of the fundamental right recognized in Roe [v.*Wade*]," and
therefore that Connecticut was not required to meet the "compelling interest"
test to justify its discrimination against elective abortion but only "the less
demanding test of rationality that applies in the absence of . . . the impingement of a fundamental right." This holding, the Court insists, "places no
obstacles—absolute or otherwise—in the pregnant woman's path to an abortion";
she is still at liberty to finance the abortion from "private sources." . . .

But a distressing insensitivity to the plight of impoverished pregnant
women is inherent in the Court's analysis. The stark reality for too many,
not just "some," indigent pregnant women is that indigency makes access to
competent licensed physicians not merely "difficult" but "impossible." As a
practical matter, many indigent women will feel they have no choice but to
carry their pregnancies to term because the State will pay for the associated
medical services, even though they would have chosen to have abortions if the
State had also provided funds for that procedure, or indeed if the State had
provided funds for neither procedure. This disparity in funding by the State
clearly operates to coerce indigent pregnant women to bear children they would
not otherwise choose to have, and just as clearly this coercion can only operate
upon the poor, who are uniquely the victims of this form of financial pressure.
Mr. Justice Frankfurter's words are apt:

> To sanction such a ruthless consequence, inevitably resulting from a money hurdle
> erected by the State, would justify a latterday Anatole France to add one more item
> to his ironic comments on the "majestic equality" of the law. "The law, in its
> majestic equality, forbids the rich as well as the poor to sleep under bridges, to beg
> in the streets, and to steal bread". . . .

None can take seriously the Court's assurance that its "conclusion signals no
retreat from Roe [v. *Wade*] or the cases applying it." That statement must
occasion great surprise among the Courts of Appeals and District Courts that,
relying upon *Roe* v. *Wade*, have held that States are constitutionally required
to fund elective abortions if they fund pregnancies carried to term. Indeed,

it cannot be gainsaid that today's decision seriously erodes the principles that Roe announced to guide the determination of what constitutes an unconstitutional infringement of the fundamental right of pregnant women to be free to decide whether to have an abortion. . . .

Roe v. Wade and cases following it hold that an area of privacy invulnerable to the State's intrusion surrounds the decision of a pregnant woman whether or not to carry her pregnancy to term. The Connecticut scheme clearly infringes upon that area of privacy by bringing financial pressures on indigent women that force them to bear children they would not otherwise have. That is an obvious impairment of the fundamental right established by Roe v. Wade. Yet the Court concludes that "the Connecticut regulation does not impinge upon [that] fundamental right." This conclusion is based on a perceived distinction, on the one hand, between the imposition of criminal penalties for the procurement of an abortion present in Roe v. Wade, and, on the other, the assertedly lesser inhibition imposed by the Connecticut scheme. Ante, at 472-474, 53 L Ed 2nd 494-495.

The last time our Brother Powell espoused the concept in an abortion case that "[t]here is a basic difference between direct state interference with a protected activity and state encouragement of an alternative activity consonant with legislative policy," ante, at 475, 53 L Ed 2d 495, the Court refused to adopt it. . . .

We have also rejected this approach in other abortion cases. Doe v. Bolton, the companion to Roe v. Wade, in addition to striking down the Georgia criminal prohibition against elective abortions, struck down the procedural requirements of certification of hospitals, of approval by a hospital committee, and of concurrence in the abortion decision by two doctors other than the woman's own doctor None of these requirements operated as an absolute bar to elective abortions in the manner of the criminal prohibitions present in the other aspect of the case or in Roe, but this was not sufficient to save them from unconstitutionality. . . .

Until today, I had not thought the nature of the fundamental right established in Roe was open to question, let alone susceptible of the interpretation advanced by the Court. The fact that the Connecticut scheme may not operate as an absolute bar preventing all indigent women from having abortions is not critical. What is critical is that the State has inhibited their fundamental right to make that choice free from state interference. . . .

Although appellant does not argue it as justification, the Court concludes that the State's interest "in protecting the potential life of the fetus" suffices.[5]

---

[5] The Court also suggests, ante, at 478 n 11, 53 L Ed 2d 497, that a "State may have legitimate demographic concerns about its rate of population growth" which might justify a choice to favor live births over abortions. While it is conceivable that under some circumstances this might be an appropriate factor to be considered as part of a State's "compelling" interest, no one contends that this is the case here, or indeed that Connecticut has any demographic concerns at all about the rate of its population growth.

Since only the first trimester of pregnancy is involved in this case, that justification is totally foreclosed if the Court is not overruling the holding of *Roe* v. *Wade* that [w]ith respect to the State's important and legitimate interest in potential life, the 'compelling' point is at viability," occurring at about the end of the second trimester. The appellant also argues a further justification not relied upon by the Court, namely, that the State needs "to control the amount of its limited public funds which will be allocated to its public welfare budget." Brief for Appellant 22. The District Court correctly held, however, that the asserted interest was "wholly chimerical" because the "state's assertion that it saves money when it declines to pay the cost of a welfare mother's abortion is simply contrary to undisputed facts."

Finally, the reasons that render the Connecticut regulation unconstitutional also render invalid, in my view, the requirement of a prior written certification by the woman's attending physician that the abortion is "medically necessary," and the requirement that the hospital submit a Request for Authorization of Professional Services including a "statement indicating the medical need for the abortion." For the same reasons, I would also strike down the requirement for prior authorization of payment by the Connecticut Department of Social Services.

ABORTION AND THE LAW

BARUCH A. BRODY

One of the most frustrating aspects of discussions about abortion is the way in which they rapidly turn into a discussion of the status of the foetus and of whether destroying the foetus constitutes the taking of a human life. Since these latter questions seem difficult, if not impossible, to resolve upon rational grounds, frustration results. It therefore seems desirable to find aspects of the abortion problem that can be resolved independently of the status of the foetus problem. One such possibility is the question of whether there should be a law against abortions performed by licensed physicians upon the request of the mother (or perhaps the parents). There are, after all, many people who, while opposed to abortion on the grounds that it involves the taking of a human life, maintain that it would still be wrong (or at least inappropriate) for a state to legislate against such abortions. If their claim can be shown to be right, then we could at least resolve the legal problem about abortion. This paper is an attempt to assess their claim.

Such a claim cannot, of course, be considered without considering, at the same time, the more general question of when it is right (or appropriate) for a state to legislate against some action. It is hoped that our discussion of this problem in the context of a specific issue may shed light upon this fundamental general problem about the law.

I

The claim that we will be considering consists of the joint assertion that

1. *It is wrong for x to perform an abortion upon y, even when x is a licensed physician and y a consenting mother (who may also have the consent of the father), and it is wrong because this act would be the taking of an innocent human life.*

and

2. *It is wrong (or at least inappropriate) for the state, in the circumstances we find ourselves in now, to have a law prohibiting such abortions.*

Reprinted by permission of the author and publisher from B. Brody, "Abortion and the Law," *The Journal of Philosophy, 68,* No. 12 (1971), pp. 357–369.

These two claims are not, by themselves, clearly incompatible. But it might be claimed that when a correct principle about what type of wrong actions ought to be prohibited by law is conjoined to these two claims, we get an inconsistent triad. If this is correct, then the position we are considering is indefensible. But is it correct? What is the principle?

One principle that would certainly do the job is

3. *It is right (or appropriate) for the state to have a law prohibiting any action that is wrong.*

The trouble with this principle is that it seems too strong for two reasons. To begin with, it implies that such laws ought to be passed even if the wrong action produces no bad consequences, or at least none for anyone but the person who is doing the action. This implication about crimes without victims certainly casts familiar doubts upon (3). But even more significantly, (3) leaves out the whole question whether the passing of a law is the right (or appropriate) means for discouraging or preventing the performance of that wrong action. Would it be right to pass a law prohibiting such actions if, because of special circumstances in the case at hand, the existence of the law would increase the performance of these wrong actions? Or would it be right to pass a law prohibiting such actions if, because of special circumstances in the case at hand, the existence of the law has side effects worse than the continued performance of the wrong actions?

Much more plausible than (3) is another principle that would do the job, the principle that

4. *It is right (or appropriate) for the state to have a law prohibiting any wrong action that results in bad consequences for someone other than the performer of the action (or someone other than him and anyone else who has voluntarily consented to his doing the action).*

(4) is much more plausible than (3) because it avoids the problem about crimes without victims. (4) does the job of destroying the claim we are considering because it, (1) and (2), and certain additional very plausible assumptions (the foetus does not consent to the abortion, and the taking of a human life is an action that has bad consequences for him whose life is being taken) do form an inconsistent set of propositions. The trouble with (4), however, is that it does not avoid the second objection against (3). Even if the wrong action does have these bad consequences, it might still be wrong (or inappropriate) to have a law prohibiting these actions if, for example, the existence of the law would, because of special circumstances in the case at hand, increase the performance of these wrong actions or produce very undesirable side effects.

A similar problem arises even for the extremely plausible principle that

5. *It is right (or appropriate) for the state to have a law prohibiting any wrong action that involves the taking of a human life.*

This principle, (1), and (2) do form an inconsistent triad. But one cannot consent even to this general principle. After all, the existence of the law still might, because of special circumstances in the case at hand, increase the performance of these wrong actions or produce overriding side effects like the loss of even more human lives.

What rapidly emerges from a consideration of principles like (3)–(5) is that questions about the rightness (or appropriateness) of a law prohibiting certain actions cannot be settled by decisions about the rightness or wrongness of the action, or even by such decisions coupled with decisions about why the action is wrong. This is true even in the extreme case where it is decided that the action is wrong because it involves the taking of an innocent human life.

We are now in a position to see that our original objection to the joint assertability of (1) and (2) will not do. It, after all, requires some true principle of the form, "It is right (or appropriate) for the state to have a law prohibiting any action of type *A*" (where abortion, if it is the taking of an innocent human life, would necessarily be of the type in question). We have now seen that all such principles are wrong, and so our initial challenge is not sustainable. In examining the question of whether there should be a law against abortions, therefore, we must go beyond the fact, if it is a fact, that abortion is the taking of a human life, to consider the results of having such a law in a given society.

II

Before turning to such considerations, however, we must first consider an important claim about law and society which, if true, might serve as the basis for the justification of the joint assertion of (1) and (2). This is the claim that citizens of a pluralistic society must forego the use of the law as a method of enforcing their private moral point of view. On the basis of this claim, it might well be argued that, in our pluralistic society, in which there are serious disagreements about the status of the foetus and about the resulting rightness or wrongness of abortion, it would be wrong (or inappropriate) to have laws against abortion.

Such claims are difficult to evaluate because of their imprecision. So let us first try to formulate some version of them more carefully. Consider the following general claim:

6. *When the citizens of a society disagree about the rightness or wrongness of a given type of action, and a considerable number think it is right, then it is*

wrong (or inappropriate) for that society to have a law prohibiting that action, even if the majority of the citizens think that the action is wrong.

There are a variety of reasons that might be offered in support of such a claim. One appeals to the right of the minority to follow its own conscience and not to be forced into following the conscience of the majority. Another appeals to the inappropriateness of a majority's doing something to a minority that it would oppose were it the minority and were that action being done to it. Still another appeals to the detrimental consequences to a society of a strong feeling on the part of a significant minority that the state has passed unjust laws and that the law is being used by the majority to coerce the minority. All these weighty considerations make it seem certain that some principle like (6) is true.

If, however, (6) is true, it seems easy to offer a defense of the joint assertability of (1) and (2). All we need are the additional obvious truths that the citizens of our society strongly disagree about the rightness and wrongness of abortion and that a significant minority think that, in at least many cases, the right thing to do is to have an abortion. From these truths and (6), (2) follows even if (1) is true.

The trouble with this argument is that it depends upon (6). I quite agree that, because of the considerations mentioned above, something like (6) must be true. But (6) is much too broad to be defensible. Consider, after all, a society in which a significant minority thinks it is OK, and perhaps even obligatory, to kill blacks, jews, etc., because they are not really human. It would seem to follow from (6) that the majority of that society, even though they thought these actions were very evil, should not pass a law prohibiting such actions, should not use the law as a means of preventing the minority from killing blacks, jews, etc. Surely this is wrong. Even if citizens of a pluralistic society should forego passing certain laws out of deference to the views of those minorities who think that the action in question is not wrong, there are some cases where, because of the extent of the evil of the action in question according to the majority conception, the law must be passed anyway. It is easy to see why this is so. If, according to the majority conception, the actions in question produce bad enough results and infringe upon the rights of enough innocent people, then the possibility of preventing this by passing and enforcing a law against such actions may well override the rights of that minority to follow its conscience.

The truth in (6) seems to be captured by a weaker principle like:

7. *When the citizens of a society strongly disagree about the rightness or wrongness of a given type of action, and a considerable number think that it is right, then it is wrong (or inappropriate) for that society to have a law prohibiting that action, even if the majority of the citizens think that the action is wrong, unless the action in question is so evil that the desirability*

of its legal prohibition outweighs the desirability of granting to the minority
the right to follow their own consciences on this issue.

(7) is, of course, rather vague. In particular, its last clause needs further clarification. But (7) is clear enough so that we can see that it cannot be used as the basis for a simple justification of the joint assertability of (1) and (2). (7), conjoined with the obvious truths that the citizens of our society strongly disagree about the rightness and wrongness of abortion and that a significant minority think that, in at least many cases, the right thing to do is to have an abortion, does not yield (2) if (1) is true. After all, if (1) is true, then the action in question is the taking of an innocent human life. Therefore, it might well fall under the last clause of (7). After all, according to (1), the destruction of a foetus is not unlike the killing of a black or a jew. They are all cases of the taking of an innocent human life.

It would seem, therefore, that an adequate account of the relation between law and morality in a pluralistic society does not easily support the joint assertability of (1) and (2). Even in a pluralistic society, the minority cannot always have the right to follow its conscience. Whether it should, in a given case, have this right depends, as (7) indicates, both on the nature of the action in question and on the results of having such a law. After all, both of these help determine "the desirability of its legal prohibition." So we are left once more with the need to consider the effects of abortion laws, and not merely the rightness and wrongness of the abortion.

III

There are a large number of arguments that are commonly offered in defense of the legalization of abortions performed by doctors upon consenting mothers. These include:

(i) The only legitimate interest the state ever had in preventing abortion, the threat to the health of the mother, is no longer present because of the safety of modern abortion techniques.

(ii) Laws prohibiting abortions interfere with a woman's right to do what she wants to do with her body.

(iii) Laws prohibiting abortions are harmful to the practice of medicine, partially because they lead to state intrusion into what should be a private relation between the doctor and his patient and partially because they prevent the doctor from practicing medicine as he sees fit.

(iv) Abortion laws that allow abortions only in a few cases (e.g., when necessary to save the life of the mother) are necessarily vague and therefore result either in a doctor's avoiding performing abortions when they should be performed, in order to play safe, or in a doctor's having to gamble that the law will uphold his decision.

(v) Abortion is a method of population control, and, with our growing population problem, we have no business outlawing any method of population control.

(vi) Laws prohibiting abortions lead to the birth of unwanted children, children who often suffer psychologically because of this, and who therefore sometimes grow up to be social problems.

(vii) Legalizing abortions is the only way of avoiding tragedies for the pregnant woman and her family, tragedies due to the cause of the pregnancy (rape, incest) or to events occurring during the pregnancy (certain types of maternal illness or certain drugs taken by the mother), or to the family's circumstances (its inability to support another child, the mother's mental or physical health).

(viii) Laws prohibiting abortions are commonly disregarded, and, like prohibition laws, all that they produce is a disrespect for the law.

(ix) Laws prohibiting abortions force pregnant women who need abortions to go to quacks, and this results in many deaths and much harm to these women's physical and mental health.

(x) Laws prohibiting abortions discriminate against the poor, who, unlike the rich, cannot get legal or safe abortions.

We are not now concerned with an evaluation of these arguments. What we want to see is whether someone who believes (1) can still use any of them as an argument for (2), i.e., whether these arguments can be used as the basis for an argument for the joint assertability of (1) and (2). We will have to ask ourselves two questions. Are the premises of these arguments compatible with (1), the claim that abortion is wrong because it is the taking of an innocent human life? And if they are compatible, does the addition to them of (1) still leave us with a good argument for legalizing abortions, an argument of the form, "Although (1), there should be no law against abortion because . . ."? If we can answer yes to both of these questions in connection with one or more of the above-mentioned arguments, or in connection with some other, as yet unmentioned, argument, then we will have a good argument in defense of the joint assertion of (1) and (2).

A good example of an argument that is not open for our use is (i). For it is clear that one of its premises, the claim that the only interest the state has in abortions is protecting the mother from a dangerous operation, is not compatible with the view that abortion is the taking of an innocent human life. After all, if abortion is the taking of an innocent human life, it would seem as though the state, as part of its general role as a protector of human life, has an interest in prohibiting abortions to protect the life of a child.

We could not use (i) because its premises are incompatible with (1). We cannot use (v) because when we conjoin (1) to its premises, the resulting statement, while consistent, is not the basis for a sound argument for legalizing abortion. Even if we do need methods of population control, and even if it's too late to talk about birth control after the woman is pregnant, the fact, if it is a fact, that abortion is the taking of an innocent human life seems to rule it out as a method of population control. At least it does, so long as we do not also allow infanticide, or even just plain killing of randomly selected adults, as methods of population control.

Argument (ii) won't do for slightly more complicated reasons. As it stands, it seems that one of its premises is that the destruction of a foetus is nothing more than the destruction of some part of a woman's body. As such, argument (ii) has a premise incompatible with (1). But I sometimes suspect that the people offering this argument (the so-called "woman's liberation argument") really only want to be arguing that women, like all other people, should be free to do what they want to do. If this is what the argument is, it still is wrong. People do not, and should not, have the right to do *anything* they want to do, and if (1) is true, then it looks as though abortion is the sort of thing that no one should have the right to do.

Argument (iii) is like argument (v). Although we may want to grant the truth of its premises that a doctor should be free to practice medicine as he sees fit and that the doctor–patient relation should be private, and although these premises are compatible with (1), the argument does not go through when we conjoin (1) with its original premises. We would not want to say, I believe, that although abortion is the taking of an innocent human life, we should have no law against it, in order to preserve the rights of the doctor and the privacy of the doctor–patient relationship. There are, after all, some limitations that will have to be placed upon these rights, like all other rights, and certainly the most obvious case for this is when these limitations are necessary to save an innocent human life.

Argument (iv) has a special type of shortcoming. It presupposes that any abortion law would allow for at least some cases of legalized abortion. It then goes on to argue that such an allowance will make any such law unfairly (and in the context of American law, unconstitutionally) vague, and concludes from this that all abortions should therefore be legal. But given (1), why should any abortions be allowed? Can we take one innocent life, the life of the child, to save another innocent life, the life of the mother? And even if we grant that we should allow this special case, it seems odd to claim that we should therefore allow all cases just to avoid a vague law. Given the problem of justifying any abortions if (1) is true, wouldn't it be more reasonable to live with this unfortunately vague law, or not allow any legal abortions at all, rather than to allow all of them?

It therefore seems to me that arguments (i)–(v) cannot be used by a believer in (1) to support (2). But these were clearly the weaker arguments, even if they are often used. The far stronger arguments are (vi) and (vii), arguments that are often used to support even the morality of abortions, and (viii)–(x). All these arguments deal with the bad consequences of not having legalized abortions; they are, therefore, the type of argument that, as was argued earlier, is most likely to support the joint assertability of (1) and (2). We turn therefore to a consideration of them.

IV

Arguments (vi) and (vii) seem to have the following structure: There are certain social problems (the problem of the unwanted child, the family that can't afford another child, the young girl pregnant because she was raped, etc.) for which abortion offers a solution; therefore, we must legalize abortion so as to make this solution available when needed. The premises of these arguments, which assert that these social problems exist and that abortion would solve them, are, of course, compatible with (1). But will we still have a good argument if we conjoin (1) to these premises; i.e., would we want to argue that, although abortion is the taking of an innocent human life, it should, by being legalized, be made available as a solution to these problems?

It might be thought that the answer to this question is unequivocally no, that we shouldn't solve our social problems by allowing some people to take the lives of other innocent people. It would seem that the sanctity of life must take precedence over the solution to these problems, and that abortions should not be allowed even if no alternative solutions are available. But, in any case, they often are available. The family who cannot afford another child can be helped financially; the unwanted child can be put up for adoption. And when an alternative solution is not available, as in the case of the young girl who has been raped, we can at least alleviate that problem by providing her in her pregnancy with an environment in which she can continue her studies, lead her life without being ridiculed or made to feel shame, and in which she can receive psychological and social counseling. It would seem, therefore, that if (1) is true, arguments (vi) and (vii) won't do.

But perhaps we are going too quickly. After all, aren't there many things that we allow, as the best solution to a problem or simply because it is convenient, which are responsible for the taking of innocent human lives? We could, for example, save many innocent human lives by banning private auto-mobiles, and yet we don't. And surely the problems we solve by allowing them are far less significant than those we can solve by legalizing abortion. This is not, however, a very persuasive analogy. In the automobile case, what we allow is, in itself, perfectly OK. It is the abuse of the right to drive a car that results in the loss of innocent human lives. But in the case of abortion, if (1) is right, then the very thing that we are allowing is the taking of innocent human lives, and this is a very different matter.

We turn now to (viii). It must be noted, to begin with, that (viii) grossly exaggerates when it claims that the only result of our abortion laws is a disrespect for the law. It surely is the case that a good percentage of contem-plated abortions are not carried out just because they are illegal (and, therefore, unsafe and expensive), even though a good percentage are carried out even though they are illegal. So what (viii) must really be arguing is that the disrespect for the law engendered by abortion laws is so great and poses such a problem that we must legalize abortions, even at the expense of an increase in the number of abortions due to the actual performance of at least some of those abortions now contemplated but not performed because of their illegality. The question we must now consider is whether one can still argue this way if (1) is true. This is indeed a difficult matter, but I am inclined to say that one cannot. After all, one must suppose that abortion is now seriously considered by a great many women who then reject it because of its illegality but who would have the abortion if it were legal. So legalized abortion would result, if (1) is right, in a great many additional cases of the taking of innocent human lives. It seems hard to believe, however, that the problem of disrespect for the law produced by abortion laws is so great that we must pay so drastic a price for its solution. The situation would be very different, of course, if (viii) were literally true, and few, if any, abortions were prevented by their being illegal—but this seems highly unlikely.

Argument (viii) derives much of its plausibility, I suppose, from the com-parison with prohibition. But these two situations are very different. We today feel that prohibition attempted to solve a social problem at much too great a price in terms of disrespect for the law because we feel that the only problem about drinking is excessive drinking. As serious a problem as that may be, it is surely far less serious than the problem posed by abortion, the problem of the taking of innocent human lives, if (1) is right. And, secondly, it seems likely that the drinking laws may have even increased the number of drinkers, and not decreased them; but this can hardly be said for the abortion laws.

(ix) is, in a way, the strongest of the arguments. It claims that we must abolish laws prohibiting abortions so as to save the lives of those unfortunate women killed by abortion quacks. It would also seem that the sanctity of human life requires the abolishment of abortion laws. But I am afraid that even this argument will not do if we grant the truth of (1). If (1) is true, this argument would be calling upon us to legalize abortions so that, by increasing the number of innocent human lives taken by abortionists, we can save the lives of some of those people, the mothers, guilty of the offense of taking these innocent human lives. This surely seems wrong. Even if, as is very unlikely, the number of human lives saved is greater if we legalize abortions, surely the innocent lives (the foetuses) should take precedence over the lives of those (the mothers) who would take them. And if, as is far more likely, the number of human lives saved would be greater if we kept the abortion laws, then this argument makes no sense at all.

Before leaving arguments (vi)–(ix), I would like to add one additional point. All I have been trying to show is that, if (1) is true, then the problems raised in (vi)–(ix) won't justify the legalization of abortions. This is not to say, however, that these are not serious problems. They are indeed extremely serious, and we must do our best to solve them, but they are not serious enough to justify the taking of innocent lives in order to solve them.

We are left with (x). (x), as a claim about the hypocrisy of society, is very powerful. There are far too many people who oppose (or do nothing for) the legalization of abortion laws because they know that the problems created by these laws will never disturb them—they are wealthy or influential enough to be able to get for themselves or for their wives, girl friends, etc. a legal or safe, if illegal, abortion. But as an argument for legalizing abortion even though (1) is true, (x) will not do. It is then, after all, arguing that, since there is an inequality about who gets away with murder, we should allow everyone to get away with it. The obvious alternative to be pursued, even if it is difficult to achieve, is the abolishment of this inequality by no one's getting away with it. Even if this can never be achieved, however, this argument will not do: no man can claim an equal right to do something if that thing is a thing, like the taking of an innocent human life, which no man has a right to do. . . .

VI

Let me end by saying a few words about how the problem now stands. It was not my intention, in this paper, to consider the truth of (1), that so difficult question which permeates the abortion issue. What was considered in this paper was the possibility of arguing for the legalization of abortion even if (1) is true. But, unfortunately, no such argument seems forthcoming; so it looks as if the legal problem about abortion cannot be resolved independently of the status of the foetus problem.

I should like to suggest, however, that there may be other aspects of the abortion problem that are resolvable independently of the status of the foetus problem. One such possible aspect is the moral justification of abortions in cases where they are necessary to save the life of the mother. But this is an issue that we will have to consider on another occasion.

A DEFENSE OF ABORTION[1]

Most opposition to abortion relies on the premise that the fetus is a human being, a person, from the moment of conception. The premise is argued for, but, as I think, not well. Take, for example, the most common argument. We are asked to notice that the development of a human being from conception through birth into childhood is continuous; then it is said that to draw a line, to choose a point in this development and say "before this point the thing is not a person, after this point it is a person" is to make an arbitrary choice, a choice for which in the nature of things no good reason can be given. It is concluded that the fetus is, or anyway that we had better say it is, a person from the moment of conception. But this conclusion does not follow. Similar things might be said about the development of an acorn into an oak tree, and it does not follow that acorns are oak trees, or that we had better say they are. Arguments of this form are sometimes called "slippery slope arguments"—the phrase is perhaps self-explanatory—and it is dismaying that opponents of abortion rely on them so heavily and uncritically.

I am inclined to agree, however, that the prospects for "drawing a line" in the development of the fetus look dim. I am inclined to think also that we shall probably have to agree that the fetus has already become a human person well before birth. Indeed, it comes as a surprise when one first learns how early in its life it begins to acquire human characteristics. By the tenth week, for example, it already has a face, arms and legs, fingers and toes; it has internal organs, and brain activity is detectable.[2] On the other hand, I think that the premise is false, that the fetus is not a person from the moment of conception. A newly fertilized

---

[1] I am very much indebted to James Thomson for discussion, criticism, and many helpful suggestions.

[2] Daniel Callahan, *Abortion: Law, Choice and Morality* (New York, 1970), p. 373. This book gives a fascinating survey of the available information on abortion. The Jewish tradition is surveyed in David M. Feldman, *Birth Control in Jewish Law* (New York, 1968), Part 5, the Catholic tradition in John T. Noonan, Jr., "An Almost Absolute Value in History," in *The Morality of Abortion*, ed. John T. Noonan, Jr. (Cambridge, Mass., 1970).

"A Defense of Abortion," by Judith Jarvis Thomson, *Philosophy and Public Affairs*, vol. 1, no. 1 (copyright © 1971 by Princeton University Press), pp. 47–66. Reprinted by permission of Princeton University Press.

ovum, a newly implanted clump of cells, is no more a person than an acorn is an oak tree. But I shall not discuss any of this. For it seems to me to be of great interest to ask what happens if, for the sake of argument, we allow the premise. How, precisely, are we supposed to get from there to the conclusion that abortion is morally impermissible? Opponents of abortion commonly spend most of their time establishing that the fetus is a person, and hardly any time explaining the step from there to the impermissibility of abortion. Perhaps they think the step too simple and obvious to require much comment. Or perhaps instead they are simply being economical in argument. Many of those who defend abortion rely on the premise that the fetus is not a person, but only a bit of tissue that will become a person at birth; and why pay out more arguments than you have to? Whatever the explanation, I suggest that the step they take is neither easy nor obvious, that it calls for closer examination than it is commonly given, and that when we do give it this closer examination we shall feel inclined to reject it.

I propose, then, that we grant that the fetus is a person from the moment of conception. How does the argument go from here? Something like this, I take it. Every person has a right to life. So the fetus has a right to life. No doubt the mother has a right to decide what shall happen in and to her body; everyone would grant that. But surely a person's right to life is stronger and more stringent than the mother's right to decide what happens in and to her body, and so outweighs it. So the fetus may not be killed; an abortion may not be performed.

It sounds plausible. But now let me ask you to imagine this. You wake up in the morning and find yourself back to back in bed with an unconscious violinist. A famous unconscious violinist. He has been found to have a fatal kidney ailment, and the Society of Music Lovers has canvassed all the available medical records and found that you alone have the right blood type to help. They have therefore kidnapped you, and last night the violinist's circulatory system was plugged into yours, so that your kidneys can be used to extract poisons from his blood as well as your own. The director of the hospital now tells you, "Look, we're sorry the Society of Music Lovers did this to you—we would never have permitted it if we had known. But still, they did it, and the violinist now is plugged into you. To unplug you would be to kill him. But never mind, it's only for nine months. By then he will have recovered from his ailment, and can safely be unplugged from you." Is it morally incumbent on you to accede to this situation? No doubt it would be very nice of you if you did, a great kindness. But do you *have* to accede to it? What if it were not nine months, but nine years? Or longer still? What if the director of the hospital says, "Tough luck, I agree, but you've now got to stay in bed, with the violinist plugged into you, for the rest of your life. Because remember this. All persons have a right to life, and violinists are persons. Granted you have a right to decide what happens in and to your body, but a person's right to life outweighs your right to decide what happens in and to your body. So you cannot ever be unplugged from him." I imagine you would regard this as outrageous, which suggests that something really is wrong with that plausible-sounding argument I mentioned a moment ago.

In this case, of course, you were kidnapped; you didn't volunteer for the operation that plugged the violinist into your kidneys. Can those who oppose abortion on the ground I mentioned make an exception for a pregnancy due to rape? Certainly. They can say that persons have a right to life only if they didn't come into existence because of rape; or they can say that all persons have a right to life, but that some have less of a right to life than others, in particular, that those who came into existence because of rape have less. But these statements have a rather unpleasant sound. Surely the question of whether you have a right to life at all, or how much of it you have, shouldn't turn on the question of whether or not you are the product of a rape. And in fact the people who oppose abortion on the ground I mentioned do not make this distinction, and hence do not make an exception in case of rape.

Nor do they make an exception for a case in which the mother has to spend the nine months of her pregnancy in bed. They would agree that would be a great pity, and hard on the mother; but all the same, all persons have a right to life, the fetus is a person, and so on. I suspect, in fact, that they would not make an exception for a case in which, miraculously enough, the pregnancy went on for nine years, or even the rest of the mother's life.

Some won't even make an exception for a case in which continuation of the pregnancy is likely to shorten the mother's life; they regard abortion as impermissible even to save the mother's life. Such cases are nowadays very rare, and many opponents of abortion do not accept this extreme view. All the same, it is a good place to begin: a number of points of interest come out in respect to it.

1. Let us call the view that abortion is impermissible even to save the mother's life "the extreme view." I want to suggest first that it does not issue from the argument I mentioned earlier without the addition of some fairly powerful premises. Suppose a woman has become pregnant, and now learns that she has a cardiac condition such that she will die if she carries the baby to term. What may be done for her? The fetus, being a person, has a right to life, but as the mother is a person too, so has she a right to life. Presumably they have an equal right to life. How is it supposed to come out that an abortion may not be performed? If mother and child have an equal right to life, shouldn't we perhaps flip a coin? Or should we add to the mother's right to life her right to decide what happens in and to her body, which everybody seems to be ready to grant—the sum of her rights now outweighing the fetus' right to life?

The most familiar argument here is the following. We are told that performing the abortion would be directly killing[3] the child, whereas doing nothing would not be killing the mother, but only letting her die. Moreover, in killing the child, one would be killing an innocent person, for the child has committed no crime, and is not aiming at his mother's death. And then there are a variety of ways in which this might be continued. (1) But as directly killing an innocent person is always and absolutely impermissible, an abortion may not be performed. Or, (2) as directly killing an innocent person is murder, and murder is always and absolutely impermissible, an abortion may not be performed.[4] Or, (3) as one's duty to refrain from directly killing an innocent person is more stringent than one's duty to keep a person from dying, an abortion may not be performed. Or, (4) if one's only options are directly killing an innocent person or letting a person die, one must prefer letting the person die, and thus an abortion may not be performed.[5]

Some people seem to have thought that these are not further premises which must be added if the conclusion is to be reached, but that they follow from the very fact that an innocent person has a right to life.[6] But this seems to me to be a mistake, and perhaps the simplest way to show this is to bring out that while we must certainly grant that innocent persons have a right to life, the theses in (1) through (4) are all false. Take (2), for example. If directly killing an innocent person is murder, and thus is impermissible, then the mother's directly killing the innocent person inside her is murder, and thus is impermissible. But it

---

[3] The term "direct" in the arguments I refer to is a technical one. Roughly, what is meant by "direct killing" is either killing as an end in itself, or killing as a means to some end, for example, the end of saving someone else's life. See note 6, below, for an example of its use.

[4] Cf. *Encyclical Letter of Pope Pius XI on Christian Marriage,* St. Paul Editions (Boston, n.d.), p. 32: "however much we may pity the mother whose health and even life is gravely imperiled in the performance of the duty allotted to her by nature, nevertheless what could ever be a sufficient reason for excusing in any way the direct murder of the innocent? This is precisely what we are dealing with here." Noonan (*The Morality of Abortion,* p. 43) reads this as follows: "What cause can ever avail to excuse in any way the direct killing of the innocent? For it is a question of that."

[5] The thesis in (4) is in an interesting way weaker than those in (1), (2), and (3): they rule out abortion even in cases in which both mother *and* child will die if the abortion is not performed. By contrast, one who held the view expressed in (4) could consistently say that one needn't prefer letting two persons die to killing one.

[6] Cf. the following passage from Pius XII, *Address to the Italian Catholic Society of Midwives:* "The baby in the maternal breast has the right to life immediately from God.—Hence there is no man, no human authority, no science, no medical, eugenic, social, economic or moral 'indication' which can establish or grant a valid juridical ground for a direct deliberate disposition of an innocent human life, that is a disposition which looks to its destruction either as an end or as a means to another end perhaps in itself not illicit.—The baby, still not born, is a man in the same degree and for the same reason as the mother" (quoted in Noonan, *The Morality of Abortion,* p. 45).

cannot seriously be thought to be murder if the mother performs an abortion on herself to save her life. It cannot seriously be said that she *must* refrain, that she *must* sit passively by and wait for her death. Let us look again at the case of you and the violinist. There you are, in bed with the violinist, and the director of the hospital says to you, "It's all most distressing, and I deeply sympathize, but you see this is putting an additional strain on your kidneys, and you'll be dead within the month. But you *have* to stay where you are all the same. Because unplugging you would be directly killing an innocent violinist, and that's murder, and that's impermissible." If anything in the world is true, it is that you do not commit murder, you do not do what is impermissible, if you reach around to your back and unplug yourself from that violinist to save your life.

The main focus of attention in writings on abortion has been on what a third party may or may not do in answer to a request from a woman for an abortion. This is in a way understandable. Things being as they are, there isn't much a woman can safely do to abort herself. So the question asked is what a third party may do, and what the mother may do, if it is mentioned at all, is deduced, almost as an afterthought, from what it is concluded that third parties may do. But it seems to me that to treat the matter in this way is to refuse to grant to the mother that very status of person which is so firmly insisted on for the fetus. For we cannot simply read off what a person may do from what a third party may do. Suppose you find yourself trapped in a tiny house with a growing child. I mean a very tiny house, and a rapidly growing child—you are already up against the wall of the house and in a few minutes you'll be crushed to death. The child on the other hand won't be crushed to death; if nothing is done to stop him from growing he'll be hurt, but in the end he'll simply burst open the house and walk out a free man. Now I could well understand it if a bystander were to say, "There's nothing we can do for you. We cannot choose between your life and his, we cannot be the ones to decide who is to live, we cannot intervene." But it cannot be concluded that you too can do nothing, that you cannot attack it to save your life. However innocent the child may be, you do not have to wait passively while it crushes you to death. Perhaps a pregnant woman is vaguely felt to have the status of house, to which we don't allow the right of self-defense. But if the woman houses the child, it should be remembered that she is a person who houses it.

I should perhaps stop to say explicitly that I am not claiming that people have a right to do anything whatever to save their lives. I think, rather, that there are drastic limits to the right of self-defense. If someone threatens you with death unless you torture someone else to death, I think you have not the right, even to save your life, to do so. But the case under consideration here is very different. In our case there are only two people involved, one whose life is threatened, and one who threatens it. Both are innocent: the one who is threatened is not threatened because of any fault, the one who threatens does not threaten because of any fault. For this reason we may feel that we bystanders cannot intervene. But the person threatened can.

In sum, a woman surely can defend her life against the threat to it posed by the unborn child, even if doing so involves its death. And this shows not merely that the theses in (1) through (4) are false; it shows also that the extreme view of abortion is false, and so we need not canvass any other possible ways of arriving at it from the argument I mentioned at the outset.

2. The extreme view could of course be weakened to say that while abortion is permissible to save the mother's life, it may not be performed by a third party, but only by the mother herself. But this cannot be right either. For what we have to keep in mind is that the mother and the unborn child are not like two tenants in a small house which has, by an unfortunate mistake, been rented to both: the mother *owns* the house. The fact that she does adds to the offensiveness of deducing that the mother can do nothing from the supposition that third parties can do nothing. But it does more than this: it casts a bright light on the supposition that third parties can do nothing. Certainly it lets us see that a third party who says "I cannot choose between you" is fooling himself if he thinks this is impartiality. If Jones has found and fastened on a certain coat, which he needs to keep him from freezing, but which Smith also needs to keep him from freezing, then it is not impartiality that says "I cannot choose between you" when Smith owns the coat. Women have said again and again "This body is *my* body!" and they have reason to feel angry, reason to feel that it has been like shouting into the wind. Smith, after all, is hardly likely to bless us if we say to him, "Of course it's your coat, anybody would grant that it is. But no ,e may choose between you and Jones who is to have it."

We should really ask what it is that says "no one may choose" in the face of the fact that the body that houses the child is the mother's body. It may be simply a failure to appreciate this fact. But it may be something more interesting, namely the sense that one has a right to refuse to lay hands on people, even where it would be just and fair to do so, even where justice seems to require that somebody do so. Thus justice might call for somebody to get Smith's coat back from Jones, and yet you have a right to refuse to be the one to lay hands on Jones, a right to refuse to do physical violence to him. This, I think, must be granted. But then what should be said is not "no one may choose," but only "*I* cannot choose," and indeed not even this, but "*I* will not *act*," leaving it open that somebody else can or should, and in particular that anyone in a position of authority, with the job of securing people's rights, both can and should. So this is no difficulty. I have not been arguing that any given third party must accede to the mother's request that he perform an abortion to save her life, but only that he may.

I suppose that in some views of human life the mother's body is only on loan to her, the loan not being one which gives her any prior claim to it. One who held this view might well think it impartiality to say "I cannot choose." But I shall simply ignore this possibility. My own view is that if a human being has any just, prior claim to anything at all, he has a just, prior claim to his own body. And perhaps this needn't be argued for here anyway, since, as I mentioned, the arguments against abortion we are looking at do grant that the woman has a right to decide what happens in and to her body.

But although they do grant it, I have tried to show that they do not take seriously what is done in granting it. I suggest the same thing will reappear even more clearly when we turn away from cases in which the mother's life is at stake, and attend, as I propose we now do, to the vastly more common cases in which a woman wants an abortion for some less weighty reason than preserving her own life.

3. Where the mother's life is not at stake, the argument I mentioned at the outset seems to have a much stronger pull. "Everyone has a right to life, so the unborn person has a right to life." And isn't the child's right to life weightier than anything other than the mother's own right to life, which she might put forward as ground for an abortion?

This argument treats the right to life as if it were unproblematic. It is not, and this seems to me to be precisely the source of the mistake.

For we should now, at long last, ask what it comes to, to have a right to life. In some views having a right to life includes having a right to be given at least the bare mimimum one needs for continued life. But suppose that what in fact *is* the bare minimum a man needs for continued life is something he has no right at all to be given? If I am sick unto death, and the only thing that will save my life is the touch of Henry Fonda's cool hand on my fevered brow, then all the same, I have no right to be given the touch of Henry Fonda's cool hand on my fevered brow. It would be frightfully nice of him to fly in from the West Coast to provide it. It would be less nice, though no doubt well meant, if my friends flew out to the West Coast and carried Henry Fonda back with them. But I have no right at all against anybody that he should do this for me. Or again, to return to the story I told earlier, the fact that for continued life that violinist needs the continued use of your kidneys does not establish that he has a right to be given the continued use of your kidneys. He certainly has no right against you that *you* should give him continued use of your kidneys. For nobody has any right to use your kidneys unless you give him such a right; and nobody has the right against you that you shall give him this right—if you do allow him to go on using your kidneys, this is a kindness on your part, and not something he can claim from you as his due. Nor has he any right against anybody else that *they* should give him continued use of your kidneys. Certainly he had no right against the Society of Music Lovers that they should plug him into you in the first place. And if you now start to unplug yourself, having learned that you will otherwise have to spend nine years in bed with him, there is nobody in the world who must try to prevent you, in order to see to it that he is given something he has a right to be given.

Some people are rather stricter about the right to life. In their view, it does not include the right to be given anything, but amounts to, and only to, the right not to be killed by anybody. But here a related difficulty arises. If everybody is to refrain from killing that violinist, then everybody must refrain from doing a great many different sorts of things. Everybody must refrain from slitting his throat, everybody must refrain from shooting him—and everybody must refrain from unplugging you from him. But does he have a right against everybody that they shall refrain from unplugging you from him? To refrain from doing this is to allow him to continue to use your kidneys. It could be argued that he has a right against us that *we* should allow him to continue to use your kidneys. That is, while he had no right against us that we should give him the use of your kidneys, it might be argued that he anyway has a right against us that we shall not now intervene and deprive him of the use of your kidneys. I shall come back to third-party interventions later. But certainly the violinist has no right against you that *you* shall allow him to continue to use your kidneys. As I said, if you do allow him to use them, it is a kindness on your part, and not something you owe him.

The difficulty I point to here is not peculiar to the right to life. It reappears in connection with all the other natural rights; and it is something which an adequate account of rights must deal with. For present purposes it is enough just to draw attention to it. But I would stress that I am not arguing that people do not have a right to life—quite to the contrary, it seems to me that the primary control we must place on the acceptability of an account of rights is that it should turn out in that account to be a truth that all persons have a right to life. I am arguing only that having a right to life does not guarantee having either a right to be given the use of or a right to be allowed continued use of another person's body—even if one needs it for life itself. So the right to life will not serve the opponents of abortion in the very simple and clear way in which they seem to have thought it would.

4. There is another way to bring out the difficulty. In the most ordinary sort of case, to deprive someone of what he has a right to is to treat him unjustly. Suppose a boy and his small brother are jointly given a box of chocolates for Christmas. If the older boy takes the box and refuses to give his brother any of the chocolates, he is unjust to him, for the brother has been given a right to half of them. But suppose that, having learned that otherwise it means nine years in bed with that violinist, you unplug yourself from him. You surely are not being unjust to him, for you gave him no right to use your kidneys, and no one else can have given him any such right. But we have to notice that in unplugging yourself, you are killing him; and violinists, like everybody else, have a right to life, and thus in the view we were considering just now, the right not

to be killed. So here you do what he supposedly has a right you shall not do, but you do not act unjustly to him in doing it.

The emendation which may be made at this point is this: the right to life consists not in the right not to be killed, but rather in the right not to be killed unjustly. This runs a risk of circularity, but never mind: it would enable us to square the fact that the violinist has a right to life with the fact that you do not act unjustly toward him in unplugging yourself, thereby killing him. For if you do not kill him unjustly, you do not violate his right to life, and so it is no wonder you do him no injustice.

But if this emendation is accepted, the gap in the argument against abortion stares us plainly in the face: it is by no means enough to show that the fetus is a person, and to remind us that all persons have a right to life—we need to be shown also that killing the fetus violates its right to life, i.e., that abortion is unjust killing. And is it?

I suppose we may take it as a datum that in a case of pregnancy due to rape the mother has not given the unborn person a right to the use of her body for food and shelter. Indeed, in what pregnancy could it be supposed that the mother has given the unborn person such a right? It is not as if there were unborn persons drifting about the world, to whom a woman who wants a child says "I invite you in."

But it might be argued that there are other ways one can have acquired a right to the use of another person's body than by having been invited to use it by that person. Suppose a woman voluntarily indulges in intercourse, knowing of the chance it will issue in pregnancy, and then she does become pregnant; is she not in part responsible for the presence, in fact the very existence, of the unborn person inside her? No doubt she did not invite it in. But doesn't her partial responsibility for its being there itself give it a right to the use of her body?[7] If so, then her aborting it would be more like the boy's taking away the chocolates, and less like your unplugging yourself from the violinist—doing so would be depriving it of what it does have a right to, and thus would be doing it an injustice.

And then, too, it might be asked whether or not she can kill it even to save her own life: If she voluntarily called it into existence, how can she now kill it, even in self-defense?

The first think to be said about this is that it is something new. Opponents of abortion have been so concerned to make out the independence of the fetus, in order to establish that it has a right to life, just as its mother does, that they have tended to overlook the possible support they might gain from making out that the fetus is *dependent* on the mother, in order to establish that she has a

[7] The need for a discussion of this argument was brought home to me by members of the Society for Ethical and Legal Philosophy, to whom this paper was originally presented.

special kind of responsibility for it, a responsibility that gives it rights against her which are not possessed by any independent person—such as an ailing violinist who is a stranger to her.

On the other hand, this argument would give the unborn person a right to its mother's body only if her pregnancy resulted from a voluntary act, undertaken in full knowledge of the chance a pregnancy might result from it. It would leave out entirely the unborn person whose existence is due to rape. Pending the availability of some further argument, then, we would be left with the conclusion that unborn persons whose existence is due to rape have no right to the use of their mothers' bodies, and thus that aborting them is not depriving them of anything they have a right to and hence is not unjust killing.

And we should also notice that it is not at all plain that this argument really does go even as far as it purports to. For there are cases and cases, and the details make a difference. If the room is stuffy, and I therefore open a window to air it, and a burglar climbs in, it would be absurd to say, "Ah, now he can stay, she's given him a right to the use of her house—for she is partially responsible for his presence there, having voluntarily done what enabled him to get in, in full knowledge that there are such things as burglars, and that burglars burgle." It would be still more absurd to say this if I had had bars installed outside my windows, precisely to prevent burglars from getting in, and a burglar got in only because of a defect in the bars. It remains equally absurd if we imagine it is not a burglar who climbs in, but an innocent person who blunders or falls in. Again, suppose it were like this: people-seeds drift about in the air like pollen, and if you open your windows, one may drift in and take root in your carpets or upholstery. You don't want children, so you fix up your windows with fine mesh screens, the very best you can buy. As can happen, however, and on very, very rare occasions does happen, one of the screens is defective; and a seed drifts in and takes root. Does the person-plant who now develops have a right to the use of your house? Surely not—despite the fact that you voluntarily opened your windows, you knowingly kept carpets and unholstered furniture, and you knew that screens were sometimes defective. Someone may argue that you are responsible for its rooting, that it does have a right to your house, because after all you *could* have lived out your life with bare floors and furniture, or with sealed windows and doors. But this won't do—for by the same token anyone can avoid a pregnancy due to rape by having a hysterectomy, or anyway by never leaving home without a (reliable!) army.

It seems to me that the argument we are looking at can establish at most that there are *some* cases in which the unborn person has a right to the use of its mother's body, and therefore *some* cases in which abortion is unjust killing. There is room for much discussion and argument as to precisely which, if any. But I think we should sidestep this issue and leave it open, for at any rate the argument certainly does not establish that all abortion is unjust killing.

5. There is room for yet another argument here, however. We surely must all grant that there may be cases in which it would be morally indecent to detach a person from your body at the cost of his life. Suppose you learn that what the violinist needs is not nine years of your life, but only one hour: all you need do to save his life is to spend one hour in that bed with him. Suppose also that letting him use your kidneys for that one hour would not affect your health in the slightest. Admittedly you were kidnapped. Admittedly you did not give anyone permission to plug him into you. Nevertheless it seems to me plain you *ought* to allow him to use your kidneys for that hour—it would be indecent to refuse.

Again, suppose pregnancy lasted only an hour, and constituted no threat to life or health. And suppose that a woman becomes pregnant as a result of rape. Admittedly she did not voluntarily do anything to bring about the existence of a child. Admittedly she did nothing at all which would give the unborn person a right to the use of her body. All the same it might well be said, as in the newly emended violinist story, that she *ought* to allow it to remain for that hour—that it would be indecent in her to refuse.

Now some people are inclined to use the term "right" in such a way that it follows from the fact that you ought to allow a person to use your body for the hour he needs, that he has a right to use your body for the hour he needs, even though he has not been given that right by any person or act. They may say that it follows also that if you refuse, you act unjustly toward him. This use of the term is perhaps so common that it cannot be called wrong; nevertheless it seems to me to be an unfortunate loosening of what we would do better to keep a tight rein on. Suppose that box of chocolates I mentioned earlier had not been given to both boys jointly, but was given only to the older boy. There he sits, stolidly eating his way through the box, his small brother watching enviously. Here we are likely to say "You ought not to be so mean. You ought to give your brother some of those chocolates." My own view is that it just does not follow from the truth of this that the brother has any right to any of the chocolates. If the boy refuses to give his brother any, he is greedy, stingy, callous—but not unjust. I suppose that the people I have in mind will say it does follow that the brother has a right to some of the chocolates, and thus that the boy does act unjustly if he refuses to give his brother any. But the effect of saying this is to obscure what we should keep distinct, namely the difference between the boy's refusal in this case and the boy's refusal in the earlier case, in which the box was given to both boys jointly, and in which the small brother thus had what was from any point of view clear title to half.

A further objection to so using the term "right" that from the fact that A ought to do a thing for B, it follows that B has a right against A that A do it for him, is that it is going to make the question of whether or not a man has a right to a thing turn on how easy it is to provide him with it; and this seems not merely unfortunate, but morally unacceptable. Take the case of Henry Fonda again. I said earlier that I had no right to the touch of his cool hand on my fevered brow, even though I needed it to save my life. I said it would be frightfully nice of him to fly in from the West Coast to provide me with it, but that I had no right against him that he should do so. But suppose he isn't on the West Coast. Suppose he has only to walk across the room, place a hand briefly on my brow—and lo, my life is saved. Then surely he ought to do it, it would be indecent to refuse. Is it to be said "Ah, well, it follows that in this case she has a right to the touch of his hand on her brow, and so it would be an injustice in him to refuse"? So that I have a right to it when it is easy for him to provide it, though no right when it's hard? It's rather a shocking idea that anyone's rights should fade away and disappear as it gets harder and harder to accord them to him.

So my own view is that even though you ought to let the violinist use your kidneys for the one hour he needs, we should not conclude that he has a right to do so—we should say that if you refuse, you are, like the boy who owns all the chocolates and will give none away, self-centered and callous, indecent in fact, but not unjust. And similarly, that even supposing a case in which a woman pregnant due to rape ought to allow the unborn person to use her body for the hour he needs, we should not conclude that he has a right to do so; we should conclude that she is self-centered, callous, indecent, but not unjust, if she refuses. The complaints are no less grave; they are just different. However, there is no need to insist on this point. If anyone does wish to deduce "he has a right" from "you ought," then all the same he must surely grant that there are cases in which it is not morally required of you that you allow that violinist to use your kidneys, and in which he does not have a right to use them, and in which you do not do him an injustice if you refuse. And so also for mother and unborn child. Except in such cases as the unborn person has a right to demand it—and we were leaving open the possibility that there may be such cases—nobody is morally *required* to make large sacrifices, of health, of all other interests and concerns, of all other duties and commitments, for nine years, or even for nine months, in order to keep another person alive.

6. We have in fact to distinguish between two kinds of Samaritan: the Good Samaritan and what we might call the Minimally Decent Samaritan. The story of the Good Samaritan, you will remember, goes like this:

> A certain man went down from Jerusalem to Jericho, and fell among thieves, which stripped him of his raiment, and wounded him, and departed, leaving him half dead.
>
> And by chance there came down a certain priest that way; and when he saw him, he passed by on the other side.
>
> And likewise a Levite, when he was at the place, came and looked on him, and passed by on the other side.

> But a certain Samaritan, as he journeyed, came where he was; and when he saw him he had compassion on him.
>
> And went to him, and bound up his wounds, pouring in oil and wine, and set him on his own beast, and brought him to an inn, and took care of him.
>
> And on the morrow, when he departed, he took out two pence, and gave them to the host, and said unto him, "Take care of him; and whatsoever thou spendest more, when I come again, I will repay thee."   *(Luke 10:30–35)*

The Good Samaritan went out of his way, at some cost to himself, to help one in need of it. We are not told what the options were, that is, whether or not the priest and the Levite could have helped by doing less than the Good Samaritan did, but assuming they could have, then the fact they did nothing at all shows they were not even Minimally Decent Samaritans, not because they were not Samaritans, but because they were not even minimally decent.

These things are a matter of degree, of course, but there is a difference, and it comes out perhaps most clearly in the story of Kitty Genovese, who, as you will remember, was murdered while thirty-eight people watched or listened, and did nothing at all to help her. A Good Samaritan would have rushed out to give direct assistance against the murderer. Or perhaps we had better allow that it would have been a Splendid Samaritan who did this, on the ground that it would have involved a risk of death for himself. But the thirty-eight not only did not do this, they did not even trouble to pick up a phone to call the police. Minimally Decent Samaritanism would call for doing at least that, and their not having done it was monstrous.

After telling the story of the Good Samaritan, Jesus said "Go, and do thou likewise." Perhaps he meant that we are morally required to act as the Good Samaritan did. Perhaps he was urging people to do more than is morally required of them. At all events it seems plain that it was not morally required of any of the thirty-eight that he rush out to give direct assistance at the risk of his own life, and that it is not morally required of anyone that he give long stretches of his life—nine years or nine months—to sustaining the life of a person who has no special right (we were leaving open the possibility of this) to demand it.

Indeed, with one rather striking class of exceptions, no one in any country of the world is *legally* required to do anywhere near as much as this for anyone else. The class of exceptions is obvious. My main concern here is not the state of the law in respect to abortion, but it is worth drawing attention to the fact that in no state in this country is any man compelled by law to be even a Minimally Decent Samaritan to any person; there is no law under which charges could be brought against the thirty-eight who stood by while Kitty Genovese died. By contrast, in most states in this country women are compelled by law to be not merely Minimally Decent Samaritans, but Good Samaritans to unborn persons inside them. This doesn't by itself settle anything one way or the other, because it may well be argued that there should be laws in this country—as there are in many European countries—compelling at least Minimally Decent Samaritanism.[8] But it does show that there is a gross injustice in the existing state of the law. And it shows also that the groups currently working against liberalization of abortion laws, in fact working toward having it declared unconstitutional for a state to permit abortion, had better start working for the adoption of Good Samaritan laws generally, or earn the charge that they are acting in bad faith.

I should think, myself, that Minimally Decent Samaritan laws would be one thing, Good Samaritan laws quite another, and in fact highly improper. But we are not here concerned with the law. What we should ask is not whether anybody should be compelled by law to be a Good Samaritan, but whether we must accede to a situation in which somebody is being compelled—by nature, perhaps—to be a Good Samaritan. We have, in other words, to look now at third-party interventions. I have been arguing that no person is morally required to make large sacrifices to sustain the life of another who has no right to demand them, and this even where the sacrifices do not include life itself; we are not morally required to be Good Samaritans or anyway Very Good Samaritans to one another. But what if a man cannot extricate himself from such a situation? What if he appeals to us to extricate him? It seems to me plain that there are cases in which we can, cases in which a Good Samaritan would extricate him. There you are, you were kidnapped, and nine years in bed with that violinist lie ahead of you. You have your own life to lead. You are sorry, but you simply cannot see giving up so much of your life to the sustaining of his. You cannot extricate yourself, and ask us to do so. I should have thought that—in light of his having no right to the use of your body—it was obvious that we do not have to accede to your being forced to give up so much. We can do what you ask. There is no injustice to the violinist in our doing so.

7. Following the lead of the opponents of abortion, I have throughout been speaking of the fetus merely as a person, and what I have been asking is whether or not the argument we began with, which proceeds only from the fetus's being a person, really does establish its conclusion. I have argued that it does not.

But of course there are arguments and arguments, and it may be said that I have simply fastened on the wrong one. It may be said that what is important is not merely the fact that the fetus is a person, but that it is a person for whom the woman has a special kind of responsibility issuing from the fact that she is its mother. And it might be argued that all my analogies are therefore irrelevant— for you do not have that special kind of responsibility for that violinist, Henry Fonda does not have that special kind of responsibility for me. And our

---

[8] For a discussion of the difficulties involved, and a survey of the European experience with such laws, see *The Good Samaritan and the Law*, ed. James M. Ratcliffe (New York, 1966).

attention might be drawn to the fact that men and women both *are* compelled by law to provide support for their children.

I have in effect dealt (briefly) with this argument in section 4 above; but a (still briefer) recapitulation now may be in order. Surely we do not have any such "special responsibility" for a person unless we have assumed it, explicitly or implicitly. If a set of parents do not try to prevent pregnancy, do not obtain an abortion, and then at the time of birth of the child do not put in out for adoption, but rather take it home with them, then they have assumed responsibility for it, they have given it rights, and they cannot *now* withdraw support from it at the cost of its life because they now find it difficult to go on providing for it. But if they have taken all reasonable precautions against having a child, they do not simply by virtue of their biological relationship to the child who comes into existence have a special responsibility for it. They may wish to assume responsibility for it, or they may not wish to. And I am suggesting that if assuming responsibility for it would require large sacrifices, then they may refuse. A Good Samaritan would not refuse—or anyway, a Splendid Samaritan, if the sacrifices that had to be made were enormous. But then so would a Good Samaritan assume responsibility for that violinist; so would Henry Fonda, if he is a Good Samaritan, fly in from the West Coast and assume responsibility for me.

8. My argument will be found unsatisfactory on two counts by many of those who want to regard abortion as morally permissible. First, while I do argue that abortion is not impermissible, I do not argue that it is always permissible. There may well be cases in which carrying the child to term requires only Minimally Decent Samaritanism of the mother, and this is a standard we must not fall below. I am inclined to think it a merit of my account precisely that it does *not* give a general yes or a general no. It allows for and supports our sense that, for example, a sick and desperately frightened fourteen-year-old schoolgirl, pregnant due to rape, may *of course* choose abortion, and that any law which rules this out is an insane law. And it also allows for and supports our sense that in other cases resort to abortion is even positively indecent. It would be indecent in the woman to request an abortion, and indecent in a doctor to perform it, if she is in her seventh month, and wants the abortion just to avoid the nuisance of postponing a trip abroad. The very fact that the arguments I have been drawing attention to treat all cases of abortion, or even all cases of abortion in which the mother's life is not at stake, as morally on a par ought to have made them suspect at the outset.

Secondly, while I am arguing for the permissibility of abortion in some cases, I am not arguing for the right to secure the death of the unborn child. It is easy to confuse these two things in that up to a certain point in the life of the fetus it is not able to survive outside the mother's body; hence removing it from her body guarantees its death. But they are importantly different. I have argued that you are not morally required to spend nine months in bed, sustaining the life of that violinist; but to say this is by no means to say that if, when you unplug yourself, there is a miracle and he survives, you then have a right to turn around and slit his throat. You may detach yourself even if this costs him his life; you have no right to be guaranteed his death, by some other means, if unplugging yourself does not kill him. There are some people who will feel dissatisfied by this feature of my argument. A woman may be utterly devastated by the thought of a child, a bit of herself, put out for adoption and never seen or heard of again. She may therefore want not merely that the child be detached from her, but more, that it die. Some opponents of abortion are inclined to regard this as beneath contempt—thereby showing insensitivity to what is surely a powerful source of despair. All the same, I agree that the desire for the child's death is not one which anybody may gratify, should it turn out to be possible to detach the child alive.

At this place, however, it should be remembered that we have only been pretending throughout that the fetus is a human being from the moment of conception. A very early abortion is surely not the killing of a person, and so is not dealt with by anything I have said here.

ABORTION

THE AVOIDABLE MORAL DILEMMA

JAMES M. HUMBER

The recent Supreme Court decision in *Roe* v. *Wade* could hardly be said to have solved the problem of abortion.[1] Grave religious and moral issues remain, and until these are settled there will be continued assaults upon the law as promulgated by the Supreme Court. Now I agree with those who hold that the Supreme Court ruling in *Roe* v. *Wade* gives legal sanction to immoral conduct. At the same time, I would urge those presently engaged in trying to change that law to give up this line of attack. There are two reasons for this. First, at this particular point in time, all avenues for change seem blocked. Given its present constitution, the Supreme Court is not going to modify its ruling; and because the majority of citizens of this country favor abortion in at least some cases,[2] movements for constitutional amendment seem unlikely to succeed. Second, even if the law could somehow be changed, it is quite certain that it would be (as it was in the past) virtually ineffectual. As long as people remain convinced that abortion is both moral and beneficial, they will continue to make use of that procedure regardless of legal sanctions. To attack the law is to attack a symptom, not the disease; and if anti-abortionists are to have any hope of eradicating abortion, they must find some way of convincing abortion advocates that this procedure is morally wrong. Now despite the many failures of the past, I think that this can be done. There are several reasons for my optimism here, but primary among them is this: unless I am mistaken, opponents of abortion have been unable to develop convincing arguments, only because they have failed to discern the true nature of their adversaries' position. Indeed, it is my belief that no party to the dispute has ever seen the abortion controversy for what it is, and that once this is done, a much more persuasive case can be made for the

---

[1] *Roe v Wade,* 410 U.S. 113 (1973).
[2] Herman Schwartz, "The Parent or the Fetus," *Humanist,* Vol. 27 (1967), p. 126.

This paper is a revised version of an essay of the same title, published in *The Journal of Value Inquiry,* Vol. IX (Winter, 1975), pp. 282–302. I am indebted to the editors of *The Journal of Value Inquiry* for their permission to republish my essay.

immorality of abortion. In order to substantiate this belief, then, I propose to argue in the following way:

First, in section I, the major defenses of abortion will be examined in detail and shown to be unsound. Further, it will be argued that abortion must always be the taking of a human life, for if we are to take seriously our ordinary ways of speaking, human life must be acknowledged to begin at conception. Next, in section II, a case will be made for the view that the arguments of the pro-abortionists are all so poor that they should not be accepted at face value, but rather should be seen as after-the-fact rationalizations for beliefs held to be true on other grounds. In addition, an attempt will be made to uncover these "other grounds." Finally, in section III it will be argued that the true basis for the abortion advocates' moral position is such that this view must be rejected out of hand. At the same time, the emotive force of the pro-abortion stance will be recognized, and the present impossibility of assuring moral behavior acknowledged. Taking these facts into consideration, then, new programs for anti-abortion action will be outlined.

I

Most of those arguing for and against abortion see the controversy as being one which can be resolved only by determining the proper use of *human*. Those opposed to the procedure, for example, usually offer into evidence biological data which, they say, clearly indicate the fetus' humanity. If prenatal beings are known to be human, they then continue, such organisms must be seen as having the right to life. And since abortion is always the violation of that right, the procedure must be considered immoral.[3] In opposition to this "conservative" position, those favoring abortion use various ploys. Some try to show that *human* is ordinarily being used in such a way that it excludes at least some prenatal beings (e.g., zygotes and/or embryos) from its extension. Unfortunately, all such attempts fail, for with each definition offered, some commonly recognized group of human beings is denied human status.[4] Recognizing this fact, other abortion advocates seek to defend their view by appealing to the arbitrary character of definition. Basically, the argument takes two forms. The

[3] Two of the chief proponents of this view are: Paul Ramsey, "The Morality of Abortion," in *Life or Death: Ethics and Options* (Seattle: 1968), and John T. Noonan Jr., "Abortion and the Catholic Church: A Summary History," *Natural Law Forum*, Vol. 12 (1967). For a complete discussion of the failures of these analyses, see D. Callahan, Abortion: *Law Choice, and Morality* (London: 1970), pp. 378–384.

[4] For example, Herman Schwartz (*op. cit.*, p. 126), contends that abortion is moral because the fetus is not "a rational creature, with unique emotions and feelings, intellect and personality, a being with whom we can identify." But this definition excludes (at least) newborn babies, and thus allows for infanticide.

most radical position is represented by Mr. Garret Hardin: "Whether the fetus is or is not a human being is a matter of definition, not fact; and we can define any way we wish. In terms of the human problem involved, it would be unwise to define the fetus as human."[5]

The difficulty with this view is all too apparent. That is, if definition is *purely* arbitrary, we may classify any group of persons as non-human, just so long as we believe the procedure is warranted by the presence of some "human problem." Alcoholics, the senile, those on welfare, *any* group legitimately may be classed as nonhuman and dealt with as we please. Hardin recognizes the problem, but refused to acknowledge its force: "This is, of course, the well-known argument of 'the camel's nose' —which says that if we let the camel put his nose in the tent, we will be unable to keep him from forcing his whole body inside. The argument is false. It is *always* possible to draw arbitrary lines *and enforce them.*"[6]

Seemingly, Hardin wants prenatal beings *alone* to be arbitrarily classed as non-human. But upon what basis can this preference be supported? It is obvious that he could not seriously assert that embryonic organisms constitute the only group of beings posing a "human problem." What we are left with, then, is simply Hardin's "bare feeling" that arbitrary definition is proper if and only if the beings to be classified are *in utero*. But what makes this feeling more proper than the feeling, say, that alcoholics should be classed as non-human and exterminated? Hardin gives us no answer.

A less radical version of the arbitrary definition defense of abortion has been developed by Glanville Williams. Sensing Hardin's problem, Williams attempts to give rational support for Hardin's "feeling" that it is with prenatal beings alone that arbitrary non-human classification is legitimate: "Do you wish to regard the microscopic fertilized ovum as a human being? You can if you want to. . . . But there are most important social arguments for *not* adopting this language. Moreover, *if you look at actual beliefs and behavior, you will find almost unanimous rejection of it.*"[7]

In effect, the arbitrary classification of fetuses is now held to be proper, not merely because there are social arguments which make such action desirable, but even more importantly, because society's behavior indicates that the majority does not believe such entities are human anyway (e.g., women do not mourn the loss of spontaneously aborted zygotes as they do the death of children, etc.)

The first thing which must be noted about Williams' attenuated version of the arbitrary definition defense is that it is not entirely clear. Is Williams

[5] Garrett Hardin, "Abortion—or Compulsory Pregnancy?" *Journal of Marriage and the Family,* Vol. 30 (May, 1968), pp. 250–251

[6] Garrett Hardin, "Semantic Aspects of Abortion," *ETC,* (Sept., 1967), p. 264.

[7] Glanville Williams, "The Legalization of Medical Abortion," *The Eugenics Review,* Vol. 56 (April, 1964), p. 21.

claiming that, society's attitudes and behavior being what they are, fertilized ova have *already* been classified as non-human, and that it would be improper to disagree with majority opinion? Or is his view merely that the classificatory status of such organisms is in doubt, and that the available "social arguments," together with majority consent, provide us with good reasons for grouping prenatal beings as non-human? Let us examine each possibility in turn.

If the first interpretation of Williams' meaning is accepted his position must be rejected out of hand, for what it amounts to is simply the assertion that the majority is always right. But whether or not the proposition "*x* is human" is true or not, is not something to be resolved by an appeal to majority opinion. In the late Middle Ages, for example, the majority's "actual beliefs and behavior" were such that children were not considered fully human.[8] Would Williams want to admit that one who killed a troublesome child in those days was acting in a morally acceptable manner? And what of the Salem witch hunts? Was witch killing "right for them," but not for us? Surely not; indeed, if the fact that the majority of the residents of Salem thought witch killing proper indicates any-thing, it is only that the majority of the people of that city were ignorant. The conclusion, then, seems clear: if Williams wants to show that fertilized ova are non-human (i.e., if he wants to prove that it is improper today to disagree with the majority concerning the status of prenatal beings), he must provide us with some reasoned argument which demonstrates that fact. But no such argument is offered. Consequently, this interpretation of his position must be rejected.

Although the second construction of Williams' argument is stronger than the first, there seem to be two good reasons for concluding that it is unsound. First, if Williams takes majority doubt concerning classification plus the availability of "social arguments" as together providing a moral justification for dealing with certain groups of beings as non-human, various undesirable consequences follow. In both word and deed, for instance, we everyday illustrate that the majority view in this country is that there are at least some criminals who are subhuman. Rapists and murderers are often referred to as "animals" and "mad dogs"; and when these men are caught, they are housed like animals in a zoo. Then too, the social arguments for getting rid of such misanthropes are numerous. Would Williams want to use these insights to develop a new argument for capital punishment?[9]

Although it is not likely that he would do so, it could be that Williams would be willing to accept the logical implications of his argument, and admit that capital punishment, euthanasia, the killing of mental defectives, etc. are

---

[8] See Phillippe Aries, *Centuries of Childhood,* trans., Robert Baldick (New York: 1965), pp. 38–39.

[9] My choice of criminals here was purely arbitrary. The argument would apply with equal force to the senile, children born with mental defects, etc.

indubitably moral. But even if this were done, Williams' defense of abortion must be rejected as it stands, for unless it is modified in some significant way, it can only be seen as fostering morally irresponsible action. To illustrate: let us say that we are deer hunting with some friends. One of our colleagues sees a movement in the bushes and fires. When we ask him why he acted as he did, he replies: (1) although he was not sure what had moved in the bushes, it was much more probable that it was a deer than a man, and (2) if it were a deer he did not want it to get away, for his family needed the food, and the deer in this region had overpopulated and were destroying the crops of local farmers. Now even if we grant the truth of (1) and (2), I doubt that anyone would accept these facts as a justification for our trigger-happy friend's behavior. True, we would not call our hunter immoral; but we *would* think him careless, and insist that he not be allowed to carry a loaded gun. And in the same vein, a woman who was not sure that the fertilized ovum within her was human, and thus decided to have an abortion simply because she wanted no more children, or would be subject to economic and/or pyschological hardship given the child's birth, should not be held responsible enough to make that life and death decision.

In order to buttress Williams' argument, defenders of abortion could object to our hunter analogy on two grounds: (a) It could be said that it does not cover two very important cases, viz., that in which the life of the mother, and that in which the lives of the mother and her fetus are endangered; or (b) it could be objected that it fails to note that there is a special relationship between a woman and the organism developing within her. Even if modified in the ways suggested, however, Williams' argument must be rejected.

First, *if* it were true that we could never be sure that prenatal beings were human, abortion would have to be considered morally acceptable whenever the conditions of (a) were in evidence. But the reason abortion would be permitted in these two special instances is not what Williams would have us believe. That is to say, in neither case would we arbitrarily define individual fetuses as non-human in order to legitimatize particular abortions. On the contrary, if only the mother's life were in jeopardy we would reason that we *have* to act in order to save her, and that since the fetus is not known to be human, we would be justified in "playing the odds," hoping all the while that our actions were not destructive of a human being. If, on the other hand, the lives of both the mother and her fetus were endangered, the argument for abortion would be stronger—indeed, abortion in this case might be warranted even if the fetus were known to be human, for our only choice here would be between saving one life, or letting two persons die. If one were to accept Williams' version of the argument, however, he would be led to one of two ridiculous results: either fetuses would be non-human (in the two cases mentioned) and not non-human (in all other cases); or, because there would sometimes be good reasons for classifying fetuses as non-human, it could be argued that they should always be so categorized.

Now the first alternative is just blatantly inconsistent. As for the second, it leads to moral absurdities. For example, an advocate of this view would have to claim that since a *starving* hunter is justified in arbitrarily classifying anything moving in the bushes as non-human and shooting, *all* movements in bushes may be thought of as being due to non-human causes, and all hunters may "fire at will."

Before a proper evaluation of (b) can be made, we must first get as clear to the exact nature of the "special relationship" to which it alludes. Surely it is not simply that of mother to child, for if our hunter analogy is amended so that the careless hunter is a woman who, at the moment of shooting, knew that the motion in the bushes must have been caused either by a deer or her child, we would think her *more* careless rather than less so in firing. If there is anything "special" about the relationship, then, it can only be that the embryonic organism exists as a parasite, and that when an abortion is effected, conditions which are both necessary for the continued life of the fetus, and in some sense possessed (or "owned") by the mother, are removed.

Having clarified the nature of the relationship referred to in (b), a second question arises: how could abortion advocates use knowledge of this relationship's existence in order to demonstrate that persons seeking abortions are not morally irresponsible? Two alternatives present themselves. First, it could be argued that the parasitic status of the conceptus shows that it is not a "separate human being endowed with human rights."[10] Now although it may well be true that the fetus' total dependence upon the mother is one factor causing some to doubt its humanity, dependency can hardly be taken to prove that the fetus is non-human and without the right to life. To hold otherwise, one should have to accept the contention that it would be morally proper for a mother to kill her newborn baby anytime prior to the severing of its umbilical cord. But this is clearly ridiculous. If knowledge of the parasitic status of the fetus is of any importance at all, then, it can only be in helping us to understand why some people doubt prenatal organisms' humanity. But our hunter analogy has all along assumed that the status of fetal beings is dubious; and the reasons for this doubt are (at least at this point in the development of our thesis) of no consequence. As a result, the first interpretation of (b) contains nothing which could allow Williams to avoid the charge of fostering moral irresponsibility.

The second version of (b) is better founded than the first, and it has been defended in detail by Professor Judith Jarvis Thomson.[11] Women have the right to abort, she says, because they have the right to control their own bodies. And *even if the fetus is a human and possessed of human rights,* "having a right to life

---

[10] Although their arguments are not clear, when feminists argue for abortion on demand, they seem to be reasoning along these lines.

[11] Judith Jarvis Thomson, "A Defense of Abortion," *Philosophy and Public Affairs,* Vol. 1 (1971), pp. 47–66.

does not guarantee having either a right to be given the use of or a right to be allowed continued use of another person's body—even if one needs it for life itself."[12]

Because Thomson assumed from the first that prenatal beings are human, I am, by conjoining her argument with that of Williams, strengthening it considerably. In addition, this action gives us a new defense of abortion—one which, I believe, makes the strongest possible case for abortion's morality. If, as Williams holds, we could never be sure that fetuses were human, and if, as Thomson says, women have a right to control their bodies, then *perhaps* an appeal to the right to control one's body would justify abortion. Quite frankly, I am not sure. Luckily, we need not face this issue, for the combined thesis may be invalidated on other grounds. Specifically, Williams' assumption concerning the uncertain classificatory status of embryonic organisms can be shown to be false; and with this demonstration, the two theses will be separated, Thomson's argument then having to stand or fall on its own.

As previously noted, most of the discussion surrounding abortion has centered upon attempts to determine the proper use of "human." Not only has this procedure been particularly unproductive, it has also failed to explain why those who oppose abortion usually wish to hold that human life begins at conception, rather than at some other point in gestation.[13] Both these failures can be overcome, however, if only one is willing to shift his focus of attention. What, after all, is the meaning of "conception"? As employed in ordinary language, the term appears to have three uses: (1) Sometimes it is used to mean "beginning," "start," or "creation" (as when we say, "The design has been faulty since its conception."). (2) Sometimes it is used to mean "act of conceiving," where "conceiving" means "to imagine" or "to form a notion or idea" (e.g., "Conception of his meaning was possible for me only after he gave an example."). (3) And finally, "conception" is often used to mean "notion" or "idea" (e.g., "I now have a conception of what must have happened yesterday."). Now which of these three uses is being employed when we discuss human conception? Surely it is the first; for when I say (p) "My conception occurred approximately nine months before I was born," I do not mean to say (as with use 2) that I imagined or thought of something at that time. Similarly, I do not mean to hold (as use 3 would require) that someone else—presumably my parents—had an idea or notion of me. Well then, if uses (2) and (3) are excluded, what else could (p) mean than that I had my beginning, start, or creation about nine months before I was born? And note, it is *I* who got his start at the point

---

[12] *Ibid.*, p. 56.

[13] This preference is evident even among those who admit that there is no proof that human life begins at conception. See Paul Ramsey, "Abortion: A Review Article," *The Thomist*, Vol. XXXVII (1973).

thus denominated. This is extremely important, for if it is essential for me to be me that I be human (as surely it is), then what I am asserting when I assert (p) is that my creation *as a human* occurred nine months before my birth. And if this is so, the rationale for the anti-abortion position becomes clear: one can deny that human beings are created at conception, only by denying that they begin to exist when they begin to exist.

Having demonstrated that from conception on embryonic organisms are human, we can only conclude that Williams is in error when he holds that the classificatory status of these beings is uncertain. This being so, the combined Williams—Thomson argument must be rejected, and we are left with Thomson's argument alone. Now, can that reasoning stand by itself once the humanity of organisms *in utero* is admitted? In arguing that it can, Thomson constructs the following example: Assume, she says, that you are kidnapped by the Society of Music Lovers and connected *via* some medical equipment to a sick, unconscious virtuoso violinist. The violinist has a rare, potentially fatal disease, which can be cured only if he remains connected to you for nine months. Only you can perform the life-giving function, because you alone have the proper blood type. Given this as the situation, then, Thomson asks: "Is it morally incumbant on you to accede to this situation? No doubt it would be very nice of you if you did. . . . But do you *have* to accede to it? What if it were not nine months, but nine years? Or longer still? . . . I imagine you would regard this as out-rageous. . . ."[14]

The conclusion seems clear: if the right to control one's body justifies "unplugging" the violinist, it must also legitimatize abortion—and this holds true regardless of whether the fetus is human or not.

Although Thomson's argument has immediate appeal, it is a relatively easy matter to show that her reasoning rests upon a confusion.[15] Consider the following counterexample: Let us say that I am involved in a shipwreck. After being thrown overboard, I manage to tie myself securely to a large piece of flotsam. As I am bobbing around in the water, a non-swimmer grabs my arm and asks that I help him get onto the piece of floating debris to which I have tied myself. To this I answer, "Having a right to life does not guarantee having either a right to be given the use of or a right to be allowed continued use of another person's body." With that, I shake him loose from my arm and watch him go under for the third time.

---

[14] Thomson, *op. cit.*, p. 49.

[15] Baruch Brody has challenged Professor Thomson's position by pointing out that she fails to distinguish between our duty to save someone's life, and our duty not to take it (B. Brody, "Thomson on Abortion," *Philosophy and Public Affairs*, Vol. 1 (1972), pp. 339–340.) There is some doubt, however, that this distinction is ever properly made in morals (See R.B. Brandt, "The Morality of Abortion," p. 157, in *Abortion: Pro and Con*, ed. by Robert L. Perkins (Cambridge: 1974), pp. 151–169).

Surely no one will doubt that in my example, I acted in an immoral manner. But why does the immorality show up so clearly here, and not in Thomson's paradigm? The answer, I think, lies in the degree of hardship being imposed upon the persons whose bodies are being used. In my example, it would have required very little effort for the one shipwrecked person to have saved the life of the other. In Thomson's analogy, however, we are asked to consider ourselves bedridden for months, even years. And as Aristotle long ago realized, anyone can "break" under pressure and do something which he realizes is morally wrong. Now in certain cases (viz., when the pressure is so great that the average person could not reasonably be expected to withstand it), the man who "breaks" and acts immorally is said to have an excuse for his actions. But to excuse an act is not to say that it is morally right. Indeed, just the opposite is true, for unless an act is morally wrong, it hardly stands in need of an excuse. And if this is granted, two conclusions seem mandated: First, if Thomson's reasoning has some "convincing power," it is only because the reader has followed her in failing to distinguish between excused acts, and acts which are morally right. And second, if Thomson's argument shows anything at all about abortion, it is only that it is a morally wrong act which, like all other morally wrong acts, may sometimes be excused.

Professor Thomson's argument is not the only defense of abortion which proceeds upon the assumption that fetal beings are human. Some pro-abortionists admit this fact, but argue that there is a distinction to be drawn between "human" and "human person"[16] That is, even if human life begins at conception, these people say, no person is present until sometime late in gestation. And if this is so, ". . . then under some circumstances the welfare of actually existing persons might supersede the welfare of developing human tissue."[17]

Now there are two reasons why any defense constructed along these lines must fail. First, if there are formidable difficulties involved in trying to define "human," these problems must simply re-arise in attempts to define "human person;" and if this is so, it must be virtually impossible to distinguish a human from a human person. Even if we ignore this apparently irresolvable problem, however, what possibly could serve to justify the belief that an individual's rights may "supersede" those of a human? That is, since the right to life is a human right rather than a personal one, fetuses must be seen as possessing that right even if they are held to be non-persons. Why, then, do these proponents of abortion feel that a human's right to life may be negated whenever it conflicts with some right or rights possessed by a person? There seems to be only one

---

[16] Thomas L. Hayes, "A Biological View," *Commonweal*, Vol. 85 (March, 1967); Rudolph Ehrensing, "When is it Really Abortion?" *The National Catholic Reporter* (May, 1966).
[17] Ehrensing, *op. cit.*, p. 4.

answer, viz., these pro-abortionists must be assuming that it is more valuable, important, or worthy, to be a human person than to be human. But how could this presupposition be shown to be true? In some circumstances, perhaps (as when the mother-to-be is, say, a doctor on the verge of discovering a cure for cancer), a good case could be made that this woman should be allowed to abort rather than having to risk her life in childbirth. But what if the expectant mother is an alcoholic, on welfare, and a general burden to society? Would the abortion advocate allow us to turn the argument around and insist that this woman should not be allowed to abort her "innocent" fetus, even if her own life were in jeopardy? This seems highly unlikely. But if this is so, the question simply re-arises: what is there about being a person which, in itself, makes one better or more worthy than a being who is merely human?

II

If my analysis is correct, none of the major defenses of abortion succeeds in its purpose. Still, in reviewing the literature as we have done, one is struck not so much by the arguments' failures, as by the reasons for those failures. That is to say, if we have represented the pro-abortion arguments fairly, it is not just that they are unsound, they are unsound for simple, almost foolish reasons. But this is not the worst of it. Sometimes proponents of abortion are aware of their mistakes; and whenever this happens, reasoned inquiry simply ends with the abortion advocate dogmatically insisting that although the criticism in question may be, in principle, applicable to his argument, in practice it will never constitute a problem (e.g., above, p. 73). Now how can these facts be explained? One thing is clear. Unless one is willing to claim that abortion advocates are both inconsistent and confused, he must hold that members of this group do not believe as they do for the reasons cited in their arguments. But if this is so, a further question arises: what is the true basis (or bases) for the pro-abortion position? It is this question to which I will now address myself. In doing so, the thesis that I shall argue for is briefly this: although abortion advocates find it impossible to identify or empathize with a fetus, they can and do sympathize with a suffering mother-to-be, and hence simply *feel* that abortion is moral. This view is not without support. Consider the following facts.

First, if our identification hypothesis is accepted, a full explanation can be given for each of the abortion advocate's errors. In general, these errors flow from one of two causes: either the proponent of abortion allows his identifications and sympathies to affect his judgment concerning what is and what is not human, or he tacitly assumes that a human's value or worth is properly determined by another's feelings toward him. In order to see how these causes have been operative in determining abortion advocates' errors, we must briefly reconsider the various pro-abortion arguments discussed above.

Those who defend abortion by trying to show that "human" is ordinarily used in such a way that it excludes prenatal beings from its extension, obviously believe that fetal organisms are non-human. Yet, all of their attempts to specify the proper use of "human" fail. If consciousness is taken as the touchstone for humanity, persons in a coma may be killed. If abortion is warranted because the fertilized ovum is not "viable," then one may kill all those persons being kept alive on heart-lung machines. And so it goes. The failures are legion, but proponents of lexical definition remain undaunted. They "know" that fetuses are not human, and so they continue seeking linguistic support for their views, despite constant frustration. Now how can this be explained? Given our analysis of "conception," we know that the elusive definition they seek will never be found. If their position cannot be given factual support, then, the only possible explanation for the abortion advocate's unwavering belief in the non-human status of fetal organisms is that this view is founded, not upon reason or fact at all, but rather upon emotively distorted "fact." Simply put, proponents of lexical definition cannot bring themselves to *feel* that prenatal beings are human. No empathy, no identification, no sympathy for such beings is present; hence, this "developing tissue" is considered by them to be non-human and without the right to life.

Aside from the above, there is another fact which operates in favor of our view. That is, if our identification hypothesis is accepted, not only are we able to explain why proponents of lexical definition persist in their efforts despite repeated failure, we can also explain why it is that different abortion advocates have favored different definitions of "human." Those who identify with thinking organisms opt for a definition of terms of sentience or rationality. Those who empathize with beings who look human hold out for a definition in terms of some specific form, etc. In each case, however, the abortion advocate is guilty of confusing the *reason* he has for *feeling* that the term "human" may be applied to a certain being, with the *meaning* of the term itself. But these pro-abortionists should not be judged too harshly; others have fallen victim to the same error. Is it at all surprising, for instance, that the ancient Greeks, enamored of reason, found man's essence in his rationality? And why is it that doctors speak of viability, while anthropologists stress the importance of tool making, family organization, and cultural forms? Why is it not the other way around?

As we have seen, the main problem faced by those defenders of abortion who are proponents of arbitrary definition is to show that their "justification" of abortion cannot be extended so as to make legitimate acts which are commonly recognized as immoral. In order to avoid this trap, then, these pro-abortionists have argued that arbitrary non-human classification should be permitted only in the case of prenatal beings. Try as they will, however, no proponent of arbitrary definition has ever been able to give a reasoned defense of this view. But if this is the case, one can only wonder why it is that fetal organisms alone have been selected for "special" treatment. Accepting our identification hypothesis, a ready answer presents itself: proponents of arbitrary definition believe that fetuses alone should be classified as non-human, because they cannot help but *feel* that these beings really fall outside the class of things we call human. In short, pro-abortionists of this sort are not truly advocates of arbitrary definition at all; rather, they are continually assuming that one's classificatory status is properly determined by another's feelings toward him. And if this is so, there is no significant difference between the so-called arbitrary definition defenses of abortion, and those which attempt to argue from some ordinary use of "human."

The reasoning of Professor Thomson, as well as the arguments of those who seek to distinguish between "human" and "human person," reflect a second way in which pro-abortionists have allowed their passions to affect their moral judgments. In both these cases, the abortion advocates admit (at least tacitly) that fetuses are humans possessed of the right to life. Still, they hold, this right may be "negated" when it comes into conflict with some personal right— say, an individual's right to control her body. But we ordinarily do not think in this way (e.g., we do not believe that a human may be killed simply because his existence gives someone else great psychological pain.) What, then, can be the process whereby these proponents of abortion arrive at their extreme conclusion? Surely the answer is clear: because they identify or empathize with a suffering mother-to-be, and not with the unconscious fetus within her, these defenders of abortion feel that the former is more valuable or important than the latter. Thus, whenever the rights of the two beings conflict, the mother's rights are held to "supersede" those of her child. If added evidence is needed for the truth of this hypothesis, it may be found simply by contrasting Thomson's violinist example with my case of the shipwrecked sailor. If this is done, it readily becomes apparent that the only difference between the two examples is that, in the latter case, the locus of sympathy has been shifted from the person whose body is being used to the one who is doing the using.[18]

---

[18] Although there are numerous other facts supporting my identification hypothesis, most cannot be discussed in an essay of this length. There is one, however, which does bear mentioning. That is, accepting our thesis, one can explain why it is that certain "extremist" members of the feminist movement are virtually alone in defending abortion on demand. Most abortion advocates do not favor this view because they find themselves able to identify with developed fetal organisms—e.g., seven-month-old fetuses hear sounds, move, hiccup, suck their thumbs, etc., and are thus thought to be human (they are often referred to as "unborn children," for instance). On the other hand, zealous

III

If the considerations argued for in the first three sections of this work are accepted, certain conclusions seem mandated. First, having uncovered the real reasons for the abortion advocates' belief, we must now reject that position as being without proper support. Surely no one will deny that it is essential to morality that our emotions be allowed to have some influence upon our determinations of right and wrong. But admitting this, it is equally true that in seeking to discriminate between right and wrong, one's passions should never be allowed to enter into his determinations of matters of fact. This kind of "method" for resolving ethical disputes has been used in the past; and invariably, the conclusions reached were anything but moral. When African blacks were enslaved and American Indians exterminated, for example, the justifications given for these actions were twofold: either these beings were said to be not fully human (savages), or they were held to be of little worth (uncivilized beings whose rights were able to be "superseded" whenever they came into conflict with our "more enlightened and worthy" desires). If Americans and Europeans found this kind of reasoning appealing, however, it was only because they could not identify with the life-styles of the beings in question. And when this lack of identification was coupled with the desire to exploit, the morality of slavery and Indian killing was assured. Today, the same kind of thing appears to be happening in the minds of abortion advocates. Of course, there is a difference in that those who defend abortion desire to help rather than to exploit some group. Still, the fact that these people operate from praiseworthy motives does nothing to guarantee the morality of their conclusions. And insofar as proponents of abortion allow their inability to sympathize with a prenatal human being support their desire to kill it, they are just as mistaken in their reasoning as were those who earlier argued for slavery or Indian killing.

Second, because our analysis focuses upon "conception" rather than "human," the objectivity of our determination of the facts is guaranteed. As we have seen, "human" is an "emotionally charged" term, and it may well be that its proper use will forever remain a subject of dispute. "Conception," however, does not suffer from this difficulty; and in discussing its various uses, we need not worry that our subjective biases have influenced our view of the facts. Indeed, because it is true that we cannot identify with fertilized ova, the objectivity of our analysis is put beyond doubt. That is, with the possible exception of those who blindly defend Catholic dogma (and as against these a modified version of my argument could easily be directed) no one can really *feel* that zygotes are human. Then too, we all empathize with suffering mothers-to-

---

devotion to their "cause" so biases some feminists that they find it impossible to emphatize even with the most developed fetal beings.

be. If we were not bound by reason to do otherwise, then, our desires would incline us to defend abortion—at least abortion performed in the first trimester of pregnancy. What better guarantee of objectivity could we have?

Third, given that we have a full and complete demonstration of the fact that human life begins at conception, there is no escaping the conclusion that abortion can be justified only when the circumstances are such that we would think it proper to take the life of a human being. Now we have allowed that there is one such case, namely, abortion must be permitted whenever the continuation of pregnancy would put in danger the lives of both the mother and her fetus. Could a case be made for the morality of abortion in any other instance? Certainly there is nothing in the abortion advocates' arguments which would incline us to believe so. Further, Professor Baruch Brody has argued convincingly that it would be morally wrong to perform an abortion, even if it were necessary to save the life of the mother.[19] And if this is true, how could any of the weaker defenses succeed? But apart from these specific claims, there are more general considerations which lead us to the same conclusion. That is, whether we like it or not, the fetus is a human being of a special kind. Because he is human, he has all human rights; yet, because he can intend no action, it makes no sense to say that he has any of the duties or obligations possessed by the rest of us. He is much like a newborn baby, unconscious since birth, and kept in isolation from everyone save his mother. How could one hope to argue for the morality of killing such a being? True, there are some instances in which a mother who killed such a baby could hope to be excused (e.g., the infant had a disease which, though it caused the baby no harm, would kill the mother if she contracted it). But even here, no argument could be made for the view that the mother who killed such a child would have acted in a morally right way.

Finally, if it is true that there is no rational or factual basis upon which one can construct a sound defense of abortion, it is also true that the strength of our emotions cannot be denied. For example, what man can honestly say that he would attempt to stop his wife from having an abortion if it were clear that she would die or become psychotic given the continuation of her pregnancy? In cases such as these we are caught in a real moral dilemma: reason tells us one thing, the passions another. And even if one cannot agree that the passions should rule reason in deciding moral issues, he must acknowledge that (in the case of abortion at least), the emotions *do* rule. Apparently some opponents of abortion have realized this. Attempting to combat the emotions' force, then, they ask their readers to empathize with the fetus—to "feel" its desire for life.[20]

---

[19] B. Brody, "Abortion and the Sanctity of Human Life," *American Philosophical Quarterly*, Vol. X (1973).

[20] Germain Grisez, *Abortion: The Myths, The Realities, and the Arguments* (New York: 1970), pp. 277–287.

But all such injunctions fall on deaf ears, for it is simply impossible for a normal person to identify with a zygote or embryo. If this is granted, however, what possible hope is there for fostering moral conduct? Unless I am mistaken, the anti-abortionist has only one choice: he must find some way of convincing women that abortion is both undesirable and unnecessary. Can this be done? In order to support the belief that it can, I now wish to offer for consideration a general set of guidelines which, though admittedly incomplete and sketchy, do offer some hope for escape from the dilemma of abortion.

First, before any substantive changes can be affected, abortion advocates must be made to see that their moral judgment rests upon an emotionally distorted view of the facts; for unless this is done, there will be no impetus for change. After all, why should proponents of abortion not rest content with the *status quo*? They feel that their position is morally right, and now the law allows that it is legally right. If anything at all is to get done, then, these people must be made to see that abortion presents us with a moral dilemma of sorts—one in which we cannot help but *feel* that the immoral course of action is right, and the moral course of action wrong.

Once people are educated to the point that their desire to be rational will (hopefully) cause them to want to avoid the abortion dilemma, action on several fronts is possible. If the statistics are to be believed, most women who seek abortions do so because they find themselves with unwanted pregnancies.[21] And women who have unwanted pregnancies turn to abortion for one or more of the following three reasons: (1) The woman is unmarried, the child is illegitimate, and the mother wants to avoid showing her "sin" to society. (2) The woman (especially the married woman) would agree to have the child and give it up for adoption, except that there is a social stigma attached to such action. And (3), the mother simply does not want to put up with pregnancy and childbirth. Given these as the primary causes for abortion, then, anti-abortion action along the following lines would seem to be indicated:

1. If it is true that we today consider illegitimacy a "sin," it need not be so. In certain Scandinavian countries, for example, illegitimacy is not frowned upon as it is here. And if our attitudes could be so modified, one of the prime motivations women now have for seeking abortions would be undercut. Indeed, if people could only be made aware of the fact that abortion is the killing of a human being, more should be able to be accomplished than a simple change in attitude concerning illegitimacy. The unwed mother who elected to carry her child to term could become a person of respect—one to whom praise was due. After all, for the sake of another human being, this woman is putting her life on the line. Why not praise her? Surely changes of this sort are not impos.ible. And

[21] Callahan, *op. cit.*, pp. 292–294.

if the Catholic Church is sincere in its opposition to abortion, it should do its utmost to see that they *do* come about.

2. If our attitudes concerning illegitimacy can be changed, so too can our feelings toward a mother who "gives away" her child. What better expression of motherly love could there be than to give up one's baby for adoption when it was apparent that such a course of action was in the best interest of the child? Is abortion a more moral course? Is is better to keep the child out of some sense of duty, and thereby condemn it to a life without love or proper care? Surely we cannot believe so. In fact, a mother who follows either of the latter two courses must be operating out of self-interest and not love. And if people could only be made to realize this, another of the major reasons women have for seeking abortions would be nullified.

3. Some women, it is true, simply do not want to suffer through pregnancy and childbirth. And where this is the case, our hope lies, not in changing social attitudes, but in doing our best to advance scientific research. At present, the process is being developed whereby a fertilized egg can be transplanted from one woman's womb into another's. If this procedure could be perfected so that it was both successful and relatively inexpensive, women—all women—would have a viable alternative to abortion.[22] Instead of abortion clinics, we could have transplant clinics. Women who wanted children could register, just as they now register for adoption; and when the need arose, they could be called up for service. Now what could be the objections to such a procedure?[23] Certainly the formation of transplant clinics would raise various new moral and legal problems. But could the new moral problems be as grave as those we now face in abortion? And why could we not simply look upon transplantation as early adoption, thus minimizing the need for new legislation? Of course, there are also practical matters to be considered. Before uterine transplants could be used, for example, it would have to be shown that the procedure was safe, not only for the transplanted egg, but also for both the women involved. But if we are willing to spend the money for research, such safety could be secured. There remains, then, the matter of cost. How expensive would such an operation be? Frankly, I do not know. But it need not be as inexpensive as an abortion, for the cost could be split between the donor and donee. Also, why should it not be possible to

---

[22] There is one possible exception to this statement. If a woman wanted an abortion because she knew that her child would be born deformed, it is almost certain that she would find no one willing to be a transplant recipient. The only way we can rid ourselves of abortions sought on these grounds, then, is to find the causes of birth defects and eradicate them.

[23] For my defense of the view that experimentation to develop interuterine transplantation is morally proper see: J. Humber, "Abortion, Fetal Research, and the Law," *Social Theory and Practice*, Vol. 4 (Spring, 1977).

obtain a small federal subsidy for such procedures? All in all, there appears to be nothing which would make it impossible in principle for uterine transplants to serve as an alternative to abortion.

Although the above three changes seem to hold out the most hope of success for the anti-abortionist, action along other lines would also be efficacious. First, a concerted effort should be made to overcome the Catholic Church's ridiculous opposition to birth control.[24] And second, those who are sincere in their opposition to abortion should do their utmost to make sex education mandatory in the schools. And perhaps a "refresher" course could be required for all those wishing to take out a marriage license. Further, pressure should be brought to bear for the development of more effective male contraceptives. Work is currently being done in this area—a pill is being developed—but the more procedures the better.

I harbor no illusions concerning the difficulties involved in getting something like the above program put into effect. Yet, it does provide hope. Indeed, if only the process of uterine transplants could be perfected, the possibility of eradicating abortion would be much increased. If women knew that there was a viable alternative to abortion, they would find it much easier to follow the dictates of reason. And if this state of affairs ever came into being, the time *would* be right for opponents of abortion to press for legal change. Of course, whether this point will ever be reached is doubtful. But even if there are good grounds for pessimism, we must try to bring about the needed changes. After all, there are human lives at stake.

---

[24] I cannot use this forum to argue for the view that the Catholic Church's position on birth control is "ridiculous." I see no escape from this conclusion, however, and hold that except for those devices which operate as abortive mechanisms (e.g., intra-uterine devices), all contraceptive procedures should be condoned.

FURTHER READINGS

Bibliographies

Clouser, Danner K. (with Arthur Zucker). *Abortion and Euthanasia: An Annotated Bibliography*. Philadelphia: Society for Health and Human Values; 1974.

Dollen, Charles. *Abortion in Context: A Select Bibliography*. Metuchen, N.J.: Scarecrow Press, 1970.

Floyd, Mary K., comp. *Abortion Bibliography for 1970*. Troy, N.Y.: Whitston, 1972.

——. *Abortion Bibliography for 1971*. Troy, N.Y.: Whitston, 1973.

——. *Abortion Bibliography for 1972*. Troy, N.Y.: Whitston, 1973.

——. *Abortion Bibliography for 1973*. Troy, N.Y.: Whitston, 1974.

——. *Abortion Bibliography for 1974*. Troy, N.Y.: Whitston, 1975.

——. *Abortion Bibliography for 1975*. Troy, N.Y.: Whitston, 1976.

Pinson, William M. *Resource Guide to Current Social Issues*. Waco, Tex.: Word Books, 1968.

Sollito, Sharmon, and Veatch, Robert M., comps. *Bibliography of Society, Ethics and the Life Sciences*. Hastings-on-Hudson, N.Y.: Institute of Society, Ethics and the Life Sciences, 1974–1977.

Walters, LeRoy, ed. *Bibliography of Bioethics*. Vols. 1– , Detroit: Gale Research Co. Issued annually.

Woytcichovsky, Stephen. *Ethical-Social-Legal Annotated Bibliography of English Language Studies on Abortion* (1967–1972). Toronto: Toronto Institute of Public Communications, 1973.

Books

Bajema, Clifford. *Abortion and the Meaning of Personhood*. Grand Rapids, Mich.: Baker Book House, 1974.

Brody, Baruch. *Abortion and the Sanctity of Human Life: A Philosophical View*. Cambridge, Mass.: MIT Press, 1975.

Callahan, Daniel. *Abortion: Law, Choice, and Morality*. New York: Macmillan, 1970.

Chartier, Michel. *Avortement et respect de la vie humaine*. Paris: Editions du Sueil, 1972.

Cohen, Marshall, Nagel, Thomas, and Scanlon, Thomas, eds. *The Rights and Wrongs of Abortion*. Princeton: Princeton University Press, 1974.

Committee on Psychiatry and Law of the Group for the Advancement of Psychiatry. *The Right to Abortion: A Psychiatric View*. New York: Charles Scribners, 1970.

Connery, John. *Abortion: The Development of the Roman Catholic Perspective*. Chicago: Loyola University Press, 1977.

Cooke, Robert E. *The Terrible Choice: The Abortion Dilemma*. New York: Bantam Books, 1968.

Curran, Charles E. *Contraception: Authority and Dissent*. New York: Herder and Herder, 1969.

Cutler, Donald R. *Updating Life and Death: Essays in Ethics and Medicine*. Boston: Beacon Press, 1969.

Dedek, J. F. *Human Life: Some Moral Issues*. New York: Sheed & Ward, 1972.

Ebon, Martin. *Every Woman's Guide to Abortion*. New York: Universe Books, 1971.

Eisenberg, John, and Borne, Paula. *The Right to Live and Die*. Toronto: Ontario Institute for Studies in Education, 1973.

Falik, Marilyn M. *Ideology and Abortion Policy Politics*. Ann Arbor: University Microfilms, 1975.

Feinberg, Joel, ed. *The Problem of Abortion*. Belmont, Calif.: Wadsworth, 1973.

Feldman, David M. *Birth Control in Jewish Law*. New York: University Press, 1968.

Finnis, John, *et al. The Rights and Wrongs of Abortion*. Princeton: Princeton University Press, 1974.

Fletcher, Joseph. *Morals and Medicine*. Boston: Beacon Press, 1960.

Frazier, Claude A. *Should Doctors Play God?* Nashville: Broadman Press, 1971.

Galbally, J. *The Right to Be Born*. Melbourne: A.C.T.S. Publications, 1970.

Granfield, David. *The Abortion Decision*. New York: Doubleday, 1969.

Greenwell, James R. *The Morality of Abortion*. Ann Arbor: University Microfilms, 1975.

Grisez, Germain G. *Abortion: The Myths, the Realities and Arguments*. New York: Corpus Books, 1970.

Guttmacher, Alan Frank. *The Case for Legalized Abortion Now*. Berkeley, Calif.: Diablo Press, 1967.

Hall, Robert E. *Abortion in a Changing World*, two volumes. New York: Columbia University Press, 1970.

Hanink, James G. *Persons, Rights and the Problem of Abortion*. Ann Arbor: University Microfilms, 1975.

Hilgers, T., and Horan, D. J., eds. *Abortion and Social Justice*. New York: Sheed and Ward, 1973.

Horden, Anthony. *Legal Abortion: The English Experience*. Oxford: Pergamon Press, 1971.

Joyce, Robert E., and Rosera, Mary. *Let Us Be Born: The Inhumanity of Abortion*. Chicago: Franciscan Herald Press, 1970.

Klotz, John W. *A Christian View of Abortion*. St. Louis: Concordia, 1973.

Kummer, Jerome M. *Legal and Illegal: A Dialogue between Attorneys and Psychiatrists*, second edition. Santa Monica: J. M. Kummer, 1969.

Labby, Daniel H. *Life or Death, Ethics and Options*. Seattle: University of Washington Press, 1968.

Lader, Lawrence. *Abortion*. Indianapolis: Bobbs-Merrill, 1966.

——. *Abortion II: Revolution in the Making*. Boston: Beacon Press, 1973.

Lee, Nancy Howell. *The Search for an Abortionist*. Chicago: University of Chicago Press, 1969.

Lowe, David. *Abortion and the Law*. New York: Pocket Books, 1966.

McFadden, C. J. *Medical Ethics*. London: F.A. Davis, 1962.

Mondrone, Demenico. *Mamma, Why Did You Kill Us?*, Translated by Dino Soria. Baltimore: 1970.

Monsma, John Clover. *Religion and Birth Control*. New York: Doubleday, 1963.

Noonan, John T., Jr. *The Morality of Abortion: Legal and Historical Perspectives*. Cambridge: Harvard University Press, 1970.

Osofsky, Howard, and Osofsky, Joy D. *The Abortion Experience: Psychological and Medical Impact*. Hagerstown, Md.: Medical Department, Harper & Row, 1973.

Perkins, Robert L. *Abortion: Pro and Con*. Cambridge: Schenkman Publishing Co., 1974.

Rachels, James. *Moral Problems*. New York: Harper & Row, 1971.

Ransil, Bernard Jerome. *Abortion*. Paramus, N.J.: Paulist Press, 1969.

Rosen, Harold. *Abortion in America*. Originally published as *Therapeutic Abortion*. Boston: Beacon Press, 1967.

Sarvis, Betty, and Rodman, Hyman. *The Abortion Controversy*. New York: Columbia University Press, 1973.

Schulder, Diane, and Kenndy, Florynce. *Abortion Rap—Shirley Chisholm, Member of Congress*. New York: McGraw-Hill, 1971.

Schur, Edwin M. *Crimes Without Victims: Deviant Behavior and Public Policy: Abortion, Homosexuality, Drug Addiction*. Englewood Cliffs, N.J.: Prentice-Hall, 1965.

Shaw, Russel B. *Abortion on Trial*. London: Hale, 1969.

Smith, David T. *Abortion and the Law*. Cleveland: Western Reserve University, 1967.

Spitzer, Walter A., and Saylor, Caryle. *Symposium on the Control of Human Reproduction*. Wheaton, Ill.: Tyndale House, 1969.

St. John-Stevas, N. *The Right to Life*. London: Hodder and Soughton, 1963.

Tarnesby, Herman Peter. *Abortion Explained*. London: Sphere Books, 1969.

Walter, David F., and Butler, Douglas J., eds. *Abortion, Society and the Law.* Cleveland: The Press of Case Western Reserve University, 1973.

Williams, Glanville. *The Sanctity of Life and Criminal Law.* New York: Knopf, 1968.

Wynn, Margaret, and Wynn, Arthur. *Some Consequences of Induced Abortion to Children Born Subsequently.* London: Foundation for Education and Research in Childbearing, 1972.

Wittgenstein, Ludwig. *Philosophical Investigation*, Translated by G.E.M. Anscombe. New York: Macmillan, 1953.

Articles

Alpern, David M. "Abortion and the Law." *Newsweek* 85 (3 March, 1975): 18-19.

Anderson, Stephen G. "Abortion and the Husband's Consent." *Journal of Family Law* 13 (1973-1974): 311-331.

Annas, George T. "Abortion and the Supreme Court: Round Two." *Hastings Center Report* 6 (October 1976): 15-17.

"A Review of State Abortion Laws Enacted Since January 1973." *Family Planning Population Reporter* 4 (December 1975): 108-113.

Atkinson, Gary M. "The Morality of Abortion." *International Philosophical Quarterly* 14 (September 1974): 347-362.

Becker, Lawrence C. "Human Being: The Boundaries of the Concept." *Philosophy and Public Affairs* 4 (Summer 1975): 334-359.

Beinaert, Louis. "L' avortement est-il infanticide." *Etudes*, 337 (1970): 547-561.

Bennett, J. "Whatever the Consequences." *Analysis* 26 (1966): 83-102.

Blake, Judith, "Abortion and Public Opinion: The 1960-1970 Decade." *Science* 171 (1971): 540-549.

Blackwood, Rich, and Blackwood, Robin. "What Are the Father's Rights in Abortion." *Journal of Legal Medicine* 3 (October 1975): 28-36.

Bluford, Robert, and Peters, Robert E. "The Medical and Moral Aspects of Abortion." In *Unwanted Pregnancy: The Medical and Ethical Implications.* New York: Harper & Row, 1973.

Bok, Sissela. "Ethical Problems of Abortion." *Hastings Center Studies* 2 (January 1974): 33-52.

———. "Who Shall Count as a Human Being? A Treacherous Question in the Abortion Discussion." In *Abortion: Pro and Con*, edited by Robert L. Perkins. Cambridge, Mass.: Schenkman, 1974, pp. 91-105.

———. "The Unwanted Child: Caring for the Fetus Born Alive after an Abortion." *Hastings Center Report* 6 (October 1976): 10-11.

———. "Ethical Problems of Abortion." In *Raising Children in Modern Urban America*, edited by Nathan Talbot, M.D. Boston: Little, Brown, 1976.

———. "The Leading Edge of the Wedge." *The Hastings Center Report* 3 (1971): 9-11.

Brandt, Richard B. "The Morality of Abortion." In *Biomedical Ethics and the Law*, 1st ed., edited by James M. Humber and Robert F. Almeder. New York: Plenum Press, 1976, pp. 50-70.

———. "The Morality of Abortion." *The Monist* 56 (1972): 504-526.

Brockway, Allan R. "Abortion: A Misplaced Debate." *Engage/Social Action* 2 (February 1974): 33-47.

Brody, B. A. "Abortion and the Law." *Philosophy Journal* 68 (1971): 357-369.

———. "Abortion and the Sanctity of Human Life." *American Philosophical Quarterly* 10 (1973): 133-140.

———. "Thomson on Abortion." *Philosophy and Public Affairs* 1 (1972): 335-340.

Brody, Baruch. "On the Humanity of the Fetus." In *Abortion: Pro and Con*, edited by Robert L. Perkins. Cambridge, Mass.: Schenkman, 1974, pp. 69-90.

———. "Fetal Humanity and the Theory of Essentialism." In *Philosophy and Sex*, edited by Robert Baker and Frederick Elliston. Buffalo: Prometheus Books, 1975.

———. "Abortion: For Whose Sake?" *Hastings Center Report* 6 (August, 1976): 31-32.

Brown, Harold O. "What the Supreme Court Didn't Know: Ancient and Early Christian Views on Abortion." *Human Life Review* 1 (Spring 1975): 5-21.

Budner, Stanley. "Value Conflicts and the Uses of Research: The Example of Abortion." *Man and Medicine: The Journal of Values and Ethics in Health Care* 1 (Autumn 1975): 42-49.

Buss, M. J. "Beginnings of Human Life as an Ethical Problem." *Journal of Religion* 47 (1967): 244-255.

Byrn, Robert M. "The Abortion Amendments: Policy in the Light of Precedent." *St. Louis University Law Journal* 18 (Spring 1974): 380-406.

———. Goodbye to the Judeo Christian Era in Law." *America* 128 (2 June, 1973): 511-514.

Callahan, Daniel. "Abortion: A Summary of the Arguments." In *Aspects of Population Growth Policy*, edited by Robert Parke and Charles F. Westoff. Washington: U.S. Government Printing Office, 1973, pp. 249-259.

———. "Abortion: Thinking and Experiencing." *Christianity and Crisis* 32 (8 January, 1973): 295-298.

———. "Abortion: Some Ethical Issues." In *Abortion, Society and the Law*, edited by David F. Walbert and J. Douglas Butler. Cleveland: Case Western Reserve University Press, 1973, pp. 89-101.

———. "The Sanctity of Life." In *Updating Life and Death: Essays in Ethics and Medicine*, edited by Donald Cutler. Boston: Beacon Press, 1969.

———. "Contraception and Abortion: American Catholic Response." *Annals of the American Academy of Political and Social Science* 387 (1970): 109-117.

Callahan, Sidney. "The Court and a Conflict of Principles." *Hastings Center Report* 7 (Aug. 1977): 7-8.

Camenisch, Paul F. "Abortion for the Fetus's Own Sake?" *Hastings Center Report* 6 (April 1976): 38-41.

Capron, Alexander M. "Legal Issues in Foetal Diagnosis and Abortion." In *Genetics and the Quality of Life*, edited by Charles Birch and Paul Abrecht. Elmsford, N.Y.: Pergamon Press, 1975, pp. 120-129.

Childress, James F. "A Response to Ronald Green: 'Confered Rights and the Fetus.'" *Journal of Religious Ethics* 2 (Spring 1974): 77-83.

Clouser, Danner K. "Abortion, Classification, and Competing Rights." *Christian Century* (1971): 626-628.

———. "The Sanctity of Life: An Analysis of a Concept." *Annals of Internal Medicine* (1973): 119-125.

Coffey, Patrick J. "Toward a Sound Moral Policy on Abortion." *New Scholasticism* 47 (1973): 105-112.

Coriden, James A. "Church Law and Abortion." *Jurist* 33 (Spring 1973): 184-198.

Currier, L. S. "Abortion and the Right to Life." *Social Theory and Practice* (Fall 1975): 381-401.

Dellums, Ronald V. "Public Supports Right to Abortion." *Congressional Record* (Daily Edition) 120 (23 Jan. 1974): E93-E101.

DeMarco, Donald. "Abortion: Legal and Philosophical Considerations." *American Ecclesiastical Review* 168 (April 1974): 251-267.

———. "The Philosophical Roots in Western Culture for the Pro-Abortion Stand." *Linacre Quarterly* 41 (May 1974): 87-99.

Destro, Robert A. "Abortion and the Constitution: The Need for a Life-Protective Amendment." *California Law Review* 63 (Sept. 1975): 1250-1351.

Diamond, James J. "Pro-Life Amendments and Due Process." *America* 130 (19 Jan. 1974): 27-29.

Di Ianni, Albert R. "Is the Fetus a Person?" *American Ecclesiastical Review* 168 (May 1974): 309-326.

Donceel, Joseph. "Abortion: Mediate and Immediate Animation." *Continuum* 5 (1969): 167-171.

Drinan, Robert F. "The Inviolability of the Right to Be Born." In *Abortion, Society and the Law*, edited by David F. Walbert and J. Douglas Butler. Cleveland: Case Western Reserve University Press, 1973.

Dumas, Andre. "An Ethical View of Abortion." In *Genetics and the Quality of*

Life, edited by Charles Birch and Paul Abrecht. New York: Pergamon Press, 1975, pp. 92-108.

Dupre, Louis. "A New Approach to the Abortion Problem." *Theological Studies* 34 (Sept. 1973): 481-488.

Dyck, Henry. "Perplexities of the Would-Be Liberal in Abortion." *Journal of Reproductive Medicine* 8 (1972): 351-354.

Engelhardt, H. Tristram. "Bioethics and the Process of Embodiement." *Perspectives in Biology and Medicine* 18 (Summer 1975): 486-500.

———. "Viability, Abortion and the Difference between a Fetus and an Infant." *American Journal of Obstetrics and Gynecology* 116 (1 June 1973): 429-434.

———. "The Ontology of Abortion." *Ethics* 84 (April 1974): 217-234.

English, Jane. "Abortion and the Concept of a Person." *Canadian Journal of Philosophy* 5 (Oct. 1975): 233-243.

Finnis, John. "The Rights and Wrongs of Abortion: A Reply to Judith Thomson." *Philosophy and Public Affairs* 2 (Winter 1973): 117-145.

———. "Three Schemes of Regulations." In *The Morality of Abortion*, edited by John T. Noonan, Jr. Cambridge: Harvard University Press, 1970.

Fletcher, Joseph. "Four Indicators of Humanhood: The Enquiry Matures." *Hastings Center Report* 4 (Dec. 1974): 4-7.

———. "Medicine and the Nature of Man." In *The Teaching of Medical Ethics*, edited by Robert M. Veatch, Willard Gaylin, and Councilman Morgan. Hastings-on-Hudson, N.Y.: Institute of Society, Ethics and the Life Sciences, 1973, pp. 47-58.

———. "Abortion and the True Believer: Private Opinions Should Not Be Imposed by Law." *Christian Century* 91 (27 Nov. 1974): 1126-1127.

Foot, Philippa. "The Problem of Abortion and the Doctrine of the Double Effect." *Oxford Review* 5 (1967): 5-15.

Forman, Howard M. "*Doe* v. *Doe:* The Wife's Right to an Abortion over Her Husband's Objections." *New England Law Review* 11 (Fall 1975): 205-224.

Fortman, Stephen P. "Abortion and Medicine." *Pharos* 38 (Jan. 1975): 25-29.

Fost, Norman. "Our Curious Attitude toward the Fetus." *Hastings Center Report* 4 (Feb. 1974): 4-5.

Freeman, Harrop A. "Population Control and Abortion." *Santa Clara Lawyer* 13 (Summer 1973): 698-719.

Friedman, Theodore. "Conflicting Rights and Human Life." In *Rights in the Light of Scientific and Technological Progress in Biology and Medicine*, edited by Simon Btesh. Geneva: World Health Organization, 1974, pp. 160-180.

Gaffney, James. "Respect for Life: The Abortion Controversy." In his *Moral Questions*, New York: Paulist Press, 1974, pp. 28-38.

Gardner, E. Clinton. "The Public Regulation of Abortion." In *The Population*

Crisis and Moral Responsibility, edited by Philip J. Wogaman. Washington: Public Affairs Press, 1973, pp. 274-291.

———. "The Sacredness of All Human Life." *Engage/Social Action* 2 (Feb. 1974): 15-28.

Gardner, R. F. R. "A New Ethical Approach to Abortion and Its Implications for the Euthanasia Dispute." *Journal of Medical Ethics* 1 (Sept. 1975): 127-131.

Geddes, Leonard. "On the Intrinsic Wrongness of Killing Innocent People." *Analysis* 33 (Jan. 1973): 93-97.

George, B. James. "The Evolving Law of Abortion." In *Abortion, Society and the Law*, edited by David F. Walbert and J. Douglas Butler. Cleveland: Case Western Reserve University Press, 1973, pp. 3-62.

Gerber, D. "Abortion: The Uptake Argument." *Ethics* 83 (1972): 80-83.

Gerber, Rudof, J. "Abortion: Parameters for Decision." *International Philosophical Quarterly* 11 (1971): 561-584.

Gillespie, Norman C. "Abortion and Human Rights." *Ethics* 87 (April 1977): 237-243.

Glenn, Gary D. "Abortion and Inalienable Rights in Classical Liberalism." *American Journal of Jurisprudence* 20 (1975): 62-80.

Glenn, H. Patrick. "The Constitutional Validity of Abortion Legislation: A Comparative Note." *McGill Law Journal* 21 (Winter 1975): 673-684.

Goldenberg, David. "The Right to Abortion: Expansion of the Right to Privacy through the Fourteenth Amendment." *Catholic Lawyer* 19 (Winter 1973): 36-57.

Graves, Frances A. "Abortion: For Whose Sake?" *Hastings Center Report* 6 (August 1976): 31.

Green, Ronald M. "Conferred Rights and the Fetus." *Journal of Religious Ethics* 2 (Spring 1974): 55-75.

Greenwell, James R. "Abortion and Moral Safety." *Critics* 9 (December 1977): 35-48.

———. "Catholic Inconsistency on Intentional Killing." *Humanist* 36 (January-February 1976): 20-23.

Grisez, Germain G. "Toward a Consistent Natural Law Ethics of Killing." *American Journal of Jurisprudence* 15 (1970): 64-96.

Gustafson, James W. "A Protestant Ethical Approach." In *The Morality of Abortion*, edited by John T. Noonan, Jr. Cambridge: Harvard University Press, 1970.

Guttmacher, A. F., and Pilpee, H. F. "Abortion and the Unwanted Child." *Family Planning Perspectives* 2 (1970): 16-24.

Guttmacher, Alan F. "A Defense of the Supreme Court's Abortion Decision." *Humanist* 33 (May-June 1973): 6-7.

Hardin, G. "Abortion or Compulsory Pregnancy." *Marriage and the Family* 30 (1968): 246-251.

Hardon, John A. "Euthanasia and Abortion: A Catholic View." *Human Life Review* 1 (Fall 1975): 88-100.

Hare, R. M. "Abortion and the Golden Rule." *Philosophy and Public Affairs* 4 (Spring 1975): 201-222.

Haring, Bernard. "A Theological Evaluation." *The Morality of Abortion*, edited by John T. Noonan, Jr. Cambridge: Harvard University Press, 1970, pp. 123-145.

Harrison, Stanley M. "The Supreme Court and Abortional Reform: Means to an End." *New York Law Forum* 19 (Winter 1974): 685-701.

Heer, D. M. "Abortion, Contraception, and Population Policy in the Soviet Union." *Soviet Studies* 17 (1965): 76-83.

Hellegers, Andre E. "Fetal Development." In *Contemporary Issues in Bioethics*. edited by Tom L. Beaychamp and LeRoy Walters. Encino, California: Dickenson Publishing Co., 1978, pp. 194-198.

———. "Abortion: 'Another Form of Birth Control'?" *Human Life Review* 1 (Winter 1975): 21-25.

Helms, Jesse. "Statement on the Rights to Life Amendment." *Congressional Record* (Daily Edition) 119 (23 January, 1973).

Herbenick, Raymond M. "Remarks on Abortion, Abandonment, and Adoption Opportunities." *Philosophy and Public Affairs* 5 (Fall 1975): 98-104.

Humber, James. "Abortion: The Avoidable Moral Dilemma." *The Journal of Value Inquiry* 9 (1975): 282-303.

———. "The Case against Abortion." *The Thomist* 39 (1975): 65-84.

Humber, James M. "Abortion, Fetal Research and the Law." *Social Theory and Practice* 4 (Spring 1977): 127-147.

Ingram, I. M. "Abortion Games: An Inquiry into the Working of the Act." *The Lancet* (1971): 969-970.

Jaggar, Alison. "Abortion and a Woman's Right to Decide." *Philosophical Forum* 5 (Fall-Winter 1973-1974): 347-360.

Jacobivitz, Immanuel. "Jewish Views on Abortion." *Human Life Review* 1 (Winter 1975): 78-84.

Joling, Robert J. "Abortion-the Breath of Life." *Medical Trial Technique Quarterly* 21 (Fall 1974): 199-232.

Kluge, Eike-Henner W. "Abortion." In his *The Practice of Death*. New Haven: Yale University Press, 1975, pp. 1-100.

Kohl, Marvin. "Abortion and the Argument from Innocence." *Inquiry* 14 (1977): 147-151.

Koop, C. Everett. "The Right to Live." *Human Life Review* 1 (Fall 1975): 65-87.

Lappe, Marc. "The Moral Claims of the Wanted Fetus." *Hastings Center Report* 5 (April 1975): 11-13.

Leavy, Z., and Kummer, J. "Criminal Abortion: Human Hardship and Unyielding Laws." *Southern California Law Review* 35 (1962): 123-218.

Leebensohn, Zigmond M. "Abortion, Psychiatry and the Quality of Life." *American Journal of Psychiatry* 128 (1972): 946-954.

Lenhardt, Wayne A. "Abortion and Pre-Natal Injury: A Legal and Philosophical Analysis." *Western Ontario Law Review* 13 (1974): 97-123.

Levine, Robert J. "Viability and Death of the Human Fetus: Biologic Definitions." *Clinical Research* 23 (October 1975): 211-216.

Lewis, Joseph L. "Homo Sapienism: Critique of *Roe* v. *Wade* and Abortion." *Albany Law Review* 39 (1975): 856-893.

Lincoln, C. Eric. "Why I Reversed My Stand on Laissez-Faire Abortion." *Christian Century* (1973): 477-479.

Louisell, David W., and Noonan, John T., Jr. "Constitutional Balance." In *The Morality of Abortion*, edited by John T. Noonan, Jr. Cambridge: Harvard University Press, 1970, pp. 220-260.

Macaluso, Chris. "Viability and Abortion." *Kentucky Law Journal* 64 (Fall 1975): 146-164.

MacDougal, Douglas, and Nasser, Wayne P. "The Abortion Decision and Evolving Limits on State Intervention." *Hawaii Bar Journal* 11 (Fall 1975): 51-72.

Margolis, Joseph. "*Abortion.*" Ethics 84 (1973): 51-61.

———. "Abortion." In his *Negativities: The Limits of Life.* Columbus, Ohio: Charles E. Merrill, 1975. pp. 37-48.

May, William E. "Abortion and Man's Moral Being." In *Abortion: Pro and Con*, edited by Robert L. Perkins. Cambridge, Mass.: Schenkman, 1974. pp. 13-35.

———. "Abortion as Indicative of Personal and Social Identity." *Jurist* 33 (Spring 1973): 199-217.

———. "The Morality of Abortion." *Linacre Quarterly* 41 (February 1974): 66-78.

McCormick, Richard A. "Past Church Teaching on Abortion." *Proceedings of the Catholic Theological Society of America* (Yonkers, N.Y., 1968), 23: 131-151.

———. "Notes on Moral Theology." *Theological Studies* 33 (1972): 68-78.

———. "Life-Saving and Life-Taking: A Comment." *Linacre Quarterly* 42 (May 1975): 110-115.

———. "Notes on Moral Theology: The Abortion Dossier." *Theological Studies* 35 (June 1974): 312-359.

McLachlan, Hugh V. "Must We Accept Either the Conservative or the Liberal View on Abortion." *Analysis* 37 (June 1977): 197-204.

Mead, Margaret. "Rights to Life." *Christianity and Crisis* 32 (8 January, 1973): 288-292.

Mileti, D. S., and Barnett, L. D. "Nine Demographic Factors and Their Relationship toward Abortion Legalization." *Social Biology* 19 (1972): 43-50.

Moore, Elizabeth N. "Moral Sentiment in Judicial Opinions on Abortion." *Santa Clara Lawyer* 15 (Spring 1975): 591-634.

Moore, Harold F. "Abortion and the Logic of Moral Justification." *Journal of Value Inquiry* 9 (Summer 1975): 140-151.

Mulhauser, Karen. "Abortion: For Whose Sake?" *Hastings Center Report* 6 (August 1976): 32.

Myrna, Frances. "Abortion: A Philosophical Analysis." *Feminist Studies* 1 (Fall 1972): 49-62.

Nardone, Roland M. "The Nexus of Biology and the Abortion Issue." *Jurist* 33 (Spring 1973): 153-161.

Nathan, David C. "The Unwanted Child: Caring for a Fetus Born Alive after an Abortion." *Hastings Center Report* 6 (October 1976): 12-13.

Nelson, James B. "The Humanity in Abortion." In his *Human Medicine: Ethical Perspectives on New Medical Issues.* Minneapolis: Augsburg Publishing House, 1973, pp. 31-58.

Nelson, Robert J. "What Does Theology Say about Abortion?" *Christian Century* 90 (31 January, 1973): 124-128.

Newman, Jay. "An Empirical Argument against Abortion." *New Scholasticism* 51 (Summer 1977):384-395.

Newton, Lisa. "Humans and Persons: A Reply to Tristram Engelhardt." *Ethics* 85 (July 1975): 332-336.

Noonan, John T., Jr. "An Almost Absolute Value in History." *The Morality of Abortion.* Cambridge: Harvard University Press, 1970.

———. "Abortion and the Catholic Church: A Summary History." National Law Forum 12 (1967): 85-131.

———. "How to Argue about Abortion." In *Contemporary Issues in Bioethics*, edited by Tom L. Beauchamp and LeRoy Walters. Encino, Calif.: Dickenson Publishing, 1978, pp. 210-217.

———. "Responding to Persons: Methods of Moral Argument in Debate over Abortion." *Theology Digest* 21 (Winter 1973): 291-307.

Novak, David. "A Jewish View of Abortion." In his *Law and Theology in Judaism.* New York: Ktav Publishing House, 1974.

Novak, Michael. "Abortion is Not Enough." *Christian Century* 84 (1967): 430-431.

O'Conner, John. "On Humanity and Abortion." *National Law Forum* 13 (1968): 127-133.

Packwood, Robert W. "The Wisdom of the Supreme Court Decision on Abortion." *Congressional Record* (Daily Edition) 121 (11 March 1975) S3644-S3668.

Patton, Dorothy E. "*Roe* v. *Wade:* Its Impact on Rights of Choice in Human Reproduction." *Columbia Human Rights Law Review* 5 (Fall 1973): 497-521.

Perez de Aguello, Maribel. "The Abortion Polemic: A Restatement of Pros and Cons." *Revista Juridica de la Universidad de Puerto Rico* (1973): 247-276.

Pole, Nelson. "To Respect Human Life." *Philosophy in Context* 2 (1973): 16-22.

Potter, Ralph. "The Abortion Debate." *Updating Life and Death: Essays in Ethics and Medicine*, edited by Donald R. Cutler. Boston: Beacon Press, 1969.

Power, Anthony P. "Abortion and the Philosophy of Human Biology." *Australian Quarterly* 45 (June 1973): 4-17.

Prescott, James W. "Abortion or the Unwanted Child: A Choice for a Humanistic Society." *Humanist* 35 (March-April 1975): 11-15.

Pulgini, Linda M. "The Case of Abortion." *Journal of Urban Law* 52 (November 1974): 277-338.

Purdy, Laura M. "Abortion: For Whose Sake?" *Hastings Center Report* 6 (August 1976): 31.

Purdy, Laura, and Tooley, Michael. "Is Abortion Murder?" In *Abortion: Pro and Con*, edited by Robert L. Perkins. Cambridge, Mass.: Schenkman, 1974, pp. 129-149.

Quay, Eugene. "Justifiable Abortion." *Georgetown Law Journal* 49 (1961): 173-256.

Ramsey, Paul. "The Sanctity of Life." *Dublin Review* 241 (1967): 3-21.

——. "Feticide/Infanticide upon Request." *Religion in Life* 39 (1970): 170-186.

——. "Reference Points in Deciding about Abortion." In *The Morality of Abortion*, edited by John T. Noonan, Jr. Cambridge: Harvard University Press, 1970.

——. "The Morality of Abortion." *Moral Problems.* New York: Harper and Row, 1971.

——. "Abortion: A Review Article." *The Thomist* 37 (1973): 174-226.

——. "The Morality of Abortion." In *Ethics for Modern Life*, edited by Razial Abelson and Marie Louis Friguegnon, New York: St. Martin's Press, 1975.

——. "Protecting the Unborn." *Commonweal* 100 (31 May, 1974): 308-314.

Robertson, John A. "Medical Ethics in the Courtroom: The Role of Law vs. Professional Self-Discipline." *Hastings Center Report* 4 (September 1974): 1-3.

——. "After Edelin: Little Guidance." *Hastings Center Report* 7 (June 1977): 15-17.

Rosner, Fred. "The Jewish Attitude toward Abortion." *Tradition* 10 (1968): 48-71.

Rostand, Jean. "The Limit of the Human." In his *Humanly Possible: A Biologist's Notes on the Future of Mankind.* New York: Saturday Review Press, 1973, pp. 64-93.

Rubin, Eva R. "The Abortion Cases: A Study in Law and Social Change." *North Carolina Central Law Journal* 5 (Spring 1974): 215-253.

Rudinow, Joel. "On 'the Slippery Slope'." *Analysis* 43 (April 1974): 173-176.

Ryle, Edward J. "Some Sociological and Psychological Reflections on the Abortion Decisions." *Jurist* 53 (Spring 1973): 218-229.

Sauer, R. "Attitudes to Abortion in America, 1800- ." *Population Studies* 28 (March 1974): 53-67.

Schall, James V. "The 'Conditional' Right to Life." *Furrow* 26 (August 1975): 455-461.

Schulte, Eugene J. "Tax-Supported Abortions: The Legal Issues." *Catholic Lawyer* 21 (Winter 1975): 1-7.

Schultz, William L. "The Father's Right in the Abortion Decision." *Texas Tech Law Review* 6 (Spring 1975): 1075-1094.

Schwartz, Herman. "The Parent or the Fetus." *Humanist* 27 (1967): 123-126.

Schuller, Bruno. "Typen ethischer Argumentation in der katholischen Moraltheologie." *Theologie und Philosphie* 45 (1970): 526-550.

Scwartz, Richard A. "Abortion on Request: The Psychiatric Implications." In *Abortion, Society and the Law*, edited by David F. Walbert and J. Douglas Butler. Cleveland: Case Western Reserve University Press, 1973, pp. 139-178.

Segers, Mary C. "Abortion and the Supreme Court: Some Are More Equal than Others." *Hastings Center Report* 7 (August 1977): 5-6.

Shainess, Natalie. "Abortion: Inalienable Right." *New York State Journal of Medicine* (1972): 1772-1775.

Shils, Edward. "The Sanctity of Life." In *Life or Death: Ethics and Opinions*, edited by Edward Shils *et al.* Seattle: University of Washington Press, 1968, pp. 2-38.

Shapiro, Sheldon R. "Validity, under Federal Constitution, of Abortion Laws." *United States Supreme Court, Lawyers' Edition*, 2nd Series, 35 (1974): 735-769.

Sher, George. "Hare, Abortion and the Golden Rule." *Philosophy and Public Affairs* 6 (Winter 1977): 185-190.

Sherain, Howard. "Beyond Roe and Doe: The Rights of the Father." *Notre Dame Lawyer* 50 (February 1975): 483-495.

Shibles, Warren. "Abortion." In his *Death: An Interdisciplinary Analysis*. Whitewater, Wisconsin: Language Press, 1974, pp. 299-324.

Shinn, Roger L. "Personal Decisions and Social Policies in a Pluralist Society." *Perkins Journal* 27 (Fall 1973): 58-63.

Simms, M. "Abortion Act after Three Years." *Political Quarterly* 42 (1971): 269-286.

Simms, Madeleine. "Abortion Law and Medical Freedom." *British Journal of Criminology* 14 (April 1974): 118-131.

Smith, Harmon L. "Abortion, Death, and the Sanctity of Life." *Social Science and Medicine* 5 (1971): 211-218.

———. "Life as Relationship: Insight on Abortion." *Christian Advocate* 14 (1970): 7-8.

——. "Religious and Moral Aspects of Population Control." *Religion in Life* 34 (1970): 193-204.

——. "Abortion and the Right to Life." In his *Ethics and the New Medicine*. Nashville: Abingdon Press, 1970, pp. 17-54.

——. "Abortion: The Theological Tradition." In *Abortion: Pro and Con*, edited by Robert L. Perkins. Cambridge, Mass.: Schenkman, 1974, pp. 37-51.

Smith, H. L., and Hodges, Louis W. "The Human Shape of Life." In their *The Christian and His Decisions*. Nashville: Abingdon Press, 1969, pp. 233-252.

Smith, Richard T., *et al*. "An Exchange of Views: 'Moral Consistency and Abortion'." *Commonweal* 100 (17 May 1974): 261-264.

Stone, Alan A. "Abortion and the Supreme Court: What Now?" *Modern Medicine* 41 (30 April, 1973): 30-37.

Sumner, L. W. "Toward a Credible View of Abortion." *Canadian Journal of Philosophy* 4 (September 1974): 163-181.

Swartz, Donald P. "The Impact of Voluntary Abortion on American Obstetrics and Gynecology." *Mount Sinai Journal of Medicine* 42 (September–October 1975): 468-478.

Swyhart, Barbara A. "Reshaping the 'Religious' toward Bioethics and Abortion." In her *Bioethical Decision-Making: Releasing Religion from the Spiritual*. Philadelphia: Fortress Press, 1975, pp. 77-125.

Teo, Wesley D. "Abortion: The Husband's Constitutional Rights." *Ethics* 85 (July 1975): 337-342.

Thimmesch, Nick. "The Abortion Culture." *Newsweek* 82 (9 July, 1973): 7.

Thomson, Judith Jarvis. "A Defense of Abortion." In *Philosophy and Public Affairs*, edited by Marshall Cohen. Princeton: Princeton University Press, 1971, pp. 47-66.

Thomson, Judith J. "Rights and Deaths." *Philosophy and Public Affairs* 2 (Winter 1975): 146-159.

Tooley, Michael. "A Defense of Abortion and Infanticide." *Philosophy and Public Affairs* 2 (1972): 37-65.

——. "A Defense of Abortion and Infanticide." In *The Problem of Abortion*, edited by Joel Feinberg. Belmont, Calif.: Wadsworth, 1973.

——. "Michael Tooley Replies." *Philosophy and Public Affairs* 2 (1973): 37-65.

——. "Abortion and Infanticide." *Philosophy and Public Affairs* 2 (Winter 1973): 146-159.

Van der Poel, Cornelius. "The Principle of Double Effect." In *Absolutes in Moral Theology?*, edited by Charles E. Curren. Washington: Corpus Books, 1968, pp. 186-210.

VanDeVeer, Donald. "Justifying Wholesale Slaughter." *Canadian Journal of Philosophy* 5 (October 1975): 245-258.

Veatch, Robert. "When Does Life Begin?" *Face to Face* 1 (1969): 18-19.
———. "Taxing of Childbearing: Can It Be Just?" Hastings-on-Hudson, New York: Institute of Society, Ethics and the Life Sciences Working Paper Series No. 4, 1971.
———. "What about Abortion on Demand?" *Social Action* (1971): 26-34.
Wade, Francis C. "Potentiality in the Abortion Discussion." *Review of Metaphysics* 29 (December 1975): 240-255.
Walberg, Rachel Conrad. "The Woman and the Fetus." In *New Theology 10*, edited by Martin E. Martin and Dean Peerman. New York: Macmillan, 1973.
Walker, Dan. "Abortion: For Whose Sake?" *Hastings Center Report* 6 (August 1976): 4, 30-31.
Warren, Mary Anne. "On the Moral and Legal Status of Abortion." *Monist* 57 (January 1973): 43-61.
———. "Do Potential People Have Moral Rights?" *Canadian Journal of Philosophy* (June 1977): 275-289.
Watt, Robert L. "Constitutional Law—A New Constitutional Right to an Abortion." *North Carolina Law Review* 51 (October 1973): 1573-1584.
Weber, Melva. "Middlemen in the Definition of Life." *Medical World News* 15 (22 November, 1974): 55-62.
Wellman, Carl. "Abortion." In his *Morals and Ethics*. Glenview, Ill.: Scott, Foresman, 1975, pp. 188-190.
Werner, Richard. "Hare on Abortion." *Analysis* 36 (June 1976): 177-181.
———. "Abortion: The Moral Status of the Unborn." *Social Theory and Practice* 3 (Fall 1974): 201-222.
Wertheimer, Roger. "Understanding the Abortion Argument." *Philosophy and Public Affairs* 1 (1971): 67-95.
Williams, B. A., and Whelan, C. M. "Abortion." In *New Catholic Encyclopedia*, edited by David Eggenberger, Vol. 16, Supplement 1967-1974. New York: McGraw-Hill, 1974, pp. 1-4.
Williams, G. H. "The Sacred Condominium." In *The Morality of Abortion*, edited by John T. Noonan, Jr. Cambridge: Harvard University Press, 1970, pp. 146-171.
———. "Religious Residues and Presuppositions in the American Debate on Abortion." *Theological Studies* 31 (1970): 10-75.
Witherspoon, Joseph P. "Impact of Abortion Decisions upon the Father's Role." *Jurist* 35 (1975): 32-65.
Zenrich, Judith H. "Constitutional Law—Abortion—Father's Rights." *Duquesne Law Review* 13 (Spring 1975): 599-610.
Zuckerman, Ruth Jane. "Abortion and the Constitutional Rights of Minors." *American Civil Liberties Union Reports*, Juvenile Rights Project, 1973.

For additional lists of sources see:

Clouser, Danner K. (with Zucker, Arthur). *Abortion and Euthanasia: An Annotated Bibliography*. Philadelphia: Society for Health and Human Values, 1974.

Dollen, Charles. *Abortion in Context: A Select Bibliography*. Metuchen, N.J.: Scarecrow Press, 1970.

Pinson, William M. *Resource Guide to Current Social Issues*. Waco, Tex.: Word Books, 1968.

PART II: MENTAL ILLNESS

INTRODUCTION

The conceptual perplexity encountered in any serious attempt to understand the nature of mental illness, as well as the unique moral and legal problems resulting from the ways we deal with the mentally ill, invites close examination of both the nature of mental illness and the ways society customarily treats the mentally ill. The essays assembled in this chapter focus on the more prominent conceptual, moral, and legal problems met in any reasonably adequate discussion on mental illness and its proper treatment. Moreover, it seems clear that the legal problems, as well as the moral problems, attending our treatment of the mentally ill derive in no small measure from an apparent lack of agreement on the nature of mental illness itself.

Leon Eisenberg's "Psychiatric Intervention" depicts what is essentially the majority opinion on the nature and proper treatment of mental illness. But in "The Myth of Mental Illness" Thomas Szasz attacks the majority view and argues that mental illness (as we have come to know it) is a myth because mental illness is not a medical problem at all. For Szasz, terms generally used to designate various forms of mental illness only designate forms of behavior deviating from currently acceptable social, moral, or legal norms; and although such deviant ways of coping with stress may require the counsel of the "psychotherapist," still, there is no reason for thinking that the behavior is irresponsible or not the product of human free choice. Although Szasz's thesis on the nature and treatment of mental illness is frequently accorded the status of a minority opinion in the field of psychiatry, Ruth Macklin's essay "Mental Health and Mental Illness: Some Problems of Definition and Concept Formation" would appear to lend substantial support to the view that the opinion of the majority on the nature of mental illness is by no means free of deep-seated conceptual difficulties. She also offers her own evaluation of the merits of Szasz's general position.

In further pursuing the origin and nature of mental illness, Arthur Falek argues in "Genetic Aspects of Schizophrenia" that current genetic research indicates that there is a strong genetic basis for schizophrenia, although the evidence has not yet shown schizophrenia to be a purely genetic disease similar to Huntington's disease. Of equal interest in seeking to define mental illness is

107

R. A. Duff's "Psychopathy and Moral Understanding." Basically, Duff claims that whatever the cause (genetic or otherwise), the distinguishing characteristic of psychotic behavior is a definable *lack* of moral understanding not to be confused with a *rejection* of morality or specific moral rules generally regarded as essential for any moral existence.

Confusion over the nature of mental illness and, consequently, the extent to which the mentally ill may or may not be held responsible for their behavior, creates serious problems for legal practice with respect to the mentally ill. In his "Psychiatrists and the Adversary Process" Judge David Bazelon traces the history of his court rulings on the nature of the insanity plea as it relates to criminal responsibility. He also discusses the reasons for, as well as the problems relevant to, the court's recent attempts to subject expert psychiatric testimony to cross-examination. The difficulties involved in substantiating a plea of insanity, along with Szasz's urging that the plea be dropped altogether from the law, raise serious questions about the viability of the plea and its place in any system of jurisprudence.

PSYCHIATRIC INTERVENTION

LEON EISENBERG

The course and outcome of the major mental disorders of man have been profoundly altered by the advent of drug treatment and by changes in the methods of delivering health care. These gains have been made in spite of our continuing ignorance of the basic causes and mechanisms of mental disorders. The remarkable efficacy of chemotherapy has provided a major spur to basic research into the biochemical and genetic mechanisms underlying psychiatric illness, and recent discoveries hold great promise for new and better means of diminishing the misery associated with disorders of the mind. The potential power of this developing "psychotechnology" is, however, creating concern about unwarranted intrusions into personal privacy and individual rights.

Even though large gains have been made, there remain major areas that await the impetus of new ideas and better methods. Psychotherapy (the psychological treatment of mental disorders) has many sources, but in the U.S. it took root in the soil provided by psychoanalysis. Whatever its future evolution, dynamic psychotherapy has had a powerful humanizing influence on medicine. It requires the physician to listen and to try to understand the patient rather than merely to categorize his foibles while remaining indifferent to his suffering.

The majority of patients with neuroses (disorders characterized by anxiety or psychic defenses that seek to ward off anxiety) describe themselves as being improved after psychotherapy. The symptomatic changes, however, appear to be nonspecific. Similar rates of improvement are found following treatments based on theories in complete contradiction to one another, and sometimes following the mere anticipation of treatment.

Psychoanalysis has undergone many changes since Freud's original formulations. Its theories, however, rest on argument, in the philosophical sense, rather than on evidence that meets the canons of science. Behavior therapy (based on conditioning theory) has shaken psychiatric traditionalism. Its usefulness for particular symptoms such as phobias would now be acknowledged by most psychiatrists, but its more general applicability remains to be demonstrated.

Family-therapy methods have administered another jolt to conventional psychiatric thought. Its practitioners reformulate the problem from one "in" the patient to one "between" the patient and his family. The designated patient may merely be the scapegoat. The illness to be treated lies in distorted interpersonal relationships in the family. These concepts have broadened the psychiatrist's frame of reference. Family therapy, however, has spread more as a messianic movement and not because of convincing evidence from well-designed therapeutic trials.

Whether the psychological treatment of neurotic patients is an exclusive medical specialty is dubious. Such studies as we have provide no evidence that psychiatrists are no more effective therapists than psychologists, social workers and counselors. Therefore in this article I concentrate on the major responsibility of psychiatry: the care and treatment of serious mental illness. It must be emphasized, however, that psychological judgment and personal sensitivity are indispensable to the effective function of the psychiatrist as a physician.

The severe mental disorders we have learned to deal with more effectively are the psychoses, the most prominent of which are schizophrenia and manic-depressive psychosis. Psychoses are severe disorders characterized by profound and pervasive alterations of mood, disorganization of thought, and withdrawal from social interactions into fantasy. Schizophrenia is a psychosis with disturbances in the evaluation of reality and in conceptual thinking that are often accompanied by hallucinations and delusions. It usually becomes manifest in late adolescence or young adulthood. Manic-depressive psychosis is marked by severe disturbances in mood that are self-limited in time but are recurrent and frequently cyclic. Mania is manifested by psychic elation, increased motor activity, rapid speech, and the quick flight of ideas. The stigmata of depression are melancholia, the slowing of thought, unusual thought content (for example overwhelming guilt over imagined transgressions and delusions of rotting away), motor retardation, sleep disturbances, and preoccupation with bodily complaints.

The most obvious indicator of the extent of the recent change in psychiatric practices is evident in the number of resident patients in the state and county mental hospitals of the U.S. . . . The number of patients peaked at about 560,000 in 1955. Over the preceding decade the number of patients had increased at the rate of 3 percent per year, almost twice the rate of growth of the population. Then the trend reversed sharply. The resident state and county mental-hospital population fell to 276,000 by 1972, in spite of general population growth and increased rates for both first admissions and readmissions. From 1962 to 1969 first-admission rates rose from 130,000 to 164,000 and readmission rates from 150,000 to 216,000 as the number of resident patients fell from 516,000 to 370,000. These figures reflect the dramatic decline in the average length of stay.

Although these data convey an overall picture of national trends, they fail to portray the extent of change in some areas. At present California has only some 5,400 patients in its state hospitals, a reduction of 80 percent since 1961, and it plans to eliminate all state-hospital beds for mental patients by 1977. Lest this be mistaken for the elimination of mental illness in California, or even the elimination of inpatient care as a mode of treatment, it should be noted that the state plan projects the transfer of care of mental patients to the counties. California counties now operate, in more or less adequate fashion, programs for the mentally ill, including psychiatric inpatient units in general hospitals and beds in nursing homes.

The total number of patient-care episodes (inpatient plus outpatient) in the U.S. increased from 1,675,000 in 1955 to 4,038,000 in 1971. In that period the number of inpatient episodes rose from 1,296,000 to 1,721,000 and the number of outpatient episodes zoomed from 379,000 to 2,317,000. Placed in relation to population growth, inpatient episodes per 100,000 population rose marginally from 799 to 847, whereas outpatient episodes increased from 234 to 1,134. The locus of care has shifted from the isolated and neglected wards of the state hospital to newly created but not always adequate facilities in the community. There is growing evidence that some of the former hospital patients are not cared for by anyone; they live in single-room-occupancy units, kinless and friendless, subsisting marginally on welfare allotments. Given what most state mental hospitals once were and what many still are, most patients are better off out of them than in them. This, however, does not excuse our failure to provide for the patients lost in the shuffle from one pattern of care to another.

The net change in patient treatment has been enormous, with the number of patients in state and county mental hospitals reduced by half, with the great majority of patients spending less time in the hospital for a given episode of illness, and with far fewer of those admitted being condemned to an endless hospital stay. What factors account for these dramatic changes? Although a complete explanation is lacking, two important transformations in psychiatric care have played the major roles. They are the rediscovery of the principles of moral (that is, humane) treatment and the development of effective psychotropic drugs.

Responding to the humanistic ideas of the revolutionary era of the 18th century, Vincenzo Chiarugi of Italy, Philippe Pinel of France and William Tuke of England pioneered in the recognition that the way mental patients are treated affects the way they behave. Chiarugi wrote into the regulations of the Bonifacio hospital in Florence in 1788 the statement: "It is a supreme moral duty and medical obligation to respect the insane person as an individual." The famous engraving of Pinel striking the chains from the insane at the Bicêtre (an accomplishment he modestly credited to his nonmedical hospital governor, Jean-Baptiste Pussin) symbolizes, if it also mythologizes, his accomplishment. In

Pinel's words: "In lunatic hospitals, as in despotic governments, it is no doubt possible to maintain, by unlimited confinement and barbarous treatment, the appearance of order and loyalty. The stillness of the grave and the silence of death, however, are not to be expected in a residence consecrated for the reception of madmen. A degree of liberty, sufficient to maintain order, dictated not by weak but enlightened humanity and calculated to spread a few charms over the unhappy existence of maniacs, contributes in most instances to diminish the violence of symptoms and in some to remove the complaint altogether."

In England, Tuke and the Society of Friends founded The Retreat at York. They chose the name to suggest "a quiet haven in which the shattered bark might find the means of reparation or of safety." Samuel Tuke, grandson of the founder, wrote in a description of the moral treatment of the insane: "If it be true, that oppression makes a wise man mad, is it to be supposed that stripes, and insults, and injuries, for which the receiver knows no cause, are calculated to make a madman wise? Or would they not exasperate his disease, and excite his resentment?"

These quotations convey the extent to which convictions about the centrality of human liberty gave rise to a therapeutic philosophy that came to replace confinement and punishment. Succeeding waves of neglect, reform, and neglect of institutional patient treatment led a century and a half later to state mental hospitals that were unmanageably large, poorly staffed and grossly underfunded. These self-contained worlds became dedicated to self-perpetuation rather than to the patients to whom they were ostensibly dedicated.

In the late 1940s and early 1950s there were two significant developments. First, sociologists began to examine the nature of mental institutions and the interactions of patients and staff as these influenced the behavior of the patient. Second, innovative hospital superintendents, first in Britain and then in the U.S., opened locked doors, introduced a measure of patient self-government, and re-established bonds with the surrounding community. It soon became evident that the apparently deteriorated behavior of chronic mental patients was not a simple result of the mental disorder that had led to admission but of what has been termed the social-breakdown syndrome, that is, the alienation and dehumanization produced by the "total institution" the mental hospital had become. With a reconceptualization of the hospital as a therapeutic community (the new name for moral treatment), many of the chronic inpatients were able to be returned to the community, even after years of continuous hospitalization, and far fewer first admissions became chronic.

The reversal of the continuous growth of the inpatient population began with the reordering of the institutional environment, the development of community-care alternatives, changes in administrative policy favoring early discharge, and hard-won battles for community acceptance of the mentally ill. Although the first decrease of the inpatient population preceded the large-scale introduction of drug treatment, the continued and much higher rate of change would not have been possible unless effective chemotherapeutic means of managing acute psychotic disorders had become available at the same time.

The history of psychopharmacology can readily be made to fit Horace Walpole's parable of the "Three Princes of Serendip," but it may be more instructive to recall Louis Pasteur's aphorism that chance favors the prepared mind. Chlorpromazine, the prime example of the new psychotherapeutic drugs, resulted from efforts to synthesize a more effective antihistamine. In 1949 Henri-Marie Laborit of France used chlorpromazine to produce a "hibernation syndrome" in patients undergoing prolonged surgery, and he noticed that a side effect was a striking indifference to environmental stimuli. Then in 1952 Jean Delay and Pierre Deniker of France discovered the drug's remarkable effectiveness in aborting acute psychotic episodes, both in schizophrenia and in the manic phase of manic-depressive disorders. The confirmation of chlorpromazine's quite extraordinary value by controlled clinical trials led to its widespread use throughout the world and to an organized search for related families of compounds, a search that required close interaction of organic chemists, pharmacologists, and clinicians. New classes of drugs now termed major tranquilizers or neuroleptics were discovered.

In spite of the similarity of these drugs in pharmacologic properties, they vary in chemical structure, milligram-for-milligram potency, in frequency of side effects and in their utility for the treatment of clinical subtypes within the schizophrenic spectrum. (For example, trifluoperazine is thought to be more useful for the inhibited schizophrenic and chlorpromazine for the overactive schizophrenic.) Extensive clinical research has documented the effectiveness of the phenothazine class of drugs (which includes chlorpromazine and trifluoperazine) in terminating an episode of schizophrenia. The natural history of the disorder, however, indicates a substantial risk of recurrence and little residue of benefit from prior treatment. Studies of maintenance therapy, when the patient is willing and able to take an appropriate drug over a long period of time, indicate a definite attenuation in the rate of subsequent attacks. Unfortunately unpleasant side effects (sedation and symptoms resembling Parkinson's disease) are a problem for some patients and serious toxicity (persistent rhythmical, involuntary movements of tongue and face, abnormal pigmentation, low white-cell count, and jaundice) afflicts a substantial minority.

Ayurvedic medicine in India had for thousands of years made use of the snakeroot plant, *Rauwolfia serpentina*, for its sedative properties. When rauwolfia was introduced as an antihypertensive agent in the late 1940s and early 1950s, its active principle, reserpine, was identified. One serious side effect was the production of severe depression in some patients. The introduction of reserpine into psychiatry led to the discovery of the drug's effectiveness in aborting acute psychotic episodes in schizophrenia. Once widely used, reserpine has been replaced by the phenothiazines because of the greater frequency of reserpine's serious side effects. It continues, however, to play an important role in the experimental pharmacology of the psychoses.

In the same year that chlorpromazine was introduced into psychiatry alert clinicians treating tuberculosis with iproniazid noted that many of their patients displayed a marked euphoria well before there was any major improvement in their pulmonary disease. Subsequent trials in depressed patients established the power of this agent in relieving depression. It was also discovered that iproniazid acted to inhibit the enzyme monamine oxidase. (Monamines, such as serotonin, norepinephrine, and dopamine, are believed to act as chemical transmitters between nerve cells in the brain.) At about the same time organic chemists synthesized the drug imipramine by replacing the sulfur atom in the phenothiazine structure with a dimethyl bridge, thereby changing a six-member ring into a seven-member ring. Tests with animals had suggested that imipramine should have properties similar to the parent compound, but the drug proved relatively ineffective in schizophrenics.

In 1957, however, R. Kuhn of Switzerland, observing that depressed schizophrenics did seem to show some improvement on being given imipramine, demonstrated that patients suffering from psychotic depression displayed marked improvement. Imipramine was the prototype of the tricyclic antidepressants. The chemical structures of these two classes of antidepressants—the monamine oxidase inhibitors and the tricyclics—are quite different. . . . The drugs are effective in the management of from 70 to 80 percent of depressive episodes and have much reduced the reliance on electroconvulsive therapy, which was once the only known effective treatment for depressive illness. In Australia J. F. J. Cade was pursuing the hypothesis that mania was the result of a toxic state that he sought to detect by searching for metabolic products in the urine. Having employed lithium because of the solubility of its urate salt, he noted that the lithium given to laboratory animals acted as a sedative. He then used it in clinical trials that indicated the element could control mania. Cade's lead was ignored for more than a decade because of concern about lithium toxicity, which had become disturbingly evident when its salts were imprudently administered in high doses as a substitute for sodium in the treatment of hypertension. With proper attention to dosage and careful monitoring of levels in the blood serum, lithium has now been shown to be a safe agent for the treatment of mania, although it is not as prompt in its action as chlorpromazine. The most exciting development has been the demonstration by the Danish group headed by Mogens Schou that lithium is an effective prophylactic agent against the recurrence of psychotic episodes in patients with manic-depressive disease. For the first time we have an agent with acceptably low levels of toxicity (under close medical supervision), low cost, and ease of administration that prevents to a significant degree the otherwise inevitable recurrent attacks of a major psychosis.

Studies of the biochemistry of the brain, which were stimulated in large part by the desire to understand how the psychoactive drugs worked, indicate that selective errors in the metabolism of the monamines in specific areas of the brain may be the pathophysiological basis for psychotic disorders. Chemical and histological studies indicate that these substances are located in certain nerve cells and the ends of their long fibers. The biogenic amines (including serotonin, norepinephrine, and dopamine) most likely function in specific regions of the central nervous system as chemical transmitters between nerve cells or as modulators of transmission by other substances (such as acetylcholine).

There appears to be a close relation between the effects of the psychoactive drugs on monamine levels and on affective and behavioral states. Drugs that result in an inactivation and depletion of norepinephrine in the brain (such as reserpine and lithium) produce sedation and depression. Drugs such as imipramine, together with monamine oxidase inhibitors that increase or potentiate norepinephrine, are associated with behavioral stimulation and usually have an antidepressant effect in man. Therefore abnormally high or low levels of norepinephrine in functionally specialized areas of the brain may be responsible for at least some types of elation and depression.

There is growing evidence that the metabolic substance cyclic AMP mediates some of the effects of norepinephrine and dopamine in the brain. For example, in the brain structure called the caudate nucleus dopamine stimulates the activity of adenylate cyclase, the enzyme that catalyzes the synthesis of cyclic AMP from adenosine triphosphate. Cyclic AMP is present in large concentrations in the central nervous system and is known to be important in the induction of enzymes and the synthesis of other proteins. Recent experiments have indicated that protein synthesis may play an important role in long-term memory. When chemicals that inhibit protein synthesis are injected into the brain of an experimental animal, the formation of long-term memories is suppressed. Drugs that release or enhance norepinephrine in the brain counteract this suppression. These findings, made by Seymour S. Kety of the Harvard Medical School, support a tentative model of memory in which protein synthesis stimulated by the release of norepinephrine serves as the biochemical basis for the consolidation of learning. Although there are no completely adequate theories to account for the correlation between biochemical change, nerve-cell activity, and behavior, the exciting pace of interchange between clinical studies and laboratory investigations promises major gains in our understanding of the fundamental mechanisms.

Evidence has been accumulating that points toward a genetic basis for schizophrenia and for manic-depressive disorders. The risk of schizophrenia for a child with one schizophrenic parent is about 10 times greater than it is in the general population, and the risk for a child with two schizophrenic parents is about 40 times greater. This empirical finding can be explained on either a genetic basis or an environmental one. Research on twins, however, has shown that schizophrenia in both twins is much commoner (with a range of 35 to 70 percent) in monozygotic (identical) pairs than it is (with a range of 10 to 26 percent) in dizygotic (fraternal) pairs.

A continuing American-Danish study conducted by Kety, D. Rosenthal, P. H. Wender, and F. Schulsinger has provided independent evidence for a hereditary basis for schizophrenia. They have been studying people who as children were adopted and as adults became schizophrenic. A comparison of the prevalence of schizophrenia among the biological relatives of such people and among the adopting families makes it possible to separate the genetic component from the environmental one. The investigators have found more instances of schizophrenia and related disorders in biological relatives than in the adopting families, which offers strong support for genetic (although not Mendelian) transmission.

The emergence of these mental disorders probably requires a predisposition involving more than one gene (polygenic transmission) and still unspecified environmental precipitants. Studies of manic-depressive disorders in families indicate the need to differentiate bipolar disorders (with both manic and depressive episodes) from unipolar ones (with only depressive episodes). The prevalence of such disorders in the parents and extended family of bipolar patients is significantly greater than it is in the families of unipolar patients. The rates for families in both groups, however, are higher than they are for the general population.

Psychiatry, like the representation of the Roman god Janus, has two faces, one represented by treatment at the psychosocial level and the other by treatment at the pharmacologic level. The two forms of treatment often act to reinforce each other. Yet on the one hand the responsiveness of psychotic states to factors in the social environment has been taken to support contemporary views that mental illness is a "myth" arising from labels applied by psychiatrists in order to rationalize the segregation of people who exhibit disturbing (rather than disturbed) behavior. On the other, the power of psychotherapeutic drugs has been used to support a vulgarized medical model that views psychoses as nothing more than biochemical derangements to be corrected by a realignment of the biochemical machinery. Neither conclusion is warranted. The fundamental task of psychiatry is to understand behavior that results from interaction of stimulus (environmental) conditions and the response (psychobiological) capacities of the organism, capacities that reflect the organism's genetic endowment as well as its history (experience).

The notion that psychiatrists create insanity simply by labeling objectionable people as being insane has a certain charm. It implies that we can legislate mental illnesses out of existence by abolishing the myth that they are real.

However, either this myth in one form or another has mysteriously proved to be necessary in every society or mental illnesses are in fact endemic in every population known to us. Studies of the lifetime expectancy for schizophrenia in Switzerland, Iceland, and Japan reveal rates that vary only slightly: from .73 percent to 1.23 percent. The modal figure for all nations reporting is $1 \pm .2$ percent.

Some have argued that the frantic pace of industrialization increases psychotic behavior. H. Goldhammer and A. W. Marshall of the Rand Corporation compared the hospital rates for the psychoses of early and middle adult life in Massachusetts from 1840 to 1940. They found no substantial change.

The major psychoses are identifiable in preindustrial societies, although the local terms for them and the theories on which the terms are based differ sharply from our own. Both psychiatrists with Western training and native healers nonetheless identify a person with a psychosis as being abnormal. Mental disorders are identifiable even when the indigenous language has no verbal label for them and even when they are not defined as illness, as in senility. The signs and symptoms of mental deterioration are known to the community, but they are ascribed to the natural course of aging. The absence of the label does not abolish the behavior, but it does reflect a difference in social management; the patient's family, rather than some other community institution, assumes the burden of the affected person's care and protection.

Whatever the cause of a psychotic disorder, be it biological or psychogenic, the mental content of the psychosis must reflect the input to the mind and how that input is refracted by the mind's history and functional state. A patient suffering from a psychosis secondary to drug intoxication can only verbalize his hallucinations in the language he knows; he employs the images of his culture in expressing his terror. A schizophrenic with delusions of grandeur will think himself Jesus in one society and Mohammed in another. This does not say that the delusions were caused by the society but rather that the metaphors for grandeur are social in their origin. Moreover, if the psychotic abandons his insistence on being the deity in response to sympathy and support, that in itself does not tell us anything about the pathogenesis of the autistic thought.

Whether the patient is wildly delusional or rigidly catatonic, he remains a person in need of human satisfactions and he is always responsive to cues in his environment. Physicians quite regularly observe that the perceived pain of cancer, the visible tremor of neurological disease, the symptomatic malfunction of the lungs in emphysema increase or decrease in response to social transactions, which have awesome power to diminish or augment stress. The capacity of sedatives to diminish anxiety by damping physiological oscillations does not deny that the source of the anxiety lies in a psychological threat to personal esteem. The signs and symptoms of disordered function are a result of the state of the organism and the psychobiological forces acting on it.

The interactions among drug effects, psychobiological state, and social setting indicate the complexity of the determinants of human behavior. Amphetamines, which for most of us are stimulants and euphoriants, are almost totally ineffective in the treatment of psychotic depression. Tricyclics, in spite of their potency in relieving depressed patients, produce nothing more than sedation and unpleasant side effects (dry mouth, blurring of vision, and the like) in normal people. Lithium, which limits the swings of mood in manic-depressives, is without detectable effects in normal volunteers. An acutely psychotic patient may require for therapeutic benefit an amount of chlorpromazine capable of producing coma in a normal person. The perception of side effects, such as the dry mouth a patient has been warned to expect, may convince him of the potency and predictability of the drug and enhance favorable outcomes. For others a side effect such as sedation may arouse fears of losing self-control and result in refusal to continue treatment.

Social context affects a person's subjective response to drugs. Hallucinogens evoke different experiences when they are given as a hallowed act in a religious ceremony, when they are part of a carefully monitored laboratory experiment, or when they are taken in the search for "expanded consciousness." The effect depends on what the seeker expects and on whether he is alone or with others (the set and setting). Epinephrine (adrenaline) has been shown to produce irritation and anger when it is injected into a volunteer who does not know what he is receiving and is then exposed to a provocative and unpleasant situation. It generates feelings of well-being when it is injected into a person who is then exposed to a situation that is cheerful and humorous.

What transforms a troubled person into a patient (someone identified by himself, or his community, and a physician as being sick) is a complex social process influenced by cultural attitudes, medical knowledge and the availability of treatment facilities. It has long been observed that proximity to a state mental hospital, belief in the efficacy of psychiatric treatment, and administrative policy facilitating easy access all lead to higher admission rates. Conversely, shame about mental illness, guilt about its cause, and fear of long-term confinement are deterrents to acknowledging the need for help. Neither set of factors alters the actual prevalence of mental disorder, but they have a marked influence on the cases officially tabulated. Community-wide surveys always find disturbed individuals who are maintaining a marginal social existence; they indicate that statistics based only on hospital and clinic records underestimate the actual prevalence of mental disorders in the general population. A person is as likely to seek psychiatric help because of a family crisis, an economic misfortune, or a chance encounter with a public agency as because of the nature of his disorder. Thus single, divorced, widowed, or otherwise isolated persons are more likely to be hospitalized than those with family support. Life stress as a precipitant of perceived illness and prolonged hospitalization is a phenomenon of medical and surgical, as well as mental, illnesses.

With medical progress disorders once crudely lumped together as insanity have been separated into discrete entities. One type of insanity, a dementia accompanied by general paralysis, is now known to be the result of pathological changes in the central nervous system caused by the spirochete of syphilis; it can be prevented by the effective treatment of primary syphilis. The complex of mental disturbances associated with pellagra was shown to be the result of a dietary deficiency of B-complex vitamins (tryptophan, nicotinic acid, and pyridoxine). Similar disturbances in the absence of dietary inadequacy have now been shown to be the result of an inherited metabolic defect (Hartnup's disease) that leads to an inability to absorb tryptophan from the gut.

The fact that the remedies for schizophrenia and manic-depressive disorders are different has given added significance to the diagnostic differentiation of the two. Studies have shown that American and British psychiatrists have tended to make quite different diagnoses when they are given the same set of symptoms for disorders that could be schizophrenic or manic-depressive. A joint American-British diagnostic study has made it evident that the term *schizophrenia* has been used much more broadly by American psychiatrists. With more precise attention to the details of the psychiatric examination, because of the therapeutic importance of the diagnostic differentiation, higher degrees of replicability among psychiatrists can be attained. As long as we must rely on clinical judgments made by psychiatrists, in contrast to more objective laboratory indicators, differences of opinion will be inevitable.

It is these characteristics of a mental disorder—its changing definitions, the variability of its course, its responsiveness to the social environment, and imprecision in its diagnosis—that make psychiatry a center of controversy. If the recognition and appropriate treatment of psychosis can benefit the afflicted, it is also true that error can harm them. Hospitalization, particularly when it is involuntary, deprives the patient of his personal liberties. It can be misused by civil authorities and by disaffected families to remove unwanted persons from the community.

In the past five years commitment laws in many states have been rewritten to protect civil rights, but the laws will be only as effective as the vigilance of the community, the courts, and physicians guarantees. There is, however, a nagging question that should not be forgotten: Are we legislating a justification for indifference to human welfare? If we wish to avoid a paternalistic society, must we settle for an atomistic one? When someone is grossly disturbed but refuses to seek help, what is our responsibility toward him? The law recognizes the legitimacy of intervention when the patient is suicidal or homicidal. Under what other circumstances is intervention warranted? That is a major issue for parents with a disturbed adolescent, for children with a disturbed parent, and for friends helplessly watching a life being wasted. It may be that such casualties are the necessary price for the benefits of individual freedom, but the matter deserves more thought than it is being given.

Current psychiatric knowledge is compatible with a stress-diathesis model for the genesis of psychoses: Psychobiological stress acts on an individual with a genetic predisposition to psychosis and eventually leads to abnormal metabolic processes that cause disorders of mood and thought. Predisposition probably varies on a continuum. Although genetic factors are a prerequisite, it is unlikely that they are sufficient to evoke psychosis in themselves. The behavior of the mentally disturbed person may cause others to reject him, so that he experiences additional severe psychological stress.

At any given time the power of psychiatric remedies and their accessibility to the patient are major determinants of the outcome of an acute mental breakdown. Therapeutic drugs not only presumably restore metabolic equilibrium but also may directly affect the patient's perception of stress. The probability of further personality deterioration and the duration of the disorder is a function of the social environment provided for the patient by the health-care system. The degree of organization or disorganization of the community where a psychotic person finds himself will influence his mood and thought directly.

Our ability to identify the significant psychobiological stressors is limited, and it is still not possible to estimate degrees of genetic predisposition accurately enough to take preventive measures. There have nonetheless been major advances in our capacity for controlling or aborting mental disorders when they do occur. Moreover, we appear to be on the verge of answering some of the basic questions about the functioning of the brain. Psychiatric research is a fragile enterprise, yet it is currently argued in ruling government circles that it should receive not more public support but less. It would be the height of folly to stifle fundamental investigation just at the time when it holds so much promise for revealing the basic mechanisms of psychotic disorders and for developing rational therapies aimed at the causes of psychoses and not merely at their symptoms.

THE MYTH
OF MENTAL ILLNESS

THOMAS SZASZ

I

At the core of virtually all contemporary psychiatric theories and practices lies the concept of mental illness. A critical examination of this concept is therefore indispensable for understanding the ideas, institutions, and interventions of psychiatrists.

My aim in this essay is to ask if there is such a thing as mental illness and to argue that there is not. Of course, mental illness is not a thing or physical object; hence it can exist only in the same sort of way as do other theoretical concepts. Yet, to those who believe in them, familiar theories are likely to appear, sooner or later, as "objective truths" or "facts." During certain historical periods, explanatory concepts such as deities, witches, and instincts appeared not only as theories but as *self-evident causes* of a vast number of events. Today mental illness is widely regarded in a similar fashion, that is, as the cause of innumerable diverse happenings.

As an antidote to the complacent use of the notion of mental illness—as a self-evident phenomenon, theory, or cause—let us ask: What is meant when it is asserted that someone is mentally ill? In this essay I shall describe the main uses of the concept of mental illness, and I shall argue that this notion has outlived whatever cognitive usefulness it might have had and that it now functions as a myth.

II

The notion of mental illness derives its main support from such phenomena as syphilis of the brain or delirious conditions—intoxications, for instance—in which persons may manifest certain disorders of thinking and behavior. Correctly speaking, however, these are diseases of the brain, not of the mind.

This paper originally appeared in vol. 15 of *The American Psychologist* and is reprinted here by permission of the author and *The American Psychological Association.*

According to one school of thought, *all* so-called mental illness is of this type. The assumption is made that some neurological defect, perhaps a very subtle one, will ultimately be found to explain all the disorders of thinking and behavior. Many contemporary physicians, psychiatrists, and other scientists hold this view, which implies that people's troubles cannot be caused by conflicting personal needs, opinions, social aspirations, values, and so forth. These difficulties—which I think we may simply call *problems in living*—are thus attributed to physicochemical processes that in due time will be discovered (and no doubt corrected) by medical research.

Mental illnesses are thus regarded as basically similar to other diseases. The only difference, in this view, between mental and bodily disease is that the former, affecting the brain, manifests itself by means of mental symptoms; whereas the latter, affecting other organ systems—for example, the skin, liver, and so on—manifests itself by means of symptoms referable to those parts of the body.

In my opinion, this view is based on two fundamental errors. In the first place, a disease of the brain, analogous to a disease of the skin or bone, is a neurological defect, not a problem in living. For example, a *defect* in a person's visual field may be explained by correlating it with certain lesions in the nervous system. On the other hand, a person's *belief*—whether it be in Christianity, in Communism, or in the idea that his internal organs are rotting and that his body is already dead—cannot be explained by a defect or disease of the nervous system. Explanations of this sort of occurrence—assuming that one is interested in the belief itself and does not regard it simply as a symptom or expression of something else that is more interesting—must be sought along different lines.

The second error is epistemological. It consists of interpreting communications about ourselves and the world around us as symptoms of neurological functioning. This is an error not in observation or reasoning, but rather in the organization and expression of knowledge. In the present case, the error lies in making a dualism between mental and physical symptoms, a dualism that is a habit of speech and not the result of known observations. Let us see if this is so.

In medical practice, when we speak of physical disturbances we mean either signs (for example, fever) or symptoms (for example, pain). We speak of mental symptoms, on the other hand, when we refer to a patient's communications about himself, others, and the world about him. The patient might assert that he is Napoleon or that he is being persecuted by the Communists. These would be considered mental symptoms only if the observer believed that the patient was *not* Napoleon or that he was *not* being persecuted by the Communists. This makes it apparent that the statement "*X* is a mental symptom" involves rendering a judgment that entails a covert comparison between the patient's ideas, concepts, or beliefs and those of the observer and the society in which they live. The notion of mental symptom is therefore inextricably tied to the social, and particularly the ethical, context in which it is made, just as the notion of bodily symptom is tied to an anatomical and genetic context.[1]

To sum up: For those who regard mental symptoms as signs of brain disease, the concept of mental illness is unnecessary and misleading. If they mean that people so labeled suffer from diseases of the brain, it would seem better, for the sake of clarity, to say that and not something else.

III

The term "mental illness" is also widely used to describe something quite different from a disease of the brain. Many people today take it for granted that living is an arduous affair. Its hardship for modern man derives, moreover, not so much from a struggle for biological survival as from the stresses and strains inherent in the social intercourse of complex human personalities. In this context, the notion of mental illness is used to identify or describe some feature of an invididual's so-called personality. Mental illness—as a deformity of the personality, so to speak—is then regarded as the cause of human disharmony. It is implicit in this view that social intercourse between people is regarded as something inherently harmonious, its disturbance being due solely to the presence of "mental illness" in many people. Clearly, this is faulty reasoning, for it makes the abstraction "mental illness" into a cause of, even though this abstraction was originally created to serve only as a shorthand expression for, certain types of human behavior. It now becomes necessary to ask: What kinds of behavior are regarded as indicative of mental illness, and by whom?

The concept of illness, whether bodily or mental, implies deviation from some clearly defined norm. In the case of physical illness, the norm is the structural and functional integrity of the human body. Thus, although the desirability of physical health, as such, is an ethical value, what health is can be stated in anatomical and physiological terms. What is the norm, deviation from which is regarded as mental illness? This question cannot be easily answered. But whatever this norm may be, we can be certain of only one thing: namely, that it must be stated in terms of psychosocial, ethical, and legal concepts. For example, notions such as "excessive repression" and "acting out an unconscious impulse" illustrate the use of psychological concepts for judging so-called mental health and illness. The idea that chronic hostility, vengefulness, or divorce are indicative of mental illness is an illustration of the use of ethical norms (that is, the desirability of love, kindness, and a stable marriage relationship). Finally, the

[1] See Szasz, T. S.: *Pain and Pleasure: A Study of Bodily Feelings* (New York: Basic Books, 1957), especially pp. 70–81; "The problem of psychiatric nosology." *Amer. J. Psychiatry, 114*:405–13 (Nov.), 1957.

widespread psychiatric opinion that only a mentally ill person would commit homicide illustrates the use of a legal concept as a norm of mental health. In short, when one speaks of mental illness, the norm from which deviation is measured is a *psychosocial and ethical* standard. Yet, the remedy is sought in terms of *medical* measures that—it is hoped and assumed—are free from wide differences of ethical value. The definition of the disorder and the terms in which its remedy are sought are therefore at serious odds with one another. The practical significance of this covert conflict between the alleged nature of the defect and the actual remedy can hardly be exaggerated.

Having identified the norms used for measuring deviations in cases of mental illness, we shall now turn to the question, Who defines the norms and hence the deviation? Two basic answers may be offered: First, it may be the person himself—that is, the patient—who decides that he deviates from a norm; for example, an artist may believe that he suffers from a work inhibition; and he may implement this conclusion by seeking help *for himself* from a psychotherapist. Second, it may be someone other than the "patient" who decides that the latter is deviant—for example, relatives, physicians, legal authorities, society generally; a psychiatrist may then be hired by persons other than the "patient" to do something *to him* in order to correct the deviation.

These considerations underscore the importance of asking the question, Whose agent is the psychiatrist? and of giving a candid answer to it. The psychiatrist (or non-medical mental health worker) may be the agent of the patient, the relatives, the school, the military services, a business organization, a court of law, and so forth. In speaking of the psychiatrist as the agent of these persons or organizations, it is not implied that his moral values, or his ideas and aims concerning the proper nature of remedial action, must coincide exactly with those of his employer. For example, a patient in individual psychotherapy may believe that his salvation lies in a new marriage; his psychotherapist need not share this hypothesis. As the patient's agent, however, he must not resort to social or legal force to prevent the patient from putting his beliefs into action. If his *contract* is with the patient, the psychiatrist (psychotherapist) may disagree with him or stop his treatment, but he cannot engage others to obstruct the patient's aspirations.[2] Similarly, if a psychiatrist is retained by a court to determine the sanity of an offender, he need not fully share the legal authorities' values and intentions in regard to the criminal, nor the means deemed appropriate for dealing with him; such a psychiatrist cannot testify, however, that the accused is not insane, but that the legislators are—for passing the law that decrees the offender's actions illegal.[3] This sort of opinion could be voiced, of

---

[2] See Szasz, T. S.: *The Ethics of Psychoanalysis: The Theory and Method of Autonomous Psychotherapy* (New York: Basic Books, 1965).

[3] See Szasz, T. S.: *Law, Liberty, and Psychiatry: An Inquiry into the Social Uses of Mental Health Practices* (New York: Macmillan, 1963).

course—but not in a courtroom, and not by a psychiatrist who is there to assist the court in performing its daily work.

To recapitulate: In contemporary social usage, the finding of mental illness is made by establishing a deviance in behavior from certain psychosocial, ethical, or legal norms. The judgment may be made, as in medicine, by the patient, the physician (psychiatrist), or others. Remedial action, finally, tends to be sought in a therapeutic—or covertly medical—framework. This creates a situation in which it is claimed that psychosocial, ethical, and legal deviations can be corrected by medical action. Since medical interventions are designed to remedy only medical problems, it is logically absurd to expect that they will help solve problems whose very existence have been defined and established on non-medical grounds.

IV

Anything that people *do*—in contrast to things that *happen* to them[4]—takes place in a context of value. Hence, no human activity is devoid of moral implications. When the values underlying certain activities are widely shared, those who participate in their pursuit often lose sight of them altogether. The discipline of medicine—both as a pure science (for example, research) and as an applied science or technology (for example, therapy)—contains many ethical considerations and judgments. Unfortunately, these are often denied, minimized, or obscured, for the ideal of the medical profession as well as of the people whom it serves is to have an ostensibly value-free system of medical care. This sentimental notion is expressed by such things as the doctor's willingness to treat patients regardless of their religious or political beliefs. But such claims only serve to obscure the fact that ethical considerations encompass a vast range of human affairs. Making medical practice neutral with respect to some specific issues of moral value (such as race or sex) need not mean, and indeed does not mean, that it can be kept free from others (such as control over pregnancy or regulation of sex relations). Thus, birth control, abortion, homosexuality, suicide, and euthanasia continue to pose major problems in medical ethics.

Psychiatry is much more intimately related to problems of ethics than is medicine in general. I use the word "psychiatry" here to refer to the contemporary discipline concerned with problems in living, and not with diseases of the brain, which belong to neurology. Difficulties in human relations can be analyzed, interpreted, and given meaning only within specific social and ethical contexts. Accordingly, the psychiatrist's socioethical orientations will influence his ideas on what is wrong with the patient, on what deserves comment or interpretation, in what directions change might be desirable, and so forth. Even

[4] Peters, R.S.: *The Concept of Motivation* (London: Routledge & Kegan Paul, 1958), especially pp. 12–15.

in medicine proper, these factors play a role, as illustrated by the divergent orientations that physicians, depending on their religious affiliations, have toward such things as birth control and therapeutic abortion. Can anyone really believe that a psychotherapist's ideas on religion, politics, and related issues play no role in his practical work? If, on the other hand, they do matter, what are we to infer from it? Does it not seem reasonable that perhaps we ought to have different psychiatric therapies—each recognized for the ethical positions that it embodies—for, say, Catholics and Jews, religious persons and atheists, democrats and Communists, white supremacists and Negroes, and so on? Indeed, if we look at the way psychiatry is actually practiced today, especially in the United States, we find that the psychiatric interventions people seek and receive depend more on their socioeconomic status and moral beliefs than on the "mental illnesses" from which they ostensibly suffer.[5] This fact should occasion no greater surprise than that practicing Catholics rarely frequent birth-control clinics, or that Christian Scientists rarely consult psychoanalysts.

V

The position outlined above, according to which contemporary psychotherapists deal with problems in living, not with mental illnesses and their cures, stands in sharp opposition to the currently prevalent position, according to which psychiatrists treat mental diseases, which are just as "real" and "objective" as bodily diseases. I submit that the holders of the latter view have no evidence whatever to justify their claim, which is actually a kind of psychiatric propaganda: their aim is to create in the popular mind a confident belief that mental illness is some sort of disease entity, like an infection or a malignancy. If this were true, one could *catch* or *get* a mental illness, one might *have* or *harbor* it, one might *transmit* it to others, and finally one could *get rid* of it. Not only is there not a shred of evidence to support this idea, but, on the contrary, all the evidence is the other way and supports the view that what people now call mental illnesses are, for the most part, *communications* expressing unacceptable ideas, often framed in an unusual idiom.

This is not the place to consider in detail the similarities and differences between bodily and mental illnesses. It should suffice to emphasize that whereas the term "bodily illness" refers to psysicochemical occurrences that are not affected by being made public, the term "mental illness" refers to sociopsychological events that are crucially affected by being made public. The psychiatrist thus cannot, and does not, stand apart from the person he observes, as the pathologist can and often does. The psychiatrist is committed to some picture of

[5] Hollingshead, A. B. and Redlich, F. C.: *Social Class and Mental Illness* (New York: Wiley, 1958).

what he considers reality, and to what he thinks society considers reality, and he observes and judges the patient's behavior in the light of these beliefs. The very notion of "mental symptom" or "mental illness" thus implies a covert comparison, and often conflict, between observer and observed, psychiatrist and patient. Though obvious, this fact needs to be re-emphasized, if one wishes, as I do here, to counter the prevailing tendency to deny the moral aspects of psychiatry and to substitute for them allegedly value-free medical concepts and interventions.

Psychotherapy is thus widely practiced as though it entailed nothing other than restoring the patient from a state of mental sickness to one of mental health. While it is generally accepted that mental illness has something to do with man's social or interpersonal relations, it is paradoxically maintained that problems of values—that is, of ethics—do not arise in this process. Freud himself went so far as to assert: "I consider ethics to be taken for granted. Actually I have never done a mean thing."[6] This is an astounding thing to say, especially for someone who had studied man as a social being as deeply as Freud had. I mention it here to show how the notion of "illness"—in the case of psychoanalysis, "psychopathology," or "mental illness"—was used by Freud, and by most of his followers, as a means of classifying certain types of human behavior as falling within the scope of medicine, and hence, by fiat, outside that of ethics. Nevertheless, the stubborn fact remains that, in a sense, much of psychotherapy revolves around nothing other than the elucidation and weighing of goals and values—many of which may be mutually contradictory—and the means whereby they might best be harmonized, realized, or relinquished.

Because the range of human values and of the methods by which they may be attained is so vast, and because many such ends and means are persistently unacknowledged, conflicts among values are the main source of conflicts in human relations. Indeed, to say that human relations at all levels—from mother to child, through husband and wife, to nation and nation—are fraught with stress, strain, and disharmony is, once again, to make the obvious explicit. Yet, what may be obvious may be also poorly understood. This, I think, is the case here. For it seems to me that in our scientific theories of behavior we have failed to accept the simple fact that human relations are inherently fraught with difficulties, and to make them even relatively harmonious requires much patience and hard work. I submit that the idea of mental illness is now being put to work to obscure certain difficulties that at present may be inherent—not that they need to be unmodifiable—in the social intercourse of persons. If this is true, the concept functions as a disguise: Instead of calling attention to conflicting human needs, aspirations, and values, the concept of mental illness provides an amoral and impersonal "thing"—an "illness"—as an explanation for problems in living. We may recall in this connection that not so long ago it was devils and

[6]Quoted in Jones, E.: *The Life and Work of Sigmund Freud* (New York: Basic Books, 1957), Vol. III, p. 247.

witches that were held responsible for man's problems in living. The belief in mental illness, as something other than man's trouble in getting along with his fellow man, is the proper heir to the belief in demonology and witchcraft. Mental illness thus exists or is "real" in exactly the same sense in which witches existed or were "real."

VI

While I maintain that mental illnesses do not exist, I obviously do not imply or mean that the social and psychological occurrences to which this label is attached also do not exist. Like the personal and social troubles that people had in the Middle Ages, contemporary human problems are real enough. It is the labels we give them that concern me, and, having labeled them, what we do about them. The demonologic concept of problems in living gave rise to therapy along theological lines. Today, a belief in mental illness implies—nay, requires— therapy along medical or psychotherapeutic lines.

I do not here propose to offer a new conception of "psychiatric illness" or a new form of "therapy." My aim is more modest and yet also more ambitious. It is to suggest that the phenomena now called mental illnesses be looked at afresh and more simply, that they be removed from the category of illnesses, and that they be regarded as the expressions of man's struggle with *the problem of how he should live*. This problem is obviously a vast one, its enormity reflecting not only man's inability to cope with his environment, but even more his increasing self-reflectiveness.

By problems in living, then, I refer to that explosive chain reaction that began with man's fall from divine grace by partaking of the fruit of the tree of knowledge. Man's awareness of himself and of the world about him seems to be a steadily expanding one, bringing in its wake an even larger *burden of understanding*.[7] This burden is to be expected and must not be misinterpreted. Our only rational means for easing it is more understanding, and appropriate action based on such understanding. The main alternative lies in acting as though the burden were not what in fact we perceive it to be, and taking refuge in an outmoded theological view of man. In such a view, man does not fashion his life and much of his world about him, but merely lives out his fate in a world created by superior beings. This may logically lead to pleading non-responsibility in the face of seemingly unfathomable problems and insurmountable difficulties. Yet, if man fails to take increasing responsibility for his actions, individually as well as collectively, it seems unlikely that some higher power or being would

[7] In this connection, see Langer, S. K.: *Philosophy in a New Key* (1942) (New York: Mentor Books, 1953), especially Chaps. 5 and 10.

assume this task and carry this burden for him. Moreover, this seems hardly a propitious time in human history for obscuring the issue of man's responsibility for his actions by hiding it behind the skirt of an all-explaining conception of mental illness.

VII

I have tried to show that the notion of mental illness has outlived whatever usefulness it may have had and that it now functions as a myth. As such, it is a true heir to religious myths in general, and to the belief in witchcraft in particular. It was the function of these belief-systems to act as social tranquilizers, fostering hope that mastery of certain problems may be achieved by means of substitutive, symbolic-magical, operations. The concept of mental illness thus serves mainly to obscure the everyday fact that life for most people is a continuous struggle, not for biological survival, but for a "place in the sun," "peace of mind," or some other meaning or value. Once the needs of preserving the body, and perhaps of the race, are satisfied, man faces the problem of personal significance: What should he do with himself? For what should he live? Sustained adherence to the myth of mental illness allows people to avoid facing this problem, believing that mental health, conceived as the absence of mental illness, automatically insures the making of right and safe choices in the conduct of life. But the facts are all the other way. It is the making of wise choices in life that people regard, retrospectively, as evidence of good mental health!

When I assert that mental illness is a myth, I am not saying that personal unhappiness and socially deviant behavior do not exist; what I am saying is that we categorize them as diseases at our own peril.

The expression "mental illness" is a metaphor that we have come to mistake for a fact. We call people physically ill when their body-functioning violates certain anatomical and physiological norms; similarly, we call people mentally ill when their personal conduct violates certain ethical, political, and social norms. This explains why many historical figures, from Jesus to Castro, and from Job to Hitler, have been diagnosed as suffering from this or that psychiatric malady.

Finally, the myth of mental illness encourages us to believe in its logical corollary: that social intercourse would be harmonious, satisfying, and the secure basis of a good life were it not for the disrupting influences of mental illness, or psychopathology. However, universal human happiness, in this form at least, is but another example of a wishful fantasy. I believe that human happiness, or well-being, is possible—not just for a select few, but on a scale hitherto unimaginable. But this can be achieved only if many men, not just a few, are willing and able to confront frankly, and tackle courageously, their ethical, personal, and social conflicts. This means having the courage and integrity to forego waging battles on false fronts, finding solutions for substitute problems—for instance, fighting the battle of stomach acid and chronic fatigue instead of facing up to a marital conflict.

Our adversaries are not demons, witches, fate, or mental illness. We have no enemy that we can fight, exorcise, or dispel by "cure." What we do have are problems in living—whether these be biologic, economic, political, or socio-psychological. In this essay I was concerned only with problems belonging in the last-mentioned category, and within this group mainly with those pertaining to moral values. The field to which modern psychiatry addresses itself is vast, and I made no effort to encompass it all. My argument was limited to the proposition that mental illness is a myth, whose function it is to disguise and thus render more palatable the bitter pill of moral conflicts in human relations.

MENTAL HEALTH AND MENTAL ILLNESS

SOME PROBLEMS OF DEFINITION AND CONCEPT FORMATION

RUTH MACKLIN

1. Introduction

In recent years there has been considerable discussion and controversy concerning the concepts of mental health and mental illness. The controversy has centered around the problem of providing criteria for an adequate conception of mental health and illness, as well as difficulties in specifying a clear and workable system for the classification, understanding, and treatment of psychological and emotional disorders. In this paper I shall examine a cluster of these complex and important issues, focusing on attempts to define "mental health" and "mental illness"; diverse factors influencing the ascription of the predicates "is mentally ill" and "is mentally healthy"; and some specific problems concerning these concepts as they appear in various theories of psychopathology. The approach here will be in the nature of a survey, directed at the specification of a number of problems—conceptual, methodological, and pragmatic—as they arise in various attempts to define and to provide criteria for applying the concepts of mental health and mental illness.

Closely related to the above-noted issues—indeed, an integral part of them—is a concern which has engendered much discussion and controversy among professionals in the past decade: the appropriateness of the "medical model," or health–disease conception of psychological disorders and emotional problems. The question arises as to whether or not the medical model of physical health and disease is the appropriate, correct, or most useful model for classifying, understanding, and treating the various emotional difficulties and behavior disorders which persons manifest. Space does not permit a detailed examination

This essay originally appeared in *Philosophy of Science*, vol. 39 (September 1972), and is reprinted with the kind permission of the author and the editor of *Philosophy of Science*.

here of this controversial and interesting issue, but some remarks will be addressed to the problem in the final section of the paper.

In the words of one recent writer, "There is hardly a term in current psychological thought as vague, elusive, and ambiguous as the term "mental health" ([5], p. 3).[1] There appears to be increasing recognition—even on the part of those who are not unhappy with the health-disease model—that some conceptual clarification is needed. Nevertheless, one psychologist claims that "The definition of mental illness is not especially difficult, though a number of problems need to be considered in certain peripheral areas of breakdown in normal human behavior. Ordinarily, we think of mental illness as an unusually persistent pattern of behavior over which the individual has little or no voluntary control; it differentiates him from his fellows; it incapacitates him; it interferes with his normal participation in life" ([1], p. 37).

It is immediately obvious that this conception of mental illness is too broad, since it fails to distinguish mental illness from physical illness—a task which most writers in this area consider crucial. It should be noted that attempts to provide an acceptable definition of these concepts and a systematic set of criteria for their application have implications beyond the concerns of psychological or psychiatric theory. There are consequences, as well, for the direction of social and institutional practices such as therapy, civil commitment proceedings, legal and judicial concerns with the "criminally insane," and other social issues concerned with antisocial and deviant behavior. In addition, given a situation where need exceeds availability of psychotherapeutic time and personnel (both inside and outside hospital and institutional settings), it seems important to have a precise conception according to which comparative judgments ("is sicker than," "is more healthy than") can be made. Such judgments—if made according to some systematic and uncontroversial professional conception of health and illness—would facilitate decision-making problems in the area of assigning priorities for private, outpatient, and inpatient treatment of persons afflicted with psychological disorders of various sorts. So there seem to be crucial practical concerns, as well as more narrowly theoretical issues, which could benefit from greater clarification and systematization in this domain.

A word should be said at this point about the enterprise of defining. The difficulties of attempting to provide a definition of a term in natural language or a set of necessary and sufficient conditions for its application are well known, and there is much philosophical literature on the subject. The generally acknowledged "open texture" of terms in natural languages (and even in scientific theories), in addition to multiple and possibly conflicting criteria of application, have led some philosophers to give up all attempts to provide such definitions.

---

[1] Numbers in brackets refer to references listed in the section at the end of this paper, p. 157.

But psychologists and psychiatrists do not seem to have given up, even if their efforts are bent towards abandoning old conceptions or models in favor of new ones ([11], [16]). In addition, the pragmatic necessity for the enterprise in the area of mental illness and psychotherapy is dictated by the need to identify persons for treatment and to decide when they are "well," and to have some more precise criteria for commitment to and release from mental hospitals. The existing state of affairs is that in general, "mental illness is regarded usually as a residual category for deviant behavior having no clearly specified label" ([10], p. 26). So a partial justification for the inquiry conducted here—the objections of some philosophers and psychiatrists notwithstanding—lies in the stated needs and attempts on the part of many theorists and clinicians at further clarification and provision of a set of criteria for an adequate conception of mental health and mental illness.

One chief difficulty lies in the vagueness and ambiguity of the concept of mental illness as construed even by professional groups presumably committed to similar theoretical orientations and diagnostic procedures. In one recent study, the authors write:

> One need only glance at the diagnostic manual of the American Psychiatric Association to learn what an elastic concept mental illness is. It ranges from the massive functional inhibition characteristic of one form of catatonic schizophrenia to those seemingly slight aberrancies associated with an unstable personality, but which are so close to conduct in which we all engage as to define the entire continuum involved.... And, because of the unavoidably ambiguous generalities in which the American Psychiatric Association describes its diagnostic categories, the diagnostician has the ability to shoehorn into the mentally diseased class almost any person he wishes, for whatever reason, to put there ([6], p. 80).

The authors point out that different norms of adjustment are employed by different users of the term "mental illness," and that "usually the use of the phrase 'mental illness' effectively masks the actual norms being applied" ([6], p. 80). The acuteness of the situation is evidenced by the recognition that the group in question here is the American Psychiatric Association, whose members we might expect, presystematically, to share a body of norms and a roughly similar theoretical background. That this is not the case is readily apparent, and the above-noted authors claim that "the usual reason for variance in diagnosis is a variance in the theoretical orientation of the diagnosticians" ([6], p. 80, n. 18). So if such variation exists even within a circumscribed group of professionals, it is not surprising that a great deal of confusion and inconsistency obtains in the entire field of mental health workers, including clinical psychologists, social psychologists, social workers, and psychiatric nurses, as well as medically trained psychiatrists and psychoanalysts. When we consider the further fact that at least some professionals in all these groups (psychiatrists included) explicitly reject the medical model and the attendant notion of "disease entities," the hope for unanimity or even some widespread agreement on the definition of "mental illness" becomes slim indeed.

In the light of these and other difficulties (a number of which will be discussed in the subsequent sections), Karl Menninger favors a "nonspecific, essentially unitary concept of mental illness" ([11], p. 87). In a brief historical review, Menninger notes that two systems of classification developed—the specific entity concept of mental illness and the unitary concept, the former of which prevailed in American Psychiatry. He writes:

> In the minds of many young doctors and in the minds of vast numbers of laymen, mental illness and particularly schizophrenia is a definite, specific, evil thing which invades the unsuspecting like a fungus or a tapeworm. The word schizophrenia becomes a damning designation. . . . A name implies a concept; and if this concept is unsound, the diagnosis can ruin the treatment; the very naming it can damage the patient whom we essay to help ([11], p. 88).

In formulating his unitary concept of mental illness, Menninger emphasizes the degree of disorganization of the ego and its course or trend of development; his system is based largely on the theoretical concept of the ego—its failures and attempts at survival and optimal adaptation under stress. He holds that there are no *natural* mental disease entities, but that "an ordering of clinical phenomena on the basis of the economics of adaptation does justice to the essential unity of sickness and health; at the same time it leaves room for recognizing the latent potentials of every individual" (p. 89).[7]

While Menninger departs from the official psychiatric nosology, still he retains the conception of psychological disorders as instances of illness—a fact which marks him as an adherent of the medical model. Other psychiatrists and many psychologists argue for a more radical departure from the traditional schema, holding that we need to drop the notions of health and illness altogether in forming a conception of emotional problems and behavior disorders. Limitations of space in this paper preclude a detailed study of these increasing efforts to abandon the medical model, but a thorough account must include an examination of the arguments for and against the model, as well as a study of alternative approaches currently in practice (e.g., behavior modification therapy, existential psychiatry, and others).

In the next four sections I shall examine some problems related to definition and concept formation, as falling under the following categories: attempts to define "mental health" in terms of the notion of mental illness; attempts to define "mental health" and "mental illness" in terms of normality and abnormality; obstacles to a clear conception of health or illness arising within or between specific theories of psychopathology; and, finally, problems with the conception of psychological disorders and malfunctioning as "disease" or "illness." There is an additional set of problems of a pragmatic sort: the identification of specific cases as instances of mental illness; conflicts between lay and professional definitions; the fact that different groups within society operate on the basis of different conceptions of mental health and illness; and the surprising fact that "the basic decision about illness is usually made by community members and *not professional personnel.* . . . Community persons are brought to the hospital on the basis of lay definitions, and once they arrive, their appearance alone is usually regarded as sufficient evidence of 'illness'" ([10], p. 27). Although these practical issues are interesting and relevant to the conceptual and theoretical concerns of this paper, unfortunately space does not permit an examination of them here.

Before proceeding to examine the problems falling under the categories cited above, one general point needs to be noted. There is an ambiguity in the terms "sick" and "healthy" as they are employed in contexts of physical as well as mental health and illness. Marie Jahoda characterizes this ambiguity as follows. The concept of mental health can be defined "as a *relatively constant and enduring function of personality,* leading to predictable differences in behavior and feelings depending on the stresses and strains of the situation in which a person finds himself; or as a *momentary function of personality and situation*" ([5], p. 8). According to the first conception, individuals will be classified as more or less healthy. On the second conception, actions will be classified as more or less healthy. There is an analogue in the context of physical health, as Jahoda notes: according to the first conception, a strong man with a bad cold is healthy; according to the second conception, he is sick. Other examples can be given to illustrate the distinction, and the point is an important one in avoiding sources of error that are often overlooked. Jahoda claims that "much of the confusion in the area of mental health stems from the failure to establish whether one is talking about mental health as an enduring attribute of a person or as a momentary attribute of functioning" ([5], p. 8). One area in which the relevance and importance of this distinction is crucial is that of the legal defense of persons charged with a criminal offense on grounds of insanity, temporary insanity, and the like. Still further implications exist for the selection of criteria according to which persons are committed to and released from mental hospitals. We now turn to an examination of some specific conceptual and theoretical problems in the area of mental health and illness.

2. *Attempts to Define "Health" in Terms of "Disease"*

The concept of disease is itself problematic, in somatic medicine as well as in the realm of psychological disorders. Two preliminary considerations will be noted briefly before examining specific problems in attempts to define the notion of health in terms of disease. Firstly, within the accepted framework of the medical model itself, there may be some difficulty in specifying relevant similarities in degree and kind between acknowledged cases of physical disease and putative instances of mental illness. This is the familiar problem of extending a concept from its standard or accepted usage to cover a new range of cases—a task first faced by Freud and others who were engaged in the process of noting affinities between the traditional cases of physical disease and the new cases (e.g., hysteria) which were being subsumed under a new, broadened concept of illness. But the familiarity of the enterprise of extending a concept does not render the issue any the less problematic (see the discussion in section 5 below).

Secondly, if one chooses to abandon or to circumvent the medical model, there is still the problem of specifying a different set of criteria from those which proceed by analogy with physical disease. While there are some guidelines according to which we can classify mental illness or psychological disorders— antisocial or socially deviant behavior, malfunctioning behavior, self-destructive behavior, and the like—these guidelines are extremely rough and may result in a category that is too *broad* to specify what we want presystematically to count as mental illness or personality disorder (cf. Albee's definition cited above). For example, an attempt along these lines may fail to distinguish between the mentally ill and the criminal. Or, it may result in classes of individuals—who by other psychological criteria would be considered "healthy," or "normal"—being classed as psychologically aberrant or emotionally disturbed, e.g., recluses, civil disobedients, radical revolutionaries, etc. On the other side of the coin, appeal to a specific theory of psychopathology might result in a definition of "mental illness" that is too *narrow* to cover the range of cases which ought to be included under the category.

It should be noted, in this connection, that even among theorists and practitioners operating within the medical model, the current emphasis is on behavior disorders rather than on internal states of illness or on mental disease entities. In an influential and widely used textbook for students and practitioners of psychiatry, the authors write:

> In older texts and in current lay parlance, psychiatry is often defined as the science dealing with mental diseases and illnesses of the mind or psyche. Since these are terms reminiscent of the metaphysical concepts of soul and spirit, we prefer to speak of behavior disorder. Behavior refers to objective data that are accessible to observation, plausible inference, hypothesis-making, and experimentation. The term disorder, although vague, is descriptive of malfunctioning of behavior without specifying etiology or underlying mechanisms. Only some of the behavior disorders are caused by diseases of the brain or are accompanied by somatic reactions. Whereas many cerebral diseases produce a behavior disorder, and while we believe that cerebral processes must be related fundamentally to behavior, *medically* recognizable diseases of the brain cannot, for the most part, be demonstrated in behavior disorders ([13], p. 2).

This position appears eminently sound, both in its emphasis on behavior and also in its presupposition that brain processes and other neurophysiological events underlie molar behavior. Behaviorists and other opponents of the medical model would do well to note the former point, while tough-minded philosophers who reject Cartesian dualism or other forms of "mentalism" (especially proponents of the neural identity thesis or modern materialism) should recognize the physicalist assumptions of at least some contemporary scientifically oriented psychiatrists. The fact that *medically* recognizable diseases of the brain cannot be demonstrated in most behavior disorders at the present time is no barrier to future progress in discovering such correlations and developing systematic psychophysical laws.

Turning now to the relationship between mental health and mental illness, we find that there is some disagreement on the matter. One writer points out the obvious fact that "consensus regarding positive mental health (or even mental abnormality) is far from unanimous" ([14], p. 3). He concludes, from an examination of several different conceptions, that the "criterion for mental health thus is simply the absence of mental illness" ([14], pp. 3–4). This view might be considered the standard conception, even among professionals in the field, as reflected in the words of Kenneth E. Appel, the 1954 president of the American Psychiatric Association: "mental illness is the opposite side of the coin of mental health" ([1], p. 38).

On the other hand, theorists such as Marie Jahoda, who are concerned to provide a workable *positive* conception of mental health, explicitly reject any attempt to define "mental health" as "the absence of mental illness or disease." She notes that at present "knowledge about deviations, illness, and malfunctioning far exceeds knowledge of healthy functioning" ([5], p. 6), and it is apparent that the emphasis in this area has been on the study of disease and malfunctioning with the result that the health–disease model has prevailed, influencing theoretical developments and providing a framework according to which treatment and therapy have proceeded. In Jahoda's view, the assumption that health and illness are different only in degree needs to be tested. She is, herself, a proponent of the view that "mental health" and "mental illness" are *not* correlative terms, each denoting a state of the organism to be understood in terms of the absence of the other. She claims that a definition of psychological health as the absence of mental disease "is based on the assumption that health is the opposite of disease, or that health and disease form the extreme poles of a continuum. What if this assumption should turn out to be unjustified and misleading? Some psychiatrists now speak of different health potentials in seemingly equally sick patients, as if they were dealing with two qualitatively different continua. . ."([5], p. 14).

Jahoda believes that this issue requires a good deal of further research, especially since there is difficulty in clearly circumscribing the notion of mental disease itself. So it would seem to be more fruitful to concentrate on "the concept of mental health in its more positive connotation, noting, however, that the absence of disease may constitute a necessary, but not a sufficient criterion for mental health" (p. 15).[15]

Among the theorists whose conceptions of mental health are not formulated in terms of the absence of disease are a number of self-realization or self-actualization theorists, as well as proponents of existential psychiatry. Rollo May, for one, claims that the carryover of concepts from physical to psychological science is often unsuitable, as in the term "health." "In the common popular meaning, physical health means the absence of infection and organic damage. In psychological therapy the term should mean something very different: "health" refers to dynamic processes; a person is healthy psychologically and emotionally to the extent that he can use all his capacities in day-to-day living" ([9], p. 167). May stresses the *active* role of the individual in relating to himself and to others in his environment—a view which supports a conception of mental health as being something different from or over and above the mere absence of illness or disease.

Jahoda cites a number of theorists who oppose the traditional view ([5], pp. 73–75), one of whom holds that the category of positive health "applies when there is evidence that the individual fully utilizes a capacity or is working in that direction" (p. 74). We shall return later in another connection to a brief examination of self-realization and self-actualization theories of psychopathology. The point to note in the present context is that the notion of *positive* mental health appears to be embedded in some theoretical conceptions while it is absent from others. To this extent, we might expect divergent views to be held on the relationship between mental health and illness by adherents of different theoretical systems in psychology and psychiatry. Jahoda points out that the relation between mental health and mental disease is still exceedingly complex, despite recent efforts at clarification, and that this relation remains one of the most urgent areas for future research.

3. Problems with Attempts to Define "Mental Health" and "Mental Illness" in Terms of Normality and Abnormality

In this category, a number of problematic issues can be delineated. As Redlich and Freedman point out, "The concepts of normality and abnormality are more complex in psychiatry than in general medicine, and some people have suggested abandoning the concepts of normal and abnormal behavior entirely because simple concepts of health and disease do not apply" ([13], p. 112). One of the sources of difficulty with these concepts is the familiar issue of cultural relativism. We turn now to an examination of that issue.

A. *Cultural Relativism*

Jahoda notes that the evidence presented by cultural anthropologists is sufficient to demonstrate the vast range of what can be regarded as normal. Cultural anthropologists "have convincingly demonstrated a great variety of social norms and institutions in different cultures in different parts of the world; and that in different cultures different forms of behavior are regarded as normal" ([5], p. 15). It should be added that even within our own culture, the different norms and standards of behavior vary greatly among different age groups, socio-economic classes, and sub-groups of the population including religious, racial, and ethnic minorities. Thus, what may be considered "normal" sexual behavior for a twenty-eight-year-old divorcée who is a professional woman living in New York City will be considered "abnormal" for her fourteen-year-old sister living in Hudson, Ohio. Similarly, what is "normal" behavior for a black youth living in a crime-infested ghetto will be considered abnormal for a white, upper-middle-class boy from Scarsdale.

Similar problems arise if we try to focus on the concept of abnormality as a criterion of mental *disease*. Again, Jahoda claims that anthropological studies throw doubt on the use of some symptoms for the diagnosis of mental disease: "According to Ruth Benedict (1934), the Kwakiutl Indians of British Columbia engage in behavior that is, by our standards, paranoid and megalomaniacal. Their view of the world is similar to a delusion of grandeur in our culture" ([5], p. 12). Other examples are given to support the view that "whereas identical observable symptoms are regarded in one culture as achievement, in another they are regarded as severe debility" ([5], p. 12). It is not clear, however, that the only conclusion to be drawn is that varying customs and accepted behavior in different cultures necessarily preclude a universally applicable conception of mental illness. Rather, it seems that in the absence of an overall psychological theory, or a well-developed personality theory that is acceptable to most, if not all, professionals and scientists in the field, no set of criteria can be agreed upon for making cross-cultural judgments of mental illness. The belief that a comprehensive psychological theory will be forthcoming someday may reflect an optimistic expression of faith in the progress and development of the science of psychology and related fields, but abundant evidence from the historical development of other sciences shows that such faith may not be wholly unwarranted. It is not unreasonable to hope that a more comprehensive and well-developed science of psychology (normal as well as abnormal) will provide us with a

systematic approach to cultural and individual differences among people, en-
abling competent professionals to specify a workable set of parameters for
formulating clear, univocal concepts of mental health and mental illness.

Redlich and Freedman address the issue of cultural relativism, claiming that
abnormality depends on the cultural values of defining persons. They note that
there is no agreement on what is normal drinking, that prostitution is accepted
in some cultures but not in others, and that "there are remarkable differences in
aggression, sexuality, and dependency needs in the different social classes of a
single culture . . ." ([13], p. 114). They point out that despite the denial of
relativism on the part of some social scientists, it is only extreme forms of
behavior such as indiscriminate murder, cannibalism, or absolute disregard for
property that are almost universally rejected. Severe behavior disorders are likely
to be considered abnormal, no matter what the cultural setting. The authors
write:

> In actual practice, psychiatrists use a composite approach; they diagnose behavior as
> clearly abnormal when it is seriously disabling, frustrating, deviates from established
> cultural norms, hence occurs relatively rarely; however, in borderline cases such an
> approach does not work well. . . .
>
> Only gross deviations are clearly recognized and agreed upon in all civilized
> societies; borderlines of normal and abnormal behavior are fuzzy and overlapping.
> Cultural relativism with respect to milder disorders is the rule. The judgments of
> psychiatrists cannot in reality be far removed from those of the common man of the
> societies and cultures in which psychiatrists and patients live. At present we cannot
> make precise statements about normal and abnormal. . . ([13], pp. 114–115).

Problems of cultural relativism constitute only a partial barrier to providing
a clear and uncontroversial conception of normality and abnormality. Another
set of difficulties lies in the way in which the terms *normality* and *abnormality*
are to be construed, an inquiry to which we turn next.

B. Normality and Abnormality as Normative and as Statistical Concepts

It should be noted at the outset that if "mental health" and "mental illness"
are not properly to be viewed as correlative terms (see section 2 above), then
even *given* some acceptable account of normality and abnormality, we may be
faced with the task of specifying an independent set of parameters for assessing
types and degrees of mental health and mental illness. But apart from this,
another set of problems emerges relating to the fact that normality is sometimes
construed as a normative concept and sometimes as a statistical one. Jahoda
rejects the attempt to provide a criterion for mental health based on normality
on a number of grounds. One such ground is that of the problems presented by
cultural relativity, as discussed above, and the second reason is as follows.

Noting that normality can be viewed either as a statistical frequency concept or as a normative idea of how people ought to function, Jahoda points out that a coincidence of statistical and normative correctness is, at best, fortuitous.

> To believe that the two connotations always coincide leads to the assertion that whatever exists in the majority of cases is right by virtue of its existence. The failure to keep the two connotations of normality separate leads straight back into an extreme cultural relativism according to which the storm trooper, for example, must be considered as the prototype of integrative adjustment in Nazi culture ([5], pp. 15–16).

The issue is now identified as the old problem in philosophical ethics: the is–ought gap. Although I am not concerned to argue here about whether there is or is not, or should or should not be such a gap, it seems that the significance of the distinction for the problem of defining "mental health" in terms of some conception of normality is clear. As Jahoda correctly points out, "insofar as normality is used in the normative sense, it is a synonym for mental health, and the problems of concept definition are, of course, identical" ([5], p. 16).

Another difficulty with "normality" as construed in the normative sense is that the concept tends to function as an "ideal type," so that the actual behavior of persons is, at best, an approximation to some optimal conditions. The problem is, then, that according to some psychological theoretical frameworks it may be extraordinarily difficult or even impossible to draw the line between normality and abnormality (and, consequently, following Jahoda's insight, impossible to draw the line between mental illness and mental health). This issue will be brought up again in connection with a problem to be discussed below: considerations *within* certain theories which preclude the possiblity of a precise definition of mental health and illness. Let it suffice to note at this point that an attempt to define "mental health" in terms of a normative conception of normality appears to lead either to circularity (as Jahoda claims), or else directly back to cultural relativism. We shall next examine the frequency concept of normality to see if it fares any better.

The most obvious difficulty with a statistical frequency concept of normality is that a majority of people may do many things we hesitate to call mentally healthy. Thus, "psychological health may, but need not be, the status of the majority of the people" ([5], p. 16). That this is so might be illustrated by considering the case of physical illness and health. No one would be likely to urge a definition of "physical health" based on statistical considerations, for it might turn out that a majority of the population is suffering from some form or other of physical ailment or disease (whether temporary or enduring). As Livermore, Malmquist, and Meehl point out in this connection:

> From a biological viewpoint, it is not inconsistent to assert that a sizable proportion—conceivably a majority—of persons in a given population are abnormal or aberrant. Thus if an epidemiologist found that 60% of the persons in a society were afflicted with plague or avitaminosis, he would (quite correctly) reject an argument that "Since most of them have it, they are okay, i.e. not pathological and not in need of treatment." It is admittedly easier to defend this nonstatistical, biological-fitness approach in the domain of physical disease, but its application in the domain of behavior is fraught with difficulties ([6], pp. 78–79, n. 11).

It is true, of course, that there are much more systematic and comprehensive biological and physiological theories on the basis of which the concept of physical or bodily health may be constructed in medicine than now exist in the realm of psychological or psychiatric theory. But the inadequacy of a statistical conception of normality for physical health provides an instructive comparison for present purposes. It may be objected here that the example just given presupposes the applicability of the medical model and a conception of mental health based on the analog of physical health. Although this is so, the reasons for questioning the adequacy of the frequency concept of normality for defining "mental health" do not depend on the analogy with physical health.

An additional difficulty with the statistical approach is noted by Redlich and Freedman. This difficulty constitutes a methodological problem rather than an objection in principle, but presents obstacles nevertheless. "Few exact data . . . are available on the frequency and distribution of behavior traits. Such an approach presupposes that behavior is quantifiable and measurable, but obviously many forms of behavior are not. . . . Few data . . . exist on the prevalence and the incidence of psychiatric symptoms, such as anxiety, hallucinations, phobias, and so forth" ([13], p. 113). The authors acknowledge that there are some good examples of the statistical approach in the data supplied by Kinsey et al. on sexual behavior, in the area of socio-economic data, and in the broad investigations of intelligence. However, the need for assessing the *relevance* of various sorts of behavioral data for the task of defining "mental health" and "mental illness" points to still another problem inherent in the statistical approach to normality and abnormality. This is the selection of a reference population—a procedure that involves nonstatistical considerations. Jahoda notes that "the choice of population inevitably contains, at least implicitly, a nonstatistical concept of health" ([5], p. 17), a factor which indicates the inadequacy of an attempt to define "mental health" and "mental illness" on the basis of a purely statistical concept of normality.

Moreover, even when the relevant reference population has been delineated, equal weight would not be given to all measurable psychological functions in developing a set of norms against which to evaluate the mental health status of individuals. "We thus find again that some, at least tacit, nonstatistical considerations must precede the application of the statistical approach" ([5], pp. 17–18).

This is borne out once again by the example of physical health and disease where purely statistical considerations are insufficient for formulating a conception of health. In the domain of mental health, the most that a statistical approach can achieve is a specification of which behaviors and traits are "abnormal" in the general population. But we still require some nonstatistical parameters for deciding which "abnormalities" are to count as illness and which "normalities" should be construed as healthy. The selection of such parameters would appear to depend partly on considerations which are contingent upon the progress and development of a comprehensive psychological theory, and also on a range of value questions which, although relevant and important, cannot be gone into here (in this connection, see [3] and [8]). The above-noted difficulties with both the normative and statistical concepts of normality point to their inadequacy (at least if taken singly) as a basis for defining "mental health" and "mental illness." Redlich and Freedman identify one further approach to normality which will be discussed briefly in the next section: the clinical approach.

C. The Clinical Approach

It was noted in subsection *B* above (p. 132 ff.), that when construed in the normative sense, the concept of normality tends to function as an "ideal type" according to whatever theory is being employed. This is not the case, however, in the clinical approach, as Redlich and Freedman point out: "In general terms, clinical normality is not ideal performance but minimal performance, just above the level of pathological performance for a given individual" ([13], p. 113). But now the problem is to identify such "levels of performance," a task which is not only clinically difficult, but also depends on some theoretical assumptions on the part of the clinician. Indeed, according to Redlich and Freedman: "The clinical approach defines as abnormal anything that does not function according to its design. This approach is useful in somatic illness, including brain disease, but it is less helpful in behavior disorders, because all too often we do not know what design or function a certain behavior pattern serves" ([13], p. 113). Some criteria for normality which have been employed in the clinical approach are adaptation, maturity, "average expectable environment," and "predominance of conscious and preconscious motivations over unconscious motivation of behavioral acts" ([13], p. 113). But Redlich and Freedman find the concept of adaptation, "which is supposed to explain just about everything, only of very limited use in differentiating normal and abnormal behavior" ([13], p. 113); the conscious–unconscious criterion fails to apply to many forms of abnormal behavior determined by brain disease and ignores the fact that in many types of normal and socially desirable behavior, unconscious and preconscious motivations occur ([13], pp. 113–114). The criteria of "average expectable environment" and maturity are viewed more favorably, but the authors fail to note that "maturity" and "immaturity" are themselves value-laden terms, depending for their application not only on the theoretical orientation of the clinician but also on a set of cultural and sub-cultural norms espoused by him.

One final problem in connection with the clinical approach lies in the unwitting conflation of a number of different criteria on the part of professionals. These criteria may encompass those already cited here, in addition to the personal, subjective conceptions of the psychiatrist or clinical psychologist. The situation has been described as follows:

> It is especially tempting to the psychiatrist or clinical psychologist, given his usual clinical orientation, to slip unconsciously from the idea of "sickness," where treatment of a so-called "patient" is the model, to an application that justifies at most a statistical or ideological or psychological-adjustment usage of the word "norm." Probably the most pernicious error is committed by those who classify as "sick" behavior that is aberrant in *neither* a statistical sense *nor* in terms of any defensible biological or medical criterion, but solely on the basis of the clinician's personal ideology of mental health and interpersonal relationships. Examples might be the current psychiatric stereotype of what a good mother or a healthy family must be like, or the rejection as "perverse" of forms of sexual behavior that are not biologically harmful, are found in many infra-human mammals and in diverse human cultures, and have a high statistical frequency in our own society ([6], p. 79, n. 11).

This situation not only complicates the process of diagnosing mental illness in individual persons, but also, if widespread or typical, precludes the use of the clinical approach as an effective means of defining "normality" and "abnormality."

4. Obstacles to a Clear Conception Arising within or between Specific Theories of Psychopathology

This section will be devoted to an examination of some of the difficulties posed by different theories or theoretical conceptions—difficulties that stand in the way of a clear and precise concept of mental health or mental illness. The inquiry will be divided into two main areas: problems *within* theories (intratheoretical); and disparity or conflict *between* or *among* theories (intertheoretical).

A. Intratheoretical Problems

While it is likely that many different theories or theoretical systems contain tacit assumptions or explicit premises which create difficulties for attempts to provide criteria for the concepts of mental health and illness, we shall limit our inquiry here to two of these: Freudian and neo-Freudian psychoanalytic theories; and self-realization or self-actualization theories. It was noted above in connection with normality construed as a normative concept (p. 350), that according to some psychological theoretical frameworks it may be extraordinarily difficult or even impossible to draw the line between sickness and health. One such theory is the classical Freudian account, and one writer points out that if a psychiatrist is trained in the more orthodox psychoanalytic notions, "his belief system makes it impossible to determine the "sickness" or "wellness" of the patient, since the classical theories assume that all people have unconscious drives which interfere with optimal functioning, and no clear practical criteria are provided for judging the "sick" from the "well" ([10], p. 27). We shall not raise questions here about the nature of the theoretical entities to which Freudian theory is committed, nor about the testability of many propositions embedded in that theory. Although such questions are legitimate and interesting, they have been examined at great length by philosophers, psychologists, and psychiatrists alike, and are peripheral to the concerns of this paper. The question here is whether, *given* an initial acceptance of the Freudian notion of the Unconscious and all that it entails, a distinction can be made between healthy and unhealthy behavior. Jahoda seconds the view cited just above, noting that it has not been demonstrated that there are any human beings who are free from unconscious conflicts. "If it is reasonable to assume that such conflicts are universal, we are all sick in different degrees. Actually, the difference between anyone and a psychotic may lie in the way he handles his conflicts and in the appearance or lack of certain symptoms. If this is so, mental disease must inevitably be inferred from behavior. But, apart from extremes, there is no agreement on the types of behavior which it is reasonable to call "sick" ([5], p. 13). So according to this objection, the theory itself precludes any workable, clear distinction between instances of mental health and cases of mental illness. The most we can hope for, according to this theoretical framework, is the provision of *comparative* judgments of health and illness—a conclusion which would be welcomed by many Freudians and non-Freudians alike on this issue.

But this is not the end of the Freudian story. As Joseph Margolis contends, it appears that Freud himself employed a "mixed model that shows clear affinities with the models that obtain in physical medicine and at the same time with the models of happiness and well-being that obtain in the ethical domain" ([7], pp. 81–82). This further complicates the issue since the "mixed model" is really a combination of two different models, each having its own set of parameters along which health and disease, good and poor functioning, desirable and undesirable traits and behavior are identified. Margolis specifies further just how Freud's development of psychoanalytic medicine runs along two converging lines:

> In one, as in the studies of hysteria, Freud was extending case by case the medical concept of illness, by working out striking and undeniable affinities between physical illnesses and counterpart cases, for which the aetiology would have had to be radically different. And, in the other, Freud inevitably assimilated the concept of

mental health to concepts of happiness—in particular, to his genital ideal. The result is that, *given* some version of this (or another such) ideal, deviation from the ideal tends to be viewed in terms of malady and disease, even though there are no strong analogical affinities between the pattern in question and clear-cut models of physical illness. Hence, patterns as significantly different as hysteria and homosexuality tend both to be assimilated to the concepts of health and disease ([7], pp. 75–76).

There is little doubt that Margolis's analysis here is correct. Indeed, on the Freudian account, the failure of an individual to pass successfully through the three developmental stages of sexuality in infancy and childhood (the oral phase, the anal phase, and the phallic phase) can lead to such diverse patterns of adult "illness" as those represented in the neuroses and those constituting the character disorders. In any case, successful passage (without "fixation," "regression," "arrest") through the early developmental stages is a necessary condition (although not sufficient) for the "healthy" adult, achieving or approximating the "genital ideal." The adult genital character is the *mature* individual; failure to attain the ideal results in varying degrees of "immaturity." Thus on the Freudian account, the concept of the "genital (ideal) character," which denotes the mature individual, is intimately bound up with the descriptive-explanatory theory of infant—childhood development. The interlacing of descriptive and normative components in this account, while not in itself pernicious, must be made explicit if there is to be any progress in providing criteria for the concepts of health and illness.

One need not, of course, accept the specific Freudian precepts concerning the developmental stages in infancy and childhood and the related notions of fixation at one level or another, regression to a previous stage, etc. Indeed, the refusal to accept this particular framework may result in different judgments as to the mental health or illness of a person who fails to live up to the "genital ideal." The fact that there are other ideals of health, happiness, and well-being which may be and are, in fact, postulated by different theorists leads not only to the presence of multiple criteria, but also to possibly conflicting ones. Even if we allow the legitimacy of a "mixed model" such as Freud's, it must be acknowledged that there exist multiple and possibly conflicting norms of health, happiness, and well-being. Consequently, deviation from one such norm might count as mental illness, while the same person might be termed mentally healthy according to some different set of norms whose ideal he fulfills or closely approximates.

We turn next to a brief look at some problems inherent in another set of influential theories: the self-realization or self-actualization theories. Mention was made earlier of these theories (above) in discussing the failure of attempts to define "mental health" in terms of the absence of disease or illness. The concepts of self-realization and self-actualization play a dual role in a number of psychopathological theories (notably, those of Karen Horney, Erich Fromm, Kurt Goldstein, and Abraham H. Maslow), functioning as a characterization of the healthy individual and also specifying the goal of psychotherapy (for a more detailed account, see [3]). Redlich and Freedman note that "in highly individualized cultures, self-actualization or self-realization is seen as the goal of certain psychotherapies. The goal of realizing one's human potential is encountered in Buddhism, particularly in the practices of Zen Buddhism, which fascinated and stimulated Karen Horney, Erich Fromm, and Alan Watts. . . . The behavioral changes . . . should be defined in rationally and operationally verifiable terms. There is no place in psychiatry for mystical, irrational, or suprarational approaches" ([13], p. 270).

Leaving aside the methodological issues connected with the goals and practice of psychotherapy, we may note that even in its role as characterizing the healthy person (a positive conception of mental health), the concept of self-realization is problematic. The difficulty is an old one in philosophy, harking back to Aristotelian notions of potentiality and essence. Indeed, Fromm cites Aristotle in his account of "activity" as "the exercise of the functions and capacities peculiar to man" and his emphasis on "the full development of our powers within the limitations set by the laws of our existence" ([3], p. 58).

Kurt Goldstein "speaks of a 'drive' that enables and impels the organism to actualize in further activities, according to its nature," emphasizing that "optimal self-actualization also means health" ([3], pp. 58–59). Karen Horney refers to "the real self as that central inner force common to all human beings and yet unique in each, which is the deep source of growth" ([3], p. 58). What all these theories—and others of this type—have in common is their emphasis on man's "inner nature" which he seeks to fulfill, his "potentialities" which need to be "actualized," and the "inner self" which develops and unfolds successfully through "self-realization." Both as goals of psychotherapy and as characterizations of positive mental health, these concepts are problematic. The assumptions about man's nature or essence cannot be accepted uncritically, and the difficulties of formulating a testable concept of man's "potentiality" (as a generic trait) are well-known. To the extent that a concept of mental health adopted by these theories rests on the foregoing assumptions, we cannot expect much in the way of criteria that meet the requirements of empirical testability and confirmability. Such theories may achieve a high degree of methodological adequacy in cases where a sensitive and insightful therapist can assess the specific "potentialities" or "natural inclinations" of a particular patient. But as attempts to provide a basis for constructing a clear and workable *concept* of mental health, the self-realization theories fail to satisfy the demands of conceptual clarity and empirical testability.

B. Intertheoretical Problems

A set of problems which naturally arises from the proliferation of theories in this area relates to the likelihood of multiple—possibly even conflicting—

criteria for mental health and mental illness. Especially among theories which are couched in terms of some normative ideal of health, happiness, or well-being, we may expect that deviations from the ideal might be construed as "sick" on one theory, while no decision might be forthcoming according to another. This raises the question of whether deviation from some *normative ideal* should properly be counted as sickness or illness, on the model of physical disease. In any case, an obvious consequence of the present situation is that the *general* concepts of mental health and mental illness can only be understood in terms of some *specific* theory of psychopathology.

Enough has been said in the preceding section to indicate the divergence between the concepts of health and illness as conceived by classical Freudian theorists, on the one hand, and self-realization theorists, on the other. Both conceptions are embedded in the theoretical systems themselves, and professional judgments concerning the health or illness of particular individuals may vary depending on which system the diagnostician espouses. The number of different theories is legion, and no attempt will be made here to survey them. Instead, a few general points will be noted.

Following Freud's tripartite division of the psyche into id, ego, and super-ego, much emphasis was placed by psychoanalytically oriented practitioners on the relationship among these and the relation of all of them to unconscious processes. Recent developments in the area known as ego psychology have tried to correct what some theorists held to be a bias in Freudian theory, attempting to replace the "one-sided emphasis on unconscious processes with a stronger acknowledgment of the importance of *conscious* experiences" ([3], p. xiii). It is apparent that with different norms of well-functioning and different emphases even in theories which accept many of the basic Freudian precepts, there is a broad scope of conceptions concerning what is to count as healthy or sick behavior.

Marie Jahoda favors a "multiple criterion" approach to problems of mental health. The value of this approach to the concepts of health and illness is that it has the requisite breadth and flexibility to comprehend a wide variety of human behavior without being so general as to become empty. Commenting on various criteria adopted by different theorists who propound different concepts of positive mental health and also on the various ways of using a multiple criterion, Jahoda writes: "There is no incompatibility between the idea of diverse types of health and the use of such a criterion. . . . At the present state of our knowledge it may well be best to combine the idea of various types of health with the use of a multiple criterion for each. The former will prevent over-generalizations; the latter will permit us to do justice to the complexity of human functioning" ([5], p. 73).

It is evident that the work of providing criteria for the concepts of mental health and illness, as well as the task of evaluating proposed definitions needs to be done by theorists and practioners in the fields of psychiatry and psychology. The task is partly conceptual and partly empirical, involving policy decisions as well as theoretical considerations. In this and the preceding sections, I have tried to specify a number of the problems which exist in this area and to note some of the issues that need clarification and careful scrutiny.

Finally, one large problem should be noted—a problem which might best be viewed as one that encompasses and gives rise to most of those already discussed. This is the absence of an overall scientific theory on which to base conceptions of mental health and illness, well-functioning and maladaptive behavior. It should be noted, however, that in this regard the concepts of health and disease face a number of similar problems in the domain of somatic medicine (i.e. the concepts are vague, there are multiple criteria for their application—criteria which may conflict occasionally, etc.). There is no general, well-integrated theory of the sort that exists in, say, physics, interconnecting the well-developed fields in medicine of physiology, anatomy, pathology, neurology, immunology, etc., with current developments in the biological sciences. The absence of bridging laws between these branches of medical and biological science, as well as the divergent theoretical and methodological approaches of experimental biologists, on the one hand, and medical scientists oriented towards pathology, on the other, all contribute to the present lack of systematization in the total field of biological science. So the absence of well-confirmed fundamental laws, from which other laws are derivable, and the absence of a systematic, general theory result in the situation that within medicine itself, there are no clear or precise formulations of the basic concepts of health and disease, and no set of necessary and sufficient conditions for their application.

These facts concerning the present stage of scientific development of somatic medicine may offer little consolation to the theorist in psychology or psychiatry who is looking to provide a clear, workable concept of mental health or mental illness. But it would seem that the clarity and precision of the basic concepts in this field—as in any other—go hand in hand with the related theoretical developments of formulating general laws, providing systematic interconnections among the various branches of the field, and relating all of these to existing, well-confirmed theories in the other sciences. The science of psychology is a long way from this goal, but there do not seem to be any good arguments that have been offered to show that the goal is unattainable, *in principle.* Some writers have attempted an operational reformulation of some of the basic psychoanalytic concepts [4], [15], and while the merits of such endeavors need to be assessed critically, these efforts point to the attempt to render more precise and testable concepts which have been found fruitful in psychotherapeutic practice. Moreover, it is not the case that all existing psychological and psychiatric theories should be viewed as competing with one another, or in some sense mutually incompatible. Rather, we might reasonably expect that with the further development of the science of psychology, bridging laws (perhaps of a very complex sort) will be formulated and theories at various levels (e.g. macro-behavior, physiological psychology, etc.) will be systematically integrated.

To show that the views expressed here do not reflect a philosopher's unwarranted optimism about the methods and goals of this field, it is appropriate to cite once again the views of Drs. Redlich and Freedman.

> As a technology based on the behavioral and biological sciences, psychiatry takes a deterministic point of view. This does not mean that all phenomena in our field can be explained, or that there is no uncertainty. It merely commits us to a scientific search for reliable and significant relationships. We assume causation—by which we mean that a *range* of similar antecedents in *both* the organism and environment produces a similar *set* of consequences. In general, we follow the procedures of basic sciences and attempt to determine the limits within which a range of antecedents has a high probability of producing similar results. . . .
>
> The principles and basic methods of studying normal and abnormal behavior in individuals and in populations, in clinical practice, as well as under experimental conditions, are the same as in other naturalistic sciences ([13], pp. 79–80).

To the extent that individual practitioners in the field—whether clinicians or theorists—depart from the above-noted principles and methods, psychiatry and psychology are not to be faulted, any more than physics is impugned by poor methodology or unsound theoretical conclusions on the part of some of its practitioners.

5. Problems with the Conception of Psychological Disorders as "Disease" or "Illness"

A number of arguments have been put forth by some influential psychologists and psychiatrists who hold that the conceptualization of psychological disorders in terms of illness represents an adherence to a mistaken model—the medical model of health and disease. These criticisms of the continued use of the medical model rest partly on conceptual and theoretical grounds and partly on pragmatic considerations relating to the consequences for the individual and society of adhering to this model. There is, however, a good deal of confusion surrounding these issues confusion which stems largely from a tendency to conflate epistemological, conceptual, and pragmatic problems and attempts at solution to such problems. I shall concentrate on only a few of these issues here, specifically, those which relate most directly to the concerns of definition and concept formation.

The most outspoken opponent of the medical model is Dr. Thomas Szasz, a psychiatrist who holds the M.D. degree. Szasz claims that "although the notion of mental illness made good *historical* sense—stemming as it does from the historical identity of medicine and psychiatry—it made no *rational* sense. Although mental illness might have been a useful concept in the nineteenth century, today it is scientifically worthless and socially harmful" ([16], p. ix).

Thus he argues that it is inappropriate or logically mistaken to construe emotional problems and psychological disorders as a species of illness, on an analogy with bodily disease. On Szasz's view, there exists a *"major logical and procedural error in the evolution of modern psychiatry"* ([16], p. 26). One "error" lay in decreeing that some malingerers be called "hysterics," which led to obscuring the similarities and differences between organic neurological diseases and phenomena that only looked like them ([16], p. 26). But it does not follow from the fact that hysteria (and other psychological disorders) are called "illness" that the similarities and differences between organic and nonorganic illness cannot be duly noted and treated accordingly. Indeed, the very introduction of the notion of *mental* illness to cover phenomena such as hysteria marks a decision to treat a class of seeming bodily disorders as different in relevant respects from organic neurological disease. The labeling itself need not involve a failure to attend to the relevant similarities and differences for the purpose of diagnosis, explanation, or treatment.

In general, the precise nature of Szasz's objection to construing psychological disorders as illnesses is not always clear. Sometimes he writes as though the reclassification and introduction of a set of "new rules of the medical game" consist in a sort of logical or conceptual error: "During [the past sixty or seventy years] a vast number of occurrences were reclassified as 'illnesses.' We have thus come to regard phobias, delinquencies, divorce, homicide, addiction, and so on almost without limit as psychiatric illnesses. This is a colossal and costly mistake" ([16], p. 43).

In answer to the question, "from what point of view is it a mistake to classify non-illnesses as illnesses?" Szasz replies that "it is a mistake from the point of view of science and intellectual integrity." This would seem to imply that a proper scientific conception and a generally accepted classificatory schema preclude treating psychological disorders as illnesses. But there is no compelling evidence—either from Szasz's own account, or revealed in our inquiry in the preceding sections—to show that it is indeed the case that a clear "error" or "mistake" is involved in this type of classification. The consequence of the medical model approach and resulting reclassifications, according to Szasz, has been that although "some members of suffering humanity were promoted . . . to higher social rank, this was attained at the cost of obscuring the logical character of the observed phenomena" ([16], p. 295).

It is evident from the passages just cited that at least sometimes Szasz construes the reclassification of psychological disorders as illnesses to be a sort of error or mistake (logical or conceptual). At other times, however, he writes as though the change is "merely linguistic" and a matter of choice or preference of one classificatory schema rather than another. Thus he holds that it is "a matter of scientific and social choice whether we prefer to emphasize the similarities and, hence, place hysteria in the category of illness, or whether we prefer to emphasize the differences and place hysteria in a category of nonillness" ([16], p. 29). This view construes the issue as one of scientific and practical utility, rather than conceptual or logical error, and is borne out by Szasz's subsequent discussion. In a later passage, he reiterates this same view:

> From the standpoint of our present analysis, the entire change in renaming certain illnesslike forms of behavior from "malingering" to "hysteria" (and "mental illness") can be understood as nothing but a linguistic change employed for the purpose of achieving a new type of action-orientedness in the listener. The verbal change . . . served to command those charged with dealing with "hysterics" to abandon their moral-condemnatory attitude toward them and to adopt instead a solicitous and benevolent attitude, such as befitted the physician vis-a-vis his patient ([16], p. 132).

It appears from the above passages and others which could be cited, that Szasz's position is at the very least, unclear, and at worst, inconsistent, with regard to the question of what is wrong with classifying behavioral disorders and disabling psychological difficulties as forms of "illness." We now turn to a brief discussion of Szasz's own view of what properly constitutes illness and some criticisms of his charge against those who have been engaged in reclassifying certain nonbodily disorders as forms of illness.

It is at least an implicit assumption of Szasz's—one which he sometimes makes explicit—that the only proper candidates for the notion of disease are those which refer to genuine *bodily* (organic or functional) ailments or involve a physical lesion. We need to examine this assumption in order to evaluate Szasz's contention that it is a mistake or error to construe nonbodily disorders as illness. The issue then becomes, on what grounds does Szasz reject mental "illnesses" as instances of some sort of disease, and are those grounds justifiable? He writes:

> The adjectives "mental," "emotional," and "neurotic" are simply devices to codify— and at the same time obscure—the differences between two classes of disabilities or "problems" in meeting life. One category consists of bodily diseases—say, leprosy, tuberculosis, or cancer—which, by rendering imperfect the functioning of the human body as a machine, produce difficulties in social adaptation. In contrast to the first, the second category is characterized by difficulties in social adaptation not attributable to malfunctioning machinery but "caused" rather by the purposes the machine was made to serve . . . ([16], pp. 41–42).

This view sets up two mutually exclusive categories of disability, such that an instance of the one category can never be construed as falling also under the second category. An antireductionist bias is evident in Szasz's remarks here and elsewhere, and it is legitimate to ask whether a clear distinction can be made between "the functioning of the human body as a machine" and "the purposes the machine was made to serve."

Moreover, it is certainly true, as Szasz contends ([16], pp. 79 ff.), that Freud continued to seek organic or physico-chemical *causes* of the psychological disorders and malfunctioning which he observed in his patients. But the question remains, *even if* Freud was mistaken in his continued search for neurological or some other physical bases for these behavioral disorders, does it follow that such disorders cannot properly be construed as forms of disease or illness nonetheless? Szasz's position seems to be that the absence of identifiable or probable physiological causes disqualifies a disorder or disability from the category of disease. Consequently, construing nonorganically based behavioral and personality disorders as diseases turns out to be *both* a logical and a scientific error. It is a logical error because the two categories of problems in facing life are mutually exclusive; and it is a scientific mistake because it erroneously presupposes an organic or neurological cause for every psychological, social, or ethical problem resulting from the malfunctioning of persons. Szasz wishes, therefore, to eliminate the entire notion of mental illness, claiming that "mental illness is a myth. Psychiatrists are not concerned with mental illnesses and their treatments. In actual practice they deal with personal, social, and ethical problems in living" ([16], p. 296).

Whereas Szasz chooses to *close* the concept of disease or illness, requiring as a necessary condition that there be a known or probable physiological basis, another view of the matter holds that the labors of Freud and others resulted in a legitimate *extension* of the then existing concept of disease or illness. The strategy in replying to Szasz's position would thus consist in the following two-stage argument: (1) showing that Freud and his followers were not making a logical or conceptual *mistake* in treating psychological disorders as illnesses, but were rather engaged in the enterprise of extending or widening the concept of disease or illness; (2) showing that such extension in this case is *legitimate,* that is, can be justified by noting relevant and important similarities between cases of mental illness and cases of physical illness. I shall take the question, "Is it *ever* legitimate to extend or enlarge a concept?" as admitting of an uncontroversial affirmative answer. Accordingly, one reply to Szasz is given in the words of Joseph Margolis:

> Szasz is absolutely right in holding that Freud reclassified types of suffering. But what he fails to see is that this is a perfectly legitimate (and even necessary) maneuver. In fact, this enlargement of the concept of illness does not obscure the differences between physical and mental illness—and the differences themselves are quite gradual, as psychosomatic disorder and hysterical conversion attest. On the contrary, these differences are preserved and respected in the very idea of an *enlargement* of the concept of illness ([7], p. 73).

This passage serves not only to make the point about the legitimacy of enlarging the concept of illness to cover cases of mental or psychological illness, it also emphasizes that there is no clear and obvious line—as Szasz appears to think there is—between physical and mental illness, or between the "two categories" of problems in facing life. Indeed, it is apparent that Margolis has drawn this line in a different place from Szasz. While Szasz considers hysteria a nonbodily illness (hence, not an "illness" at all) on the grounds that it has no organic or neurological *causes,* Margolis construes hysterical conversion and other psychosomatic ailments at least as borderline cases, presumably on the grounds that such disorders are manifested in terms of observable and clear-cut bodily *symptoms* and *malfunctioning.* So it appears that there may be some genuine dispute as to the selection of criteria for an adequate or uncontroversial characterization of *physical* or *bodily* illness itself.

Once it is acknowledged that there are good reasons for construing Freud's maneuver as one of extending a concept rather than as a sort of logical or conceptual error, we may proceed to the second stage of the argument in reply to Szasz: the justification of the extension of the concept of illness to cover psychological problems and personality disorders. Margolis suggests the following, in answer to the question "Should mental 'disorders' be allowed, in a medical sense, to count as diseases or illnesses?"

> If I were to describe a condition in which a patient suffers great pain in walking and is quickly overcome by fatigue, a condition which lasts for several years, and we were to find that there is an organic cause for this pattern, we should be strongly inclined to regard what we have before us as a *physical illness.* Now, if we have the same sort of pattern but are unable to find any organic cause, and begin to suspect that, in some inexplained way, the condition is due to the emotional or psychical life of the patient, we may have a reason for insisting that the pattern is still a *pattern of illness* ([7], p. 74).

The reasonableness of this conclusion—Szasz's view notwithstanding—is shown by observing the affinities between the new cases and the standard ones. It should be noted, further, that the existence of unexplained phenomena and the absence at present of psycho-physical laws (covering normal as well as abnormal behavior) do not in themselves compel theoretical conclusions and conceptual decisions of the sort that Szasz is prone to make.

There is a line of argument different from that employed by Margolis which can serve to show the relevant similarities between cases of physical disease and cases of putative mental illness. Whereas Margolis's method is a case by case approach, proceeding by comparison of new (mental) cases to old (physical) instances of disease and noting the affinities between them, the alternative method distinguishes general *categories* of behavioral symptoms and demonstrates that these categories are common both to bodily diseases and to disorders commonly construed as mental illness. David Ausubel uses this approach in arguing that "the plausibility of subsuming abnormal behavioral reactions to stress under the general rubric of disease is further enhanced by the fact that these reactions include the same three principal categories of symptoms found in physical illness" ([2], p. 262). Ausubel characterizes these categories as manifestations of impaired functioning, adaptive compensation, and defensive overreaction, and cites examples of both physical and mental diseases falling under each category, noting the relevant similarities between them. He concludes that there is no inherent contradiction in regarding mental symptoms *both* as expressions of "problems in living" (Szasz's preferred locution) *and* as manifestations of illness. "The latter situation results when individuals are for various reasons unable to cope with such problems, and react with seriously distorted or maladaptive behavior" ([2], p. 265). So according to some opponents of Szasz, the position is taken that in order to qualify as a genuine manifestation of disease, a symptom need not reflect a physical lesion.

We may conclude from the inquiry in this section that there appears to be no compelling reason to adopt Szasz's view that mental illness is a "myth" and that personality disorders and psychological problems are inappropriately viewed as illness and properly to be construed as "problems in living." In sum, there appear to be no logical or conceptual reasons why such difficulties cannot or should not be subsumed under the category of "illness." Moreover, whatever is gained in terms of social utility by viewing these problems as "problems in living" is not precluded by viewing them *also* as manifestations of disease, as Ausubel suggests. So whatever merits Szasz's position may have in terms of pragmatic consequences, these same results can be achieved if we retain the concept of mental *illness* along with the present classificatory schema.

By way of summary and conclusion, it would be well to note where the rejection of Szasz's antimedical model position leads us. Most of the problems discussed in this paper can be seen to re-emerge upon consideration of a brief quotation from Ausubel's paper. Arguing specifically against Szasz's contention that to qualify as a genuine manifestation of disease a given symptom must be caused by a physical lesion, Ausubel writes: "Adoption of such a criterion would be arbitrary and inconsistent both with medical and lay connotations of the term "disease," which in current usage is generally regarded as including any marked deviation, physical, mental, or behavioral, from normally desirable standards of structural and functional integrity" ([2], p. 259).

While this statement may appear sufficiently general to escape controversy, upon closer analysis a range of familiar problems can be identified in connection with the phrase *normally desirable standards*. The immediate difficulty concerns whether the phrase is to be construed descriptively or normatively, but even if this question is decided, further problems remain.

Construed descriptively, *normally desirable standards* denotes those standards which people (the issue of just *which* people will be put aside for the moment) actually desire for themselves or others. The question of whether or not this is an adequate account of the general notion of desirability has been raised at least since John Stuart Mill wrote, in his essay *Utilitarianism:* "The only proof capable of being given that an object is visible, is that people actually see it. The only proof that a sound is audible, is that people hear it: and so of the other sources of our experience. In like manner, I apprehend, the sole evidence it is possible to produce that anything is desirable, is that people do actually desire it" ([12], p. 221).

Critical views contend that the notion of desirability is properly to be explicated in terms of what *ought* to be desired, or what it is *rational* to desire, and that Mill's purely descriptive account fails to capture the normative force of the term *desirable.*

Construed normatively (in terms of which standards ought to be adopted or are worthy of being maintained), the phrase generates a number of problems noted in detail above—chief among which is the cultural relativity of values. The questions "desirable *for* whom?" "desirable *according* to whom?" and "desirable for what ends or aims or purposes?" all need to be answered satisfactorily before Ausubel's general statement can serve to provide even a rough and ready criterion for the notions of mental health and illness. Moreover, it may emerge that there is no set of "normally desirable standards" that will be accepted without controversy by all individuals or groups because of the differing ideologies and value systems and differing background experiences in a society as large and diverse as ours (not to mention those of other societies and cultures).

It may be, however, that we need to emphasize the further phrase: "of structural and functional integrity" in analyzing Ausubel's statement. On this view, the appeal to "normally desirable standards of structural and functional integrity" presupposes some general theory which provides an account of an integrated, well-functioning system. Such an account is given, for the most part, in biological (anatomical and physiological) theories so that the notion of physical disease, although not without a number of problems, can be specified without engendering a great deal of controversy. With regard to mental health and illness, however, not only is there no generally accepted psychological or personality theory that can be presupposed, but the search for criteria of application for the basic concepts is itself an attempt to fill out such a theory and provide the very parameters which enable us to judge that a personality system possesses "structural and functional integrity."

In the words of Redlich and Freedman, "a completely acceptable super-theory on which psychiatry can generally rest its work does not exist" ([13], p. 79). But these authors would be quick to note that progress in the behavioral and biological sciences has been rapid and steadily advancing in recent years. So whatever pessimism may accrue to the observations made in this study about the concepts of mental health and mental illness as currently understood and employed by professionals and laymen alike, a measure of optimism exists in the belief that fruitful and systematic developments will continue to be forthcoming in the experimental, theoretical, and clinical areas of psychology and psychiatry.

References

[1] Albee, G. "Definition of Mental Illness and Mental Health Manpower Trends." *Psychopathology Today.* Edited by William S. Sahakian. Itasca, Ill.: F. E. Peacock Publishers, 1970.

[2] Ausubel, D. P. "Personality Disorder *Is* Disease." *Mental Illness and Social Processes.* Edited by Thomas J. Scheff. New York: Harper & Row, 1967.

[3] Buhler, C. *Values in Psychotherapy.* New York: The Free Press of Glencoe, 1962.

[4] Ellis, A. "An Operational Reformulation of Some of the Basic Principles of Psychoanalysis." *Minnesota Studies in the Philosophy of Science.* vol. 1. Edited by Herbert Feigl and Michael Scriven. Minneapolis: University of Minnesota Press, 1956.

[5] Jahoda, M. *Current Concepts of Positive Mental Health* New York: Basic Books, 1958.

[6] Livermore, J. M.; Malmquist, C. P.; and Meehl, P. E. "On the Justifications for Civil Commitment." *University of Pennsylvania Law Review 117* (1968): 75–96.

[7] Margolis, J. *Psychotherapy and Morality.* New York: Random House, 1966.

[8] Masserman, J. H., ed. *Psychoanalysis and Human Values.* New York: Grune and Stratton, 1960.

[9] May, R. "The Work and Training of the Psychological Therapist." *Psychology, Psychiatry, and the Public Interest.* Edited by Maurice H. Krout. Minneapolis: University of Minnesota Press, 1956.

[10] Mechanic, D. "Some Factors in Identifying and Defining Mental Illness." *Mental Illness and Social Processes.* Edited by Thomas J. Scheff. New York: Harper & Row, 1967.

[11] Menninger, K. "Unitary Concept of Mental Illness." *Psychopathology Today.* Edited by William S. Sahakian. Itasca, Ill.: F. E. Peacock Publishers, 1970.

[12] Mill, J. S. "Utilitarianism." *Essential Works of John Stuart Mill.* New York: Bantam Books, 1961.

[13] Redlich, F. C. and Freedman, D. X. *The Theory and Practice of Psychiatry.* New York: Basic Books, 1966.

[14] Sahakian, W. S., ed. *Psychopathology Today,* Itasca, Ill.: F. E. Peacock Publishers, 1970.

[15] Skinner, B. F. *Science and Human Behavior.* New York: Macmillan Company, 1953.

[16] Szasz, T. S. *The Myth of Mental Illness.* New York: Harper & Row, 1961.

GENETIC ASPECTS OF SCHIZOPHRENIA

ARTHUR FALEK

Since the early years of this century, many studies concerned with the biological and vital statistics aspects of schizophrenia have been conducted based on the definition of this disorder according to the Kraepelin-Bleuler classification. This classification model has four major subtypes of schizophrenia: the catatonic, the paranoid, the hebephrenic, and the simple. There have been many concerns about the definitiveness of this diagnostic scheme, and some of these have been discussed in publications edited by Rosenthal and Kety,[1] Kaplan,[2] as well as in a monograph by Rosenthal.[3]   Of particular interest are those aspects that deal with the finding that, while affected family members are more likely to display the same subtype of schizophrenia, there are family constellations in which affected members present more than one subtype. There is also evidence that some individuals, at a particular time, exhibit one subtype of the schizophrenia and, at another point in time, have the clinical picture of one of the other subtypes. Both the finding of differences in subtypes among relatives and the observation of changes in diagnostic subtype in individuals, over a period of time, have been pointed to as evidence that the unified clinical model of schizophrenia is not a viable entity.

It should be noted, however, that a similar fourfold classification model has been presented for the definitive neuropsychiatric genetic disorder, Huntington's disease. This disorder is one of the presenile psychoses with a mean age of onset in the early 40s, strong evidence of a history of the disorder in direct family members, and clinical findings of progressive choreatic motor movements as well as mental deterioration resulting in early death. For over a century, on the basis of such symptomatology and family history, this disorder has been identified as a single-disease entity with a dominant mode of inheritance. It has been found that Huntington's disease can be divided into four major subtypes: the achoreatic, the akinetic, the rigid, and the hyperkinetic forms. It was noted that

---

[1] D. Rosenthal and S. S. Kety, *The Transmission of Schizophrenia* (New York: Pergamon Press, 1968).

[2] A. R. Kaplan, *Genetic Factors in Schizophrenia* (Springfield, Ill.: Charles C Thomas, 1972).

[3] D. Rosenthal, *Genetic Theory and Abnormal Behavior* (New York: McGraw-Hill, 1970).

in many families with Huntington's disease, affected individuals often have one or the other of the four subtypes and, indeed, over a period of time often display more than one of the subtypes. The observation of four subtypes in this well-known disease entity was an attempt to refine the diagnosis and certainly did not dilute the concept of Huntington's disease as a definitive neuropsychiatric disorder.

In similar fashion, it is suggested that the classification model described initially by Kraepelin and modified by Bleuler does not weaken the concept of a unified, diagnostic classification of schizophrenia. Of course, it may be possible, in the future, to subdivide the present symptomatologically derived classification of schizophrenia into two or more biochemical disorders, when findings are obtained similar to those now being reported for infantile amaurotic idiocy, Tay Sachs disease, phenylketonuria, and the hemoglobinopathies.

Currently, we appear to be a long way from this potential, and the only evidence of heterogeneity from a genetic point of view is a statistical one.[4] The inability to establish a simple genetic model to account for all cases of schizophrenia indicates that current knowledge to classify this disorder is based on phenotypic definition. To determine whether there are genetic aspects to the disorder, it is first necessary to evaluate the frequency of schizophrenia in family members from a variety of selected nonschizophrenic populations. These studies were conducted in central Europe between 1926 and 1938.[5] Investigations were conducted of the family members of spouses of patients with late onset organic psychoses, among relatives of patients with physical and surgical disorders as well as family members from specific groups in the general population. The reason the studies were conducted in families with late onset organic disorders was to prevent the bias of limited marital opportunities that could have occurred to members of families with early onset organic disorders. In addition, late onset studies have a population of siblings available for analysis either within or past the age range established for the onset of schizophrenia (15–45 years of age). The siblings of spouses, rather than those of the hospitalized patients, were studied in order to eliminate any possible bias resulting from the initial selection of a mental hospital population. The age correction was instituted in these morbidity risk studies, since an adjustment was found necessary to correct for those in the population sample below as well as within the age of onset for the disorder. For correction, those whose ages at the time of ascertainment were below the youngest age accepted for the onset of schizophrenia were eliminated from the total population sample. That number was further reduced by counting only a portion of those ascertained within the age of onset in order to correct

[4] I. I. Gottesman and J. Shields, "A Polygenic Theory of Schizophrenia." *Proceedings of the National Academy of Science 58:*199–205, 1967.
[5] A. Falek and H. M. Moser, "Classification in Schizophrenia." *Archives of General Psychiatry 32:*59–67, 1975.

for those with late as well as early onset of the disorder. Even with this age-corrected, morbidity risk analysis, which produced the highest estimate of this disorder in these family members, the highest risk found in members of families from nonschizophrenic populations was 1.75%. It needs to be pointed out that the often quoted schizophrenia, morbidity risk frequency of 0.85% for siblings of selected nonschizophrenic populations is, in fact, based on the combined data of two of these investigators who reported in 1928 on the siblings of spouses with cerebral arteriosclerosis and general paresis. Of interest is the fact that, although no definition of schizophrenia is presented by these early European investigators other than to refer back to the Kraepelin-Bleuler diagnostic scheme, apparently they were trained to identify the disorder in similar fashion. This is evidenced by the data in which they all found low frequencies of schizophrenia. An additional 20 studies on populations in North America, Europe, and Asia were reported by Yolles and Kramer.[6] In spite of the limitations of this series of studies because of variations in case finding methods, differences in demographic characteristics of the population, and apparent lack of a consistent diagnostic procedure, the findings in these 20 studies are very similar to those reported for the first 18 studies. At its highest prevalence is no more than 1%, and the age-uncorrected mean morbidity risk for schizophrenia for both studies is 0.35%. Unfortunately, no age-corrected data are available for comparative purposes. Furthermore, studies in which the frequency of schizophrenia is measured in a total population followed for their lifetimes reveals that in such populations the mean frequency for schizophrenia is approximately 1% with a range between 0.71 and 1.40%.

By contrast, in the fourteen investigations of siblings of schizophrenia index cases conducted in Europe, England, Scandinavia, and the United States,[5] the mean age-corrected morbidity risk was found to be 8.7% with a range from 4.9 to 14.3%. The morbidity risk in siblings is, therefore, eight times that reported for members of unaffected families in the general population. Although there is much criticism regarding the method for the diagnosis of schizophrenia, this classification scheme has apparently been sufficiently clear throughout this century to yield very similar estimates of a low frequency of the disorder in 50 studies in the general population. In comparison, 14 studies in the families with a schizophrenic index case have shown consistently higher morbidity among the relatives of affected individuals.

According to Gottesman and Shields,[7] twin studies were first undertaken to determine the rate of occurrence of the genetic factor for schizophrenia rather than the relative importance of nature or nurture in the development of the dis-

[6]S. F. Yolles and M. Kramer, "Vital Statistics." In *The Schizophrenia Syndrome* (New York: Grune and Stratton, 1969), pp. 66–114.

[7]II. Gottesman and J. Shields, *Schizophrenia and Genetics* (New York: Academic Press, 1972).

order. In the late 1920s and early 1930s, it was believed that gene expression was a biological constant and not something dynamic depending on multiple factors both external and internal. For most scientists, however, the principal object of the monozygotic versus dizygotic twin comparison was to test the hypothesis that genes really made the difference and that familial aggregation of schizophrenia was not simply due to the shared family environment. The twin studies reported by Kallmann in 1946[8] and Slater in 1953[9] as well as the many other early twin studies clearly showed that monozygotic twins had a much higher concordance rate than dizygotic twins, as high as 86% in one study for the monozygotic twins as compared to 14% for the dizygotic twins.

The strongest criticisms of the twin studies started in the late 1950s and early 1960s. Concern was first voiced that the biological and psychological peculiarity of monozygotic twins resulted in the more frequent concordance for schizophrenia in these twin pairs. It has been possible to show that schizophrenia in monozygotic twins is no more frequent than in dizygotic twins and that the twins do not need to be reared together to be concordant with the disorder. The other area of criticism was that monozygotic twin pairs encountered more similar environments than dizygotic twin pairs and that the concordance rates for monozygotic twin pairs was misleadingly high for a number of methodological reasons. As the nature/nurture argument became more shrill, it became more and more difficult for persons in this controversy to remember that from the genetic point of view both genetic and environmental factors were involved.

For a number of years there seemed to be no way to resolve this controversy. Then, in 1966, Heston[10] reported the first adoption study in schizophrenia in which he showed a higher prevalence of schizophrenia and other disorders in children born of mothers with a hospitalized diagnosis of schizophrenia. These children had been separated from their mothers within the first three days of life and reared in institutions or foster homes without contact with their mothers or their mothers' families. The controls were also children adopted shortly after birth and matched for type of rearing but with a nonpsychotic parentage. No schizophrenia and significantly less psychopathology were found in the control group with the nonpsychotic parentage. Adoption studies have also been conducted by Rosenthal, Kety, Schulsinger, and Wender in population samples obtained in Denmark.[11] In these studies, the frequency of schizophrenia in the

[8] F. J. Kallmann, "The Genetic Theory of Schizophrenia: An Analysis of 691 Schizophrenic Twin Index Families. *American Journal of Psychiatry 103:* 309–322, 1946.

[9] E. Slater, "Psychotic and Neurotic Illnesses in Twins." *Medical Research Council Special Report No. 278* (Her Majesty's Stationary Office, London, 1953).

[10] L. L. Heston, "Psychiatric Disorders in Foster Home Reared Children of Schizophrenic Mothers." *British Journal of Psychiatry 112:* 819–825, 1966.

[11] S. S. Kety, D. Rosenthal, P. H. Wender, and F. Schulsinger, "The Types and Prevalence of Mental Illness in the Biological and Adoptive Families of Adoptive Families of Adop-

biological relatives of adoptees with a diagnosis of schizophrenia were compared with the frequency of schizophrenia in the biological relatives of a matched sample of control adoptees who did not have a diagnosis of schizophrenia or any other severe mental health problem. These data confirm the finding of Heston of an increased frequency of schizophrenia in the families of patients with this disorder. This appears to be particularly so for patients with chronic schizophrenia as compared with patients with a diagnosis of acute schizophrenia with evidence of only one short episode of the disorder in a lifetime. Furthermore, Kety was able to demonstrate in a small population of adoptees, in which the father was the affected parent and the mother showed no evidence of psychiatric disorder (so that the maternal environment during pregnancy had little, if anything, to do with the development or occurrence of this disorder in the offspring), a marked increase in the frequency of schizophrenia. Wender and his colleagues,[12] in a study of normal children adopted into families with a schizophrenia foster parent, presented evidence that such an environmental situation did not increase the frequency of schizophrenia in these children whose natural parents and their families had no evidence of this disorder.

While all of these studies have added strength to the early finding of a genetic basis for the occurrence of schizophrenia in individuals, current data do not clarify the mode of inheritance of this disorder or the heterogeneity of the diagnosis. Current thinking is that there is strong likelihood that this is a polygenic trait and that diagnostic assessment permits phenotypic heterogeneity as well as environmental phenocopies of the genetic disorder(s). Based on the most recent analyses, the incidence of schizophrenia is approximately 1% in the general population, about 10% in the siblings and children of a schizophrenic patient, about 40% in the children of two schizophrenic patients, and almost 50% in monozygotic co-twins.

Studies conducted in recent decades indicate that fertility among schizophrenic women is rising.[13] While earlier studies revealed lower reproductive rates for schizophrenic men and women, current research suggests that reproduction in this population is at least as high as that of the normal reproductive population. In part, this is due to the reduction in offspring in the general popu-

---

tive Schizophrenics." In D. Rosenthal and S. S. Kety (eds.), *The Transmission of Schizophrenia* (Oxford: Pergamon Press, 1968), pp. 345–362; "Mental Illness in the Biological and Adoptive Families of Adopted Schizophrenics, *American Journal of Psychiatry 128:*302–306, 1971; and in R. R. Fieve, D. Rosenthal, and H. Brill (eds.), *Genetic Research in Psychiatry* (Baltimore: Johns Hopkins University Press, 1975), pp. 135–145.

[12]P. H. Wender, D. Rosenthal, S. S. Kety, F. Schulsinger, and J. Welner, "Cross-Fostering: A Research Strategy for Clarifying the Role of Genetic and Experiential Factors in the Etiology of Schizophrenia. *Archives of General Psychiatry 30:*121–128, 1974.

[13]W. A. Burr, A. Falek, L. T. Strauss, and S. B. Brown, "Fertility in Psychiatric Outpatients." Paper presented at the 33rd Annual Meeting of the Society of Biological Psychiatry, Atlanta, 1978. *Hospital and Community Psychiatry*, in press.

lation, and for schizophrenic patients the short-term institutional policies, community mental health programs, and new drug therapies that have enabled them to spend most of their lifetime in outpatient treatment programs rather than in inpatient institutionalization. This has resulted in a change in the sexual activity of schizophrenic persons, and in schizophrenic women this is accompanied by high frequencies of unprotected coitus, unplanned fertility, and unwanted delivery. The data lend support to the clinical impression that unwanted or unplanned pregnancies in psychiatric populations are detrimental to both the parents and the children involved. It must be pointed out that while women seen in psychiatric facilities do not differ from the population at large in their desire to have birth-control assistance available to them, family-planning services are not being provided on a regular basis to such patients either in inpatient or outpatient facilities. Whether one believes the etiology of schizophrenia to be largely genetic or, in addition, to have a large environmental component, there is, at present, an unmet need for the provision of voluntary family-planning programs to affected individuals desiring such services. Without such services, it is expected that from either the genetic or environmental basis there will be an increase in the need to treat many more patients with a diagnosis of schizophrenia in the future.

PSYCHOPATHY AND
MORAL UNDERSTANDING

ANTONY DUFF

I

Critics of contemporary psychiatry argue that concepts of mental disorder are wrongly used to exclude from ordinary human rights and relationships people who are fully rational and responsible; that the pseudomedical terminology of disorder gives a spurious air of objectivity to our *value* judgements on those whose conduct we find unacceptable and disguises the fact that we are *imposing* on them our own moral and social values.[1] Criticism has been fiercest of the concept of "psychopathy": even critics who allow the concept of mental disorder to be legitimately extended beyond the narrow limits of the M'Naghten Rules dismiss "psychopathy" as a pseudomedical moral judgment.[2] They argue that this "diagnosis," based solely on the antisocial conduct it is meant to explain, is vacuously circular; that it marks only our disapproval of the conduct, not the medical discovery of its origin in a disordered condition of mind; that we cannot distinguish a disordered psychopath from a rational criminal or rebel.

My aim is not to defend current usage of the term "psychopathy"—it is certainly too often used to ascribe disorder to those whom we should rather call immoral or unusual—but to show that it *can* be used to identify a kind of disorder not captured by the more readily accepted criteria, and thus that critics who argue, not just that it is abused in practice, but that it has *no* legitimate use, are wrong. The argument is also relevant to wider philosophical and moral issues. As part of a more general attempt to understand the problematic concepts of mental health and disorder, it should help to provide a sounder theoretical basis

---

[1] Cf. Barbara Wootton, *Social Science and Social Pathology* (London, 1959), chs. 7–8; Thomas Szasz, *The Myth of Mental Illness* (New York, 1961); Antony Flew, *Crime or Disease?* (London, 1973).

[2] Besides those noted above cf. Anthony Kenny, "Mental Health in Plato's Republic," *Proceedings of the British Academy 55:* 249–253, 1969; Nigel Walker and Sarah McCabe, *Crime and Insanity in England* (Edinburgh, 1973), ch. 10.

Reprinted from *American Philosophical Quarterly*, *14* (3):189–200, July 1977, with the kind permission of the author and the editor.

for our treatment of the disordered. It is relevant too to philosophical discussions of responsibility and rationality: an account of mental disorder, as a condition in which a person's rational capacities, and thus his status as a rational agent, are impaired, requires a correlative account of what it is to *be* a rational and responsible agent. More directly, a discussion of psychopathy will demonstrate the inadequacy of one traditional philosophical account of practical rationality, which underlies many criticisms of the concept of psychopathy. I hope to show at least that these ambitious claims are well founded.

An account of psychopathy as a disorder should begin with a general account of the concept of mental disorder. I can here only assert what should be argued: that a person is mentally disordered insofar as he suffers some abnormal and harmful impairment of his rational capacities.[3] The identification of impaired capacities provides the "objective" basis of judgments of disorder: the requirement of harmfulness indicates the evaluative aspect of such judgments.[4] We must thus identify the capacities essential for a rational human life and provide criteria for their assessment. Two such capacities can be readily identified: the intellectual capacity for reasoning about the empirical features of one's environment, one's actions, and their consequences; and the capacity to control one's actions and resist contrary impulses, in the light of one's rational purposes. We can thus identify two kinds of disorder, involving the impairment of these capacities. Serious intellectual incapacity, typical of severe mental deficiency and delusional psychoses, brings the agent under the strictest interpretation of the M'Naghten Rules: he is "labouring under such a defect of reason . . . as not to know the nature and quality of the act he was doing."[5] An impaired capacity for control subjects the agent to "irresistible impulses"—to compulsive actions which he rationally rejects but cannot prevent himself doing.[6] The abnormal impairment of these essential human capacities constitutes a disorder.

To focus on our central problem, I will define a psychopath, negatively, as one in whom *these* capacities are unimpaired: he can discover the empirical features of his environment and actions, and he acts as he want to. I will argue later that we can legitimately extend the notions of rational understanding and

---

[3] For accounts of disorder based on the notion of incapacity, cf. Antony Flew, *op. cit.;* Jonathan Glover, *Responsibility* (London, 1970), ch. 7.

[4] I would argue that we can give a parallel, and equally evaluative, account of the concept of physical disorder, in terms of the harmful impairment of capacities: cf. Antony Flew, *op. cit.* pp. 35–53; Jonathan Glover, *op cit.*, ch. 6.

[5] The Rules are quoted in full in the *Report of the Royal Commission on Capital Punishment 1949–53* (London, 1953), Appendix 8: this strictly intellectualist interpretation is the one which has been officially adopted by English courts; cf. *R.* v. *Codere* (1916) 12 C. A. R. 21; *R.* v. *Windle* (1952)2 Q.B. 826.

[6] There are, however, more problems with this category of disorder than is sometimes recognized: cf. Antony Flew, *op cit.*, pp. 59–60; Jonathan Glover, *op. cit.*, pp. 97–101 and 135–140, for discussions that are not really adequate.

control and say that a psychopath *is* unable to understand the nature and quality of his acts, or to control them rationally: but this extension must be justified. I will try to construct an account of psychopathy as a disorder, partly by showing the inadequacies of some suggested accounts and partly by showing how the inadequacies of traditional empiricist accounts of the notions of understanding and rationality in moral and emotional contexts may hinder the recognition of this kind of disorder.

II

Accounts of psychopathy usually begin, and sometimes end, with accounts of psychopathic behavior.

> The psychopath . . . is constantly getting into trouble with neighbors, "friends," family, and police. Periods of socially acceptable conduct alternate erratically with destructive pranks, petty thefts, forgeries, fights, intoxication, miscellaneous other minor and often pointless crimes. Inexplicable minor cruelties, humiliations, inconveniences are dealt out freely by him. He knows the probable consequences of his acts . . . but does not care—very often does not care even enough to try to protect his liberty by concealing his doings. [7]

But such accounts of criminal and antisocial behavior, injurious to others and apparently to himself, provide by themselves no proof of disorder. Persistent criminality, for instance, could be a criterion of disorder only within a determinist perspective which, denying responsibility to anyone, takes the fact of crime as proof that "something has gone wrong." But the sense of "disorder" is now radically changed; for we cannot assume that all criminals are less capable of rational understanding and control than the rest of us. Furthermore, if crime is *the* criterion of psychopathy, the label becomes utterly uninformative: it neither explains nor illuminatingly redescribes criminal conduct, but simply marks its occurrence; it precludes any distinction between psychopathic and other criminals. [8]

Nor will it help to provide a fuller account of "psychopathic" patterns of behavior, specifying the kinds of offense committed—violent, sexual, etc.; adding that his conduct is generally antisocial, not just criminal; that he exhibits no concern either for his own interests or for those of others, acting without any recognizably rational motive, making no attempt to avoid detection, and destroying the ends which prudence is thought to dictate, and the relationships which men value; that, in short, his conduct is by our standards grossly immoral,

[7]Herbert Fingarette, *On Responsibility* (New York, 1967), pp. 25-26. Cf. also Hervey Cleckley, *The Mask of Sanity* (St. Louis, 1964); D. K. Henderson, *Psychopathic States* (London, 1939); William McCord and Joan McCord, *The Psychopath* (New York, 1964).
[8]Cf. Antony Flew, *op. cit.*, pp. 73-78; Barbara Wootton, *op. cit.*, pp. 249-250.

imprudent, and irrational. This distinguishes a psychopath from other criminals: and *if* we can suppose that he shares our conceptions of prudence and value, he must be disordered; conduct so obviously destructive of the agent's own ends must be attributed to an inability either to realize its obvious consequences, or to resist impulses which *he* sees as irrational. But why suppose this? He clearly *knows* what he is doing (he can tell us) and is *not* trying to resist his impulses: he just has values very different from ours.[9] Human values, both moral and prudential, are irreducibly diverse: a man can rationally live by values very different from, and perhaps repugnant to, our own. An adequate concept of disorder must allow a distinction between the rebel against conventional values and a disordered psychopath: mere difference, in conduct or values, precludes this distinction.

But could the psychopath help acquiring his perverse values; could he now change them? This test, if intelligible, will not distinguish a psychopath from other criminals or rebels.[10] If it means "could he acquire other values *if* he wanted to?", it asks whether he can modify his derivative purposes in the light of his more basic desires: could he lead a law-abiding and conventional life if he thought it better to do so? But the psychopath, *if* he wanted to, could change his ways as easily, or as arduously, as anyone else. And it is meaningless to ask whether he could *want* to change: any intelligible notion of capacity must be explained hypothetically, as a capacity to do something *if* I want to; at the level of those basic desires from which all others, including the desire to change, are derived, notions of capacity and incapacity become meaningless. Responsibility cannot require the capacity to change our *basic* desires or values: for we try to change desires, and thus reveal a capacity or incapacity to do so, only on the basis of more basic desires, which are the unchosen *given* of all practical reason and rational action.[11]

Two other suggestions may be mentioned. First, that the fact that the psychopath is not deterred from crime by punishment, or from antisocial and irresponsible conduct by rational criticism, provides good utilitarian grounds for holding him nonresponsible: for a man is responsible insofar as we can usefully modify his conduct by rational deterrence and criticism; if these persistently fail, we must seek other ways of controlling his conduct, such as therapy or detention, and count him disordered—as insusceptible to rational persuasion.[12] This suggestion may serve the utilitarian goals of deterrence and prevention, so long as the alternative to prison is enforced psychiatric treatment: but it does not

[9]Cf. Vinit Haksar, "The Responsibility of Psychopaths," *The Philosophical Quarterly 15:* 140-143, 1965.
[10]Cf. Vinit Haksar, "Aristotle and the Punishment of Psychopaths," *Philosophy 39:* 81-88, 1964.
[11]Cf. P. H. Nowell-Smith, *Ethics* (Harmondsworth, 1954), ch. 19.
[12]Cf. William Kneale, "The Responsibility of Criminals" in H. B. Acton (ed.), *The Philosophy of Punishment* (London, 1969), pp. 185-190.

provide an adequate criterion of disorder. We must distinguish the man who is undeterred or unpersuaded because he is rationally unconvinced by our arguments, or is committed to some principle which justifies his actions, from the man who is rationally incapacitated, and thus disordered: that we cannot *in fact* deter or persuade a man does not show him to be incapacitated or less than fully rational; persistent crime may still be rational.[13]

Secondly, it has been suggested that the correlations between behavior independently identified as psychopathic and the presense of certain physiological abnormalities (an extra Y chromosome; abnormalities in EEG patterns and capillary loop formations) can justify a diagnosis of disorder.[14] But even a 100% correlation between such behavior and such statistical abnormalities could provide evidence of disorder *only* if the abnormalities could also be correlated with some independently identifiable incapacity.[15]

These preliminary attempts to provide criteria by which a psychopath can be judged disordered are inadequate. But some point toward the truth: it is by asking whether a psychopath exhibits any intelligible values in his own life; how he is related to those values of ours which he does not share; how far any rational argument is possible with him (though not just whether we can in fact persuade him by such means); that we will identify his disorder and the crucial differences between him and the rational rebel or criminal.

I will argue that we cannot find in a psychopath's life any intelligible dimension of value, emotion, or rational concern: and that this lack is logically connected to an inability to understand this dimension of the lives of others; the values, interests, and emotions which inform their lives and actions; the moral, prudential, and emotional aspects of his own actions. I will thus be arguing that there is a close logical connection between two commonly identified features of psychopathy: first, that it involves an incapacity for such emotional and moral responses as love, remorse, and concern for others:

> He can commit the most appalling acts, yet view them without remorse. The psychopath has a warped capacity for love. His emotional relationships, when they exist,

---

[13]This suggests that a strictly utilitarian account of responsibility will be inadequate: indeed, I would argue that a strictly utilitarian approach must lead us to abandon the notion of responsibility altogether, and with it the related distinctions between punishment and therapeutic treatment. Cf. Barbara Wootton, *Crime and the Criminal Law* (London, 1963) for a consistent working out of such an approach.

[14]CF. D. K. Henderson and R. D. Gillespie, *Textbook of Psychiatry*, 10th edition, revised I. R. Batchelor (London, 1969), p. 531; David Stafford-Clark, *Psychiatry Today*, 2nd edition (Harmondsworth, 1963), p. 117; *Evidence of Dr. Stafford-Clark and Dr. Hill to the Royal Commission on Capital Punishment* (1949-53), *Minutes of Evidence*, vol. XIII, 297ff.

[15]Cf. Antony Flew, *op. cit.*, pp. 76-78. We should note though that these data may at least be *suggestive*, since the EEG patterns and capillary loop formations of psychopaths are very like those of children, which may lead us to look for some kind immaturity or deficiency in the psychopath.

are meager, fleeting, and designed to satisfy his own desires. These last two traits, guiltlessness and lovelessness, conspiciously mark the psychopath as different from other men.[16]

Second, that a psychopath, although not intellectually incompetent, is unable properly to understand the "nature and quality" of his acts, since he cannot grasp those emotional and moral aspects which are as much a part of them as their empirical features.[17] A psychopath is not a rebel, who *rejects* more conventional values and emotions in the light of some favored conception of the good: he is a man who has never come to understand, or to share in, this dimension of human life.

Here, however, we face a familiar philosophical argument, based on an empiricist account of practical reasoning and on the supposed distinctions between fact and value, reason and emotion, and designed to show that we can call a man disordered *only* if he is intellectually incompetent or suffering some strictly irresistible impulse.[18] On this account, the values, wants, and emotions which determine and explain a man's actions are analyzable into sets of factual beliefs about the world, his actions, and their consequences, to which are joined certain attitudes or reactions—of approval or disapproval, liking or disliking. Rational assessment, and thus a judgment of disorder (which must rest on the discovery of some serious irrationality or rational incapacity), is possible only of factual beliefs, or of the *internal* consistency of a man's wants and values: we can regard him as rationally defective, or disordered, only if we can identify some irrationality of factual belief, or some radical conflict between his actions and his wants, or between the wants on which he acts and other wants which we can say are more important to him. But no such rational criticism is possible of those basic reactions and attitudes which form his basic wants and values: for they are neither true nor false, nor are they means to any further end. A man is rational and responsible just so long as he knows, factually, what he is doing, and is doing what he wants.

On this account there is nothing wrong with a psychopath: he knows, factually, what he is doing; he does what he wants and would not do it if he did not want to; he has emotions, values, and wants since he clearly has pro- and anti-attitudes toward actions and states of affairs. He does not *share* our values and emotions: but since we cannot say that he wants, but is unable, to share

[16]William McCord and Joan McCord, *Psychopathy and Delinquency* (New York, 1965), p. 14; quoted by M. S. Pritchard, "Responsibility, Understanding, and Psychopathology," *Monist 58:* 631, 1974.

[17]Cf. Hervey Cleckley, *op cit.;* compare too the extended interpretation of the M'Naghten Rules favored by Australian courts: Norval Morris, "The Defenses of Insanity in Australia" in Gerhard Mueller (ed.), *Essays in Criminal Science* (New Jersey, 1960), pp. 273–298.

[18]Such an account clearly underlies Flew's argument (Antony Flew, *op. cit.*), and is closely related to the argument about capacities mentioned above, p. 168.

them, we cannot regard him as either irrational or incapacitated on this basis; for these basic values and emotions are neither rational nor irrational—they simply *are*. Nor can we say that he cannot understand our values and emotions: for understanding requires only that he be able to grasp our factual beliefs and observe what our pro- and anti-attitudes are; and this an intellectually competent psychopath, who has pro- and anti-attitudes of his own, can do. If someone claims that "real" understanding of values and emotions requires that we actually share them, then a psychopath cannot understand ours, nor we his: but the same will be true of anyone whose values and emotions we do not share; thus we cannot distinguish a psychopath, as disordered, from a rational rebel or criminal. In any sense which could be relevant to the ascription of responsibility or disorder, a psychopath can understand his actions and our values.

My aim in the rest of this paper will be to show that, although a psychopath satisfies *these* criteria of practical rationality, he is still disordered, because incapable of a proper understanding of those values, interests, and emotions which he so conspicuously does not share: in showing this, I will also be showing the inadequacy of this account of practical reasoning and understanding.

III

A more detailed example will assist this task. Meursault, in Camus's *L'Etranger*, seems a paradigm example of a psychopath.[19] Although the prosecutor portrays him as a callous and cold-blooded criminal, and the defense counsel as a "decent hard-working young man" who "for one tragic moment lost his self-control," it is clear that they both read into his conduct purposes, interests, and values which are not there. He does not help Raymond, or kill the Arab, in pursuit of a calculated vendetta: he helps because he is asked, and can see no good reasons for or against it; the killing is almost something that happens to him, not something he does with any intention or purpose. Nor does he exhibit the kinds of concern appropriate either to a rational egoist or to a "decent hard-working young man": he has no interest in promotion at work, or in developing lasting emotional relationships of love or friendship—indeed, he finds these notions meaningless; he makes no effort to avoid conviction or sentence; he feels neither remorse for his crime nor pity for himself. His life lacks that dimension of emotion, value, and interest which gives cohesion and intelligibility to other lives, connecting a man's actions to each other and to him.[20] It consists

---

[19] Albert Camus, *L'Etranger*, translated as *The Outsider* (tr. Stuart Gilbert) (Harmondsworth, 1961); cf. J. G. Murphy, "Moral Death: A Kantian Essay on Psychopathy," *Ethics 82:* 288–89, 1972.

[20] My understanding of *L'Etranger* has been much helped by S. R. Sutherland, "Imagination in Literature and Philosophy," *British Journal of Aesthetics 10:* 261–274, 1970.

of discrete episodes and impulses, limited to the present moment and the immediate context; the absence of recognizably rational purposes and values makes
it difficult sometimes even to say that he *acts*, rather than that events and acts
happen to and through him.

However, it may be suggested that Camus shows Meursault's to be an intelligible life, lived by a rational, though unusual, conception of human life and its
possibilities: for Meursault's revelation at the end of *L'Etranger*, supplemented
by *The Myth of Sisyphus*, provides an intelligible metaphysical and ethical
background to such a life. Given his account of human life as a solitary movement toward death; of the impossibility of discovering any meaning within or
without the world: given a fundamental ethic of honesty—of living in the light
of the truth, however harsh: we can understand someone who regards as illusory
the concerns of others for marriage, jobs, and the future; who, abandoning the
futile attempt to build lasting relationships and regarding others as of no more
significance than himself, lives strictly for the moment, seeking only to extract
the maximum intensity from each passing experience. Meursault has *seen
through* the illusory concerns with which others surround and support themselves: it is honesty, not incomprehension, which explains his failure to act as
others expect, or to exhibit the kinds of concern—for his mother, for Marie,
for his victim, for himself—whose absence we find so puzzling or repugnant.
He is a rational rebel: we may condemn or admire him, but cannot call him
disordered.[21]

This attempt to show a life like Meursault's to be intelligible can succeed
only if it can connect such a life to a shared metaphysical and ethical tradition,
showing his beliefs and values to form an intelligible extension, development, or
modification of concepts and values within a tradition we share with him.[22]
But, even if Camus succeeds in providing an intelligible background which
could thus make sense of a life like Meursault's, he still fails to render Meursault's
life intelligible. For we *cannot* find in Meursault's life the kind of understanding,
insight, and concern for honesty which, at the end of the book, we are asked to
see in it: he exhibits, not an insight into a truth which others conceal from
themselves and a dedication to living in the light of that truth, but rather a blank
incomprehension of the values, interests, and emotions which inform the lives
of those around him, and a complete absence of any conception of truth or
value of his own.

He is not intellectually defective: he can give a factual account of his actions;
he can see that others find such matters as death, love, friendship, career, important, and that they are irritated or annoyed by his actions and responses. But his
understanding is still deficient: for he cannot see *how* these things can be impor-

[21] Compare Mailer's account of the "White Negro's" psychopathic life: Norman Mailer,
"The White Negro," *Advertisements for Myself* (London, 1969), pp. 269–289.
[22] Cf. R. W. Beardsmore, *Moral Reasoning* (London, 1969), ch. 5.

tant, how they can provide reasons for action and judgment; he cannot understand the emotional and moral significance these aspects of life have for others.
And thus he cannot understand the "nature and quality" of his actions, since
he has no grasp of these aspects of them. He has not *seen through* the illusions
of others, since he lacks the understanding of them which that would require:
it is not a concern for honesty—a refusal to lie—which explains his refusal to
cooperate with his counsel, since he is incapable of the moral understanding
which such an ethical stance requires. He is not a man living by unconventional
or unusual values: for he has no rational values, concerns, or interests at all;
that dimension of thought and experience which he cannot understand in the
lives of others is equally missing from his own life. He is more like a mental
defective than a psychotic: his grasp of values and concepts is *lacking*, not
distorted.

My claim is that Meursault's life is psychopathic, and must remain so unless
we can show, not just that a life *like* that could be rendered intelligible by
providing an appropriate background, but that *his* life, as lived by him, has that
kind of meaning. To substantiate this claim, I will try first to explicate the kind
of understanding of moral values which Meursault lacks, and the connection
between such understanding and an acceptance of, or concern for, these values,
which will involve expanding my brief comments above on the conditions for
the intelligibility of moral beliefs. I will then discuss the way in which this lack
of moral understanding is logically connected to his failure to understand the
more generally practical and emotional aspects of his actions and of the lives
of others, and the logical connections between this lack of understanding of, and
concern for, others and the absence in his own life of any conception of, or
concern for, values and interests of his own, and the related absence of emotional responses and concerns.

IV

Psychiatrists and philosophers sometimes identify a psychopath's "lack of
conscience" as grounds for calling him disordered.[23] Of course, most of us are
at various times more or less indifferent to the moral aspects of our actions and
to the interests of others—for which we are properly blamed. But a psychopath
is not just *sometimes* thoughtless or indifferent: he *never* exhibits any sincere
concern for the interests of others, or remorse for his actions. But why should
this render him disordered, rather than just more callous or wicked than others?

Can we say that such *complete* lack of concern for the values we recognize
is by itself enough to render him disordered: that our moral reactions to, and

[23]Cf. the works cited above by Cleckley, McCord and McCord, Fingarette, and Pritchard;
also G. M. Stephenson, *The Development of Conscience* (London, 1966).

relationships with, each other as responsible moral agents are possible only within a common form of life, based on shared values; that we cannot enter into such moral relationships with a man whose values are so alien to ours and thus cannot properly hold him responsible?[24] But to avoid the response that lack of concern is grounds for, not a defense against, condemnation, we must also show how a psychopath's lack of concern involves a lack of understanding, which is connected to the absence in his own life of *any* intelligible values. M. S. Pritchard has argued that such a lack of concern for moral values *amounts* to an inability to understand them.[25] He claims that moral communication and understanding are possible only within a shared form of life, which involves "agreement not only in definitions but also in . . . judgments," reactions, and emotions: and thus that an understanding of moral concepts and values requires not just an intellectual recognition of the criteria by which others make moral judgments, but a *concern* for such values, which enables me to understand these judgments as *practical.*[26] His argument points the way to a better understanding of psychopathy as a disorder, but he gives a misleading account both of the kind of concern required for moral understanding and of the kind of "intellectual" understanding possible for a psychopath.

We must allow that we can understand not only values with which we profoundly disagree, but also values belonging within forms of life other than our own, such as those of historical or alien cultures, with which there is no question of either agreement or disagreement: we can gain not only an "intellectual" understanding of such values, but a moral understanding of their meaning, and of how they can intelligibly provide reasons of action. Understanding requires neither a common form of life nor any *identity* of moral concerns with those we wish to understand. It *does* require that we have moral values, and a moral language, of our own; *and* that we can find logical connections between our concepts and values and theirs: we come to understand them by tracing out these connections. Unless we can understand their concepts and values in terms of our own (which may involve extending, stretching, and modifying ours), we cannot understand them at all: unless we have moral concerns of our own, values to which we are practically committed, we cannot understand their values as practical.

Pritchard rightly emphasizes that coming to understand values must involve coming to care for *some* values: a child learns moral concepts and the language of values, as an agent and participant; not just as an observer. He does not (and this is a logical, not a psychological, point) learn first to identify a class of actions

---

[24]Cf. Herbert Fingarette, *op. cit.*

[25]Pritchard, *op. cit.*

[26]Pritchard draws on Wittgenstein and A. E. Murphy for his account of practical reason: Ludwig Wittgenstein, *Philosophical Investigations* (Oxford, 1958); A. E. Murphy, *Theory of Practical Reason* (LaSalle, 1965).

under some neutral description and *then* discover that people also adopt a (logically distinct) attitude of approval or disapproval towards such actions: he is taught to identify them *as* right or wrong, as actions which he has reason to do or not to do.[27] The major defect of empiricist accounts of moral concepts is that they suppose we can distinguish moral attitudes from the kinds of action toward which they are directed; and thus that an understanding of a moral view requires only a grasp of the descriptive criteria through which the attitude is directed toward a class of actions. But Pritchard's insistence on concern as a requirement of understanding ignores the fact that, having learned to understand (in part by learning to care for) certain values, a rational agent becomes able not only to criticize and modify the values he has been taught, but also to understand values very different from them.

Moral understanding is not a purely intellectual matter: but it can be exhibited by someone who remains unmoved by the values he seeks to understand. Indeed, the kind of "intellectual" understanding which Prichard allows to the man "lacking a sense of justice," *is*, as he describes it, a moral understanding:

> If he is sufficiently observant and cautious in his behaviour, he might acquire a reputation as an astute judge of issues of justice. He might learn very well what others count as relevant in settling these issues. He could feign guilt feelings or act apologetic when criticised for acting unfairly. He could appear indignant when injustices are done to others by others and resentful when they are done to him. And he could put on a show of other-regard and positive concern to be just. Still, since all of this is only mimicry, he would lack a sense of justice. And, although he would not lack "information" or "data" that others have, he would not see what they see.[28]

It is often said that an intelligent psychopath can purvey an impression of moral understanding and concern; that it is only his unguarded actions and responses which give him away.[29] But what Pritchard describes *is* a moral understanding, requiring more than purely intellectual capacities, though less than an actual concern for *those* values: it requires emotional and imaginative capacities which a psychopath lacks. To call it a purely intellectual understanding, requiring only a grasp of the *descriptive* criteria by which the application of moral terms, and the propriety of moral responses, are determined, revives the very distinction between fact and value which this argument should lay to rest.

For what does the competent and astute discussion of moral issues involve? It involves more than the ability to apply learned formulas which provide descriptive criteria for the identification of actions to which moral labels can then be attached—of this an intelligent psychopath may well be capable. A person who is to exhibit moral understanding must also be able to explain and

[27]Cf. D. Z. Phillips and H. O. Mounce, *Moral Practices* (London, 1969), ch. 1; Richard Norman, *Reasons for Actions* (Oxford, 1971), ch. 3.
[28]Pritchard, *op. cit.*, p. 640.
[29]Cf. Stephenson, *op. cit.*, pp. 19–20.

criticize these moral rules—which involves more than showing how they do or do not derive from other formulas; he must be able to show how these rules may or may not be *extended* to cover new cases, which do not fall exactly under any specified set of descriptive criteria; to discuss rationally the resolution, or the impossibility of resolving, cases of conflict. Following moral rules, the ability to "go on in the same way,"[30] requires more than the intellectual capacity to acquire and apply fixed formula: it requires a *creative* capacity to understand the significance of the value in question, and to discuss, extend, and criticize its application.

This capacity, or its lack, can be exhibited in detached discussion of values which we do not share: its exhibition, in creative and imaginative discussion, *constitutes* a moral understanding of those values. But it requires a kind of sensitivity and imagination possible only for someone who already shares in some form of moral and emotional life, whose life includes values and emotions logically connected to those he is trying to understand: it is this which a psychopath, like Meursault, lacks. He may learn, for instance, that it is wrong to hurt people and notice that this word, and this moral label are applied not only to physical assaults, but also to some ways of talking to others, and to failures to do what we said we would do. He may thus build up a set of descriptive criteria for the application of the term "hurting" and for the judgment that it is wrong. But understanding requires that he also be able to explain the connections between these criteria; and to see how the term could be extended to cover new cases which do not fall under this list—which will count as cases of hurting not (just) because of their empirical or descriptive resemblances to the more central cases, but because of the emotional and moral connections we can see between them. And of this a psychopath is incapable: lacking any dimension of emotion or value in his own life, he cannot see how, though he may be told that, it can be hurtful to someone, and a kind of dishonesty, not just to fail to do what you explicitly said you would do, but also to fail to do something you know they have come, tacitly, to rely on you to do; nor could he argue that this is morally different from other kinds of injury.

A psychopath's incapacity, his lack of understanding, is revealed by the fact that he is capable of no more than a sterotyped and rigid application of moral formulas he has learned.[31] His relation to moral concepts is like that to aesthetic concepts of a person lacking in aesthetic sensitivity (which is distinct from an actual concern for the artistic objects he is discussing): he can parrot certain stereotyped judgments, and apply them to new cases which fall under such

[30] Cf. Wittgenstein, *op. cit.*, I. 185ff; Peter Winch, *The Idea of a Social Science and its Relation to Philosophy* (London, 1970), pp. 24–33.
[31] Cf. Stephenson, *op. cit.*, ch. II.

descriptive criteria as he has learned; but he can neither understand, nor intelligently discuss, criticize, or extend the rules he has picked up.

I have been trying in this section to steer a way between two untenable extremes: the view that moral understanding requires only an intellectual grasp of the descriptive criteria for the application of moral labels, which are themselves logically distinct from these criteria; and the view that "real" understanding requires an actual concern for the values in question. The latter ignores the fact that we can understand values we do not share, and which we might be unable to see ourselves ever accepting. The former, wrongly supposing that we could provide purely descriptive criteria for the application of moral terms, and that we can separate attitudes from the features of actions toward which they are directed, ignores the kind of sensitivity and imagination required for even a nonparticipant understanding of values—of how they can provide reasons for action, of how they are to be applied and developed in particular cases. My own account insists that a concern for *some* values—a participant understanding of them—is essential for understanding *any* values; and that the attitudes, emotions, and values I am to understand must be logically related to those which I share myself: only thus can I come to see, not just *that* others have pro- and anti-attitudes toward actions I can identify by some descriptive criteria, but what these attitudes amount to, *and* what the actions are toward which they are directed.

A psychopath, who shares in no values himself, is incapable of such understanding, as even detached moral discussion with him will reveal. He does not just fail to appreciate the moral implications of actions which he can independently understand and identify: he cannot even understand what these actions are—what dishonesty, or injury, *are*, as kinds of human action. It is in this sense that he does "not see what they see": he does not see the same actions, any more than an aesthetically insensitive person sees the same pictures as the man who can understand their aesthetic dimensions.

V

However, I must try, albeit briefly, to say more, both about the connection between participation in some values and the capacity for understanding any values, and about the dimension of human life and thought which a psychopath can neither understand nor share.

A psychopath's lack of understanding cannot be limited to some distinct set of concepts, or some distinct aspects of human action, identified as *moral*: in denying the empiricist distinction between fact and value, I am also insisting on the close logical connections between moral and nonmoral aspects of action and language; it is not fortuitous that Meursault is as incapable of understanding the emotions and interests of others as he is of understanding the specifically moral features of his actions. These connections can be brought out by showing, first, how moral thought and judgment must involve concepts which are not specifically moral, and, second, how many of our nonmoral concerns involve concepts and attitudes closely related to moral notions.

I argued above that a psychopath cannot understand the nature and quality of his actions, since he cannot identify or understand them in terms of the concepts relevant to moral assessment: but these must include that whole range of concepts, not themselves specifically moral concepts, by which we identify and describe human interests, concerns, and emotions. If we are to understand, for instance, how it is wrong to hurt someone, we must be able to understand what it *is* to hurt someone: and this requires an understanding of the kinds of interest and concern people can have, in the light of which actions will be seen as hurtful. We can hurt someone by physical injury; by injuring or insulting someone he loves; by destroying or denigrating his achievements; by ignoring or frustrating his wishes and ambitions; by denying him responses and relationships which matter to him—gratitude, trust, love, friendship. Unless we can understand the significance of such interests, emotions, and relationships in a man's life, we cannot understand what it is to hurt him, or how it can be wrong. An understanding of the moral aspects of my actions, and of the moral values of others, requires an understanding of that dimension of human life which includes both moral values and those interests and emotions which make our actions morally significant: it is this which a psychopath lacks. Meursault was unable to grasp the moral aspects of his conduct *because* he could not understand the meaning of love or friendship, or those concerns of others which reach beyond the immediate moment and its immediate impact on me.

Furthermore, many of the interests, concerns, emotions, and relationships which give moral significance to our actions can themselves by explained only in terms which connect them closely to *moral* concerns. Relationships of love and friendship, for instance, which may play an important part in a man's conception of his own interests, involve a concern for the interests and well-being of the other as having an independent significance, not just as means to some satisfaction of my own. Similarly, many of our ambitions and aims are important to us because we ascribe to the goal or the activity pursued a significance independent of, and indeed basic to, our interest in them. A philosopher may devote time and effort to philosophy not just because he happens to enjoy it, or sees it as an easy way to earn a living, but because he sees the subject and its problems as important—as something he *ought* to be concerned about. Such relationships, to people or activities, are very close to moral relationships: the agent's conception of his own interests as lying in such relationships is based on a *non*-self-interested concern for, and conception of, the significance of someone or something other than himself. And within such relationships a part will be played by more obviously moral notions—of a duty owed, which may conflict with present inclination; of the honesty and respect which is required by my concern for the other; of the kind of failure which consists not just in failing to achieve what I want but in letting the person or the subject down.[32]

I am suggesting, not that there is *no* distinction between moral and non-moral values, concerns, and concepts, but that there are close and complex connections between specifically moral concepts and the concepts in terms of which we must explain the interests, concerns, and emotions which matter to people; and thus that a psychopath will be unable to understand not only moral notions, but also these further aspects of the lives of others. He also lacks this dimension to his own life. Meursault not only lacks any understanding of the interests and emotions of others: he exhibits no conception of interests of his own which reach beyond his present moment to other people or other times; no emotional responses or concerns on any level deeper than that of immediate feeling.[33] It is not just that he does not share our particular concerns: he has *none* that we can understand. We cannot say that he is pursuing his own interests, except in the minimal sense that he does what he feels like doing at the time; or that he acts or reacts on the basis of emotions of love, ambition, pride, self-love, or hatred; or that he has any conception of activities, goals, or people as being important to him. He lacks the kind of conception of himself and others which would make this possible.

I have emphasized the absence in a psychopath's own life of that dimension which he cannot understand in the lives of others for two reasons. First, it shows that a psychopath does not have a "form of life" of his own, radically different from our own, since he has nothing we can identify as a *form* of life. Of course, were we faced by a group of alien beings, in whose lives we could discover as little as we can in the psychopath's, we would not call *them* disordered: we *might* suppose that they have a form of life which we cannot (yet) understand, though we would do better to say nothing at all. But with the psychopath we are not reduced to that despairing silence, which would *not* allow us to call him disordered.[34] For he has been brought up within our own culture and language, within forms of life we share: and it makes no sense to suggest that from such a basis a man could develop a form of life, a set of values and concepts, of his own which have no intelligible connection with those within which he was brought up (just as it would make no sense to suppose that a man

---

[32]On these and other features of caring for others, cf. Milton Mayerhoff, *On Caring* (New York, 1972).

[33]The distinction between emotions and feelings is clearly crucial here: cf. Sutherland, *op. cit.*, p. 271.

[34]This is a further defect in accounts like Fingarette's, and perhaps Haksar's, which seem to allow that the psychopath *has* values, or a form of life, of his own.

could develop his own empirical perspective on, and beliefs about, the world, having no intelligible logical connections with the beliefs and concepts with which, and through which, he first learned to see the world.

The moral rebel develops, extends, and modifies both the values and the concepts of the tradition within which he was brought up: but if his rebellion is to be intelligible as such, there must be a logical continuity between that public, shared, tradition and his present beliefs: we must be able to see (which may require an imaginative effort) how his present values and concepts form an intelligible development of that tradition.[35] This is why Camus can make sense of Meursault's life only by showing how it can be understood in terms of concepts and values belonging within an existing, and shared, tradition of thought. But a psychopath does not have his own, revolutionary, values: for he does not share in, and cannot be seen to be modifying, any such tradition, any common form of life. He is *defective*: he has never come to share in a common form of moral or emotional life and thus can neither understand these dimensions to the lives of others nor develop them in his own life. His relation to concepts of values and emotion is like that of the intellectually defective to the concepts in terms of which we come to understand and describe the empirical world: having failed to develop a participant understanding of such concepts and language, he cannot be said to have developed his own, different, beliefs and concepts.

Second, the absence in a psychopath's own life of any dimension of value and emotion is logically connected to his inability to understand this dimension of the lives of others. We could understand *his* life in terms of values and interests by tracing logical connections between our values and concepts and his: but such connections would also provide the basis for him to understand *us*. If he exhibits some conception of, and concern for, interests of his own, he is in a position to understand the interests of others, as providing them with reasons for action; if he displays love or friendship for another, he is in a position to understand the significance of such relationships for others, and already has the kind of concern for another which is closely related to a moral concern;[36] if he feels resentment, indignation, gratitude, we must ascribe to him a moral understanding of the actions of others, and thus the capacity for a moral understanding of his own actions.

This is not to say that I can understand the values and interests of others only on the basis of a *prior* understanding of values and interests of my own: if that were so, we could imagine someone who acquires a rational conception of his own interests, but never comes to see that there are other people around

[35] Cf. Beardsmore, *op. cit.*
[36] Cf. Bernard Williams, *Morality* (Harmondsworth, 1973), pp. 23–26.

him with interests and values of their own.[37] But one reason for insisting on participation in a *common* form of life, as an essential basis for developing both values and interests of one's own and an understanding of those of others, is to rule out just this kind of possibility. A child does not, and logically could not, come first to feel certain emotions, have certain wants and interests; then learn to describe these in a language; and then discover that there are other people in the world with emotions, wants, and interests like his own. He comes, or learns, to feel emotions, to have wants and interests, in and through coming to share in a form of life with other people—a form of life which includes not just a language, but modes of experience, emotion, and interest. It is by such a process that he comes to be, and to see himself as, a person; to understand and to share in characteristically human activities, experiences, and relationships. And this process is one of coming to see myself as a person among other persons, with whom I share this form of life. An understanding of others, and of the emotions, wants, and interests which inform their lives, is an integral part of coming to understand, and to have, emotions, wants, and interests of my own.[38]

VI

I have been arguing that a psychopath is disordered insofar as he is unable to understand, or to participate in, a significant dimension of human life and thought, which includes both moral concepts and values and conceptions of self-interest, of emotion, and of concerns other than the strictly moral. Such an understanding, while distinct from a concern for the particular values or interests in question, is not just a matter of an intellectual grasp of the descriptive criteria by which people determine the application of evaluative terms, or identify the objects of their emotions: thus accounts of practical rationality based on the fact-value distinction, in terms of an intellectual understanding to which is added some affective response, are inadequate. A psychopath is seriously defective in practical understanding and rationality: he is cut off by his deficiency from a central dimension of human life, just as the intellectually defective are cut off from the dimension of intellectual understanding and thought. This deficiency is clearly a *disorder*: a psychopath cannot understand the nature and quality of his actions, or the lives and interests of those around him: he cannot

---

[37]This might sound something like the "partial psychopath" defined by Cleckley (*op. cit.*, pp. 195-234), who unlike the complete psychopath, at least pursues his own interests rationally. I would argue against this that his conception of his own interests will be as limited as his conception of the interests of others; but the question of the nature, possibilities, and limitations of egoism would be a topic for another paper.

[38]Cf. Norman, *op cit.*; P. F. Strawson, *Individuals* (London, 1964), ch. 3.

control his actions in the light of any rational concerns or values, not because his impulses are strictly irresistible, but because he has no conception of rational values as providing reasons for action.[39]   We cannot hold him answerable for his actions, any more than we can a young child; we cannot impose on him the duties or expectations we impose on others, allow him the rights we allow others, or hope to share with him the kinds of relationship we share with others: he does not, and cannot, participate in a common life with us.

We can now make more sense of the question of whether a psychopath *could* accept our values and see the proper basis to the utilitarian requirement that a responsible agent be open to rational persuasion.[40]   The question, and the requirement, must be taken as logical, not practical. We should ask, not whether the agent will *in fact* change, or be persuaded to change, his values and actions (for that test would be failed by many who we would condemn as wicked, or admire as principled rebels), but rather whether it is *conceivable* that he should come, *rationally*, to accept our values and see his own as wrong; whether we could imagine a rational process of reform, conversion, or moral change, however unlikely we think it that this will in fact occur. Such a change is conceivable for a person living by intelligible values of his own, who *can* thus understand, whether he bothers to or not, the values and interests in the light of which we assess his actions: for he can understand his actions and our responses to them; he can understand how and why we are blaming and punishing him.[41]   But a psychopath is incapable of such understanding: nor does his own life exhibit that basis, of values, concerns, and understanding, from which we could imagine any rational reform developing; and *that* is why he is disordered.

The argument in this paper has been, of necessity, schematic and incomplete: it should provide, at best, the program for a fuller and more adequate work. Such a work would need to include a more detailed examination of further examples of psychopathy: it would also need to provide a more adequate explication of the account of practical rationality, of moral understanding, and of the connections between moral and nonmoral thought and concepts, which is here outlined in the most skeletal of forms. More needs to be said about the role of emotion and emotional capacities in moral development and understanding; about the kinds of logical connections which must be found with, or within, a shared form of life if we are to ascribe intelligible values to a man; about the nature and extent of the connections between moral and nonmoral concepts

---

[39]It has sometimes been suggested that the M'Naghten Rules can and should be interpreted in such a way as to cover these kinds of defect of understanding and control: cf. the *Royal Commission on Capital Punishment* (1949–53), ch. 4; Morris, *op. cit.*

[40]Cf. above, pp. 168–169.

[41]The moral requirement that a criminal be able to understand that he is being *punished* helps to explain the legal practice of refusing to try, punish, or execute those who have become disordered *since* their offense.

and values. This last point is of particular relevance to the topic of egoism: philosophers have often talked about "the egoist"—the man for whom only his own interests provide final reasons for action, and whose interests are specified purely in terms of what *he* wants—as if his life provided an intelligible, and even attractive, human possibility; but it would be instructive to compare such a "pure egoist" with a psychopath, as I have described him. We would need to ask what kind of conception of his own interests such a person could have, and what kinds of interest are possible for him; what kind of understanding of other people, their interests, and their values, we can ascribe to him; and how far a life like his is parasitic, conceptually as well as practically, on nonegoistical forms of life.

These would be the subjects for a monograph, not an article: I hope at least to have shown that an examination of psychopathy provides a fruitful approach to them, fruitful both for an understanding of mental disorder itself and for philosophical discussions of practical rationality. For if we can see that and how a psychopath, as I have described him, is disordered, we will also see the inadequacy of any account of practical reason according to which he is fully competent and rational and begin to see the outlines of a more adequate account.[42]

[42] Besides thanking colleagues at Stirling with whom I have discussed the topics of this paper, I must record my special gratitude to Sandra Marshall, whose philosophical co-operation and assistance has been invaluable.

PSYCHIATRISTS AND
THE ADVERSARY PROCESS

DAVID L. BAZELON

In our society part of the task of scrutinizing the decisional process involving experts in a great many disciplines has fallen to the judiciary. With public issues increasingly conditioned by scientific discovery and technological change, courts often confront technical questions with legal and moral implications for society. As a judge on the United States Court of Appeals for the District of Columbia Circuit for the past 25 years, I have been exposed to almost every sensitive scientific and medical question that has legal, moral, and ethical implications for our society. Arguments before our court, where the Federal Government is often a party, have ranged over the spectrum from abortion and blood transfusions to the underground-nuclear-explosion experiment in the Aleutian Islands and the safety of nuclear reactors. It is my duty to approach these questions not as a surgeon, a physicist, an ecologist, or any other technical expert does but as one charged with monitoring the decisional process. In scrutinizing the decision-making process of experts I have seen our familiar judicial procedures attempt to bring the most arcane sciences and technologies under public surveillance.

Psychiatry, I suppose, is the ultimate wizardry. My experience has shown that in no case is it more difficult to elicit productive and reliable expert testimony than in cases that call on the knowledge and practice of psychiatry. Such cases turn up in every jurisdiction. They raise fundamental questions: Who can be morally convicted of a crime? Who can be ordered into a hospital for compulsory treatment, and for how long? What kinds of treatment can be imposed without the consent of the patient? These questions engage the overriding question of the balance of power between the state and the individual. The effort by the courts to strike that balance requires the knowledge and expertise of the experts in the behavioral sciences, particularly psychiatry.

The discipline of psychiatry has direct relevance to cases involving human behavior. One might hope that psychiatrists would open up their reservoirs of knowledge in the courtroom. Unfortunately in my experience they try to limit their testimony to conclusory statements couched in psychiatric terminology.

Thereafter they take shelter in a defensive resistance to questions about the facts that are or ought to be in their possession. They thus refuse to submit their opinions to the scrutiny that the adversary process demands.

Psychiatrists are not alone, of course, in their failure to comprehend the nature and the importance of the adversary process. A word of explanation about what I mean when I use the term is in order here. The adversary process is the central feature of the system of legal institutions and procedures set up by our society to resolve controversies that arise between contending interests, values, and ideologies. The adversity—to use the word in its old dictionary meaning—is supplied not by the process but by the parties to the conflict; the adversary process is merely the decisional mechanism for resolving their conflict. Decisions must be reached even in the absence of any source of perfect information or wisdom. We therefore arrange an orderly contest of the parties in the courtroom, in which adversary roles are assigned to reflect the reality of the underlying dispute. Those of us who are engaged in conducting these proceedings have an awed awareness of the risk of arriving at an imperfect decision often with enormous consequences for the individual and for our society.

Cases always present conflicts over both facts and values since they arise on petitions for redress of grievances. To find facts we rely on an exhaustive inquiry. Parties and counsel must make the best case for themselves; they must check and correct the material offered by their adversary. Specific rules make the system at once skeptical and objective. These rules of evidence presuppose that men are biased and that their testimony is invariably shaped by their background, personality, interests, and values. Cross-examination challenges witnesses' veracity, accuracy, and bias. The inquiry is conducted in the presence of fact finders—the jury—chosen by measures that it is hoped will ensure their impartiality. Counsel are expected to be sensitive to their own conflicts of interest and to take care they do not serve more than one master.

We might be able to develop better rules to bring out facts in the courtroom and to dispel the excesses in the proceedings that excite hostile charges from those who are subjected to rigorous cross-examination. With full awareness of its weaknesses as well as its strengths, however, we still rely on the adversary process to uncover as many of the relevant facts as possible.

The law must also reconcile competing values that seem irreconcilable. In this task it does not seek final solutions; it recognizes the ongoing nature of deep-rooted conflicts. A judge reviews and develops criteria for resolving each case as it comes before him. The criteria are made known to the public in written opinions in which the competing values are ventilated. The court's decisions are never fixed and frozen; they are altered in response to new information, new understanding and new public demands. The law of itself does not provide wisdom. It offers a method for seeking wisdom.

In this system the expert witness has a special role. He is the only witness who is allowed to testify to a conclusion ("The defendant was intoxicated") as well as to the facts ("The defendant had two drinks last night"). Precisely because the expert testifies to a conclusion, and to one that almost inevitably favors one side, he must be open to cross-examination by the other side on the facts and premises on which he rests his conclusion. To the court and to the great aim of the proceeding he owes all the insight and information that his knowledge and training can offer.

My first exposure to psychiatry inside the courtroom concerned the expert opinions that psychiatrists were asked to render in criminal trials. In the early 1950s psychiatry and the law were deadlocked on the same issue of criminal responsibility, the so-called insanity defense. The traditional legal test for insanity, in use in virtually every American jurisdiction, was the M'Naghten test. According to this holding of a British court in 1843, the accused could not be found morally responsible if it was shown that he was suffering such "a defect of reason, from disease of the mind, as not to know the nature and the quality of the act he was doing, or, if he did know it, that he did not know he was doing what was wrong."

The M'Naghten rule thus betrayed its origins in a period when the dominant perception of human behavior was that people, as rational beings, made free choices informed by conscious consideration. The psychiatric profession was outspokenly critical of this model of the human psyche. It ignored, they said, modern dynamic understanding of man as an integrated personality, manifesting nonrational and irrational as well as rational, compulsive as well as volitional, behavior. The M'Naghten rule recognized only one aspect of that personality—cognitive reasoning—as the determinant of conduct.

Psychiatrists declared that, if the law would let them, they could give a more adequate account of realities. They complained that the M'Naghten test forced the physician to testify on whether or not the accused knew right from wrong and hence to decide the ultimate issue of moral responsibility, which should be left to the jury. Some urged their colleagues to refuse to speak to the question of "right or wrong, by virtue of reason alone." If psychiatrists were to be qualified as experts in criminal cases, they should be allowed to address the issue of responsibility in terms appropriate to their medical discipline.

Now, the law recognizes that the question of guilt or innocence is essentially a moral one. I believe the morality of a person's actions cannot be determined solely by abstract philosophical principles without regard to the facts that condition human behavior in the real world. To obtain these facts I wrote the opinion in the *Durham* case, in 1954, in which our court formulated a new test of criminal responsibility. *Durham* held that an accused man is not criminally responsible if it is shown that his unlawful act was the product of a mental disease or defect. *Durham* was not based on any notion that psychiatrists know everything there is to know about behavior. Its purpose was to bring into the courtroom the knowledge they do have and to restore to the jury its traditional function of applying "our inherited ideas of moral responsibility" to those accused of crime.

The response of the psychiatric profession to the new rule was enthusiastic. Here was the chance they had asked for to bring their expertise into the courtroom. Karl Menninger described the decision as "more revolutionary" than the *Brown* decision, also given in 1954, that outlawed racial segregation in the public schools. If the *Durham* "revolution" comes with the same "deliberate speed" as the desegregation ordered by the United States Supreme Court in *Brown,* however, only our great-grandchildren will be able to validate the Menninger appraisal.

Gregory Zilboorg had this to say about *Durham:* "[The *Durham* rule] might require of the psychiatrist that he study offenders and examine them clinically with much greater care than has often been the custom. . . . But at least . . . psychiatry is permitted to take the witness stand with all the dignity, medical and professional, which is due it. . . . The old unpleasantness of the 'adversary proceeding' in which psychiatric expert testimony has so often been engulfed . . . is bound to disappear."

Zilboorg's appraisal can be evaluated now. He was wrong. Psychiatrists continued to limit their testimony to conclusions—applying conclusory labels to the defendant—without explaining the origin, development, or manifestation of a disease in terms comprehensible to the jury. They began to wage a war of words in the courtroom, arguing about whether a defendant had a "personality defect," a "personality problem," a "personality disorder," a "disease," an "illness," or simply a "type of personality." Even more disturbing, they began to speak conclusively to the question of whether the criminal act was the "product" of mental disorder. The word "product" in their testimony conveyed no more clinical meaning than "right" or "wrong."

From St. Elizabeths, the Federal Government's well-known mental hospital in the District of Columbia, from which many cases come before our court, there came this insight into the response of the profession to the *Durham* test.

"Our psychiatric staff became alarmed that the courts would equate personality disorders with the psychoses and because of this anxiety, we erroneously—although in good faith—decided to add the words 'without mental disorder' in parenthesis immediately following the diagnosis . . . of personality disorder."

What psychiatrists have not understood is that conclusory labels are no substitute in judicial proceedings for facts derived from disciplined investigation. Labeling a person "schizophrenic" does not make him so! Although the law must settle for an "educated guess," that guess is only as good as the investigation, the facts, and the reasoning that underpin it.

The sterility of the profession's response to *Durham,* I now conclude, was due to the fact that its observance was bound to make the psychiatrist's task in the courtroom much more demanding than before. The late Winfred Overholser, superintendent of St. Elizabeths, once told me that the breadth of information I envisioned being placed before the jury would require from 50 to 100 man-hours of interviewing and investigation; he declared that a public hospital simply could not afford it. If that were the case, I replied, psychiatrists should frankly explain on the witness stand that their opinions are thus qualified by lack of time and resources. It was no service to the administration of justice for them to create the false impression that they had learned substantially all that could be known about someone on the basis of study they knew was inadequate.

The jury is equally entitled to know the differences of opinion and outright conflicts involved in psychiatric diagnosis. Consider this case reported by a leading forensic psychiatrist:

"A 17-year-old boy, confined as a patient in a state hospital, strangled another patient. He was sent to another hospital for medical-legal observation. The diagnostic choices lay between schizophrenia and schizoid personality disorder. Which diagnosis was made would naturally have great bearing on his criminal responsibility. When the case was presented to the staff conference, there was a great division of opinion. . . . After repeated medical conferences over a period of a year, it was agreed that further observation was futile, and that a diagnosis would have to be agreed on. The vote was five to four in favor of psychopathy [that is, personality disorder]. A report was then sent to the court stating that this diagnosis had been made, following a year's observation, and that he was now sane and could stand trial. The wording of the report clearly implied that the diagnosis was definitely established and that there was full agreement."

In the words of the psychiatrist reporting this incident: "What we have here, of course, is nothing else than the familiar star-chamber proceeding. The hospital staff usurped the function of the jury . . . and the court was then deprived of the full evidence, the conflict of medical opinion."

Attempts by my court to obtain records or tapes of just such clinical conferences have consistently been opposed and thwarted by the psychiatric staff at St. Elizabeths. In asking the profession to open up its opinions and decisions, we were asking no more than that psychiatric expertise should submit to the process by which the shortcomings of all opinion evidence are tested. The status of court-appointed "impartial" expert is not open to any profession. The potential for bias, distortion, and deviation from the truth is unavoidable. Like any other man, a physician acquires an emotional identification with an opinion that comes down on one side of a conflict; he has an inescapable, prideful conviction in the accuracy of his own findings. These realities belie the myth that a medical expert can speak from above or outside the legal adversary system.

In the end, after 18 years, I favored the abandonment of the *Durham* rule because in practice it had failed to take the issue of criminal responsibility away from the experts. Psychiatrists continued to testify to the naked conclusion instead of providing information about the accused so that the jury could render the ultimate moral judgment about blameworthiness. *Durham* had secured little improvement over M'Naghten.

In 1972, in the *Brawner* case, our court unanimously set aside the *Durham* rule. Essentially we replaced it with the insanity test that had been proposed by the American Law Institute:

"A person is not responsible for criminal conduct if at the time of such conduct as a result of mental disease or defect he lacks substantial capacity either to appreciate the wrongfulness of his conduct or to conform his conduct to the requirements of the law."

The *Brawner* formulation was designed in large part to end the expert's dominance over the question of moral responsibility. Psychiatrists will nonetheless still be able to take away the jury's function by presenting conclusory testimony. Thus they will testify that a defendant lacked capacity "as a result," just as under *Durham* they testified to whether the act was "the product" of a mental disorder.

Although no phrase will magically solve the problem of expert dominance, my own separate opinion in *Brawner* suggested the jury be instructed that a defendant is not responsible "if at the time of his unlawful conduct his mental or emotional processes or behavior controls were impaired to such an extent that he cannot justly be held responsible." This approach envisions that the jury will be provided with a broad range of information about the accused from a variety of sources including but not necessarily limited to psychiatrists. Other disciplines with special skills and knowledge in the field of human behavior would not be precluded from the opportunity to show the relevance of their data in the courtroom. Moreover, experts will be less likely to address the ultimate issue: whether the accused can be "justly held responsible." Even the promise of this approach, however, will be broken unless means are provided for the defendant, who is virtually always indigent, to obtain and present the required broad spectrum of information.

The form of words by which we call the insanity defense is not crucial, but the provision to the jury of all arguably relevant information about the accused's freedom of choice is. As I said in my opinion in *Brawner,* "while [we] generals are designing inspiring new insignia for the standard, the battle is being lost in the trenches."

In the *Jenkins* case, in 1962, spokesmen for the psychiatric profession betrayed a further misunderstanding of the role of the psychiatric witness that must have been widely shared among their colleagues. The trial court in this case had excluded the testimony of highly qualified and certified clinical psychologists, on the ground that "a psychologist is not competent to give a medical opinion." In the appeal to our court the American Psychiatric Association supported the lower court's decision. It asserted that in medical problems medical opinion can be the only guide. It chose to overlook the fact that the problem of criminal responsibility is not the exclusive terrain of psychiatry. I wrote the opinion for our court rejecting such guild mentality.

The "right to treatment" cases, in the 1960s, brought the issues under consideration here into sharper focus. In the *Rouse* case, in 1966, a patient confined without his consent sued for release or for adequate treatment of his disability. For our court I wrote that the plaintiff had a right to treatment, founded on a statute passed by Congress for the District of Columbia. This placed a more difficult question before us: How to establish whether this theoretical right was violated in actual practice. We held that adequacy of treatment is reviewable in court. In view of the inherent lack of certainty in psychiatric (as in other scientific) decisions, we held that the question of adequacy must be weighed on the basis of the "state of the art." We imposed no artificial criteria of success or failure, nor did we suggest we would overturn informed medical judgments. Independent experts should be enlisted, we said, to establish the parameters of acceptable treatment, and we urged that the American Psychiatric Association, which had published standards of medical care, be consulted.

The American Psychiatric Association responded to *Rouse* with an adamant statement of what I must call professional mystique: "The definition of treatment and the appraisal of its adequacy are matters for medical determination." This declaration ignored the explicit message in *Rouse* that the court does not presume to assess the quality of anyone's performance, unless that performance is patently arbitrary and capricious. As in all administrative law, the task of the court is to ensure that the administrative process itself controls abuse of discretion, that a factual record is established, that alternatives are considered and that reasons for decisions are set forth.

The instant opposition to *Rouse* was a clue to a deeper discordance between the professional and the judicial outlook. Plainly the profession was blind to or was concealing the conflict between the imposition of treatment and the human and civil rights of patients. In the view of most members medical decisions are by definition made in the best interests of the patient. If a physician says a man is sick, he must be sick; if he says the man must be treated or confined, that must be what is best for him. Such bootstrap reasoning comes under scrutiny only when, in the case of psychiatric prescriptions, it calls for involuntary treatment. The patient's interest in release, in less restrictive confinement or in adequate treatment cannot be matters solely "for medical determination."

Bringing these matters into court does not impose an artificial adversary relationship between the patient and his keepers; it reflects an adversity that already exists. This proposition comes as a surprise, of course, to the psychiatrist engaged exclusively in office practice and to his voluntary patient. In the public sector the adversity of interests that confronts the psychiatrist and his involuntary patient—although it does not encompass the entire relationship—must be recognized as an inescapable reality.

What is more, it should be recognized that the physician–patient relationship in the public sector is compromised by the interests of third parties and the pressures from hidden agendas. At the state hospital in Napa, Calif., the superintendent told me a few years ago in a public meeting that the staff had "Sacramento looking over its shoulder." Psychiatric decisions—to confine or release—are influenced by public outcry for "law and order." In some hospitals the shortage of beds and manpower has been known to override medical determinations; in Veterans Administration hospitals the need to fill empty beds also presses medical determinations, but in the opposite direction. Psychiatrists have justified fudging their testimony on "dangerousness"—a ground for involuntary confinement—when they were convinced that an individual was too sick to seek help voluntarily.

What is disturbing about these situations is not that they impute venality or frailty to merely human practitioners, nor that conflicting societal interests can dictate different and not necessarily the best medical results. It is rather that the psychiatric profession should resist facing these conflicts in the open. Serious legal challenges have been needed to surface its hidden agendas.

The hazard implicit in professional resistance to public scrutiny is well illustrated by the use in the U.S.S.R. of psychiatric facilities for the suppression of political dissenters. I had occasion to read the Russian case studies as a member of an *ad hoc* committee set up by the American Psychiatric Association. The studies showed how the medical model of "sickness" could be perverted to encompass judgment of what is socially and politically unacceptable behavior. On the record the physicians did not seem to be acting in their patients' best interests, or even in their own direct self-interest, but were using psychiatric terminology and techniques in the service of state policy. Yet when I was in the U.S.S.R., the Russian psychiatrists steadfastly insisted that they follow the medical model, much as their American colleagues are known to do.

As I read these case studies, however, I was impressed to realize how, in many analogous situations in this country, I had had occasion to find psychiatrists making decisions for motives and under pressures from outside their professional role. Whenever psychiatrists enter the public sector to apply their knowledge in the service of public institutions—the military, state hospitals, schools and penal institutions, to name only a few—they face conflicts between the therapeutic interests of their patients and the institutional interests of their employers. Needless to say I found the leadership of the profession in America not nearly as eager to investigate such conflicts in their own ranks as they were to look into evidence of malpractice in the U.S.S.R. To make a not very pleasant story short, when our *ad hoc* committee turned its attention to the American scene, at first with official approval, its charter was soon revoked. The need for examination remains. The American Bar Association and the Institute of Medicine of the National Academy of Sciences plan studies of these conflicts. The American Psychiatric Association apparently recognizes the importance of acting itself; it now has commissioned an inquiry by the Institute of Society, Ethics and the Life Sciences in Hastings, N.Y.

Such guild self-protection is not, of course, peculiar to the psychiatric profession. Business enterprises, labor unions and government agencies all exhibit the same penchant for privacy. The usual counter to the call for public scrutiny is the promise of "self-regulation." Whereas peer review is a much praised and not much observed principle of the medical profession, it has been largely foreign to the practice of psychiatry. Its practitioners work alone with their patients, behind ritually locked doors. For medical practitioners of all kinds peer review is now required, however, for the validation of professional performance paid for by Medicaid and Medicare funds. Curiously, this requirement was imposed not out of professional agreement that self-evaluation is in order but because of Congressional concern at rising medical costs.

For monitoring the performance of a profession there is no substitute, in the end, for the adversary process. This discussion has focused on psychiatry because decisions grounded on this discipline and on counsel from its practitioners are employed by the state to confine people against their will and to treat people in ways they do not ask for. As such the discipline is of concern to those of us whose judicial duty is to scrutinize governmental intrusions on liberty. Much of what I have said, however, applies equally well to the public surveillance of other highly specialized professions on which the operation of our complex civilization depends. Today every profession is being challenged by those who believe that trust should rest not on mystique but rather on what the public knows about its exercise of its expertise. Challenging the expert and digging into the facts behind his opinion is the lifeblood of our legal system, whether it is a psychiatrist characterizing a mental disturbance, a physicist testifying on the environmental impact of a nuclear power plant or a Detroit engineer insisting on the impossibility of meeting legislated automobile exhaust-emission standards by 1975. It is the only way a judge or a jury—or the public—can decide whom to trust.

FURTHER READINGS

Bibliographies

"Behavior Control Bibliography." *American Criminal Law Review* 13 (Summer 1975): 101–113.

Hall, Jacquelyn H., and Shore, Milton F. "Selected Bibliography." In *Current Ethical Issues in Mental Health*, edited by Milton F. Shore and Stuart E. Golann. Washington, D.C.: U.S. Government Printing Office, 1973, pp. 47–53.

Sollittom, Sharmon, and Veatch, Robert M., comps. *Bibliography of Society, Ethics and the Life Sciences*. Hastings-on-Hudson, N.Y.: Institute of Society, Ethics and the Life Sciences, 1974–1977.

Wade, Michael D. "Mental Health Law Bibliography." *University of Toledo Law Review* 6 (Fall 1974): 314–340.

Walters, LeRoy, ed. *Bibliography of Bioethics*. Vols. 1– . Detroit: Gale Research Co. Issued Annually.

Books

American Psychological Association. Ad Hoc Committee on Ethical Standards in Psychological Research. *Ethical Principles in the Conduct of Research with Human Participants*. Washington: American Psychological Association, 1973.

Ayd, Frank J., ed. *Medical, Moral, and Legal Issues in Mental Health Care*. Baltimore: Williams & Wilkins, 1974.

Bootzin, Richard R. *Modification and Therapy: An Introduction*. Cambridge, Massachusetts: Winthrop, 1975.

Cooper, D. C. *Psychiatry and Anti-Psychiatry*. London: Tavistock, 1967.

Dershowitz, Joseph Goldstein, and Katz, Jay. *Psychoanalysis, Psychiatry, and Law*. New York: Free Press, 1967.

Douglas Jack D., ed. *Deviance and Respectability: The Social Construction of Moral Meanings*. New York: Basic Books, 1970.

Eliade, M. *Shamanism, Archaic Technique of Ecstasy*. New York: Bollingen Foundation, 1964.

Ennis, Bruce. *Prisoners of Psychiatry.* New York: Harcourt, Brace, Jovanovich, 1972.

Ennis, Bruce, and Siegel, Loren. *The Rights of Mental Patients.* New York: Avon Books, 1973.

Ennis, Bruce R., Friedman, P. R., with Gitlin, Bonnie, eds. *Legal Rights of the Mentally Handicapped.* Three volumes. Criminal Law and Urban Problems Course Handbook Series No. 57. Practicing Law Institute. The Mental Health Law Project. 1973.

Fox, S. J. *Science and Justice: The Massachusetts Witchcraft Trials.* Baltimore: Johns Hopkins Press, 1968.

Gaylin, Willard, Meister, Joel S., and Neville, Robert C., eds. *Operating on the Mind: The Psychosurgery Conflict.* New York: Basic Books, 1975.

Gaylin, Willard, Carr, A., and Hendrin, H., eds. *Psychoanalysis and Social Research.* New York: Doubleday, 1965.

Goffman, Ervin. *Asylums.* New York: Doubleday Anchor, 1961.

Greenfield, N. S., Miller, H. M., and Roberts, C. M., eds. *Comprehensive Mental Health.* Madison: University of Wisconsin Press, 1968.

Group for the Advancement of Psychiatry, Criminal Responsibility and Psychiatric Expert Testimony, Rep. No. 26. New York: Gap Publication Office, 1954.

Halleck, Seymour L. *The Politics of Therapy.* New York: Science House, 1971.

Hartmann, H. *Psychoanalysis and Moral Values.* New York: International Universities Press, 1960.

Katz, Jay, *et al.*, eds. *Psychoanalysis, Psychiatry and Law.* New York: Free Press, 1967.

Kennedy, Eugene C., ed. *Human Rights and Psychological Research: A Debate on Psychology and Ethics.* New York: Thomas Y. Crowell, 1975.

Kittrie, Nicholas N. *The Right to Be Different: Deviance and Enforced Therapy.* Baltimore: Johns Hopkins Press, 1971.

London, Perry. *Behavior Control.* New York: Harper & Row, 1971.

——. *Modes and Morals of Psychotherapy.* New York: Holt, Rinehart & Winston. 1964.

Lowe, C. M. *Value Orientation in Counseling and Psychotherapy: The Meaning of Mental Health.* San Francisco: Chandler, 1969.

Margolis, Joseph. *Psychotherapy and Morality.* New York: Random House, 1966.

Martindale, Don, and Martindale, Edith. *Psychiatry and the Law: The Crusade Against Involuntary Hospitalization.* St. Paul: Windflower, 1973.

Medvedev, Roy, and Zhores, A. *The Question of Madness.* New York: Knopf, 1971.

Mitford, Jessica. *Kind and Usual Punishment.* New York: Knopf, 1973.

Osmond, Humphrey, and Siegler, Miriam. *Models of Madness, Models of Medicine.* New York: Macmillan, 1974.

Pearlstein, Stanley. *Psychiatry, the Law, and Mental Health*. Dobbs Ferry, N.Y.: Oceana Publications, 1967.

Peszke, Michael A. *Involuntary Treatment of the Mentally Ill: The Problem of Autonomy*. Springfield, Ill.: Charles C Thomas, 1975.

Potter, V. R. *Bioethics: Bridge to the Future*. Englewood Cliffs, N.J.: Prentice-Hall, 1971.

Rieff, Philip. *The Triumph of the Therapeutic: Uses of Faith After Freud*. New York: Harper Torchbooks, 1968.

Robitscher, Jonas. *Pursuit of Agreement: Psychiatry and the Law*. Philadelphia: Lippincott, 1966.

Rosen, G. *Madness in Society: Chapters in the Historical Sociology of Mental Illness*. New York: Harper & Row, 1968.

Rothman, David J. *The Discovery of the Asylum*. Boston: Little, Brown, 1971.

Rudovsky, David. *The Rights of Prisoners*. New York: Avon Books, 1973.

Scheff, T. J. *Being Mentally Ill: A Sociological Theory*. Chicago: Aldine Publishing, 1966.

Schoenfeld, C. G. *Psychoanalysis and the Law*. Springfield, Ill.: Charles C Thomas, 1973.

Schoolar, Joseph C., and Gaitz, Charles M., eds. *Research and the Psychiatric Patient*. New York: Brunner/Mazel, 1975.

Shore, Milton F., and Golann, Stuart E., eds. *Current Ethical Issues in Mental Health*. Washington, D.C.: U.S. Government Printing Office, 1973.

Skinner, B. F. *Beyond Freedom and Dignity*. New York: Knopf, 1971.

Slovenko, Ralph. *Psychiatry and the Law*, first edition. Boston: Little, Brown, 1973.

Szasz, Thomas S. *The Ethics of Psychoanalysis*. New York: Basic Books, 1965.

——. *Ideology and Insanity*. New York: Doubleday Anchor, 1970.

——. *Law, Liberty, and Psychiatry*. New York: Macmillan, 1963.

——. *The Manufacture of Madness: A Comparative Study of the Inquisition and the Mental Health Movement*. New York: Dell, 1970.

——. *Psychiatric Injustice*. New York: Macmillan, 1965.

Tancredi, Laurence R., Lieb, Julian, and Slaby, Andrew E. *Legal Issues in Psychiatric Care*. Hagerstown, Md.: Harper & Row, Medical Department, 1975.

Torrey, E. Fuller. *The Death of Psychiatry*. Radnor, Penn.: Chilton Book Co., 1974.

——. *Ethical Issues in Medicine: The Role of the Physician in Today's Society*. Boston: Little, Brown, 1968.

——. *The Mind Game: Witchdoctors and Psychiatrists*, New York: Bantam Books, 1972.

U.S. National Commision for the Protection of Human Subjects. *Psychosurgery: Report and Recommendations and Appendix*. Washington, D.C.: U.S. Department of Health, Education and Welfare, 1977.

Valenstein, Elliot S. *Brain Control: A Critical Examination of Brain Stimulation and Psychosurgery.* New York: Wiley, 1973.

For extensive lists of sources see: Slovenko, Ralph. *Psychiatry and Law*, first edition. Boston: Little, Brown, 1973, p. 611; and Torrey, E. Fuller. *The Death of Psychiatry.* Radnor, Penn.: Chilton, 1974, p. 213.

Articles and Addresses

American Psychiatric Association. "Position Statement on Involuntary Hospitalization of the Mentally Ill" (revised). *American Journal of Psychiatry* 130 (March 1973): 392.

Andy, O. J. "The Decision-Making Process in Psychosurgery." *Duquesne Law Review* 13 (Summer 1975): 783–818.

Annas, George J., *"O'Connor v. Donaldson:* Insanity Inside Out." *Hastings Center Report* 6 (August 1976): 11–12.

——. "Psychosurgery: Procedural Safeguards." *Hastings Center Report* 7 (October 1977): 4.

Annas, George J., and Glantz, Leonard H. "Psychosurgery: The Law's Response." *Boston University Law Review* 54 (March 1974): 249–267.

Appel, Kenneth. "Constitutional Law—Due Process Requires a Standard of Proof beyond a Reasonable Doubt for Involuntary Civil Commitment." *Catholic University Law Review* 23 (Winter 1973): 409–416.

Arrington, Robert L. "Practical Reason, Responsibility and the Psychopath." *Journal for the Theory of Social Behavior*, forthcoming.

Barrish, I. J. "Ethical Issues and Answers to Behavior Modification." *Corrective and Social Psychiatry and Journal of Behavior Technology Methods and Therapy* 20 (April 1974): 30–37.

Bazelon, David L. "The Adversary Process in Psychiatry." Address delivered to The Southern California Psychiatric Society (April 21, 1973).

——. "Follow the Yellow Brick Road." *American Journal of Orthopsychiatry* 40: 4 (1970): 562–567.

——. "Institutionalization, Deinstitutionalization and the Adversary Process." *Columbia Law Review* 75 (June 1975): 897–912.

——. "Institutional Psychiatry—The Self-Inflicted Wound." Address delivered to the Conference on Mental Health and the Law, the Catholic University of America (January 19, 1974).

——. "Psychiatry's Fear of Analysis." *Washington Post* (June 24, 1973).

——. "The Right to Treatment: The Court's Role." *Hospital and Community Psychiatry* 20 (1969): 129–135.

——. "A Statement to the President of the American Psychiatric Association, The Board of Trustees of the APA, and to the Members of the Ad Hoc

Committee on the Use of Psychiatric Institutions for the Commitment of Political Dissenters" (April 30, 1972).

Begelman, D. A. "Ethical and Legal Issues of Behavior Modification." In *Progress in Behavior Modification*, edited by Michel Hersen, Richard M. Eisler and Peter M. Miller. New York: Academic Press, 1975, pp. 159-189.

——. "Ethical Issues in Behavioral Control." *Journal of Nervous and Mental Disease* 156 (January 1973): 412-419.

Bell, James E. "Ethical Issues in New Group Procedures." In *Current Ethical Issues in Mental Health*, edited by Milton F. Shore and Stuart E. Golann. Washington, D.C.: U.S. Government Printing Office, 1973, pp. 3-11.

Bernal y Del Rio, Victor. "Psychiatric Ethics." In *Comprehensive Textbook of Psychiatry—II*, edited by Alfred M. Freedman, Harold I. Kaplan, and Benjamin J. Sadock. Baltimore, MD.: Williams & Wilkins, 1975, pp. 2543-2552.

Birbaum, M. "A Rationale for the Right." *Georgetown Law Journal* 57 (1969): 752.

——. "The Right to Treatment." *A.B.A.J.* 46 (1969): 499.

Black, Peter McL. "The Rationale for Psychosurgery." *Humanist* 37 (July-August 1977): 6, 8-9.

Blatte, Helen. "Evaluating Psychotherapies." *Hastings Center Report* 3 (September 1973): 4-6.

Boorse, Christopher. "What a Theory of Mental Health Should Be." *Journal for the Theory of Social Behavior* 6 (April 1976): 61-84.

Bootzin, Richard R. "Philosophical and Ethical Issues." In his *Behavior Modification and Therapy: An Introduction*. Cambridge, Mass.: Winthrop, 1975, pp. 147-157.

Braun, Stephen H. "Ethical Issues in Behavior Modification." *Behavior Therapy* 6 (January 1975): 51-62.

Breggin, Peter R. "Psychosurgery for Political Purposes." *Duquesne Law Review* 13 (Summer 1975): 841-862.

——. "Psychotherapy as Applied Ethics." *Psychiatry* 34 (1971): 59-74.

Brent, David J. "Civil Commitment—Due Process and the Standard of Proof." *DePaul Law Review* 23 (Summer 1974): 1500-1511.

Brody, Eugene B. "On the Legal Control of Psychosurgery." *Journal of Nervous and Mental Disease* 157 (September 1973): 151-153.

Brody, Jane E. "Psychosurgery: Myriad Tough Questions." *The New York Times* 18 (March 1973): 14.

Brownfield, Allan C. "Psychosurgery: Mental Progress of Medical Nightmare." *Private Practice* 5 (June 1973): 46-50.

Burrell, Garland E. "Mental Privacy: An International Safeguard to Governmental Intrusions into Mental Processes." *California Western International Law Journal* 6 (Winter 1975): 110-128.

Burt, Robert A. "Why We Should Keep Prisoners from the Doctors." *Hastings Center Report* 5 (February 1975): 25-34.

Callahan, D. M., and Lorr, M. "Therapist 'Type' and Patient Response to Psychotherapy." *Journal of Consulting Psychology* 26 (1962): 425-429.

Campbell, Ross. "Progress in Voluntary Commitment." *Washington Law Review* 49 (February 1974): 617-646.

Capron, Alex. Book Review of N. N. Kittrie, "The Right to Be Different." *Columbia Law Review* 73 (1973): 893-913.

Carrera, Frank, and Adams, P. L. "An Ethical Perspective on Operant Conditioning." *Journal of the American Academy of Child Psychiatry* 9 (1970): 607-623.

Chodoff, Paul. "The Case for Involuntary Hospitalization of the Mentally Ill." *American Journal of Psychiatry* 133 (May 1976): 496-501.

Chorover, Stephan L. "Psychosurgery: A Neuropsychological Perspective." *Boston University Law Review* 52 (March 1974): 231-248.

Cooke, Robert E. "Ethics and Law on Behalf of the Mentally Retarded." *Pediatric Clinics of North America* 20 (February 1973): 259-268.

Cooke, Thomas P., and Cooke, Sharon. "Behavior Modification: Answers to Some Ethical Questions." *Psychology in the Schools* 11 (January 1974): 5-10.

Cotter, Lloyd H. "Operant Conditioning in a Vietnamese Mental Hospital." *American Journal of Psychiatry* 124 (1967): 23-28.

"The 'Crime' of Mental Illness: Extension of 'Criminal' Procedural Safeguards to Involuntary Civil Commitments." *Journal of Criminal Law and Criminology* 66 (September 1975): 255-270.

Curran, W. J. "Community Mental Health and the Commitment Laws: A Radical New Approach Is Needed." *American Journal of Public Health* 57 (1967): 1565-1570.

——. "Ethical and Legal Considerations in High-Risk Studies of Schizophrenia." *Schizophrenia Bulletin* 10 (Fall 1974): 74-92.

Damich, Edward J. "The Right against Treatment: Behavior Modification and the Involuntary Committed." *Catholic University Law Review* 23 (Summer 1974): 774-787.

Davison, Gerald C., and Stuart, Richard B. "Behavior Therapy and Civil Liberties." *American Psychologist* 30 (July 1975): 755-763.

Dedek, John F. "Two Moral Cases: Psychosurgery and Behavior Control: Grossly Malformed Infants." *Chicago Studies* 14 (Spring 1975): 19-35.

——. "Developments in the Law: Civil Commitment of the Mentally Ill." *Harvard Law Review* 87 (April 1974): 1190-1406.

Deschin, C. S. "Knowledge Is Neither Neutral Nor Apolitical." *American Journal of Orthopsychiatry* 41 (1971): 344-347.

Dietz, Park E. "Mental Health, Criminal Justice and Social Control." In *Medical, Moral, and Legal Issues in Mental Health Care.* edited by Frank J. Ayd. Baltimore: Williams & Wilkins, 1974, pp. 204-210.

Dunham, H. Warren. "Psychiatry, Sociology and Civil Liberties." *Man and Medicine* 2 (1976-1977): 263-274.

Dworkin, Gerald. "Autonomy and Behavior Control." *Hastings Center Report* 6 (February 1976): 23-28.

Edgar, Harold. "Regulating Psychosurgery: Issues of Public Policy and Law." In *Operating on the Mind: The Psychosurgery Conflict.* edited by Willard M. Gaylin, Joel S. Meister, and Robert C. Neville. New York: Basic Books, 1975, pp. 117-168.

Edson, Lee. "The Psyche and the Surgeon." *The New York Times Magazine* 30 (September 1973): 14-15.

Eisenberg, Leon. "The Future of Psychiatry." *Lancet* 7842 (1973): 1371.

Erienmeyer-Kimling, L. "Schizophrenia: A Bag of Dilemmas." *Social Biology* (Summer 1976): 123-134.

Farber, L. H. "Psychoanalysis and Morality." *Commentary* 40 (1965): 69-74.

Felix, R. H. "The Image of the Psychiatrist: Past, Present and Future." *American Journal of Psychiatry* 121 (October 1964): 318-322.

Ferleger, David. "Loosing the Chains: In-Hospital Civil Liberties of Mental Patients." *Santa Clara Lawyer* (Spring 1973): 447-500.

Field, L. H., Rollin, Henry, and Watts, C. A. H. "Changing the Patient's Personality." *British Medical Journal* 2 (9 June 1973): 594-598.

Flaschner, Franklin N. "Constitutional Requirements in the Commitment of the Mentally Ill in the U.S.A.: Rights to Liberty and Therapy." *International Journal of Offender Therapy and Comparative Criminology* 18 (1974): 283-301.

Fleming, John G., and Maximer, Bruce. "The Patient or His Victim: The Therapist's Dilemma." *California Law Review* 62 (May 1974): 1025-1068.

Fornasero, Joseph M. "Substantive Constitutional Rights of the Mentally Ill." *Davis Law Review* 7 (1974): 128-149.

Foster, Henry H. "The Conflict and Reconciliation of the Ethical Interest of Therapist and Patient." *Journal of Psychiatry and Law* 3 (Spring 1975): 39-61.

Friedman, M. J. "The Place of Drugs in Psychotherapy." In *Psychotherapy—The Promised Land*, edited by M. Dinoft, M. E. Beil, and R. L. Vosburg. University, Ala.: University of Alabama Press, 1977, pp. 101-111.

Friedman, Paul R. "Behind the Institutional Wall." *Trial* 11 (November-December 1975): 29-31.

———. "Legal Regulation of Applied Behavior Analysis in Mental Institutions and Prisons." *Arizona Law Review* 17 (1975): 39-94.

Gaylin, Willard. "Psychiatry and the Law: Partners in Crime." *Columbia Forum* (1965): 23-27.

———. "What's Normal—Mental Illness and Public Office." *The New York Times Sunday Magazine* (April 1 1973).

——. "Skinner Redux." *Harpers Magazine* (October 1973): 48–56.

——. "On the Borders of Persuasion: A Psychoanalytic Look at Coercion." *Psychiatry* 37 (February 1974): 1–9.

Gaylin, Willard and Callahan, Daniel. "The Psychiatrist as Double Agent." *Hastings Center Report* 4 (February 1974): 11–14.

German, June R. "Involuntary Treatment—Its Legal Limitations." *Bulletin of the American Academy of Psychiatry and the Law* 3 (1975): 66–69.

Glaser, F. G. " The Dichotomy Game: A Further Consideration of the Writings of Dr. Thomas Szasz." *American Journal of Psychiatry* 2 (May 1965): 1069–1074.

Gobert, James J. "Psychosurgery, Conditioning, and the Prisoner's Right to Refuse 'Rehabilitation.'" *Virginia Law Review* 61 (February 1975): 155–196.

Gordon, James S. "The Uses of Madness." *Social Policy* 4 (September/October 1973): 37–43.

Greenberg, David F. "Involuntary Psychiatric Commitments to Prevent Suicide." *New York University Law Review* 49 (May–June 1974): 227–269.

Gustafson, James M., and Pizzulli, Francis C. "Ain't Nobody Gonna Cut on My Head!" *Hastings Center Report* 5 (February 1975): 49–51.

Guttmacher, M. S. "Critique of Views of Thomas Szasz on Legal Psychiatry." *AMA Archives of General Psychiatry* 10 (March 1964): 238–245.

Halleck, Seymour L. "Legal and Ethical Aspects of Behavior Control." *American Journal of Psychiatry* 131 (April 1974): 381–385.

Hauerwas, Stanley. "The Retarded and the Criteria for the Human." *Linacre Quarterly* 40 (November 1973): 217–222.

Himmelstein, Jack, and Michels, Robert "Case Studies in Bioethics: The Right to Refuse Psychoactive Drugs." *Hastings Center Report* 3 (June 1973): 8–11.

Holden, Constance. "Psychosurgery: Legitimate Therapy or Laundered Lobotomy?" *Science* 179 (16 March 1973): 1109–1112.

Holland, James G. "Ethical Considerations in Behavior Modification." In *Current Ethical Issues in Mental Health*, edited by Milton F. Shore and Stuart E. Golann. Washington, D.C.: U.S. Government Printing Office, 1973, pp. 24–30.

Horton, Paul C. "Normality—Toward a Meaningful Construct." *Comprehensive Psychiatry* 12 (1971): 54–66.

Jeffery, C. R., and Jeffery, Ina A. "Psychosurgery and Behavior Modification: Legal Control Techniques versus Behavior Control Techniques." *American Behavioral Scientist* 18 (May–June 1975): 685–722.

Johnson, Maile. "Due Process—Commitment—Due Process Requires Proof of Mental Disability beyond a Reasonable Doubt." *University of Cincinnati Law Review* 42 (October 1973): 751–760.

Jones, D. G. "Psychosurgery—The Handmaiden of the Technological Society." *Medical Journal of Australia* 1 (25 January 1975): 108–112.

Katz, Barbara F. "The Legal Control of Psychosurgery." *Medical Trial Quarterly* 21 (Spring 1975): 407-443.

Katz, Jay. "The Right to Treatment—An Enchanting Legal Fiction?" *University of Chicago Law Review* 36 (1969): 755-783.

Klerman, Gerald L. "Behavior Control and the Limits of Reform." *Hastings Center Report* 5 (August 1975): 40-45.

———. "Psychotropic Drugs as Therapeutic Agents," and with Veatch, Robert M. "Drugs and Competing Drug Ethics." *Hastings Center Studies* 2 (January 1974): 68-93.

Kunasaka, Y., *et al.* "Criteria for Involuntary Hospitalization." *Archives of General Psychiatry* 26 (1972): 399-404.

Knowles, Steve. "Beyond the 'Cuckoo's Nest': A Proposal for Federal Regulation of Psychosurgery." *Harvard Journal on Legislation* 12 (June 1975): 610-667.

Krouner, Leonard W. "Shock Therapy and Psychiatric Malpractice: The Legal Accommodation to a Controversial Treatment." *Forensic Science* 2 (1973): 397-439.

Lansdell, Herbert. "Psychosurgery: Some Ethical Considerations." In *Protection of Human Rights in the Light of Scientific and Technological Progress in Biology and Medicine*, edited by Simon Btesh. Geneva: World Health Organization, 1974, pp. 264-275.

Laves, Rona G. "The Prediction of 'Dangerousness' as a Criterion for Involuntary Civil Commitment: Constitutional Considerations." *Journal of Psychiatry and Law* 3 (Autumn 1975): 291-326.

Lazare, Aston. "Hidden Conceptual Models in Clinical Psychiatry." *New England Journal of Medicine* 228 (1973): 345-351.

Lowe, C. M. "Value Orientations: An Ethical Dilemma." *American Psychologist* 14 (1959): 687-693.

Macklin, Ruth. "The Medical Model in Psychoanalysis and Psychotherapy." *Comprehensive Psychiatry* 14 (January-February 1973): 49-69.

———. "Mental Health and Mental Illness: Some Problems of Definition and Concept Formation." *Philosophy in Science* 39 (September 1972): 341-365.

Maisel, R. "Decision-Making in a Commitment Court." *Psychiatry* 33 (1970): 352.

Margolis, Joseph. "Insanity." In his *Negativities: The Limits of Life*. Columbus, Ohio: Charles E. Merrill, 1975, pp. 107-117.

———. "The Question of Insanity." *Wayne Law Review* XIX (1973): 1007-1022.

———. "The Myths of Psychoanalysis." *The Monist* LVI (1972): 361-375.

Mark, Vernon H. "A Psychosurgeon's Case for Psychosurgery." *Psychology Today* 8 (February 1974): 28.

Masserman, J. "Is Mental Illness a Medicosocial 'Myth'?" *Archives of General Psychiatry* 9 (1963): 1975.

Mathews, A. R. "Mental Illness and the Criminal Law: Is Community Mental

Health an Answer?" *American Journal of Public Health* 57:9 (1967): 1571–1579.

McCollough, Thomas E. "Mental Illness and Public Policy." *Journal of Religion and Health* 13 (October 1974): 251–258.

McDonald, Robert K. "Constitutional Law—Mental Health—Procedural Due Process and Involuntary Commitment." *Missouri Law Review* 38 (Fall 1973): 645–652.

McGarry, A. L., and Greenblatt, M. "Conditional Voluntary Mental Hospital Admission." *New England Journal of Medicine* 287 (1972): 279.

McGarry, Louis A., and Kaplan, Honora A. "Overview: Current Trends in Mental Health Law." *American Journal of Psychiatry* 130 (1973): 621–630.

McLemove, C. W. "Religion and Psychotherapy—Ethics, Civil Liberties and Clinical Savvy: A Critique." *Journal of Consulting and Clinical Psychology* 45 (December 1977): 1172–1175.

McMorris, S. C. "Can We Punish for the Acts of Addiction?" *Bulletin on Narcotics* 22:3 (1970): 43–48.

McNeil, J. N., *et al.* "Community Psychiatry and Ethics." *American Journal of Orthopsychiatry* 40:1 (1970): 22–29.

Mearns, Edward A. "Law and the Physical Control of the Mind: Experimentation in Psychosurgery." *Case Western Reserve Law Review* 25 (Spring 1975): 565–603.

Mendel, W. M. "On the Abolition of the Psychiatric Hospital." In *Comprehensive Mental Health*, edited by C. M. Roberts, N. S. Greenfield, and M. H. Miller. Madison: University of Wisconsin, 1968.

———. "Responsibility in Health, Illness, and Treatment." *Archives of General Psychiatry* 18 (1968): 697–705.

Michels, Robert. "Ethical Issues of Psychological and Psychotherapeutic Means of Behavior Control: Is the Moral Contract Being Observed?" *Hastings Center Report* 3 (April 1973): 11–13.

Miller, M. H., and Halleck, S. L. "The Critics of Psychiatry: A Review of Contemporary Critical Attitudes." *American Journal of Psychiatry* 119 (1963): 705.

Milton, Teresa T. "Constitutional Law: Mental Patients and Court Ordered Standards of Treatment." *University of Florida Law Review* 25 (Spring 1973): 614–619.

Mischel, Theodore. "The Concept of Mental Health and Disease: An Analysis of the Controversy between Behavioral and Psychodynamic Approaches." *Journal of Medicine and Philosophy* 2 (September 1977): 197–219.

Moore, Erin. "Legislative Control of Shock Treatment." *University of San Francisco Law Review* 9 (Spring 1975): 738–777.

Moraczewski, Albert A. "Scientific Methodology and Ethical Imperatives." In *Research and the Psychiatric Patient*, edited by Joseph C. Schoolar and Charles M. Gaitz. New York: Brunner/Mazel, 1975, pp. 142–149.

Muller, D. J. "Involuntary Mental Hospitalization." *Comprehensive Psychiatry* 9 (1968): 187.

Muller, Michael J. *"O'Connor* v. *Donaldson*: A Right to Liberty for the Non-Dangerous Mentally Ill." *Ohio Northern University Law Review* 3 (1975): 550-562.

Murphy, Jeffrie G. "Total Institutions and the Possibility of Consent to Organic Therapies." *Human Rights* 5 (Fall 1975): 25-45.

National Association for Mental Health. "Psychosurgery: An NAMH Position Statement." *Mental Health* 58 (Winter 1974): 22-23.

Neville, Robert. "Ethical and Philosophical Issues of Behavior Control." Paper presented at the American Association for the Advancement of Science meeting, 1973.

——. "Posts and Black Kettles: A Philosopher's Perspective on Psychosurgery." *Boston University Law Review* 57 (March 1974): 340-353.

O'Donnell, Clifford R. "The Struggle for Patients' Right in a State Hospital: Issues and Implications." *International Journal of Social Psychiatry* 19 (1973): 286-287.

Oelbaum, L. R. "Clinical and Moral Views of Madness: Laing and Goffman Compared." *Bulletin of the Menninger Clinic* 36 (1972): 487.

Offir, Carole W. "Civil Rights and the Mentally Ill: Revolution in Bedlam." *Psychology Today* 8 (October 1974): 60-62+.

Older, Jules. "Psychosurgery: Ethical Issues and a Proposal for Control." *American Journal of Orthopsychiatry* 44 (October 1974): 661-674.

Osmond, H. "The Medical Model in Psychiatry: Love It or Leave It." *Medical Annals of District of Columbia* 41 (1972): 171-175.

Ostrow, David E., and Lehmann, Heinz E. "Quizzing the Expert: Clinical Criteria for Psychosurgery." *Hospital Physician* 9 (February 1973): 24-31.

Page, Stewart. "Power, Professionals, and Arguments against Civil Commitment." *Professional Psychology* 6 (November 1975): 381-393.

Parker, Laurence. "Psychotherapy and Ethics." *Cornell Journal of Social Relations* 9 (Fall 1974): 207-216.

Parry, Hugh J., *et al.* "National Patterns of Psychotherapeutic Drug Use." *Archives of General Psychiatry* 28 (June 1973): 769-783.

Parsons, Talcott. "Definitions of Health and Illness in the Light of American Values and Social Structure." In *Patients, Physicians and Illness*, edited by E. G. Jaco. New York: Free Press, 1970.

Peck, Connie L. "Current Legislative Issues concerning the Right to Refuse versus the Right to Choose Hospitalization and Treatment." *Psychiatry* 38 (November 1975): 303-317.

Peszke, Michael. "Is Dangerousness an Issue for Physicians in Emergency Commitment?" *American Journal of Psychiatry* 132 (August 1975): 825-828.

"Physical Manipulation of the Brain." The *Hastings Center Report* Special Supplement 9 (March 1973).

Platt, John. "The Skinnerian Revolution." In *Beyond the Punitive Society*, edited by Harvey Wheeler. San Francisco: W. H. Freeman, 1973, pp. 22–56.

Prettyman, E. Barrett. "The Indeterminate Sentence and the Right to Treatment." *American Criminal Law Review* 11 (1972): 7–37.

"The Principles of Medical Ethics with Annotations Especially Applicable to Psychiatry." *American Journal of Psychiatry* 130 (September 1973): 1058–1064.

Rachlin, Stephen, Pam, Alvin, and Milton, Janet, "Civil Liberties versus Involuntary Hospitalization." *American Journal of Psychiatry* 132 (February 1975): 189–192.

Rada, Richard T. "Psychosurgery and the Psychiatric Implications of the Kaimowitz Case." *Bulletin of the American Academy of Psychiatry and the Law* 2 (June 1974): 96–100.

Rainer, John D. "Genetic Knowledge and Heredity Counseling: New Responsibilities for Psychiatry." In *Proceedings of the Sixty-Third Annual Meeting of the American Psychopathological Association*, edited by Ronald R. Fieve, David Rosenthal, and Henry Brill. Baltimore: Johns Hopkins University Press, 1975, pp. 289–295.

Rastatter, Patrick C. "The Rights of the Mentally Ill during Incarceration: The Developing Law." *University of Florida Law Review* 25 (Spring 1973): 425–520.

Redlich, Fritz, and Mollica, Richard F. "Overview: Ethical Issues in Contemporary Psychiatry." *American Journal of Psychiatry* 133 (February 1975): 125–136.

Resnick, Jerome H., and Schwartz, Thomas. "Ethical Standards as an Independent Variable in Psychological Research." *American Psychologist* 28 (February 1973): 134–139.

Restak, R. "The Promise and Peril of Psychosurgery." *Saturday Review/World* 54 (September 25, 1973).

Ricketts, Henry T. "The New Psychosurgery." *Journal of the American Medical Association* 226 (12 November, 1973): 779.

Robitscher, Jonas. "Controversial Crusaders: The Mentally Ill and Psychiatric Reform." *Medical Opinion and Review* 4 (1968): 54–67.

——. "Courts, State Hospitals and the Right to Treatment." *American Journal of Psychiatry* 129 (1972): 298–304.

——. "The Right to Treatment: A Social-Legal Approach to the Plight of the State Hospital Patient." *Villanova Law Review* 18 (1972): 11–36.

——. "Social Legal Psychiatry." Address to the Annual Meeting, American College of Legal Medicine (1972).

——. "The Impact of New Legal Standards on Psychiatry or Who Are David Bazelon and Thomas Szasz and Why Are They Saying Such Terrible Things about Us?" *Journal of Psychiatry and Law* 3 (Summer 1975): 151–174.

———. "Psychosurgery and Other Somatic Means of Altering Behavior." *Bulletin of the American Academy of Psychiatry and the Law* 11 (March 1974): 7-33.

———. "Implementing the Right of the Mentally Disabled: Judicial, Legislative and Psychiatric Action." In *Medical, Moral and Legal Issues in Mental Health Care*, edited by Frank J. Ayd. Baltimore: Williams & Wilkins, 1974, pp. 142-178.

———. "The New Face of Legal Psychiatry." *American Journal of Psychiatry* 129 (September 1972): 315-321; reprinted in *Readings in Law and Psychiatry*, 2nd edition, edited by Elyce Zenoff Ferster and Jesse G. Rubin. Baltimore: Johns Hopkins, 1975, pp. 15-21.

———. "Medical Limits of Criminality." Editorial, *Annals of Internal Medicine* 73 (1970): 849-851.

———. "The Use and Abuses of Psychiatry." (The 1976 Isaac Ray Award Lectures), *The Journal of Psychiatry and Law* 5 (Fall 1977): 331-404.

Robitscher, Jonas, with Brady, Sister Madeleine. "Case Studies in Bioethics: Informed Consent: When Can It Be Withdrawn?" *Hastings Center Report* 2 (June 1972): 10-11.

Rogers, Rita R. "Psychiatric Hospitalization of Political Dissenters." *Psychiatric Opinion* 11 (February 1974): 20-24.

Rokeach, Milton. "Long Range Experimental Modification of Values, Attitudes and Behavior." *American Psychologist* 26 (1971): 453-459.

Rosen, G. "Social Attitude to Irrationality and Madness in 17th and 18th Century Europe." *Journal of History, Medicine and Allied Science* 18 (1963): 220-240.

Rosenhan, D. L. "On Being Sane in Insane Places." *Science* 179 (1973): 250-258.

Rosenzweig, S. "Compulsory Hospitalization of the Mentally Ill." *American Journal of Public Health* 61 (1971): 121.

Ryan, Kenneth J., and Yesley, Michael. "Psychosurgery: Clarification from the National Commission." *The Hastings Center Report* 7 (October 1977): 4.

Sabshin, M. "Psychiatric Perspectives on Normality." *Archives of General Psychiatry* 17(3) (1967): 258-264.

Sarbin, T. R. "On the Futility of the Proposition That Some People Be Labeled Mentally Ill." *Journal of Consulting Psychology* 31 (1967): 447.

Schatzman, Morton. "Madness and Morals." *Radical Therapist* 1 (October/November 1970): 11-15.

Schreiber, Aaron. "Indeterminate Therapeutic Incarceration of Dangerous Criminals: Perspectives and Problems." *Virginia Law Review* 56 (1970): 602-634.

Shah, Saleem A. "Dangerousness and Civil Commitment of the Mentally Ill: Some Public Policy Considerations." *American Journal of Psychiatry* 132 (May 1975): 501-505.

Shakow, David. "Ethics for a Scientific Age: Some Moral Aspects of Psychoanalysis." *Psychoanalytic Review* 52 (Fall 1965): 5-18.

Shestack, Jerome J. "Psychiatry and the Dilemmas of Dual Loyalities." In *Medical, Moral and Legal Issues in Mental Health Care*, edited by Frank J. Ayd. Baltimore: Williams & Wilkins, 1974, pp. 7-17.

Shuman, S. I. "The Emotional, Medical and Legal Reasons for the Special Concern about Psychosurgery." In *Medical, Moral and Legal Issues in Mental Health Care*, edited by Frank J. Ayd. Baltimore: Williams & Wilkins, 1974, pp. 48-80.

Siegler, M., and Osmond, H. "Models of Madness." *British Journal of Psychiatry* 112 (December 1966): 1193-1203.

———. "Laing's Models of Madness." *British Journal of Psychiatry* 115 (August 1969): 947-958.

Sitnick, Stanley A. "Major Tranquilizers in Prision: Drug Therapy and the Unconsenting Inmate." *Williamette Law Journal* 11 (Summer 1975): 378-397.

Slovenko, Ralph. "Psychotherapy and Confidentiality." *Cleveland State Law Review* 24 (1975): 375-396.

———. "On Psychosurgery." *Hastings Center Report* 5 (October 1975): 19-22.

Smith, J. Sydney, and Kiloh, L. G. "Psychosurgery and Society." *Medical Journal of Australia* 1 (25 January 1975): 117-119.

Smith, James M. "Madness, Innovation, and Social Policy," *Hastings Center Report* 7 (October 1977): 8-9.

Spece, Roy G., Jr. "Conditioning and Other Technologies Used to 'Treat'? 'Rehabilitate'? 'Demolish'? Prisoners and Mental Patients." *Southern California Law Review* 45 (Spring 1972): 616-684.

Stolz, Stephanie B. "Ethical Issues in Research on Behavior Therapy." In *Issues in Evaluating Behavior Modification*, edited by W. Scott Wood. Champaign, Ill.: Research Press, 1975, pp. 239-256.

Stone, Alan A. "Psychiatry and the Law." *Psychiatric Annals* (October 1971): 18-44.

Stone, I. F. "Betrayal by Psychiatry." *The New York Review* (February 19, 1972): 8.

"Symposium Psychosurgery." *Boston University Law Review* 54 (March 1974).

Szasz, Thomas S. "Criminal Responsibility and Psychiatry." In *Legal and Criminal Psychology*, edited by H. Toch. New York: Holt, Rinehart & Winston, 1961.

———. "The Ethics of Addiction." *American Journal of Psychiatry* 128 (1971): 541-546.

———. "Justice and Psychiatry." *Atlantic* 222 (1968): 127.

———. "The Problem of Psychiatric Nosology." *American Journal of Psychiatry* 114:5 (1957): 405-413.

———. "Problems Facing Psychiatry: The Psychiatrist as Party to Conflict." In

Ethical Issues in Medicine: The Role of the Physician in Today's Society, edited by E. F. Torrey. Boston: Little, Brown, 1968.

——. "Psychiatry as a Social Institution." In *Psychiatry and Responsibility*, edited by H. Schoeck and J. W. Wiggins. Princeton, N.J.: Van Nostrand, 1962.

——. "Psychiatry, Psychotherapy, and Psychology." *Archives of General Psychiatry* 4 (1959): 455.

——. "Psychoanalysis and Suggestion." *Comprehensive Psychiatry* 4 (1963): 271-280.

——. "Psychoanalysis and Taxation." *American Journal of Psychotherapy* 18 (1964): 635-643.

——. "Psychoanalytic Treatment as Education." *Archives of General Psychiatry* 9(1) (1963): 46-52.

——. "The Sane Slave: Social Control and Legal Psychiatry." *American Criminal Law Review* 10 (1972): 337.

——. "Involuntary Mental Hospitalization: An Unacknowledged Practice of Medical Fraud." *New England Journal of Medicine* 287(6) (1972): 277-278.

——. "Wither Psychiatry?" *Social Research* 33(3) (1966): 439-462.

——. "Commitment of the Mentally Ill: Treatment or Social Restraint?" *Journal of Nervous and Mental Disorders* 125 (April-June 1957): 293-307.

——. "The Danger of Coercive Psychiatry." *American Bar Association Journal* 61 (October 1975): 1246-1248.

——. "Involuntary Mental Hospitalization: A Crime against Humanity." In *Biomedical Ethics and the Law*, 1st ed., edited by James M. Humber and Robert F. Almeder. Plenum Press, 1976, pp. 151-171.

——. "Aborting Unwanted Behavior." *Humanist* 37 (July-August 1977): 67-72.

Szasz, Thomas, and Alexander, G. J. "Law, Property and Psychiatry." *American Journal of Orthopsychiatry* 42(4) (1972): 610-626.

——. "Mental Illness as Excuse for Civil Wrongs." *Journal of Nervous and Mental Disease* 147 (1968): 113-123.

Szasz, Thomas, and Hollender, M. H. "A Contribution to the Philosophy of Medicine." *Archives of Internal Medicine* 97 (1956): 585.

Szasz, Thomas, Hollender, M. H., and Knoff, W. F. "The Doctor-Patient Relationship and Its Historical Context." *American Journal of Psychiatry* 115 (1958): 522-528.

Stone, Alan A., *et al.* "Psychosurgery in Massachusetts: A Task Force Report." *Massachusetts Journal of Mental Health* 5 (Spring 1975): 26-54.

Tancredi, Laurence, and Clark, Diana. "Psychiatry and the Legal Rights of Patients." *American Journal of Psychiatry* 129 (1972): 320-328.

Tapp, L. J. "Psychology and the Law: The Dilema." American Bar Foundation Pamphlet No. 2 (1969).

Thompson, George H. "Involuntary Commitment and Individual Rights." *Biological Psychiatry* 8 (February 1974): 3-4.

Trotter, Robert J. "Open Sesame: The Constitution and Mental Institutions." *Science News* 108 (12 July 1975): 30-31.

U.S. Supreme Court. *"O'Conner* v. *Donaldson."* *United States Reports* 422 (26 June 1975): 563-589.

Vater, Joseph A. "Revising Pennsylvania's Involuntary Civil Commitment Statute." *University of Pittsburgh Law Review* 37 (Fall 1975): 180-193.

Vaux, Kenneth. "Look What They've Done to My Brain Ma!: Ethical Issues in Brain and Behavior Control." *Duquesne Law Review* 13 (Summer 1975): 907-918.

Washington, Judith E. "John Doe's Dilemma: Legal Resistance to Psychology." *North Carolina Central Law Journal* 5 (Fall 1973): 97-110.

Waterman, Alan S. "The Civil Liberties of the Participants in Psychological Research." *American Psychologist* 29 (June 1974): 470-471.

Weintraub, W., and Aronson, H. "Is Classical Psychoanalysis a Danger Procedure?" *Journal of Nervous and Mental Disease* 149 (1969): 224-229.

West, L. J. "Psychiatry, 'Brainwashing,' and the American Character." *American Journal of Psychiatry* 120 (1964): 842-850.

Wexler, Daniel B. "Token Taboo: Behavior Modification, Token Economics and the Law." *California Law Review* 61 (1973): 81-109.

Wiehl, Gerald W. "Involuntary Civil Commitment of the Non-Dangerous Mentally Ill: Substantive Limitations." *South Dakota Law Review* 18 (Spring 1973): 407-422.

Wilkins, Leslie T. "Putting 'Treatment' on Trial." *Hastings Center Report* 5 (February 1975): 35-48.

Wiseman, F. "Psychiatry and Law: Use and Abuse of Psychiatry in a Murder Case." *American Journal of Psychiatry* 118 (1961): 289-299.

Wohl, Julian. "Third Parties and Individual Psychotherapy." *American Journal of Psychotherapy* 28 (October 1974): 527-542.

Yeo, Clayton. "Psychiatry, The Law and Dissent in the Soviet Union." *Review of the International Commission of Jurists* 14 (June 1975): 34-41.

Zwerdling, Zachary E. "Informed Consent and the Mental Patient: California Recognizes a Mental Patient's Right to Refuse Psychosurgery and Shock Treatment." *Santa Clara Lawyer* 15 (Spring 1975): 725-759.

PART III: HUMAN EXPERIMENTATION

INTRODUCTION

In his now-classic piece, "Ethics and Clinical Research," Dr. Henry K. Beecher introduces the problem of human experimentation by citing twenty-two examples of unethical or questionably ethical studies with human subjects. Although Beecher affirms his belief in the soundness of American medicine, he contends that, unless steps are taken to correct activities of the sort he has noted, great harm will be done to medicine in the United States.

In order to ensure that the proprieties are followed by an investigator in any experiment, Beecher proposes that professional journals refuse to publish data which have been improperly obtained. Still, he admits that the most reliable safeguard will always be the presence of an intelligent, informed, conscientious, compassionate, and responsible investigator.

Dr. Michael Shimkin represents the medical research worker's viewpoint. He rejects the idea that professional journals refuse to publish data which have been obtained under questionable circumstances, contending that "we learn by our mistakes as well as our successes, and there are few situations in which ignorance or the hiding of facts are desirable solutions."

Dr. Shimkin outlines a list of items for a protocol to be followed in investigations on human beings. In order to ensure that subjects' rights are not subverted, he suggests (1) that a technically qualified and objective counselor act in a continued advisory capacity to the subject in an experiment, and (2) that there be a review board, not made up exclusively of medical personnel, to judge protocols of proposed research, justifications for experimental studies, etc. Still, he insists, members of review boards should be sympathetic to research and should not include individuals having "emotional blocks" to human experimentation. Further, he contends that there are cases in which the subjects in an experiment should perhaps be given no information at all concerning the experiment, as where the possession of such information would bias or negate the results.

Finally, Shimkin insists upon a fact often overlooked in the literature, viz., the rights of the investigator. He notes four such rights and spells out the need for mechanisms by which the investigator can defend himself and exact penalties for unfounded charges.

The issue with which Hans Jonas is primarily concerned in his essay is that of determining a proper method of selection for experimental subjects. Jonas argues that neither the social contract theory of the state, nor the moral law, imposes an obligation upon one to offer himself up as the subject of experimental study. But if individuals must be asked to commit themselves to participation in experimental studies, to whom should the appeal be addressed? Contrary to established practice, Jonas argues for what may be called an "elitist" standard. For Jonas, it is proper that the issuer of the call, viz., the researcher himself, be the first addressee. Still, Jonas realizes that it is impossible to keep the issue of human experimentation within the research community: "Neither in numbers nor in variety of material would its [the research community's] potential suffice for. . . the continual attack on disease. . . . " Thus, the aid of other persons must be sought. And in soliciting such aid, Jonas contends, the qualifications of the members of the scientific fraternity should be taken as the general criteria for selection. That is to say, researchers should look for additional subjects among the most highly motivated, most highly educated, and least "captive" members of our society.

Jonas realizes that his recommendations, if taken seriously by the scientific community, would restrict the pool of potential subjects for experimental study and so perhaps work for a slower rate of progress in the conquest of disease. But Jonas contends that progress in overcoming disease is only an optional goal—one which, if not achieved with the greatest possible haste, would not threaten society. For Jonas, a far greater danger to society lies in the possible erosion of moral values which could be one of the side effects of too ruthless a pursuit of scientific progress.

Proper design of an experiment and determination of a just procedure of selection for experimental subjects do not, in and of themselves, guarantee the morality of any experiment. If an experiment using human subjects is to be morally proper, the subjects used in that research must have consented freely to serve as experimental subjects. But consent can be free if, and only if, (1) the potential subject is informed as to all the facts that are material to a knowledgeable decision, and (2) the subject's decision is in no way forced or coerced. Together, (1) and (2) constitute the requirement of informed consent. Both the essays of Franz Ingelfinger and John Fletcher deal with the difficulties involved in securing truly informed consent from potential experimental subjects. Ingelfinger contends that it is in practice impossible to inform a potential subject as to all the facts material to a knowledgeable decision, and that even if all pertinent facts could be provided, the subject—or most subjects—would fail to comprehend their significance. Fletcher, on the other hand, is most concerned with the danger of coercion in the consent situation. Conducting a series of interviews with patient-volunteers, Fletcher discovers that, although the persons he interviewed did not feel that their decision to participate in an experiment was coerced, they did show indications of having had their consent "engineered." That is to say, Fletcher finds that patients tend to tie their participation in experimentation with continued treatment of their disease. Furthermore, everything that happens seems to be filtered through illness; and arrangements at the institution of study tend to diminish the patient's willingness to complain or question. In order to combat these "engineering" forces, then, Fletcher suggests that research institutions act to designate a "physician-friend," who would bear the responsibility of advocating for the patient. Such a step would be particularly desirable, he says, whenever especially necessitous groups, such as prisoners, children, or the mentally ill, were involved in research.

As Fletcher observes, certain classes of humans have limited capacity to consent to their involvement in experimental activities; and where individuals of this sort are used in research, special problems arise. Two such classes of individuals are fetuses and children. Richard Wasserstrom considers the moral issues involved in experimentation on nonviable human fetuses and hesitatingly concludes (1) that experimentation on fetuses *ex utero* may be permissible provided certain conditions are met, and (2) that experiments *in utero* should not be permitted where those experiments involve a substantial risk of injury to the fetus.

While Wasserstrom is concerned with experimentation upon nonviable fetuses, Richard McCormick is concerned with the question of whether or not it is morally proper to experiment upon children, when consent for such experimentation must be given by parents or guardians. After some deliberation, McCormick concludes (with some qualifications) that proxy consent to experiment upon children is morally legitimate (1) if the experiment is well designed and possibly beneficial, (2) if the experiment cannot succeed unless children are used, and (3) if there is no discernible risk or undue discomfort for the child.

ETHICS AND
CLINICAL RESEARCH*

HENRY K. BEECHER‡

Human experimentation since World War II has created some difficult problems with the increasing employment of patients as experimental subjects when it must be apparent that they would not have been available if they had been truly aware of the uses that would be made of them. Evidence is at hand that many of the patients in the examples to follow never had the risk satisfactorily explained to them, and it seems obvious that further hundreds have not known that they were the subjects of an experiment although grave consequences have been suffered as a direct result of experiments described here. There is a belief prevalent in some sophisticated circles that attention to these matters would "block progress." But, according to Pope Pius XII,[1] "... science is not the highest value to which all other orders of values ... should be subordinated."

I am aware that these are troubling charges. They have grown out of troubling practices. They can be documented, as I propose to do, by examples from leading medical schools, university hospitals, private hospitals, governmental military departments (the Army, the Navy and the Air Force), governmental institutes (the National Institutes of Health), Veterans Administration hospitals and industry. The basis for the charges is broad.[2]

[1] Pope Pius XII. Address. Presented at First International Congress on Histopathology of Nervous System, Rome, Italy, September 14, 1952.

[2] At the Brook Lodge Conference on "Problems and Complexities of Clinical Research" I commented that "what seem to be breaches of ethical conduct in experimentation are by no means rare, but are almost, one fears, universal." I thought it was obvious that I was by "universal" referring to the fact that examples could easily be found in *all* categories where research in man takes place to any significant extent. Judging by press comments, that was not obvious; hence, this note.

* Printed with permission of the author and *The New England Journal of Medicine, 274:* 1354–1360 (June 16, 1966). © 1966 by the Massachusetts Medical Society. From the Anaesthesia Laboratory of the Harvard Medical School at the Massachusetts General Hospital.

‡ Dorr Professor of Research in Anaesthesia, Harvard Medical School.

I should like to affirm that American medicine is sound, and most progress in it soundly attained. There is, however, a reason for concern in certain areas, and I believe the type of activities to be mentioned will do great harm to medicine unless soon corrected. It will certainly be charged that any mention of these matters does a disservice to medicine, but not one so great, I believe, as a continuation of the practices to be cited.

Experimentation in man takes place in several areas: in self-experimentation; in patient volunteers and normal subjects; in therapy; and in the different areas of *experimentation on a patient not for his benefit but for that, at least in theory, of patients in general.* The present study is limited to this last category.

Reasons for Urgency of Study

Ethical errors are increasing not only in numbers but in variety—for example, in the recently added problems arising in transplantation of organs.

There are a number of reasons why serious attention to the general problem is urgent.

Of transcendent importance is the enormous and continuing increase in available funds, as shown below.

Money Available for Research Each Year

	Massachusetts General Hospital	National Institutes of Health[a]
1945	$ 500,000[b]	$ 701,800
1955	2,222,816	36,063,200
1965	8,384,342	436,600,000

[a]National Institutes of Health figures based upon decade averages, excluding funds for construction, kindly supplied by Dr. John Sherman, of National Institutes of Health.
[b]Approximation, supplied by Mr. David C. Crockett, of Massachusetts General Hospital.

Since World War II the annual expenditure for research (in large part in man) in the Massachusetts General Hospital has increased a remarkagle 17-fold. At the National Institutes of Health, the increase has been a gigantic 624-fold. This "national" rate of increase is over 36 times that of the Massachusetts General Hospital. These data, rough as they are, illustrate vast opportunities and concomitantly expanded responsibilities.

Taking into account the sound and increasing emphasis of recent years that experimentation in man must precede general application of new procedures in therapy, plus the great sums of money available, there is reason to fear that these requirements and these resources may be greater than the supply of responsible investigators. All this heightens the problems under discussion.

Medical schools and university hospitals are increasingly dominated by investigators. Every young man knows that he will never be promoted to a tenure post, to a professorship in a major medical school, unless he has proved himself as an investigator. If the ready availability of money for condcting research is added to this fact, one can see how great the pressures are on ambitious young physicians.

Implementation of the recommendations of the President's Commission on Heart Disease, Cancer and Stroke means that further astronomical sums of money will become available for research in man.

In addition to the foregoing three practical points there are others that Sir Robert Platt[3] has pointed out: a general awakening of social conscience; greater power for good or harm in new remedies, new operations, and new investigative procedures than was formerly the case; new methods of preventive treatment with their advantages and dangers that are now applied to communities as a whole as well as to individuals, with multiplication of the possibilities for injury; medical science has shown how valuable human experimentation can be in solving problems of disease and its treatment; one can therefore anticipate an increase in experimentation; and the newly developed concept of clinical re-search as a profession (for example, clinical pharmacology)—and this, of course, can lead to unfortunate separation between the interests of science and the interests of the patient.

Frequency of Unethical or Questionably Ethical Procedures

Nearly everyone agrees that ethical violations do occur. The practical question is, how often? A preliminary examination of the matter was based on 17 examples, which were easily increased to 50. These 50 studies contained references to 186 further likely examples, on the average 3.7 leads per study; they at times overlapped from paper to paper, but this figure indicates how conveniently one can proceed in a search for such material. The data are suggestive of widespread problems but there is need for another kind of information, which was obtained by examination of 100 consecutive human studies

[3] Platt (Sir Robert), 1st part. *Doctor and Patient: Ethics, morals, government.* 87 pp. London: Nuffield provincial hospitals trust, 1963. Pp. 62 and 63.

published in 1964, in an excellent journal; 12 of these seemed to be unethical. If only one quarter of them is truly unethical, this still indicates the existence of a serious situation. Pappworth,[4] in England, has collected, he says, more than 500 papers based upon unethical experimentation. It is evident from such observations that unethical or questionably ethical procedures are not uncommon.

The Problem of Consent

All so-called codes are based on the bland assumption that meaningful or informed consent is readily available for the asking. As pointed out elsewhere,[5] this is very often not the case. Consent in any fully informed sense may not be obtainable. Nevertheless, except, possibly, in the most trivial situations, it remains a goal toward which one must strive for sociologic, ethical, and clear-cut legal reasons. There is no choice in the matter.

If suitably approached, patients will accede, on the basis of trust, to about any request their physician may make. At the same time, every experienced clinician investigator knows that patients will often submit to inconvenience and some discomfort, if they do not last very long, but the usual patient will never agree to jeopardize seriously his health or his life for the sake of "science."

In only 2 of the 50[6] examples originally compiled for this study was consent mentioned. Actually, it should be emphasized in all cases for obvious moral and legal reasons, but it would be unrealistic to place much dependence on it. In any precise sense statements regarding consent are meaningless unless one knows how fully the patient was informed of all risks, and if these are not known, the fact should also be made clear. A far more dependable safeguard than consent is the presence of a truly *responsible* investigator.

Examples of Unethical or Questionably Ethical Studies

These examples are not cited for the condemnation of individuals; they are recorded to call attention to a variety of ethical problems found in experimental medicine, for it is hoped that calling attention to them will help to correct abuses present. During ten years of study of these matters it has become apparent that thoughtlessness and carelessness, not a willful disregard of the patient's rights, account for most of the cases encountered. Nonetheless, it is

[4] Pappworth, M. H. Personal communication.
[5] Beecher, H. K. Consent in clinical experimentation: Myth and reality. *J.A.M.A. 195:*34, 1966.
[6] Reduced here to 22 for reasons of space.

evident that in many of the examples presented, the investigators have risked the health or the life of their subjects. No attempt has been made to present the "worst" possible examples; rather, the aim has been to show the variety of problems encountered.

References to the examples presented are not given, for there is no intention of pointing to individuals, but rather, a wish to call attention to widespread practices. All, however, are documented to the satisfaction of the editors of the *Journal*.

Known Effective Treatment Withheld

Example 1. It is known that rheumatic fever can usually be prevented by adequate treatment of streptococcal respiratory infections by the parenteral administration of penicillin. Nevertheless, definitive treatment was withheld, and placebos were given to a group of 109 men in service, while benzathine penicillin G was given to others.

The therapy that each patient received was determined automatically by his military serial number arranged so that more men received penicillin than received placebo. In the small group of patients studied 2 cases of acute rheumatic fever and 1 of acute nephritis developed in the control patients, whereas these complications did not occur among those who received the benzathine penicillin G.

Example 2. The sulfonamides were for many years the only antibacterial drugs effective in shortening the duration of acute streptococcal pharyngitis and in reducing its suppurative complications. The investigators in this study undertook to determine if the occurrence of the serious nonsuppurative complications, rheumatic fever, and acute glomerulonephritis, would be reduced by this treatment. This study was made despite the general experience that certain antibiotics, including penicillin, will prevent the development of rheumatic fever.

The subjects were a large group of hospital patients; a control group of approximately the same size, also with exudative Group A streptococcus, was included. The latter group received only nonspecific therapy (no sulfadiazine). The total group denied the effective penicillin comprised over 500 men.

Rheumatic fever was diagnosed in 5.4 percent of those treated with sulfadiazine. In the control group rheumatic fever developed in 4.2 percent.

In reference to this study a medical officer stated in writing that the subjects were not informed, did not consent and were not aware that they had been involved in an experiment, and yet admittedly 25 acquired rheumatic fever. According to this same medical officer *more than 70* who had had known definitive treatment withheld were on the wards with rheumatic fever when he was there.

Example 3. This involved a study of the relapse rate in typhoid fever treated in two ways. In an earlier study by the present investigators chloramphenicol had been recognized as an effective treatment for typhoid fever, being attended by half the mortality that was experienced when this agent was not used. Others had made the same observations, indicating that to withhold this effective remedy can be a life-or-death decision. The present study was carried out to determine the relapse rate under the two methods of treatment; of 408 charity patients 251 were treated with chloramphenicol, of whom 20, or 7.97 percent, died. Symptomatic treatment was given, but chloramphenicol was withheld in 157, of whom 36, or 22.9 percent, died. According to the data presented, 23 patients died in the course of this study who would not have been expected to succumb if they had received specific therapy.

Study of Therapy

Example 4. TriA (triacetyloleandomycin) was originally introduced for the treatment of infection with gram-positive organisms. Spotty evidence of hepatic dysfunction emerged, especially in children, and so the present study was undertaken on 50 patients, including mental defectives or juvenile delinquents who were inmates of a children's center. No disease other than acne was present; the drug was given for treatment of this. The ages of the subjects ranged from thirteen to thirty-nine years. "By the time half the patients had received the drug for four weeks, the high incidence of significant hepatic dysfunction . . . led to the discontinuation of administration to the remainder of the group at three weeks." (However, only two weeks after the start of the administration of the drug, 54 percent of the patients showed abnormal excretion of bromsulfalein.) Eight patients with marked hepatic dysfunction were transferred to the hospital "for more intensive study." Liver biopsy was carried out in these 8 patients and repeated in 4 of them. Liver damage was evident. Four of these hospitalized patients, after their liver-function tests returned to normal limits, received a "challenge" dose of the drug. Within two days hepatic dysfunction was evident in 3 of the 4 patients. In 1 patient a second challenge dose was given after the first challenge and again led to evidence of abnormal liver function. Flocculation tests remained abnormal in some patients as long as five weeks after discontinuance of the drug.

Physiologic Studies

Example 5. In this controlled, double-blind study of the hematologic toxicity of chloramphenicol, it was recognized that chloramphenicol is "well known as a cause of aplastic anemia" and that there is a "prolonged morbidity and high mortality of asplastic anemia" and that "chloramphenicol-induced aplastic anemia can be related to dose......" The aim of the study was "further definition of the toxicology of the drug......"

Forty-one randomly chosen patients were given either 2 or 6 gm. of chloramphenicol per day; 12 control patients were used. "Toxic bone-marrow depression, predominantly affecting erythropoiesis, developed in 2 of 20 patients given 2.0 gm. and in 18 of 21 given 6 gm. of chloramphenicol daily." The smaller dose is recommended for routine use.

Example 6. In a study of the effect of thymectomy on the survival of skin homografts 18 children, three and a half months to eighteen years of age, about to undergo surgery for congenital heart disease, were selected. Eleven were to have total thymectomy as part of the operation, and 7 were to serve as controls. As part of the experiment, full-thickness skin homografts from an unrelated adult donor were sutured to the chest wall in each case. (Total thymectomy is occasionally, although not usually part of the primary cardiovascular surgery involved, and whereas it may not greatly add to the hazards of the necessary operation, its eventual effects in children are not known.) This work was proposed as part of a long-range study of "the growth and development of these children over the years." No difference in the survival of the skin homograft was observed in the 2 groups.

Example 7. This study of cyclopropane anesthesia and cardiac arrhythmias consisted of 31 patients. The average duration of the study was three hours, ranging from two to four and a half hours. "Minor surgical procedures" were carried out in all but 1 subject. Moderate to deep anesthesia, with endotracheal intubation and controlled respiration, was used. Carbon dioxide was injected into the closed respiratory system until cardiac arrhythmias appeared. Toxic levels of carbon dioxide were achieved and maintained for considerable periods. During the cyclopropane anesthesia a variety of pathologic cardiac arrhythmias occurred. When the carbon dioxide tension was elevated above normal, ventricular extrasystoles were more numerous than when the carbon dioxide tension was normal, ventricular arrhythmias being continuous in 1 subject for ninety minutes. (This can lead to fatal fibrillation.)

Example 8. Since the minimum blood-flow requirements of the cerebral circulation are not accurately known, this study was carried out to determine "cerebral hemodynamic and metabolic changes ... before and during acute reductions in arterial pressure induced by drug administration and/or postural adjustments." Forty-four patients whose ages varied from the second to the tenth decade were involved. They included normotensive subjects, those with essential hypertension and finally a group with malignant hypertension. Fifteen had abnormal electrocardiograms. Few details about the reasons for hospitalization are given.

Signs of cerebral circulatory insufficiency, which were easily recognized, included confusion and in some cases a nonresponsive state. By alteration in the tilt of the patient "the clinical state of the subject could be changed in a matter of seconds from one of alertness to confusion, and for the remainder of the flow, the subject was maintained in the latter state." The femoral arteries were cannulated in all subjects, and the internal jugular veins in 14.

The mean arterial pressure fell in 37 subjects from 109 to 48 mm. of mercury, with signs of cerebral ischemia. "With the onset of collapse, cardiac output and right ventricular pressures decreased sharply."

Since signs of cerebral insufficiency developed without evidence of coronary insufficiency the authors concluded that "the brain may be more sensitive to acute hypotension than is the heart."

Example 9. This is a study of the adverse circulatory responses elicited by intra-abdominal maneuvers:

> When the peritoneal cavity was entered, a deliberate series of maneuvers was carried out [in 68 patients] to ascertain the effective stimuli and the areas responsible for development of the expected circulatory changes. Accordingly, the surgeon rubbed localized areas of the parietal and visceral peritoneum with a small ball sponge as discretely as possible. Traction on the mesenteries, pressure in the area of the celiac plexus, traction on the gallbladder and stomach, and occlusion of the portal and caval veins were the other stimuli applied.

Thirty-four of the patients were sixty years of age or older; 11 were seventy or older. In 44 patients the hypotension produced by the deliberate stimulation was "moderate to marked." The maximum fall produced by manipulation was from 200 systolic, 105 diastolic, to 42 systolic, 20 diastolic; the average fall in mean pressure in 26 patients was 53 mm. of mercury.

Of the 50 patients studied, 17 showed either atrioventricular dissociation with nodal rhythm or nodal rhythm alone. A decrease in the amplitude of the T wave and elevation or depression of the ST segment were noted in 25 cases in association with manipulation and hypotension or, at other times, in the course of anesthesia and operation. In only 1 case was the change pronounced enough to suggest myocardial ischemia. No case of myocardial infarction was noted in the group studied although routine electrocardiograms were not taken after operation to detect silent infarcts. Two cases in which electrocardiograms were taken after operation showed T-wave and ST-segment changes that had not been present before.

These authors refer to a similar study in which more alarming electrocardiographic changes were observed. Four patients in the series sustained silent myocardial infarctions; most of their patients were undergoing gallbladder surgery because of associated heart disease. It can be added further that in the 34 patients referred to above as being sixty years of age or older, some doubtless had heart disease that could have made risky the maneuvers carried out. In any event, this possibility might have been a deterrent.

Example 10. Starling's law—"that the heart output per beat is directly proportional to the diastolic filling"—was studied in 30 adult patients with atrial fibrillation and mitral stenosis sufficiently severe to require valvulotomy. "Continuous alterations of the length of a segment of left ventricular muscle were recorded simultaneously in 13 of these patients by means of a mercury-filled resistance gauge sutured to the surface of the left ventricle." Pressures in the left ventricle were determined by direct puncture simultaneously with the segment length in 13 patients and without the segment length in an additional 13 patients. Four similar unanesthetized patients were studied through catheterization of the left side of the heart transeptally. In all 30 patients arterial pressure was measured through the catheterized brachial artery.

Example 11. To study the sequence of ventricular contraction in human bundle-branch block, simultaneous catheterization of both ventricles was performed in 22 subjects; catheterization of the right side of the heart was carried out in the usual manner; the left side was catheterized transbronchially. Extrasystoles were produced by tapping on the epicardium in subjects with normal myocardium while they were undergoing thoracotomy. Simultaneous pressures were measured in both ventricles through needle puncture of this group.

The purpose of this study was to gain increased insight into the psysiology involved.

Example 12. This investigation was carried out to examine the possible effect of vagal stimulation on cardiac arrest. The authors had in recent years transected the homolateral vagus nerve immediately below the origin of the recurrent laryngeal nerve as palliation against cough and pain in bronchogenic carcinoma. Having been impressed with the number of reports of cardiac arrest that seemed to follow vagal stimulation, they tested the effects of intrathoracic vagal stimulation during 30 of their surgical procedures, concluding, from these observations in patients under satisfactory anesthesia, that cardiac irregularities and cardiac arrest due to vagovagal reflex were less common than had previously been supposed.

Example 13. This study presented a technic for determining portal circulation time and hepatic blood flow. It involved the transcutaneous injection of the spleen and catheterization of the hepatic vein. This was carried out in 43 subjects, of whom 14 were normal; 16 had cirrhosis (varying degrees), 9 acute hepatitis, and 4 hemolytic anemia.

No mention is made of what information was divulged to the subjects, some of whom were seriously ill. This study consisted in the development of a technic, not of therapy, in the 14 normal subjects.

Studies to Improve the Understanding of Disease

Example 14. In this study of the syndrome of impending hepatic coma in patients with cirrhosis of the liver certain nitrogenous substances were administered to 9 patients with chronic alcoholism and advanced cirrhosis: ammonium chloride, di-ammonium citrate, urea or dietary protein. In all patients a reaction that included mental disturbances, a "flapping tremor," and electroencephalographic changes developed. Similar signs had occurred in only 1 of the patients before these substances were administered:

> The first sign noted was usually clouding of the consciousness. Three patients had a second or a third course of administration of a nitrogenous substance with the same results. It was concluded that marked resemblance between this reaction and impending hepatic coma, implied that the administration of these [nitrogenous] substances to patients with cirrhosis may be hazardous.

Example 15. The relation of the effects of ingested ammonia to liver disease were investigated in 11 normal subjects, 6 with acute virus hepatitis, 26 with cirrhosis, and 8 miscellaneous patients. Ten of these patients had neurologic changes associated with either hepatitis or cirrhosis.

The hepatic and renal veins were cannulated. Ammonium chloride was administered by mouth. After this, a tremor that lasted for three days developed in 1 patient. When ammonium chloride was ingested by 4 cirrhotic patients with tremor and mental confusion the symptoms were exaggerated during the test. The same thing was true of a fifth patient in another group.

Example 16. This study was directed toward determining the period of infectivity of infectious hepatitis. Artifical induction of hepatitis was carried out in an institution for mentally defective children in which a mild form of hepatitis was endemic. The parents gave consent for the intramuscular injection or oral administration of the virus, but nothing is said regarding what was told them concerning the appreciable hazards involved.

A resolution adopted by the World Medical Association states explicitly: "Under no circumstances is a doctor permitted to do anything which would weaken the physical or mental resistance of a human being except from strictly therapeutic or prophylactic indications imposed in the interest of the patient." There is no right to risk an injury to 1 person for the benefit of others.

Example 17. Live cancer cells were injected into 22 human subjects as part of a study of immunity to cancer. According to a recent review, the subjects (hospitalized patients) were "merely told they would be receiving 'some cells'"— "... the word cancer was entirely omitted...."

Example 18. Melanoma was transplanted from a daughter to her volunteering and informed mother, "in the hope of gaining a little better understanding of cancer immunity and in the hope that the production of tumor antibodies might be helpful in the treatment of the cancer patient." Since the daughter died on the day after the transplantation of the tumor into her mother, the hope expressed seems to have been more theoretical than practical, and the daughter's condition was described as "terminal" at the time the mother volunteered to be a recipient. The primary implant was widely excised on the twenty-fourth day after it had been placed in the mother. She died from metastatic melanoma on the four hundred and fifty-first day after transplantation. The evidence that this patient died of diffuse melanoma that metastasized from a small piece of transplanted tumor was considered conclusive.

Technical Study of Disease

Example 19. During bronchoscopy a special needle was inserted through a bronchus into the left atrium of the heart. This was done in an unspecified number of subjects, both with cardiac disease and with normal hearts.

The technic was a new approach whose hazards were at the beginning quite unknown. The subjects with normal hearts were used, not for their possible benefit but for that of patients in general.

Example 20. The percutaneous method of catheterization of the left side of the heart has, it is reported, led to 8 deaths (1.09 percent death rate) and other serious accidents in 732 cases. There was, therefore, need for another method, the transbronchial approach, which was carried out in the present study in more than 500 cases, with no deaths.

Granted that a delicate problem arises regarding how much should be discussed with the patients involved in the use of a new method, nevertheless where the method is employed in a given patient for *his* benefit, the ethical problems are far less than when this potentially extremely dangerous method is used "in 15 patients with normal hearts, undergoing bronchoscopy for other reasons." Nothing was said about what was told any of the subjects, and nothing was said about the granting of permission, which was certainly indicated in the 15 normal subjects used.

Example 21. This was a study of the effect of exercise on cardiac output and pulmonary-artery pressure in 8 "normal" persons (that is, patients whose diseases were not related to the cardiovascular system), in 8 with congestive heart failure severe enough to have recently required complete bed rest, in 6 with hypertension, and 2 with aortic insufficiency, in 7 with mitral stenosis, and in 5 with pulmonary emphysema.

Intracardiac catheterization was carried out, and the catheter then inserted into the right or left main branch of the pulmonary artery. The brachial artery was usually catheterized; sometimes, the radial or femoral arteries were catheterized. The subjects exercised in a supine position by pushing their feet against weighted pedals. "The ability of these patients to carry on sustained work was severely limited by weakness and dyspnea." Several were in severe failure. This was not a therapeutic attempt but rather a physiologic study.

Bizarre Study

Example 22. There is a question whether ureteral reflux can occur in the normal bladder. With this in mind, vesicourethrography was carried out on 26 normal babies less than forty-eight hours old. The infants were exposed to x-rays while the bladder was filling and during voiding. Multiple spot films were made to record the presence or absence of ureteral reflux. None was found in this group, and fortunately no infection followed the catheterization. What the results of the extensive x-ray exposure may be, no one can yet say.

Comment on Death Rates

In the foregoing examples a number of procedures, some with their own demonstrated death rates, were carried out. The following data were provided by 3 distinguished investigators in the field and represent widely held views.

Cardiac catheterization: right side of the heart, about 1 death per 1000 cases; left side, 5 deaths per 1000 cases. "Probably considerably higher in some places, depending on the portal of entry." (One investigator had 15 deaths in his first 150 cases.) It is possible that catheterization of a hepatic vein or the renal vein would have a lower death rate than that of catheterization of the right side of the heart, for if it is properly carried out, only the atrium is entered en route to the liver or the kidney, not the right ventricle, which can lead to serious cardiac irregularities. There is always the possibility, however, that the ventricle will be entered inadvertently. This occurs in at least half the cases, according to 1 expert—"but if properly done is too transient to be of importance."

Liver biopsy: the death rate here is estimated at 2 to 3 per 1000, depending in considerable part on the condition of the subject.

Anesthesia: the anesthesia death rate can be placed in general at about 1 death per 2000 cases. The hazard is doubtless higher when certain practices such as deliberate evocation of ventricular extrasystoles under cyclopropane are involved.

Publication

In the view of the British Medical Research Council[7] it is not enough to ensure that all investigation is carried out in an ethical manner: it must be made unmistakably clear in the publications that the proprieties have been observed. This implies editorial responsibility in addition to the investigator's. The question rises, then, about valuable data that have been improperly obtained.[8] It is

[7] Great Britain, Medical Research Council. *Memorandum,* 1953.
[8] As far as principle goes, a parallel can be seen in the recent Mapp decision by the United States Supreme Court. It was stated there that evidence unconstitutionally obtained cannot be used in any judicial decision, no matter how important the evidence is to the ends of justice.

my view that such material should not be published (see footnote 7). There is a practical aspect to the matter: failure to obtain publication would discourage unethical experimentation. How many would carry out such experimentation if they *knew* its results would never be published? Even though suppression of such data (by not publishing it) would constitute a loss to medicine, in a specific localized sense, this loss, it seems, would be less important than the far-reaching moral loss to medicine if the data thus obtained were to be published. Admittedly, there is room for debate. Others believe that such data, because of their intrinsic value, obtained at a cost of great risk or damage to the subjects, should not be wasted but should be published with stern editorial comment. This would have to be done with exceptional skill, to avoid an odor of hypocrisy.

Summary and Conclusions

The ethical approach to experimentation in man has several components; two are more important than the others, the first being informed consent. The difficulty of obtaining this is discussed in detail. But it is absolutely essential to *strive* for it for moral, sociologic, and legal reasons. The statement that consent has been obtained has little meaning unless the subject or his guardian is capable of understanding what is to be undertaken and unless all hazards are made clear. If these are not known this, too, should be stated. In such a situation the subject at least knows that he is to be a participant in an experiment. Secondly, there is the more reliable safeguard provided by the presence of an intelligent, informed, conscientious, compassionate, responsible investigator.

Ordinary patients will not knowingly risk their health or their life for the sake of "science." Every experienced clinician investigator knows this. When such risks are taken and a considerable number of patients are involved, it may be assumed that informed consent has not been obtained in all cases.

The gain anticipated from an experiment must be commensurate with the risk involved.

An experiment is ethical or not at its inception; it does not become ethical *post hoc*—ends do not justify means. There is no ethical distinction between ends and means.

In the publication of experimental results it must be made unmistakably clear that the proprieties have been observed. It is debatable whether data obtained unethically should be published even with stern editorial comment.

SCIENTIFIC INVESTIGATIONS ON MAN

A MEDICAL RESEARCH WORKER'S VIEWPOINT

MICHAEL B. SHIMKIN

Scientific investigations on human beings have a rich tradition, have yielded many important advances for the betterment of man, and will continue to have an increasingly larger role in biomedical research.

The expanding dimensions of human investigations also have expanded the vexing but inescapable moral and legal problems such investigations entail. The timeliness and the importance of the problems are suggested by the recent medical writings such as those of Beecher,[1] their public recognition,[2] and the official governmental actions.[3] For purposes of this discussion, we must assume that the extent and seriousness of the problems are commensurate with the concern they have evinced.

Scientific research is usually directed toward obtaining precise information on specific, defined questions. Scientists become uneasy when they are asked to deal with generalities and abstractions. They, as well as the public, are also susceptible to emotional reactions when confronted with semantic subtleties and reactive labels. For this reason the word *investigation* appears to me to be a desirable substitute for its emotion-laden synonym, *experimentation*. But call it what we will, when the hiatus between morals, which embody the aspirations of man, and mores, the actual conduct of man, becomes too wide, it must be

[1] H. K. Beecher, "Ethics and Clinical Research," *New Engl. J. Med., 274,* 1354–1360 (1966).
[2] P. Lear, "Experiments on People–The Growing Debate," *Saturday Rev.,* pp. 41–50 (July 2, 1966).
[3] W. H. Stewart, "Memorandum on Revised Procedure on Clinical Research and Investigation Involving Human Subjects," Public Health Service, Dept. of Health, Education and Welfare. Washington, D.C. (July 1, 1966).

From M. Shimkin, "Scientific Investigations on Man: A Medical Research Worker's Viewpoint," in *Use of Human Subjects in Safety Evaluation of Food Chemicals–Proceedings of a Conference.* National Academy of Sciences and National Research Council, Pub. 1491 (Wash., D.C., 1967), pp. 217–227. Reproduced with permission of the author and the National Academy of Sciences.

narrowed in one way or another.[4] Such a hiatus seems to have appeared in the expanded investigations on man in the United States.

The problems as they now exist must be defined and then considered despite the absence of absolute, immutable criteria for human conduct. Scientific research, morals, and laws are creations of man and are thus defined as aspects of human behavior in our period of a space–time continuum.[5]

Resolutions to the problems, it is hoped, will emerge from discussions of specific questions, such as: How and when should human investigations be undertaken? What principles and rules should guide such investigations? What measures will reduce to a minimum the consequences of human frailty and misconduct, yet impose minimum restrictions upon useful investigations? The considerations of these and similar questions must be modified by experience and new information and relevant to specific conditions of each situation and its temporal occurrence. The aim is to seek workable methods of successive approximations, rather than nonexistent final solutions.

The Conduct of Investigations on Man

Existing moral and legal concepts governing investigations on man are derived to a great extent from past experiences in clinical research. The compilation of this material by Ladimer and Newman[6] is an essential basis for further discussion. It is evident that clinical considerations are also of direct relevance to investigations on healthy individuals and on human populations.

Table I outlines a functional sequence that applies to most projects for investigations involving human beings. The outline provides no surprises, for it includes essentially the same points and steps as are entailed in most biomedical research, although some are of particular importance when man is involved. Many of the points are interrelated, the value judgments are inescapable.

I. As in all research, perhaps the most important items are the primary question or hypothesis and the quality of the investigator who proposes to conduct the research.

The question must be valid and approachable by existent methods. The background requires documentation on the importance of the problem, scientifically and practically, and an analytical review of preceding basic and applied

[4] H. F. Pilpel, "Morals, Mores and Mandates," *Vassar Alumnae Magazine, 51* (5), 18–21 (June 1966).

[5] E. Goldberger, *How Physicians Think,* Charles C Thomas, Springfield, Ill. (1965).

[6] I. Ladimer, and R. W. Newman, editors, *Clinical Investigation in Medicine: Legal, Ethical, and Moral Aspects,* Law-Medicine Research Institute, Boston University, Boston, Mass. (1963).

*Table I. Items for a Protocol Involving Investigation
on Human Beings*

I. The Question (Problem, Hypothesis)
   A. Is it valid and substantive?
   B. Is it approachable scientifically?
   C. Review of relevant knowledge, basic and applied
   D. Who proposes the question?
      1. Qualifications of investigator(s)
      2. Facilities and consultations available

II. Type of Research Proposed
   A. Observational
      1. Retrospective
      2. Prospective
   B. Manipulative (experimental)
      1. Episodic
      2. Repetitive or continual

III. Materials Needed
   A. Type of individuals
      1. With defined characteristics (e.g., patients)
      2. Normal individuals
      3. Contratests (controls)
   B. Type of facilities
      1. Field
      2. Institutional
      3. Special
   C. Type of instruments, laboratories

IV. Methods Proposed
   A. Type of data to be gathered
      1. Surveys of existing data
      2. Questionnaires, interviews
      3. Psychological tests
      4. Physical measurements
      5. Physiological measurements
         a. Basal
         b. Under stress (surgical, etc.)
      6. Pharmacological tests
   B. Type of specimens required
      1. Excretory (urine, etc.)
      2. Blood
      3. Tissues
      4. Organs

V. Investigative Procedure
   A. Pilot phase
      1. Safety of procedures

continued

Table I. continued.

---

      2. Validation of data-procurement procedures
      3. Validation of test procedures
  B. Biometric considerations
      1. Number of individuals required
      2. Number and type of observations required
      3. Randomization, double-blinding, sequential trials
  C. Practical considerations
      1. Cost
      2. Time
  D. Formal investigation

VI. Control and Analysis
  A. During investigation
  B. Final analysis and conclusions
  C. Publication or other dissemination

---

research relating to the problem with special justification of its extension to man.

Particularly when human populations are involved, the topic must be substantive and of interest to the subject-participants as well as to the investigators, and to the community as well as to those involved in the study, in order that the investigation be initiated and pursued at all. It must also be able to attract and to hold capable scientific personnel, thus helping to assure competent planning and performance.

As for the investigator, there must be confidence in his judgment, integrity, and technical competence. This confidence must extend to his associates and his institution. It is necessarily based on past performance.

II. Research on man, like other scientific research, can be divided into two general types. One type is *observational,* in which findings are compared and analyzed, without active participation of, or procedures on, the subjects. Even in this type of inquiry, there will be differences of opinion regarding the proper use of records, especially those involving confidential information. Clinical records are the usual problem, but so are data on occupation, income, habits, or legal entanglements. Observational research may extend to data on the future status of the subjects, requiring examinations and follow-up procedures, or the gathering of specimens of excreta, blood, and various tissues. The latter type of research extends beyond simple passive observations and analyses for interrelations.

Our chief concern is with the second type of research, *manipulative* or experimental research, in which some deliberate procedure is imposed upon the subjects. This may involve the addition of an agent to or its removal from the environment, or some physiological or pharmacological procedure and the study of the effects of this manipulation on the subjects.

III. It is also necessary to categorize research on man by the type of subject to be used in the research. One type is exemplified by patients with disease upon whom new procedures are instituted for diagnostic or therapeutic aims, and are therefore of potential benefit to the patient. Most of us accept the thought that in patients with rapidly progressing fatal afflictions, more risk is justified than in, say, the treatment of an annoying allergy.

The other type of research involves either patients or normal individuals on whom procedures are contemplated that do not aim to be of direct benefit to that individual. The two categories may overlap, and the latter may be rationalized into the former. However, limiting human research to clinical aims is neither realistic nor desirable. Man's aspirations and interests include adventure, discovery, contribution to society, and the recognition and honors that may result. These drives are not limited to healthy individuals, and they exist in the potential subjects as well as in the potential investigators. Perhaps we should recognize the subjects in research more often as our co-workers. The initial participation of the investigator as one of the subjects in research reinforces the equality of their roles.

IV. The methods specify procedures to be performed on the human subjects. These extend from simple observations to complex physiological and pharmacological situations in which stress and risk are unavoidable. Risk must be commensurate with the importance of the potential discovery, and the estimate of the risk must be revised with experience. An extreme example is afforded by the current explorations of space, in which disaster is a possibility at each step, while the importance of potential discoveries remains unknown.

Possible effects of external environmental stresses are now equalled by the potential dangers of changes in man's internal milieu. Chemical agents with therapeutic effects may also transform genetic material, produce fetal abnormalities, block cellular metabolic pathways, and affect personality. In pharmacological investigations, the exposure of man should come only after a series of laboratory studies, culminating with animals, have been performed and evaluated. But at some point data on nonhuman material have to be transposed to man. Complex investigational systems have been devised to achieve proper therapeutic trials, yet, with each new drug, different problems arise. The consequences of chemical agents in trace amounts over long periods and the cumulative effects and interactions between such agents require much more laboratory and animal data, as well as observations on man.

V. When the question has been specified and the appropriate materials and methods selected, the next step is the experimental design. In modern times, this involves biometric considerations of the choice of the samples to be compared, the criteria by which individuals are selected, and the numbers required to establish differences or to test nondifferences at predetermined levels of statistical significance. It involves strict definitions and interpretative criteria for the observations to be made. Randomized assignment of individuals to the groups to be compared, double-blinding wherever possible, and sequential analysis of data are among techniques useful for economy and as safety measures. The words *randomization, double-blind,* and *control* sometimes meet emotional resistance, and their scientific meaning requires careful, specific explanation. In the case of control, the concept in human investigations is perhaps better expressed by a substitute word, *contratest.*[7]

Formal studies on man in almost all instances require a pilot phase, directed toward further establishing safety and feasibility for the investigation. The pilot phase also provides additional data for biometric design and final considerations of cost.

VI. The last item relates research to communications. Research should start and end in the library, and research is not completed if it is not reported and disseminated. The history of man is in his written records, and those who do not read history are condemned to repeating it. We learn by mistakes as well as by successes, and there are few situations in which ignorance or the hiding of facts are desirable solutions.

The Rights of the Human Subject

Recognized human rights are the unique feature that separates investigations on man from all other research. Table II suggests four such features. Again, all are relative and involve subjective reactions and judgments.

There appears to be a consensus that informed consent of the subjects is essential for manipulative investigations. But what is informed consent? How can one convey "all" relevant information, especially when the investigator himself cannot predict the course or the outcome of a research situation?

The usual practice in clinical research is to accept patients who are referred by other physicians. This, in effect, provides the subject with a professional counselor who assists him toward arriving at a decision. It has been suggested[8] that this may be developed into a more formal arrangement in which a "physician-friend" would act in a continued advisory capacity to the patient. Perhaps

---

[7] M. B. Shimkin, "The Numerical Method in Therapeutic Medicine," *Public Health Repts., 79,* 1–12 (1964).

[8] O. Guttentag, "The Problem of Experimentation on Human Beings: II. The Physician's Point of View," *Science, 117,* 207–210 (1953).

Table II. The Rights of the Human Subject

I. Informed consent
II. Volunteer participation
III. Review of proposal and conduct by board of peers
IV. Recourse to religious and other counsel

this can be usefully extended to nonclinical situations, by providing technically qualified but presumably objective counselors to the potential subject.

In many specific therapeutic situations detailed discussion with a patient is not called for and may even be harmful to the patient. For nontherapeutically oriented investigations, however, the procedure, the possible risks, and the aims should be available to the prospective subject and his counselors. How much to tell and how to convey the information depend on specific circumstances. This may vary from full participation in the actual research to no information in situations where the possession of such information would bias or negate the results.

There also appears to be a consensus regarding the principle that the subjects in manipulative investigations, whether they be patients or normal individuals, must be volunteers in a strict sense. This implies an untrammeled option to reject as well as to accept the proposition. All human beings have equal, inalienable rights, and their role as subjects or as investigators does not modify such rights.[9]

In order to assure these rights, prior review mechanisms as well as remedies in courts of law must be available for the protection of both the investigators and the subjects. In therapeutic research, this can be relatively simple and informal, perhaps by the investigator's peers in the institution or of the professional group. For human volunteers, sick or healthy, more rigorous and formal review may be required, depending on the potential dangers of the experimental design. Protocols of the proposed research, its justification, and its need appear unavoidable.

And here again we are faced with the Socratic question, "Who selects the judges?" For patients and for medical institutions, physicians must bear the responsibility. But for many other types of human investigations, an exclusively medical jury is parochial. Legal and religious viewpoints, as well as technical proficiency in the contemplated techniques, are desirable for the protection of the subjects and the investigators. Of course, members of review boards should

[9]M. B. Shimkin, "The Problem of Experimentation on Human Beings: The Research Worker's Point of View," *Science, 117,* 205–207 (1953).

be sympathetic to research, and should not include individuals with emotional blocks to human experimentation.

A sticky point confronts us regarding individuals who are legally incapable of giving consent, especially children or mental defectives. There seems to be no alternative to placing the burden of consent on the legal guardians. But this only begs the question, since the aspect of volunteer participation would still be lacking. This assigns additional responsibility to the judgment of the review mechanism.

The last item of Table II emphasizes the equality of human rights in all situations and man's need for recourse to forces beyond his limitations. The subjects of investigation, as well as the investigators, should have ready access to theological and other counsel.

All these precautions are susceptible to the formulation of memoranda, codes, and laws. How far these should go at any stage, and how detailed they should be, are crucial questions that will determine how human investigations will and should progress.

The Rights of the Investigator

This brings us to another aspect of the dynamic equilibrium between the subject, the investigator, and society that is represented in human investigations.

In order to perform investigations, there must be investigators. The investigators must be motivated to plan and to pursue the work. Most good research is self-motivated, meaning that the idea stems primarily from the investigator, is considered to be important by the investigator, and, despite frustrations and difficulties, remains rewarding to the investigator.

Truly novel ideas, the most important elements for scientific advance, are born in individual minds. New ideas are stimulated by an environment of sufficient freedom to allow unorthodoxy and possible error. They are not encouraged by reviews and restrictions.

Scientists do not differ from other individuals in their responsibilities and their commitments to human values. They also have rights, as real as those of the subjects who may be involved in the investigation. And research, with its yields to society, will not flourish unless these rights are also recognized and reasonably met.

Table III lists four such rights, which must be placed in correct relationship with the rights of the subjects, and of society, including its ethics and its laws.

Privacy of ideas and of preliminary investigations is the first item. It is unrealistic to expect investigators to divulge original ideas. Moreover, without actual data, somehow obtained, such ideas have an excellent chance of being

Table III. The Rights of the Investigator

I. Privacy of own ideas and investigations
II. Freedom to reject ideas and assignments of others
III. Protection against excessive detail of plans, reports, records
IV. Appeal and defense, with confrontation, against accusations

---

rejected just because they are unsupported. To get out of this circular trap requires opportunity for the investigator to generate some data.

Plans presented in writing to committees, and examined by clerical and scientific assistants, seldom remain confidential. The better qualified the reviewers, the more opportunity there is for the transfer of ideas, consciously or subconsciously, with possible loss of priority and claim for discovery.

The second point is the right to reject ideas and assignments of others, be they other scientists, committees, industrial concerns, or governmental agencies. Such rejection, just as for the potential subject, should not carry implied penalties for the investigator. He should be free to voice his objections, but must allow identical freedom to others who might wish to proceed despite his criticisms.

Research on man should be substantive from scientific as well as from practical standpoints. It may be of considerable commercial importance to provide data on the safety and utility of some product. Whether an actual study is to be performed, however, requires consideration of its scientific interest and priority.

The most precious commodity of an investigator is his time. A substantial proportion of his time is already devoted to composing plans, forwarding reports, and filling out forms on fiscal and administrative matters. Operations research is highly desirable to develop methods that would meet these responsibilities with a minimum of paper work. Funding agencies, governmental or private, are not owners but stewards of funds that are in their custody to meet defined objectives. Mechanisms that preclude or make difficult the meeting of the objectives should be revised. Otherwise investigators best qualified to do the work will find other outlets for their drives, to the detriment of all.

The fourth point is seldom openly discussed. Review committees, funding agencies, and university faculties reach many of their decisions *in camera*. Rejection of a proposal may carry only theoretical right to reconsideration; seldom is there actual confrontation between the body that makes the decision and the investigator. The subjects of human investigation require protection, we all admit. Investigators who are accused of unethical practices, openly or by innuendo, also need mechanisms through which they can defend themselves and exact penalties for unfounded charges.

One of the problems facing us, in all aspects of life, is the proliferation of laws and their interpretations. Most of these mandates are promulgated for worthy reasons, but their effect *en masse* is not without drawbacks. Rules and regulations produce records and restrictions in a never-ending cycle. In an area as complex and as varied as research on human beings, all rules are imperfect and susceptible to many interpretations, and these are not made perfect by additional rules. But neither are they made useless by the presence of imperfections.

Discussions such as these should be helpful in the pragmatic resolution of the problems inherent in scientific investigations on human beings. Yet it is difficult to improve upon the conclusion written by Claude Bernard[10] almost a century ago: "So, among the experiments that may be tried on man, those that can only harm are forbidden, those that are innocent are permissible, and those that may do good are obligatory." Surely this is in keeping with the pivotal moral and ethical guide of our major religions, stated many times in the Bible: "Thou shalt love thy neighbor as thyself."[11]

Acknowledgment

I am indebted to Dr. Nathaniel I. Berlin, of Bethesda, Maryland, to Dr. Otto E. Guttentag and Mr. Stillman Drake of San Francisco, and to Mrs. Mary N. Shimkin for their thoughtful suggestions and comments.

[10] C. Bernard, *An Introduction to the Study of Experimental Medicine,* 1878, transl. by H. C. Greene, Henry Schuman, New York (1949), p. 102.
[11] *The Bible,* Leviticus, 19:18, Matthew, 22:39; Mark, 12:31.

PHILOSOPHICAL REFLECTIONS ON EXPERIMENTING WITH HUMAN SUBJECTS

HANS JONAS

Experimenting with human subjects is going on in many fields of scientific and technological progress. It is designed to replace the overall instruction by natural, occasional, and cumulative experience with the selective information from artificial, systematic experiment which physicial science has found so effective in dealing with inanimate nature. Of the new experimentation with man, medical is surely the most legitimate; psychological, the most dubious; biological (still to come), the most dangerous. I have chosen here to deal with the first only, where the case *for* it is strongest and the task of adjudicating conflicting claims hardest. When I was first asked[1] to comment "philo-sophically" on it, I had all the hesitation natural to a layman in the face of matters on which experts of the highest competence have had their say and still carry on their dialogue. As I familiarized myself with the material,[2] any initial feeling of moral rectitude that might have facilitated my task quickly dissipated before the awesome complexity of the problem, and a state of great humility took its place. The awareness of the problem in all its shadings and ramifications

[1] The American Academy of Arts and Sciences invited me to participate in a conference on the Ethical Aspects of Experimentation on Human Subjects, sponsored by the Academy journal *Daedalus* and the National Institutes of Health. The conference was held September 26–28, 1968, in Boston, Massachusetts, and all papers were subsequently published in *Daedalus*. A previous conference of the same title and under the same auspices is documented in *Proceedings of the Conference on the Ethical Aspects of Experimentation on Human Subjects,* Nov. 3–4, 1967 (Boston; hereafter called *Proceedings*).

[2] Since the time of writing this essay (1968), the literature on the subject has grown so much that listing what was then available to me would be of no more than historical interest.

Originally published in *Daedalus* 98 (Spring 1969), and in its present revised version, with a comment by Arthur J. Dyck, in *Experimentation with Human Subjects,* ed. Paul A. Freund (New York: Braziller, 1970). The article as it appears here is from *Philosophical Essays: From Ancient Creed To Technological Man,* ed. Hans Jonas (Englewood Cliffs, N.J.: Pren-tice-Hall, 1974). Reprinted by permission of *DAEDALUS,* Journal of The American Academy of Arts and Sciences, Boston, Mass. Spring, 1969, *Ethical Aspects of Experi-mentation with Human Subjects.*

speaks out with such authority, perception, and sophistication in the published discussions of the researchers themselves that it would be foolish of me to hope that I, an onlooker on the sidelines, could tell those battling in the arena anything they have not pondered themselves. Still, since the matter is obscure by its nature and involves very fundamental, transtechnical issues, anyone's attempt at clarification can be of use, even without novelty. And even if the philosophical reflection should in the end achieve no more than the realization that in the dialectics of this area we must sin and fall into guilt, this insight may not be without its own gains.

I. The Peculiarity of Human Experimentation

Experimentation was originally sanctioned by natural science. There it is performed on inanimate objects, and this raises no moral problems. But as soon as animate, feeling beings become the subject of experiment, as they do in the life sciences and especially in medical research, this innocence of the search for knowledge is lost, and questions of conscience arise. The depth to which moral and religious sensibilities can become aroused over these questions is shown by the vivisection issue. Human experimentation must sharpen the issue as it involves ultimate questions of personal dignity and sacrosanctity. One profound difference between the human experiment and the physical (beside that between animate and inanimate, feeling and unfeeling nature) is this: The physical experiment employs small-scale, artificially devised substitutes for that about which knowledge is to be obtained, and the experimenter extrapolates from these models and simulated conditions to nature at large. Something deputizes for the "real thing"—balls rolling down an inclined plane for sun and planets, electric discharges from a condenser for real lightning, and so on. For the most part, no such substitution is possible in the biological sphere. We must operate on the original itself, the real thing in the fullest sense, and perhaps affect it irreversibly. No simulacrum can take its place. Especially in the human sphere, experimentation loses entirely the advantage of the clear division between vicarious model and true object. Up to a point, animals may fulfill the proxy role of the classical physical experiment. But in the end man himself must furnish knowledge about himself, and the comfortable separation of noncommittal experiment and definitive action vanishes. An experiment in education affects the lives of its subjects, perhaps a whole generation of schoolchildren. Human experimentation for whatever purpose is always *also* a responsible, nonexperimental, definitive dealing with the subject himself. And not even the noblest purpose abrogates the obligations this involves.

This is the root of the problem with which we are faced: Can both that purpose and this obligation be satisfied? It not, what would be a just compromise? Which side should give way to the other? The question is inherently philosophical as it concerns not merely pragmatic difficulties and their arbitration, but a genuine conflict of values involving principles of a high order. May I put the conflict in these terms. On principle, it is felt, human beings *ought not* to be dealt with in that way (the "guinea pig" protest); on the other hand, such dealings are increasingly urged on us by considerations, in turn appealing to principle, that claim to override those objections. Such a claim must be carefully assessed, especially when it is swept along by a mighty tide. Putting the matter thus, we have already made one important assumption rooted in our "Western" cultural tradition: The prohibitive rule is, to that way of thinking, the primary and axiomatic one; the permissive counter-rule, as qualifying the first, is secondary and stands in need of justification. We must justify the infringement of a primary inviolability, which needs no justification itself; and the justification of its infringement must be by values and needs of a dignity commensurate with those to be sacrificed.

Before going any further, we should give some more articulate voice to the resistance we feel against a merely utilitarian view of the matter. It has to do with a peculiarity of human experimentation quite independent of the question of possible injury to the subject. What is wrong with making a person an experimental subject is not so much that we make him thereby a means (which happens in social contexts of all kinds), as that we make him a thing—a passive thing merely to be acted on, and passive not even for real action, but for token action whose token object he is. His being is reduced to that of a mere token or "sample." This is different from even the most exploitative situations of social life: there the business is real, not fictitious. The subject, however much abused, remains an agent and thus a "subject" in the other sense of the word. The soldier's case is instructive: Subject to most unilateral discipline, forced to risk mutilation and death, conscripted without, perhaps against, his will—he is still conscripted with his capacities to act, to hold his own or fail in situations, to meet real challenges for real stakes. Though a mere "number" to the High Command, he is not a token and not a thing. (Imagine what he would say if it turned out that the war was a game staged to sample observations on his endurance, courage, or cowardice.)

These compensations of personhood are denied to the subject of experimentation, who is acted upon for an extraneous end without being engaged in a real relation where he would be the counterpoint to the other or to circumstance. Mere "consent" (mostly amounting to no more than permission) does not right this reification. Only genuine authenticity of volunteering can possibly redeem the condition of "thinghood" to which the subject submits. Of this we shall speak later. Let us now look at the nature of the conflict, and especially at the nature of the claims countering in this matter those on behalf of personal sacrosanctity.

II. "Individual Versus Society" as the Conceptual Framework

The setting for the conflict most consistently invoked in the literature is the polarity of individual versus society—the possible tension between the individual good and the common good, between private and public welfare. Thus, W. Wolfensberger speaks of "the tension between the long-range interests of society, science, and progress, on one hand, and the rights of the individual on the other."[3] Walsh McDermott says: "In essence, this is a problem of the rights of the individual versus the rights of society."[4] Somewhere I found the "social contract" invoked in support of claims that science may make on individuals in the matter of experimentation. I have grave doubts about the adequacy of this frame of reference, but I will go along with it part of the way. It does apply to some extent, and it has the advantage of being familiar. We concede, as a matter of course, to the common good some pragmatically determined measure of precedence over the individual good. In terms of rights, we let some of the basic rights of the individual be overruled by the acknowledged rights of society—as a matter of right and moral justness and not of mere force or dire necessity (much as such necessity may be adduced in defense of that right). But in making that concession, we require careful clarification of what the needs, interests, and rights of society are, for society—as distinct from any plurality of individuals—is an abstract and, as such, is subject to our definition, and his basic good is more or less known. Thus the unknown in our problem is the so-called common or public good and its potentially superior claims, to which the individual good must or might sometimes be sacrificed, in circumstances that in turn must also be counted among the unknowns of our question. Note that in putting the matter in this way—that is, in asking about the right of society to individual sacrifice—the consent of the sacrificial subject is no necessary part of the *basic* question.

"Consent," however, is the other most consistently emphasized and examined concept in discussions of this issue. This attention betrays a feeling that the "social" angle is not fully satisfactory. If society has a right, its exercise is not contingent on volunteering. On the other hand, if volunteering is fully genuine, no public right to the volunteered act need be construed. There is a difference between the moral or emotional appeal of a cause that elicits volunteering and a right that demands compliance—for example, with particular reference to the social sphere, between the *moral claim* of a common good and society's *right* to that good and to the means of its realization. A moral claim cannot be met without consent; a right can do without it. Where consent is present anyway, the

---

[3] Wolfensberger, "Ethical Issues in Research with Human Subjects," *World Science 155* (Jan. 6, 1967), p. 48.
[4] *Proceedings*, p. 29.

distinction may become immaterial. But the awareness of the many ambiguities besetting the "consent" actually available and used in medical research[5] prompts recourse to the idea of a public right conceived independently of (and valid prior to) consent; and, vice versa, the awareness of the problematic nature of such a right makes even its advocates still insist on the idea of consent with all its ambiguities: an uneasy situation either way.

Nor does it help much to replace the language of "rights" by that of "interests" and then argue the sheer cumulative weight of the interest of the many over against those of the few or the single individual. "Interests" range all the way from the most marginal and optional to the most vital and imperative, and only those sanctioned by particular importance and merit will be admitted to count in such a calculus—which simply brings us back to the question of right or moral claim. Moreover, the appeal to numbers is dangerous. Is the number of those afflicted with a particular disease great enough to warrant violating the interests of the nonafflicted? Since the number of the latter is usually so much greater, the argument can actually turn around to the contention that the cumulative weight of interest is on *their* side. Finally, it may well be the case that the individual's interest in his own inviolability is itself a public interest, such that its publicly condoned violation, irrespective of numbers, violates the interest of all. In that case, its protection in *each* instance would be a paramount interest, and the comparison of numbers will not avail.

These are some of the difficulties hidden in the conceptual framework indicated by the terms *society-individual, interest,* and *rights.* But we also spoke of a moral call, and this points to another dimension—not indeed divorced from the social sphere, but transcending it. And there is something even beyond that: true sacrifice from highest devotion, for which there are no laws or rules except that it must be absolutely free. "No one has the right to choose martyrs for science" was a statement repeatedly quoted in the November 1967 *Daedalus* conference. But no scientist can be prevented from making himself a martyr for his science. At all times, dedicated explorers, thinkers, and artists have immolated themselves on the altar of their vocation, and creative genius most often pays the price of happiness, health, and life for its own consummation. But no one, not even society, has the shred of a right to expect and ask these things in the normal course of events. They come to the rest of us as a *gratia gratis data.*

III. The Sacrificial Theme

Yet we must face the somber truth that the *ultima ratio* of communal life is and has always been the compulsory, vicarious sacrifice of individual lives. The

---

[5] See M. H. Pappworth, "Ethical Issues in Experimental Medicine" in D. R. Cutler, ed., *Updating Life and Death* (Boston: Beacon Press, 1969), pp. 64–69.

primordial sacrificial situation is that of outright human sacrifices in early communities. These were not acts of blood-lust or gleeful savagery; they were the solemn execution of a supreme, sacral necessity. One of the fellowship of men had to die so that all could live, the earth be fertile, the cycle of nature renewed. The victim often was not a captured enemy, but a select member of the group: "The king must die." If there was cruelty here, it was not that of men, but that of the gods, or rather of the stern order of things, which was believed to exact that price for the bounty of life. To assure it for the community, and to assure it ever again, the awesome *quid pro quo* had to be paid over and over.

Far should it be from us to belittle, from the height of our enlightened knowledge, the majesty of the underlying conception. The particular *causal* views that prompted our ancestors have long since been relegated to the realm of superstition. But in moments of national danger we still send the flower of our young manhood to offer their lives for the continued life of the community, and if it is a just war, we see them go forth as consecrated and strangely ennobled by a sacrificial role. Nor do we make their going forth depend on their own will and consent, much as we may desire and foster these. We conscript them according to law. We conscript the best and feel morally disturbed if the draft, either by design or in effect, works so that mainly the disadvantaged, socially less useful, more expendable, make up those whose lives are to buy ours. No rational persuasion of the pragmatic necessity here at work can do away with the feeling, a mixture of gratitude and guilt, that the sphere of the sacred is touched with the vicarious offering of life for life. Quite apart from these dramatic occasions, there is, it appears, a persistent and constitutive aspect of human immolation to the very being and prospering of human society—an immolation in terms of life and happiness, imposed or voluntary, of the few for the many. What Goethe has said of the rise of Christianity may well apply to the nature of civilization in general: *"Opfer fallen hier, / Weder Lamm noch Stier, / Aber Menschenopfer unerhört."*[6] We can never rest comfortably in the belief that the soil from which our satisfactions sprout is not watered with the blood of martyrs. But a troubled conscience compels us, the undeserving beneficiaries, to ask: Who is to be martyred? In the service of what cause and by whose choice?

Not for a moment do I wish to suggest that medical experimentation on human subjects, sick or healthy, is to be likened to primeval human sacrifices. Yet something sacrificial is involved in the selective abrogation of personal inviolability and the ritualized exposure to gratuitous risk of health and life,

---

[6]"Victims do fall here, /Neither lamb nor steer, / Nay, but human offerings untold." —*Die Braut von Korinth.*

justified by a presumed greater, social good. My examples from the sphere of stark sacrifice were intended to sharpen the issues implied in that context and to set them off clearly from the kinds of obligation and constraint imposed on the citizen in the normal course of things or generally demanded of the individual in exchange for the advantages of civil society.

IV. The "Social Contract" Theme

The first thing to say in such a setting-off is that the sacrificial area is not covered by what is called the "social contract." This fiction of political theory, premised on the primacy of the individual, was designed to supply a rationale for the *limitation* of individual freedom and power required for the existence of the body politic, whose existence in turn is for the benefit of the individuals. The principle of these limitations is that their *general* observance profits all, and that therefore the individual observant, assuring this general observance for his part, profits by it himself. I observe property rights because their general observance assures my own; I observe traffic rules because their general observance assures my own safety; and so on. The obligations here are mutual and general; no one is singled out for special sacrifice. Moreover, for the most part, *qua* limitations of my liberty, the laws thus deducible from the hypothetical "social contract" enjoin me from certain actions rather than obligate me to positive actions (as did the laws of feudal society). Even where the latter is the case, as in the duty to pay taxes, the rationale is that I am myself a beneficiary of the services financed through these payments. Even the contributions levied by the welfare state, though not originally contemplated in the liberal version of the social contract theory, can be interpreted as a personal insurance policy of one sort or another— be it against the contingency of my own indigence, be it against the dangers of disaffection from the laws in consequence of widespread unrelieved destitution, be it even against the disadvantages of a diminished consumer market. Thus, by some stretch, such contributions can still be subsumed under the principle of enlightened self-interest. But no complete abrogation of self-interest at any time is in the terms of the social contract, and so pure sacrifice falls outside it. Under the putative terms of the contract alone, I cannot be required to die for the public good. (Thomas Hobbes made this forcibly clear.) Even short of this extreme, we like to think that nobody is entirely and one-sidedly the victim in any of the renunciations exacted under normal circumstances by society "in the general interest"—that is, for the benefit of others. "Under normal circumstances," as we shall see, is a necessary qualification. Moreover, the "contract" can legitimize claims only on our overt, public actions and not on our invisible, private being. Our powers, not our persons, are beholden to the common weal.

In one important respect, it is true, public interest and control do extend to the private sphere by general consent: in the compulsory education of our children. Even there, the assumption is that the learning and what is learned, apart from all future social usefulness, are also for the benefit of the individual in his own being. We would not tolerate education to degenerate into the conditioning of useful robots for the social machine.

Both restrictions of public claim in behalf of the "common good"—that concerning one-sided sacrifice and that concerning the private sphere—are valid only, let us remember, on the premise of the primacy of the individual, upon which the whole idea of the "social contract" rests. This primacy is itself a metaphysical axiom or option peculiar to our Western tradition, and the whittling away of its force would threaten the tradition's whole foundation. In passing, I may remark that systems adopting the alternative primacy of the community as their axiom are naturally less bound by the restrictions we postulate. Whereas we reject the idea of "expendables" and regard those not useful or even recalcitrant to the social purpose as a burden that society must carry (since their individual claim to existence is as absolute as that of the most useful), a truly totalitarian regime, Communist or other, may deem it right for the collective to rid itself of such encumbrances or to make them forcibly serve some social end by conscripting their persons (and there are effective combinations of both). We do not normally—that is, in nonemergency conditions—give the state the right to conscript labor, while we do give it the right to "conscript" money, for money is detachable from the person as labor is not. Even less than forced labor do we countenance forced risk, injury, and indignity.

But in time of war our society itself supersedes the nice balance of the social contract with an almost absolute precedence of public necessities over individual rights. In this and similar emergencies, the sacrosanctity of the individual is abrogated, and what for all practical purposes amounts to a near-totalitarian, quasi-communist state of affairs is *temporarily* permitted to pervail. In such situations, the community is conceded the right to make calls on its members, or certain of its members, entirely different in magnitude and kind from the calls normally allowed. It is deemed right that a part of the population bears a disproportionate burden of risk of a disproportionate gravity; and it is deemed right that the rest of the community accepts this sacrifice, whether voluntary or enforced, and reaps its benefits—difficult as we find it to justify this acceptance and this benefit by any normal ethical standards. We justify it transethically, as it were, by the supreme collective emergency, formalized, for example, by the declaration of a state of war.

Medical experimentation on human subjects falls somewhere between this overpowering case and the normal transactions of the social contract. On the one hand, no comparable extreme issue of social survival is (by and large) at stake.

And no comparable extreme sacrifice or foreseeable risk is (by and large) asked. On the other hand, what is asked goes decidedly beyond, even runs counter to, what it is otherwise deemed fair to let the individual sign over of his person to the benefit of the "common good." Indeed, our sensitivity to the kind of intrusion and use involved is such that only an end of transcendent value or overriding urgency can make it arguable and possibly acceptable in our eyes.

V. Health as a Public Good

The cause invoked is health and, in its more critical aspect, life itself—clearly superlative goods that the physician serves directly by curing and the researcher indirectly by the knowledge gained through his experiments. There is no question about the good served nor about the evil fought—disease and premature death. But a good to whom and an evil to whom? Here the issue tends to become somewhat clouded. In the attempt to give experimentation the proper dignity (on the problematic view that a value becomes greater by being "social" instead of merely individual), the health in question or the disease in question is somehow predicated of the social whole, as if it were society that, in the persons of its members, enjoyed the one and suffered the other. For the purposes of our problem, public interest can then be pitted against private interest, the common good against the individual good. Indeed, I have found health called a national resource, which of course it is, but surely not in the first place.

In trying to resolve some of the complexities and ambiguities lurking in these conceptualizations, I have pondered a particular statement, made in the form of a question, which I found in the *Proceedings* of the earlier *Daedalus* conference: "Can society afford to discard the tissues and organs of the hopelessly unconscious patient when they could be used to restore the otherwise hopelessly ill, but still salvageable, individual?" And somewhat later: "A strong case can be made that society can ill afford to discard the tissues and organs of the hopelessly unconscious patient; they are greatly needed for study and experimental trial to help those who can be salvaged."[7] I hasten to add that any suspicion of callousness that the "commodity" language of these statements may suggest is immediately dispelled by the name of the speaker, Dr. Henry K. Beecher, for whose humanity and moral sensibility there can be nothing but admiration. But the use, in all innocence, of this language gives food for thought. Let me, for a moment, take the question literally. "Discarding" implies proprietary rights—nobody can discard what does not belong to him in the first place. Does society then own my body? "Salvaging" implies the same and,

[7]*Proceedings,* pp. 50–51.

moreover, a use-value to the owner. Is the life-extension of certain individuals then a public interest? "Affording" implies a critically vital level of such an interest—that is, of the loss or gain involved. And "society" itself—what is it? When does a need, an aim, an obligation become social? Let us reflect on some of these terms.

VI. What Society Can Afford

"Can society afford . . .?" Afford what? To let people die intact, thereby withholding something from other people who desperately need it, who in consequence will have to die too? These other, unfortunate people indeed cannot afford not to have a kidney, heart, or other organ of the dying patient, on which they depend for an extension of their lease on life; but does that give them a right to it? And does it oblige society to procure it for them? What is it that *society* can or cannot afford—leaving aside for the moment the question of what it has a *right* to? It surely can afford to lose members through death; more than that, it is built on the balance of death and birth decreed by the order of life. This is too general, of course, for our question, but perhaps it is well to remember. The specific question seems to be whether society can afford to let some people die whose death might be deferred by particular means if these were authorized by society. Again, if it is merely a question of what society can or cannot afford, rather than of what it ought or ought not to do, the answer must be: Of course, it can. If cancer, heart disease, and other organic, noncontagious ills, especially those tending to strike the old more than the young, continue to exact their toll at the normal rate of incidence (including the toll of private anguish and misery), society can go on flourishing in every way.

Here, by contrast, are some examples of what, in sober truth, society cannot afford. It cannot afford to let an epidemic rage unchecked; a persistent excess of deaths over births, but neither—we must add—too great an excess of births over deaths; too low an average life expectancy even if demographically balanced by fertility, but neither too great a longevity with the necessitated correlative dearth of youth in the social body; a debilitating state of general health; and things of this kind. These are plain cases where the whole condition of society is critically affected, and the public interest can make its imperative claims. The Black Death of the Middle Ages was a *public* calamity of the acute kind; the life-sapping ravages of endemic malaria or sleeping sickness in certain areas are a public calamity of the chronic kind. Such situations a society as a whole can truly not "afford," and they may call for extraordinary remedies, including, perhaps, the invasion of private sacrosanctities.

This is not entirely a matter of numbers and numerical ratios. Society, in a subtler sense, cannot "afford" a single miscarriage of justice, a single inequity in the dispensation of its laws, the violation of the rights of even the tiniest minority, because these undermine the moral basis on which society's existence rests. Nor can it, for a similar reason, afford the absence or atrophy in its midst of compassion and of the effort to alleviate suffering—be it widespread or rare—one form of which is the effort to conquer disease of any kind, whether "socially" significant (by reason of number) or not. And in short, society cannot afford the absence among its members of *virtue* with its readiness for sacrifice beyond defined duty. Since its presence—that is to say, that of personal ideal-ism—is a matter of grace and not of decree, we have the paradox that society depends for its existence on intangibles of nothing less than a religious order, for which it can hope, but which it cannot enforce. All the more must it protect this most precious capital from abuse.

For what objectives connected with the medico-biological sphere should this reserve be drawn upon—for example, in the form of accepting, soliciting, perhaps even imposing the submission of human subjects to experimentation? We postu-late that this must be not just a worthy cause, as any promotion of the health of anybody doubtlessly is, but a cause qualifying for transcendent social sanction. Here one thinks first of those cases critically affecting the whole condition, present and future, of the community we have illustrated. Something equivalent to what in the political sphere is called "clear and present danger" may be invoked and a state of emergency proclaimed, thereby suspending certain other-wise inviolable prohibitions and taboos. We may observe that averting a disaster always carries greater weight than promoting a good. Extraordinary danger excuses extraordinary means. This covers human experimentation, which we would like to count, as far as possible, among the extraordinary rather than the ordinary means of serving the common good under public auspices. Naturally, since foresight and responsibility for the future are of the essence of institutional society, averting disaster extends into long-term prevention, although the lesser urgency will warrant less sweeping licenses.

VII. Society and the Cause of Progress

Much weaker is the case where it is a matter not of saving but of improving society. Much of medical research falls into this category. As stated before, a permanent death rate from heart failure or cancer does not threaten society. So long as certain statistical ratios are maintained, the incidence of disease and of disease-induced mortality is not (in the strict sense) a "social" misfortune. I hasten to add that it is not therefore less of a human misfortune, and the call for relief issuing with silent eloquence from each victim and all potential victims is of no lesser dignity. But it is misleading to equate the fundamentally human response to it with what is owed to society: it is owed by man to man—and it is thereby owed by society to the individuals as soon as the adequate ministering to these concerns outgrows (as it progressively does) the scope of private spontaneity and is made a public mandate. It is thus that society assumes responsibility for medical care, research, old age, and innumerable other things not originally of the public realm (in the original "social contract"), and they become duties toward "society" (rather than directly toward one's fellow man) by the fact that they are socially operated.

Indeed, we expect from organized society no longer mere protection against harm and the securing of the conditions of our preservation, but active and constant improvement in all the domains of life: the waging of the battle against nature, the enhancement of the human estate—in short, the promotion of progress. This is an expansive goal, one far surpassing the disaster norm of our previous reflections. It lacks the urgency of the latter, but has the nobility of the free, forward thrust. It surely is worth sacrifices. It is not at all a question of what society can afford, but of what it is committed to, beyond all necessity, by our mandate. Its trusteeship has become an established, ongoing, institutionalized business of the body politic. As eager beneficiaries of its gains, we now owe to "society," as its chief agent, our individual contributions toward its *continued* pursuit. I emphasize "continued pursuit." Maintaining the existing level requires no more than the orthodox means of taxation and enforcement of professional standards that raise no problems. The more optional goal of pushing forward is also more exacting. We have this syndrome: Progress is by our choosing an acknowledged interest of society, in which we have a stake in various degrees; science is a necessary instrument of progress; research is a necessary instrument of science; and in medical science experimentation on human subjects is a necessary instrument of research. Therefore, human experimentation has come to be of societal interest.

The destination of research is essentially melioristic. It does not serve the preservation of the existing good from which I profit myself and to which I am obligated. Unless the present state is intolerable, the melioristic goal is in a sense gratuitous, and this not only from the vantage point of the present. Our descendants have a right to be left an unplundered planet; they do not have a right to new miracle cures. We have sinned against them, if by our doing we have destroyed their inheritance—which we are doing at full blast; we have not sinned against them, if by the time they come around arthritis has not yet been conquered (unless by sheer neglect). And generally, in the matter of progress, as humanity had no claim on a Newton, a Michelangelo, or a St. Francis to appear, and no right to the blessings of their unscheduled deeds, so progress, with all our methodical labor for it, cannot be budgeted in advance and its fruits received as a due. Its coming-about at all and its turning out for good (of which we can never be sure) must rather be regarded as something akin to grace.

VIII. The Melioristic Goal, Medical Research, and Individual Duty

Nowhere is the melioristic goal more inherent than in medicine. To the physician, it is not gratuitous. He is committed to curing and thus to improving the power to cure. Gratuitous we called it (outside disaster conditions) as a *social* goal, but noble at the same time. Both the nobility and the gratuitousness must influence the manner in which self-sacrifice for it is elicited, and even its free offer accepted. Freedom is certainly the first condition to be observed here. The surrender of one's body to medical experimentation is entirely outside the enforceable "social contract."

Or can it be construed to fall within its terms—namely, as repayment for benefits from past experimentation that I have enjoyed myself? But I am indebted for these benefits not to society, but to the past "martyrs," to whom society is indebted itself, and society has no right to call in my personal debt by way of adding new to its own. Moreover, gratitude is not an enforceable social obligation; it anyway does not mean that I must emulate the deed. Most of all, if it was wrong to exact such sacrifice in the first place, it does not become right to exact it again with the plea of the profit it has brought me. If, however, it was not exacted, but entirely free, as it ought to have been, then it should remain so, and its precedence must not be used as a social pressure on others for doing the same under the sign of duty.

Indeed, we must look outside the sphere of the social contract, outside the whole realm of public rights and duties, for the motivations and norms by which we can expect ever again the upwelling of a will to give what nobody—neither society, nor fellow man, nor posterity—is entitled to. There are such dimensions in man with trans-social wellsprings of conduct, and I have already pointed to the paradox, or mystery, that society cannot prosper without them, that it must draw on them, but cannot command them.

What about the moral law as such a transcendent motivation of conduct? It goes considerably beyond the public law of the social contract. The latter, we saw, is founded on the rule of enlightened self-interest: *Do ut des*—I give so that I be given to. The law of individual conscience asks more. Under the Golden Rule, for example, I am required to give as I wish to be given to under like circumstances, but not in order that I be given to and not in expectation of return. Reciprocity, essential to the social law, is not a condition of the moral law. One subtle "expectation" and "self-interest," but of the moral order itself, may even then be in my mind: I prefer the environment of a moral society and can expect to contribute to the general morality by my own example. But even if I should always be the dupe, the Golden Rule holds. (If the social law breaks faith with me, I am released from its claim.)

IX. Moral Law and Transmoral Dedication

Can I, then, be called upon to offer myself for medical experimentation in the name of the moral law? *Prima facie,* the Golden Rule seems to apply. I should wish, were I dying of a disease, that enough volunteers in the past had provided enough knowledge through the gift of their bodies that I could now be saved. I should wish, were I desperately in need of a transplant, that the dying patient next door had agreed to a definition of death by which his organs would become available to me in the freshest possible condition. I surely should also wish, were I drowning, that somebody would risk his life, even sacrifice his life, for mine.

But the last example reminds us that only the negative form of the Golden Rule ("Do not do unto others what you do not want done unto yourself") is fully prescriptive. The positive form ("Do unto others as you would wish them to do unto you"), in whose compass our issue falls, points into an infinite, open horizon where prescriptive force soon ceases. We may well say of somebody that he ought to have come to the succor of B, to have shared with him in his need, and the like. But we may not say that he ought to have given his life for him. To have done so would be praiseworthy; not to have done so is not blameworthy. It cannot be asked of him; if he fails to do so, he reneges on no duty. But *he* may say of himself, and only he, that he ought to have given his life. *This* "ought" is strictly between him and himself, or between him and God; no outside party— fellow man or society—can appropriate its voice. It can humbly receive the superogatory gifts from the free enactment of it.

We must, in other words, distinguish between moral obligation and the much larger sphere of moral value. (This, incidentally, shows up the error in the widely held view of value theory that the higher a value, the stronger its claim and the greater the duty to realize it. The highest are in a region beyond duty and claim.) The ethical dimension far exceeds that of the moral law and reaches into the sublime solitude of dedication and ultimate commitment, away from all reckoning and rule—in short, into the sphere of the *holy.* From there alone can the offer of self-sacrifice genuinely spring, and this source of it must be honored religiously. How? The first duty here falling on the research community, when it enlists and uses this source, is the safeguarding of true authenticity and spontaneity.

X. The "Conscription" of Consent

But here we must realize that the mere issuing of the appeal, the calling for volunteers, with the moral and social pressures it inevitably generates, amounts even under the most meticulous rules of consent to a sort of *conscripting*. And some soliciting is necessarily involved. This was in part meant by the earlier remark that in this area sin and guilt can perhaps not be wholly avoided. And this is why "consent," surely a non-negotiable minimum requirement, is not the full answer to the problem. Granting then that soliciting and therefore some degree of conscripting are part of the situation, who may conscript and who may be conscripted? Or less harshly expressed: Who should issue appeals and to whom?

The naturally qualified issuer of the appeal is the research scientist himself, collectively the main carrier of the impulse and the only one with the technical competence to judge. But his being very much an interested party (with vested interests, indeed, not purely in the public good, but in the scientific enterprise as such, in "his" project, and even in his career) makes him also suspect. The ineradicable dialectic of this situation—a delicate incompatibility problem—calls for particular controls by the research community and by public authority that we need not discuss. They can mitigate, but not eliminate the problem. We have to live with the ambiguity, the treacherous impurity of everything human.

XI. Self-Recruitment of the Scientific Community

To whom should the appeal be addressed? The natural issuer of the call is also the first natural addressee: the physician-researcher himself and the scientific confraternity at large. With such a coincidence—indeed, the noble tradition with which the whole business of human experimentation started—almost all of the associated legal, ethical, and metaphysical problems vanish. If it is full, autonomous identification of the subject with the purpose that is required for the dignifying of his serving as a subject—here it is; if strongest motivation—here it is; if fullest understanding—here it is; if freest decision—here it is; if greatest integration with the person's total, chosen pursuit—here it is. With the fact of self-solicitation the issue of consent in all its insoluble equivocality is bypassed *per se*. Not even the condition that the particular purpose be truly important and the project reasonably promising, which must hold in any solicitation of others, need be satisfied here. By himself, the scientist is free to obey his obsession, to play his hunch, to wager on chance, to follow the lure of ambition. It is all part of the "divine madness" that somehow animates the ceaseless pressing against frontiers. For the rest of society, which has a deep-seated disposition to look with reverence and awe upon the guardians of the mysteries of life, the profession assumes with this proof of its devotion the role of a self-chosen, consecrated fraternity, not unlike the monastic orders of the past, and this would come nearest to the actual, religious origins of the art of healing.

It would be the ideal, but is not a real solution, to keep the issue of human experimentation within the research community itself. Neither in numbers nor in variety of material would its potential suffice for the many-pronged, systematic, continual attack on disease into which the lonely exploits of the early investigators have grown. Statistical requirements alone make their voracious demands; and were it not for what I have called the essentially "gratuitous" nature of the whole enterprise of progress, as against the mandatory respect for invasion-proof self-hood, the simplest answer would be to keep the whole population enrolled, and let the lot, or an equivalent of draft boards, decide which of each category will at any one time be called up for "service." It is not difficult to picture societies with whose philosophy this would be consonant. We are agreed that ours is not one such and should not become one. The specter of it is indeed among the threatening utopias on our own horizon from which we should recoil, and of whose advent by imperceptible steps we must beware. How then can our mandatory faith be honored when the recruitment for experimentation goes outside the scientific community, as it must in honoring another commitment of no mean dignity? We simply repeat the former question: To whom should the call be addressed?

XII. "Identification" as the Principle of Recruitment in General

If the properties we adduced as the particular qualifications of the members of the scientific fraternity itself are taken as general criteria of selection, then one should look for additional subjects where a maximum of identification, understanding, and spontaneity can be expected—that is, among the most highly motivated, and most highly educated, and the least "captive" members of the community. From this naturally scarce resource, a descending order of permissibility leads to greater abundance and ease of supply, whose use should become proportionately more hesitant as the exculpating criteria are relaxed. An inversion of normal "market" behavior is demanded here—namely, to accept the lowest quotation last (and excused only by the greatest pressure of need); to pay the highest price first.

The ruling principle in our considerations is that the "wrong" of reification can only be made "right" by such authentic identification with the cause that it is the subject's as well as the researcher's cause—whereby his role in its service is not just permitted by him, but *willed*. That sovereign will of his which embraces the end as his own restores his personhood to the otherwise depersonalizing context. To be valid it must be autonomous and informed. The latter condition can, outside the research community, only be fulfilled by degrees; but the higher the degree of the understanding regarding the purpose and the technique, the more valid becomes the endorsement of the will. A margin of mere trust inevitably remains. Ultimately, the appeal for volunteers should seek this free and generous endorsement, the appropriation of the research purpose into the person's own scheme of ends. Thus, the appeal is in truth addressed to the one, mysterious, and sacred source of any such generosity of the will—"devotion," whose forms and objects of commitment are various and may invest different motivations in different individuals. The following, for instance, may be responsive to the "call" we are discussing: compassion with human suffering, zeal for humanity, reverence for the Golden Rule, enthusiasm for progress, homage to the cause of knowledge, even longing for sacrificial justification (do not call that "masochism," please). On all these, I say, it is defensible and right to draw when the research objective is worthy enough; and it is a prime duty of the research community (especially in view of what we called the "margin of trust") to see that this sacred source is never abused for frivolous ends. For a less than adequate cause, not even the freest, unsolicited offer should be accepted.

XIII. The Rule of the "Descending Order" and Its Counter-Utility Sense

We have laid down what must seem to be a forbidding rule to the number-hungry research industry. Having faith in the transcendent potential of man, I do not fear that the "source" will ever fail a society that does not destroy it—and only such a one is worthy of the blessings of progress. But "elitistic" the rule is (as is the enterprise of progress itself), and elites are by nature small. The combined attribute of motivation and information, plus the absence of external pressures, tends to be socially so circumscribed that strict adherence to the rule might numerically starve the research process. This is why I spoke of a descending order of permissibility, which is itself permissive, but where the realization that it is a *descending* order is not without pragmatic import. Departing from the august norm, the appeal must needs shift from idealism to docility, from high-mindedness to compliance, from judgment to trust. Consent spreads over the whole spectrum. I will not go into the casuistics of this penumbral area. I merely indicate the principle of the order of preference: The poorer in knowledge, motivation, and freedom of decision (and that, alas, means the more readily available in terms of numbers and possible manipulation), the more sparingly and indeed reluctantly should the reservoir be used, and the more compelling must therefore become the countervailing justification.

Let us note that this is the opposite of a social utility standard, the reverse of the order by "availability and expendability": The most valuable and scarcest, the least expendable elements of the social organism, are to be the first candidates for risk and sacrifice. It is the standard of *noblesse oblige;* and with all its counter-utility and seeming "wastefulness," we feel a rightness about it and perhaps even a higher "utility," for the soul of the community lives by this spirit.[8] It is also the opposite of what the day-to-day interests of research clamor for, and for the scientific community to honor it will mean that it will have to fight a strong temptation to go by routine to the readiest sources of supply—the suggestible, the ignorant, the dependent, the "captive" in various senses.[9] I do not believe that heightened resistance here must cripple research, which cannot be permitted; but it may indeed slow it down by the smaller numbers fed into experimentation in consequence. This price—a possibly slower rate of progress—may have to be paid for the preservation of the most precious capital of higher communal life.

XIV. Experimentation on Patients

So far we have been speaking on the tacit assumption that the subjects of experimentation are recruited from among the healthy. To the question "Who is conscriptable?" the spontaneous answer is: least and last of all the sick—the most available of all as they are under treatment and observation anyway. That the afflicted should not be called upon to bear additional burden and risk, that they are society's special trust and the physician's trust in particular—these are elementary responses of our moral sense. Yet the very destination of medical research, the conquest of disease, requires at the crucial stage trial and verification on precisely the sufferers from the disease, and their total exemption would defeat the purpose itself. In acknowledging this inescapable necessity, we enter the most sensitive area of the whole complex, the one most keenly felt and most searchingly discussed by the practitioners themselves. No wonder, for it touches the heart of the doctor—patient relation, putting its most solemn obligations to the test. There is nothing new in what I have to say about the ethics of the

---

[8] Socially, everyone is expendable relatively—that is, in different degrees; religiously, no one is expendable absolutely: the "image of God" is in all. If it can be enhanced, then not by anyone being expended, but by someone expending himself.

[9] This refers to captives of circumstance, not of justice. Prison inmates are, with respect to our problem, in a special class. If we hold to some idea of guilt, and to the supposition that our judicial system is not entirely at fault, they may be held to stand in a special debt to society, and their offer to serve—from whatever motive—may be accepted with a minimum of qualms as a means of reparation.

doctor—patient relation, but for the purpose of confronting it with the issue of experimentation some of the oldest verities must be recalled.

A. The Fundamental Privilege of the Sick

In the course of treatment, the physician is obligated to the patient and to no one else. He is not the agent of society, nor of the interests of medical science, nor of the patient's family, nor of his cosufferers, or future sufferers from the same disease. The patient alone counts when he is under the physician's care. By the simple law of bilateral contract (analogous, for example, to the relation of lawyer to client and its "conflict of interest" rule), the physician is bound not to let any other interest interfere with that of the patient in being cured. But, manifestly, more sublime norms than contractual ones are involved. We may speak of a sacred trust; strictly by its terms, the doctor is, as it were, alone with his patient and God.

There is one normal exception to this—that is, to the doctor's not being the agent of society vis-à-vis the patient, but the trustee of his interests alone: the quarantining of the contagious sick. This is plainly not for the patient's interest, but for that of others threatened by him. (In vaccination, we have a combination of both: protection of the individual and others.) But preventing the patient from causing harm to others is not the same as exploiting him for the advantage of others. And there is, of course, the abnormal exception of collective catastrophe, the analog to a state of war. The physician who desperately battles a raging epidemic is under a unique dispensation that suspends in a nonspecifiable way some of the strictures of normal practice, including possibly those against experimental liberties with his patients. No rules can be devised for the waiving of rules in extremities. And as with the famous shipwreck examples of ethical theory, the less said about it the better. But what is allowable there and may later be passed over in forgiving silence cannot serve as a precedent. We are concerned with nonextreme, nonemergency conditions where the voice of principle can be heard and claims can be adjudicated free from duress. We have conceded that there are such claims, and that if there is to be medical advance at all, not even the superlative privilege of the suffering and the sick can be kept wholly intact from the intrusion of its needs. About this least palatable, most disquieting part of our subject, I have to offer only groping, inconclusive remarks.

B. The Principle of "Identification" Applied to Patients

On the whole, the same principles would seem to hold here as are found to hold with "normal subjects": motivation, identification, understanding on the part of the subject. But it is clear that these conditions are peculiarly difficult to satisfy with regard to a patient. His physical state, psychic preoccupation, dependent relation to the doctor, the submissive attitude induced by treatment—everything connected with his condition and situation makes the sick person inherently less of a sovereign person than the healthy one. Spontaneity of self-offering has almost to be ruled out; consent is marred by lower resistance or captive circumstance, and so on. In fact, all the factors that make the patient, as a category, particularly accessible and welcome for experimentation at the same time compromise the quality of the responding affirmation that must morally redeem the making use of them. This, in addition to the primacy of the physician's duty, puts a heightened onus on the physician-researcher to limit his undue power to the most important and defensible research objectives and, of course, to keep persuasion at a minimum.

Still, with all the disabilities noted, there is scope among patients for observing the rule of the "descending order of permissibility" that we have laid down for normal subjects, in vexing inversion of the utility order of quantitative abundance and qualitative "expendability." By the principle of this order, those patients who most identify with and are cognizant of the cause of research—members of the medical profession (who after all are sometimes patients themselves)—come first; the highly motivated and educated, also least dependent, among the lay patients come next; and so on down the line. An added consideration here is seriousness of condition, which again operates in inverse proportion. Here the profession must fight the tempting sophistry that the hopeless case is expendable (because in prospect already expended) and therefore especially usable; and generally the attitude that the poorer the chances of the patient the more justifiable his recruitment for experimentation (other than for his own benefit). The opposite is true.

C. Nondisclosure as a Borderline Case

Then there is the case where ignorance of the subject, sometimes even of the experimenter, is of the essence of the experiment (the "double blind"-control group-placebo syndrome). It is said to be a necessary element of the scientific process. Whatever may be said about its ethics in regard to normal subjects, especially volunteers, it is an outright betrayal of trust in regard to the patient who believes that he is receiving treatment. Only supreme importance of the objective can exonerate it, without making it less of a transgression. The patient is definitely wronged even when not harmed. And ethics apart, the practice of such deception holds the danger of undermining the faith in the bona fides of treatment, the beneficial intent of the physician—the very basis of the doctor—patient relationship. In every respect, it follows that concealed experiment on patients—that is, experiment under the guise of treatment—should be the rarest exception, at best, if it cannot be wholly avoided.

This has still the merit of a borderline problem. The same is not true of the other case of necessary ignorance of the subject—that of the unconscious patient. Drafting him for nontherapeutic experiments is simply and unquali-fiedly impermissible; progress or not, he must never be used, on the inflexible principle that utter helplessness demands utter protection.

When preparing this paper, I filled pages with a casuistics of this harrowing field, but then scrapped most of it, realizing my dilettante status. The shadings are endless, and only the physician-researcher can discern them properly as the cases arise. Into his lap the decision is thrown. The philosophical rule, once it has admitted into itself the idea of a sliding scale, cannot really specify its own application. It can only impress on the practitioner a general maxim or attitude for the exercise of his judgment and conscience in the concrete occasions of his work. In our case, I am afraid, it means making life more difficult for him.

It will also be noted that, somewhat at variance with the emphasis in the literature, I have not dwelt on the element of "risk" and very little on that of "consent." Discussion of the first is beyond the layman's competence; the emphasis on the second has been lessened because of its equivocal character. It is a truism to say that one should strive to minimize the risk and to maximize the consent. The more demanding concept of "identification," which I have used, includes "consent" in its maximal or authentic form, and the assumption of risk is its privilege.

XV. No Experiments on Patients Unrelated to Their Own Disease

Although my ponderings have, on the whole, yielded points of view rather than definite prescriptions, premises rather than conclusions, they have led me to a few unequivocal yeses and noes. The first is the emphatic rule that patients should be experimented upon, if at all, *only* with reference to *their disease*. Never should there be added to the gratuitousness of the experiment as such the gratuitousness of service to an unrelated cause. This follows simply from what we have found to be the *only* excuse for infracting the special exemption of the sick at all—namely, that the scientific war on disease cannot accomplish its goal without drawing the sufferers from disease into the investigative process. If under this excuse they become subjects of experiment, they do so *because,* and only because, of *their* disease.

This is the fundamental and self-sufficient consideration. That the patient cannot possibly benefit from the unrelated experiment therapeutically, while he might from experiment related to his condition, is also true, but lies beyond the problem area of pure experiment. I am in any case discussing nontherapeutic experimentation only, where *ex hypothesi* the patient does not benefit. Experiment as part of therapy—that is, directed toward helping the subject himself—is a different matter altogether and raises its own problems, but hardly philosophical ones. As long as a doctor can say, even if only in his own thought: "There is no known cure for your condition (or: you have responded to none); but there is promise in a new treatment still under investigation, not quite tested yet as to effectiveness and safety; you will be taking a chance, but all things considered, I judge it in your best interest to let me try it on you"—as long as he can speak thus, he speaks as the patient's physician and may err, but does not transform the patient into a subject of experimentation. Introduction of an untried therapy into the treatment where the tried ones have failed is not "experimentation on the patient."

Generally, and almost needless to say, with all the rules of the book, there is something "experimental" (because tentative) about every individual treatment, beginning with the diagnosis itself; and he would be a poor doctor who would not learn from every case for the benefit of future cases, and a poor member of the profession who would not make any new insights gained from his treatments available to the profession at large. Thus, knowledge may be advanced in the treatment of any patient, and the interest of the medical art and sufferers from the same affliction as well as the patient himself may be served if something happens to be learned from his case. But this gain to knowledge and future therapy is incidental to the bona fide service to the present patient. He has the right to expect that the doctor does nothing to him just in order to learn.

In that case, the doctor's imaginary speech would run, for instance, like this: "There is nothing more I can do for you. But you can do something for me. Speaking no longer as your physician but on behalf of medical science, we could learn a great deal about future cases of this kind if you would permit me to perform certain experiments on you. It is understood that you yourself would not benefit from any knowledge we might gain; but future patients would." This statement would express the purely experimental situation, assumedly here with the subject's concurrence and with all cards on the table. In Alexander Bickel's words: "It is a different situation when the doctor is no longer trying to make [the patient] well, but is trying to find out how to make others well in the future.[10]"

---

[10] *Proceedings*, p. 33. To spell out the difference between the two cases: In the first case, the patient himself is meant to be the beneficiary of the experiment, and directly so; the "subject" of the experiment is at the same time its object, its end. It is performed not for gaining knowledge, but for helping him—and helping him in the *act* of performing it, even if by its results it also contributes to a broader testing process currently under way. It is in fact part of the treatment itself and an "experiment" only in the loose sense of being untried and highly tentative. But whatever the degree of uncertainty, the motivating

But even in the second case, that of the nontherapeutic experiment where the patient does not benefit, at least the patient's own disease is enlisted in the cause of fighting that disease, even if only in others. It is yet another thing to say or think: "Since you are here—in the hospital with its facilities—anyway, under our care and observation anyway, away from your job (or, perhaps, doomed) anyway, we wish to profit from your being available for some other research of great interest we are presently engaged in." From the standpoint of merely medical ethics, which has only to consider risk, consent, and the worth of the objective, there may be no cardinal difference between this case and the last one. I hope that the medical reader will not think I am making too fine a point when I say that from the standpoint of the subject and his dignity there is a cardinal difference that crosses the line between the permissible and the impermissible, and this by the same principle of "identification" I have been invoking all along. Whatever the rights and wrongs of any experimentation on any patient—in the one case, at least that residue of identification is left him that it is his own affliction by which he can contribute to the conquest of the affliction, his own kind of suffering which he helps to alleviate in others; and so in a sense it is his own cause. It is totally indefensible to rob the unfortunate of this intimacy with the purpose and make his misfortune a convenience for the furtherance of alien concerns. The observance of this rule is essential, I think, to at least attenuate the wrong that nontherapeutic experimenting on patients commits in any case.

XVI. On the Redefinition of Death

My other emphatic verdict concerns the question of the redefinition of death—that is, acknowledging "irreversible coma as a new definition for death."[11] I wish not to be misunderstood. As long as it is merely a question of when it is permitted to cease the artificial prolongation of certain functions (like heartbeat) traditionally regarded as signs of life, I do not see anything ominous in the notion of "brain death." Indeed, a new definition of death is not even

---

anticipation (the wager, if you like) is for success, and success here means the subject's own good. To a pure experiment, by contrast, undertaken to gain knowledge, the difference of success and failure is not germane, only that of conclusiveness and inconclusiveness. The "negative" result has as much to teach as the "positive." Also, the true experiment is an act distinct from the uses later made of the findings. And, most important, the subject experimented on is distinct from the eventual beneficiaries of those findings: He lets himself be used as a means toward an end external to himself (even if he should at some later time happen to be among the beneficiaries himself). With respect to his own present needs and his own good, the act is gratuitous.

[11] "A Definition of Irreversible Coma," Report of the *Ad Hoc* Committee of the Harvard Medical School to Examine the Definition of Brain Death, *Journal of the American Mental Association* 205, no. 6 (August 5, 1968), pp. 337–40.

necessary to legitimize the same result if one adopts the position of the Roman Catholic Church, which here at least is eminently reasonable—namely that "when deep unconsciousness is judged to be permanent, extraordinary means to maintain life are not obligatory. They can be terminated and the patient allowed to die."[12] Given a clearly defined negative condition of the brain, the physician is allowed to allow the patient to die his own death by *any* definition, which of itself will lead through the gamut of all possible definitions. But a disquietingly contradictory purpose is combined with this purpose in the quest for a new definition of death—that is, in the will to *advance* the moment of declaring him dead: Permission not to turn off the respirator, but, on the contrary, to keep it on and thereby maintain the body in a state of what would have been "life" by the older definition (but is only a "simulacrum" of life by the new)—so as to get at his organs and tissues under the ideal conditions of what would previously have been "vivisection."[13]

Now this, whether done for research or transplant purposes, seems to me to overstep what the definition can warrant. Surely it is one thing when to cease delaying death, another when to start doing violence to the body; one thing when to desist from protracting the process of dying, another when to regard that process as complete and thereby the body as a cadaver free for inflicting on it what would be torture and death to any living body. For the first purpose, we need not know the exact borderline between life and death—we leave it to nature to cross it wherever it is, or to traverse the whole spectrum if there is not just one line. All we need to know is that coma is irreversible. For the second purpose we must know the borderline with absolute certainty; and to use any definition short of the maximal for perpetrating on a *possibly* penultimate state what only the ultimate state can permit is to arrogate a knowledge which, I think, we cannot possibly have. *Since we do not know the exact borderline between life and death,* nothing less than the maximum definition of death will do—brain death plus heart death plus any other indication that may be pertinent—before final violence is allowed to be done.

---

[12] As rendered by Dr. Beecher in *Proceedings,* p. 50.

[13] The Report of the *Ad Hoc* Committee no more than indicates this possibility with the second of the "two reasons why there is need for a definition"; "(2) Obsolete criteria for the definition of death can lead to controversy in obtaining organs for transplantation." The first reason is relief from the burden of indefinitely drawn out coma. The report wisely confines its recommendations on application to what falls under this first reason— namely, turning off the respirator—and remains silent on the possible use of the definition under the second reason. But when "the patient is declared dead on the basis of these criteria," the road to the other use has theoretically been opened and will be taken (if I remember rightly, it has even been taken once, in a much debated case in England), unless it is blocked by a special barrier in good time. The above is my feeble attempt to help in doing so.

It would follow then, for this layman at least, that the use of the definition should itself be defined, and this in a restrictive sense. When only permanent coma can be gained with the artificial sustaining of functions, by all means turn off the respirator, the stimulator, any sustaining artifice, and let the patient die; but let him die all the way. Do not, instead, arrest the process and start using him as a mine while, with your own help and cunning, he is still kept this side of what may in truth be the final line. Who is to say that a shock, a final trauma, is not administered to a sensitivity diffusely situated elsewhere than in the brain and still vulnerable to suffering, a sensitivity that we ourselves have been keeping alive. No fiat of definition can settle this question.[14] But I wish to emphasize that the question of possible suffering (easily brushed aside by a sufficient show of reassuring expert consensus) is merely a subsidiary and not the real point of my argument; this, to reiterate, turns on the indeterminacy of the boundaries between *life and death,* not between sensitivity and insensitivity, and bids us to lean toward a maximal rather than a minimal determination of death in an area of basic uncertainty.

There is also this to consider: The patient must be absolutely sure that his doctor does not become his executioner, and that no definition authorizes him ever to become one. His right to this certainty is absolute, and so is his right to his own body with all its organs. Absolute respect for these rights violates no one else's right, for no one has a right to another's body. Speaking in still another, religious vein: The expiring moments should be watched over with piety and be safe from exploitation.

I strongly feel, therefore, that it should be made quite clear that the proposed new definition of death is to authorize *only* the one and *not* the other of the two opposing things: only to break off a sustaining intervention and let things take their course, not to keep up the sustaining intervention for a final intervention of the most destructive kind.

XVII. Conclusion

There would now have to be said something about nonmedical experiments on human subjects, notably psychological and genetic, of which I have not lost sight. But I must leave this for another occasion. I wish only to say in conclusion that if some of the practical implications of my reasonings are felt to work out toward a slower rate of progress, this should not cause too great dismay. Let us

---

[14] Only a Cartesian view of the "animal machine," which I somehow see lingering here, could set the mind at rest, as in historical fact it did at its time in the matter of vivisection. But its truth is surely not established by definition.

not forget that progress is an optional goal, not an unconditional commitment, and that its tempo in particular, compulsive as it may become, has nothing sacred about it. Let us also remember that a slower progress in the conquest of disease would not threaten society, grievous as it is to those who have to deplore that their particular disease be not yet conquered, but that society would indeed be threatened by the erosion of those moral values whose loss, possibly caused by too ruthless a pursuit of scientific progress, would make its most dazzling triumphs not worth having. Let us finally remember that it cannot be the aim of progress to abolish the lot of mortality. Of some ill or other, each of us will die. Our mortal condition is upon us with its harshness but also its wisdom—because without it there would not be the eternally renewed promise of the freshness, immediacy, and eagerness of youth; nor would there be for any of us the incentive to number our days and make them count. With all our striving to wrest from our mortality what we can, we should bear its burden with patience and dignity.

INFORMED (BUT UNEDUCATED) CONSENT

FRANZ J. INGELFINGER

The trouble with informed consent is that it is not educated consent. Let us assume that the experimental subject, whether a patient, a volunteer, or otherwise enlisted, is exposed to a completely honest array of factual detail. He is told of the medical uncertainty that exists and that must be resolved by research endeavors, of the time and discomfort involved, and of the tiny percentage risk of some serious consequences of the test procedure. He is also reassured of his rights and given a formal, quasilegal statement to read. No exculpatory language is used. With his written signature, the subject then caps the transaction, and whether he sees himself as a heroic martyr for the sake of mankind, or as a reluctant guinea pig dragooned for the benefit of science, or whether, perhaps, he is merely bewildered, he obviously has given his "informed consent." Because established routines have been scrupulously observed, the doctor, the lawyer, and the ethicist are content.

But the chances are remote that the subject really understands what he has consented to—in the sense that the responsible medical investigator understands the goals, nature, and hazards of his study. How can the layman comprehend the importance of his perhaps not receiving, as determined by the luck of the draw, the highly touted new treatment that his roommate will get? How can he appreciate the sensation of living for days with a multilumen intestinal tube passing through his mouth and pharynx? How can he interpret the information that an intravascular catheter and radiopaque dye injection have an 0.01% probability of leading to a dangerous thrombosis or cardiac arrhythmia? It is moreover quite unlikely that any patient–subject can see himself accurately within the broad context of the situation, to weigh the inconveniences and hazards that he will have to undergo against the improvements that the research project may bring to the management of his disease in general and to his own case in particular. The difficulty that the public has in understanding information that is both medical and stressful is exemplified by [a] report [in the *New*

Reprinted with permission from *The New England Journal of Medicine, 287* (9):465–466, Aug. 31, 1972.

England Journal of Medicine, August 31, 1972, page 433]—only half the families given genetic counseling grasped its impact.

Nor can the information given to the experimental subject be in any sense totally complete. It would be impractical and probably unethical for the investigator to present the nearly endless list of all possible contingencies; in fact, he may not himself be aware of every untoward thing that might happen. Extensive detail, moreover, usually enhances the subject's confusion. Epstein and Lasagna showed that comprehension of medical information given to untutored subjects is inversely correlated with the elaborateness of the material presented.[1] The inconsiderate investigator, indeed, conceivably could exploit his authority and knowledge and extract "informed consent" by overwhelming the candidate-subject with information.

Ideally, the subject should give his consent freely, under no duress whatsoever. The facts are that some element of coercion is instrumental in any investigator-subject transaction. Volunteers for experiments will usually be influenced by hopes of obtaining better grades, earlier parole, more substantial egos, or just mundane cash. These pressures, however, are but fractional shadows of those enclosing the patient-subject. Incapacitated and hospitalized because of illness, frightened by strange and impersonal routines, and fearful for his health and perhaps life, he is far from exercising a free power of choice when the person to whom he anchors all his hopes asks, "Say, you wouldn't mind, would you, if you joined some of the other patients on this floor and helped us to carry out some very important research we are doing?" When "informed consent" is obtained, it is not the student, the destitute bum, or the prisoner to whom, by virtue of his condition, the thumb screws of coercion are most relentlessly applied; it is the most used and useful of all experimental subjects, the patient with disease.

When a man or woman agrees to act as an experimental subject, therefore, his or her consent is marked by neither adequate understanding nor total freedom of choice. The conditions of the agreement are a far cry from those visualized as ideal. Jonas would have the subject identify with the investigative endeavor so that he and the researcher would be seeking a common cause: "Ultimately, the appeal for volunteers should seek . . . free and generous endorsement, the appropriation of the research purpose into the person's [i.e., the subject's] own scheme of ends."[2] For Ramsey, "informed consent" should represent a "convenantal bond between consenting man and consenting man [that] makes them . . . joint adventurers in medical care and progress."[3] Clearly,

---

[1] L. C. Epstein and L. Lasagna, "Obtaining Informed Consent: Form or Substance," *Archieves of Internal Medicine 123:* 682–688, 1969.

[2] H. Jonas, "Philosophical Reflections on Experimenting with Human Subjects," *Daedalus 98:* 219–247, Spring, 1969.

[3] P. Ramsey, "The Ethics of a Cottage Industry in an Age of Community and Research Medicine," *New England Journal of Medicine 284:* 700–706, 1971.

to achieve motivations and attitudes of this lofty type, an educated and under-standing, rather than merely informed, consent is necessary.

Although it is unlikely that the goals of Jonas and of Ramsey will ever be achieved, and that human research subjects will spontaneously volunteer rather than be "conscripted,"[4] efforts to promote educated consent are in order. In view of the current emphasis on involving "the community" in such activities as regional planning, operation of clinics, and assignment of priorities, the gen-eral public and its political leaders are showing an increased awareness and under-standing of medical affairs. But the orientation of this public interest in medi-cine is chiefly socioeconomic. Little has been done to give the public a basic understanding of medical research and its requirements not only for the people's money but also for their participation. The public, to be sure, is being subjected to a bombardment of sensation-mongering news stories and books that feature "break-throughs," or that reveal real or alleged exploitations—horror stories of Nazi-type experimentation on abused human minds and bodies. Muckraking is essential to expose malpractices, but unless accompanied by efforts to promote a broader appreciation of medical research and its methods, it merely com-pounds the difficulties for both the investigator and the subject when "informed consent" is solicited.

The procedure currently approved in the United States for enlisting human experimental subjects has one great virtue: patient–subjects are put on notice that their management is, in part, at least an experiment. The deceptions of the past are no longer tolerated. Beyond this accomplishment, however, the pro-cess of obtaining "informed consent," with all its regulations and conditions, is no more than elaborate ritual, a device that, when the subject is uneducated and uncomprehending, confers no more than the semblance of propriety on human experimentation. The subject's only real protection, the public as well as the medical profession must recognize, depends on the conscience and compassion of the investigator and his peers.

---

[4] Jonas, *op. cit.*

REALITIES OF PATIENT CONSENT TO MEDICAL RESEARCH

JOHN FLETCHER

I

The theme of coercion and freedom is at the center of moral concern about the ethics of medical research in human beings. Intense efforts by groups in government, medical societies, and related professions have produced interpretations, codes, and regulations in the conduct of research.[1] Among the many valued objectives clustered around the discussion of morality in medical research, obtaining informed consent from the subject in an experiment is emphasized most. The literature on the principles of informed consent is enormous. Ninety-nine percent of it considers what ought to be; only a small fraction contains reports of what *happens* when consent is given by patient to investigator. A handful of studies by Renée Fox, Henry K. Beecher, and Fellner and Marshall expose the fragility of the consent contract and lay bare many "myths" about the supposed freedom and rationality in informed consent.[2] Due to the considerable doubts about the possibility of obtaining informed consent in many

---

[1] John Fletcher, "Human Experimentation: Ethics in the Consent Situation," *Law and Contemporary Problems 34:*620–649, 1967; and "A Study of Ethics of Medical Research," Th.D. thesis, Union Theological Seminary, New York, 1969.

[2] Renée C. Fox, *Experiment Perilous* (Glencoe, Illinois: The Free Press, 1959); Henry K. Beecher, "Ethics and Clinical Research," *New England Journal of Medicine 274:*1354–1360, 1966, and "Some Guiding Principles for Clinical Investigation," *Journal of the American Medical Association 195:* 1135–1136, 1966; W. J. Curran and Henry K. Beecher, "Expérimentation in Children," *Journal of the American Medical Association 210:* 71–73, 1969; C. H. Fellner and J. R. Marshall, "Kidney Donors—The Myth of Informed Consent," *American Journal of Psychiatry 126:*1245–1251, 1970.

Reprinted from John Fletcher, "Realities of Patient Consent to Medical Research," *Hastings Center Studies, 1,* No. 1 (1973), pp. 39–49 by permission of the author and the Institute of Society, Ethics and the Life Sciences, Hastings-on-Hudson, New York.

circumstances, a fresh treatment of the actualities of giving consent in medical experiments is in order.

The most rewarding inquiry in ethics takes place between the "ought" and the "is." The dangers in the debate on informed consent are a too legalistic approach from the side of those who uphold the law and a too secretive approach from those who practice. H. Richard Niebuhr[3] noted that the two purposes of ethics are self-understanding and guidance in the concrete problems of using our freedom. Researchers need to know more about the ways they and their subjects actually make decisions, and those who are charged with regulating research need to keep rules within the reach of obedience.

In order to inquire into the dynamics of the consent situation in practice, I first interviewed twenty clinical investigators at the Clinical Center, National Institutes of Health, Bethesda, Maryland, to discern the major moral problems confronting them in their work. A majority named the difficulty of obtaining a truly informed consent from a sick person to do research for nontherapeutic purposes. Those interviewed felt morally compelled to seek a highly qualitative consent for studies which carried no benefit to the patient, but felt equally that in practice high standards could not be attained. A study of the relationship of subject and investigator was designed which would allow me to interview patient and doctor both before and after visits for consent to nontherapeutic studies were made. I participated in the conduct of four such studies and interviewed eighteen patient-volunteers extensively after they entered the studies.[4] Each had signed a consent document and had been given an explanation of the study.

The Clinical Center is a unique medical research institution controlled by the government. Investigators often contact patients in different parts of the country, or have patients referred to them, who suffer from the diseases the Institutes exist to study. Thus, the "consent situation" begins in most cases before the patient enters the hospital. Fellner and Marshall discovered that kidney donors actually made a decision to donate long before they were ever interviewed by physicians and "informed" about the risks of donating. My findings were similar in that the decision to enter research was made prior to entering the hospital, though decisions about particular studies and their related demands were not made until after admission. Patients made decisions agreeing to the importance of human studies before they arrived. Consenting must be defined dynamically to include all of those encounters between investigator and subject in which the expectations of the research agreement are being built, maintained, or repaired.

---

[3] H. Richard Niebuhr, *The Responsible Self* (New York: Harper and Row, 1963), p. 48.
[4] Fletcher, "A Study of Ethics of Medical Research."

II

When consent is being sought for medical research, a human encounter involving decisions to take risks occurs between an investigator and a subject. I assume that in the majority of these encounters little discussion of whether the investigator is *really* justified in pursuing his study takes place. Usually, he has already had to justify his plan with a group of his peers. Further, I assume that it would be rare, if ever, that a question would be raised by either party as to whether the subject were *really* free to choose to participate, or whether there is an authentic condition called "freedom" anyway. As Henry D. Aiken, a moral philosopher, pointed out, these sorts of questions usually occur some distance from practice and are occasioned by changing social conditions or a severe conflict of rules.[5] I am not claiming that the raw materials for such questions are not present in the consent encounter, for wherever one self puts a claim on another and risk is a factor, ethical and theological questions are implicit. I am claiming that one observing the consent process would seldom hear self-conscious discussions of the ethics of consent.

I did assume, however, in approaching a field study of the consent process, that patient-volunteers in medical research would be able to reflect upon their impressions of the possibilities and limits of their freedom of choice. Since individualism or the sense of autonomy is the primary value orientation within which these patients might be expected to speak of their sense of freedom,[6] one might expect that when the patient reflects on his sense of being a "person" or being denied such a status, the issue of his freedom would be to the forefront. Thus, as an ethicist studying the issue of freedom in research, my research was designed to test the hypothesis that the conduct of the consent situation was decisive for the patient's sense of being treated as a "person."

Reading and interviews had convinced me that many investigators and administrators maintained a ritualistic attitude toward informed consent. That is, working from the assumption that a sick person will do almost anything a physician suggests, and feeling that the signing of a consent form entailed a ritual which covered over the impossibility of informed consent, many investigators went about their practice having despaired of attaining genuine informed consent from their patients. Several early interviews had opened with an investigator remarking that patients are so dependent on physicians that they would not be seriously affected by anything the physician did in his explanation of a study. These interviews were also spiced with a heavy antipathy to the legal profession

---

[5] Henry D. Aiken, *Reason and Conduct* (New York: Knopf, 1962), p. 75.
[6] C. Kluckhohm, H. A. Murray, and D. M. Schneider, *Personality in Nature, Society, and Culture* (New York: Knopf, 1964), p. 352.

and administrators who, according to several physicians intereviewed, were interested only in protecting the reputation of the institution.

In short, it appeared to me that many people supposed that patients who entered the research situation left their sense of personhood behind, having surrendered their autonomy to the "white coat" world. From a deep professional interest in inquiring into dependency relations between "laymen" and experts who control valuable yet risky techniques, I expected that these patients would give signs, gestures, and verbal expression to show how their experience in a risk-taking study reflected on their sense of having the status of a "person." I assumed, with those who have labored on the concept of informed consent, that the real meaning of the rule was to protect the status of personhood which is enshrined in the traditions of law, morality, and religion surrounding the concept of consent. Arthur Dyck and Herbert Richardson have expressed better than anyone the social-structural values which nourish the need for consent: freedom, justice, truth-telling, and equality.[7] They affirmed that unless these values were responded to in the actual practice of medical research no one would interpret the progress of medical science in terms of social "benefits." If being socialized in institutions which are maintained by such values creates the capacity (or status) of perceiving that one is a "person," then would he divest himself of this status, lower himself, when he came within the orbit of medical investigators? Here was an opportunity to test the relation between a theory of the ethics of informed consent and the practice of investigator and subject in the process of consent-giving.

What does the "sense of being treated as a person" mean? Three norms were accepted which nourish the basis of the symbolic status of "person."

1. The patient might perceive himself as a being who was addressable as "never merely as means . . . but at the same time as ends in themselves."[8] To use more religious terms to describe this sense, one may perceive himself as a "thou and not an it"; as Buber stated: "Without *It* man cannot live. But he who lives with It alone is not a man."[9]

2. He might give signs of perceiving himself as a responsible being, capable of choice, exercising some control over his body and general welfare. To quote Tillich: "As a centered self and individual, man can respond in knowledge and action to the stimuli that reach him from the world to which he belongs; but because he also *confronts* his world, and in this sense is free from it, he can

---

[7] Arthur J. Dyck and Herbert W. Richardson, "The Moral Justification for Research Using Human Subjects," *Uses of Human Subjects in Safety Evaluation of Food Chemicals* (National Academy of Sciences, 1967), p. 231.

[8] I. Kant, "The Metaphysics of Morals," *Great Books of the Western World,* edited by R. M. Hutchins, Vol. 42 (Chicago: Encyclopedia Britannica, Inc., 1952), p. 274.

[9] Martin Buber, *I and Thou* (New York: Scribner's Sons, 1958), p. 34.

respond "responsibly," namely, after deliberation and decision rather than through a determined compulsion."[10]

3. The patient might give signs of including himself as a member of a community in which the transcendence of self-interest is an ever-present possibility. Both psychologist Jean Piaget and theologian Reinhold Niebuhr agree that social relations of cooperation, involving the transcendence of one's own interests, are the hallmark of personal life.[11]

These three norms can be shown to be embodied in the law and morality surrounding human experimentation. Moreover, they can be shown to arise, at the deepest level, from a confidence that we are related to reality in a way that calls forth actions based on these norms which can be trusted to survive. In short, as a theologian, I am interested in pressing to uncover the sources of morality in human encounter of great risk. Persons disagree on the final source of morality. A theological perspective is one of several ways of exploring the depths of human encounters. Because medical research is an encounter of persons with persons, and not I's and It's, one final court of appeal to establish the limits of that encounter is a moral imperative derived from an unconditional source establishing our personhood beyond any threat of destruction.

When one examines all of the possible perspectives within which to answer the question of why investigators should be moral at all in their consent relations with subjects, he finds that an answer can only arise from the actual commitments in decisions made by those who practice. Persons are ultimately accountable only in the light of their decisions and that to which they are committed beneath their decisions. The reason why a theologian should be interested in inquiring into the ethics of informed consent is that when pushed to its final justification, the morality of any action rests upon some form of commitment and loyalty. The task of a theologian in all times and places is to clarify the forms of commitment, for upon them rests the substance of culture and science.

A description of two studies and their chief investigators will illustrate my conclusion that patient-volunteers in this setting maintained their relation to personhood, but that several gave signs of having to defend themselves against their consent being "engineered" rather than "coerced."

Study of Dyslipoproteinemia

The physician-investigator in this study was a twenty-eight-year-old Clinical Associate interested in discovering the basic causes of dyslipoproteinemias.

---

[10] Paul Tillich, *Morality and Beyond* (New York: Harper and Row, 1963), p. 19.
[11] Jean Piaget, *The Moral Judgment of the Child* (Glencoe, Ill.: The Free Press, 1965), p. 395; Reinhold Niebuhr, *Man's Nature and His Communities* (New York: Scribner's Sons, 1965), p. 107.

These genetically inherited conditions result in a radically high blood cholesterol level for those who suffer from one form of this disease. Dr. A. had prepared the design of his study for one year, doing preliminary studies in animals. His work was designed to investigate the metabolism of labeled lipoproteins in these disease states. He explained that if the production and destruction rate of the lipoproteins could be determined, as these proteins are essential to the transportation of cholesterol in the body, physicians could better attack the control of this problem through drugs as well as understand the basic mechanisms of these diseases.

The method of implementation was as follows: blood would be collected from each subject, plasma separated and lipoproteins isolated by ultracentrifugation. The lipoproteins would then be labeled with a radioactive iodine tracer, sterilized, and tested extensively for pyrogenicity. This preparation would be injected intravenously into each subject and small samples of blood collected ten minutes later and then daily or every other day for 14–21 days. Complete urine collections would be made. The blood and urine collections would enable a complete study of the rate at which the labeled lipoproteins were being destroyed. A special safety measure included doses of potassium iodide to protect the thyroid. Dr. A described the risks of radiation in these cases as less than that received from a standard X ray. Other than the discomfort of an injection and the regimen of diet and collections, there would be no real risks in this study. The risk of hepatitis had been greatly reduced by using the patient's own blood for isolating lipoproteins.

Dr. A.'s study had been approved, after careful scrutiny, by (1) group consideration of his peers, (2) a radiation committee of the Center, and (3) the clinical research committee of his Institute.

Dr. A. had visited each patient-volunteer several times prior to his call to get consent forms signed. During these visits he had given a complete explanation of the study and had tried to answer questions. He showed that he knew a great deal about each subject personally, as well as physiologically. Dr. A. described this study as "investigative," one in which the possibility of therapeutic value might be indirect. All of his patients had children who had inherited the same disease, and each had been involved in research prior to this study.

It is important to note here that Dr. A.'s study was carried out in the context of his patient's participation in another drug study which carried possible therapeutic benefits. A double-blind drug study, designed to test a particular preparation and its effect on plasma cholesterol levels, was accepted by the patient volunteers Dr. A. also intended to study. Each patient was told *before* and *after* entry to the Center that their hospitalization would be prolonged to allow Dr. A.'s study to be integrated with the drug study.

Study of Biogenic Amines

Dr. C. is a thirty-five-year-old neurologist. He works on several projects with patients who have diseases of the brain or disorders which affect the central nervous system. His interest lay in studying a group of chemicals, the biogenic amines, believed to play a central role in synaptic transmission in the brain. Dopamine is an example of one main subgroup of these chemicals, the catecholamines. He had designed a study, after a year of animal testing, to investigate the difference in the metabolism of dopamine in the brain as contrasted to its metabolism in the body. He explained that neurologists did not know if there were a difference; if there were, they will know more about dopamine's nature and the uses drug therapy can have in treating brain disease.

The following experiment was designed: patients with indwelling intraventricular catheters would be chosen as subjects. Some patients with brain tumors have such catheters to permit safer and easier treatment with chemotherapeutic agents. Radioactively labeled dopamine would be injected intravenously *or* intraventricularly in these patients, in a very small dose. By testing urine collections for four days following the injection, Dr. C. hoped to study the difference in metabolism.

He explained that the study carried no direct benefit to the patient-volunteer, although the potential information to be gained was within proportion to the risks. Animal tests showed no pharmacologic effect. The major risk of any injection, he stated, was infection, but every known precaution had been taken. Ninety-eight percent of injected radioactivity would be passed in the urine of each patient. His study has been approved by a group of his peers and by a radiation committee.

Dr. C. mentioned more than once the possibility that what transpires in the consent situation can be a "charade." He defined this term as the disappointment of society's expectation that the investigator will always obtain an informed consent, and that the patient will fully understand the risks and benefits. He frankly admitted that some patients are, through serious illness, unable to measure up to these expectations, even after serious attempts to communicate. In such cases, he stressed, he always sought third-party consent.

Dr. C. had chosen two female patients, both of whom had had nursing educations, as participants in dopamine infusion. Both had come to the Center expecting research with treatment for brain tumor. Since they were roommates, he had met with them together several times prior to obtaining signed consent, six hours in all, and he showed he was very aware of their limitations. He had gradually unfolded his explanations for them, giving them ample time to discuss it. Dr. C. had noticed that Mrs. S., who was somewhat aphasic as a result of her brain tumor and had difficulty understanding others and expressing herself, had become very dependent upon Mrs. N. for interpretation and cues. Following the session in which both had signed forms, Dr. C. said that in his opinion Mrs. N. had given informed consent, but if strict standards were applied, Mrs. S. had not. "Her illness is so pronounced." He observed that "Mrs. N. really understands what is going on," but that Mrs. S. "kept looking at the other lady to find out what the right thing to do was." Under the circumstances, he concluded that Mrs. N. had given an authentic third-party consent for Mrs. S., and that the previous sessions had indicated to him that this was an acceptable route to follow.

It is seriously debatable as to whether one should choose a third party who is participating in the same experiment to authenticate the consent of another. In principle, such should never be the case. As the following interview shows, Mrs. S. gives dramatic signs that she felt treated humanely and as a person. Yet several hard questions should be raised here about the conclusion of Dr. C. that she could be included in the study on the basis of Mrs. N.'s consent. The two patient-volunteers made the following comments after each had already received an injection:

Q.: *You had met with the doctor several times before yesterday?*

Mrs. N.: *Yes. He saw us four or five times, no ... every day last week. Then one day he just sat down, for about an hour, and talked and talked. He told us all about the project. He explained everything. He told us that this chemical he was studying was in the body anyway, so it wouldn't put anything new into us.*

Q.: *How do you feel about Dr. C.?*

Mrs. S.: *He talks to you like you are a human being and not a glass. He has a lot of warmth. He took our anxieties away. The doctor is the most important thing in something like this. If he talks to you then you know what is happening.*

Q.: *Then you liked that part of it?*

Mrs. S.: *Oh, yes. I like being told what is going on. It isn't that often a doctor will talk to you that long. Dr. C. took his time and answered all of our questions.*

Q.: *What do you understand about the purpose of this study?*

Mrs. N.: *Well, they are going to study how this chemical acts ... maybe they will be able to use it on others.*

Q.: *Will your participating in this study help you?*

Mrs. N.: *It won't help the illness I have. Maybe it will help someone else someday, or the world of medicine.*

Mrs. S.: *At least we have contributed something. So much of the time you are just like a robot; now you can do something, you can give. Everyone is doing something for us all the time, now we can repay them in this way.*

Q.: *Did any questions occur to you after we met yesterday?*

Mrs. N.: *No, no questions. We had them all answered before. Mainly, we were concerned about how long it would last and if it would do any harm. Since it was just a teeny bit of radioactivity, and they would get that later, it didn't seem that it would do any harm.*

When the three norms of the presence of personhood discussed above are applied, each appears clearly confirmed here. Being treated as an end and not a means only is affirmed by Mrs. S. (the aphasic patient) as being a "human being and not a glass." Her metaphor is possibly a more apt description of personhood in this age than the "thou–it" terminology. Mrs. N. showed that she understood the meaning of a nontherapeutic study, that she had had her questions answered, and had exercised her capacity to choose. Mrs. N. also answered all of the "technical" questions, showing the special role Dr. C. had used with her. Mrs. S. perceived that she was a member of a community in which the consuming self-interest of illness can be transcended; her use of the term *robot* is especially compelling to describe the dehumanization of being ill in a hospital. When contrasted with her *"now* you can give," a clear picture of membership in a special community emerges.

When one contrasts Mrs. S.'s warm statements with the probability that there is no firm basis for assuming that Dr. C. got consent in this case, he can understand how complex a moral judgment there is to render in this case. First, there is Dr. C.'s own estimate that Mrs. S. was too ill to speak for herself. Secondly, Mrs. N. was never told that she was acting as a third party to consent for her roommate. Thirdly, even if Mrs. N. had been told, there is the likelihood that she was a poor choice, since she was a fellow-participant in the same study. In my opinion, a more independent third-party consent should have been obtained by Dr. C. To the extent that I played that role unknowingly in discussion with Dr. C. about Mrs. S., I would have said yes. Yet I must conclude that the wrong third party was used and that his choice did not constitute a sound basis for including Mrs. S. in the study. Dr. C.'s conduct of the consent situation was decisive for Mrs. S.'s sense of being treated as a person, but it was not sufficient to provide a firm moral basis for consent when studied by an independent party. Thus, the sense of "personhood" on the part of the patient is not sufficient evidence that all is well. A physician can be compassionate and extraordinarily informative, as was Dr. C., and his patient can feel quite free about his choices; yet each be found in serious legal and moral question. This case is an excellent prism for the problems of informed consent and a good illustration of the "finite freedom" of men.

Two additional matters can be pointed out about these two patients. The guilt of illness, and especially of the very ill, as commented on by Otto Guttentag and Beecher,[12] may be present in Mrs. S.'s great need to "give." At any rate, the guilt of illness and the need to sacrifice may be exploited by insensitive investigators. Secondly, I asked no questions of these two patients about their understanding of their right to withdraw, since each had already received an injection and one had felt somewhat dizzy as a result.

Dr. A's patient-volunteers also showed signs of maintaining their status as persons during participation in research. Mr. J., a Navy veteran with an eighth-grade education:

Q.: *How do you feel about being here in such a study?*

Mr. J.: *Well, it makes me feel good. Everybody is here for a purpose. I just happen to be part of discovery. Like I say, I have two children who have this, and I feel obligated to them to do something. If my life had been different, and I hadn't had any children maybe I wouldn't feel this way.*

Q.: *I can see you feel strongly about it.*

Mr. J.: *You've go to. Even if nothing comes of it, you are still part of something.*

Mr. J. put special emphasis on being part of a community of "discovery," where everyone is there for a "purpose." To have purposes is a particularly human activity, and he joins nicely the first and third norms.

Mrs. B. in her early sixties, whose daughter had died as a result of the same inherited condition, complained in her interview with me that she lacked knowledge about the purpose of Dr. A.'s study, and that she had difficulty understanding the technical parts. When I reminded her that she did have ample opportunity in the consent process to ask such questions of Dr. A., she said, "Well, I didn't want him to think I was stupid!" She had pretended to understand some things and did not question Dr. A. as much as she wanted. This action might be taken as a negative confirmation of the hypothesis. That is, Mrs. B. was *pretending* to be a person who understood and chose rationally. She in fact withheld her questions and capacity to control for fear of alienating the doctor. It is debatable whether a pretense at personhood is better, in the moral sense, than no attempt at all; I tend to believe so. At least, Mrs. B. gives evidence that she was aware of the possibility of exercising more autonomy.

Another example of negative confirmation came from Mr. C., who after saying that he had been in the Navy for twenty-one years and had learned to take orders from officers (whom he compared to doctors), stated: "My philos-

---

[12] Otto Guttentag, "The Problem of Experimentation on Human Beings: The Physician's Point of View," *Science 117:*209, 1953; Beecher, "Some Guiding Principles," p. 1135.

ophy in the Navy was 'yours not to reason why, yours but to do or die.' You will find that people who have been in the service for a long time think my way. *That may not be a good outlook,* but it is the way I have been raised." [Emphasis added.] In the process of "lowering" himself from the status of a responsible person who asks questions, Mr. C. acknowledged his wrongdoing, appealing in a negative way to values which might restore him to a relation with his own best sense of himself.

The term *guinea pig* when applied to human subjects represents the ultimate lowering of humans from personal to animal status. Mrs. F., a forty-year-old patient-volunteer, showed how she defends against it:

Q.: *Had you met with Dr. X. (principal investigator) before?*

Mrs. F.: *No, that was my first time. I have confidence in him and had it the first time I saw him. I have trust in him, and I have been around enough doctors to know something about it. He knows his business, and he takes his time.* (She mentions another doctor who appears to her to be always in a hurry.) *Dr. X. sat and talked with me. My family does not understand my illness at all, and they call me a "guinea pig." I wish I could change their minds about that, but they would have to go through what I have to understand, and be a part of what I know to feel different.*

In short, one would have to be a member of the community of Mrs. F. to maintain the sense of being a person. Persons are creatures who, when they perceive that their stature in that role is being limited, threatened, or coerced, will respond to values which promise to restore them to their sense of occupying a special and unique capacity in their relationships.

One could not conclude, from these examples, that these patients in research leave their personhood behind. Ample signs were shown that the sense of freedom in a patient is related to being part of a community of healing in which his own contribution might be ultimately valuable. At the same time, research patients will require assistance in keeping them open to ask questions of physicians and themselves, for there are many diverse forces at work in the consent process.

III

Many factors impinge on the patient-volunteer to limit or reduce his autonomy. First, serious illness is threatening and limiting. Patients tend to believe that the slightest change in the arrangements, such as the introduction of a tape recorder, will make them better. Almost everything that happens is filtered through illness, including consent to research. Bennett, a social worker in an experimental therapeutics ward of the Clinical Center, corroborated my findings in her study of twenty-three patients, and observed that "patients do not conceptualize the principal investigator as a scientist and equate treatment and research as one and the same."[13] Park and others reported on the same phenomenon in psychiatric patients.[14]

Secondly, the arrangements at an imposing institution like the Clinical Center tend to diminish the patient's willingness to complain or question. Surely the fact that treatment is free, and that each has a serious disease for which no cure has yet been found, limits a patient's freedom to question. Savard, also a social worker, reports for the whole social work staff: "One of the functions the social work staff sees for itself is to help the patient work through this conflict (guilt over being ungrateful when the wish to gripe crosses their minds). This could include second thoughts about continued participation in a research project."[15]

Thirdly, the expectations of the investigator for the subject are a strong force which may operate often to limit the subject's freedom. Dr. A. actually believed Mrs. B. to be very well informed and highly curious about the technical side of medicine. He spent much time on his explanation, but at the same time she was embarrassed to ask more questions. Patients are also aware from the attitudes shown by investigators that they have much of their own prestige invested in studies. They are eager not to disappoint. The investigator's knowledge of human behavior has become as important for his work as his skill in carrying out his studies.

None of the three restrictions on freedom of the patient to question or withdraw mentioned above are comparable to outright examples of coercion. No investigator I observed ever used force, threat, or his authority to make a patient submit to research. Patients come to the Center knowing that they will be in studies, even though they tend to confuse research and treatment. The particular question of coercion and freedom in human studies revolves in part around the right of the patient to withdraw at any time. Mr. H., a thirty-eight-year-old patient in Dr. A.'s study, declared that he had a right to withdraw but that the subject had not come up. "It is something I knew about. I never signed any agreement to be held to, and they can't hold anyone against his will. . . . The choice was really made when they called me on the telephone and asked me to come."

[13] C. M. Bennett, "Motivation, Expectations and Adjustment of Patients on an Experimental Therapeutics Service," 1970. Available from Social Work Department, Clinical Center, NIH.

[14] L. C. Park et al., "The Subjective Experience of the Research Patient," Journal of Nervous and Mental Disease 143:199–206, 1966.

[15] R. J. Savard, "Serving Investigator, Patient and Community in Research Studies," Annals of the New York Academy of Science 169:429–434, 1970.

Coercion can be normally defined as the act of influencing others against their will. It has been said that the ultimate in coercion is manipulating another's emotions, "forcing him to will that which you will." If an entire will had to be created *ex nihilo* for the subject in research, this definition might hold; however, patients come prepared for research by cultural, medical, and institutional conditions. It is more true to say that a specific will to do a particular study has to be developed in the patient; he must be persuaded. A more capacious concept than "coercion" must be sought to describe the *pressure,* bordering on coercion, which some patients felt to accept research. I observed that some patients found an opportunity to defend themselves against their consent to research being "engineered," a term used by Cahn to describe the control of the conditions of consent by experts controlling information and technique.[16]

The participants in Dr. A.'s study were asked to discuss their right of withdrawal, should they so choose. Mr. J. said that he wanted to participate and was "wide open for suggestions." He discussed the question of his freedom of choice, and his right of withdrawal, without distinguishing between Dr. A.'s study and the double-blind drug study. He made it clear that if he were inclined to leave the nontherapeutic study he would risk continuing in treatment. Smiling wryly, he commented, "that is pretty strong pressure." Mrs. B. also discussed her freedom to say yes or no in association with the risk of continuing in treatment. "Since I came here for treatment," she said, "if I didn't cooperate, it would mean ending treatment." She strongly wanted treatment, since she felt the drug might be helping her for the first time. The apprehension of the patients was that the condition of the right of withdrawal had been severely weakened by the risk of losing treatment.

When I reported these interpretations to Dr. A. in writing, he immediately responded, along with his colleague who was in charge of the drug study. They assured me and the patients that there was no intention of tying research to treatment. Under the arrangements which had been made for the two studies, if these patients had chosen to withdraw, they would not have been excluded from treatment, even though their hospitalization would have been shorter, excluding the time necessary to complete Dr. A.'s study. In reviewing the process of this feedback, Dr. A. stated: "These patients were aware that they were brought in to do two studies. They were aware that the 'turnover' study was superimposed on the drug study. What wasn't made clear to them was that they didn't have to do the second study."

He also affirmed that the most important finding, for him, in participating in our study of consent, was the effect of not informing the patient-volunteer as to his right of withdrawal from nontherapeutic studies. He reported that he had

[16] E. Cahn, "The Lawyer as Scientist and Scoundrel: Reflections on Francis Bacon's Quadricentennial," *New York University Law Review 36:*8, 1961.

not encountered the same sense of pressure in patients who had been informed of the right to withdraw.

I would attribute this sense of pressure to accept research "tied" to treatment, in these patients, as a result of institutional arrangements plus the unfinished business of a consent process. The patients entered an impressive research center for therapeutic and nontherapeutic studies. They knew that they had a right to withdraw, but they had not discussed it with their physician. One of the most important findings of the study, in my estimation, was the opportunity the presence of my inquiry gave to the physician and subject to maintain, build and repair their agreement. Savard and Bennett also report such effects. Although I did not present myself as an "ombudsman" or advocate for the patient to physicians, the implication of my position was similar. An intermediary person who has access to the consent process might function to enhance the freedom of patient and investigator to change the terms of an unfinished agreement. The range of options open to an individual constitutes his sphere of freedom. Whenever a third party enters, there may be new options available.

What is needed to remedy the possibility of coercion is not more exhortation, but more practical action within the consent process to insure a maximum number of options for improving qualitative consent between physician and patient. The addition of institutional review committees in grantee institutions funded by the government, obligated to assure the rights of subjects in research carried out by their own institutions, seems a creative step. The following table indicates a reduction in the number of "problem projects," deferrable on scientific or ethical grounds, proposed through the NIH system.

Table I is concrete evidence that unpromising studies, or studies involving unethical risks, are being screened at a much more elementary level so far as those studies funded through public funds are concerned. Further evaluation of the actual effectiveness of institutional review committees, and their composition, should be eagerly anticipated.

In view of the increasing demand for medical research, it is past the time when research institutions should act concretely on Guttentag's proposal of the provision of a "physician-friend" to supplement the physician-investigator for purposes of advocacy for the patient.[17] In my experience, a busy investigator cannot sort out the many signals he or she receives from needy patients in research, and he or she requires assistance from one who is not invested in the project. In some institutions this role may be played by social workers or psychiatrists who are delegated to represent the total welfare of the patient. The part psychiatrists have played in screening organ donors is an important pre-

[17] Guttentag, "The Problem of Experimentation on Human Beings," p. 210.

Table I. Two-Year Study of Relation of Problem Projects to Applications

Council	Total applications	"At Risk" human subject applications	Problem projects		
			No.	% total applica.	% "at risk"
June '66	4,100	1,230	93	2.24	7.4
June '67	3,931	1,180	38	0.96	3.2
Nov. '67	3,677	1,100	38	1.03	3.4
Mar. '68	4,001	1,200	27	0.67	2.2
June '68	4,078	1,250	21	0.52	1.7

Source: Office of Associate Director for Extramural Programs, National Institutes of Health. "Status Report of Experience with PPO #129," May 31, 1968 (Memorandum).

cursor of the emerging role of medical "ombudsman."[18] In other institutions where chaplains are charged with such duties their roles might be enlarged to include special relations with investigators and patients attendant to conflicts over research demands. Special training and sensitivity to the complexities of medical research are definitely required of such a figure, whether he be a medical or paramedical person. However, the time has arrived for all medical institutions which engage in human research to consider the step of designating one or more persons to bear the responsibility of advocating *for* the patient, to assure him and the public that consent is within the reach of obedience. Such steps definitely need to be taken wherever especially necessitous groups are involved in research such as prisoners, children and the mentally ill. The principal investigator in each human study is charged with the responsibility to be the final judge of the quality of consent obtained. My proposal would not shift that responsibility. It would help assure him that every step had been taken by providing maximum feedback between himself and the subject. The issue of informed consent has become too socially charged to relegate to the realm of goals alone. New moral initiatives should be taken by those responsible for regulating medical research to invent a flexible role for one working between what ought to be and what is in each research institution.

---

[18] Fellner and Marshall, "Kidney Donors"; J. P. Kemph, "Renal Failure, Artificial Kidney and Kidney Transplants," *American Journal of Psychiatry 122:*1270–1274, 1966, and "Psychotherapy with Patients Receiving Kidney Transplant," *American Journal of Psychiatry 124:*623–629, 1967.

A proposal for a special representative of the subject in research may find its most productive work in the study done with poor or otherwise deprived persons who possess the least defenses for maintaining their moral status. As the history of human experimentation shows, the poor have been a "captive group" for medical experiments. A review of the policy of municipal hospitals in New York City cited evidence that research exploitation of the poor was a common occurrence known to city health officials.[19] A familiar method of exploitation is to make the receiving of continued treatment in outpatient clinics conditional upon participation in experimental drug trials.

Every moral resource in the religious traditions urges special attention to the needs of the sick, the defenseless, and the poor. Lying behind this moral concern is an ethic of universal responsibility, inhering in the double-love commandment. Yet, love has not yet become visible until it is embodied in concrete human relations which establish the "weighty matters" of justice and mercy. Now that the period of concern about the principle of informed consent has crested, and lest this concern be found to be mere sentimentality, more thorough steps to institutionalize and embody the value of personhood in medical research are required.

[19] R. Burlage, *New York City's Municipal Hospitals* (Washington, D.C.: Institute for Policy Studies, 1967), p. 329.

ETHICAL ISSUES INVOLVED IN EXPERIMENTATION ON THE NONVIABLE HUMAN FETUS

RICHARD WASSERSTROM

The Status of the Fetus

I do not believe that the question of the morality of experimentation on living, nonviable fetuses can be sensibly considered without some attention being paid at the outset to the question of what kind of an entity a human fetus is. Although some of the relevant arguments do not depend, even implicitly, upon an answer to this question, the great majority of them do. That this is so can be seen, I think, from the fact that the question of experimentation is a very different one if the fetus is thought to be fundamentally like a piece of human tissue or organ, e.g., an appendix, than if the fetus is thought to be fundamentally like a fully developed, adult human being with normal capacities and abilities.

There are four different views that tend to be held concerning the status of the human fetus. They are: (a) that the fetus is in most if not all morally relevant respects like a fully developed, adult human being. At least two major arguments can be given in support of this position. The first is a theological argument which fixes conception as the time at which the entity acquires a soul. And since possession of a soul is what matters morally and what distinguishes human beings from other entities, the fetus is properly regarded as like all other persons. The second argument focuses upon the similarities between a developing fetus and a newly born infant. In briefest form, the argument goes as follows. It is clear that we regard a newly born infant as like an adult in all morally relevant respects. Infants as well as adults are regarded as persons who are entitled to the same sorts of protection, respect, etc. But there are no significant differences between newly born infants and fetuses which are quite fully developed and about to be born. What is more, there is no point in the developmental life of

Reprinted from National Commission for the Protection of Human Subjects of Biomedical and Behavioral Research, *Research on the Fetus: Appendix* (Washington, D.C.: U.S. Department of Health, Education, and Welfare, 1975).

the fetus which can be singled out as the morally significant point at which to distinguish a fetus not yet at that point from one which has developed beyond it and hence is now to be regarded as a person. Therefore, fetuses are properly regarded from the moment of conception as having the same basic status as an infant. And since infants are properly regarded as having the same basic status as adults, fetuses should also be so regarded.

Now, of course, on this view abortion, whether before or after viability, raises enormous moral problems, since it is morally comparable to infanticide and homicide, generally. And the morality of abortion *per se* is beyond the scope of the present inquiry. This view is nonetheless directly relevant, even on the assumption that abortion prior to viability is morally permissible. For on this view, for instance, experimentation *ex utero* upon a nonviable living fetus is to be seen as analogous to experimentation upon, say, an adult human being who is in a coma and who will die within the next few hours. Thus, on this view, the moral problems of experimentation *ex utero* would be thought to be similar to those of experimentation upon adults whose deaths were imminent and who were themselves unconscious.

(b) That the fetus is in most if not all morally relevant respects like a piece of tissue or a discrete human organ, e.g., a bunch of hair or a kidney. The argument in support of this view focuses upon all the ways in which fetuses are different from typical adults with typical abilities. In particular, the absence of an ability to communicate, to act autonomously (morally as well as physically), to be aware of one's own existence, and/or experience sensations of pain and pleasure, would singly and collectively be taken to be sufficient grounds for regarding the fetus as more like an organ growing within the woman's body than like any other kind of entity. It should be noted, too, that for our purposes this view includes all those positions which regard the status of the fetus as changing from something like a human organ to something else only at or after the moment of viability has been reached. For this inquiry is concerned only with experimentation upon nonviable fetuses.

On this view there are, I think, virtually no arguments against experimentation *ex utero* and only a few arguments against experimentation *in utero*. Whatever, for example, can properly be done to a severed human organ which still has certain life capacities—e.g., it is capable of being transplanted into another human, or it still maintains some of its organ function—can properly be done to the nonviable fetus *ex utero* in those few hours before its life functions have ceased.

(c) That the fetus is in most if not all morally relevant respects like an animal, such as a dog or a monkey. The fetus is, on this view, clearly not a person, nor is it just a collection of tissue or an organ. It is an entity which is at most entitled only to the same kind of respect that many (but not necessarily all) persons think is due to the "higher" animals. It is wrong to inflict needless cruelty on animals—perhaps because they do suffer or perhaps because of what this reveals about the character of the human imposing the cruelty. And fetuses are, basically, in the same class.

On this view, too, there are comparatively few worries about experimentation *ex utero* on nonviable fetuses. At most, the worries are of the same sort that apply to experimentation upon living animals. For the most part, it is proper to regard them as objects to be controlled, altered, killed, or otherwise used for the benefit of humans—subject only to concerns relating to the infliction of needless and perhaps intentional pain and suffering upon the entities being experimented upon, and (in the case of those higher animals we most identify with) to prohibitions upon their consumption as food.

(d) That the fetus is in a distinctive, relatively unique moral category, in which its status is close to but not identical with that of a typical adult. On this view the status of the fetus is both different from and superior to that of the "higher" animals. It is, perhaps, closest to the status of the newly born infant in a culture in which infanticide is regarded as a very different activity from murder or to the status of the insane, the mentally defective, or slaves—again in cultures which see them as less than persons but as clearly superior to animals. The case for regarding fetuses as belonging to a special, discrete class of entities rests, I think, largely on the fetus's potential to become in the usual case a fully developed adult human being. Conceding that the fetus is significantly different from an adult in respect to such things as its present capacity to act autonomously, to experience self-consciousness, and perhaps even to experience pain, this view emphasizes the distinctiveness of the human fetus as the entity capable in the ordinary course of events of becoming a fully developed person. This view sees the value of human life in the things of genuine value or worth that persons are capable of producing, creating, enjoying, and being, e.g., works of art, interpersonal relations of love, trust and benevolence, and scientific and humanistic inquiries and reflections. Correspondingly, it sees the distinctive value of the fetus as being alone the kind of entity that can some day produce, create, enjoy, and be these things of genuine value and worth.

It is, I think, especially important to notice the implications of this view for the morality of experimentation upon nonviable fetuses *ex utero*. For it is the nonviability of the fetus that goes, I believe, a long way toward making experimentation a substantially less troublesome act than it would otherwise be. That is to say, it is evident, I think, that on this view abortion is a morally worrisome act because it involves the destruction of an entity that possesses the potential to produce and be things of the highest value. However, if an abortion has been performed and if the fetus is still nonviable, then experimentation upon the fetus in no way affects the fetus's ability, or lack thereof, ever to realize any of its existing potential. On this view especially, abortion, not experimentation upon the nonviable fetus, is the fundamental, morally problematic activity.

Specific Issues Relating to Experimentation Ex Utero

I propose now to turn to an examination of what seem to me to be the specific issues that arise in thinking about the morality of experimentation upon nonviable, living, human fetuses *ex utero*. The examination will be divided into four parts: (a) an enumeration and analysis of the arguments against experimentation; (b) an enumeration and analysis of the arguments in favor of experimentation; (c) an enumeration and discussion of some specific problems that arise in respect to the question of consent; and (d) a statement of my own view about the permissibility of experimentation.

The Major Arguments against Experimentation upon Nonviable, Living, Human Fetuses Ex Utero

The arguments can be divided in a rough fashion into two groups: those that, on the one hand, oppose experimentation because of the possible, deleterious consequences that are thought to follow from the legitimization of such a practice; and those that, on the other hand, oppose experimentation because of some feature of the situation that is seen to be itself wrong or improper. I begin with the former collection of arguments—those that concentrate on the possible, deleterious consequences.

Possible, Deleterious, Consequences of Permitting a Practice of Fetal Experimentation. One general argument here is that if such a practice is permitted and well publicized, then individuals and, in some related sense, the society will become less sensitive to values and claims which are entitled to the greatest respect. Thus, one specific version of this general line of attack is the argument that individuals will become less sensitive than they ought to be to the value of human life. Another specific claim is that individuals will become less sensitive than they ought to be to the rights and needs of persons who are, for one reason or other, incapable of looking after themselves, e.g., infants, the aged, and the seriously ill or retarded. Still a third, related worry is that individuals will become less sensitive than they ought to be to the claims of those persons whose deaths are reasonably thought to be certain and imminent, e.g., persons in the last stages of terminal illnesses. And a fourth, consequential concern is that individuals will become less sensitive than they ought to be to the rights of persons not to be the unwilling subjects of experimentation.

I think one thing that is of interest about all four of these arguments is that they can retain some, if not all, of their force irrespective of what is thought in fact to be the correct view about the kind of entity a fetus is. That is to say, consider the claim that permitting fetal research may lead individuals to become less sensitive than they ought to be to the rights and needs of persons who are, for one reason or another, incapable of looking after themselves. Even someone who is convinced that a fetus is basically like a human organ might nonetheless legitimately worry about the inferences that individuals would mistakenly draw from the permissibility of a practice of fetal research. As long as it is reasonable to believe that persons, in any significant number, might mistakenly suppose that the principle which justified fetal experimentation was a principle which justified experimentation upon any entity that was incapable of keeping itself alive without substantial human assistance, this is a deleterious consequence of a practice of fetal experimentation which would have to be taken into account. Of course, the more one thinks that a fetus is like other persons in most significant respects, the more one is also apt to think that individuals generally may confuse the case of the fetus with the case of those other entities whose claims to morally more sensitive treatment are nonetheless distinguishable.

A rather different consequential argument goes like this. Once it becomes permissible for experiments to be done on living, nonviable fetuses, such fetuses will come to be regarded as extremely useful in medical research. The increased demand for fetuses within the scientific community will lead to the creation of a variety of subtle as well as obvious incentives for persons both to have abortions and to have them in such a way that the fetus can be a useful object of experimentation. And this is undesirable for several reasons. To begin with, unless it is the case that abortion is a morally unproblematic action, it is wrong to develop a social practice which will encourage persons to have abortions. In addition, the fact that fetuses are useful objects of experimentation might lead members of the scientific and medical community unconsciously to distort or alter their views of when persons should have abortions. Doctors might in this way take into account nonmedical reasons for advising patients to have abortions. And, finally, there is always the danger that the pressures and inducements would operate unequally throughout the society—persons from a low socioeconomic status would be the ones who were more likely to be attracted by the incentives and subjected to the pressures.

Still a third argument, which may or may not be consequentialist, points to the fact that many individuals will experience revulsion and will be in psychic turmoil when they learn of fetuses being treated in this way, i.e., as objects of experimentation. The revulsion and turmoil are comparable, although less universal, to that encountered at the thought of such things as cannibalism and the desecration of graves. If a large number of persons respond this way, then one argument against experimentation is that it will substantially impair social peace and harmony. Because they care so strongly, they will be led to act antagonistically toward the source of their discomfort. In addition, even if the numbers are not large, the severe quality of their reactions may justify prohibition simply on the ground that the gains of experimentation do not overbalance the pain and discomfort experienced by those who are so affected.

Arguments for the Intrinsic or Direct Wrongness of Fetal Experimentation. I can identify approximately a half-dozen arguments that in some direct, non-consequential way call into question the morality of fetal experimentation upon nonviable, living fetuses. More so than in the case of the consequential arguments, the force of these arguments often depends upon the status that, it is thought, ought properly be accorded the fetus.

The first two arguments relate to the principle involved in fetal experimentation. One such argument is this: to permit fetal experimentation is at least to commit oneself to the principle that it is permissible to perform comparable experiments upon any living person, provided only that we have good reason to believe that the person will die very soon, i.e., within a few hours, anyway. But since it is surely wrong to experiment on persons just because they will die anyway within a few hours, experimentation on nonviable, living fetuses lacks a coherent principle of support.

The other argument is similar: to permit fetal experimentation is to commit oneself to the principle that it is permissible to perform comparable experiments on all living persons, provided only that are no longer conscious and will not regain their consciousness before they die. But since it is surely wrong to experiment on all such persons, experimentation on nonviable living fetuses lacks a coherent principle of support.

In both cases it is, I think, clear that the force of the argument depends upon the claim that fetuses are sufficiently like other human persons so that there are no plausible, reasonably persuasive grounds upon which to distinguish the way in which the fetus is treated from the way in which other persons, e.g., the terminally ill or the unconscious, could also properly be treated. The argument appeals both to a claim that it would be wrong to treat other persons in this way and to a claim that the case of fetal experimentation cannot be readily or convincingly distinguished.

A third argument concerns the concept of viability. It is this. The concept of viability is anything but a precise one, even within medical science. It is fundamentally the idea that the fewer the number of weeks of gestation the less likely it is that any medical means presently exists by which the fetus could be kept alive until it could function without artificial support. The problem is not just one of imaginary, theoretical possibilities. Given the present state of medical technology there will, at best, be a range within which it is relatively likely or unlikely that the fetus could be kept alive, i.e., is viable. This means that it is not the case that all fetuses classified as nonviable for purposes of experimentation would necessarily have died no matter what steps has been taken to try to maintain their lives. Now it is clear that once a fetus is viable it is wrong to experiment upon it in ways that are potentially harmful to it. But if this is so, then in some significant number of cases comparable experiments will be performed on fetuses classified "nonviable" but perhaps really viable.

The plausibility of this argument depends both upon the claim that deleterious experimentation upon viable fetuses would be wrong and upon the claim that a significant number of moderately developed fetuses determined to be nonviable might, in fact, have proved to have been viable, if they had not been the subjects of experimentation.

A fourth argument is this: we believe that fetal experiments which directly terminate either respiration or heartbeat are wrong; see, e.g., DHEW, "Protection of Human Subjects: Policies and Procedures." But there is no real difference between that and engaging in experiments in which the risk of terminating respiration or heartbeat is substantially increased. Hence, if the former is wrong, the latter must be too.

I think this argument is surely correct in its insistence upon the absence of any convincing way to distinguish experiments which directly terminate either respiration or heartbeat from those that increase the risk of termination significantly. What remains the open question, however, is whether there is any good moral reason to regard as improper experiments which directly terminate the respiration or heartbeat of a nonviable fetus.

The fifth argument concerns the general question of the relationship between means and ends in morality. Let it be conceded, so this argument goes, that good ends, e.g., the prevention of premature births, are sought to be achieved through this kind of fetal experimentation. Nonetheless, if the means used to achieve that end are morally unacceptable, it is wrong to seek that end in this way. Hence the pursuit of a good end cannot justify experimentation on nonviable fetuses.

This argument leaves two questions unanswered. To begin with, the argument assumes, rather than explains, the immorality of this kind of experimentation on nonviable fetuses. Unless independent grounds are offered to establish the impropriety of such experiments, the argument is at best hypothetical: if such grounds exist, they cannot be overridden by the worth of the end that is sought. In addition, the argument assumes both the possibility of separating clearly means from ends and the wrongness of using bad means to achieve a good end. Neither assumption seems to me to be unproblematic, and both would require discussion and analysis of a sort which lies beyond the scope of this inquiry.

The remaining argument relates especially to those experiments which prolong the life of the nonviable fetus, but also to some experiments which do not. The argument is that all experiments which cause the fetus more pain than it would otherwise experience are bad just in virtue of this fact. I do think that it always counts against the doing of an action that it increases the amount of pain in the world, and it always counts substantially against the doing of an action that it increases the amount of pain experienced by human beings. Thus, this argument would, I think, be a relevant argument if it were the case that it was reasonable to think that the nonviable fetus had the present capacity to experience pain, even in the sense, say, that we think animals like dogs and horses do. And the argument would be an especially important one if it were the case that it was reasonable to think that the nonviable fetus possessed the present capacity to experience pain in roughly the same sense or way in which fully developed persons do.

The Major Arguments in Favor of the Permissibility of Experimentation upon Nonviable, Living Fetuses Ex Utero

As has already been indicated, some of the arguments depend quite directly upon what view is held concerning the status of the fetus, and others do not. More specifically, if the nonviable fetus is properly regarded as basically a human organ or piece of tissue, little if anything more than scientific curiosity is needed to justify experimentation. In the same way, if the nonviable fetus is properly regarded as basically like a higher animal, e.g., a monkey, genuine scientific curiosity coupled with the avoidance of unnecessary suffering, if any, is all that is required.

The chief argument that applies, even if the nonviable fetus enjoys some other, more significant status, consists in a threefold claim. First, things of great usefulness vis-à-vis the preservation and improvement of human lives can be learned from these experiments. Second, things of great usefulness vis-à-vis the preservation and improvement of human lives can only be learned from these experiments. And third, to describe the fetus as nonviable is to concede that no matter what is done, all signs of life will disappear from the fetus within a very short period of time, i.e., not more than four or five hours. Thus, it is claimed, the conjunction of utility, need, and inevitability combine to establish the legitimacy of this kind of experimentation, irrespective of the status of the fetus.

One important objection that this argument must confront is this: if experimentation is justifiable under these conditions, then it is also justifiable in the case of a person who is unconscious, and who will die soon without regaining consciousness, e.g., because he or she is in the last stages of a terminal illness. But because it is wrong to experiment on adults who are in this state, it cannot consistently be maintained that it is right to experiment on the fetus.

At least two responses are possible. First, it might be argued that fetuses are just in a different class from adults. To be sure, there may not be anything intrinsically wrong with experimenting on an adult in the circumstances just described. However, to permit experimentation would be an unwise exception to the doctrine of the sanctity of human life. Because fetuses are perceived to be different entities from fully developed persons, to permit experimentation on them is not to create the same kind of dangerous exception.

Second, it might be argued that the two cases are distinguishable in that there is no analogue to the concept of nonviability in the case of the adult. That is to say, medical science cannot identify with confidence those cases in which an individual will die soon without regaining consciousness, in the same way in which it can identify with confidence those fetuses that are not yet viable.

There is one other argument in favor of experimentation that is worth noting. It is that if there is no good, moral reason to prohibit experimentation, then a decision to prohibit it encourages the practice of making social decisions on nonrational if not irrational grounds. And this is a generally unwise thing to do. That is to say, it might be maintained that experimentation should be prohibited just because it seems wrong or offensive even though no one can give a plausible account of why it ought to be so regarded. This argument is an answer to that way to proceeding. It is an argument for the importance of restricting scientific inquiry only if there are good reasons and not, for example, irrational or superstitious objections to the investigations.

The Issue of Consent

There is a general problem of consent that arises: namely, that the fetus will not have consented to anything. The question is whether that should make a difference. It might be argued, of course, that an experiment is always improper unless the subject of the experiment agrees or consents to being a subject. Since the fetus did not consent to being a subject, any experimentation upon the fetus is improper. The difficulty with this position is that there is no obvious way to decide whether the principle should apply to entities who are not capable of consenting, and if so, to which kinds of entities. It will depend upon the view that is taken of the status of the fetus, and the possible answers will parallel those discussed above in the first part of the paper. If the fetus is a person, then consent will be required (but so, *a fortiori*, should consent have been required for the abortion). I conclude, therefore, that no new general problem is raised by the absence of the consent of the fetus to being the subject of experimentation.

There is, however, a related isssue that is worth mentioning. It is possible, I think, to hold a variety of views about the status of the fetus and still believe that the mother, or perhaps both parents, have a legitimate claim to have their consent secured before any fetal experimentation occurs. The justification cannot, of course, be that to require the consent of the parents will protect the fetus from harm. This is because, having elected to terminate the pregnancy, the parents are already in a nontraditional, atypical relationship vis-à-vis the offspring. So it cannot be that the consent of the parents should be required as a means of protecting the fetus, or looking after its interests. Still, the parents may have sensibilities, attitudes, etc., that are deserving of respect—sensibilities, etc., that correspond to those of living persons toward a deceased relative. It is not exactly that they "own" the deceased, but that they do have a legitimate claim to decide how the body of the deceased shall be dealt with. In the same way, I think, parents of an aborted fetus could still quite often see themselves as being in a similar relationship to the fetus, such that they would feel themselves injured in serious ways were the fetus to become the subject of experimentation without their agreement. For this reason, I believe that the consent of the mother (in the case of an unmarried woman) or of both parents to any experimentation should be required before the abortion occurs, and that the nature of the proposed experiments should be explained carefully and fully to them.

Recommendations Concerning Experimentation Ex Utero

My own view is that the fetus enjoys the kind of unique moral status described in (d) above. Hence, abortion on demand seems to me to be a very troublesome moral issue. If the morality of the abortion is not in question, however, then I somewhat uncertainly conclude that experimentation *ex utero* may be permissible provided the following conditions are satisfied:

1. The consent of the mother (if unmarried) or of both parents should be procured before the abortion, and the experiments clearly described to those whose consent is required.

2. It should be determined by a body independent of those proposing the experiments that the experiments can reasonably be expected to yield important information or knowledge concerning the prevention of harm or the treatment of illness in other human beings. That same body should also determine that the desired information or knowledge is not reasonably obtainable in other ways.

3. Those medical persons who counsel a woman concerning abortion and secure the requisite consent should not be the same persons—or affiliated directly with those persons—who will be involved in the experimentation.

4. No experiments should be permitted on an aborted fetus which might, in fact, be viable, given the state of present medical ability.

Specific Issues Relating to Experimentation in Utero

The cases that seem to me to be problematic are those in which there is a reasonable risk that the experiment will be harmful to the fetus and in which the experiments are not undertaken in order to benefit the particular fetus. Much of what has been said about experimentation *ex utero* applies to these cases as well. In addition, however, there are several new arguments that are relevant only in these cases.

The most significant one against experimentation *in utero* is that the fetus's nonviability has not yet been established in the same way in which it has been in the case of experimentation *ex utero*. That is to say, in the latter case, the abortion has already occured and *ex hypothesis* the fetus cannot survive no matter what is done. In the former case, however, the abortion has yet to take place, and until it does there is always the genuine possibility that the mother may change her mind and decide not to have the abortion at all.

Because this is so, the possibility of intervening injury resulting from the experimentation creates the following dilemma. On the one hand, if the mother changes her mind and decides not to have the abortion, the chances have thereby been increased that she will give birth to a child who is unnecessarily injured. It seems unfair to the child, the society, and the parents to bring into the world a child with defects or disabilities that could have been prevented.

On the other hand, if the mother is required to proceed with the abortion because the experiments have been undertaken, the state is regarding the original consent to the abortion as irrevocable and it is, in essence, requiring her to submit to the abortion against her will.

There is, in addition, a related matter. The fact that potentially damaging experiments have been performed on the fetus will itself constitute an added inducement to the mother to go through with the abortion and not change her mind. That is to say, experimentation itself makes abortion more likely because the belief that the fetus has been injured will make the mother less likely to change her mind. If abortion is viewed as the kind of serious act that ought not be "artificially" encouraged, then the intervening experimentation may be objected to as just such an "artificial" inducement or encouragement to stay with the original decision to have the abortion.

For the above (and other) reasons I think it important that the decision to have an abortion be kept easily revocable, up until the time of the abortion. And for this reason I do not think that any experiments *in utero* should be permitted, where those experiments involve a substantial risk of injury to the fetus.

PROXY CONSENT IN THE EXPERIMENTATION SITUATION

RICHARD A. McCORMICK

It is widely admitted within the research community that if there is to be continuing and proportionate progress in pediatric medicine, experimentation is utterly essential. This conviction rests on two closely interrelated facts. First, as Alexander Capron has pointed out,[1] "Children cannot be regarded simply as 'little people' pharmacologically. Their metabolism, enzymatic and excretory systems, skeletal development and so forth differ so markedly from adults' that drug tests for the latter provide inadequate information about dosage, efficacy, toxicity, side effects, and contraindications for children." Second, and consequently, there is a limit to the usefulness of prior experimentation with animals and adults. At some point or other experimentation with children becomes necessary.

Legal Consideration

At this point, however, a severe problem arises. The legal and moral legitimacy of experimentation (understood here as procedures involving no direct benefit to the person participating in the experiment) is founded above all on the informed consent of the subject. But in many instances, the young subject is either legally or factually incapable of consent. Furthermore, it is argued, the parents are neither legally nor morally capable of supplying this consent for the child. As Dr. Donald T. Chalkley of the National Institutes of Health puts it: "A parent has no legal right to give consent for the involvement of his child in an activity not for the benefit of that child. No legal guardian, no person standing *in loco parentis*, has that right."[2] It would seem to follow that infants and

---

[1] A. Capron, *Clinical Research 21:*141, 1973.
[2] *Medical World News*, June 8, 1973, p. 41.

Reprinted with permission of the author and the publisher from *Perspectives in Biology and Medicine 18* (1):2–20, Autumn, 1974. Copyright 1974 by The University of Chicago Press.

some minors are simply out of bounds where clinical research is concerned. Indeed, this conclusion has been explicitly drawn by the well-known ethician Paul Ramsey. He notes: "If children are incapable of truly consenting to experiments having unknown hazards for the sake of good to come, and if no one else should consent for them in cases unrelated to their own treatment, then medical research and society in general must choose a perhaps more difficult course of action to gain the benefits we seek from medical investigations."[3]

Does the consent requirement taken seriously exclude all experiments on children? If it does, then children themselves will be the ultimate sufferers. If it does not, what is the moral justification for the experimental procedures? The problem is serious, for, as Ramsey notes, an investigation involving children as subjects is "a prismatic case in which to tell whether we mean to take seriously the consent-requirement."[4]

Before concluding with Shirkey that those incompetent of consent are "therapeutic orphans,"[5] I should like to explore the notion and validity of proxy consent. More specifically, the interest here is in the question, Can and may parents consent, and to what extent, to experiments on their children where the procedures are nonbeneficial for the child involved? Before approaching this question, it is necessary to point out the genuine if restricted input of the ethician in such matters. Ramsey has rightly pointed up the difference between the ethics of consent and ethics in the consent situation. This latter refers to the meaning and practical applications of the requirement of an informed consent. It is the work of prudence and pertains to the competence and responsibility of physicians and investigators. The former, on the other hand, refers to the principle requiring an informed consent, the ethics of consent itself. Such moral principles are elaborated out of competences broader than those associated with the medical community.

A brief review of the literature will reveal that the question raised above remains in something of a legal and moral limbo. The *Nuremberg Code* states only that "the voluntary consent of the human subject is absolutely essential. This means that the person involved should have legal capacity to give consent.[6] Nothing specific is said about infants or those who are mentally incompetent. Dr. Leo Alexander, who aided in drafting the first version of the *Nuremberg Code*, explained subsequently that his provision for valid consent from next of kin where mentally ill patients are concerned was dropped by the Nuremberg judges, "probably because [it] did not apply in the specific cases under trial."[7]

---

[3] P. Ramsey, *The Patient as Person* (New Haven: Yale University Press), 1970, p. 17.
[4] *Ibid.*, p. 28.
[5] H. Shirkey, *Journal of Pediatrics 72:*119, 1968.
[6] H. K. Beecher, *Research and the Individual* (Boston: Little, Brown), 1970.
[7] P. Ramsey, *op. cit.*, p. 26. See also L. Alexander, *Diseases of the Nervous System 27:*62, 1966.

Be that as it may, it has been pointed out by Beecher[8] that a strict observance of Nuremberg's Rule 1 would effectively cripple study of mental disease and would simply prohibit all experimentation on children.

The *International Code of Medical Ethics* (General Assembly of the World Medical Association, 1949) states simply: "Under no circumstances is a doctor permitted to do anything that would weaken the physical or mental resistance of a human being except from strictly therapeutic or prophylactic indications imposed in the interest of his patient."[9] This statement is categorical and if taken literally means that "young children and the mentally incompetent are categorically excluded from all investigations except those that directly may benefit the subjects."[10] However, in 1954 the General Assembly of the World Medical Association (in *Principles for Those in Research and Experimentation*) stated: "It should be required that each person who submits to experimentation be informed of the nature, the reason for, and the risk of the proposed experiment. If the patient is irresponsible, consent should be obtained from the individual who is legally responsible for the individual."[11] In the context it is somewhat ambiguous whether this statement is meant to apply beyond experimental procedures that are performed for the patient's good.

The *Declaration of Helsinki* (1964) is much clearer on the point. After distinguishing "clinical research combined with professional care" and "nontherapeutic clinical research," it states of this latter: "Clinical research on a human being cannot be undertaken without his free consent, after he has been fully informed; if he is legally incompetent the consent of the legal guardian should be procured."[12] In 1966 the American Medical Association, in its *Principles of Medical Ethics*, endorsed the Helsinki statement. It distinguished clinical investigation "primarily for treatment" and clinical investigation "primarily for the accumulation of scientific knowledge." With regard to this latter, it noted that "consent, in writing, should be obtained from the subject, or from his legally authorized representative if the subject lacks the capacity to consent." More specifically, with regard to minors or mentally incompetent persons, the AMA statement reads: "Consent, in writing is given by a legally authorized representative of the subject under circumstances in which an informed and prudent adult would reasonably be expected to volunteer himself or his child as a subject."[13]

In 1963, the Medical Research Council of Great Britain issued its *Responsibility in Investigations on Human Subjects.*[14] Under title of "Procedures Not of

[8] H. K. Beecher, *op. cit.*, p. 231.
[9] *Ibid.*, p. 236.
[10] F. J. Ingelfinger, *New England Journal of Medicine 228:*791, 1973.
[11] H. K. Beecher, *op. cit.*, p. 240.
[12] *Ibid.*, p. 278.
[13] *Ibid.*, p. 223.
[14] *Ibid.*, p. 262 ff.

Direct Benefit to the Individual" the Council stated: "The situation in respect of minors and mentally subnormal or mentally disordered persons is of particular difficulty. In the strict view of the law parents and guardians of minors cannot give consent on their behalf to any procedures which are of no particular benefit to them and which may carry some risk of harm." Then, after discussing consent as involving a full understanding of "the implications to himself of the procedures to which he was consenting," the Council concluded: "When true consent in this sense cannot be obtained, procedures which are of no direct benefit and which might carry a risk of harm to the subject should not be undertaken." If it is granted that every experiment involves some risk, then the MRC statement would exclude any experiment on children. Curran and Beecher[15] have pointed out that this strict reading of English law is based on the advice of Sir Harvey Druitt, though there is no statute or case law to support it. Nevertheless, it has gone relatively unchallenged.

Statements of the validity of proxy consent similar to those of the *Declaration of Helsinki* and the American Medical Association have been issued by the American Psychological Association[16] and the Food and Drug Administration.[17] The most recent formulation touching on proxy consent is that of the Department of Health, Education, and Welfare in its *Protection of Human Subjects: Policies and Procedures.*[18] In situations where the subject cannot himself give consent, the document refers to "supplementary judgment." It states: "For the purposes of this document, supplementary judgment will refer to judgements made by local committees in addition to the subject's consent (when possible) and that of the parents or legal guardian (where applicable), as to whether or not a subject may participate in clinical research." The DHEW proposed guidelines admit that the law on parental consent is not clear in all respects. Proxy consent is valid with regard to established and generally accepted thereapeutic procedures; it is, in practice, valid for therapeutic research. However, the guidelines state that "when research might expose a subject to risk without defined therapeutic benefit or other positive effect on the subject's well-being, parental or guardian consent appears to be insufficient." These statements about validity concern law, in the sense (I would judge) of what would happen should a case determination be provoked on the basis of existing precedent.

Medical Ethics

After this review of the legal validity of proxy consent and its limitations, the DHEW guidelines go on to draw two ethical conclusions. First, "When the

---

[15] W. J. Curran and H. K. Beecher *Journal of the American Medical Association 210:*77, 1969.

[16] H. K. Beecher, *op. cit.*, p. 256 ff.

[17] *Ibid.*, p. 299 ff.

[18] Department of Health, Education, and Welfare, *Federal Register 38:*31738, 1973.

risk of a proposed study is generally considered not significant, and the potential benefit is explicit, the ethical issues need not preclude the participation of children in biomedical research." Presumably, this means that where there is risk, ethical issues do preclude the use of children. However, the DHEW document did not draw this conclusion. Rather, its second ethical conclusion states: "An investigator proposing research activities which expose children to risk must document, as part of the application for support, that the information to be gained can be obtained in no other way. The investigator must also stipulate either that the risk to the subjects will be insignificant or that, although some risk exists, the potential benefit is significant and far outweighs that risk. In no case will research activities be approved which entail substantial risk except in the cases of clearly therapeutic procedures." These proposed guidelines admit, therefore, three levels of risk within the ethical calculus: insignificant risk, some risk, and substantial risk. Proxy consent is, by inference, ethically acceptable for the first two levels but not for the third.

The documents cited move almost imperceptibly back and forth between legal and moral considerations, so that it is often difficult to know whether the major concern is one or the other, or even how the relationship of the legal and ethical is conceived. Nevertheless, it can be said that there has been a gradual move away from the absolutism represented in the *Nuremberg Code* to the acceptance of proxy consent, possibly because the *Nuremberg Code* is viewed as containing, to some extent, elements of a reaction to the Nazi experiments.

Medical literature of the noncodal variety has revealed this same pattern or ambiguity. For instance, writing in the *Lancet*, Dr. R. E. W. Fisher reacted to the reports of the use of children in research procedures as follows: "No medical procedure involving the slightest risk or accompanied by the slightest physical or mental pain may be inflicted on a child for experimental purposes unless there is a reasonable chance, or at least a hope, that the child may benefit thereby."[19] On the other hand, Franz J. Ingelfinger, editor of the *New England Journal of Medicine*, contends that the World Medical Association's statement ("Under no circumstances . . ."[above]) is an extremist position that must be modified.[20] His suggested modification reads: "Only when the risks are small and justifiable is a doctor permitted. . . ." It is difficult to know from Ingelfinger's wording whether he means small and therefore justifiable or whether "justifiable" refers to the hoped-for benefit. Responses to this editorial were contradictory. N. Baumslag and R. E. Yodaiken state: "In our opinion there are no conditions under which any children may be used for experimentation not primarily designed for their benefit."[21] Ian Shine, John Howieson, and Ward Griffen, Jr.,

[19]R. E. W. Fisher, *Lancet* (Letters), Nov. 7, 1953, p. 993.

[20]F. J. Ingelfinger, *op. cit.*, p. 791.

[21]N. Baumslag and R. W. Yodaiken, *New England Journal of Medicine* (Letters) *288:*1247, 1973.

came to the opposite conclusion: "We strongly support his [Ingelfinger's] proposals provided that one criterion of 'small and justifiable risks' is the willingness of the experimentor to be an experimentee, or to offer a spouse or child when appropriate."[22]

Curran and Beecher had earlier disagreed strongly with the rigid interpretation given the statement of the Medical Research Council through Druitt's influence. Their own conclusion was the "children under 14 may participate in clinical investigation which is not for their benefit where the studies are sound, promise important new knowledge for mankind, and there is no discernible risk."[23] The editors of *Archives of Disease in Childhood* recently endorsed this same conclusion, adding only "necessity of informed parental consent."[24] Discussing relatively minor procedures such as weighing a baby, skin pricks, venipunctures, etc., they contend that "whether or not these procedures are acceptable must depend, it seems to us, on whether the potential gain to others is commensurate with the discomfort to the individual." They see the Medical Research Council's statement as an understandable but exaggerated reaction to the shocking disclosures of the Nazi era. A new value judgment is required in our time, one based on the low risk/benefit ratio.

This same attitude is proposed by Alan M. W. Porter.[25] He argues that there are grounds "for believing that it may be permissible and reasonable to undertake minor procedures on children for experimental purposes with the permission of the parents." The low risk/benefit ratio is the ultimate justification. Interestingly, Porter reports the reactions of colleagues and the public to a research protocol he had drawn up. He desired to study the siblings of children who had succumbed to "cot death." The research involved venipuncture. A pediatric authority told Porter that venipuncture was inadmissible under the Medical Research Council code. Astonished, Porter showed the protocol to the first 10 colleagues he met. The instinctive reaction of 9 out of 10 was "Of course you may." Similarly, a professional market researcher asked (for Porter) 10 laymen about the procedure, and all responded that he could proceed. In other words, Porter argues that public opinion (and therefore, presumably, moral common sense) stands behind the low risk/benefit ratio approach to experimentation on children.

This sampling is sufficient indication of the variety of reactions likely to be encountered when research on children is discussed.

---

[22] I. Shine, J. Howieson, and W. Griffen, Jr., *New England Journal of Medicine* (Letters) *288:*1248, 1973.

[23] W. J. Curran and H. K. Beecher, *op. cit.*, p. 81.

[24] Editorial, *Archives of Disease in Children 48:*751, 1973.

[25] A. W. Franklin, A. M. Porter, and D. N. Raine, *British Medical Journal*, May 19, 1973, p. 402.

The Views of Ethicians

The professional ethicians who have written on this subject have also drawn rather different conclusions. John Fletcher argues that a middle path between autonomy (of the physician) and heteronomy (external control) must be discovered.[26] The Nuremberg rule "does not take account of exceptions which can be controlled and makes no allowance whatsoever for the exercise of professional judgment." It is clear that Fletcher would accept proxy consent in some instances, though he has not fully specified what these would be.

Thomas J. O'Donnell, S.J., notes that, besides informed consent, we also speak of three other modalities of consent.[27] First, there is presumed consent. Life-saving measures that are done on an unconscious patient in an emergency room are done with presumed consent. Second, there is implied consent. The various tests done on a person who undergoes a general checkup are done with implied consent, the consent being contained and implied in the very fact of his coming for a checkup. Finally, there is vicarious consent. This is the case of the parent who consents for therapy on an infant. O'Donnell wonders whether these modalities of consent, already accepted in the therapeutic context, can be extended to the context of clinical investigation (and by this he means research not to the direct benefit of the child). It is his conclusion that vicarious consent can be ethically operative "provided it is contained within the strict limits of a presumed consent (on the part of the subject) proper to clinical research and much narrower than the presumptions that might be valid in a therapeutic context." Practically, this means that O'Donnell would accept the validity of vicarious consent only where "danger is so remote and discomfort so minimal that a normal and informed individual would be presupposed to give ready consent." O'Donnell discusses neither the criteria nor the analysis that would set the "strict limits of a presumed consent."

Princeton's Paul Ramsey is the ethician who has discussed this problem at greatest length.[28] He is in clear disagreement with the positions of Fletcher and O'Donnell. Ramsey denies the validity of proxy consent in nonbeneficial (to the child) experiments simply and without qualification. Why? We may not, he argues, submit a child either to procedures that involve any measure of risk of harm or to procedures that involve no harm but simply "offensive touching," "A subject can be wronged without being harmed," he writes. This occurs whenever he is used as an object, or as a means only rather than also as an end in himself. Parents cannot consent to this type of thing, regardless of the significance of the experiment. Ramsey sees the morality of experimentation on

[26] J. Fletcher, *Law and Contemporary Problems 32:*620, 1967.
[27] T. J. O'Donnell, *Journal of the American Medical Association 227:*73, 1974.
[28] P. Ramsey, *op. cit.*

children to be exactly what Paul Freund has described as the law on the matter: "The law here is that parents may consent for the child if the invasion of the child's body is for the child's welfare or benefit."[29]

In pursuit of his point, Ramsey argues as follows: "To attempt to consent for a child to be made an experimental subject is to treat a child as not a child. It is to treat him as if he were an adult person who has consented to become a joint adventurer in the common cause of medical research. If the grounds for this are alleged to be the presumptive or implied consent of the child, that must simply be characterized as a violent and a false presumption." Thus, he concludes simply that "no parent is morally competent to consent that his child shall be submitted to hazardous *or other experiments* having no diagnostic or therapeutic significance for the child himself" (emphasis added). Though he does not say so. Ramsey would certainly conclude that a law that tolerates proxy consent to any purely experimental procedure is one without moral warrants, indeed, is immoral because it legitimates (or tries to) treating a human being as a means only.

A careful study, then, of the legal, medical, and ethical literature on proxy consent for nontherapeutic research on children reveals profoundly diverging views. Generally, the pros and cons are spelled out in terms of two important values: individual integrity and societal good through medical benefits. Furthermore, in attempting to balance these two values, this literature by and large either affirms or denies the moral legitimacy of a risk/benefit ratio, what ethicians refer to as a teleological calculus. It seems to me that in doing this, current literature has not faced this tremendously important and paradigmatic issue at its most fundamental level. For instance, Ramsey bases his prohibitive position on the contention that nonbeneficial experimental procedures make an "object" of an individual. In these cases, he contends, parents cannot consent for the individual. Consent is the heart of the matter. If the parents could legitimately consent for the child, then presumably experimental procedures would not make an object of the infant and would be permissible. Therefore, the basic question seems to be, Why cannot the parents provide consent for the child? Why is their consent considered null here while it is accepted when procedures are therapeutic? To say that the child would be treated as an object does not answer this question; it seems that it presupposes the answer and announces it under this formulation.

Traditional Moral Theology

There is in traditional moral theology a handle that may allow us to take hold of this problem at a deeper root and arrive at a principled and consistent position, one that takes account of all the values without arbitrarily softening or

[29] P. Freund, *New England Journal of Medicine 273:*691, 1965; *idem, Trial 2:*48, 1966.

suppressing any of them. That handle is the notion of parental consent, particularly the theoretical implications underlying it. If this can be unpacked a bit, perhaps a more satisfying analysis will emerge. Parental consent is required and sufficient for therapy directed at the child's own good. We refer to this as vicarious consent. It is closely related to presumed consent. That is, it is morally valid precisely insofar as it is a resonable presumption of the child's wishes, a construction of what the child would wish could he consent for himself. But here the notion of "what the child would wish" must be pushed further if we are to avoid a simple imposition of the adult world on the child. Why *would* the child so wish? The answer seems to be that he would choose this if he were capable of choice because he *ought* to do so. This statement roots in a traditional natural-law understanding of human moral obligations.

The natural-law tradition argues that there are certain identifiable values that we *ought* to support, attempt to realize, and never directly suppress because they are definitive of our flourishing and well-being. It further argues that knowledge of these values and of the prescriptions and proscriptions associated with them is, in principle, available to human reason. That is, they require for their discovery no divine revelation.

Moral Legitimacy of Proxy Consent

What does all this have to do with the moral legitimacy of proxy consent? It was noted that parental (proxy, vicarious) consent is required and sufficient for therapy directed to the child's own good. It was further noted that it is morally valid precisely insofar as it is a reasonable presumption of the child's wishes, a construction of what the child would wish could he do so. Finally, it was suggested that the child *would* wish this therapy because he *ought* to do so. In other words, a construction of what the child *would* wish (presumed consent) is not an exercise in adult capriciousness and arbitrariness, subject to an equally carpicious denial or challenge when the child comes of age. It is based, rather, on two assertions: (a) that there are certain values (in this case life itself) definitive of our good and flourishing, hence values that we *ought* to choose and support if we want to become and stay human, and that, therefore, these are good also for the child; and (b) that these "ought" judgments, at least in their more general formulations, are a common patronage available to all men, and hence form the basis on which policies can be built.

Specifically, then, I would argue that parental consent is morally legitimate where therapy on the child is involved precisely because we know that life and health are goods for the child, that he *would* choose them because he *ought* to choose the good of life, his own self-preservation as long as this life remains, all things considered, a human good. To see whether and to what extent this type of moral analysis applies to experimentation, we must ask, "Are there other things that the child *ought*, as a human being, to choose precisely because and insofar as they are goods definitive of his growth and flourishing?" Concretely, *ought* he to choose his own involvement in nontherapeutic experimentation, and to what extent? Certainly there are goods or benefits, at least potential, involved. But are they goods that the child *ought* to choose? Or again, if we can argue that a certain level of involvement in nontherapeutic experimentation is good for the child and therefore that he *ought* to choose it, then there are grounds for saying that parental consent for this is morally legitimate and should be recognized as such.

Perhaps a beginning can be made as follows. To pursue the good that is human life means not only to choose and support this value in one's own case, but also in the case of others when the opportunity arises. In other words, the individual *ought* also to take into account, realize, make efforts in behalf of the lives of others also, for we are social beings and the goods that define our growth and invite to it are goods that reside also in others. It can be good for one to pursue and support this good in others. Therefore, when it factually is good, we may say that one *ought* to do so (as opposed to not doing so). If this is true of all of us up to a point and within limits, it is no less true of the infant. He would choose to do so because he *ought* to do so. Now, to support and realize the value that is life means to support and realize health, the cure of disease, and so on. Therefore, up to a point, this support and realization is good for all of us individually. To share in the general effort and burden of health maintenance and disease control is part of our flourishing and growth as humans. To the extent that it is good for all of us to share this burden, we all *ought* to do so. And to the extent that we *ought* to do so, it is a reasonable construction or presumption of our wishes to say that we would do so. The reasonableness of this presumption validates vicarious consent.

It was just noted that sharing in the common burden of progress in medicine constitutes an individual good for all of us *up to a point.* That qualification is crucially important. It suggests that there are limits beyond which sharing is not or might not be a good. What might be the limits of this sharing? When might it no longer be a good for all individuals and therefore something that all need not choose to do? I would develop the matter as follows.

Adults may donate (*inter vivos*) an organ precisely because their personal good is not to be conceived individualistically but socially, that is, there is a natural order to other human persons which is in the very notion of the human personality itself. The personal being and good of an individual do have a relationship to the being and good of others, difficult as it may be to keep this in a balanced perspective. For this reason, an individual can become (in carefully delimited circumstances) more fully a person by donation of an organ, for by communicating to another of his very being he has more fully integrated himself into the mysterious unity between person and person.

Something similar can be said of participation in nontherapeutic experimentation. It can be an affirmation of one's solidarity and Christian concern for others (through advancement of medicine). Becoming an experimental subject can involve any or all of three things: some degree of risk (at least of complications), pain, and associated inconvenience (e.g., prolonging hospital stay, delaying recovery, etc.). To accept these for the good of others could be an act of charitable concern.

There are two qualifications to these general statements that must immediately be made, and these qualifications explain the phrase "up to a point." First, whether it is personally good for an individual to donate an organ or participate in experimentation is a very circumstantial and therefore highly individual affair. For some individuals, these undertakings could be or prove to be humanly destructive. Much depends on their personalities, past family life, maturity, future position in life, etc. The second and more important qualification is that these procedures become human goods for the donor or subject precisely because and therefore only when they are voluntary, for the personal good under discussion is the good of expressed charity. For these two reasons I would conclude that no one else can make such decisions for an individual, that is, reasonably presume his consent. He has a right to make them for himself. In other words, whether a person *ought* to do such things is a highly individual affair and cannot be generalized in the way the good of self-preservation can be. And if we cannot say of an individual that he ought to do these things, proxy consent has no reasonable presumptive basis.

But are there situations where such considerations are not involved and where the presumption of consent is reasonable, because we may continue to say of all individuals that (other things being equal) they *ought* to be willing? I believe so. For instance, where organ donation is involved, if the only way a young child could be saved were by a blood transfusion from another child, I suspect that few would find such blood donation an unreasonable presumption on the child's wishes. The reason for the presumption is, I believe, that a great good is provided for another at almost no cost to the child. As the scholastics put it, *parum pro nihilo reputatur* ("very little counts for nothing"). For this reason we may say, lacking countervailing individual evidence, that the individual *ought* to do this.

Could the same reasoning apply to experimentation? Concretely, when a particular experiment would involve no discernible risks, no notable pain, no notable inconvenience, and yet hold promise of considerable benefit, should not the child be constructed to wish this in the same way we presume he chooses his own life, because he *ought* to? I believe so. He *ought* to want this not because it is in any way for his own medical good, but because it is not in any realistic way to his harm, and represents a potentially great benefit for others. He *ought* to want these benefits for others.

What They Ought to Want

If this is a defensible account of the meaning and limits of presumed consent where those incompetent to consent are concerned, it means that proxy consent can be morally legitimate in some experimentations. Which? Those that are scientifically well designed (and therefore offer hope of genuine benefit), that cannot succeed unless children are used (because there are dangers involved in interpreting terms such as "discernible" and "negligible," the child should not unnecessarily be exposed to these even minimal risks), that contain no discernible risk or undue discomfort for the child. Here it must be granted that the notions of "discernible risk" and "undue discomfort" are themselves slippery and difficult, and probably somewhat relative. They certainly involve a value judgment and one that is the heavy responsibility of the medical profession (not the moral theologian) to make. For example, perhaps it can be debated whether venipuncture involves "discernible risks" or "undue discomfort" or not. But if it can be concluded that, in human terms, the risk involved or the discomfort is negligible or insignificant, then I believe there are sound reasons in moral analysis for saying that parental consent to this type of invasion can be justified.

Practically, then, I think there are good moral warrants for adopting the position espoused by Curran, Beecher, Ingelfinger, the *Helsinki Declaration*, the *Archives of Disease in Childhood*, and others. Some who have adopted this position have argued it in terms of a low risk/benefit ratio. This is acceptable if properly understood, that is, if "low risk" means for all practical purposes and in human judgment "no realistic risk." If it is interpreted in any other way, it opens the door wide to a utilitarian subordination of the individual to the collectivity. It goes beyond what individuals would want because they *ought* to. For instance, in light of the above analysis, I find totally unacceptable the DHEW statement that "the investigator must also stipulate either that the risk to the subjects will be insignificant, or that *although some risk exists, the potential benefit is significant and far outweighs that risk.*" This goes beyond what all of us, as members of the community, necessarily *ought* to do. Therefore, it is an invalid basis for proxy consent. For analogous reasons, in light of the foregoing analysis I would conclude that parental consent for a kidney transplant from one noncompetent 3-year-old to another is without moral justification.

These considerations do not mean that all noncompetents (where consent is concerned) may be treated in the same way, that the same presumptions are morally legitimate in all cases. For if the circumstances of the infant or child differ markedly, then it is possible that there are appropriate modifications in our construction of what he *ought* to choose. For instance, I believe that institutionalized infants demand special consideration. They are in a situation of peculiar danger for several reasons. First, they are often in a disadvantaged condition physically or mentally so that there is a temptation to regard them as "lesser human beings." Medical history shows our vulnerability to this type of judgment. Second, as institutionalized, they are a controlled group, making them particularly tempting as research subjects. Third, experimentation in such infants is less exposed to public scrutiny. These and other considerations suggest that there is a real danger of overstepping the line between what we all ought to want and what only the individual might want out of heroic, self-sacrificial charity. If such a real danger exists, then what the infant is construed as wanting because he *ought* must be modified. He need not *ought to want* if this involves him in real dangers of going beyond this point.

The editor of the *Journal of the American Medical Association*, Robert H. Moser, in the course of an editorial touching on, among other things, the problem of experimentation, asks whether we are ever justified in the use of children. His answer: "It is an insoluble dilemma. All one can ask is that each situation be studied with consummate circumspection and be approached rationally and compassionately."[30] If circumspection in each situation is to be truly consummate, and if the approach is to be rational and compassionate, then the situation alone cannot be the decisional guide. If the situation alone is the guide, if everything else is a "dilemma," then the qualities Moser seeks in the situation are in jeopardy, and along with them human rights. One can indeed, to paraphrase Moser, ask more than that each situation be studied. He can ask that a genuine ethics of consent be brought to the situation so that ethics in the consent situation will have some chance of surviving human enthusiasms. And an ethics of consent finds its roots in a solid natural-law tradition which maintains that there are basic values that define our potential as human beings; that we ought (within limits and with qualifications) to choose, support, and never directly suppress these values in our conduct; that we can know, therefore, what others would choose (up to a point) because they ought; and that this knowledge is the basis for a soundly grounded and rather precisely limited proxy consent.

---

[30] R. H. Moser, *Journal of the American Medical Association 277:*432, 1974.

•

FURTHER READINGS

Bibliographies

Sollito, Sharmon, and Veatch, Robert M., comps. *Bibliography of Society, Ethics and the Life Sciences.* Hastings-on-Hudson, New York: Institute of Society, Ethics and the Life Sciences, 1974-1977.

Walters, LeRoy., ed. *Bibliography of Bioethics.* Vols. 1- . Detroit: Gale Research Co. Issued Annually.

For lists of further sources see: The National Library of Medicine, Literature Search: #5-69 "Heart Transplantation", #73-4 "Human Expermentation"; #6-69 "Kidney Transplantation in Man"; #70-35 "Psychological Aspects of Transplantation"; #70-32 "Psychological Response to Hemodialysis"; #71-3 "Transplantation in the Therapy of Hearing Disorders"; and #73-6 "Transplantation-Ethical, Legal and Religious." All these lists are obtainable from the Literature Search Program, National Library of Medicine, Bethesda, Maryland 20014.

Books

Adair, Alvis V. *Human Experimentation: An Ancient Notion in a Modern Technology.* Washington: Institute for Urban Affairs and Research, Howard University, 1974.

Annas, George J. *The Rights of Hospital Patients: The Basic ACLU Guide to a Hospital Patient's Rights.* New York: Avon, 1975.

———. *Informed Consent to Human Experimentation: The Subject's Dilemma.* Cambridge, Mass.: Ballinger, 1977.

Arellano-Galdames, F. Jaime. *Some Ethical Problems in Research on Human Subjects.* Ann Arbor: University Microfilms, 1973.

Barber, Bernard, *et al. Research on Human Subjects: Problems of Social Control in Medical Experimentation.* New York: Russell Sage Foundation, 1973.

Beecher, Henry K. *Experimentation in Man.* Springfield, Ill.: Charles C Thomas, 1959.

———. *Research and the Individual: Human Studies.* Boston: Little, Brown, 1970.

Bernard, Claude. *An Introduction to the Study of Experimental Medicine*, Translated by Henry Copley Green. New York: Dover, 1957.

Bogomolny, Robert L. *Human Experimentation, Symposium on Human Experimentation, 1975*. Dallas: SMU Press, 1976.

Branson, Roy, and Veatch, Robert M. *Ethics and Health Policy*. Cambridge, Mass.: Ballinger, 1976.

Copper, I. S. *The Victim Is Always the Same*. New York: Harper & Row, 1973.

Dunstan, G. R. *The Artifice of Ethics*. London: S.C.M. Press, 1974.

Eastwood, R. T. *Cardiac Replacement: Medical, Ethical, Psychological and Economic Implications*. A report by the Ad Hoc Task Force on Cardiac Replacement. National Heart and Lung Institute, National Institutes of Health. Washington, D.C.: U.S. Government Printing Office, 1969.

Fattorusso, V., ed. *Biomedical Science and the Dilemma of Human Experimentation*. Paris: Council for International Organization of Medical Sciences, UNESCO House, 1967.

Freund, Paul A., ed. *Experimentation with Human Subjects*. New York: Braziller, 1970.

Fox, Renée, and Swazey, Judith P. *The Courage to Fail: A Social View of Organ Transplants and Dialysis*. Chicago: University of Chicago Press, 1974.

Fried, Charles. *Medical Experimentation: Personal Integrity and Social Policy*. New York: Elsevier, 1974.

Gray, Bradford. *Human Subjects in Medical Experimentation: A Sociological Study of the Conduct and Regulation of Clinical Research*. New York: Wiley, 1975.

Haring, Bernard. *Medical Ethics*. Notre Dame, Indiana: Fides Publications, 1972.

——. *Ethics of Manipulation: Issues in Medicine, Behavior Control and Genetics*. New York: Seabury Press, 1975.

Hershey, Nathan, and Miller, Robert D. *Human Experimentation and the Law*. Germantown, Md.: Aspen Systems Corporation, 1976.

Jonsen, Albert R., *et al. Biomedical Experimentation on Prisoners: Review of Practices and Problems of Proposal of a New Regulatory Approach*. San Francisco: University of California, School of Medicine, 1975.

Katz, Jay, with Capron, Alexander M., and Glass, Eleanor Swift. *Experimentation with Human Beings*. New York: Russell Sage Foundation, 1972.

Kelman, Herbert. *A Time to Speak: On Human Values and Social Research*. San Francisco: Jossey-Bass, 1968.

Kevorkian, Jack. *Capital Punishment or Capital Gain*. New York: Philosophical Library, 1962.

——. *Medical Research and the Death Penalty*. New York: Vantage Press, 1960.

Ladimer, Irving, and Mewman, Roger, eds. *Clinical Investigation in Medicine: Legal, Ethical and Moral Aspects*. Boston: Law-Medicine Research Institute, Boston University, 1963.

Levy, Charlotte L. *The Human Body and the Law: Legal and Ethical Considerations in Human Experimentation.* Dobbs Ferry, N.Y.: Oceana Publications, 1975.

Longmore, Donald. *Spare-Part Surgery: The Surgical Practice of the Future.* Garden City, N.Y.: Doubleday & Co., 1968.

Lyons, Catherine. *Organ Transplants: The Moral Issues.* Philadelphia: Westminster Press, 1970.

Makarushka, Julia L. *Learning to Be Ethical: Patterns of Socialization and Their Variable Consequences for the Ethical Standards of Bio-Medical Researches.* Ann Arbor: University Microfilms, 1974.

Merlis, Sidney, ed. *Non-Scientific Constraints on Medical Research.* New York: Raven Press, 1970.

Meyers, David W. *The Human Body and the Law.* Chicago: Aldine Press, 1970.

Milgram, Stanley. *Obedience to Authority.* New York: Harper & Row, 1973.

Miller, George W. *Moral and Ethical Implications of Human Organ Transplants.* Springfield, Ill.: Charles C Thomas, 1971.

Mitscherlich, Alexander, and Mielke, Fred *Doctors Of Infamy: The Story of the Nazi Medical Crimes.* New York: Henry Schuman, 1949.

New York University School of Medicine, The Student Council. *Ethical Issues in Human Experimentation: The Case of Willowbrook State Hospital Research.* New York: New York University Medical Center, The Urban Affairs Program, 1973.

Pappworth, M. H. *Human Guinea Pigs: Experimentation on Man.* Boston: Beacon Press, 1968.

Quimby, Freeman H., McKenzie, Susan R., and Chapman, Cynthia B. *Federal Regulation of Human Experimentation, 1975.* Washington: U.S. Government Printing Office, May 1975.

Ramsey, Paul. *The Ethics of Fetal Research.* New Haven: Yale University Press, 1975.

———. *The Patient as a Person.* New Haven: Yale University Press, 1970.

Rapaport, Felix T., ed. *A Second Look at Life.* New York: Grune & Stratton, 1973.

Reagan, C. *Ethics for Scientific Researchers*, second edition. Springfield, Ill.: Charles C Thomas, 1971.

Regan, Tom, and Singer, Peter *Animal Rights and Human Obligation.* Englewood Cliffs, N.J.: Prentice-Hall, 1976.

Rivlin, Alice M., and Timpane, Michael P., eds. *Ethical and Legal Issues of Social Experimentation.* Washington: Brookings Institution, 1975.

Sadler, Alfred M., and Sadler, Blair L. *Organ Transplantation: Current Medical and Medical-Legal Status: The Problems of an Opportunity.* Washington, D.C.: U.S. Government Printing Office, 1970.

Shaw, Bernard. *The Doctor's Dilemma: A Tragedy*. Baltimore: Penguin Books, 1965.

Smith, Harmon L. *Ethics and the New Medicine*. Nashville: Abingdon Press, 1970.

Titmuss, Richard. *The Gift Relationship: From Human Blood to Social Policy*. New York: Pantheon, 1971.

Visscher, Maurice B. *Ethical Constraints and Imperatives in Medical Research*. Springfield, Ill.: Charles C Thomas, 1975.

Weber, Hans-Reudi, ed. *Experiments with Man: Report of an Ecumenical Consultation*. World Council of Churches Studies, No. 6. New York: Friendship Press, 1969.

Wolstenholme, G. E. W., and O'Connor, Maeve. *Ethics in Medical Progress: With Special Reference to Transplantation*. Boston: Little, Brown, 1966.

Articles

Adams, Bernard, and Shea-Stonum, Marilyn. "Toward a Theory of Control of Medical Experimentation with Human Subjects: The Role of Compensation." *Case Western Reserve Law Review* 25 (Spring 1975): 604-648.

Alexander, Leo. "Medical Science under Dictatorship." *New England Journal of Medicine* 241 (July 14, 1949): 39-47.

Alfidi, Ralph J. "Informed Consent: A Study of Patient Reaction." *Journal of the American Medical Association* 216 (1971): 1325-1329.

Altman, Lawrence K. "Auto-Experimentation: An Unappreciated Tradition in Medical Science." *New England Journal of Medicine* 286 (1972): 346-352.

American College of Surgeons/National Institutes of Health Organ Transplant Registry, Advisory Committee to the Registry. "Third Scientific Report." *Journal of the American Medical Association* 226 (December 3, 1973): 1211-1216.

American Medical Association. "Human Experimentation: Statement of the American Medical Association." *Connecticut Medicine* 37 (July 1973): 365-366.

American Medical Association House of Delegates. "Statement on Heart Transplantation." *Journal of the American Medical Association* 207 (March 3, 1969): 1704-1705.

American Medical Association Judicial Council. "Ethical Guidelines for Organ Transplantation." *Journal of the American Medical Association* 205 (August 5, 1968): 341-342.

Aptheker, Herbert. "Racism and Human Experimentation." *Political Affairs* 53 (February 1974): 46-59.

Baker, James A. "Court Ordered Non-Emergency Medical Care for Infants." *Cleveland Marshall Law Review* 18 (1969): 296-307.

Barber, Bernard. "The Ethics of Experimentation with Human Subjects." *Scientific American* 234 (February 1976): 25-31.

——. "Research on Research on Human Subjects: Problems of Access to a Powerful Profession." *Social Problems* 2 (Summer 1973): 103-112.

Bartholeme, William G. "Parents, Children and the Moral Benefits of Research." *Hastings Center Report* 6 (December 1976): 44-45.

Baumrind, Diana. "Metaethical and Normative Considerations Covering the Treatment of Human Subjects in the Behavioral Sciences." In *Human Rights and Psychological Research: A Debate on Psychology and Ethics*, edited by Eugene C. Kennedy. New York: Thomas Y. Crowell, 1975.

Beard, B. H. "Fear of Death and Fear of Life: The Dilemma in Chronic Renal Failures, Hemodialysis, and Kidney Transplantation." *Archives of General Psychiatry* 21 (1969): 373-380.

Beaven, D. W. "Morals and Ethics in Medical Research." *New Zealand Medical Journal* 81 (June 1975): 519-524.

Beecher, Henry K. "Experimentation in Man." *Journal of the American Medical Association* 169 (January 31, 1959): 461-478.

Beecher, Henry K. "Scarce Resources and Medical Advancement." In *Experimentation with Human Subjects*, edited by Paul Freund. New York: George Braziller, 1970, pp. 66-104.

——. "Some Guiding Principles for Clinical Investigation." *Journal of the American Medical Association* 195 (March 28, 1966): 1135-1136.

Berman, Emile Z. "The Legal Problems of Organ Transplantation." *Villanova Law Review* 13 (1968): 751-758.

Bernstein, Arthur H. "Consent to Operate, to Live, or to Die." *Hospitals: J. A. H. A.* (October 1, 1972): 124-128.

Bernstein, Joel E. "Ethical Considerations in Human Experimentation." *Journal of Clinical Pharmacology* 15 (August-September, 1975): 579-590.

Bernstein, Joel E., and Nelson, Kirk F. "Medical Experimentation in the Elderly." *Journal of the American Geriatrics Society* 23 (July 1975): 327-329.

Black, M. M., and Riley, C. "Moral Issues and Priorities in Biomedical Engineering." *Science, Medicine and Man* 1 (April 1973): 67-74.

Blackstone, William T. "The American Psychological Association's Code of Ethics for Research Involving Human Participants: An Appraisal." *The Southern Journal of Philosophy* 13 (1975): 407-418.

Blomquist, Clarence. "Ethical Guidelines for Biomedical Research." *Annals of Clinical Research* 7 (October 1975): 291-294.

Bloom, Michael J. "Non-Therapeutic Medical Research Involving Human Subjects." *Syracuse Law Review* 24 (Summer 1973): 1067-1099.

Board on Medicine of the National Academy of Sciences. "Cardiac Transplant-ation in Man." *Journal of the American Medical Association* 204 (May 27, 1968): 805-806.

Branson, Roy. "Prison Research: National Commission Says 'No Unless. . . .'" *Hastings Center Report* 7 (February 1977): 15-21.

Brant, Jonathan. "Behavioral Modification as a Potential Infringement on Pris-oners' Right to Privacy." *New England Journal on Prison Law* 1 (Fall 1974): 180-202.

British Medical Association. "New Horizons in Medical Ethics: Research Investi-gations in Adults." *British Medical Journal* (April 28, 1973): 220-224.

———. "Report of the Special Committee on Organ Transplantation." *British Medical Journal* (March 21, 1970): 750-751.

Brown, Harold O. "Fetal Research II: The Ethical Question." *Human Life Re-view* 1 (Fall 1975): 118-128.

Budner, Stanley. "Value Conflicts and the Uses of Research: The Example of Abortion." *Man and Medicine* 1 (1975-1976): 29-41.

Capron, Alexander. "Legal Consideration Affecting Clinical Pharmacological Studies in Children." *Clinical Research* 21 (February 1973): 141-150.

Capron, Alexander M. "Medical Research in Prisons: Should a Moratorium Be Called?" *Hastings Center Report* 3 (June 1973): 4-6.

Chalmers, Thomas, *et al.* "Controlled Studies in Clinical Cancer Research." *New England Journal of Medicine* 287 (July 13, 1972): 75-78.

Childress, James F. "Who Shall Live When Not All Can Live?" *Readings on Ethical and Social Issues in Biomedicine*, edited by Richard W. Wertz, Engle-wood Cliffs, N.J.: Prentice-Hall, 1973.

Childress, James F. "Compensating Injured Research Subjects: I. The Moral Argument." *Hastings Center Report* 6 (December 1976): 21-27.

Clothier, C. M. "Consent to Medical Experiment." *Lancet* (March 1977): 642-643.

Coene, Roger E. "Dialysis or Transplant: One Patient's Choice." *Hastings Center Report* 8 (April 1978): 5-7.

Cournard, Andre, *et al.* "Symposium on Organ Transplantation in Man." *Pro-ceedings of the National Academy of Sciences* 63 (August 1969): 1018-1038.

Cowan, Dale H. "Human Experimentation: The Review Process in Practice." *Case Western Reserve Law Review* 25 (Spring 1975): 533-564.

Curran, Charles E. "Ethical Considerations in Human Experimentation." *Du-quesne Law Review* 13 (Summer 1975): 819-840.

Curran, W. J. "A Problem of Consent: Kidney Transplantation in Minors." *New York University Law Review* 34 (1959): 891ff.

———. "Kidney Transplantation in Identical Twin Minors." *New England Journal of Medicine* 287 (July 6, 1972): 26-27.

———. The Law and Human Experimentation." *New England Journal of Medicine* 275 (August 11, 1966): 323-325.

Curran, W. J., with Henry K. Beecher. "Experimentation in Children." *Journal of the American Medical Association* 210 (October 6, 1969): 77-83.

Cutter, Fred. "Transplants and Psychological Survival in the Treatment of Kidney Disease." *Omega* 3 (February 1973): 57-65.

Dalton, Elizabeth, Hooper, Kim, and Reiner, Susan. "Ethical Issues in Behavior Control: A Preliminary Examination." *Man and Medicine* 2 (1976-1977): 1-40.

Delahunt, William D. "Biomedical Research: A View from the State Legislature." *Hastings Center Report* 6 (April 1976): 25-26.

Department of Health, Education and Welfare. "Protection of Human Subjects." Code of Federal Regulations (January 1978): 1-12.

Dickens, Bernard M. "Information for Consent in Human Experimentation." *University of Toronto Law Journal* (Autumn, 1974): 381-410.

———. "The Use of Children in Medical Experimentation." *Medico-Legal Journal* 43 (1975): 166-172.

———. "Contractual Aspects of Human Medical Experimentation." *University of Toronto Law Journal* 25 (Fall 1975): 406-438.

———. "What is a Medical Experiment?" *Canadian Medical Association Journal* 113 (October 1975): 635-639.

Donagan, Alan. "Informed Consent in Therapy and Experimentation." *Journal of Medicine and Philosophy* 2 (December 1977): 307-329.

Donovan, Patricia. "Sterilizing the Poor and Incompetent." *The Hastings Center Report* (October 1976): 6-7.

Dorn, Dean S., and Long, Gary L. "Brief Remarks on the Association's Code of Ethics." *The American Sociologist* 9 (February 1974): 31-35.

Duffy, John C. "Research with Children: The Rights of Children." *Child Psychiatry and Human Development* 4 (Winter 1973): 67-70.

Dukeminier, J., Jr. "Supplying Organs for Transplantation." *Michigan Law Review* 68 (1970): 811-866.

Dukeminier, J., Jr., with D. Sanders. "Organ Transplantation: A Proposal for Routine Salvaging of Cadaver Organs." *New England Journal of Medicine* 279 (August 22, 1968): 413-419.

Dworkin, Gerald. "Autonomy and Behavior Control." *Hastings Center Report* 6 (February 1976): 23-28.

Dyck, A. J., and Richardson, H. W. "The Moral Justification for Research Using Human Subjects." *Use of Human Subjects on Safety Evaluation of Food Chemicals*, Proceedings of a Conference of the National Academy of Sciences and National Research Council (1967): 229-247.

Dyer, Gary S. "Kidney Transplant—Mentally Incompetent Donor." *Missouri Law Review* 85 (Fall 1970): 538-544.

Elkinton, J. R. "Moral Problems in the Use of Borrowed Organs, Artificial and Transplanted." *Annals of Internal Medicine* 60 (1964): 309-313.

Emma, Lawrence. "Informed Consent and Human Experimentation." *North Carolina Central Law Journal* 5 (Spring 1974): 254-262.

Ervin, Frank. "Biological Intervention Technologies and Social Control." *American Behavioral Scientist* 18 (May-June 1975): 617-635.

Fay, Charles. "Behavior Control: A Moral Imperative." *Religious Humanism* 7 (Winter 1973): 26-28.

Feinberg, Irwin. "Behavior Control: Man's Concern." In *The Teaching of Medical Ethics*, edited by Robert M. Veatch, Willard Gaylin, and Morgan Councilman. Hastings-on-Hudson, N.Y.: Institute of Society, Ethics and the Life Sciences, 1973, pp. 129-132.

Fellner, Carl H. "Altruism in Disrepute." *New England Journal of Medicine* 284 (March 18, 1971): 582-585.

——. "Kidney Donors–the Myth of Informed Consent." *American Journal of Psychiatry* 126 (March 1970): 9.

——. "Selection of Living Kidney Donors and the Problem of Informed Consent." *Seminars in Psychiatry* 3 (February 1971): 79-85.

——. "Twelve Kidney Donors." *Journal of the American Medical Association* 206 (December 16, 1968): 2703.

Fishbein, Morns. "The Ethics of Biomedical Engineering." *Medical World News* 14 (October 1973): 80.

Fletcher, John C. "Dialogue between Medicine and Theology: Death and Transplantation." In *Should Doctors Play God?*, edited by Claude A. Frazier. Nashville: Broadman Press, 1971, pp. 150-163.

——. "Human Experimentation: Ethics in the Consent Situation." *Law and Contemporary Problems* 32 (1967): 620-649.

——. "Our Shameful Waste of Human Tissue." In *Updating Life and Death*, edited by Donald Cutler. Boston: Beacon Press, 1969, Chapter 1.

——. "Realities of Patient Consent to Medical Research." *Hastings Center Studies* 1 (No. 1, 1973): 39-49.

——. "Ethical Options in Fetal Research." *Clinical Research* 23 (October 1975): 217-222.

Frankel, Mark S. "The Development of Policy Guidelines Governing Human Experimentation in the United States: A Case Study of Public Policy-Making for Science and Technology." *Ethics in Science and Medicine* 2 (May 1975): 43-59.

Frederickson, Donald S., *et al.* "Human Experimentation." *Science* 188 (June 1975): 1062.

Freedman, Benjamin. "A Normal Theory of Informed Consent." *Hastings Center Report* 5 (August 1975): 32-39.

Freund, Paul A. "Ethical Problems in Human Experimentation." *New England Journal of Medicine* 273 (1965): 687-692.

Fried, Charles. "The Legal Context of Medical Experimentation." In his *Medical Experimentation: Personal Integrity and Social Policy*. New York: Elsevier, 1974, pp. 13-43.

Friedman, Paul R. "Legal Regulation of Applied Behavior Analysis in Mental Institutions and Prisons." *Arizona Law Review* 17 (1975):39-104.

Galdston, Iago. "The History of Research, with Particular Regard to Medical Research." *Ciba Symposium* 8 (1946): 338-372.

Galliher, John F. "The Protection of Human Subjects: A Reexamination of the Professional Code of Ethics." *The American Sociologist* 8 (August 1973): 93-100.

Garnham, J. C. "Some Observations on Informed Consent in Non-Therapeutic Research." *Journal of Medical Ethics* 1 (September 1975): 138-145.

Gaylin, Willard, and Blatte, Helen "Behavior Modification in Prisons." *American Criminal Law Review* 13 (Summer 1975): 11-35.

Gaylin, Willard, and Lappe, Marc. "Fetal Politics: The Debate on Experimenting with the Unborn." *Atlantic Monthly* 235 (May 1975): 66-71.

Goldiamond, Israel. "Singling Out Behavior Modification for Legal Regulations: Some Effects on Patient Care, Psychotherapy, and Research in General." *Arizona Law Review* 17 (1975): 105-126.

Grant, C. K. "Experiments on Human Beings." *Philosophy* 48 (July 1973): 284-287.

Gray, Bradford H. "An Assessment of Institutional Review Committees in Human Experimentation." *Medical Care* 13 (April 1975): 318-328.

Greenberg, Roger, *et al.* "The Psychological Evaluation of Patients for a Kidney Transplant and Hemodialysis Program." *American Journal of Psychiatry* 130 (March 1973): 274-277.

Grisez, Germain G. "Rational Ethics Says 'No.'" *Commonweal* 86 (April 14, 1967): 112-125.

Grundel, J. "Ethics of Organ Transplantation." In *Organ Transplantation Today*, edited by N. A. Mitchison, J. M. Greep, and J. C. M. Hattina Verschure. Amsterdam: Excerpta Medica Foundation, 1969.

Guttentag, O. E. "Ethical Problems in Human Experimentation." In *Ethical Issues in Medicine*, edited by E. Fuller Torrey. Boston: Little, Brown, 1968, pp. 195-226.

Hamburger, J., and Crosnier, J. "Moral and Ethical Problems in Transplantation." In *Human Transplantation*, edited by Felix T. Rapaport and Jean Dausset. New York: Grune & Stratton, 1968.

Havinghurst, C. C. "Compensating Persons Injured in Human Experimentation." *Science* 169 (July 10, 1969): 154.

Hofmann, Adele, and Pilpel, Harriet F. "The Legal Rights of Minors." *Pediatric Clinics of North America* 20 (November 1973): 989-1004.

Holder, Angela R. "Transplant Problems." *Journal of the American Medical Association* 223 (March 12, 1973): 1315-1316.

Hollander, Rachelle. "Patients' Rights Still Not Established." *Hastings Center Report* 6 (August 1976): 10-11.

Hollister, Leo E. "The Use of Psychiatric Patients as Experimental Subjects." In *Medical, Moral and Legal Issues in Mental Health Care*, edited by Frank J. Ayd. Baltimore: Williams & Wilkins, 1974, pp. 28-36.

Horowitz, Lawrence C. "The Issues as Viewed by the Legislature." *Clinical Research* 21 (October 1973): 782-784.

"Human Experimentation." *Medical World News* (June 8, 1973): 37-51.

Hussey, Hugh H. "Human Experimentation." *Journal of the American Medical Association* 226 (October 1973): 561.

Ingelfinger, F. J. "Ethics of Experiments on Children." *New England Journal of Medicine* 288 (April 1973): 791-792.

Jamali, Naseem A. "Compulsory Sterilization." *Hastings Center Report* 7 (April 1977): 4.

Jonas, Hans. "Philosophical Reflections on Experimenting with Human Subjects." In *Experimentation with Human Subjects*, edited by Paul A. Freund. New York: Braziller, 1970, pp. 1-31.

Jonas, Hans. "Freedom of Scientific Inquiry and the Public Interest." *Hastings Center Report* 6 (August 1976): 15-17.

Jonsen, Albert R. "The Totally Implantable Artificial Heart." *Hastings Center Report* 3 (November 1973): 1-4.

Kass, Leon R. "Babies by Means of *In Vitro* Fertilization: Unethical Experiments on the Unborn?" *New England Journal of Medicine* (November 1971): 1174-1179.

Kidd, Alexander M. "Limits of the Right of a Person to Consent to Experimentation on Himself." *Science* 117 (February 27, 1953): 211-212.

Kindregan, Charles P. "Fetal Research IV: The Living Fetus and the Law—the State's Role." *Human Life Review* 1 (Fall 1975): 133-144.

Klein, Marc. "Problems Arising from Biological Experimentation in Prisons." In *Medical Care of Prisoners and Detainees*, edited by G. E. W. Wolstenholme and Maeve O'Connor, New York: Elsevier, 1973, pp. 65-78.

Klerman, Gerald. "Behavior Control and the Limits of Reform." *Hastings Center Report* 5 (August 1975): 40-45.

Knutson, A. L. "Body Transplants and Ethical Values." *Social Science and Medicine* 2 (1968-1969): 393-414.

Ladimer, Irving, ed. "New Dimensions in Legal and Ethical Concepts for Human Research." *Annals of the New York Academy of Sciences* 169 (1970): 293-593.

Lasagna, Louis. "Some Ethical Problems in Clinical Investigation." In *Human Aspects of Biomedical Innovation*, edited by E. Mendelsohn, J. P. Swazey, and I. Taviss. Cambridge: Harvard University Press, 1971, pp. 98-111.

Leeper, E. M. "Fetal Research: Commission Sets Guidelines for Experimentation." *Bioscience* 25 (June 1975): 357-360.

Leonard, Martha F. "Does Research Stigmatize?" *Hastings Center Report* 6 (February 1976): 4, 37.

Levine, Carol. "Dialysis or Transplant: Values and Choices." *Hastings Center Report* 8 (April 1978): 8-11.

Levine, Robert J. "Symposium—Ethics of Human Experimentation." *Clinical Research* 21 (October 1973): 774-776.

———. "Guidelines for Negotiating Informed Consent with Prospective Subjects of Experimentation." *Clinical Research* 22 (February 1974): 42-46.

———. "Ethical Consideration in the Publication of the Results of Research Involving Human Subjects." *Clinical Research* 21 (October 1973): 763-767.

Liley, A. W. "Codes of Ethics in Research and Experimentation in Man." *Linacre Quarterly* 40 (February 1973): 34-43.

Mabe, Alan R. "Coerced Therapy, Social Protection, and Moral Autonomy." *American Behavioral Scientist* 18 (May-June, 1975): 599-616.

Macklin, Ruth, and Sherwin, Susan. "Experimenting on Human Subjects: Philosophical Perspectives." *Case Western Reserve Law Review* 25 (Spring 1975): 434-471.

Marston, Robert Q. "Medical Science, the Clinical Trail and Society." *Hastings Center Report* 3 (April 1973): 1-4.

Martin, Daniel, *et al.* "Human Subjects in Clinical Research—A Report of Three Studies." *New England Journal of Medicine* 279 (1968): 1426-1431.

Martin, Michael M. "Ethical Standards for Fetal Experimentation." *Fordham Law Review* 43 (March 1975): 547-570.

May, William E. "Experimenting on Human Subjects." *Linacre Quarterly* 41 (November 1974): 238-252.

McCormick, Richard A. "Experimentation in Children: Sharing in Sociality." *Hastings Center Report* 6 (December 1976): 41-46.

———. "Fetal Research, Morality, and Public Policy." *Hastings Center Report* 5 (June 1975): 26-31.

McCormick, Richard A., and Walters, LeRoy "Fetal Research and Public Policy." *America* 132 (June 1975): 473-476.

Milgram, Stanley. "Problems of Ethics in Research." In his *Obedience to Authority*. New York: Harper & Row, 1974, pp. 193-202.

———. "Subject Reaction: The Neglected Factor in the Ethics of Experimentation." *Hastings Center Report* 7 (October 1977): 19-24.

Mills, Michael, and Morris, Norval "Prisoners as Laboratory Animals." *Society* 11 (July-August 1974): 60-66.

Morison, Robert, and Twiss, Sumner B., Jr. "The Human Fetus as Useful Research Material." *Hastings Center Report* 3 (April 1973): 8-10.

Morris, Curtis R., *et al.* "Guidelines for Accepting Volunteers: Consent, Ethical Implications, and the Function of Peer Review." *Clinical Pharmacology and Therapeutics* 13 (September 1972): 782-802.

Morse, Howard N. "Legal Implications of Clinical Investigation." *Vanderbilt Law Review* 20 (1967): 747.

Munson, Judith W. "Fetal Research: A View from Right to Life to Wrongful Birth." *Chicago-Kent Law Review* 52 (1975): 133-156.

Nathan, David G. "Ethical Problems in Fetal Research." *Journal of General Education* 29 (Fall 1975): 165-175.

Nelson, James G. "Human Experimentation." In his *Human Medicine: Ethical Perspectives on New Medical Issues.* Minneapolis: Augsburg Publishing House, 1973, pp. 79-95.

Neville, Robert C., and Steinfels, Peter, commentators. "Case Studies in Bioethics: Blood Money: Should a Rich Nation Buy Plasma from the Poor?" *Hastings Center Report* 2 (December 1972): 8-10.

O'Rourke, Kevin D. "Fetal Experimentation: An Evaluation of the New Federal Norms." *Hospital Progress* 56 (September 1975): 60-69.

Ottenberg, Perry. "Dehumanization and Human Experimentation." In *Research and Psychiatric Patients*, edited by Joseph C. Schoolar and Charles M. Gaitz. New York: Brunner-Mazel, 1975, pp. 87-103.

Pappworth, M. H. "Ethical Issues in Experimental Medicine." In *Updating Life and Death*, edited by D. R. Cutler. Boston: Beacon Press, 1969, pp. 64-69.

Perlman, David. "A Layman's Look at Human Experimentation." *American Review of Respiratory Disease* 110 (October 1974): 387-389.

Perlman, Judy L. "Human Experimentation." *Journal of Legal Medicine* 2 (January-February 1974): 40-50.

Patten, Steven C. "The Case That Milgram Makes." *The Philosophical Review* (July 1977): 350-364.

Pilpel, Harriet F. "Minors' Rights to Medical Care." *Albany Law Review* 36 (1972): 462-487.

Powledge, Tabitha M. "Fetal Experimentation: Trying to Sort Out the Issues." *Hastings Center Report* 5 (April 1975): 8-10.

Prescott, James W. "Ethical Issues in Fetal Research." *Humanist* 35 (May-June 1975): 37-38.

Ramsey, Paul. "The Ethics of a Cottage Industry in an Age of Community and Research Medicine." *New England Journal of Medicine* 284 (April 1, 1971): 700-706.

———. "Children as Research Subjects: A Reply." *Hastings Center Report* 7 (April 1977): 40-41.

———. "The Enforcement of Morals: Nontherapeutic Research on Children." *Hastings Center Report* 6 (August 1976): 21-30.

Ratnoff, Marian F. "Who Shall Decide When Doctors Disagree? A Review of the Legal Development of Informed Consent and the Implications of Proposed Lay Review of Human Experimentation." *Case Western Reserve Law Review* 25 (Spring 1975): 472-532.

Reback, Gary. "Fetal Experimentation: Moral, Legal and Medical Implications." *Stanford Law Review* 26 (May 1974): 1191-1207.

Reed, James. "Knowledge, Power, Man and Justice: Ethical Problems in Biomedical Research." *Canadian Journal of Genetics and Cytology* 17 (September 1975): 297-304.

Rescher, Nicholas. "The Allocation of Exotic Medical Lifesaving Therapy." *Ethics* 79 (April 1969): 173-186.

Reynolds, Paul Davidson. "On the Protection of Human Subjects and Social Science." *International Social Science Journal* 24 (1972): 693-719.

Reynolds, Paul D. "The Protection of Human Subjects: An Open Letter to NIH." *American Sociologist* 9 (November 1974): 221-225.

———. "Value Dilemmas in the Professional Conduct of Social Science." *International Social Science Journal* 27 (1975): 563-612.

Riecken, Henry W., *et al.* "Human Values and Social Experimentation." In *Social Experimentation: A Method for Planning and Evaluating Social Intervention*, edited by Henry W. Riecken and Robert F. Boruch. New York: Academic Press, 1974, pp. 245-269.

Robertson, John. "Compensating Injured Research Subjects: II. The Law." *Hastings Center Report* 6 (December 1976): 29-31.

Rosner, Fred. "Modern Medicine, Religion, and Law: Human Experimentation." *New York State Journal of Medicine* 75 (April 1975): 758-764.

Roth, Russell. "The Dilemmas of Human Experimentation." *Modern Medicine* 43 (February 1975): 56-61.

Sadler, Alfred M., Jr., and Sadler, Blair L. "Transplantation and the Law: The Need for Organized Sensitivity." *Georgetown Law Review* 57 (1968): 5.

———. "Transplantation and the Law: Progress toward Uniformity." *New England Journal of Medicine* 282 (March 26, 1970): 717-723.

———. "Recent Developments in the Legal Aspects of Transplantation in the United States." *Transplantation Proceedings* 3 (March 1971): 293-297.

Sadler, Alfred M., Jr., Sadler, Blair L., and Stason, E. B. "The Uniform Anatomical Gift Act: A Model for Reform" *Journal of the American Medical Association* 206 (December 9, 1968): 2501-2506.

"Scarce Medical Resources." *Columbia Law Review* 69 (April 1969): 620-692.

Schmeck, Harold M. "Playing God: Necessary and Fearful." *The New York Times* 15 (July 1973): 6.

Schroeder, Oliver C. "Research on Human Subjects: The Developing Law." *Postgraduate Medicine* 54 (July 1973): 175-176+.

Schwartz, Herbert A. "Children's Concepts of Research Hospitalization." *New England Journal of Medicine* 287 (September 21, 1972): 589-592.

Schwitzgebel, Ralph K., Kolb, David A., and Gergen, Kenneth J. "Toward an Ethic for Research on Human Behavior." In *Changing Human Behavior:*

Principles of Planned Intervention, edited by Ralph K. Schwitzgebel and David A. Kolb, New York: McGraw-Hill, 1974, pp. 253-272.

Shapiro, Michael H. "Legislating the Control of Behavior Control: Autonomy and the Coercive Use of Organic Therapies." *Southern California Law Review* 47 (February 1974): 237-356.

Simonaitis, Joseph E. "Recent Decisions on Informed Consent." *Journal of the American Medical Association* 221 (July 24, 1972): 441-442.

——. "More about Informed Consent." *Journal of the American Medical Association* 224 (June 25, 1973): 1831-1832.

Smodish, Susan D. "Recent Legislation Prohibiting the Use of Prison Inmates as Subjects in Medical Research." *New England Journal on Prison Law* 1 (Fall 1974): 220-243.

Stetlen, De Witt. "Freedom of Inquiry." *Genetics* 81 (November 1975): 415-425.

Strauss, Maurice B. "Ethics of Experimental Therapeutics." *New England Journal of Medicine* 288 (May 1973): 1183-1184.

Strunk v. *Strunk*, Ky., 445 S. W. 2d. 145 (1969).

Surgenor, D., *et al.* "Blood Services: Prices and Public Policy." *Science* 180 (April 27, 1973): 384-389.

"The Ethics of Human Experimentation." *Science News* 107 (March 1975): 134-135.

Toole, James F. "Certain Aspects of Biomedical Research: Evolution of Concepts of Ethical Standards." *North Carolina Medical Journal* 35 (August 1974): 475-478.

Toulmin, Stephen. "Exploring the Moderate Consensus." *Hastings Center Report* 5 (June 1975): 31-40.

Travitzky, Daniel E. "Volunteering a Vacaville." *Hastings Center Report* 7 (February 1977): 13.

Veatch, Robert M. "Ethical Principles in Medical Experimentation." In *Ethical and Legal Issues of Social Experimentation*, edited by Alice M. Rivlin and Michael P. Timpane. Washington: Brookings Institution, 1975, pp. 21-78.

——. "Human Experimentation Committees: Professional or Representative?" *Hastings Center Report* 5 (October 1975): 31-40.

——. "Why Get Consent?" *Hospital Physician* 11 (December 1975): 30-31.

Veatch, Robert M., and Sollitto, Sharman. "Human Experimentation—The Ethical Questions Persist." *Hastings Center Report* 3 (June 1973): 1-3.

Wallwork, Ernest. "Ethical Issues in Research Involving Human Subjects." In *Human Rights and Psychological Research: A Debate on Psychology and Ethics*, edited by Eugene Kennedy. New York: Thomas Y. Crowell, 1975, pp. 69-81.

Walters, LeRoy. "Sterilizing the Retarded Child." *Hastings Center Report* 6 (April 1976): 13-16.

——. "Fetal Research and Ethical Issues." *Hastings Center Report* 5 (June 1975): 13-18.

Warwick, Donald. "Tearoom Trade: Means and Ends in Social Research." *Hastings Center Studies* 1 (1973): 27-38.

Wasserstrom, Richard. "The Status of the Fetus." *Hastings Center Report* 5 (June 1975): 18-22.

Wax, Murray L. "Fieldworker and Research Subjects: Who Needs Protection?" *Hastings Center Report* 7 (August 1977): 29-32.

Weinstein, Milton C. "Allocation of Subjects in Medical Experiments." *New England Journal of Medicine* 291 (December 1974): 1278-1285.

Wells, Stephen H., *et al.* "We Feel Free, But. . . ." *Journal of Current Social Issues* 12 (Fall 1975): 43-47.

Wexler, David B. "Behavior Modification and Legal Developments." *American Behavioral Scientist* 18 (May-June 1975): 679-684.

Wing, J. K. "The Ethics of Clinical Trials." *Journal of Medical Ethics* 1 (December 1975): 174-175.

Wolfenberger, Wolf. "Ethical Issues in Research with Human Subjects." *Science* 155 (1967): 47-51.

Wolpaw, Jonathan R., *et al.* "Ethics of Human Experimentation." *New England Journal of Medicine* 292 (February 1975): 320-322.

Zimbardo, Philip G. "On the Ethics of Investigation in Human Psychological Research: With Special Reference to the Stanford Prison Experiment." *Cognition* 2 (1973): 243-256.

PART IV:
HUMAN GENETICS

INTRODUCTION

This section deals with the unique moral and legal problems attending the acquisition and possible uses of genetic knowledge.

Tracy Sonneborne's opening essay, "Ethical Issues Arising from the Possible Uses of Genetic Knowledge," presents a panoramic view of the more pressing moral problems emerging from the uses of genetic information and raises very basic questions pertinent to the possibility of achieving moral agreement.

Probing the ethical issues of genetic counseling and prenatal diagnosis, Leon Kass's "Implications of Prenatal Diagnosis for the Human Right to Life" focuses on the moral problems centering on the abortion of the genetically defective fetus. Although sympathetic to the practice of abortion for reasons of severe genetic defect, the author argues that there are no reasons which can morally justify such a procedure without simultaneously justifying the killing of "defective" infants, children, and adults. Robert Morison, however, argues against this latter view in his "Implications of Prenatal Diagnosis for the Quality of, and Right to Human Life: Society as a Standard."

Turning from the more specific questions on abortion for reasons of severe genetic defect, Kurt Hirschhorn's paper, "Practical and Ethical Problems in Human Genetics," urges that the current methods of positive and negative eugenics cannot significantly improve the gene pool of the population and allow for adequate evolutionary improvement of the race.

In "Reproductive Rights and Genetic Disease" Lawrence Ulrich treats the question of whether or not a person's moral right to reproduce is subject to encroachment or repeal on the part of society. He argues that reproductive rights are not absolute and that those who are a high risk for passing on clearly identifiable severely deleterious genes and debilitating genetic disease should not be allowed to exercise their reproductive prerogative. The general reasoning behind this latter view is rejected by Thomas Beauchamp in his "On Justifications For Coercive Genetic Control."

The next two essays in the section deal extensively with the legal problems generated by current practice in genetic counseling and improvement. In "Legal Rights and Moral Rights" Alexander Capron argues, in part, that the genetic counselor has a clear legal duty to give competent advice so as to place parents in the position of informed decision-makers. If a counselor's negligence results in the birth of a defective child, parents and child alike have a valid claim for damages against him. The essay describes in detail not only current legal attitude and practice but also the problems the law will need to solve in order to have an effective legal code dealing with the rights of individuals in the face of current techniques and practice employed for the genetic improvement of the species. Pursuing the legal dimension further, Herbert Lub's paper "Privacy and Genetic Information," reexamines the concept of privacy and seeks to provoke thought about what test cases might be most suitable to clarify the issues of medical ethics in relation to human genetics. He also discusses what new laws may be desirable.

The final three articles in the section deal with the recent controversy over recombinant DNA research. John Madden begins the discussion by describing the experimental procedure and briefly outlining some of the potential hazards and rewards of such research. In the following essay Stephen Stich considers some of the arguments commonly used against recombinant DNA research, and after some discussion concludes that it would be unwise to impose a ban upon this form of experimentation. James Humber agrees with Stich's conclusion (although for reasons different from those cited by Stich), and then argues that the general public ought to have no voice in determining when and how safeguards should be employed in recombinant DNA research.

ETHICAL ISSUES ARISING FROM THE POSSIBLE USES OF GENETIC KNOWLEDGE

TRACY M. SONNEBORN

I realize that I am probably a fool to rush into the ethical domain where angels—the philosphers, ethicists, theologians, and lawyers—do not fear to tread. But these ethical problems concern us all, and not the least among us, the geneticists. I submit that after we listen carefully to what the professional theologians, ethicists, and philosophers have to say, as many of us have, then we, too, may speak up and tell about our own attempts to see our way through the difficult problems that beset us. This dialogue has now been going on with increasing frequency during the last eight years, and some of my fellow scientists have written and spoken very thoughtfully on the subject. They are not in complete agreement, but neither are the theologians, ethicists, and philosophers. I assume that the purpose of this conference is to encourage further communication between physicians and geneticists, on the one hand, and philosophers, theologians, ethicists, and lawyers on the other hand. Perhaps it is significant that a geneticist has been given the opening spot at the conference, but that lawyers and a historian will have the last words.

The present and potential uses of genetic knowledge and technology are, in a general way, widely known. They have been frequently presented to the public by the popular press and other mass communication media. So, I think it is not necessary for me to do more than recall them briefly. Most of the major ethical issues arise directly or indirectly from the genetic knowledge and correlated technologies that are concerned with human procreation. Genetic knowledge permits a degree of counseling to prospective parents in regard to the probabilities for the occurrence of certain traits among their future children. Perhaps the most spectacular technological advances along these lines have been those that

This paper originally appeared in *Ethical Issues in Human Genetics*, Bruce Hilton *et al.*, eds. (New York: Plenum Press, 1973). Reprinted with permission of the author and Plenum Publishing Corporation.

are useful in predicting characteristics of a developing baby a considerable time before it is due to be born. Certain abnormal genes and chromosomal conditions can be detected by this technology with virtually 100 percent accuracy. The number of conditions that can be predicted prenatally and the accuracy with which these predictions can be made is increasing every year. Many ethical issues arise in connection with the interrelations among the genetic counselor, the physician, the pregnant woman, and her spouse. These will doubtless be brought out in some of the later papers and discussions. But the major ethical issue is whether abortion is justified when the child is found to have defective or abnormal genes or chromosomes. In a beautiful and eminently humane paper known to many of us, Dr. Lejeune—who has been a pioneer and remains a leader in the field of human chromosomal abnormalities—has presented many reasons for doubting the justification of such induced abortions. Later I shall come back to this problem.

A second and very different set of ethical issues arises from the possibility of using for genetic purposes forms of procreation other than the normal one of sexual intercourse between husband and wife. Among these forms of procreation, only one is at present feasible; artificial insemination of the woman with sperm from a donor other than her husband. The other forms of procreation have been carried out with higher animals; although not yet possible in man, research toward this objective is in progress. One of them is fertilization outside of the body, using eggs from any female and sperm from any male; the fertilized egg, after proceeding to a very early developmental stage, is then implanted into the uterus of any properly prepared female. As Arno Motulsky vividly phrased it, this raises among other ethical problems the problem of "wombs for rent." The other form of procreation is to remove the nucleus from any female's egg and replace it by a nucleus obtained from a body cell of the same or any other individual. This, theoretically, should result in the development of an individual whose heredity is identical with that of the individual who provided the donor nucleus. As you are well aware, this is called cloning and can be used to produce as many genetically identical individuals as desired—not merely twins or triplets, but multiplets. Cloning has been subjected to searching ethical analysis by Kass, Ramsey, and others.

Finally, a third set of ethical issues is raised by genetic surgery, which lies still further in the future. Genetic surgery refers to anticipated possibilities of changing the genetic constitution of the reproductive cells in a person, or by changing it in the initial or very early stage of development of a new individual. Doubtless Dr. Sinsheimer will have much to say about this.

All of the possibilities mentioned, along with simple differential amounts of normal procreation by people with different genetic endowments, are components of a vision held in some quarters that foresees man consciously and purposefully guiding his own future evolution or, as some like to characterize it, trying to play God. Clearly the ethical issues that arise from these possibilities are among the most important that could be envisaged. They all deal with problems of life and death, with the character or quality of life, with the active interference of human beings in deciding who shall live and who shall die, and with what kinds of people shall live or die. These decisions could affect not only those now living and their children but our successors many generations hence.

These, then, are the major questions, problems, and ethical issues that have been and will continue to be discussed. Yet there is, I believe, a deeper and more encompassing question. The way we answer this question largely determines how we will answer all the others. It is a touchy and highly sensitive question, which is bound to annoy, anger, or infuriate many of us. Perhaps that is why it is so seldom put explicitly and clearly at the center of discussion where it really belongs, although answers to it are tacitly implied by our actions and the principles of action to which we adhere. It is, therefore, with fear and trembling that I put the question before you: Who or what decides what is right or good? By what authority? What do we really mean when we ask about anything—"Is it ethical?" In spite of not being a professional ethicist, I cannot avoid coming always to that central question. Do we assume that there are eternal verities—universal, self-evident, absolute truths about right and good human conduct? Do we assume that they have been transmitted to us from a supernatural divine authority via his mortal servants? Do we assume that knowledge of them is an inherent characteristic of man, knowledge that he can obtain by turning to his conscience? Or does ethics take a different form and have a different authority? If so, what? Or is ethics a chaotic no-man's land without authority of any kind?

The answers given by human beings to these central questions are by no means uniform. Some of us, though profoundly awed by the universe as we apprehend it, do not believe in a supernatural God and we reject divine authority for an ethical code. Nor can we accept the idea of an eternal, universal, absolute ethics imprinted in the conscience of man. We find in comparative religion, in anthropology, and in history the record of diverse ethical codes. We see them as man-made and variable from time to time, from culture to culture. We see them as codes of conduct authorized by common consent, or imposed to regulate particular social orders. Although, as Waddington and others have argued, man is an ethical animal and even an authority acceptor (as well as challenger), the particulars of his conceptions of right and good are varied and changeable. Even within one overall culture, different groups profess different ethical codes—for example, physicians, corporation executives, lawyers, congressmen, and presidents. It seems to me, therefore, that the authority for ethical decisions, for decisions as to what is right and good, comes from man himself, from his own choices, individually and in groups. The function then of conferences such as this is to debate what is right and what is good for man as part of the process of crystallizing individual and group choices which will become the authority for ethical decisions.

Viewing the general situation in this way, I should like now to apply this view to the ethical problems of life and death, of human procreation, that arises from present and potential uses of genetic knowledge. The first problem is abortion. Two opposed solutions to the problem are indicated by news reports. Superior Court Judge Jack G. Marks of Tucson, Arizona, is reported to have appointed a guardian of a nine-week old fetus on the ground that "the fetus has the rights of equal protection of this court." The suit was reported to have been filed by the Planned Parenthood Center of Tucson and by ten physicians in a challenge of the state's abortion laws. According to the papers, the suit claims that the mother of the fetus will probably not die if she gives birth to the child, but that she will be permanently injured. I have seen no mention of whether abnormality of the child is involved; presumably it is not. The issue that appears to be drawn is simply conformity to existing laws, based on the sanctity of life versus modification of the law to conform to changing public opinion about the range of applicability of the adversary principle.

The adversary principle has been recognized as valid even by the Judaeo-Christian tradition. Abortion is right if the choice is death of the fetus or death of the mother. Killing has also been justified—albeit regrettably—in self-defense against a life-threatening adversary, both at the level of the individual and, in the case of war, at the level of a nation. The ethical question at issue now is whether the adversary principle should be extended, in the case of a fetus, to situations in which the fetus is deemed to be an adversary against not necessarily the life, but merely the well-being of the parents or society. In the past, man's ethical judgments have changed on the basis of discussion and experience as new situations have arisen—as, for example, in the case of contraception when new methods were developed and new social conditions came into being. At first, argument centered about the right to prevent the initiation of a new life by interposing mechanical blocks between sperm and egg. After long and bitter battles agains the law and previous ethical judgments, the issue was in effect decided by widespread practice. More recently the pill, working on a different principle, has been widely accepted. The intrauterine device, which may operate on what amounts to very early abortion, is also accepted by many. Extension to somewhat later abortion is now at issue, as well as the question of how late.

The great numbers and heterogeneity of mankind, as well as the existence of many adventurous, nonconformist or simply desperate people, make it highly unlikely that new possibilities will be tried by some people regardless of how they stand in the light of current civil, moral, or sacred law. Some of these trials will fail to win general acceptance; others will succeed. Acceptance may at first be limited to special cases and later become more general and comprehensive.

Submission to the test of public opinion and practice is sometimes a slow method of change. But a slow pace, permitting time for testing and weighing, affords some protection against precipitous unwise choices. Individuals and society thus have ways of sanctioning uses of new knowledge and technology and, in fact, they do so even if these uses initially conflict with current legal, moral, and religious codes. If the new ethics are eventually judged to operate contrary to the good of man, readjustments can be made. We went through that reversal, for example, in the adoption and then repeal of Prohibition. The touchstone of man's choices, of his ethical choices, is simply his judgment of whether it is right and good for man. Man is the measure of all things.

This I believe to be the way that all of the ethical issues mentioned earlier—abortion, methods of procreation, guiding human evolution—will be decided. I doubt whether man's present choices will be guided by long-range considerations of human evolution, at least not by enough people to have an appreciable effect. Actually, however, that doesn't greatly matter. What does matter are the choices made in each generation with regard only to the procreation of the next generation. People greatly desire not to have defective or abnormal children. Because this hits home hard, I believe man will eventually decide that it is right and good to use for this purpose means offered by genetic knowledge and procreative technology, including the techniques of genetic surgery if and when they become available. I believe that man will, in short, adopt as ethical Bentley Glass' dictum that every child has the right to be free of genetic defect and abnormality insofar as this can be achieved. If people come to desire to have above-average or outstanding children, however defined, with anything like the strength of their desire to avoid having defective and abnormal children, they will find it as easy, or as difficult, to resolve the ethical problem in the one case as in the other, for the problems have much in common. The conscious guiding of human evolution would then be in progress simply by active concern for one's children, without looking further ahead; the guidance could continually adjust to changing conditions and new knowledge.

My thesis, then, is that man develops his ethics by the method of public discussion, by individual decisions and actions, by public acceptance of what appears to be right and good for man, and by rejection of what appears to be wrong or bad. We agree that it is right and good to reduce misery and improve the quality of life for all those who live, by using environmental and social means. We now debate whether it is right and good to use genetic means. Our conceptions of what is ethical, right, and good change in the light of new knowledge and new conditions. What we lack is neither flexibility of mind nor adventurous spirits, but knowledge and experience. If the future can be judged by the present and the past, we shall get that knowledge and experience and eventually authorize the ethics that permits doing what is believed to be right and good for man.

If I have glossed over the pitfalls and difficulties in the process of arriving at particular ethical judgments about specific details of the uses of genetic knowledge and technology, it is not because I am unaware of them. But this, I am happy to say, is not my assignment. These tough problems will occupy us during the next four days—and beyond.* As we approach that task, we have no basis for being cocky. We are still full of ignorance in spite of the spectacular increase of knowledge. It would be both unwise and inhumane to proceed without the utmost humility and compassion.

*All papers in this section, taken from *Ethical Issues in Human Genetics,* were part of a symposium sponsored by The John E. Fogarty International Center For Advanced Study in The Health Sciences and The Institute of Society, Ethics and the Life Sciences, October 10–14, 1971.

IMPLICATIONS OF PRENATAL DIAGNOSIS FOR THE HUMAN RIGHT TO LIFE

LEON R. KASS

It is especially fitting on this occasion to begin by acknowledging how pleased I am to be a participant in this symposium. I suspect that I am not alone among the assembled in considering myself fortunate to be here. For I was conceived after antibiotics yet before amniocentesis, late enough to have benefited from medicine's ability to prevent and control fatal infectious diseases, yet early enough to have escaped from medicine's ability to prevent me from living to suffer from my genetic diseases. To be sure, my genetic vices are, as far as I know them, rather modest, taken individually—myopia, asthma and other allergies, bilateral forefoot adduction, bowleggedness, loquaciousness, and pessimism, plus some four to eight as yet undiagnosed recessive lethal genes in the heterozygous condition—but, taken together, and if diagnosable prenatally, I might never have made it.

Just as I am happy to be here, so am I unhappy with what I shall have to say. Little did I realize when I first conceived the topic, "Implications of Prenatal Diagnosis for the Human Right to Life," what a painful and difficult labor it would lead to. More than once while this paper was gestating, I considered obtaining permission to abort it, on the grounds that, by prenatal diagnosis, I knew it to be defective. My lawyer told me that I was legally in the clear, but my conscience reminded me that I had made a commitment to deliver myself to this paper, flawed or not. Next time, I shall practice better contraception.

Any discussion of the ethical issues of genetic counseling and prenatal diagnosis is unavoidably haunted by a ghost called the morality of abortion. This ghost I shall not vex. More precisely, I shall not vex the reader by telling ghost stories. However, I would be neither surprised nor disappointed if my discussion

This paper originally appeared in *Ethical Issues in Human Genetics*, Bruce Hilton *et al.*, eds. (New York: Plenum Press, 1973). Reprinted with permission of the author and Plenum Publishing Corporation.

of an admittedly related matter, the ethics of aborting the genetically defective, summons that hovering spirit to the reader's mind. For the morality of abortion is a matter not easily laid to rest, recent efforts to do so notwithstanding. A vote by the legislature of the State of New York can indeed legitimatize the disposal of fetuses, but not of the moral questions. But though the questions remain, there is likely to be little new that can be said about them, and certainly not by me.

Yet before leaving the general question of abortion, let me pause to drop some anchors for the discussion that follows. Despite great differences of opinion both as to what to think and how to reason about abortion, nearly everyone agrees that abortion is a moral issue.[1] What does this mean? Formally it means that a woman seeking or refusing an abortion can expect to be asked to justify her action. And we can expect that she should be able to give reasons for her choice other than "I like it" or "I don't like it." Substantively, it means that, in the absence of good reasons for intervention, there is some presumption in favor of allowing the pregnancy to continue once it has begun. A common way of expressing this presumption is to say that "the fetus has a right to continued life."[2] In this context, disagreement concerning the moral permissibility of abortion concerns what rights (or interests or needs), and whose, override (take precedence over, or outweigh) this fetal "right." Even most of the "opponents" of abortion agree that the mother's right to live takes precedence, and that abortion to save her life is permissible, perhaps obligatory. Some believe that a woman's right to determine the number and spacing of her children takes precedence, while yet others argue that the need to curb population growth is, at least at this time overriding.

Hopefully, this brief analysis of what it means to say that abortion is a moral issue is sufficient to establish two points. First, that the fetus is a living

---

[1] This strikes me as by far the most important inference to be drawn from the fact that men in different times and cultures have answered the abortion question differently. Seen in this light, the differing and changing answers themselves suggest that it is a question not easily put under, at least not for very long.

[2] Other ways include: one should not do violence to living or growing things; life is sacred; respect nature; fetal life has value; refrain from taking innocent life; protect and preserve life. As some have pointed out, the terms chosen are of different weight, and would require reasons of different weight to tip the balance in favor of abortion. My choice of the "rights" terminlogy is not meant to beg the questions of whether such rights really exist, or of where they come from. However, the notion of a "fetal right to life" presents only a little more difficulty in this regard than does the notion of a "human right to life," since the former does not depend on a claim that the human fetus is already "human." In my sense of terms "right" and "life," we might even say that a dog or a fetal dog has a "right to life," and that it would be cruel and immoral for a man to go around performing abortions even on dogs for no good reason.

thing with some moral claim on us not to do it violence, and therefore, second, that justification must be given for destroying it.

Turning now from the general questions of the ethics of abortion, I wish to focus on the special ethical issues raised by the abortion of "defective" fetuses (so-called "abortion for fetal indications"). I shall consider only the cleanest cases, those cases where well-characterized genetic diseases are diagnosed with a high degree of certainty by means of amniocentesis, in order to sidestep the added moral dilemmas posed when the diagnosis is suspected or possible, but unconfirmed. However, many of the questions I shall discuss could also be raised about cases where genetic analysis gives only a statistical prediction about the genotype of the fetus, and also about cases where the defect has an infectious or chemical rather than a genetic cause (e.g., rubella, thalidomide).

My first and possibly most difficult task is to show that there is anything left to discuss once we have agreed not to discuss the morality of abortion in general. There is a sense in which abortion for genetic defect is, after abortion to save the life of the mother, perhaps the most defensible kind of abortion. Certainly, it is a serious and not a frivolous reason for abortion, defended by its proponents in sober and rational speech—unlike justifications based upon the false notion that a fetus is a mere part of a woman's body, to be used and abused at her pleasure. Standing behind genetic abortion are serious and well-intentioned people, with reasonable ends in view: the prevention of genetic diseases, the elimination of suffering in families, the preservation of precious financial and medical resources, the protection of our genetic heritage. No profiteers, no sex-ploiters, no racists. No arguments about the connection of abortion with promiscuity and licentiousness, no perjured testimony about the mental health of the mother, no arguments about the seriousness of the population problem. In short, clear objective data, a worthy cause, decent men and women. If abortion, what better reason for it?

Yet if genetic abortion is but a happily wagging tail on the dog of abortion, it is simultaneously the nose of a camel protruding under a rather different tent. Precisely because the quality of the fetus is central to the decision to abort, the practice of genetic abortion has implications which go beyond those raised by abortion in general. What may be at stake here is the belief in the radical moral equality of all human beings, the belief that all human beings possess equally and independent of merit certain fundamental rights, one among which is, of course, the right to life.

To be sure, the belief that fundamental human rights belong equally to all human beings has been but an ideal, never realized, often ignored, sometimes shamelessly. Yet is has been perhaps the most powerful moral idea at work in the world for at least two centuries. It is this idea and ideal that animates most of the current political and social criticism around the globe. It is ironic that we should acquire the power to detect and eliminate the genetically unequal at a time when we have finally succeeded in removing much of the stigma and disgrace previously attached to victims of congenital illness, in providing them with improved care and support, and in preventing, by means of education, feelings of guilt on the part of their parents. One might even wonder whether the development of aminocentesis and prenatal diagnosis may represent a backlash against these same humanitarian and egalitarian tendencies in the practice of medicine, which by helping to sustain to the age of reproduction persons with genetic disease has itself contributed to the increasing incidence of genetic disease, and with it, to increased pressures for genetic screening, genetic counseling, and genetic abortion.

No doubt our humanitarian and egalitarian principles and practices have caused us some new difficulties, but if we mean to weaken or turn our backs on them, we should do so consciously and thoughtfully. If, as I believe, the idea and practice of genetic abortion points in that direction, we should make ourselves aware of it. And if, as I believe, the way in which genetic abortion is described, discussed, and justified is perhaps of even greater consequence than its practice for our notions of human rights and of their equal possession by all human beings, we should pay special attention to questions of language and, in particular, to the question of justification. Before turning full attention to these matters, two points should be clarified.

First, my question "What decision, and why?" is to be distinguished from the question "Who decides, and why?" There is a tendency to blur this distinction and to discuss only the latter, and with it, the underlying question of private freedom versus public good. I will say nothing about this, since I am more interested in exploring what constitutes "good," both public and private. Accordingly, I would emphasize that the moral question—What decision and why?—does not disappear simply because the decision is left in the hands of each pregnant woman. It is the moral question she faces. I would add that the moral health of the community and of each of its members is as likely to be affected by the aggregate of purely private and voluntary decisions on genetic abortion as by a uniform policy imposed by statute. We physicians and scientists especially should refuse to finesse the moral question of genetic abortion and its implications and to take refuge behind the issue, "Who decides?" For it is we who are responsible for choosing to develop the technology of prenatal diagnosis, for informing and promoting this technology among the public, and for the actual counseling of patients.

Second, I wish to distinguish my discussion of what ought to be done from a descriptive account of what in fact is being done, and especially from a consideration of what I myself might do, faced with the difficult decision. I cannot know with certainty what I would think, feel, do, or want done, faced with the knowledge that my wife was carrying a child branded with Down's syndrome or Tay-Sachs disease. But an understanding of the issues is not advanced by personal anecdote or confession. We all know that what we and others actually do is often done out of weakness, rather than conviction. It is all too human to make an exception in one's own case (consider, e.g., the extra car, the "extra" child, income tax, the draft, the flight from the cities). For what it is worth, I confess to feeling more than a little sympathy with parents who choose abortions for severe genetic defect. Nevertheless, as I shall indicate later, in seeking for reasons to justify this practice, I can find none that are in themselves fully satisfactory and none that do not simultaneously justify the killing of "defective" infants, children, and adults. I am mindful that my arguments will fall far from the middle of the stream, yet I hope that the oarsmen of the flagship will pause and row more slowly, while we all consider whither we are going.

Genetic Abortion and the Living Defective

The practice of abortion of the genetically defective will no doubt affect our view of and our behavior toward those abnormals who escape the net of detection and abortion. A child with Down's syndrome or with hemophilia or with muscular dystrophy born at a time when most of his (potential) fellow sufferers were destroyed prenatally is liable to be looked upon by the community as one unfit to be alive, as a second-class (or even lower) human type. He may be seen as a person who need not have been, and who would not have been, if only someone had gotten to him in time.

The parents of such children are also likely to treat them differently, especially if the mother would have wished but failed to get an amniocentesis because of ignorance, poverty, or distance from the testing station, or if the prenatal diagnosis was in error. In such cases, parents are especially likely to resent the child. They may be disinclined to give it the kind of care they might have before the advent of amniocentesis and genetic abortion, rationalizing that a second-class specimen is not entitled to first-class treatment. If pressed to do so, say by physicians, the parents might refuse, and the courts may become involved. This has already begun to happen.

In Maryland, parents of a child with Down's syndrome refused permission to have the child operated on for an intestinal obstruction present at birth. The physicians and the hospital sought an injunction to require the parents to allow surgery. The judge ruled in favor of the parents, despite what I understand to be the weight of precedent to the contrary, on the grounds that the child was Mongoloid; that is, had the child been "normal," the decision would have gone the other way. Although the decision was not appealed to and hence not affirmed by a higher court, we can see through the prism of this case the possibility that the new powers of human genetics will strip the blindfold from the lady of justice and will make official the dangerous doctrine that some men are more equal than others.

The abnormal child may also feel resentful. A child with Down's syndrome or Tay-Sachs disease will probably never know or care, but what about a child with hemophilia or with Turner's syndrome? In the past decade, with medical knowledge and power over the prenatal child increasing and with parental authority over the postnatal child decreasing, we have seen the appearance of a new type of legal action, suits for wrongful life. Children have brought suit against their parents (and others) seeking to recover damages for physical and social handicaps inextricably tied to their birth (e.g., congenital deformities, congenital syphilis, illegitimacy). In some of the American cases, the courts have recognized the justice of the child's claim (that he was injured due to parental negligence), although they have so far refused to award damages, due to policy considerations. In other countries, e.g., in Germany, judgments with compensation have gone for the plaintiffs. With the spread of amniocentesis and genetic abortion, we can only expect such cases to increase. And here it will be the soft-heated rather than the hard-hearted judges who will establish the doctrine of second-class human beings, out of compassion for the mutants who escaped the traps set out for them.

It may be argued that I am dealing with a problem which, even if it is real, will affect very few people. It may be suggested that very few will escape the traps once we have set them properly and widely, once people are informed about aminocentesis, once the power to detect prenatally grows to its full capacity, and once our "superstitious" opposition to abortion dies out or is extirpated. But in order even to come close to this vision of success, amniocentesis will have to become part of every pregnancy—either by making it mandatory, like the test for syphilis, or by making it "routine medical practice," like the Pap smear. Leaving aside the other problems with universal amniocentesis, we could expect that the problem for the few who escape is likely to be even worse precisely because they will be few.

The point, however, should be generalized. How will we come to view and act toward the many "abnormals" that will remain among us—the retarded, the crippled, the senile, the deformed, and the true mutants—once we embark on a program to root out genetic abnormality? For it must be remembered that we shall always have abnormals—some who escape detection or whose disease is undetectable *in utero,* others as a result of new mutations, birth injuries, accidents, maltreatment, or disease—who will require our care and protection. The existence of "defectives" cannot be fully prevented, not even by totalitarian breeding and weeding programs. Is it not likely that our principle with respect to these people will change from "We try harder" to "Why accept second best?" The idea of "the unwanted because abnormal child" may become a self-fulfilling prophecy, whose consequences may be worse than those of the abnormality itself.

Genetic and Other Defectives

The mention of other abnormals points to a second danger of the practice of genetic abortion. Genetic abortion may come to be seen not so much as the prevention of genetic disease, but as the prevention of birth of defective or abnormal children—and, in a way, understandably so. For in the case of what other diseases does preventive medicine consist in the elimination of the patient-at-risk? Moreover, the very language used to discuss genetic disease leads us to the easy but wrong conclusion that the afflicted fetus or person is rather than has a disease. True, one is partly defined by his genotype, but only partly. A person is more than his disease. And yet we slide easily from the language of possession to the language of identity, from "He has hemophilia" to "He is a hemophiliac," from "She has diabetes" through "She is diabetic" to "She is a diabetic," from "The fetus had Down's syndrome" to "The fetus is a Down's." This way of speaking supports the belief that it is defective persons (or potential persons) that are being eliminated, rather than diseases.

If this is so, then it becomes simply accidental that the defect has a genetic cause. Surely, it is only because of the high regard for medicine and science, and for the accuracy of genetic diagnosis, that genotypic defectives are likely to be the first to go. But once the principle, "Defectives should not be born," is established, grounds other than cytological and biochemical may very well be sought. Even ignoring racialists and others equally misguided—of course, they cannot be ignored—we should know that there are social scientists, for example, who believe that one can predict with a high degree of accuracy how a child will turn out from a careful, systematic study of the socio-economic and psycho-dynamic environment into which he is born and in which he grows up. They might press for the prevention of socio-psychological disease, even of "crimi-nality," by means of prenatal environmental diagnosis and abortion. I have heard rumor that a crude, unscientific form of eliminating potential "phenotypic defectives" is already being practiced in some cities, in that submission to abortion is allegedly being made a condition for the receipt of welfare payments. "Defectives should not be born" is a principle without limits. We can ill afford to have it established.

Up to this point, I have been discussing the possible implications of the practices of genetic abortion for our belief in and adherence to the idea that, at least in fundamental human matters such as life and liberty, all men are to be considered as equals, that for these matters we should ignore as irrelevant the real qualitative differences amongst men, however important these differences may be for other purposes. Those who are concerned about abortion fear that the permissible time of eliminating the unwanted will be moved forward along the time continuum, against newborns, infants, and children. Similarly, I suggest that we should be concerned lest the attack on gross genetic inequality in fetuses be advanced along the continuum of quality and into the later stages of life.

I am not engaged in predicting the future; I am not saying that amniocentesis and genetic abortion will lead down the road to Nazi Germany. Rather, I am suggesting that the principles underlying genetic abortion simultaneously justify many further steps down that road. The point was very well made by Abraham Lincoln (1854)[3] :

> If A can prove, however conclusively, that he may, of right, enslave B—Why may not B snatch the same argument and prove equally, that he may enslave A?
>
> You say A is white, and B is black. It is color, then; the lighter having the right to enslave the darker? Take care. By this rule, you are to be slave to the first man you meet with a fairer skin than your own.
>
> You do not mean color exactly? You mean the whites are intellectually the superiors of the blacks, and, therefore have the right to enslave them? Take care again. By this rule, you are to be slave to the first man you meet with an intellect superior to your own.
>
> But, say you, it is a question of interest; and, if you can make it your interest, you have the right to enslave another. Very well. And if he can make it his interest, he has the right to enslave you.

Perhaps I have exaggerated the dangers; perhaps we will not abandon our inexplicable preference for generous humanitarianism over consistency. But we should indeed be cautious and move slowly as we give serious consideration to the question "What price the perfect baby?"[4]

Standards for Justifying Genetic Abortion

The rest of this paper deals with the problem of justification. What would constitute an adequate justification of the decision to abort a genetically defective fetus? Let me suggest the following formal characteristics, each of which still begs many questions. (1) The reasons given should be logically consistent, and should lead to relatively unambiguous guidelines—note that I do not say "rules"—for action in most cases. (2) The justification should make

[3] Lincoln, A. (1854). In *The Collected Works of Abraham Lincoln,* R. P. Basler, editor. New Brunswick, New Jersey, Rutgers University Press, Vol. II, p. 222.

[4] For a discussion of the possible biological rather than moral price of attempts to prevent the birth of defective children see Motulsky, A. G., G. R. Fraser, and J. Felsenstein (1971). In Symposium on Intrauterine Diagnosis, D. Bergsma, editor. *Birth Defects: Original Article Series,* Vol. 7, No. 5; Neel, J. (1972). In Early Diagnosis of Human Genetic Defects: *Scientific and Ethical Considerations,* M. Harris, editor. Washington, D.C. U.S. Government Printing Office, pp. 366–380.

evident to a reasonable person that the interest or need or right being served by abortion is sufficient to override the otherwise presumptive claim on us to protect and preserve the life of the fetus. (3) Hopefully, the justification would be such as to help provide intellectual support for drawing distinctions between acceptable and unacceptable kinds of genetic abortion and between genetic abortion itself and the further practices we would all find abhorrent. (4) The justification ought to be capable of generalization to all persons in identical circumstances. (5) The justification should not lead to different actions from month to month or from year to year. (6) The justification should be grounded on standards that can, both in principle and in fact, sustain and support our actions in the case of genetic abortion and our notions of human rights in general.

Though I would ask the reader to consider all these criteria, I shall focus primarily on the last. According to what standards can and should we judge a fetus with genetic abnormalities unfit to live, i.e., abortable? It seems to me that there are at least three dominant standards to which we are likely to repair.

The first is societal good. The needs and interests of society are often invoked to justify the practices of prenatal diagnosis and abortion of the genetically abnormal. The argument, full blown, runs something like this. Society has an interest in the genetic fitness of its members. It is foolish for society to squander its precious resources ministering to and caring for the unfit, especially for those who will never become "productive," or who will never in any way "benefit" society. Therefore, the interests of society are best served by the elimination of the genetically defective prior to their birth.

The societal standard is all too often reduced to its lowest common denominator: money. Thus one physician, claiming that he has "made a cost-benefit analysis of Tay-Sachs disease," notes that "the total cost of carrier detection, prenatal diagnosis and termination of at-risk pregnancies for all Jewish individuals in the United States under 30 who will marry is $5,730,281. If the program is set up to screen only one married partner, the cost is $3,122,695. The hospital costs for the 990 cases of Tay-Sachs disease these individuals would produce over a thirty-year period in the United States is $34,650,000.[5] Another physician, apparently less interested or able to make such a precise audit has written: "Cost-benefit analyses have been made for the total prospective detection and monitoring of Tay-Sachs disease, cystic fibrosis (when prenatal detection becomes available for cystric fibrosis) and other disorders, and in most cases, the expenditures for hospitalization and medical care far exceed the cost of prenatal detection in properly selected risk populations, followed by selective abortion." Yet a third physician has calculated that the costs to the state of caring for children with Down's syndrome is more than three times that of detecting and aborting them. (These authors all acknowledge the additional

[5] I assume this calculation ignores the possibilities of inflation, devaluation, and revolution.

non-societal "costs" of personal suffering, but insofar as they consider society, the costs are purely economic.)

There are many questions that can be raised about this approach. First, there are questions about the accuracy of the calculations. Not all the costs have been reckoned. The aborted defective child will be "replaced" by a "normal" child. In keeping the ledger, the "costs" to society of his care and maintenance cannot be ignored—costs of educating him, or removing his wastes and pollutions, not to mention the "costs" in non-replaceable natural resources that he consumes. Who is a greater drain on society's precious resources, the average inmate of a home for the retarded or the average graduate of Harvard College? I am not sure we know or can even find out. Then there are the costs of training the physician, and genetic counselors, equipping their laboratories, supporting their research, and sending them and us to conferences to worry about what they are doing. An accurate economic analysis seems to me to be impossible, even in principle. And even if it were possible, one could fall back on the words of that ordinary language philosopher, Andy Capp, who, when his wife said that she was getting really worried about the cost of living, replied: "Sweet 'eart, name me one person who wants t'stop livin' on account of the cost."

A second defect of the economic analysis is that there are matters of social importance that are not reducible to financial costs, and others that may not be quantifiable at all. How does one quantitate the costs of real and potential social conflict, either between children and parents, or between the community and the "deviants" who refuse amniocentesis and continue to bear abnormal children? Can one measure the effect of racial tensions of attempting to screen for and prevent the birth of children homozygous (or heterozygous) for sickle cell anemia? What numbers does one attach to any decreased willingness or ability to take care of the less fortunate, or to cope with difficult problems? And what about the "costs" of rising expectations? Will we become increasingly dissatisfied with anything short of the "optimum baby?" How does one quantify anxiety? humiliation? guilt? Finally, might not the medical profession pay an unmeasurable price if genetic abortion and other revoluntionary activities bring about changes in medical ethics and medical practice that lead to the further erosion of trust in the physician?

An appeal to social worthiness or usefulness is a less vulgar form of the standard of societal good. It is true that great social contributions are unlikely to be forthcoming from persons who suffer from most serious genetic diseases, especially since many of them die in childhood. Yet consider the following remarks of Pearl Buck[6] on the subject of being a mother of a child retarded from phenylketonuria:

[6] Buck, P. S. (1968). Foreward to *The Terrible Choice: The Abortion Dilemma*, New York, Bantam Books, pp. ix–xi.

My child's life has not been meaningless. She has indeed brought comfort and practical help to many people who are parents of retarded children or are themselves handicapped. True, she has done it through me, yet without her I would not have had the means of learning how to accept the inevitable sorrow, and how to make that acceptance useful to others. Would I be so heartless as to say that it has been worthwhile for my child to be born retarded? Certainly not, but I am saying that even though gravely retarded it has been worthwhile for her to have lived.

It can be summed up, perhaps, by saying that in this world, where cruelty prevails so many aspects of our life, I would not add the weight of choice to kill rather than to let live. A retarded child, a handicapped person, brings its own gift to life, even to the life of normal human beings. That gift is comprehended in the lessons of patience, understanding, and mercy, lessons which we all need to receive and to practice with one another, whatever we are.

The standard of potential social worthiness is little better in deciding about abortion in particular cases than is the standard of economic cost. To drive the point home, each of us might consider retrospectively whether he would have been willing to stand trial for his life while a fetus, pleading only his worth to society as he now can evaluate it. How many of us are not socially "defective" and with none of the excuses possible for a child with phenylketonuria? If there is to be human life at all, potential social worthiness cannot be its entitlement.

Finally, we should take note of the ambiguities in the very notion of societal good. Some use the term "society" to mean their own particular political community, others to mean the whole human race, and still others speak as if they mean both simultaneously, following that all-too-human belief that what is good for me and mine is good for mankind. Who knows what is genetically best for mankind, even with respect to Down's syndrome? I would submit that the genetic heritage of the human species is largely in the care of persons who do not live along the aminocentesis frontier. If we in the industrialized West wish to be really serious about the genetic future of the species, we would concentrate our attack on mutagenesis, and especially on our large contribution to the pool of environmental mutagens.

But even the more narrow use of society is ambiguous. Do we mean our "society" as it is today? Or do we mean our "society" as it ought to be? If the former, our standards will be ephemeral, for ours is a faddish "society." (By far the most worrisome feature of the changing attitudes on abortion is the suddenness with which they change.) Any such socially determined standards are likely to provide too precarious a foundation for decisions about genetic abortion, let alone for our notions of human rights. It we mean the latter, then we have transcended the societal standard, since the "good society" is not to be found in "society" itself, nor is it likely to be discovered by taking a vote. In sum, societal good as a standard for justifying genetic abortion seems to be unsatisfactory. It is hard to define in general, difficult to apply clearly to particular cases, susceptible to overreaching and abuse (hence, very dangerous), and not sufficient unto itself if considerations of the good community are held to be automatically implied.

A second major alternative is the standard of parental or familial good. Here the argument of justification might run as follows. Parents have a right to determine, according to their own wishes and based upon their own notions of what is good for them, the qualitative as well as the quantitative character of their families. If they believe that the birth of a seriously deformed child will be the cause of great sorrow and suffering to themselves and to their other children and a drain on their time and resources, then they may ethically decide to prevent the birth of such a child, even by abortion.

This argument I would expect to be more attractive to most people than the argument appealing to the good of society. For one thing, we are more likely to trust a person's conception of what is good for him than his notion of what is good for society. Also, the number of persons involved is small, making it seem less impossible to weigh all the relevant factors in determining the good of the family. Most powerfully, one can see and appreciate the possible harm done to healthy children if the parents are obliged to devote most of their energies to caring for the afflicted child.

Yet there are ambiguities and difficulties perhaps as great as with the standard of societal good. In the first place, it is not entirely clear what would be good for the other children. In a strong family, the experience with a suffering and dying child might help the healthy siblings learn to face and cope with adversity. Some have even speculated that the lack of experience with death and serious illness in our affluent young people is an important element in their difficulty in trying to find a way of life and in responding patiently yet steadily to the serious problems of our society[7]. I suspect that one cannot generalize. In some children and in some families, experience with suffering may be strengthening, and in others, disabling. My point here is that the matter is uncertain, and that parents deciding on this basis are as likely as not to be mistaken.

The family or parental standard, like the societal standard, is unavoidably elastic because "suffering" does not come in discontinuous units, and because parental wishes and desires know no limits. Both are utterly subjective, relative, and notoriously subject to change. Some parents claim that they could not tolerate having to raise a child of the undesired sex; I know of one case where the woman in the delivery room, on being informed that her child was a son, told the physician that she did not even wish to see it and that he should get rid of it. We may judge her attitude to be pathological, but even pathological suffering is suffering. Would such suffering justify aborting her normal male fetus?

[7] Cassell, E. (1969). *Death and the Physician, Commentary,* (June) pp. 73–79.

Or take the converse case of two parents, who for their own very peculiar reasons, wish to have an abnormal child, say a child who will suffer from the same disease as grandfather or a child whose arrested development would preclude the threat of adolescent rebellion and separation. Are these acceptable grounds for the abortion of "normals"?

Granted, such cases will be rare. But they serve to show the dangers inherent in talking about the parental right to determine, according to their wishes, the quality of their children. Indeed, the whole idea of parental rights with respect to children strikes me as problematic. It suggests that children are like property, that they exist for the parents. One need only look around to see some of the results of this notion of parenthood. The language of duties to children would be more in keeping with the heavy responsibility we bear in affirming the continuity of life with life and in trying to transmit what wisdom we have acquired to the next generation. Our children are not our children. Hopefully, reflection on these matters could lead to a greater appreciation of why it is people do and should have children. No better consequence can be hoped for from the advent of amniocentesis and other technologies for controlling human reproduction.

If one speaks of familial good in terms of parental duty, one could argue that parents have an obligation to do what they can to insure that their children are born healthy and sound. But this formulation transcends the limitation of parental wishes and desires. As in the case of the good society, the idea of "healthy and sound" requires an objective standard, a standard in reality. Hard as it may be to uncover it, this is what we are seeking. Nature as a standard is the third alternative.

The justification according to the natural standard might run like this. As a result of our knowledge of genetic diseases, we know that persons afflicted with certain diseases will never be capable of living the full life of a human being. Just as a non-necked giraffe could never live a giraffe's life, or a needle-less porcupine would not attain true "porcupine-hood," so a child or fetus with Tay-Sachs disease or Down's syndrome, for example, will never be truly human. They will never be able to care for themselves, nor have they even the potential for developing the distinctively human capacities for thought or self-consciousness. Nature herself has aborted many similar cases, and has provided for the early death of many who happen to get born. There is no reason to keep them alive; instead, we should prevent their birth by contraception or sterilization if possible, and abortion if necessary.

The advantages of this approach are clear. The standards are objective and in the fetus itself, thus avoiding the relativity and ambiguity in societal and parental good. The standard can be easily generalized to cover all such cases and will be resistant to the shifting sands of public opinion.

This standard, I would suggest, is the one which most physicians and genetic counselors appeal to in their heart of hearts, no matter what they say or do about letting the parents choose. Why else would they have developed genetic counseling and amniocentesis? Indeed, the notions of disease, of abnormal, of defective, make no sense at all in the absence of a natural norm of health. This norm is the foundation of the art of the physician and of the inquiry of the health scientist. Yet, as Motulsky and others have pointed out, the standard is elusive. Ironically, we are gaining increasing power to manipulate and control our own nature at a time in which we are increasingly confused about what is normal, healthy, and fit.

Although possibly acceptable in principle, the natural standard runs into problems in application when attempts are made to fix the boundary between potentially human and potentially not human. Professor Lejeune[8] has clearly demonstrated the difficulty, if not the impossibility, of setting clear molecular, cytological, or developmental signposts for this boundary. Attempts to induce signposts by considering the phenotypes of the worst cases is equally difficult. Which features would we take to be the most relevant in, say, Tay-Sachs disease, Lesch-Nyhan syndrome, Cri du chat, Down's syndrome? Certainly, severe mental retardation. But how "severe" is "severe"? As Abraham Lincoln and I argued earlier, mental retardation admits of degree. It too is relative. Moreover it is not clear that certain other defects and deformities might not equally foreclose the possibility of a truly or fully human life. What about blindness or deafness? Quadriplegia Asphasia? Several of these in combination? Not only does each kind of defect admit of a continuous scale of severity, but it also merges with other defects on a continuous scale of defectiveness. Where on this scale is the line to be drawn: after mental retardation? blindness? muscular dystrophy? cystic fibrosis? hemophilia diabetes? galactosemia? Turner's syndrome? XYY? club foot? Moreover, the identical two continuous scales—kind and severity—are found also among the living. In fact, it is the natural standard which may be the most dangerous one in that it leads most directly to the idea that there are second-class human beings and subhuman beings.

But the story is not complete. The very idea of nature is ambiguous. According to one view, the one I have been using, nature points to or implies a peak, a perfection. According to this view, human rights depend upon attaining the status of humanness. The fetus is only potential; it has no rights, according to this view. But all kinds of people fall short of the norm: children, idiots, some adults. This understanding of nature has been used to justify not only abortion and infanticide, but also slavery.

There is another notion of nature, less splendid, more humane and, though less able to sustain a notion of health, more acceptable to the findings of modern science. Animal nature is characterized by impulses of self-preservation and by

[8] Lejeune, J. (1970). *American Journal of Human Genetics, 22,* 121.

the capacity to feel pleasure and to suffer pain. Man and other animals are alike on this understanding of nature. And the right to life is ascribed to all such self-preserving and suffering creatures. Yet on this understanding of nature, the fetus—even a defective fetus—is not potential, but actual. The right to life belongs to him. But for this reason, this understanding of nature does not provide and may even deny what it is we are seeking, namely, a justification for genetic abortion, adequate unto itself, which does not simultaneously justify infanticide, homicide, and enslavement of the genetically abnormal.

There is a third understanding of nature, akin to the second, nature as sacrosanct, nature as created by a Creator. Indeed, to speak about this reminds us that there is a fourth possible standard of judgments about genetic abortion: the religious standard. I shall leave the discussion of this standard to those who are able to speak of it in better faith.

Now that I am at the end, the reader can better share my sense of frustration. I have failed to provide myself with a satisfactory intellectual and moral justification for the practice of genetic abortion. Perhaps others more able than I can supply one. Perhaps the pragmatists can persuade me that we should abandon the search for principled justification, that if we just trust people's situational decisions or their gut reactions, everything will turn out fine. Maybe they are right. But we should not forget the sage observation of Bertrand Russell: "Pragmatism is like a warm bath that heats up so imperceptibly that you don't know when to scream." I would add that before we submerge ourselves irrevocably in amniotic fluid, we take note of the connection to our own baths, into which we have started the hot water running.

IMPLICATIONS OF PRENATAL DIAGNOSIS FOR THE QUALITY OF, AND RIGHT TO, HUMAN LIFE

SOCIETY AS A STANDARD

ROBERT S. MORISON

My framework will be one, as Dr. Kass has already predicted, of a rather crass pragmatist. I have no expertise such as is represented by the other contributors, but I once had a fairly close association with public health. And since I was given the topic of talking about amniocentesis from the standpoint of the social standard, I have drawn a little bit on my past public health experience.

Actually, I want to ally myself with the ethical attitude which relies principally on a careful weighing of the probable practical consequences of a given choice of alternatives.

In doing this, I withdraw in horror from the tendency exhibited, I am sorry to say, by Dr. Kass and others to reduce this utilitarian procedure to a cheap matter of dollars, cents, and simple linear equations. It clearly is a much more complicated matter than that and involves judgment of all kinds of values, as Dr. Kass hinted as he went through this. But he would like you to remember that it is really dollars that we use, and I don't believe that is really the case.

I am also relatively unimpressed with the camel's head argument. I don't think that looking at an ethical viewpoint from the standpoint of "You do this and inevitably this terrible thing is going to happen later on" is an acceptable way of going about it.

I have noticed that principles, whatever their logical base, are valid only over a certain limited range; when pushed toward their limit, they tend to conflict with one another or become absurd. Even Oliver Wendell Holmes could not

---

This paper originally appeared in *Ethical Issues in Human Genetics,* Bruce Hilton *et al.,* eds. (New York: Plenum Press, 1973). Reprinted with permission of the author and Plenum Publishing Corporation.

extend the principle of free speech to those who falsely cried "fire" in a crowded theatre. Even the most concerned believers in the sanctity of life do not always equate the life of a four-day-old, yet-to-be-implanted egg with the life of a Mahatma Ghandi.

Again, I follow the view that modern ethical decision-making should be guided by moral policies rather than by principles. Policies are—and indeed usually should be—developed in relation to principles, but they need not be completely bound by them. Policies do not determine decisions by themselves. There must always be a decision-maker in the background, or a group of decision-makers.

Fortunately, the decision-makers in the abortion case are already in the process of being identified for us, and we need not spend time on this problem. A steadily increasing proportion of the developed world is deciding that the principal decision-maker should be the woman carrying the fetus—assisted, perhaps, by her physician. This primacy of the prospective mother cannot be based only or even primarily on the feminist assertion of the woman's right to do what she wants with her own body. As many people have pointed out here, the biological evidence is conclusively that a fetus is something quite different from a right hand or even an eye, which even the Bible urges as to extirpate or pluck out if they are offensive. I realize the Bible is equivocal on this point, and one can quote other passages against self-mutilation. The woman in the case, however much she would like to, cannot help participating as a trustee or guardian of the developing human being. The fact that the fetus is so primitive and so helpless, far from justifying a ruthlessly destructive attitude, should be added reason for compassionate concern.

It seems to me, therefore, that society, in its capacity as protector of the weak and moderator of differences between individuals, should not become indifferent to the welfare of the fetus or to the effect that the continuance or discontinuance of its life will have on the fabric of society as a whole.

The recent worldwide move towards liberalizing the abortion laws should not be construed as reflecting the belief that such laws have no constitutional standing. The change in attitude is so sweeping and so recent, especially in this country, that it is difficult to assess all the reasons that have influenced so many different people to change their minds—including me. But it appears that the majority finally concluded that the old rules were simply not working as acceptable policies.

One way of describing what we have done with our recent legislation is to say we have converted a matter of principle into a series of individual problems in situational ethics. This by no means implies, however, that society should relinquish all interest in the question. In place of the previous formal and legal restraints, it must find informal ways of impressing the decision-makers with the gravity of the situation in which they find themselves. And—here again, I think I agree with Kass—pointing out the numerous issues which must be weighed before arriving at a decision.

In reviewing the legislative history of the new arrangements, it appears that principal attention has centered on allowing the mother to base her decision on the effect of another child on her own health, on the welfare of the other children, and on the standard of living of the entire family unit. The particular qualities of the particular fetus to be destroyed were not at issue, in part because they seemed destined to remain unknown.

It may be worthwhile to pause and note that the presumptive unknownness of the individual characteristics of the fetus may have contributed to the lack of concern that some people have felt for the right of the fetus as an individual. As long as it remained in the darkness of the womb, it could be safely dismissed as in limbo, a subhuman entity, a thing rather than a person.

What amniocentesis may have done for us, among other things, is to make it clear that the fetus is an individual with definite, identifiable characteristics. In considering whether or not to abort a fetus because of certain such characteristics we don't happen to like, we recognize her or his individuality in a way we could avoid when we talked simply about the addition of any new member, or an essentially unknown "X," to the family circle.

However much considerations of personal identity will heighten our awareness of what we are doing and increase our sense of what I have called the gravity of the situation, I believe these considerations will not keep us from weighing the finding of amniocentesis in the balance when it comes to deciding on particular abortions.

This conference is based on the assumption that we will indeed use such findings, and I understand my task to be to discuss if and how the interests of society as a whole are to be taken into account.

I will, in fact, argue that society does have substantial interest in both the quantity and quality of the children to be born into its midst, and that it is already expressing an interest in the results of amniocentesis and in the way these findings are used in arriving at individual abortion decisions.

I should explain that I am using the word *society* in a flexible and—you may think—ambiguous way. Part of the time I am thinking of society as what the mathematicians refer to as a "set" or collection of individuals with needs, interests, and rights. More often I include with this notion the formal and informal organizations and institutions through which people express, satisfy, and protect their collective interests and rights.

Any suggestion that society may have some sort of stake in the proceedings may be greeted with the prediction that such ideas lead directly and immediately to the worst abuses of Nazi Germany. Let me say at once, then, that in trying to analyze the interest of society in unborn babies, I am not for a moment suggesting that legislation be passed forcing people to have abortions or to be surgically sterilized. If it turns out that society does have defensible interests in the number and condition of the infants to be born, it can express these interests in ways that fall far short of totalitarian compulsion.

It can, for example, facilitate or ban abortion. It can develop or not develop genetic counseling and contraceptive services. It may offer bounties or impose taxes on parents for having or not having children. Purists may object to such procedures as invasions of personal liberty, as perhaps they are, but they are the kind of invasions which all societies find necessary for survival.

No modern society could long endure without making it as easy as possible for parents to send children to school. But expressions of interest in individual education do not stop there. Most societies require that children be sent to school for some years under penalty of the law. In most countries the courts have the right to protect children from physical abuse, to order ordinary medical care in opposition to the parent's wishes, and even to remove them entirely from a family environment that appears to be inadequate.

Such protection and fostering of infants and children by the state can be explained wholly in terms of an obligation to protect the child's right to life, liberty, and the pursuit of happiness. But in point of fact, this is not the only consideration. Society is also protecting its own safety and welfare by ensuring that there will be maximal numbers of people capable of protecting the goods and services and composing the songs necessary for a good society. Note that "composing songs." It is not purely a matter of dollars and cents. We want people who are able to contribute at every level. At the same time, society is minimizing the number likely to become public charges or public enemies.

Similarly, the provision of maternal and child clinics and the requiring of vaccination against disease can be explained in part as an expression of society's interest in controlling the spread of disease to third parties, and in part by the desire to ensure that each individual citizen be as healthy as possible. Part of this concern is altruistic, but public health officials can also argue that such preventive measures help society avoid the cost of caring for the incapacitated and handicapped later on.

These social concerns about individual health are not limited to persons already born. They extend back to the period of pregnancy and fetal life. Perhaps one of the earliest legal expressions of society's concern for the unborn infant was the dramatic requirement by the ancient Romans that Cesarean section be performed on all woman who died while carrying a viable fetus. Less dramatic perhaps, but far more important quantitatively, are our present procedures for encouraging prospective mothers to eat the right foods, have their blood tested for syphilis and Rh antibodies, and even to give up smoking.

This concern for the unborn extends back into time before the new individual is even conceived. Mothers are urged to check their health and to undergo such procedures as vaccination against German measles before becoming pregnant. Vaccination of young women against German measles is now so fully accepted that we may overlook how sophisticated a procedure it really is. It is not proposed as a protection of the woman, herself, against what is usually a scarcely noticeable illness; its purpose is purely and simply that of protecting an unborn, unknown individual against a small but identifiable probability that it may be born with a congenital defect.

Perhaps the foregoing examples are sufficient to establish the following points:

1. Society has an interest in the welfare of children and fetuses.
2. This interest is recognized by the general public as legitimate, and various expressions of it have the sanction of tradition and current practice.
3. In several important cases, the interest is thought to justify not only the use of educational persuasion, but even the force of law to control or shape the behavior of mothers and prospective mothers.

It is highly probable that different people have different reasons for supporting these policies, and of course there is a minority which has reasons for opposing them. Some will talk of the right of the infant to be born healthy as a part of a more general right to health, which some enthusiasts regard as having been established by the World Health Organization shortly after the close of World War II. Other more utilitarian types will simply point out that the results for both mother and child are usually "better"—and that the cost to society is less.

Still others maintain that the Christian commandment to love everyone requires society to analyze all the angles in each particular case and that, by and large, love will be maximized if society takes an intelligent interest in the welfare of infants and fetuses.

The important thing to note is not the variety of reasons, but the general agreement on the conclusions. In a pluralistic society one must never lose sight of the fact that it is much more important that people agree on a policy rather than that they agree on the reasons for agreeing.

We must now move from this all too brief discussion of how society is currently expressing its interest in the yet-unborn, to how we can build on this experience to formulate policies to guide mothers and their counselors in adding the facts revealed by amniocentesis to all the other matters in the minds and hearts as they decide whether to continue or interrupt a pregnancy.

In the first place, I will assume that a prospective mother has a right to consider the specific characteristics of a specific fetus as she weighs the probable results of carrying a given pregnancy to term. If so, it follows that a society like ours has an obligation to provide, either through public or private means, facilities for amniocentesis in the same way as it customarily provides diagnostic facilities in other areas of medicine and public health.

So far, everything seems to be in accord with normal public health practice. But as we look a little further we encounter perplexities. The major difficulty is that the facts revealed by amniocentesis do not tell us what to do as clearly as many other laboratory tests do.

When a laboratory test reveals the presence of a streptococcus or a treponema, there is not much doubt in anyone's mind that the thing to do is to get rid of it.

When amniocentesis reveals a hereditary or a congenital defect, the situation is rather different. In the first place, the object to be got rid of is not a bacterium but an incipient human being. In the second place, it is not always immediately clear what the results will be if the defective fetus is allowed to go to term. Who is to say whether a child with Down's syndrome is more or less happy than the child with an IQ of 150 who spends the first 16 years of his life competing with his peers for admission to an ivy league college? Who is to assess the complex effects on parents of coping with a handicapped child?

Most troublesome is the recognition that the interest of the individuals directly concerned may be more often at variance with those of society than is the case in most public health procedures. For example, most public health officials have little difficulty in urging or even requiring people to be vaccinated, since the risk is very small and the benefits appear to accrue more or less equally to society and to the individual concerned.

The interests of parents and the interests of society in the birth of children, however, may often be quite at odds with one another. In some rapidly growing societies, for example, the birth of additional children of any description may be looked upon with dismay by society as a whole, however much the new citizens may be welcomed by their parents. In societies where the overall rate of growth is under better control, society may properly still have an interest in maximizing the proportion of new members who can at least take care of themselves, and if possible return some net benefit. Some parents, however, may long for any child to love and to cherish. They may regard any talk of social costs and benefits as shockingly utilitarian.

Even more difficult situations could arise when the prospective child may, himself, be quite normal, a joy to his parents, and a net asset to society—except for the fact that he is a heterozygous carrier of a serious defect who would, as a matter of fact, not have been started at all had the way not been made clear for him by aborting one or more homozygous siblings.

The more one thinks of these problems in abstract, philosophical terms, the more appalled he becomes, and this is one of the reasons for meetings like this. I am beginning to suspect, however, that the situation will turn out to be less serious in practice than it is in theory.

In the first place, it seems highly improbable that the wishes of parents and the interests of society will really be at odds in cases of severe defects like Down's syndrome or Tay-Sachs disease. In other words, if the parents' views are such that abortion is an acceptable option on general grounds, they are likely to exercise it for their own reasons in the kinds of cases in which carrying the fetus to term would also be most costly and least beneficial to society. In cases where the option is unacceptable to the individual for religious or similar reasons, society, under existing and generally agreed upon policies, has no business interfering anyway.

At the other end of the spectrum, relatively mild defects which may alter only slightly the subject's chances of becoming a useful citizen, like six fingers, may be safely left to the parents to decide without comment from outside since the social costs of either outcome are likely to be negligible. There may be a number of areas where family attitudes may be quite variable. It would seem unwise to emphasize the possible conflicts between individuals and society in these gray areas until we know a lot more about them.

Particularly troublesome, of course, are those genetic conditions in which the homozygotes suffer a severe disorder while the heterozygotes show little or no deficit. There may come a day when the question of what to do about such heterozygous fetuses may indeed involve ethical problems between the long-run interest of society in its gene pool and the short-run interest of the individual in family life. At present, however, the technical difficulties of identifying hetero-zygotes in many conditions and especially of evaluating the possibly unusual "fitness" of the latter may excuse us from taking any firm position which might breathe life into a latent conflict between individuals and society.

To point out that the number of potential conflicts is probably not so large as some people have feared is not to say that there is no problem. But the realization may be of some comfort to prudent men as they start to formulate policies.

It is also true that the above analysis depends very largely on the assumption that the general public knows as much about the disorders in question as the representatives of society do and that decisions will be arrived at more or less autonomously. This, of course, is not the case, as we are thus brought to the heart of the problem that worries many moralists and men of good will.

In most instances the facts revealed by amniocentesis must be interpreted to the prospective parents. In advanced countries these interpretative services are likely to be at least partially supported by society. How are we—and perhaps equally important, how is the counselor—to be sure that he is providing the interpretation in the best interests of the patient? Alternatively, how far is he justified in presenting the interests of society, especially if these may appear from some angles to be in conflict with those of the parents? These are indeed difficult questions. But I am not persuaded that they are so difficult as some people think they are.

Some commentators appear to feel that society is making an unjustifiable invasion of personal liberties if it undertakes to persuade an individual to make any decision in the reproductive sphere other than that suggested by his uninstructed instincts. The criticism is particularly severe if the proposed learning experience is coupled with rewards and penalties. It is hard to understand this squeamishness, since societies have been rewarding people from time immemorial for doing things which benefited society and even more enthusiastically penalized its citizens for actions against the public interest.

Even without this background, it is hard to see how offering a man a transistor radio if he refrains from having a child is interfering with his personal freedom. Indeed, one would ordinarily suppose that by increasing the number of options open to him, we increase rather than restrict his freedom. Furthermore, transistor radios may be looked upon primarily as educational devices, a way of making real to a not very sophisticated mind that children impose costs on society—and that society can in turn use its resources to benefit existing individuals if they cooperate in reducing the potential competition.

Again, this increase in understanding should be considered liberating rather than confining.

If society has a definable and legitimate interest in the number of children to be born, then it is clear that it also may have an interest in their quality. This is especially true in a period of sharply reduced birth and death rates. In an earlier day when both were high, normal attrition worked differentially to eliminate the unfit. A much smaller proportion of society's resources was devoted to keeping the unfit alive. Now, when a defective child may cost the society many thousands of dollars a year for a whole lifetime without returning any benefit, it would appear inevitable that society should do what it reasonably can to assure that those children who are born can lead normal and reasonably independent lives. It goes without saying that if the model couple is to be restricted to 2.1 children, it is also more important to them that all their children be normal than it was when an abnormal child was, in effect, diluted by a large number of normal siblings. And the over-all point here again is that the interests of society and the interests of the family become coincident at this stage, when they both realize that there are a limited number of slots to be filled.

That is really the situation that we are approaching in many countries. There is a limited number of slots that human beings can occupy, and there do seem to be both social and family reasons to see that those increasingly rare slots are occupied by people with the greatest possible potential for themselves and for others.

What then can society reasonably do to work with potential parents to insure as high quality a product as possible? It certainly can encourage and support the development of research in genetics and the physiology of fetal life. It can certainly support, in the same way, work on the technique of amniocentesis. It can make abortion available under appropriate auspices and regulations. Many societies are doing some or all of these things right now.

Our problem, if there is one, centers on what society can and should do in helping the individual mother to use the available information not only in her own best interests, but also in those of the society of which she is part. And the whole assumption here is that we are not going to require any behavior. We seem to be working toward a position which gives to the mother's physician or genetic counselor the greatest possible influence. Sometimes the two functions may be discharged by the same individual. In either case, the relationship is a professional one, with the individuals giving the advice owing primary responsibility to their patient or client. I think all of us with medical training feel our first obligation in any such situation is to the patient before us.

Just what the amniocentesis counselor will say to a given client is likely to remain a professional matter, biased in favor of the client when her interests and those of society conflict. On the other hand, there seems no good reason to discourage the advisor from pointing out to the client what the interests of society are. Indeed, there seem to be several good reasons for encouraging him to do so.

In the first place it seems proper, even if it is not always precisely true, to assume that the client wishes to be a good citizen as well as a good parent. Thus, it is in some sense an insult to her intelligence and good will to withhold information about social repercussions on the grounds that such advice might curtail her Anglo-Saxon freedom to act ignorantly in her own selfish interest.

It may also be remembered that every professional man is an officer of society—although I realize not everybody agrees with this—as well as an individual counselor. True, most lawyers, clergymen, and physicians like to think of themselves as owing a paramount obligation to their patients, clients, and parishioners. But the clergyman has at least a nominal interest in the deity, the lawyer in justice, and the physician in the health of the community.

Fortunately, in medicine at least, the welfare of the patient usually coincides reasonably closely with the welfare of society. But there are well-known cases of conflicts in which the physician is supposed to act in the best interest of society even at some cost to his patients, and sometime he does.

Thus, the conscientious physician reports his cases of veneral infection and T.B. in order to protect society, even at the risk of embarrassment and inconvenience to the patient. In a similar vein he urges his epileptic patients and those with seriously defective vision not to drive automobiles. These and other examples provide ample precedent for injecting the interests of society into a counseling situation.

I hope it is obvious that when he does so, the counselor will wish to make clear exactly what he is doing and why. It would of course be totally inadmissible for a professional counselor of any kind to deceive his patient or client, in order to gain what he thinks of as a socially desirable end.

We have heard of cases where it may be necessary to deceive a patient for his own good (or what is thought to be his own good), but I don't think any of us would countenance deceiving a patient for society's good.

On the other hand, it would be almost equally reprehensible to conceal the long-term effects on the gene pool of substituting a heterozygous carrier for a homozygote of limited life expectancy, or to fail to mention social dislocations which might follow from a decision to use abortion as a method of sex determination.

In summary, the position I have described is a simple and straightforward one. Many people are likely to feel it is too simple. It is based on the fact that society has placed or is in the process of placing the burden of decision as to whether or not to have an abortion in the hands of the woman carrying the fetus.

It accepts the proposition that in arriving at that decision, she will be allowed to add to a number of already stated considerations, evidence on the probable characteristics of the child.

It does not accept the inference that society no longer has interest in the matter simply because it has released the formal decision-making power.

It suggests that the best way of expressing its interest is through the counselor-physician, who in effect has a dual responsibility to the individual whom he serves and to the society of which he and she are parts.

Finally, it holds out the hope that instances in which the interest of the individual woman are clearly seen to conflict with the interests of society will be less numerous than might be feared.

In review, I find that I must add one point. Just as I believe there are no simple principles which take precedence over all others, I believe that everything one does affects everything else. We are now all so interdependent that there are no such things as purely private acts.

There is danger that the present effort to make abortion a crime without a victim will obscure the seriousness of all such decisions.

As Dr. Kass has pointed out, we will all certainly be diminished as human beings, if not in great moral peril, if we allow ourselves to accept abortion for what are essentially trivial reasons. On the other hand we will, I fear, be in equal danger if we don't accept abortion as one means of ensuring that both the quantity and quality of the human race are kept within reasonable limits.

PRACTICAL AND ETHICAL
PROBLEMS IN HUMAN GENETICS

KURT HIRSCHHORN

The past 20 years, and more particularly, the past five or ten years have seen an exponential growth of scientific technology. The chemical structure of the hereditary material, as well as its language, have essentially been resolved. Cells can be routinely grown in test tubes by tissue culture technics. The exact biochemical mechanisms of many hereditary disorders have become clarified. Computer programs for genetic analysis are in common use. All of these advances and many others have inevitably led to discussions and suggestions for the modification of human heredity, both in individuals and in populations. This has been called genetic engineering. Among the many recent articles on this subject three of the most challenging are by the Nobel Prize winning geneticist Joshua Lederberg,(1) by the world's leading experts on evolution, Theodosius Dobzhansky,(2) and by Bernard Davis.(3)

One of the principal concerns of the pioneers in the field is the problem of the human genetic load, that is, the frequency of disadvantageous genes in the population. It is well established that each of us carries between three and eight genes which, if present in double dose in the offspring of two carriers of identical genes, would lead to severe genetic abnormality or even to death of the affected individual before or after birth. In view of the rapid medical advances in the treatment of such diseases, it is likely that affected individuals will be able to reproduce more frequently than in the past. Therefore, instead of a loss of genes due to death or sterility of the abnormal, the mutant gene will be transmitted to future generations in a slowly but steadily increasing frequency. This is leading the pessimists to predict that we will become a race of genetic cripples requiring a host of therapeutic crutches.

The optimists, on the other hand, have great faith that the forces of natural evolution will continue to select favorably those individuals who are best

This paper originally appeared in *Advances in Human Genetics and Their Impact on Society,* Birth Defects Original Article Series, D. Bergsma (ed.) Vol. VIII, No. 4, White Plains: The National Foundation, 1972, pp. 17–30. Reprinted with permission of the author and The National Foundation.

adapted to the then current environment. It is important to remember in this context that the "natural" environment necessarily includes man-made changes in the medical, technical, and social spheres. Since it appears that at least some of the aspects of evolution and a great deal of genetic planning will be in human and specifically in scientific hands, it is crucial at this relatively early stage to consider the ethical implications of these proposed maneuvers. Few scientists today doubt the feasibility of at least some forms of genetic engineering, and there is considerable danger that common use of this practice will be upon us before its ethical applications are defined.

While examining the various possibilities for genetic engineering, it will be useful to keep in mind the concepts of freedom and coercion as they may apply to the various technics. For the purpose of this paper, freedom is defined primarily as the right to make a decision with full knowledge of all available data. This definition of freedom must, however, be somehow limited so that the decisions do not impinge upon the immediate needs of or benefits to other individuals and the general population. Coercion is defined as a direct, indirect, or subliminal attempt to influence the decision of one or more individuals for an assumed, but unproved, benefit of other individuals or the general population, or secondary to a conscious bias of the counselor.

It must be recognized that these concepts apply to three groups of individuals, each quite different in their objectives and interests. The first, consisting of individuals and families, is primarily concerned with their own and their children's welfare. How open-ended is their freedom of decision to be, when the result may or will have harmful social consequences, such as the birth of a child who will remain totally dependent on society? Should society or how could society control organized voluntary practices by groups of individuals, practices known or believed to be detrimental to the genetic well-being of society, such as widespread inbreeding?

The second group, consisting of research scientists and genetic counselors, poses perhaps even greater problems of definition of limitation of freedom and coercion. How free should the investigator be in pursuing certain lines of investigation? If widespread use of some technics, eg., the utilization of frozen sperm banks, is assumed to have long-term detrimental effects, should a group be allowed to implement these on a more limited basis? Is governmental regulation required or should scientists regulate themselves? How can one (or should one) limit scientific investigation which could result in potentially harmful technics? Does the genetic counselor have the right to persuade families, to direct (or coerce) their decision, in even an obviously beneficial manner, or should he be restricted in simply presenting all the data and alternatives?

The third group is society itself or its governmental representatives. Do public authorities have the freedom to intervene, either by establishing laws or through regulatory agencies in the field of genetics, by limiting the scope of decisions by individuals and by regulating the limits of research or its applications?

I do not propose to answer these questions, but simply raise them as a background for consideration while examining the various technics suggested for genetic intervention. It is obvious that conflicts arise in the answers to these questions, when considering limitations imposed on individuals as against society.

A number of individually quite different methods have been proposed for the control and modification of human hereditary material. Some of these methods are meant to work on the population level, some on the family level and others directly on the affected individual. Interest in the alteration of the genetic pool of human populations originated shortly after the time of Mendel and Darwin in the latter part of the 19th century. The leaders were the English group of eugenicists headed by Galton. *Eugenics* is nothing more than planned breeding designed to alter the genetic makeup of future generations. This technic, of course, has been successfully used by the agricultural community in the development of hybrid breeds of cattle, corn, and numerous other food products.

Human eugenics can be divided into *positive eugenics* and *negative eugenics. Positive eugenics* is the preferential breeding of so-called superior individuals in order to improve the genetic stock of the human race. The most famous of the many proponents of positive eugenics was the late Nobel Prize winner Herman J. Muller. It was his suggestion that sperm banks be established from a relatively small number of donors, chosen by some appropriate panel, and that this frozen sperm remain in storage until some future panel had decided that the chosen donors truly represented desirable genetic studs. If the decision is favorable, a relatively large number of women would be inseminated with these samples of sperm, and it is hoped by the proponents of this method that a better world would result. The qualifications for such a donor would include high intellectual achievement and a socially desirable personality, qualities assumed to be affected by the genetic makeup of the individual, as well as an absence of obvious genetically determined physical anomalies.

A much more common effort is in the application of *negative eugenics*. This is defined as the discouragement of the legal prohibition of reproduction by individuals carrying genes leading to disease or disability. This can be achieved by genetic counseling or by sterilization, either on a voluntary or enforced basis. There are, however, quite divergent opinions as to which genetic traits are to be considered sufficiently disadvantageous to warrant the application of negative eugenics.

A diametrically opposite solution is that of *euthenics,* which is a modification of the environment in such a way as to allow the genetically abnormal individual to develop normally and to live a relatively normal life. Euthenics can be applied both medically and socially. The prescription of glasses for near-sighted individuals so that they may live normally in our automotive world is an example of medical euthenics. The provision of special schools for the deaf, a great proportion of whom are genetically abnormal, is an example of social euthenics. The humanitarianism of such efforts is obvious, but it is exactly these types of activities that have led to the concern of the pessimists who assume that evolution has selected for the best of possible variations in man and that further accumulations of genes considered abnormal can only lead to decline.

One of the most talked-about advances for the future is the possibility of altering an individual's genetic complement. Since we are well on the way to understanding the genetic code, as well as to deciphering it, it is suggested that we can alter it. This code is written in a language of 64 letters, each being determined by a special arrangement of three out of four possible nucleotide bases. A chain of these bases is called deoxyribonucleic acid or DNA and makes up the genetic material of the chromosomes. If the altered letter responsible for an abnormal gene can be located, for example in a fertilized egg, and the appropriate nucleotide base substituted, the correct message would again produce its normal product, which would be either a structurally or enzymologically functional protein. Another method of providing a proper gene, or code word, to an individual having a defect has been suggested from an analysis of viral behavior in bacteria. It has long been known that certain types of viruses can carry genetic information from one bacterium to another or instruct a bacterium carrying it to produce what is essentially a viral product. Viruses are functional only when they live in a host cell. They use the host's genetic machinery to translate their own genetic codes. Viruses living parasitically in human cells can cause diseases such a poliomyelitis and have been implicated in the causation of tumors. Other viruses have been shown to live in cells and be reproduced along with the cells without causing damage either to the cell or to the organism. If such a harmless virus either produces a protein that will serve the function of one lacking in an affected individual or if it can be made to carry the genetic material required for such functions into the cells of the affected individual, it could permanently cure the disease without additional therapy. If carried on to the next generation, it could even modify the inheritance of the disease.

An even more radical approach has been outlined by Lederberg.(1) It has become possible to transplant whole nuclei, the structures which carry the DNA, from one cell to another. It has become easy to grow cells from various tissues of any individual in tissue culture. Such tissue cultures can be examined for a variety of genetic markers and thereby screened for evidence of new mutations. Lederberg suggests that it would be possible to use nuclei from such cells derived from known human individuals, again with favorable genetic traits, for the asexual human reproduction of replicas of the individuals whose nuclei are being used. For example, a nucleus from a cell of the chosen individual could be transplanted into a human egg whose own nucleus has been removed. This egg, implanted into a womb, could then divide just like a normal fertilized egg to produce an individual genetically identical to the one whose nucleus was used. One of the proposed advantages of such a method would be that, as in positive eugenics, one could choose the traits that appear to be favorable, and one could do this with greater efficiency since one eliminates the somewhat randomly chosen female parent necessary for the sperm bank approach. Another advantage is that one can mimic what has developed in plants as a system for the preservation of genetic stability over limited periods of time. Many plants reproduce intermittently by such parthenogenetic mechanisms, always followed by periods of sexual reproduction which results in elimination of disadvantageous mutants and increase in variability.

Another possibility derives from two other technologic advances. Tissue typing, similar to blood typing, and some immunologic tricks have made it possible to transplant cells, tissues, and organs from one individual to another with reasonably long-term success. Over the past few years scientists have also succeeded in producing hybrid cells containing some of the genetic material from each of two cell types either from two different species or two different individuals from the same species. Recently Weiss and Green(4) at New York University have succeeded in hybridizing normal human cultured cells with cells from a long-established mouse tissue culture line. Different products from such fusions contain varying numbers of human chromosomes and, therefore, varying amounts of human genes. If such hybrids can be produced which carry primarily that genetic information which is lacking or abnormal in an affected individual, transplantation of these cultured cells into the individual may produce a correction of his defect.

These are the proposed methods. It is now fair to address oneself to the question of feasibility. Feasibility must be considered not only from a technical point of view; of equal importance are the effects of each of these methods on the evolution of the human population and the effect of evolution upon the efficacy of the method. It should also be remembered that adverse effects on evolution raise the question whether freedom alone is sufficient reason for attempting some of these technics. In general, it can be stated that most of the proposed methods either are now or will in the not too distant future be technically possible. We are, therefore, not dealing with hypothesis or science fiction but with scientific reality. Let us consider each of the propositions independently.

Positive eugenics by means of artificial insemination from sperm banks has been practiced successfully in cattle for many years. Artificial insemination in man is an everyday occurrence. But what are some of its effects? There is now ample evidence in many species, including man, of the advantages for the population in terms of individual genetic variation, mainly flexibility of adaptation to a changing environment. Changes in environment can produce drastic effects on some individuals, but a population which contains many genetic variations of that set of genes affected by the particular environmental change, will contain numerous individuals who can adapt. There is also good evidence that individuals who carry two different forms of the same gene, that is, are heterozygous, appear to have an advantage. This is even true if that gene in double dose, that is, in the homozygous state, produces a severe disease. For example, individuals homozygous for the gene coding for sickle-cell hemoglobin invariably develop sickle-cell anemia which is generally fatal before the reproductive years. Heterozygotes for the gene are, however, protected more than normals from the effects of the most malignant form of malaria. It has been shown that women who carry the gene in single dose have a higher fertility in malarial areas than do normals. This effect is well known to agricultural geneticists and is referred to as hybrid vigor. Fertilization of many women by sperm from few men will have an adverse effect on both of these advantages of genetic variability since the population will tend to be more and more alike in their genetic characteristics. Also, selection for a few genetically advantageous factors will carry with it selection for a host of other genes present in high numbers in the population. Therefore, the interaction between positive eugenics and evolution makes this method not desirable on its own, and raises the question of the need for limitation upon individual, or even collective freedom to engage in such efforts.

Negative eugenics is, of course, currently practiced by most human geneticists. It is possible to detect carriers of many genes, which when inherited from both parents will produce abnormal offspring. Parents, both of whom carry such a gene, can be told that they have a one in four chance of producing such an abnormal child. Individuals who carry chromosomal translocations are informed that they have a high risk of producing offspring with congenital malformations and mental retardation. But how far can one carry out such a program? Some states have laws prescribing the sterilization of individuals who are mentally retarded to a certain degree. These laws are frequently based on false information regarding the heredity of the condition. The marriage of people with reduced intelligence is forbidden in some localities, again without adequate genetic information. While the effects of negative eugenics may be quite desirable in individual families with a high risk of known hereditary disease, it is important to examine its effects on the general population. These effects must be looked at individually for conditions determined by genes that express themselves in single dose (dominant), in double dose (recessive) and those which are due to an interaction of many genes (polygenic inheritance). With a few exceptions, dominant diseases are rare and interfere severely with reproductive ability. They are generally maintained in the population by new mutations.

Therefore, there is either no need or essentially no need for discouraging these individuals from reproduction. Any discouragement, if applicable, will be useful only within that family but not have any significance for the general population. One possible exception is the severe neurologic disorder, Huntington's chorea, which does not express itself until most of the patient's children are already born. In such a situation it may be useful to advise the child of an effected individual that he has a 50% chance of developing the disease and a 25% chance of any of his children being affected. Negative eugenics in such a case would at least keep the gene frequency at the level usually maintained by new mutations.

The story is quite different for recessive conditions. Although detection of the clinically normal carriers of these genes is currently possible only for a moderate number of diseases, the technics are rapidly developing whereby most of these conditions can be diagnosed even if the gene is present only in single dose and will not cause the disease. Again, with any particular married couple it would be possible to advise them that they are both carriers of the gene and that any child of theirs would have a 25% chance of being affected. However, any attempt to decrease the gene frequency of these common genetic disorders in the population by prevention of fertility of all carriers would be doomed to failure. First, we will carry between three and eight of these genes in a single dose. Secondly, for many of these conditions, the frequency of carriers in the population is about 1 in 50 or even greater. Prevention of fertility for even one of these disorders would stop a sizable proportion of the population from reproducing and for all of these disorders would prevent the passing on to future generations of a great number of favorable genes and would, therefore, interfere with the selective aspects of evolution which can only function to improve the population within a changing environment by selecting from a gene pool containing enormous variability. It has now been shown that in fact no two individuals, with the exception of identical twins, are likely to be genetically and biochemically identical, thereby allowing the greatest possible adaptation to changing environment and the most efficient selection of the fittest.

The most complex problem is that of negative eugenics for traits determined by polygenic inheritance. Characteristics inherited in this manner include many measurements that are distributed over a wide range throughout the population, such as height, birthweight, and possibly intelligence. The latter of these can serve as a good example of the problems encountered. Severe mental retardation in a child is not infrequently associated with perfectly normal intelligence or in some cases even superior intelligence in the parents. These cases can, a priori, be assumed to be due to the homozygous state, in the child, of a gene leading to mental retardation, the parents representing heterozygous carriers. On the other hand, borderline mental retardation shows a high association with subnormal intelligence in other family members. This type of deficiency is assumed by some to be due to polygenic factors, more of the pertinent genes in these families being of the variety that tends to lower intelligence. However, among the offspring of these families there is also a high proportion of individuals with normal intelligence and a sprinkling of individuals with superior intelligence. All of these comments are made with the realization that our current measurements of intelligence are very crude and cannot be compared between different population groups. It is estimated that, on the whole, people with superior intelligence have fewer offspring than do those of average or somewhat below average intelligence, and therefore, a lack of replacement of superior individuals from the offspring of less intelligent parents would lead to a general decline of intelligence in the population.

It can be seen therefore, that neither positive nor negative eugenics can ever significantly improve the gene pool of the population and simultaneously allow for adequate evolutionary improvement of the human race. The only useful aspect of negative eugenics is in individual counseling of specific families in order to prevent some of the births of abnormal individuals. One recent advance in this sphere has important implications from both a genetic and a social point of view. It is now possible to diagnose genetic and chromosomal abnormalities in an unborn child by obtaining cells from the amniotic fluid in which the child lives in the mother.

It is now known that some 24 biochemical inborn errors of metabolism are potentially diagnosable prenatally. The chromosomal disorders can also be detected by this method, and one group that it would be particularly useful to study in this manner would be mothers over 40 who have at least 1%, and probably closer to 3%, risk of having chromosomally abnormal offspring. One could enlarge upon the number of people to be studied in this way if we were to screen populations for heterozygotes for particular biochemical defects that can be detected in utero and therefore could be prewarned when two carriers happen to get married and the wife gets pregnant. At least 40 genes in the heterozygote can now be detected and presumably these 40 genes in the homozygous state will also be diagnosable by amniocentesis. An example is Tay-Sachs disease. This disease is recessively inherited, that is, it expresses itself in the homozygote (in double dose) and happens to be frequent in Ashkenazic Jews. In this population about one in 25 individuals is asymptomatic carrier of this particular disease. It is now quite easy to detect the carrier from a simple blood sample and it is also easy to detect the disease from an amniotic fluid sample so that one knows whether two carriers in fact have produced a defective child. This is a particularly nasty genetic disease in that the child is born apparently normal and then at about eight or nine months of age begins to deteriorate and then dies a rather miserable death by two or three years of age. If one were to go to the Ashkenazic Jewish population and do universal screening for heterozygotes one could conceivably within one generation stop the birth of affected individuals. One would, of course, not eradicate the gene unless one also were to diagnose for carriers by means of prenatal diagnosis and abort the clinically normal carriers that would be born to these individuals. This, of course, raises a number of legal, religious, and ethical questions. One has to balance, however, some of these questions with the knowledge that in a relatively inbred group such as the Ashkenazic Jews where the gene frequency is as high as it is for this particular gene, abortion of the affected would be compensated for by the birth of clinically normal offspring which will lead to a slow increase in the gene frequency for the particular gene. The reason for this is that two out of three of the normal offspring of such families will be carriers. The earlier you abort, the more quickly reproductive compensation is going to happen, leading to an additional rise in the rate of increase of the gene frequency. These types of problems, of course, need to be worked out and discussed very thoroughly. There is, however, one additional aspect which must be considered. The fact is that the inbreeding of Ashkenazic Jews is rapidly decreasing and they are beginning to outbreed to the extent that there is now an increasing frequency of religious intermarriage. This, of course, would avoid the concentration of this particular gene and its increase, and will lead to a sharp decrease in the number of couples at risk.

The future may bring further advances allowing one to start treatment on the unborn child and to produce a functionally normal infant. We already have at least five or six disease such as phenylketonuria in which treatment is possible. If one starts treatment in the newborn child, it is possible to produce an intellectually normal child, whereas without treatment these children in most cases would be severely mentally retarded. Here again questions would arise for a number of genes, because in order to do this efficiently one might have to screen the parents for the heterozygous state. When should one screen? Should one screen all newborns and then give them a score card as to what genes they are carrying? Should one screen when people get married? Should one screen all pregnant women when they arrive for the first prenatal examination, and if one finds a particular carrier state, should the husband then be examined to see whether he also carries that particular gene?

There are many other problems, and not the least of these with regard to universal screening is the question of invasion of privacy, and what one does with this information beyond transmitting it to the individual who is being screened. The only currently possible solution, however, for many of these problems is restricted to termination of particular pregnancies by therapeutic abortion. This is, of course, applied negative eugenics in its most extreme form. The future may bring further advances, allowing one, then, to start treatment on the unborn child and to produce a functionally normal infant.

Euthenics, the alteration of the environment to allow aberrant individuals to develop normally and to lead a normal life, is currently in wide use. Medical examples include special diets for children with a variety of inborn errors of metabolism who would, in the absence of such diets, either die or grow up mentally retarded. Such action, of course, requires very early diagnosis of these diseases, and programs are currently in effect to routinely examine newborns for such defects. For example, PKU screening laws are in existence which provide for newborn screening in most states. Other examples of euthenics include the treatment of diabetics with insulin and the provision of special devices for children with skeletal deformities. Social measures are of extreme importance in this regard. As has many times been pointed out by Dobzhansky,(2) it is useless to plan for any type of genetic improvement if we do not provide an environment within which an individual can best use his strong qualities and obtain support for his weak qualities. One need only mention the availability of an environment conducive to artistic endeavor for Toulouse-Lautrec, who was deformed by an inherited disease.

The problem of altering an individual's genes by direct chemical change of his DNA presents technically an enormously difficult task. Even if it became possible to do this, the chance of error would be high. Such an error, of course, would have the diametrically opposite effect to that desired and would be irreversible; in other words, the individual would become even more abnormal. The introduction of corrective genetic material by viruses or transplantation of appropriately hybridized cells is technically predictable, and since it would be performed only in a single affected individual, would have no direct effect on the population. If it became widespread enough, it could, like euthenics, increase the frequency in the population of so-called abnormal genes, but if this treatment became routine, this would not develop into an evolutionarily disadvantageous situation. It must also be constantly kept in mind that medical advances are occurring at a much more rapid rate than any conceivable deterioration of the genetic endowment of man. It is, therefore, very likely that such corrective procedures will become commonplace long before there is any noticeable increase in the load of disadvantageous genes in the population.

The growing of human beings from cultured cells, while again theoretically feasible, would, on the other hand, interfere with the action of evolutionary forces. There would be an increase, just as with positive eugenics, of a number of individuals who would be alike in their genetic complement with no opportunity for the degree of genetic recombination which occurs during the formation of sperm and eggs and which becomes manifest in the resultant progeny. This would diminish the adaptability of the population to changes in the environment and, if these genetic replicas were later permitted to return to sexual reproduction, would lead to a marked increase in homozygosity for a number of genes with the disadvantages pointed out before.

We see, therefore, that many of the proposed technics are feasible although not necessarily practical in producing their desired results. We may now ask the question, which of these are ethical from a humanistic point of view? Both positive and negative eugenics when applied to populations presume a judgment of what is genetically good and what is bad. Who will be the judges and where will be the separation between good and bad? We have had at least one example of a sad experience with eugenics in its application in Nazi Germany. This alone can serve as a lesson on the inability to separate science and politics. The most difficult decisions will come in defining the borderline cases. Will we breed against tallness because space requirements become more critical? Will we breed against nearsightedness because people with glasses may not make good astronauts? Will we forbid intellectually inferior individuals from procreating despite their proved ability to produce a number of superior individuals? Or should we rather provide an adequate environment for the offspring of such individuals to realize their full genetic potential?

C. C. Li(5) in his presidential address to the American Society of Human Genetics in 1960 pointed out the real fallacy in eugenic arguments. As he points out, man has continuously improved his environment to allow so-called inferior individuals to survive and reproduce. The movement into the cave and the putting on of clothes have protected the individual unable to survive the stress of the elements. Should we then consider that we have reached the peak of man's progress, largely determined by environmental improvements designed to increase fertility and longevity, and that any future improvements designed to permit anyone to live a normal life will only lead to deterioration? Nineteenth century scientists, including such eminent biologists as Galton, firmly believed that this peak was reached in their time. As analyzed by Li, this obviously fallacious reasoning must not allow a lapse in ethical considerations by the individual and by humanity as a whole, just to placate the genetic pessimists. The tired axiom of democracy that all men are created equal must not be considered from the geneticist's point of view, since genetically all men are created unequal. Equality must be defined purely and simply as equality of opportunity to do what one is best equipped to do. When we achieve this, the forces of natural evolution will choose those individuals best adapted to this egalitarian environment. No matter how we change the genetic make-up of individuals, we cannot do away with natural selection. We must always remember that natural selection is determined by a combination of truly natural events and the artificial modifications which we are introducing into our environment at an exponentially increasing rate.

It is obvious that the possibility of coercion exists in each of the technics proposed. The false concepts of what is good or bad in the genetic makeup of an individual or population, or even the misapplication of true concepts, can lead well-meaning scientists or politicians (in the latter case occasionally not so well-meaning) to urge or decree a variety of maneuvers designed to fulfill the aims of their bias. This does not imply that, therefore, none of these methods is justified. It does mean that their application must be controlled by avoiding, as much as possible, any coercive aspects. The genetic counselor can easily fall into the trap of letting his biased opinion, good or bad, influence the decision of a family regarding procreation or abortion. Perhaps it will become necessary to submit such opinions to teams of experts in order to correct the bias, or to make clear the existence of divergent opinions. Lack of understanding that what is "bad" at this time may act quite differently in an altered environment, may lead well-meaning counselors to change the gene pool or to do away with clinical carriers for certain genes by means of selective abortion.

With these points in mind, we can try to decide what in all of these methods is both feasible and ethical. I believe that the only logical conclusion is that all maneuvers of genetic engineering must be judged for each individual and, in each case, must take primary consideration of the rights of the individual. Obviously each situation will differ as to whether we are considering the rights of present individuals or those not yet born or conceived. Consideration of individual rights is patently impossible in any attempt at positive eugenics. Negative eugenics on a population level suffers from similar problems, but applied in this form of intelligent genetic counseling is the answer for some. Our currently changing attitudes about practicing negative eugenics by means of intelligent selection for therapeutic abortion must be encouraged. Basic to this change is a more accurate definition of a living human being. Such restricted uses of negative eugenics will prevent individual tragedies. Correction of unprevented genetic disease, or that due to new mutation, by introduction of new genetic material may be one answer for the future; but until such a new world becomes universally feasible, we must on the whole restrict ourselves to environmental manipulations from both the points of view of allowing affected individuals to live normally and permitting each individual to realize his full genetic potential.

There is no question that genetic engineering in many forms, here described or not yet conceived, will come about. It is a general rule that whatever is scientifically feasible will be attempted. The application of these technics must, however, be examined from the point of view of ethics, individual freedom, and coercion. Both the scientists directly involved and, perhaps more important, the political and social leaders of our civilization must exercise utmost caution in order to prevent genetic, evolutionary, and social tragedies.

References

1. Lederberg, J.: Experimental genetics and human evolution. *American Naturalist* **100**: 519, 1966.
2. Dobzhansky, T.: Changing man. *Science* **155**:409, 1967.
3. Davis, B. D.: Prospects for genetic intervention in man. *Science* **170**:1279, 1970.
4. Weiss, M. C. and Green, H.: Human-mouse hybrid cell lines containing partial complements of human chromosomes and functioning human genes. *Proc. Nat. Acad. Sci. (Wash.)* **58**:1104, 1967.
5. Li, C. C.: The diminishing jaw of civilized people. *Amer. J. Hum. Genet.* **13**:1, 1960.

REPRODUCTIVE RIGHTS AND GENETIC DISEASE

LAWRENCE P. ULRICH

This paper attempts to examine each of the four issues contained in the title: (1) rights; (2) rights with regard to the reproductive function of human organisms; (3) disease in general; (4) disease which has a currently identifiable genetic etiology. The thesis which I wish to adopt is this: Reproductive rights are not absolute and those who are at high risk for passing on clearly identifiable, severely deleterious genes and debilitating genetic disease should not be allowed to exercise their reproductive prerogative.

I. Rights

Rights are frequently classified in two general ways: legal and human. In many ways the first are much easier to treat than the second, primarily because of their specificity and the fact that they are witten down and consciously agreed to by the society which is concerned enough about its citizens to work them out. While legal rights may be specific, they are not so specific that they do not admit of disputes in their application to particular situations. Hence the need for the legal profession.

Much less clear are those rights which some members of the human population claim under the guise of natural human rights—the most frequently quoted of which are life, (its means) liberty, and (its end) the pursuit of happiness. This is not to say that legal rights and human rights are two completely separate *kinds* of rights. They probably differ only as two parts of the same fabric of claims with the difference being that legal rights are written down while human rights are not. Because of this common bond between legal and human rights, the former are frequently taken as a reinforcement and guarantor of the latter. And in cases that are serious enough, the latter are taken as a substitute for the former.

The attempts at constitutional democracy in the last several hundred years have been largely attempts at "legalizing" fundamental human rights. This has

Research for this paper was funded by the University of Dayton's Research Council. Printed with permission of the author.

generally been done by guaranteeing that the first rights of the citizen are his rights as a person. The constitutions and legal codes were developed, among other reasons, to further guarantee what were claimed to be fundamental human rights. The Nuremburg trials exemplify the situation in which human rights are taken as a substitute for legal rights. The trials were predicated on the acknowledgement that there are such claims as fundamental human rights which every decent person and civilized nation acknowledges and that the violator of them is just as liable as the violator of a human right guaranteed by a legal code.

An important issue in this paper is whether the class of rights which we call human rights are indeed inalienable and non-negotiable. The natural rights theorist believes that certain rights are intrinsic to man and are his by reason of his nature. This position leads to a number of dubious claims for virtually any natural right. For the right that is claimed reflects the claimant's cultural heritage and specifically what he means by being a person and what he thinks will insure a better quality of life for the persons in the human condition. Can we say, then, that there are no such rights which we customarily speak of as natural human rights? Attempts at falsification here would get us no further than attempts at proof. In neither case do we have anything identifiable to use as a criterion for adjudication. Because of these stalemate I should like to advance what I take to be a reasonable account of human rights which are a great concern behind many of the medical ethical problems which we face today. The following considerations allow us to account for the addition of rights to the class of so-called human rights and the variation that we find in these rights-claims from population to population.

I suggest that the rights which we call human rights are nothing more than claims which are made with regard to the performance or prohibition of certain actions and which are acknowledged by other members of the population. Now merely to lay claim to a right does not authorize the right. The factor of social acknowledgement is absolutely central. Part of the problem here lies in the historical perspective from which we view the right. While the 18th-century liberal may have viewed liberty as a natural right, it would not have occurred to the 13th-century serf to claim such a right, much less would it have occured to the 13th-century lord to acknowledge such a right. Rights as recognized claims seem to be correlated with the state of awareness—political, economic, moral, etc.—of the claimants and their social environment. Similarly, it probably never occurred to early man to claim the right to life as a natural right. We do not know when the right to life was claimed and acknowledged but from the earliest days of civilization as we know it there seems to be agreement that the wanton killing of another human organism is a wrongful act.

What can be asserted about rights which are directly claimed as one's own is also true about rights claimed for another. This would be true of rights claimed for the infant, the fetus, the demented, the unconscious. We frequently assign to them human rights which we wish to claim for ourselves, with the hope that society at large will recognize the rights for them just as society recognizes the rights for us. But it is immediately obvious that the rights which articulate claimants assert for themselves are not always claimed for others. We can reflect on those societies where the old are cast out of the tribe to die or where the deformed infant is immediately executed. It would be useless to say that in such cases the basic human rights of such individuals have been violated. For there is no criterion for making such a judgment other than the acknowledged claims of the population as they have developed through practice and tradition. Thus it may be that a society may develop which does indeed hold the "right to life" for its citizens but does not hold it as absolute for its fetuses.

In conclusion, there is indeed a class of rights that can be called "human" but that these are to be understood as unwritten claims acknowledged by society rather than as intrinsic properties of "human nature."

II. Reproductive Rights

I would like now to turn to the matter of the rights of individual humans in the reproductive process. The right to conceive and bear offspring is seemingly implied in the right to life, liberty, and the pursuit of happiness articulated, for example, in the Declaration of Independence of the United States. And the implied claim is that such activity is a natural human right. However, the legal codes, in the United States at least, do not respect this right to reproduce as absolute. We can cite two cases: (1) marriages of close kinship and (2) marriages of parties who have not passed the venereal disease screening test. (Marriage in these cases is considered the normal vehicle for reproduction.) Society imposes this abridgment of reproductive rights for the promotion of the public good in the area of public health.

There is no intrinsic reason for prohibiting marriages of close kinship. The high risk of diseased offspring, because of the combination of recessive genes, is the only reason. The purpose of the law, then, is to protect society and the individuals involved from a situation that can easily lead to undesirable consequences. For one who would believe that reproductive rights are absolute either the law would have to be considered wrong in this case or the concession would have to be made that reproductive rights are not absolute. Of course there is the option, not advanced by society that two closely related individuals can marry but may not bear offspring. This procedure would admit the negotiability of reproductive rights.

The case is similar with the venereal disease test. Legally, society claims the right to prohibit or delay marriage until such time as a cure is verified or at least until reasonable treatment is undertaken and the individual had indicated his or her intention to continue the treatment to its successful conclusion.

There is implied in these two situations more than the right of society to guard its public health even at the sacrifice of individual liberties. Concomitant with this concern is the obligation of individuals to respect and promote public health. In this connection I would like to turn briefly to the matter of obligation.

Obligations, like rights, are not immediately deducible from actions or a series of actions. Just because one can perform an action does not mean that he has a right to perform the action. In natural biological processes, e.g., reproduction, the ability to perform the action does not make the action good nor does it confer upon the actors the right to perform the action. The action itself, the action as good, and the performance of the action as a right are three distinctly discernable features. In the case of obligations we find similar distinctions. The performance of, or ability to perform, an action does not entail an obligation to respect the carrying out of that action. Even if that action is evaluated as good, obligation to respect its performance is not attached. Only when the action is construed as a right does there follow an obligation to respect the performance of the action by either providing the means to facilitate the performance of the action or by prohibiting circumstances which might obstruct it. Thus, the acknowledgement and discharge of obligations are directly related to rights and are accredited and negotiated in a way similar to the accreditation and negotiation of rights. Just as rights are not directly deducible from actions but are mediated by acknowledged claims, so also obligations are not directly deducible from actions but are mediated by rights. Actions, then, and states of affairs only provide clues for the ultimate accrediting of rights and obligations. This accrediting is done with an eye toward actions, actions as good, and actions that fall within the range of priorities of goods. While obligations in general cannot be directly deduced from actions or states of affairs, nevertheless it would be reckless to impose or accept obligations without taking into account actions or states of affairs. Thus, there are clues to obligations which must be considered in any human context.

We can now turn to the question of species survival. In the past 100 years we have come to know that the actions of a species and the interactions of a species with other species or with its environment frequently lead to extinction. The species always "attempts" to survive and is frequently temporarily successful. Its actions, then, are survival oriented, but the end result of those actions over time is generally extinction. If rights were directly deducible from actions then the answer to the question "Does a species have the right to survive?" would be both "yes" and "no" and we would get nowhere. A reasonable case could be made for the affirmative position in view of some natural selective tendencies which select for the survival of the fit. A reasonable case could be made for the negative position because of the general end result of natural selective tendencies toward extinction. But if survival is accredited as a good as opposed to extinction, then we might be in a position to claim survival as a right and attempt to gain acknowledgement of that right. We humans are egocentric enough to think that our continued presence on the planet is important and that it is to be construed as a good to be pursued. Moreover, we humans seem to be the only species on this planet, that we know of, that can pursue its own survival as a *good*. While other animals survive instinctively, we engage in long-range actions to insure (somewhat) our survival as a good. (Many conservation groups accredit the survival of other species in the same way.) I suggest that in the past few generations, we humans have at least tacitly accepted our survival as a species as a good and even laid claim to it as a right. If we have tacitly accepted our species survival as a good and indirectly claimed it as a right, it seems appropriate to articulate the right more strongly, attempt to gain explicit acknowledgement of it, and examine the obligations that this right entails. The area of species survival and thus of species obligation with which I am particularly concerned is that of reproductive practices.

This matter is complicated by the tendency in the history of western civilization to attain individual liberty in an acceptable social context. If this social and political tendency is true, then the advent of our understanding of ourselves as a species with concomitant obligations must certainly temper our pursuit of individual liberties. However, this species awareness does not have to temper all of our actions and claimed rights. Many or our actions could be unaffected by species awareness. But reproductive activity is directly affected because, in the evolutionary context, the pivotal point upon which turns the survival of a species is its reproductive pattern. We can mention the production of more offspring than is needed for species survival, an inverse proportion between the number of offspring and the availability of parental care and the length of time of parental care. Two features that are of particular concern in this paper are the quick demise of some offspring that are genetically defective and, if the demise is not so quick, the demise of some of the genetically defective before they have the ability themselves to reproduce. The early death (or death before reproductive age) of those with serious genetic deficiencies occurs frequently enough in the natural selective process to control the passing on of deleterious genes and the burden which the genetically defective imposes on the population as a whole. With regard to the human population, modern medicine has modified these natural selective factors considerably, primarily in the area of maintenance. The result being that many of those with serious genetic defects are kept alive, even into reproductive age, with the accompanying strain on the population as a whole and the passing on of deleterious genes. We can now turn directly to this matter of genetic disease.

III. Disease

Disease, like health, is an extremely complex matter to analyze conceptually. Philosophers of medicine are only now turning to it. I shall make only a few preliminary remarks before going into the more specific matter of genetic disease. It is important at the outset to distinguish between disease and a trait. Baldness, for example, is a trait, not a disease. In the following section I am discussing genetic diseases, not genetic traits.

To discuss disease as a deviation from the "normal" is a particularly unsatisfying, but common, approach. For the norm, when it comes to many bodily functions, will vary from individual to individual. Some bodies may have a high tolerance for a particular substance while others may have a relatively low tolerance. The variances in diabetes would be a good example. Currently physicians acknowledge this phenomenon by dealing in ranges that constitute the normal. This tolerance of variation within a range retains some notion of normalcy and so we are still left to decide if the "normal" is a statistical average, the expectation of a group of experts, a medical stipulation of the optimal, or whatever. This variability is further complicated by the fact that within a given organism, changes occur which may seem to be disease but as possibly temporary or defensive in character, are ambiguous in their diagnosis. Hypertension is a case in point. It could be that an individual is undergoing a specific stressful situation of fairly long duration and his blood pressure rises to protect the organism from other forms of harm or to provide the resources to carry out its operation with optimal efficiency. Some quite compelling examples might be employed here in the area of mental disease.

At the very minimum I suggest that we call an organism "diseased" if the relative independence of its existence is jeopardized and/or its well-being needs supervised health care, e.g., chemical or mechanical support (when the latter is a part of treatment) for its restoration or maintenance. The jeopardy results from some metabolic (in the case of physical disease) malfunction whether caused by an agent external to the organism such as a virus or by a breakdown in the chemistry of the organism. Some mental disease might result in a similar malfunction but of an emotional sort. There are other cases where the relative independence of an organism is jeopardized, such as a broken limb, and in such cases the organism is said to be "ailing."

We have observed that living organisms generally enjoy a good measure of independence. They ingest food on their own, they eliminate waste products on their own, they ward off minor infections on their own, etc. This independence is designated as relative because we do rely on our natural and social environments in many ways which would not lead to designating the organism as "diseased," e.g., the need for warmth, shelter, companionship, etc.

Supervised health care is generally executed by the use of chemical means—drugs—or mechanical means—repirators, transfusion equipment, etc. Some supervised health care may be dispensed by a regimen of rest and/or exercise or some monitoring system to watch a given condition. Mechanical support may be of two kinds. (1) When the support is needed for actual treatment such as a dialysis machine we can readily identify the organism as diseased. (2) When it is needed after treatment, e.g., in the case of amputees and victims of paralysis, such support is not an indication of disease. One need not actually be treated to call the organism "diseased." Some conditions may admit of no treatment or the diseased individual may not pursue treatment.

Perhaps, in the end, there is no general characterization for disease and each kind, e.g., mental, genetic, etc. will have some characterization peculiar to it. With the acknowledgement of this open question we can now turn to the notion of genetic disease.

IV. Genetic Disease

Every disease has a genetic component whether we are referring to gross genetic defects of early manifestation, a later breakdown in the DNA coding or the quality of the response of organism to external invaders. Thus, a further specification of genetic disease must be made for present purposes. At the outset I wish to indicate that I do not take a very rigid stance against reproduction on the part of those who suffer from genetic disease in general or of those who are carriers of any deleterious genes. (It is estimated that each of us carries approximately five deleterious, but recessive, genes in our organism that will never be expressed.) My focus of concern is genetic defects which, from birth (or within a relatively short time thereafter), manifest themselves as disease conditions and can only be treated, not corrected, as great economic expense. Therefore, I am not including such genetic defects as some carcinomas, hypertension, myopia, etc. These diseases manifest themselves late in individual development and a decent quality of life can be enjoyed before the disease is expressed. Nor does it include diseases which are easily treatable even though in an untreated condition they are quite lethal, e.g., diabetes and asthma.

Genetic diseases that fall within the scope of my position are conditions such as gross chromosomal translocations, some of the trisomies, Tay Sachs, hemophilia, and possibly cystic fibrosis. These diseases are clearly grossly debilitating and cause severe economic strain on the part of those associated with the afflicted. The severe debilitation is apparent almost from birth. The individual affected can only be treated and maintained but not cured and his dependence is virtually absolute.

I do not concern myself here with the emotional ·strain caused by such defects. What is a matter of species concern and is so frequently obscured is the economic strain involved in this type of disease. We are becoming more and more aware that we are living with very limited resources. The limitation of our resources even overrides cases where parents could affort to pay high medical costs. Beyond the costs of drugs, blood, or sophisticated machinery is the cost of medical care personnel who are devoting much of their time and efforts to cases that could have been avoided instead of devoting their time to many other medical care problems that may command a higher priority in terms of species survival or the quality of life of those affected. The time of medical care personnel can be diverted to those problems which admit of cure as well as treatment. This involves a priority of goods and it is here that we meet the issue of species obligation for the first time.

There are several ways we could deal with the problem of genetic disease in the area to which I have confined myself.

1. The classical libertarian would leave the choice to the parents, even in high risk situations, and medical resources would be available to those who can pay the price.

2. An amniocentesis could be performed in each pregnancy where the parents are at risk and parents could have the option of aborting identifiable abnormalities or laws could be passed requiring that identifiable abnormalities be aborted. The former would be an outgrowth of the libertarian position, the latter would be part of a social control package. There are some risks involved in amniocentesis and some errors in extraction of samples can occur. In the case of more than one fetus in the uterus, one of which is diseased and the other not, the appropriate action is unclear. This alternative, of course, involves a positive resolution to the abortion argument.

3. The classical libertarian might suggest genetic counseling so that parents could make an informed decision concerning their reproductive practices. I suggest that genetic counseling with the libertarian attitude is most appropriate in cases (a) where the risk of disease is not exceptionally high, (b) where the disease is easily treatable but nevertheless incurable, (c) where the disease does not manifest itself until well into the growth process. Parents in such cases can be given all the genetic information, the options can be laid open to them and support and aid given in the decision-making process.

4. Reproductive controls along much the same line as our current legislation regarding marriages of close kinship and venereal disease screening are the only approach that I find satisfactory in dealing with genetic disease of the high-risk, early-appearance type within the context of species obligation. Research should

be directed to clearly and economically identifying carriers of severely debilitating diseases of the kind to which I have narrowed my remarks. This is no simple task because a variety of tests may be necessary, chemical analysis, karyotyping, pedigree analysis, etc. Premarital screening should take place to compare disease-producing genetic conditions. For those couples identified at high risk, reproductive rights should be suspended. By "high risk" I mean a chance of one in four that the offspring would be affected and a chance of two in four that the offspring would be a carrier. In other words, if parents can produce a genetically healthy noncarrier for the clearly identifiable trait in only one chance in four, then the risk is too great. I suggest that there is both legal precedent and a species obligation to suspend reproductive rights under these conditions in line with my argument in the first two parts of my paper.

Finally, research should be redoubled on safe and effective means of contraception so that no danger accrues to those involved in this situation. Techniques should also be developed for reversible sterilization so that in the case of marital breakdowns and remarriage where the risk is no longer present, reproductive practices can then be resumed.

To summarize my argument briefly: My fundamental commitment is that the survival of the human species is a good and that it is a good of such importance and value that it can be accredited as a right. From this I deduce that individuals and social units have the concomitant obligation to pursue courses of action that will foster and protect the right of species survival. Among these acknowledged and traditional courses of action is general health care. One segment of that health care involves the protection of the population from the transmission of identifiable, seriously deleterious genes and from debilitating and costly (in terms of natural, economic, and human resources) genetic disease which can neither be cured nor treated with any preservation of the quality of life and relative independence of the afflicted. Because individual human rights are negotiable according to their historical context and because there is legal precedent for restriciting the exercise of reproductive rights, those who are at high risk for passing on clearly identifiable and severely deleterious genes and debilitating genetic disease should not be allowed to exercise their reproductive prerogative.

Bibliography

Brown, Stuart. "Inalienable Rights," *Philosophical Review,* Vol. 64, No. 2 (April, 1955), 192–211.

Callahan, Daniel and Murray, Robert. "Genetic Disease and Human Health," *The Hastings Center Report,* Vol. 4, No. 4 (September, 1974), 4–7.

Feinberg, Joel. *Social Philosophy.* Englewood Cliffs: Prentice-Hall, Inc. 1973.

Frankena, William. "Natural and Inalienable Rights," *Philosophical Review,* Vol. 64, No. 2 (April, 1955), 212–232.

Harris, Maureen. (ed.) *Early Diagnosis of Human Genetic Defects.* Fogarty Symposium, 1970. International Center for Advanced Study in the Health Sciences. National Institutes of Health, Bethesda, Maryland. Washington, D.C.: Government Printing Office, 1971.

Hart, H.L.A. "Are There Any Natural Rights?" *Philosophical Review,* Vol. 64, No. 2 (April, 1955), 175–191.

Hart, H.L.A. *The Concept of Law.* Oxford: The Clarendon Press, 1961.

Hilton, Bruce, *et al.* (ed.) *Ethical Issues in Human Genetics: Genetic Counseling and the Use of Genetic Knowledge.* Fogarty Symposium, 1971. International Center for Advanced Study in the Health Sciences and the Institute of Society, Ethics and the Life Sciences. New York: Plenum Press, 1973.

Lappe, Marc. "Allegiances of Human Geneticists," *The Hastings Center Studies,* Vol. 1, No. 2, (1973), 63–78.

Lappe, Marc. "Moral Obligations and the Fallacies of Genetic Control," *Theological Studies,* Vol. 33 (September, 1972), 411–427.

Melden, A. I. *Human Rights.* Belmont, California: Wadsworth Publishing Co., 1973.

Rawls, John. *A Theory of Justice.* Cambridge, Mass.: Harvard University Press, 1971.

Rensch, Bernhard. *Biophilosophy.* Translated by C.A.M. Sym. New York: Columbia University Press, 1971.

Watson, J.D. *Molecular Biology of the Gene.* 2nd edition. Menlo Park, California: W.A. Benjamin, Inc., 1970.

ON JUSTIFICATIONS FOR COERCIVE GENETIC CONTROL

THOMAS L. BEAUCHAMP

Good laws function to safeguard individual and societal rights and liberties. But the law has two sides. By ensuring liberty to one set of persons, the law may restrict the liberty of others. A law by its very function is coercive because it places a limit on what was formerly a free exercise or action. It is often said that we trade some liberties either for the insurance of other liberties or for some form of protection by the state. The acceptability of these liberty-limiting laws ultimately depends upon the adequacy of the justification offered for them; and when an adequate justification is not forthcoming, the law can easily become an instrument of oppression. In recent years a number of proposals by doctors, moral philosophers, and legislators have been offered which focus on what we ought to do legislatively in the near future to control various health and population problems by genetic engineering. In this paper I test the adequacy of some of the more sweeping of these endorsements of coercive genetic intervention by considering the justifications offered for them.

Two independent liberty-limiting principles are most frequently employed by the supporters of genetic intervention: the harm principle and the paternalistic principle. The harm principle says that coercive interference with a person's liberty is justified if through his actions he produces harm to *other* persons or perhaps to public institutions. It is sometimes argued, for example, that failure to enact this or that genetic program will produce serious and needless suffering to proximate future generations or will lead to avoidable and highly expensive costs to the state in the form of confinement and treatment. The moral force of such claims is generated by the harm principle. The paternalistic principle is slightly but significantly different. It says that coercive interference with a person's liberty is justified if through his actions he produces harm to *himself.* It is sometimes maintained, for example, that persons ill

This article is written especially for this volume. Two predecessors, on which the argument is partially based, are "Paternalism and Bio-behavioral Control," *The Monist,* Vol. 60 (January, 1976) and "On Justifying Genetic Intervention," an address delivered at the Symposium on Rights, Ethics, and Medicine at the University of Dayton, 1974. © 1975 by Thomas L. Beauchamp.

equipped to care for themselves or potential offspring should be sterilized by the state in order to protect them from their own sexual activity. The moral force of such claims is generated by the paternalistic principle. While these two principles almost always are implicit rather than explicit in the arguments of the friends of genetic intervention, I cannot see that there are any other more basic moral principles underlying their arguments.

In this paper I argue (1) that paternalistic grounds should not be considered to provide good grounds for coercive genetic intervention, because the paternalistic principle itself is not an acceptable justifying principle, and (2) that while the harm principle is an acceptable justifying principle, those who invoke it for purposes of genetic intervention have not provided an acceptable moral justification, because they have not shown that the potential of harm to others and/or to public institutions is sufficient to warrant the loss of liberties which would accompany the adoption of coercive genetic laws. I begin with a discussion of the modern developments in biology which have created moral problems of genetic control. In the next two sections I explain further the nature of the harm and paternalistic principles, and provide examples of some of the actual proposals for genetic intervention which are at least mixed paternalistic and harm principle justifications. In the final section I argue that no such justification thus far offered ought to be accepted as satisfactory, despite the exciting and hopeful promise extended by some enthusiasts. I do not, however, argue the bolder thesis that eugenic laws which coerce persons cannot by any principles and under any conditions be justified.

Ethics and the New Biology

What are the actual and potential ethical problems which motivate us to be concerned about the possibilities for engineering people by biological means? Some problems have long been obvious: By lowering infant mortality rates and devising means of increasing fecundity, while also extending life spans, we increase population; something must be done to control the increase. Which among the possible means are we to select and/or prohibit? And, far more importantly for the purpose of this paper, should we under any circumstances allow the state to establish requirements such as mandatory sterilization for retarded persons or for those carriers of deleterious genes which might be passed on to future generations?

While these more familiar ethical problems are certainly important, they are only the beginning. Once the so-called genetic code was broken, and we began to learn the genetic processes which control human development, an area rife with possibilities for human engineering emerged. Recently, inheritable alterations in human cells (developing in tissue culture) have been produced by means such as the initiation of viral infection. This produces the possibility that both "favorable" and "unfavorable" alterations may be required by the state, or at least introduced on a massive scale. Further, medical diagnostic procedures now allow not only prenatal determination of the sex of infants, but also limited detection of crucial genetic deficiencies. This capacity will in all likelihood enormously increase. When perfected, genetic engineering will also enable us to alter and create new genetic capacities which will be transmitted to subsequent generations. We will be thus enabled to control both the sex and the genetic character of the population.

Although these projected biological possibilities stimulate great scientific interest, they are in themselves of little ethical interest. It is on the engineering side of "genetic engineering" that the specter of control emerges. Direct alteration of genes themselves is the least practicable but in some ways most exciting possibility, for it might result in the direct alteration of genotypes and ultimately in DNA artistry where new types of biological organisms are concocted. Various forms of genetic surgery on actual living persons may soon be available, and even deliberately initiated mutations may be planned. With adequate knowledge it will be tempting to require doctors to treat either infants or fetuses when diseases such as cystic fibrosis, Tay-Sachs, phenylketonuria (PKU), or sickle cell anemia have been detected. Other programs might be directed not so much at the actual living person but rather at his or her future progeny. One could in theory have women superovulated and their eggs frozen at a prime age, in order to minimize the threat of mongolism and other defects; and one could even alter the genetic structure of human ova prior to its being united with sperm. Theoretically less remote and perhaps more likely of actualization are eugenic programs where the genes themselves are not altered but where breeding ideals established criteria for marriage and reproduction. Here persons could for genetic reasons be prevented from marrying or from having offspring, perhaps by sterilization or forced abortion. Some eugenicists believe the latter program should be effected immediately. Indeed, as we shall see, some on the vanguard of the aforementioned biological contingencies contend that we can and should "improve" as a whole the human stock we breed.

In the mass of literature on genetic control an important distinction between "negative eugenics" and "positive eugenics" has been introduced. Eugenics is the technological science which promotes the improvement of hereditary qualities by preventing the transmission of genetically inferior conditions. The distinction centers around the nature of the "improvement" to be made. Negative eugenics supposedly has only the medical objective of eliminating or otherwise treating inherited genetic diseases. Since genetic diseases are both prevalent and flourishing, and since they are universally regarded as worthy of elimination, negative eugenics is generally praised as an advance in biomedical technology, though it certainly does raise a number of ethical issues. Positive eugenics raises still other issues, since its purported objective is the positive betterment of the human hereditary condition. Hermann Muller is now well known for the following sketch of the objectives he thinks could be and ought to be eugenically promoted: "a genuine warmth of fellow feeling and a cooperative disposition, a depth and breadth of intellectual capacity, moral courage and integrity, an appreciation of nature and of art, and an aptness of expression and of communication."[1] However well intentioned, comments such as these have quite naturally raised fears of gross abuse by the state.

Harm and Paternalism as Justifying Principles

On what grounds might the state be justified in adopting a coercive program of either positive or negative eugenics? As previously mentioned, most proponents finally rest their case on an appeal either to the harm principle or to the paternalistic principle. Actual examples of such arguments will be surveyed momentarily, but first it will be useful to reach a somewhat more precise understanding of the nature of these two justifying principles.

The Harm Principle

The harm principle, as I construe it,[2] says that when specific kinds of harm are caused to a person or a group of persons the state is justified in coercively intervening for the purpose of protection. In some cases the liberty of those causing the harm may be limited and in others the liberty of those harmed may be limited (at least temporarily). Harm might be produced in many ways, but certainly the fact that the harm was produced by negligence or other inadvertent means would not render coercive interference unjustified. There are also cases where an individual or group of individuals has been or will be physically or mentally harmed not directly by another party but rather by some cause or condition which is to the first party not known or not within its control or both. An earthquake or an epileptic seizure would be examples of the latter. In such cases the state is normally thought to be justified in interfering with the liberty of the persons threatened, at least in order to inform them of an impending

---

[1] "Should We Weaken or Strengthen Our Genetic Heritage?," *Daedalus,* Vol. 90 (Summer, 1961), p. 445.

[2] My construal of both principles is more elaborately explicated and defended in "Paternalism and Bio-behavioral Control," *The Monist,* Vol. 60 (January, 1976).

danger. Some think the state is justified in treating or protecting threatened persons whether or not they consent, though I would not agree to this construal of the harm principle, as the principle then incorporates elements of paternalism and no longer remains an independent liberty-limiting principle.

The role one grants to consent is a critical factor in one's interpretation of the harm principle. One may consent to actions and still be harmed (as a boxer who consents to a match and winds up in the hospital is harmed), though we might want to say that he is not *wrongfully* harmed because he consented. In my view, the state's only proper role is the prevention either of wrongful harm to persons or of conditions productive of harm which are unknown or uncontrollable by the affected persons. The state should not be in the business of preventing harm when that harm or its possibility have been consented to in an informed manner. I construe the harm principle, then, to allow the state to intervene only in the former cases and not in cases where informed consent is present.

The Paternalistic Principle

In recent years we have come to take with increasing seriousness laws which coerce human persons against their will on grounds that the coercive actions protect those persons against consequences of their own conduct. Such justifying grounds are said to be paternalistic, and statutes allowing or requiring such coercion are said to be paternalistic laws. The best known example of such practices is the nonvoluntary institutionalization of persons capable of free choice but allegedly ill mentally. However, as H. L. A. Hart has pointed out, such laws are found throughout our civil and criminal statutes.

Gerald Dworkin has provided a reasonable definition of paternalism, which I accept with only two innocuous modifications (in barackets): Paternalism is "the [coercive] interference with a person's liberty of action justified by [protective or beneficent] reasons referring exclusively to the welfare, good, happiness, needs, interests or values of the person being coerced."[3] Any supporter of the paternalistic principle will specify with care precisely which goods, needs, interests, etc. are acceptable. In most recent formulations, it has been said that the state is justified in coercively interfering with a person's liberty if by its interference it protects the person against his own actions where those actions are extremely and unreasonably risky (waterfall-rafting, e.g.), or are genuinely not in the person's own best interest when his best interest is knowable by the state (as some believe in the case of suicide), or are potentially dangerous and

[3] Gerald Dworkin, "Paternalism," *The Monist,* Vol. 56 (January, 1972), p. 65.

irreversible in effect (as some drugs are). Hart's characterization, though loose, is representative:

> Paternalism—the protection of people against themselves—is a perfectly coherent policy.... No doubt if we no longer sympathise with [Mill's] criticism this is due, in part, to a general decline in the belief that individuals know their own interests best, and to an increased awareness of a great range of factors which diminish the significance to be attached to an apparently free choice or to consent.... Harming others is something we may still seek to prevent by use of the criminal law, even when the victims consent to or assist in the acts which are harmful to them.[4]

Various qualifications are added by Hart and others—e.g., that the general presumption against coercion must be outweighed by the significance and real possibility of the danger involved. However, for our purposes the details of these qualifications are largely irrelevant.

Although controversial, I restrict use of the term *paternalism* to cases where the state coercively protects or benefits a person when his contrary choices are informed and voluntary. Intervention in cases of nonvoluntary or of uninformed conduct is not paternalism in any interesting sense, because it is not based on a liberty-limiting principle independent of the harm principle. It is important to be clear about this distinction since some interventions are both coercive and justified on what might deceptively appear to be paternalistic grounds. John Stuart Mill believed that a person ignorant of a potential danger which might befall him could justifiably be restrained, so long as the coercion was temporary and only for the purpose of rendering the person informed, in which case he would be free to choose whatever course he wished. Mill regarded this— correctly, I think—as temporary but justified coercion which is not "real infringement" of liberty: "If either a public officer or anyone else saw a person attempting to cross a bridge which had been ascertained to be unsafe, and there were no time to warn him of his danger, they might seize him and turn him back, without any real infringement of his liberty; for liberty consists in doing what one desires, and he does not desire to fall into the river."[5]

It is not a question of protecting a man *against himself* or of interfering with his liberty of action. He is not acting at all in regard to this danger. He needs protection from something which is precisely not himself, not his intended action, not in any remote sense of his own making. While I am here embellishing Mill, this seems to me clearly the direction of his argument. Mill goes on to say that once the man has been fully informed and understands the dangers of the bridge, then he should be free to traverse it, if he wishes. I shall be arguing in support of Mill's conclusion, though not by appeal to his utilitarian grounds.

---

[4] H. L. A. Hart, *Law, Liberty, and Morality* (Stanford: Stanford University Press, 1963), pp. 31–33.

[5] Mill, *On Liberty* (Indianapolis: Liberal Arts Press, 1956), p. 117.

Contemporary Justifications for Eugenic Methods

At various points in American history, eugenics has been put to some rather disconcerting purposes, only recently documented by Kenneth Ludmerer.[6] Sterilization laws and other forms of reproductive control have been the most prominent means to eugenic ends, but to contemporary eugenicists these pioneering efforts recede in significance when compared with the broader cultural controls on selective breeding which they propose. I shall discuss, as representative samples, three recent eugenic proposals. An instance of a justification for an immediately effective eugenic sterilization law will first be cited, and then two more speculatively bold programs will be discussed.

Eugenic Sterilization. Eugenic sterilization laws are still in effect in over half the states in the United States. The retarded have been a special target, since they along with criminals, epileptics, alcoholics, and other vulnerable groups have been alleged to have genetically rooted mental and physical disabilities. Since the retarded are often childlike and relatively inattentive to their responsibilities, the rearing of children is frequently a heavy burden. For such reasons it has been considered in their own best interest that they be sterilized, even if they do not agree or fail to comprehend the decision. Irvin B. Hill, writing about the sterilization of mentally deficient persons in prison, argues as follows:

> A mentally deficient person is not a suitable parent for either a normal or a subnormal child, and children would be an added burden to an already handicapped individual, who does well to support himself. It would be *unfair to the state, to the individual, and particularly to his potential children,* to permit his release without the protection of sterilization. . . . It has been the policy of the State of Oregon to sterilize mentally deficient persons before releasing them from its institution and . . . this program has been of benefit from *economic, social, and eugenic* standpoints. . . . It *assists the individual* in his transition to a non-institutional life; and it relieves the state of the financial burden. . . .[7]

This justification appeals to both the paternalistic and the harm principles. This mixture is common to most such justifications. Pure paternalistic justifications are especially rare, but once canonized into law, they can easily become purely paternalistic in coercive environments. Free and informed consent is unlikely in the context of penal institutions, especially when one is dealing with mentally deficient persons. They can be bribed with offers of freedom and intimidated by threats that their confinement will be extended. Although we now know both that many retarded persons are born from parents of normal intelligence and that the retarded often have children of normal intelligence, prison and other

---

[6] *Genetics and American Society: A Historical Appraisal* (Baltimore: The Johns Hopkins University Press, 1972).

[7] Irvin B. Hill, "Sterilizations in Oregon," *American Journal of Mental Deficiency*, Vol. 54 (1950), p. 403. Italics added.

custodial environments continue to give rise to the sort of paternalistically motivated interventions suggested by Hill.

Negative Eugenics

In a recent book-length study, *The Ethics of Genetic Control*, Joseph Fletcher trumpets the virtues of negative eugenics and throws a few kisses in the direction of positive eugenics. His arguments are tenaciously and somewhat dogmatically based on his version of the harm principle, with implicit support obliquely squeezed from the paternalistic principle. Fletcher is especially concerned about carriers of "genetic faults" who transmit genetic deficiencies and thereby "victimize" their children, their marital partners, and the general public. The following is a typical Fletcher argument:

> Each of us has a genetic "load" of three to eight defects. This could double in two hundred years if we go on spreading genetic disorders through random sexual reproduction, multiplying the illnesses and costs that result from bad genes. . . . Terrible and uncorrectable fetuses will have to be aborted or, after birth, let go; for those that *are* preserved and are able to live to reproductive maturity sterilization can prevent the spread of the bad genes and obviate the dysgenic side effect.
>
> What, then, of the "right to reproduce"? . . . Humanistic or personistic moralists will say, "A right depends on human well-being, and if the parents are both carriers of a recessive gene causing lifelong pain and misery for the child they would have, then they should not conceive—the right is null and void." The right to be parents ceases to run at the point of victimizing the offspring or society.[8]

Fletcher often seems most concerned about what present laws do not *permit*. He complains, for example, that laws force obstetricians and pediatricians to "stretch the truth" in the case of defective fetuses by "telling a woman her baby was 'stillborn' when it wasn't, after having simply not respirated the delivered fetus—out of mercy for her and her family."[9] The latter argument appears to be a harm principle justification for more permissive laws. The argument is hard to understand, however, since Fletcher approves the doctors' paternalistic treatment of the patient and the family, and presumably would continue to approve such merciful paternalism if the law were changed.

At other points Fletcher seems more concerned about what eugenic laws should *require* rather than simply about what they should permit. He advocates, for example, "preconceptive and uterine control" in the production of children in order to avoid congenital infirmities. He refers to such measures as "compassionate control" and contends that it is immoral to avoid the use of controls

---

[8] *The Ethics of Genetic Control* (Garden City: Doubleday, 1974), pp. 29f, 125f.
[9] *Ibid.*, p. 153.

when the medical knowledge is available.[10] He explicitly endorses control by the state:

> If people could be relied upon to be compassionate we would have no reason to even consider mandatory controls. But there are too many who do not control their lives out of moral concern; ... the common welfare often has to be safeguarded by compulsory control or what Garrett Hardin calls "mutual coercion mutually agreed upon." ... Ideally it is better to do the moral thing freely, but sometimes it is more compassionate to force it to be done than to sacrifice the well-being of the many to the "rights" of the few. This obviously is the ethics of a sane society. Compulsory controls on reproduction would not, of course, fit present interpretations of due process in the fifth and fourteenth amendments to the Constitution. Here, as in so many other ways, the law lags behind the ethics of modern medicine and public health knowledge.[11]

Positive Eugenics

Perhaps the best known advocate of positive eugenics in recent years has been Hermann Muller. He is, like Fletcher, mostly worried about "an increasing accumulation of deterimental mutations that occur at random" and which "adversely affect health, intellect, powers of appreciation and expression, and even the genetic bases of our cooperative disposition itself."[12] How the state rightly ought to promote eugenic reform is never extensively explored by Muller; generally he is content to allow enlightened individual decisions and social pressures to determine the course of genetic improvement. Still, he thinks the state should record the genetic "pedigrees" of its citizens, favors extensive use of AID and sperm banks for cross-family usage, and suggests that genetic selection is not to be feared if "conducted in a democratic way." If the majority seeks to "promote the diverse abilities and proclivities of specific types" he finds this control both natural and permissible.[13] Muller is also interested in more than what is merely permissible. As a eugenicist who believes that a clear and present danger exists, he thinks we cannot avoid making some hard decisions which will have to be enforced. It follows that if a democratic majority decides, for paternalistic or for harm principle reasons, to improve the genetic health of its deficient members, then this can only be regarded as a means for improving their lives (Fletcher and Hardin's "mutual coercion"?). It is to their advantage and to ours that some controls be initiated.

To be sure I have been putting some words in Muller's mouth, and it should be explicitly acknowledged that he rejects governmental controls "at this stage

[10] *Ibid.*, p. 158f.
[11] *Ibid.*, p. 180.
[12] Muller, *op. cit.*, p. 433.
[13] *Ibid.*, p. 447.

of world affairs."[14] He insists on voluntary action even in programs of negative eugenics. Nonetheless, I think any realistic appraisal of his proposals inescapably leads to the conclusion—as both Martin Golding and Bernard Davis have argued—that such eugenic controls could be achieved only by some rigorous form of state regulation.[15]

A Critical Estimate

In conclusion I shall briefly outline some arguments against the legislative enactment of the aforementioned genetic policies, whether based on the harm principle or on the paternalistic principle.

Use of the Harm Principle

It is universally acknowledged that the harm principle justifiably permits coercive state interventions. But proper application of the harm principle is always contingent upon evidence both that the quanity and quality of harm forecast will be produced unless the state intervenes and that the balance of harm will be minimized by the state intervention. Any assessment of the eugenic point of view, then, must consider the extensiveness and character of the genetic threat. It is in precisely these respects that eugenicists' arguments are lacking.

As regards positive eugenics, any proposal must *select* a set of traits which are allegedly of great positive value to the human species and therefore to be promoted. However, there are problems in regard to the wisdom of the choice of traits, in regard to the original source of the traits, and in regard to the alleged advantageousness of the traits. First, how are we to determine which traits ought to be promoted? Paul Ramsey has complained that when positive eugenicists "describe those human qualities to be selected and bred into the race of men, they write remarkably as if they were describing the attributes of mind and of character that make a good geneticist, or at least a good community of scientists."[16] While no doubt intentionally exaggerated, Ramsey's comment presses the important point that the choice of traits is a value-laden one. It is by no means obvious which traits are the most valuable to mankind, "bad" traits

[14] Muller, "What Genetic Course Will Man Steer?", in James F. Crow & James V. Neel, eds., *Proceedings of the Third International Congress of Human Genetics* (Baltimore, 1967), p. 536.

[15] Martin Golding, "Ethical Issues in Biological Engineering," 15 *UCLA Law Review* (1968), pp. 470f. reprinted in T. Beauchamp, ed., *Ethics and Public Policy* (Englewood Cliffs: Prentice-Hall, 1975). Bernard Davis, "Threat and Promise in Genetic Engineering," in *Ethical Issues in Biology and Medicine* (Cambridge, Mass.: Schenkman Publishing Co., 1973), p. 26.

being infinitely easier to ascertainment than "good" ones. And even if one were to select traits which virtually everyone admires (e.g., intellect and beauty), it would not follow that society would be improved if these traits were widely enhanced. Indeed, social problems would be enhanced if there were no employment for persons with similar talents or if we inadvertently enhanced the wrong traits.

There are many incompatible but strongly felt visions of man's future, and even those who are given to visions of social control often alter those visions in the light of new facts and theories.[17] Eugenicists generally tend to assume that we all agree or will come to agree on these traits, rather than present the required argument to this effect. I very much doubt that this argument is forthcoming, as their views seem to rest on false empirical assumptions about the extent of evaluative agreement and also appear to rest on ideological and individual-preferential bases.

Perhaps the most serious problem with positive eugenics is the assumption that the traits to be promoted in fact have a genetic rather than an environmental basis. The majority of the traits they mention involve higher cognitive and emotional capacities which are nurtured by education and which seem more subject to psychological control than genetic control.[18] This is not the place to mediate the age-old nativist—environmentalist debate, but eugenicists may fairly be accused, I think, of a simple fallacy of reasoning. They move from the perhaps acceptable premise that every human trait has *some* genetically controlled basis to the unacceptable conclusion that every trait has an *entirely* genetically controllable basis.[19] This claim not only downgrades causal consideration of environmental influence, but begs the critical question of whether the actual features of the desirable traits they promote are describable in purely genetic terms. It is not implausible to suppose that the most desirable features of their desirable traits are entirely or largely environmentally controlled, even if the traits are in some respects subject to genetic intervention. But, in any case, eugenicists have never, to my knowledge, made any serious experimental attempt to prove that the desired trait, under their description of it, can be engineered genetically.

[16] Paul Ramsey, *Fabricated Man* New Haven: Yale University Press, 1970), p. 22.
[17] Muller himself once had Marx, Lenin, and Sun Yat Sen on his list of highly valuable sperm donors, whose genetic capacities might be saved for purposes of artificial insemination. These names are absent from similar later lists which he published, while he added Einstein and Lincoln. It is hard to account for this change except (at least partially) in terms of a political evaluation of desirable traits. (I owe this comparison of lists to Martin Golding and Kenneth D. Eberhard.)
[18] Some persuasive examples of social and psychological influence are given in a commentary on Muller's *Daedalus* paper by J. P. Scott, esp. pp. 456f. Cf. also the comments by Ernst Mayr, p. 461. Both in the same volume.
[19] Muller's equivocal use of "have genetic bases" is interesting in *Daedalus, op. cit.,* p. 438.

Furthermore, most if not all of their allegedly desirable traits are subject to different and conflicting descriptions. Consider "intellectual capacity," "moral courage," and "warmth of fellow feeling"—three typical traits endorsed for enhancement by Muller. Even if such terms were not relative to cultural and individual preference, as I believe they are, they are so systematically vague that large numbers of philosophers skilled in conceptual analysis could spend careers on each without making significant headway. There is in addition an equally pressing need for an analysis of the notion of a "defective gene." L. K. Frank elliptically raises this question with an interesting example he adduces while commenting on one of Muller's papers. He asks whether the human female's loss of "the gene for heat" ought to be classified as a "genetic deterioration, or an emancipation from a strict biological control of sex."[20] Many parallel and probably unresolvable conceptual and normative problems would arise.

As regards negative eugenics, the major problem with all such proposals has been well stated by Martin Golding:

> It is not clear that a social program of negative eugenics wouldn't do more harm than good. This, of course, might depend upon the kind of defects that it would aim to eliminate. Nevertheless it is plain that "good" genes would be reduced in the process. A conflict could arise between the aims of positive and negative eugenics. Sweden has had a ban on the marriage of endogenous epileptics since 1757. This has been attacked by a Swedish geneticist not only on the grounds that the chances for an epileptic to have epileptic children are not very high, but also on the grounds "that many epileptics are highly intelligent and socially valuable members of their community, well fitted to bring up children, and that they may carry valuable genes whose transmission will be prevented by the existing law."[21]

In addition to this problem, for largely theoretical reasons, it is not clear that any program of negative eugenics, given current knowledge, is likely to be effective. The genes to be controlled often result from mutation rather than inheritance. Hence, one would need scientific knowledge of the causal laws governing mutation, as well as of the inheritance process, and science is not at this time capable of providing such knowledge. Moreover, many of the genes one would most want to monitor appear only infrequently and unpredictably. And even if this latter problem were eradicated, substantial problems of choice— paralleling the aforementioned problems in the choice of traits—would remain. According to modern genetic theory, each human person carries several recessive genetic diseases, and hence one would have to provide an order of priorities specifying which are to be combatted first. It is likely neither that this could be a value-free ordering nor that it could be linked in an unbiased way to the seriousness of the genetic threat posed by some but not by other diseases.

[20] *Daedalus, op. cit.,* p. 459.
[21] Golding, *op. cit.,* p. 475.

Use of the Paternalistic Principle

Finally, why ought paternalism to be judged an unacceptable justifying principle? The dominant reason is that paternalistic principles are intrinsically too broad and hence serve to justify too much. Robert Harris has correctly pointed out that H. L. A. Hart's description of paternalism, as above, would in principle "justify the imposition of a Spartan-like regimen requiring rigorous physical exercise and abstention from smoking, drinking, and hazardous pastimes."[22] Even the most thoughtful restrictions on paternalism known to me still leave unacceptable latitude, especially in contexts where behavioral controls are most likely to be abused. Prison environments and therapeutic agencies notoriously have thrived on the use of paternalistic justifications to confine and treat. Paternalism potentially gives prison wardens, psychosurgeons, and state officials a good reason for coercively using most any means in order to achieve ends they believe in subjects' or their offsprings' best interest. It is demonstrable that allowing this latitude of judgment is dangerous and acutely uncontrollable. Paternalistic justifications will become increasingly dangerous as genetic knowledge advances.

Most of us would surely be reluctant to allow state officials or even personal friends to judge the reasonableness of another's merely risk-running actions. The difficulty of disentangling judgments of unreasonableness and abnormality from judgments of moral attitude and evaluative outlook is notoriously difficult. We do not allow doctors coercively to give blood transfusions even in life and death situations without consent (except in certain special cases, as in an emergency, when the patient's wishes are unknown). Yet if ever there were, in the eyes of most, an extreme and unreasonable risk, surely this one qualifies.

Paternalism, then, leaves us with unresolved problems concerning the scope of the principle. Suppose, for example, that a man risks his life for the advance of medicine by submitting to an unreasonably risky genetic experiment, an act which most would think not in his own interest. Are we to commend him or coercively restrain him? Paternalism strongly suggests that it would be permissible to coercively restrain such a person. Yet if that is so, then the state is permitted to restrain coercively its morally heroic citizens, not to mention its martyrs, if they act—as such people do—in a manner "harmful" to themselves. I do not see how paternalism can be patched up by adding further conditions about the actions of heroes and martyrs. It would increasingly come to bear the marks of an ad hoc and gratuitous principle which is not genuinely independent of the harm principle, the deficiencies of which, in regard to genetic intervention, we have already surveyed.

[22] "Private Consensual Adult Behavior: The Requirement of Harm to Others in the Enforcement of Morality," 14 *UCLA Law Review* (1967), p. 585n.

LEGAL RIGHTS AND
MORAL RIGHTS

ALEXANDER M. CAPRON

The relationship of a genetic counselor and his patients is a delicate, complex and important one. Treating as it does subjects of great moment—the prevention of crippling diseases, even life and death themselves—it commands growing public interest and scrutiny, especially as the counselor's predictive skills increase. It involves not only parents but geneticists, physicians, ministers, and others, in more lengthy and careful contemplation of the conception and birth of a child than occurs in any other type of "planned parenthood." Its highly charged subject matter and deeply involved participants open it to the internal and external pressures which encumber all significant decisions. Yet when we look at the moral and legal rights of the participants in genetic counseling, the picture before us begins to grow less distinct, and we inevitably see only the sharp features, outlined in black and white and not the interesting shadings of gray.

While this difficulty is inherent in any attempt to state general rules about complicated and varied relationships, it will be particularly pronounced in what follows. There are any number of rights which could be asserted on behalf of those who play a role in the relationship—genetic counselor, parents, unborn child, other family members, and even professional and public institutions. But I have chosen, not too arbitrarily I hope you will agree, to focus on the two sets of immediate participants, counselors and parents, and on only the one right which I believe ought to be of central concern to us.

Before we get to that right, perhaps we should pause to ask: What do we mean when we say a person has a right? The term *right* is customarily used when a person has a claim on the way another person or group behaves, especially toward himself. The concept is often defined by its reciprocal: to say that A has a right is to say that B has a duty to do, or abstain from doing, something at A's prompting. Sometimes "right" and "privilege" are used interchangeably, but "right" is by far the stronger term, suggesting that B's duty is not subject to

This essay originally appeared in *Ethical Issues in Human Genetics*, Bruce Hilton *et al.*, eds. (New York: Plenum Press, 1973). Reprinted with permission of the author and Plenum Publishing Corporation.

recall without A's approval. If A has a "legal right," he can compel B to perform his duty by calling on the organized power of the state; if his right is a "moral" one, he has to rely on B's conscience (abetted perhaps by persons or groups possessing "moral authority") to compel B to fulfill his duty.

It is perhaps only a reflection of my lawyerly literalness, but I find the term *moral right* to be something of an anomaly. While we speak easily of a "moral duty," the legal unenforceability of that duty makes strained any reference to a corresponding "right." In this sense of the word, we usually say a person has a "moral right" precisely when we believe that he ought to be able to compel another's behavior (or whatever) but legally cannot. You may, for example, have no legal right to collect on a debt which you foolishly and unnecessarily forgave me, but—perhaps to make you feel better if not richer—we might say you had a "moral right" to collect, particularly if I used the loan to get rich and you are now destitute. A desire to reduce this category of "moral right" (and the perceived injustice with which it may be associated), partly explains the development of courts of equity in the English (and by transplantation, the American) legal system; such courts sat only where the plaintiff was without "legal remedy" (legal in this case being distinguished from equitable).

My premise is that in genetic counseling the parents[1] have a *legal right* to be *fully informed* decision-makers about whether to have a child; or in the terms just discussed, the genetic counselor has the duty to convey to those he advises as clear and comprehensible a picture of the options open to them, and the relative risks, benefits, and foreseeable consequences of each option, as he can. This formulation is basically a legal one, and it suggests that the parents have recourse to the authority of the state, should the counselor breach his duty by negligently or intentionally withholding options or misdescribing their risks, benefits, etc. This right can also be seen from a "moral" vantage point, however. A dominant ethic in Western culture is the importance and inviolability of each individual human being; from this derives a right to make decisions about one's life, to be "master of one's fate."[2]

Despite the broad way in which this right to be an "informed decision-maker" can be stated, it is certainly narrower than many rights which might be (and have been) asserted to arise in genetic counseling. I would defend the primacy of this right for a number of reasons. First, it is as good a reflection of the underlying moral and legal principles (the sanctity of life; the protection of each member of the community) as any other, such as "the right of every child

---

[1] For the moment, I shall use the phrase "parents' rights" to include both those they assert on their own behalf and those they assert as the representatives of others, particularly their unborn child. This point is discussed *infra* in "Rights and Duties in Genetic Counseling."

[2] Berlin, I. (1969). "Two Concepts of Liberty," in *Four Essays on Liberty*. Oxford: Clarendon Press.

to be born with a sound physical and mental constitution, based on a sound genotype."[3] Second, it avoids, at least on the legal side, the ticklish problems which other such formulations of rights raise concerning "the quality of life." Third, it limits the issues under review to those which are comprehensible given the present state of genetic knowledge.

I anticipate that this limitation on the definition of the right which should concern us will meet with some objection, since our past discussions of genetics have ranged over a host of moral principles, which I would exclude from consideration. At the risk of stirring up the hornets' nest further, then, I will challenge a premise on which those discussions sometimes proceeded: that the moral conclusions reached were necessarily translatable into legal conclusions. My purpose in doing so is to try to demonstrate two things about the legal right set forth previously: (a) that it operates in the genetic counseling situation independently of any "moral" conclusions, and (b) that, for the time being at least, it is not only a necessary, but sufficient, legal right to regulate the participants in genetic counseling.

A Connection Between Law and Morality

I would like to endorse the hypothesis that "there is no necessary connection between law and morality" as the starting point for my discussion of "Moral Rights and Legal Rights." I embark on this course with some trepidation. First, not being a moral philosopher, there is danger in my saying anything about "moral rights," and I might be better advised simply to speak only of legal rights in genetic counseling. Second, by taking on the "no necessary connection" hypothesis, I run the risk of spawning a positivist–natural law debate. Moreover, there is a great deal of evidence that suggests this position is untenable. And finally, there is a part of me which wants to reject this premise and to assert rather that law not only must but should enact a set of morals—my set, of course. Nevertheless, I shall proceed on the premise of "no necessary connection," not merely to be provocative but because I believe it is useful to see the need for building separate, albeit related, lines of argument when we discourse in the moral and legal spheres, and because I hope to demonstrate that courts in disposing of the legal issues in genetic counseling cases need not venture into the "moral thicket," to paraphrase Justice Frankfurter.

[3]Glass, B. (1971), Science: Endless Horizons or Golden Age?, *Science, 171*, 38. See also *Smith v. Brennan,* 31 N.J. 353, 364 (1960), ("the right to begin life with a sound mind and body") quoted in *Glietman v. Cosgrove, 49* N.J. 22, 28 (1967), which is discussed extensively in "Rights and Duties in Genetic Counseling" in this paper.

Let us begin our discussion by exploring the different meanings which attach to the words "connection," "law," and "morality."

Connection

The term *connection* can imply a historical relationship, a chance overlap, or a strict cause-and-effect nexus. In a historical sense, there can be no denying that our system of laws has been closely related to morality, particularly that body of conventional morality known as religion. Even when a link is not provable as a matter of historical fact, the occurence of similar rules in the legal and moral domains suggest the existence of a connection, perhaps one with an anthropological explanation. Yet neither of these meanings, nor even that of cause-and-effect, is adequate once "connection" is modified by "necessary," for we are then referring to a "but for" relationship. In this sense, to speak of a necessary "connection" between a moral right and a legal right is to argue that the ultimate rationale for the existence and validity of the legal right is to be found in the moral one.[4] Any less rigorous meaning of "necessary connection" raises the danger of *post hoc* reasoning. For even without a knowledge of the moral views of a society, one can from a careful examination of its legal system derive a statement of that system's view of man, which could be cast in moral (or psychological or political) terms; but this falls far short of demonstrating the necessity of the connection, or even of showing which way it runs.

Morality

There are two ways in which "morals" might be said to be related to the law. The first—the one which people most often have in mind when they speak of law enacting morality—is illustrated by the set of criminal laws which punish abortion, prostitution, homosexual activities, and the like. As a historical matter, it is undeniable that the felt immorality of feticide and of variant sexual practices accounts for their prohibition by statute; however, since an examination of such relationships (whether perceived as what I term "codification" or "replacement") shows them to be merely historical, the definition of "connection" previously set out has not been satisfied.

Law as Codified Morals. Over the years, ethical thinkers have contributed to the growth of society's legal system as well as having guided its conscience.

---

[4] It is often assumed that the asserted "connection between law and morality" refers to law incorporating, or resting on, morality. The opposite meaning is equally plausible, but the interesting questions it raises go beyond the scope of this paper. What is at issue is whether the Old Testament view of the law as "a lamp unto the feet and a light unto the path" should be taken as a description of law's effect on morality or merely on conduct.

Most prominently, organized religion has had profound direct and indirect impact, through ecclesiastical law and general religious precepts, on legal rules not only on the Continent but also in the common law and in our own constitutional system.[5] This influence is even reflected in the language and customs of the law: for example, the "repentence" for which a judge looks in setting the sentence of a convicted man, or the oath on the Bible by which witnesses affirm that they will tell the truth.

During the period when the Anglo-American legal system was molded by the common law judges, legal rules represented what the courts took to be the community's view of the proper relationship of moral men. In these circumstances, "the law" was merely a formal endorsement by the community of views which its members (or most of them) already held. Once legislation came to play an important, or predominant, role in the legal system however, the more complex and less simply "moral" drives of law-makers became apparent.[6] It became more difficult simply to assert that since the people (directly or through their judges and legislators) create the law and the people (judges, legislators) hold moral views, therefore the law enacts morality.[7] This syllogism fails because under it we could as well say that law enacts biology, economics, psychology, astrology, or any other set of views which people hold and often believe in strongly.

---

[5] Under our constitution, the historical connection between a statute and that body of morality known as religion can present some intriguing questions of legislative intent and legal effect, but these need not detain us now. See generally John Hart Ely, "Legislative and Administrative Motivation in Constitutional Law," 79 *Yale Law Journal 1205* (1970).

[6] Even when the framers of a law speak in moral terms ("equality," "social justice"), the law-morality connection is not patent. Take, for example, Workmen's Compensation, which makes an employer liable for job-related injuries without a showing that he is at fault for their occurrence. There was much opposition to these statutes in the early years of this century, and for a while the courts held them unconstitutional on the grounds that they deprived the employer of his property without due process of law in violation of the fourteenth amendment. See, e.g., *Ives v. South Buffalo Railway Co.,* 201 N.Y. 271, 94 N.E. 431 (1911). (To do this, the courts found the doctrines of the fault system of liability, which along with numerous exceptions they had themselves created over the preceding centuries, to be an immutable part of the concept of "due process.") But while a "moral" rationale can be thought of for or against these statutes, the basis on which they were enacted by the legislatures and eventually accepted by the courts (as a valid exercise of the "police power" of the state) was, in the words of the draftsmen of the 1910 New York law, that the existing negligence system was "economically unwise . . . wasteful, uncertain and productive of antagonism between workmen and employers." The legislators concluded (1) that if employers, particularly in "dangerous trades," had to bear at least some of the cost of injuries, they would be more likely to improve the safety of working conditions, and (2) that both the costs of the accidents and of their prevention are costs of doing business, which ought to be reflected in the price of the goods purchased.

[7] Cahn, E. (1955). *The Moral Decision.* Bloomington and London: Indiana University Press.

Law in Place of Morals. There is another sense in which law and morals might be said to be connected—a sense in which a law—biology connection would not be even facetiously asserted. This relates to the role law has as a replacement for morality. Usually, in peaceful, smoothly functioning relationships and stable societies, there is little need for "the law" to play an active role in many areas, such as the family, education, or the like. The conduct of the individuals involved is guided by the commonly accepted norms for these relationships: e.g., children obey their parents (teachers, etc.), achieving greater independence with their increased maturity; parents are responsible for the well-being of their children; old people can rely on their position within the family to provide respect and, if need be, sustenance. These norms are not only provided by custom but explicitly sanctioned by moral codes, enforced either by internally assimilated standards or by outside forces operating with moral authority. Once this system breaks down, once the "commonly accepted" view of proper behavior is more widely questioned and less commonly accepted, however, people may turn instead to the law to restore relationships. In the process, law brings along new sanctions, new actors and new modes of action; in effect, it creates new relationships, although such relationships usually are presumed to be the heirs of the traditional ones and bear their names. While it is possible to see this as just another instance of law enforcing morality (akin to a common law judge creating the crime of "larceny by trick"),[8] in fact, the operant fact here is the failure of the moral system to operate, so that the legal system's intrusion might more accurately be seen as a desertion of morals for law (seen as a set of regulations fashioned on the basis of the sciences of human behavior rather than on *a priori* principles).

Justice and Fairness. In neither of these senses ("codification" nor "replacement"), then, does it seem accurate to say there is any necessary link between law and that notion of morals with which it is commonly associated. Yet one principle is not so easily disposed of—the principle of fairness. To hold that a law does not comport with a person's standards of sexual behavior is one thing, but to declare that it does not square with his standards of fairness or justice is quite another. The standard of fairness, like the standard of sexual behavior, can be seen as a moral one but unlike the latter, its connection to law seems almost indisputable. It provides the yardstick by which individual laws and decisions as well as whole legal systems are judged; its connection with "the very notion of proceeding by rule is obviously very close."[9] In deciding on the distribution of benefits and burdens or the compensation of injuries, it is the precept to which the law turns; as Professor Hart has formulated it: "Treat like cases alike, and treat different cases differently."[10]

---

[8] *King v. Pear,* 168 Eng. Rep. 208 (1779).
[9] Hart, H. L. A. (1961). *The Concept of Law.* Oxford: Clarendon Press.
[10] Id. at 155.

All this does not, however, make out a necessary connection between law and morality. First, the "Treat like cases alike" precept is functionally incomplete; a definition of likeness must also be given, and this need not be in "moral" terms. Some would argue that other standards of judgment (e.g., "rationality" or "reasonableness") are thereby simply made part of the concept of justice and that the overall concept remains a moral one. Under this view, to state that it is unreasonable to punish blue-eyed thiefs but not brown-eyed ones is to make a moral statement.[11] It can equally well be argued that the non-moral judgment (i.e., the "rational" definition of where lines are drawn for "like" classes) is the determinative one and the principle of fairness and justice only secondary. Moreover, even the fairness principle itself can have an amoral rationale: a legal system, or a judge deciding a case, might employ the principle because to do so decreases the costs of the system or increases subjects' allegiance to their sovereign, or whatever. These rationales might in turn reduce to a utilitarian calculus on closer inspection; while as such they would be part of a moral system this is a long way from what is usually taken to be the morality with which law is assertedly connected.

Law

In order to develop the distinction between two meanings of the third word—law—which concerns us, I should like to offer some definitions, albeit tentative ones, of morality and law. A moral system serves as a guide to conduct which is considered "good" in itself or which will lead to "the good" (variously defined as happiness, holiness, etc.). The system may be seen as a discoverable natural pattern or as a strictly human creation, or somewhere in between; that does not alter the basic definition. Law can be seen as the collection of enforceable rights and responsibilities through which the members of a society relate to one another and to their society as well as the system by which the society assigns these rights and responsibilities and resolves asserted conflicts among its members.[12]

Law and morality are similar in that both attempt to prescribe human behavior according to a set of rights and duties. If one adheres to a moral or legal

---

[11] See id. at 156. Professor Hart identifies the "moral outlook" of equality as the principle underlying justice and fairness, but he acknowledges that other bases for a "just" system are possible. Id. at 160–161.

[12] Some of these rules or arrangements are described as "customs" by anthropologists. Similarly, Prof. Hart argues that primitive societies which lack "secondary rules" (roughly, procedural rules) cannot be said to have law at all. (Unlike his fellow positivist John Austin, however, Hart holds that some customs count as law even before a law-making institution recognizes them.) I would argue further that those rules at the edge of the legal system, which enjoy their non-legal status primarily because the law has foreborne incorporating them for the present, ought to be regarded as part of our concept of law. What is said hereafter is not affected by these distinctions, however.

system, he does nothing more than it gives him the right to do and nothing less than it makes it his duty to do. But these definitions also suggest some differences between morals and law. First, the definition of morality includes on its face a normative element and that of law does not. This is more than a matter of chance or of arbitrary definition—the heart of a moral system is its judgments of right and wrong, in an outward-referring sense, while the heart of the legal system is the ordering of relationships, in which only consistency with the system's own rules need be sought.

A second difference arises from this matter of "reference." If you found yourself alone on the proverbial desert island, you might find cause to employ a moral system, but you would have no use in any reasonable sense for a legal system. If, however, I were then to be washed ashore on your island, a need for laws would arise. (We might decide not to have any "laws" as such but to talk through each matter on its own merits; that decision, however, would in itself create a legal system, one of negotiation without precedent.) If I decided that I did not like a law, you would then have to make reference to some "justification" which demonstrated my obligation to obey the law.[13]

To do this, you would make reference to some principle (that I acknowledged as binding) which either justified the particular disputed rule or established my general obligation to obey all valid rules, including the one in question. Law, in other words, has two meanings: that of individual rule and that of a system of rules. The Positivists argue, convincingly I believe, that law in the narrower sense can find its justification by reference to law in the broader sense; that is, a law need not rest on moral principles to have force. In the modern formulation of Professor Hart, binding legal duties (or, more generally, legal rules) are those which meet the criteria of what Hart calls "the rule of recognition" (e.g., "a law adopted by majority vote of the legislature and signed by the chief executive"), which in turn rests on its acceptance by members of the society.[14] Thus, neither individual rules nor the system as a whole need to be traced back to a "moral" wellspring.[15] The role of morality in this system is to supply a standard of judgment or criticism.

---

[13] The question of justification is what really lies behind most discussions of the connection between law and morality. The question underlying such discussions is whether one need obey a law for which the connection is missing.

[14] In addition, some rules—or customs, really—are binding in Hart's scheme because they too arc "accepted" rather than achieving their validity by means of the master rule.

[15] Extra-legal (possilbly "moral") principles do have a place in Hart's system. When a "hard case" is not decided by an existing rule, or when an existing rule leads to a harsh result, the "rule of recognition" gives certain people (typically judges) discretion to fashion a new rule. In the exercise of their discretion, the judges may rely on extra-legal standards; consequently, some individual laws may (but need not) be grounded in moral principles. This explains the connection between morals and certain laws which was discussed under

In sum, the thesis of "no necessary connection between law and morality" is valid to a limited extent. If we adopt the positivist view, reference need not be made to moral rights or duties to justify either individual legal rights or duties or the aggregate legal system. We may sometimes invoke the moral judgment that "This law is unjust," but this is only a criticism of the law and does not reduce the law's binding force on its addressees, provided its valid pedigree is established. (Our discussion of this point would have to go into much greater detail if we were faced with deciding whether to punish a person who engages in civil disobedience against a law he believes is unjust, or conversely a person who committed what is now regarded as an unjust act in compliance with an apparently valid law which he believed was binding on him. The questions raised by our topic, while complex, are less knotty.)

Informed Decision-Making: A Legal Right?

The Legal Pedigree

Does the "informed decision-maker" rule I have suggested, then, state a legal right? There are two aspects to the right—information and decision—and both of them have been recognized by the law. The information component is of recent origin; it was developed out of recognition that knowledge is necessary to make meaningful the power to decide.[16] The doctrine of "informed consent" has been developed in cases involving malpractice claims arising out of the physician–patient relationship, which is basically the same as the relationship of genetic counselor and parents (if we assume that genetic counselors are either

---

the previous heading. Critics of the positivist model insist that the legal system is more than just a collection of individual laws. For example, Prof. Ronald Dworkin's contextualist approach attempts to supply a theory of legal obligation that squares with our social practices; particularly, he is concerned to avoid the positivists' use of "discretion" which leads to *ex post facto* results inconsistent with our social practice of blaming someone only for the breach of an existing social obligation. Unlike the positivist judge who may refer to standards outside the law as a guide to decision-making, a Dworkinian judge is bound by certain principles which as such are part of the law. In other words, Dworkin denies the dichotomy between law and morals and locates the notion of legal duty in the general practice of social obligation.

[16] See *Natanson v. Kline,* 186 Kan. 383, 350 P.2d 1093, clarified, 187 Kan. 186, 354 P.2d 670 (1960); *Salgo v. Leland Stanford,* etc., *Bd. of Trustees,* 154 Cal.App.2d 500, 317 P.2d 170 (1957). Cf. *Miranda v. Arizona,* 384 U.S. 436 (1966) (prescribing information about rights to remain silent and to confer with counsel which must be communicated to criminal suspect prior to interrogation); *Banzhaf v. F.C.C.,* 405 F.2d 1082 (D.C. Cir. 1968), *cert. denied* 396 U.S. 842 (1969) (broadcasters required to air anti-smoking information.)

physicians or fall into a special professional class of their own). The second right—the right to self-determination—has a fundamental place in Anglo-American law; its pedigree is indisputable, as reflected in the rules of consensual agreements in contracts law and consent as a defense to assault and battery in torts law. As previously suggested the two rights have come together in "the obligation of a physician to disclose and explain to the patient as simply as necessary the nature of the ailment, the nature of the proposed treatment, and probability of success or of alternatives, and perhaps the risks of unfortunate results and unforeseen conditions"[17] before obtaining the patient's consent.

Despite this rather clear rule, physicians often withhold information from their patients. Usually this reflects only an understandable desire to "keep things simple" and "move patients along" and if challenged in such a case, a physician would probably admit that he hadn't adhered to the standard of full disclosure but argue that no harm was done thereby. (If harm did occur, however, the physician would be in an unenviable position defending a malpractice or battery action.) In some instances, however, failure to disclose is based on intention rather than inadvertence. When he believes his patients' "best interests" would be served by ignorance, a physician may decide to withhold diagnosis, prognosis, or information about an impending medical intervention, as where a patient is found to have a malignant tumor but is told that the growth is benign so that "his final days can be happy ones." All the problems raised by this "therapeutic privilege," and few of its justifications, seem to be present in genetic counseling, although it is apparent that most counselors presently believe they have an unqualified right to withhold information from their patients. While the question is surely a ticklish one, I do not agree that a "therapeutic privilege" is wise or proper in this setting. I would rather that counselors proceeded on the premise, as the court said in a leading case, that "the law does not permit (the physician) to substitute his own judgment for that of the patient by any form of artifice or deception."[18]

The theoretical problems involved are highlighted by the statement that a patient's freedom is limited if knowledge (specifically, that he carries the sickle cell trait) is communicated without treatment being possible. Yet, as is so often the case, under the flag of "enhancing freedom," freedom (in the "positive" sense, of being able to make choices for oneself) has been severely limited—we deny the person before us freedom of choice (by depriving him of the knowledge which would inform, or even prompt, his choice) in order to increase his "true freedom" as we perceive it. Substituting our view of what should be done for that of the persons affected is always a dangerous course, and it is particularly so in the case of genetic counseling because of the great risk that counselors

---

[17] *Natanson v. Kline,* 186 Kan. at 417, 350 P.2d at 1106.
[18] Id. at 407, 350 P.2d at 1104.

will not choose as their patients would—or even in their patients' "best interests."

Briefly, my practical objections to the modus operandi adopted by genetic counselors are as follows. First, genetic counselors, unlike the family doctors of yore, are not intimately acquainted with their patients, their families, communities, etc. I have been impressed by the time and effort that we have heard the genetic counselors here devote to their clients, but I think this reflects qualities one would expect in men and women who are willing to come to such a conference and expose their practices to ethical and legal scrutiny. Similar sensitivity—and time—cannot be expected on the part of all counselors, particularly once the demands on counseling facilities increase substantially, as they are bound to. When counseling becomes much more routine, part of accepted practice should not be the routine withholding of information from the counselees on the spurious grounds that the counselors know what is best for patients they hardly know at all.

A second reason derives from the innumerable internal and external pressures operating on counselors which will interfere with an accurate assessment of their patient's "best interests." In efficiency/humanity terms, the really "efficient" course for most counselors is not full disclosure on a computer print-out, but the withholding of information which if disclosed would involve the counselor in a long and arduous process of truly "counseling" his patients. In short, it is more "efficient" (and certainly easier) for him to make the choices himself rather than to bring into open discussion facts (about carrier status, etc.) which are difficult to contemplate or discuss. This points toward another pressure which operates here: physicians' well-known tendency to overreact to disease. The phenomenon of regarding disease as an "enemy" to be "conquered" has its origins, I suspect, in the medical fraternity itself. As Professor Renee Fox has observed, this frame of mind may be quite necessary for physicians, particularly those working on the frontiers of medical science.[19] Whether it is necessary, or merely a reflection of doctors' training or the preexisting psychological makeup which brought them into the profession, this attitude is hardly conducive to a counselor's making a good choice for his patient. As Dr. Kaback commented yesterday, he is much more upset and distressed by the diagnosis of the Tay-Sachs trait than are the carriers to whom he communicates this fact.

Third, a physician's judgment may also be clouded by his own set of values, which will not necessarily correspond to his patient's. The potential for conflict is especially great in genetic counseling in which the options elected depend on one's opinions about such controversial matters as the importance of the traditional concept of family, the morality of divorce and of abortion, etc.

[19] Fox, R. C. (1959). *Experiment Perilous: Physicians and Patients Facing the Unknown.* Glencoe, Ill.: The Free Press.

Finally, the physician's map of social goals may differ markedly from the one held by the patient. A counselor who, for example, strongly believes in the elimination of a genetic disease for eugenic reasons, ought to convey his eugenic premises to any woman to whom he suggests an abortion for that disease, lest her choice be uninformed.[20]

To conclude this aside on "therapeutic privilege," not only do I think that withholding information is theoretically and practically unwise, but I find it unjustified in that the opposite course is perfectly acceptable. The terms in which the alternatives have been posed at this conference—revealing the "brutal truth" or keeping the patient in "benign ignorance"—give a false impression of the courses open to the counselor. They are reminiscent of the early discussions of how much dying patients should be told, discussions which also obscured much through the blinding dichotomies they employed. Only slowly did a few practicing physicians, and some enlightened sociologists, suggest that the question was not whether to tell but how to tell and how fast to tell.[21] Dr. Lejeune's description of his method of informing couples which of the marriage partners is a trait carrier illustrates the advantages of beginning with the assumption that the information should be conveyed and then applying one's creativity to devising a sensitive humane means of conveying it.[22]

Since its articulation by the courts establishes the "informed decision-maker" right as valid law (by reason of the "rule of recognition"), no moral justification for it need be given for its application to the participants before us. We may wish, however, to ask, "Is it just?" In legal terms, as we have already

---

[20] This formulation highlights the question of what "facts" must be disclosed. Ordinarily, this question may not be an easy one (how much of a diagnosis or description of risks, side-effects, etc., is "fact"?) but at least it is limited to "facts" about the patient (the results of his lab tests, etc.). But what of further information about the significance of the diagnosis, risks, etc., or about the physician's premises, etc. I believe that these too must be included in the information required to be disclosed, but while I may for economy's sake refer to "disclosing facts," I recognize that this phrase encompasses hard, factual data as well as opinions, beliefs and interpretations. Indeed, the very "non-factual" nature of the latter category suggests the great need that it be disclosed and that the disclosure include as full a statement of the competing opinions, beliefs, and interpretations as is possible.

[21] See, e.g., Glaser, B. G. and A. L. Strauss (1965), *Awareness of Dying,* Chicago: Aldine Publishing Co.; Weisman, A. D. (1967), "The Patient With a Fatal Illness: To Tell or Not to Tell," *J. Am. Med. Assn., 201,* 153.

[22] Another way of stating my thesis is that the "best interests" doctrine is acceptable to the extent it mirrors the physician's Hippocratic duty to "do no harm," but that it should be abandoned to the extent it would permit a physician to substitute his judgment for his patient's. Thus, this modified "best interests" would place a floor under the standard of acceptable conduct by physicians, by refusing to excuse intentional or reckless harm to patients, without allowing this protection against potential harm to swallow up the patient's whole right to information and consent.

noted, the right in question is an application of the same rule as that which is applied in torts and contracts law: that each person is free to govern his life as he chooses subject only to those constraints or interferences which have his voluntary assent. This principle also has its reciprocal: that each person is responsible for the consequences (sometimes limited to the foreseeable consequences) of his choices. A statement of rights in genetic counseling which denied parents "informed decision-maker" status would run afoul of the "like cases" precept on both points; the right is therefore necessary to a "just" treatment of counseling.

To conclude that the "informed decision-maker" right states a just principle of law in no wise denies that it also has moral equivalents.[23] Indeed, the very concept of man as a "moral being" is closely linked with this principle. In the view of many philosophers, as well as biologists and anthropologists, man's distinctive characteristics are his abilities to communicate, to reason, to imagine alternative possibilities so as to anticipate future events, and to act so as to alter them. Given his faculties, if man is to act morally he must take responsibility that each of his acts comports with moral rules (however conceived, i.e., "do no harm," "help thy neighbor," etc.). Giving each person power, as well as responsibility, for his own conduct also, in the view of some philosophers, assures that the good of the whole community is maximized.

The Question of Liberty

This raises a question which I have skirted. My primary interest in the "informed decision-maker" right is to identify its allocation of authority and responsibility between parents and counselor. Thus far, the state has entered the picture only as the enforcer of the right (through its courts). One implication of the right, however, is that the parents' decision takes precedence not only against the counselor's wishes but also against those of the state. I raise this point not to discuss it at any length,[24] but because it reflects one of the major forms of the law—morality debate. The view that one should have free choice

---

[23] One moralist's approach to informed consent is found in Prof. Paul Ramsey's description of the deontological dimension of consent: "The principle of an informed consent is a statement of fidelity between the man who performs medical procedures and the man on whom they are performed." Fidelity is thus an aspect of "the faithfulness that is normative for all the covenants or moral bonds of life with life." Ramsey, P. (1970), *The Patient as Person,* New Haven and London: Yale University Press.

[24] The issues involved would require lengthy treatment in a separate paper. The state's right to act against the parents' wishes would probably depend on such issues as: (a) in whose behalf is the state acting, that of the unborn child, the community, future generations, or science; (b) is its action premised on paternalism, the "common good," or the limitations which it places on the exercise of certain privileges it grants; and (c) how does it enforce its decisions, (by prohibiting abortions or commanding them, or by compulsory amniocentesis, contraception, sterilization, etc.).

about his own conduct is, of course, identified with John Stuart Mill. His critics argue that Mill's concept of liberty is not[25] and should not be accepted by society, for each member of a society owes the collectivity a duty to keep himself "physically, mentally and morally fit."[26] This argument provides another perspective on, or way into, the question of a necessary connection between law and morality. Rather than asking whether it is possible to view the legal system as a useful, justified entity, independent of morality, it asks whether one can conceive of a society operating successfully without imposing its moral views on its members. While this debate, between libertarians on the one hand and paternalists and collectivists on the other, is as fascinating as that between positivists and naturalists, I don't think we need go into it here. Suffice it to say that I defend the full implications of the "informed decision-maker" right, even against the state's authority.

Having concluded that genetic counselees do have a legal right to act on full information about the options open to them and their risks, I should like now to apply this analysis to a hypothetical situation presenting some of the potential conflicts among the rights and obligations of the participants in genetic counseling.

Rights and Duties in Genetic Counseling: A Case Analysis

Suppose that a couple who believe their potential offspring to be "at risk" for a genetically linked disorder consult a physician who specializes in genetics. The stage of the unborn child's development at the time of consultation, the type of advice, and the sorts of data used might vary greatly. Let us assume that the parents seek out the counselor after the child has been conceived but in time to terminate pregnancy safely; further assume that the data are restricted to family histories (the probabilities of the disease being calculable on that basis, but the disease not being amenable to diagnosis by amniocentesis, etc.); and finally assume that the advice given is a straightforward assertion that there is no known risk of the disease occurring. On this assumed set of facts, what consequences follow if the counselor intentionally withholds information or makes a negligent mistake in his advice and a child with the feared genetic disorder is born?

Although no such case has arisen to the best of my knowledge, analogies are available. Perhaps the closest of these is the decision of the Supreme Court of

---

[25] As Lord Devlin has observed: "Mill's doctrine has existed for over a century and no one has ever attempted to put it into practice." Devlin, P. (1965), *The Enforcement of Morals,* Oxford: Oxford University Press.

[26] Id. at 104.

New Jersey in *Gleitman v. Cosgrove*,[27] which provides us with a useful vehicle for analysis, not the least because Lord Kilbrandon takes a rather different view of the result reached from that which I take. I believe it will be worth our while to examine *Gleitman* in some detail, both because it is the leading case on this subject, and also because I believe both the New Jersey court and its critics have mistaken the rights and duties involved. Using the analysis we have developed, I believe we come inescapably to a different, and better, resolution of the contentions raised by the case.

The *Gleitman* court held that there was no cognizable claim against a physician who erroneously advised a woman that the German measles she suffered during the first month of pregnancy "would have no effect at all on her child."[28] Apparently Dr. Cosgrove knew the risk of rubella damage to be about 25 percent, but he withheld this information because he believed it unfair to abort three healthy fetuses to avoid one diseased one. By a divided vote, the justices ruled that neither parents nor child could sue for the child's substantial birth defects, because the mother had testified that if she had been properly warned of the risks she would have sought an abortion; the parents were foreclosed because at abortion even if legal (which the court assumed),[29] would have violated "the preciousness of human life," and the child was foreclosed because he would "not have been born at all" had his parents carried out the abortion. While it is not difficult to understand why the New Jersey court reached the conclusion it did, I believe its opinion rests on a misunderstanding of legal principles, a misapplication of precedent, and a misapprehension of the consequences of the result it reached as compared with the contrary result.[30]

Misunderstood Principles

The first question which arises is whether the legal rule established in this case is a just one. The reason it seems unjust is that the general rule—that (a) a person (b) who suffers injuries (c) will be made whole by (d) the person who

---

[27] 49 N.J. 22, 227 A.2d 689 (1967).

[28] *Gleitman v. Cosgrove*, 49 N.J. 22, 24 (1967).

[29] The court's assumption accords with one of the grounds for abortion proposed by American Law Institute (and now accepted in a dozen states): that a licensed physician believes there is substantial risk the child will be born with grave physical or mental defects. *Model Penal Code* Section 230.3.

[30] The discussion herein is limited to the child's right to recover, since the parents' claim is either derivative, dependent on the same theory, or governed by whether abortion is legal. The court assumed that the Gleitmans could theoretically have obtained an abortion, but cited "policy reasons" why recovery should be denied. If an abortion had been actually as well as theoretically, possible on a legal basis, the court would not have been able to rely on these policies.

caused the injuries—was not applied here. In consequence the court is open to criticism for not treating like cases alike.

As my statement of this tort rule suggests, in determining whether justice was done in the *Gleitman* case, we first inquire into the infant plaintiff's standing to sue. Is Jeffrey Gleitman, the defective child, "a person" in the eyes of the law? This question did not detain Justice Proctor of New Jersey for long. Looking to *Smith v. Brennan*,[31] in which the court upheld the right of a child to sue for injuries sustained *in utero,* he quoted that "justice requires that the principle be recognized that a child has a legal right to begin life with a sound mind and body."[32] In other words, the court relied on the principle of fairness to reach the conclusion that the protection of, and redress for, postnatal harm to "mind and body" should likewise be available to persons alleging prenatal injuries.

As to the second element of the rule—injuries—no question arose: the judges all agreed that Jeffrey suffered severe impairment. If we skip momentarily over the third element—compensation—the fourth element poses the question whether Dr. Cosgrove was "the person who caused (Jeffrey's) injuries." The physician did not cause the impairment in the sense of having given Mrs. Gleitman rubella; however, in torts parlance he was the proximate cause of the impairment because his mistaken advice prevented the Gleitmans from avoiding the manifestation of injuries. Had Jeffrey been a grown man who received negligently inaccurate advice from Dr. Cosgrove about a neurological disorder which thereafter, in absence of treatment, rendered him blind and deaf, the legal rules governing the doctor–patient relationship would require Dr. Cosgrove to compensate Jeffrey for his impairment.[33] The court's contrary conclusion that Dr. Cosgrove's conduct "was not the cause of infant plantiff's condition"[34] is nonsensical—as the court itself recognizes, the plaintiff would not have been in that condition had Dr. Cosgrove told the Gleitmans of the risk of impairment.

The reason why the New Jersey court felt constrained to deny Jeffrey a "just" application of the usual rule of recovery is not that Dr. Cosgrove did not cause the injuries, but its conclusion that there was no way to calculate how to make Jeffrey "whole" again. This aspect of *Gleitman* is very pertinent for us; given the present state of genetic counseling, the only "treatment" available in most cases is to abort the fetus.

---

[31] 31 N.J. 353 (1960).

[32] Id. at 364.

[33] Jeffrey's legal right to competent advice from an expert, and Dr. Cosgrove's duty to provide it, are paralleled by the moral rights and duties set forth in the *Principles of Medical Ethics* which state that physicians should render "to each (patient) a full measure of service and devotion."

[34] 49 N.J. at 28.

There are two grounds on which the court's holding is open to criticism. First, the conclusion that a court "cannot weigh the value of life with impairments against the nonexistence of life itself"[34] is contradicted by courts making similar subjective calculations (the value of lives cut short, of pain and suffering, and other intangibles) every day. Second, if the New Jersey court intended a broader point, that life with any handicap is per se better than no life at all, it cited no authority for this conclusion. What it did cite is Professor Tedeschi's argument that "no comparison is possible since were it not for the act of birth the infant would not exist."[35] But this adds nothing to the court's own *a priori* judgment in favor of impaired life versus abortion; it only serves to create confusion over the act for which plaintiff is suing. Jeffrey did not sue Dr. Cosgrove "for his life," although such a suit is not as illogical as Justice Proctor, relying on Professor Tedeschi, suggests.[36] Rather, Jeffrey sued the physician for his failure to give accurate advice on which a decision could be made by Jeffrey's parents, acting in their child's behalf, that for him not to be born would be preferable to being born deformed. If one objects to awarding damages for the violation of this right, it seems to me that the objection goes either to the policy of allowing abortions (the court assumed one could have been legally obtained) or to giving parents, who may have conflicting motivations, the authority to make this decision (as the law now does). The fact remains that the *Gleitman* court departed from the rule that the choice in this matter lies with the patient, not the physician,[37] and its action is no more defensible than that of a court which, faced with a patient who was ravaged by an untreated disease, were to dismiss the suit on the grounds that the standard treatment (about which the physician negligently failed to inform the patient) is highly dangerous and nearly always fatal.

[35] Tedeschi, G. (1966). "On Tort Liability for 'Wrongful Life'", *Israel Law Review, 1,* 529.
[36] Would a court throw out a suit brought by a patient who had contracted a disabling injury through a physician's negligence in administering transfusions, simply because the physician proved that but for the transfusions the patient would have died? Although the plaintiff would "owe his life" to the physician, he could, of course, still sue him.
[37] This choice may even extend to a patient's refusing "life-saving" therapy. See *In re Brooks Estate,* 32 Ill. 2d 361, 205 N.E.2d 435 (1965). The imposition of such therapy against the patient's wishes in *Application of the President and Directors of Georgetown College,* Inc., 331 F.2d 1010 (D.C. Cir.) cert. denied 377 U.S. 978 (1964), was defended by the judge there because the patient had shifted the "legal responsibility" for the choice over to the hospital. Moreover, cases involving adult patients turn on the applicability and interpretation of the policy against suicide which does not apply to cases involving fetuses under a "liberal" abortion law. And both the *Brooks Estate* and *Georgetown* lines of cases start from the position that if the patient's choice is overridden it can only be done by someone (usually a judge) officially enpowered to act as his guardian, and not by the physician alone, as in *Gleitman.*

Misapplied Precedent

If the New Jersey court's failure to heed prevailing legal doctrines led it into one sort of error, its application of prior cases led it into other errors, although certainly not all of its own making. The *Gleitman* court relied on "two cases from other states which have considered the theory of action for 'wrongful life',"[38] *Zepeda v. Zepeda,*[39] an Illinois case, and *Williams v. New York.*[40]

The New Jersey court's reliance on these cases is misplaced because, as the court observed, they "were brought by illegitimate children for damages caused by their birth out of wedlock, and in both cases policy reasons were found to deny recovery."[41] Policies relevant to illegitimacy clearly have limited, if any, application to a suit by a child made deaf and blind by rubella. Moreover, the opinions of the New York and Illinois courts are unsatisfactory on their own facts. In *Williams,* for example, the plaintiff was an infant who had been conceived when her mother, a mental defective in the custody of a state hospital, was raped by another patient. The child claimed that the state's negligence in protecting her mother had caused her (the child) to be deprived of a normal childhood and rearing and "to bear the stigma of illegitimacy."[42] The New York Court of Appeals recognized the "unfair burdens" the plaintiff would bear, as do "many other sons and daughters of shame and sorrow."[43] But, it concluded, "the law knows no cure or compensation for it, and the policy and social reasons against providing such compensation are at least as strong as those which might be thought to favor it."[43] If "the policy and social reasons" against making illegitimacy a "suable wrong" are of no assistance to the *Gleitman* court, perhaps it had in mind the arguments presented by Judge Keating's concurring opinion in *Williams.*[44] These concerned the "logico-legal" difficulty (derived by Judge Keating from Tedeschi's article) "of permitting recovery when the very act which caused the plaintiff's birth was the same one responsible for whatever damage she has suffered or will suffer."[43] We have already seen the error in the "same act" approach, which by characterizing the claim as one for "wrongful life" fails to distinguish between the act of conception and the circumstances under which it is done. Having intercourse is not a crime, but having it when unmarried is, and in this case that was the state's fault. Of course, "had the State

---

[38] 49 N.J. at 29.

[39] 41 Ill.App.2d 240, 190 N.E.2d 849 (App. Ct. 1963), cert. denied 379 U.S. 945 (1964).

[40] 18 N.Y.2d 481, 223 N.E.2d 343 (1966).

[41] 49 N.J. at 29.

[42] 18 N.Y.2d at 482.

[43] Id. at 484.

[44] The Appellate Division, whose decision was being reviewed, had based its decision in part on the Keating line of reasoning (that damages cannot be ascertained because they rest "upon the very fact of conception"). 25 App.Div.2d 907 (1966).

acted responsibly," as Judge Keating noted, the plaintiff "would not have been born at all."[45] Yet the state's failure to do so created not only the infant plaintiff but also her cause of action.

In *Williams* not only were the act (conception) and the tort (negligence in failing to protect the mother from men to whom she was not married) separable, but the latter was even partly remediable without abortion, since the illegitimacy could have been "cured" by subsequent marriage, adoption, etc. This is not so in the genetic counseling situation nor in the *Zepeda* case, where the defendant father was already married when he fraudulently induced the plaintiff's mother to have sexual relations with him by promising to marry her. Yet the *Zepeda* case is also of little comfort to the *Gleitman* court because the Illinois court agreed with plaintiff Zepeda "that the elements of a wilful tort are presented by the allegations of the complaint."[46] The *Zepeda* court saw no barrier to the suit in the tortious act or omission having occurred at, or even before, the plaintiff's conception; nor was the suit barred by the nature of the inquiry, which "is not as tangible as a physical defect but . . . is as real."[47] Yet the "radical" nature of the injury alleged—loosely, "bad" parentage—was the factor which led the court to deny recovery for the tort. If the *Gleitman* court relied at all on the "policy" set by *Zepeda,* it must be on that aspect of the opinion which held that recovery should be permitted only after the legislature had undertaken a "thorough study of the consequences."

Misapprehended Consequences

The Illinois court was not merely worried that entertaining Zepeda's suit would open the floodgates of litigation, leaving the courts inundated by the claims of the quarter million illegitimate children born each year in the United States, but also that damages would soon be sought "for being born of a certain color (or) race; . . . for being born with a hereditary disease, . . . for inheriting unfortunate family characteristics; (or) for being born into a large and destitute

---

[45] 18 N.Y.2d at 485.

[46] 41 Ill.App.2d at 259.

[47] The court built its theory of injury on a detailed review of the "lot of a child born out of wedlock." It contrasted the ignominy and hardships of illegitimacy in the past with the enlightened attitude of modern statutes, which do much to equalize the rights of bastards with those of legitimate offspring. It concluded, nonetheless, that:

Praiseworthy as they are, they do not, and no law can, make these children whole. Children born illegitimate have suffered an injury. (Id. at 258.)

Earlier in the case the court had concluded that three more specific types of injury were not made out by the complaint—mental suffering was not properly averred; defamation requires communication to third persons, which was not alleged; and no child, legitimate or illegitimate, has a legal right to love or a happy home. Id. at 253–255.

family, (or to) a parent (who) has an unsavory reputation."[48] There is a surface appeal to the court's reasoning. Being born into a minority group of a "disadvantaged" family may subject a child to burdens similar to those of illegitimacy, and hereditary disease may cause greater suffering still.

But opening the court to the infant Zepeda would not necessarily open it to the others cited by the court, for poverty, race and genetic makeup do not constitute "moral wrongs(s) and . . . criminal act(s)"[49] which the court held Mr. Zepeda's sexual relations with the plaintiff's mother to be. Being poor or carrying an hereditary disease are not crimes; procreating in these circumstances violates no legal right of the child conceived.

Nevertheless, although nothing in the "policy reasons" of *Williams* or *Zepeda* is either convincing or applicable to *Gleitman*, we owe it to the New Jersey court to puzzle through the consequences of the result we believe it should have reached before criticizing as unjust the one that it did reach. Can it be said of the *Gleitman* decision "that, regrettable though it is, the demands of justice . . . must be overridden in order to preserve something held to be of greater value, which would be jeopardized if . . . discriminations (between Jeffrey Gleitman and other plaintiffs injured by a negligent failure to give complete medical advice) were not made"?[50]

To bring one possible countervailing value into view, let us alter the facts of the Gleitman case. Suppose the child alleged that the physician gave accurate advice to the parents but that the parents disregarded the risks and did not abort, resulting in his being born deformed. If the claim against Dr. Cosgrove is good, must not that against the parents also succeed? If we assume that there is no longer intrafamilial immunity in the jurisdiction,[51] there remains the simple

---

[48] Id. at 260.

[49] Id. at 253.

[50] Hart (1961), 158.

[51] English common law permitted tort actions as well as those involving property and contracts between children and parents. "But beginning in 1891 with *Hewlett v. George* (68 Miss. 703, 9 So. 885 (1891)), a Mississippi case of false imprisonment which cited no authorities, the American courts adopted a general rule refusing to allow actions between parent and minor child for personal torts, whether they are intentional or negligent in character." Prosser, W. L. (1971), *Handbook of The Law of Torts,* Section 122, 865. This result was justified as necessary to avoid introducing "discord and contention where the laws of nature have established peace and obedience." *Wick v. Wick,* 1972 Wis. 260, 262, 212 N.W., 787, 789 (1927); the danger of "fraud" has also been stressed. The "retreat" from this rule is now "under way," as Prof. Prosser notes, and parent-child immunity for personal torts may soon be a thing of the past. See, e.g., *Gibson v. Gibson,* 92 Cal. Rptr. 288 (1971); *Gelbman v. Gelbman,* 23 N.Y.2d 434, 245 N.E.2d 192 (1969): and *Coller v. White* 20 Wis.2d 402, 122 N.W.2d 193 (1963). The courts continue immunity, however, for matters subject to "parental discretion" over the care, etc. of children, and this would serve as a further bar to suits for inherited diseases, unless they involved wanton disregard of or intentional injury to the child's health.

fact that such suits are unlikely because the child's parents, as his guardians or "next friends," actually instigate suits on the child's behalf, and it is unlikely that they would, in effect, sue themselves. Yet even if the state routinely appointed special guardians for all defective children (or all children for that matter), with instructions to bring any necessary lawsuits, such suits would be of little practical value. Parents are already legally obliged to support their children, and most do so to the limits of their ability whether the child is "normal" or not. Consequently, unlike a recovery against an outside party like Dr. Cosgrove, a recovery against the parents would just shift family funds (less lawyers' fees and court costs) from one pocket to another.[52]

While there is at least some merit to these practical reasons why a suit against parents would be unlikely to follow had *Gleitman* been differently decided, the really persuasive argument denies that there is any claim against the parents at all. For there to be a recovery, the defendant must have breached a duty legally owed the plaintiff. Dr. Cosgrove violated such a legal (and moral) duty when he failed to give competent medical advice; by contrast, parents, in choosing not to abort, have exercised their legal right to make this choice. This right of the parents has two sources: (a) one derived from the child's own right, in which case the parents are considered to be making their decision on behalf of their offspring, in what they judge to be his "best interests"; and (b) one which focuses on the parents' own right to exercise control over an event which is of major importance to their lives (directly so in the mother's case, and indirectly in the father's). The second rationale is of more recent vintage and more narrow in scope, being applicable, so far as I know, only in the choice to have an abortion to safeguard the mother's life or health or, in a few jurisdictions, for any reason the parents may have prior to 24 weeks of gestation.[53] Since the decision not to have an abortion would probably be viewed by the courts as being based on both rationales, absent proof of intentional disregard of their child's interests or gross negligence in the exercise of their discretion, such an exercise of judgment would not subject the couple to liability. In the view of the law, it is up to them to weigh the probabilities and risks and to decide whether life with any defects is better than abortion or whether in some cases life with defects is "a fate worse than death."

Conclusion

From this discussion, I would conclude that our hypothetical genetic counselor has a legal duty to give competent advice so as to place the parents

---

[52] Additional funds would be injected only in the unlikely event that an insurance policy held by the parents covered this situation.

[53] Act 1, *Hawaii Sessions Laws of 1970;* N.Y. Penal Law Section 125.05 (McKinney 1970).

into the position of informed decision-makers,[54] and that if by his negligent or intentional breach of this duty a defective child is born, the child (and its parents) have a valid claim for damages against him. This is true whether the parents come to him for advice on whether to abort or on whether to conceive in the first place. (I take the latter situation to be an easier case to establish liability for medical advice and, consequently, have addressed myself only to the former).

Unless we accept as a valid legal rule the *Gleitman* court's dictum that every child has "a legal right to begin life with a sound mind and body,"[55] however, a child who suffers a genetic disease does not have a claim against its parents because they decided to give it birth despite the risks of the disease. The *Gleitman* court did not accept this principle at face value, and neither should we. As a moral precept it states an admirable guide for conduct and aspiration; as a legal rule it is too far-reaching. The legal rule which I have suggested should be applied protects courts from the nearly impossible task of reviewing the parents' good faith judgment about the "quality of life" which a child will experience; the child is protected against intentional harm by the parents, as he would be after birth; and the parents are protected in the prudent use of the capabilities with which nature endowed them. This comports with our moral sense that it is unjust to blame someone for something (such as his genetic makeup) which he cannot (presently) control. It would be cruel to add to the injury of a defective gene (and the undeserved self-blame which is felt when the disease manifests itself in an offspring) the insult of a suit by the offspring. On the other hand, parents who knowingly and recklessly took a drug with a substantial teratogenic risk would be liable if their offspring were deformed. Similarly, major manipulations of the birth process, done in the face of adverse or incalculable risks, would expose their creators to liability for injuries suffered.

None of these eventualities are pleasant to contemplate, and one can hope that they never pass from the hypothetical to the real. But if they do, I am confident that the courts, and in some instances the legislatures, will make clear

---

[54] Our discussion has focused solely on the rights and duties relating to liability for negligent advice. Time does not permit an exploration of the myriad other rights and duties which arise from the geneticist-patient relationship or of the limitations (and their remedies, if any) which are placed on the exercise of these rights and duties by internal and external constraints. Some exploration of these problems especially concerning informed consent, appears in my "Law of Genetic Therapy" in *The New Genetics and the Future of Man*, M. Hamilton, editor, Grand Rapids, Eerdmans (1972), and see Hans Jonas, "Philosophical Reflections on Experimenting with Human Subjects," 98 *Daedalus 219* (1969); Henry K. Beecher, "Consent in Clinical Experimentation: Myth and Reality," 195 *J. Am. Med. Assn. 124* (1966).

[55] 49 N.J. at 28, quoting 31 N.J. at 364.

the right of children to recover for their injuries. *Gleitman v. Cosgrove* neither will, nor should be, the final word on the subject.

Acknowledgment

The author is grateful to Dr. Jay Katz and Miss Barbara A. Brown for their comments on this paper, which also profited from work done on a related subject under grant HSM 110-69-213, Health Services and Mental Health Administration, DHEW.

PRIVACY AND
GENETIC INFORMATION

HERBERT A. LUBS

Introduction

Privacy is a hot topic!

Invasion of privacy is decried on the streets and discussed in academic halls. The preservation of privacy is almost a holy cause in the United States and, indeed, it is somewhat un-American not to come to the vigorous defense of privacy. The other side of the coin, namely, the possible harmful effects of maintaining privacy, is less often displayed.

In this paper, I hope to provoke thought about what test cases might be most suitable to clarify the issues of medical ethics in relation to human genetics and what new laws might be desirable. However, one might ask whether we really would like to bring legal clarification to these issues. Perhaps instead a set of ethics for the medical geneticist would be more appropriate for handling this rapidly changing situation in human genetics.

One of the theses I submit is that over the next 10 to 20 years we must re-examine and possibly modify attitudes towards privacy. The geneticist must work in this sensitive area and it is critical for the future practice of medical genetics that questions of privacy be resolved. Stated succinctly, "How can optimal use of genetic data best be coupled with the maintenance of privacy?"

Genetic information may be used in three ways. A "good use" might be prevention of mental retardation by early treatment of a genetic disorder in a child known to be at risk. A "misuse" might be release of a report of an individual's abnormal chromosome complement in a way which would hinder his employment. "Nonuse," or complete privacy, would be a lost opportunity to use genetic information for the benefit of other family members.

The considerations must be made slightly more complex, however. Two levels of privacy are implicit even in these simple examples: (1) the patient's own

This paper originally appeared in *Ethical Issues in Human Genetics,* Bruce Hilton *et al.,* eds. (New York: Plenum Press, 1973). Reprinted with permission of the author and Plenum Publishing Corporation.

privacy and (2) that of other family members, including future offspring. There are also two general routes by which an individual's privacy may be invaded.

The first is through the proband (or propositus), who is the individual through whom a family comes to medical attention. This may occur in several ways. An individual with a genetic disorder may seek medical attention and the medical geneticist may subsequently seek information from or provide genetic counseling to other family members of the proband. Their privacy is therefore invaded. Similarly, geneticists interested in research may begin their clinical investigations with a group of individuals ascertained from clinics and hospital records and proceed to their families. If the investigation is on a larger scale, the genetics investigator might search health insurance records of major insuring agencies for patients with Tay-Sachs disease, for example. This would certainly be part of the "Big Brother" concern.

The second route is the identification of individuals with genetic disorders through surveys or screening programs. These may be either legally required, such as the PKU screening program, or for the purpose of medical research. The cytogenetic surveys of consecutive newborn infants are examples. In the future, medical screening of individuals in health plans will likely include certain genetic tests, such as tests for sickle and other abnormal hemoglobins. I emphasize this second route of invasion of privacy because here the individual does not come to the doctor with a medical problem. The relationship between the doctor and the patient is thus different, and he is an unusual proband. We are going to the patient and asking to help him.

Practical Problems

The majority of our work in the last five years in the Department of Pediatrics, University of Colorado Medical Center, has begun with cytogenetic studies of relatively large unselected populations of newborns or children, and we have become experts in how people react to having their privacy invaded. The range of reactions displayed by these children's mothers was enormous: from interest manifested by a letter every six months inquiring about the program of the study, to refusal to participate in the study because the mother was convinced my research nurse was really a commercial photographer. We have ventured out into several hundred of these thousands of families for more information and have experienced a wide range of reactions, often from the same person in a family. One hostile aunt of a child with a translocation, who initially resisted being studied, finally cooperated, but later again became hostile because more family studies had not been done sooner. Perhaps I oversold. Most people have been extremely cooperative and interested. Several examples will serve to illustrate certain of the problems we encountered. The names and precise pedigrees are hypothetical, but each situation has actually occurred.

Jack was found to have an XYY karyotype in a survey of newborn infants (Figure 1). Generally, the occurrence of an XYY karyotype is a sporadic event, and we are not greatly concerned with its transmission to offspring. We are concerned with the effect the XYY karyotype, as well as knowledge of this karyotype, on Jack's development and progress in life. The stereotype of the XYY "syndrome" has passed too quickly into the public domain, and the concern is what teachers, neighbors, and employers will think if they know that he is XYY. It is difficult to envision any benefit to his image, except in the eyes of an interested genetics investigator. Because of our knowledge of his karyotype, his development will be watched closely. Perhaps early referral for psychiatric help might help to prevent some of the potential psychological and social problems that appear to be associated with an XYY karyotype in some individuals. It is not known, however, that psychiatric intervention would be effective. Much has been written about the unproven association of the XYY karyotype with prisoner status, and I believe there is a real associated risk, since all surveys show a manyfold increase in frequency of the XYY karyotype in prisoners over that in newborn infants. Many XYY men, however, are normal, and the real problem is our ignorance. Jack may be the victim of this ignorance, and the question is how to safeguard him and protect society. My own temporary solution to this problem is to stall until we know more. The safest thing seems to be to withhold the information from everyone and to follow Jack closely. Ultimately, when perspective returns, society and physicians and the patient can handle the situation as it should be handled: by evaluating the particular person's performance and behavior. Privacy, ultimately, will not be so important in such cases.

What sort of informed consent should be obtained in studies such as this, which led to the detection of Jack's XYY karyotype? First, it should contain an

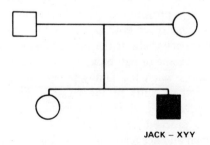

JACK – XYY

Figure 1. Ascertainment through screening programs: Problems for the individual.

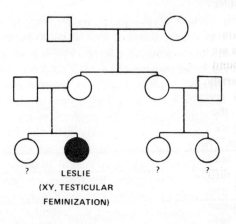

Figure 2. Ascertainment through screening programs: Problems for other family members.

assurance that the information will remain private. It should also include a statement that if important medical information is found, the investigator will inform the patient and his physician if it is felt to be helpful information. It should probably not include very much more. I do not see how we can discuss, when doing such surveys, all the possible disorders we may find and all of the implications. There are hundreds of abnormalities and we cannot possibly inform someone of each one.

Leslie was a normal appearing baby girl who showed evidence of a Y chromosome in a survey of amnions (Figure 2). This test was being done on each infant at the hospital where she was born. Further tests showed that she had an XY karyotype and the testicular feminization syndrome. She will develop as a girl and have normal intelligence, but she will have no uterus and a real risk that a tumor will develop in her abnormal gonads. Her older sister and two first cousins, all under 10 years of age, are at risk for the same problems. How are we to proceed? We do not wish to tell the whole truth (that Leslie is a chromosomal male), but we do wish to provide the best medical care for the family. Generally, we explain the risks and offer both prophylactic surgery and hormonal treatment, without being specific about the chromosomal information, and often we do not put the chromosome or pathology reports in the medical chart. The most difficult question arises when the family pursues the etiology of the problems and wants to know the results of the chromosome studies. Privacy may be essential to Leslie's psychological development and the geneticist for each family must decide how to proceed. It is a case of her privacy (on a very personal matter) versus her own and her relatives medical well being.

I believe we are obligated to offer similar chromosomal studies to others at risk in the family, and therefore to invade their privacy. Both real and imagined concerns will be introduced, but we hope we will do more good than harm. Once the issue is raised, it is critical to proceed with dispatch and return answers about the normality or abnormality of each person in question. An approach might be to wait until those at risk are age 5 or 10 and then carry out the studies. Americans are a mobile population, however, and we worry that the family will be lost to follow-up in the interval and that a tumor might develop in a family member. We do not have a nationwide medical data bank and it is likely that a relative will be lost to follow-up. Here, privacy is likely to be detrimental.

Who is the proper person to investigate, or at least to offer the possibilities of investigation, to the other family members? Is it the state, the geneticist, or the family? There is no current answer to these questions.

I believe that telling people the full truth is good and that this should be our goal, but I think it is too soon for this. People cannot yet cope with too much genetic knowledge about themselves.

The next case is presented as a complex situation involving an additional dimension, time, and should serve to caution us about rigid thinking and premature institution of laws. Hope was found to have 45 chromosomes and a D/G translocation in a survey of newborn infants five years ago (Figure 3). Her mother, grandmother, and aunt had the same translocation. No abnormal family members were found, yet it was felt at the time that a D/G translocation carrier had a significant risk of having a child with an unbalanced karyotype. The benefit from invading this family's privacy was the chance to have subsequent pregnancies monitored by amniocentesis and cytogenetic study, with therapeutic abortion of fetuses with an unbalanced translocation, as suggested by the question marks. The risk figure originally discussed with the parents was in fact a mean of several risk figures, since at least six possible combinations between D and G chromosomes were possible and at that time we could not determine

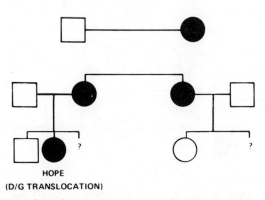

HOPE
(D/G TRANSLOCATION)

Figure 3. Ascertainment through screening programs: Problems created by imprecise methodology.

which combination was present. The family was restudied this fall with the more precise new techniques and the translocation was found to involve chromosomes 14 and 22. It is likely that there is little or no risk associated with this particular translocation and that we have caused five years of worry. We hope that by having offered amniocentesis to the involved parents that at least the worry was minimal. The point I want to illustrate here is the hazard of incomplete knowledge. The five-year interval between the initial ascertainment, nevertheless, provides an important perspective to the impact of such information on the involved families. Both the passage of time and precise information ultimately may produce a realistic acceptance and utilization of initially disturbing information. When first told that his daughter and wife had a translocation, the father responded half jokingly: "Is that grounds for divorce, Doctor?" Five years later he wrote a grateful letter, saying that they had given copies of my letters to their family physicians and were keeping a folder for each child with appropriate information to be given to them later. Lastly, he even referred to our "humane approach to research." Certain families, at least, are grateful for the invasion of privacy, even in the face of the uncertainties that may be raised in their minds.

Peter was brought to a hemophilia clinic at three months with severe bleeding and the diagnosis of hemophilia A was established (Figure 4). The family was shocked, disbelieving, and rejected the doctor's explanation of X-linked inheritance. No amount of persuasion would change their minds and they refused permission for the medical geneticist to contact relatives, even when it was explained that, by determining the sex of subsequent pregnancies in relatives at risk, it would be possible to prevent other cases of hemophilia in the family. The risks for having an affected male child are as follows (given only one affected male in the family):

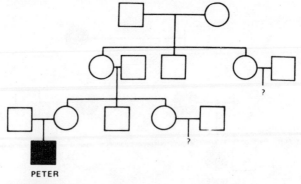

PETER

(HEMOPHILIA A)

Figure 4. Ascertainment through a proband: Refusal of permission to see other family members.

Female Relatives	Risk of Having an Affected Male Child[1]
	%
Mother	25.0
Sister	12.5
Niece	6.3
Grand niece	3.2
Maternal grandmother	25.0
Maternal grand aunt	12.5
Maternal first cousin	6.3
Maternal first cousin once removed	3.2
Maternal second cousin	1.6

Many family members have a significant risk. How then are we to proceed? To my knowledge, this situation has not been tested in court and the usual procedure is to respect the privacy of Peter and his parents and hope that other family members at risk will hear of the problem and seek genetic counseling. They seldom do. This, then, is a case of nonuse. No study has been made to determine how many relatives are aware of their risks (or lack of risks) in similar situations. When such a case does come to court, the legal case would seem to rest on how far two laws are extended: the first being the 4th Amendment which covers invasion of privacy, and the second being the State's traditional right to control transmissable disease (e.g., infectious disease). We are on the horns of a dilemma. I can envision being sued by the mother if I went to other family members or by other family members if I did not.

The Data Bank and Big Brother

What has been discussed above are my concerns as a medical geneticist. Most people's concerns, I suspect, are about other possible misuses of computerized genetic data. Will "Big Brother" decide that certain parents cannot reproduce? How can we prevent computerized control of human behavior?

Are these real concerns? At the moment there is no prospect of a nation-wide genetic data bank, but a number of genetic registries are being developed. Dr. William Kimberling has a very large family registry in Oregon, and the aim is to record in the computer registry all the families in Oregon with genetic disorders. Dr. Marie-Louise Lubs in our laboratory is beginning a similar registry for Colorado. One of our specific aims in computerizing the data is to make it relatively easy to contact each family once a year, both to provide them with information about newly available treatments and to update our records. In addition, we hope it will be a resource to which the families can continue to turn

[1] New mutations not considered.

for help and information over the years as they move about the country. We proceed, I might add, only on a voluntary basis and one of our first projects will be to determine the families' reactions to this intrusion into their privacy.

There are a number of ways of maintaining the privacy of information on tapes and discs. The primary one is to code each person's data and identification, and to keep names and addresses on separate tapes. It is also possible to garble the coded information on the tape or disc in a number of ways, but this seems to me unnecessary. It would take a rather sophisticated intruder to find the number of the desired tape (there are thousands in the computer center), the format, and the coding system, hire a programmer, and have access to a computer. The hazard is not the computerized data, no matter how extensive, but the people around it. I don't see any safeguard from an underpaid programmer who might be bought, or a crusading geneticist who wished to prove how dangerous this approach was by exposing all data to the public. Basically, we have to depend on the integrity of scientists for the maintenance of privacy.

Let us assume, for the sake of discussion, that there is a nationwide data bank and that a request for names and addresses of all individuals with hemophilia is made by an insurance company who wished to offer special high risk policies to families with hemophilia. Should this information be released? Who should decide on the "goodness" of such a request? We can get some information about this by looking at other parts of the world. In Sweden such a data bank for certain diseases does exist and is workable. Information is released to bona fide investigators and no one seems troubled by it. I mention this simply to show that we should at least consider the benefits from such an approach as well as the hazards. Perhaps a board of medical geneticists, laymen, and social scientists would be helpful in the future if such a data bank even comes to pass in the United States. It is the history of science that, if something can be done, it will be done. Our role, I believe, is to see that something is done well, not to prevent its being done at all.

Summary and Conclusions

A simple balance sheet can serve to summarize what has been presented:

Potential Hazards of Loss of Privacy
Loss of feeling of "privacy," per se.
Prejudicial use of genetic information by other persons.
Disastrous effects on the patient of "loaded" information such as chromosomal sex.
Creation of unnecessary concerns in other family members.
Control of reproduction in a biased or unsound fashion by society.

Potential Benefits of Loss of Privacy

Opportunity of realistically dealing with a high reproductive risk.

Opportunity to alleviate unnecessary fears in relatives at complications of genetic disease in relatives.

Opportunity to offer selective reproduction via therapeutic abortion to relatives at risk.

Opportunity to offer benefits of research to affected families, without the usual 5–10-year delay.

How can these problems be resolved? Time, I believe, is the most important factor. The combination of better genetic information and better education of the public about genetics will resolve most of them. Examples of abnormal human karyotypes and biochemical disorders are now in many high school biology books, and sickle cell disease is becoming a household word, albeit for the wrong reasons. Privacy need not be such a hot topic. In the interim, however, we must proceed cautiously.

Discussion

SINGER: Dr. Lubs makes a point that is important for lawyers, physicians, and philosophers to remember—facts always seem to get in the way of our nice, theoretical analyses. They resist getting shoved comfortably into the pigeonholes we design for them. For example, one who is committed to full disclosure of information cannot but be made uncomfortable by the example of the XY female.

In analyzing issues of privacy we must ask to what extent and under what circumstances is it appropriate to invade the privacy of another? This question has two parts: the acquisition of information and the disclosure of information. It is one thing to acquire genetic data from A, about A; a different question is raised when we acquire data from A about B. On the disclosure side, should disclosure be made to the donor of the information or to some related party for whom the genetic information may be relevant? Perhaps the most difficult problem is disclosure of information to an unrelated person. Whose privacy is being invaded, by whom is it being invaded, and for what purposes is the invasion made?

We may also come to the point where we ask whether there are some types of information that we do not want to have acquired. For the research community, are there some types of experiments or information that you simply do not want to get into? One example is the relationship, if any, between race and intelligence. I am not anxious to acquire that information because I think it is irrelevant to current social issues. Thus for the issue of mass screening, we must balance the need to know and the right to maintain privacy among human beings who live very closely in one society.

CAPRON: The primary harm to a patient arises in the screening process when information which was never sought by the patient is found out. Giving this information to the patient is the second point at which he is harmed. If, however, a patient comes to you asking for information about himself, this information should be conveyed to him, although in a proper psychological setting. But it does not seem to me that there are any grounds, other than a misimpression of what is in the patient's best interest, which would lead to withholding information which is sought.

MURRAY: You have exaggerated the situation. It is the exceptional case in which one withholds information, and it is certainly not routine medical practice. The kinds of cases in which I would do that are those involving emotional stability. Lawyers ought to know that you can get some of the biggest verdicts in suits relating to emotional distress. You are trying to ignore the emotions in your rule that knowledge should always be transmitted, Also, you are guessing, just as the physician is guessing, that the patient will be able to deal with the information, no matter how it is conveyed. All you need is one person who takes an overdose of barbiturates or jumps off a bridge, and the lawyers have a case against the physician or counselor. You can get in trouble whether you give the information, and a patient kills himself, or whether you withhold the information. I prefer to commit a sin of omission rather than take the chance of committing a sin of commission.

CAPRON: I have stated a rule, which I defended on both theoretical and practical grounds, and yet I admit that you may present a case to me which I will find very difficult to insist should be guided by the principle of full disclosure. I don't pretend to say that these choices are easy or that they should always be decided according to that principle.

McLAREN: Mr. Capron has raised the problem of withholding information in the interests of the patient. This is really an example of the more general category of paternalism which is, of course, traditional to the medical profession. Medical practitioners should remember that if they do err, they are likely to err in that direction.

FRIED: Several non-physicians and I share Dr. McLaren's notion that the medical profession is indeed very paternalistic. Surely, if a physician has some findings, perhaps broad, inconclusive, or even incorrect, it would be very wrong to withhold this information on the mistakenly paternalistic notion that the people involved couldn't take it.

HIMSWORTH: Lord Kilbrandon made the point that a special relationship exists between a doctor and a patient, a relationship based on the expectation that the doctor will do the best for the patient that it is possible to do. The ultimate responsibility is on the physician to decide what information to give to the patient. If you get information that a fetus is abnormal, you have got to ask yourself what will be the effect of disclosing this, however tactfully and carefully, to the mother? Can she face bringing up this child? Or when she gets away from my persuasion and smoothness of talking, will she go take an overdose of barbiturates?

CAPRON: There seems to be no question that the relationship is a complex one, and there may be many doctors who believe, as Sir Harold does, that the doctor should make many choices for his patient. However, if doctors find themselves making choices not about the medical facts, but about future psychological factors of the child and the parents, then I think doctors have overstepped their role. This is not the role of the doctor; the doctor has the responsibility of conveying the medical import of the diagnosis.

MURRAY: Mr. Capron, in your analysis of one case you considered legal justification for performing abortion, and you supported the parents' right to decide to abort a fetus based on what they thought was in the best interests of the unborn child. I know a great deal more about a patient, even though I have only talked to him for a brief time, than those parents know about an unborn fetus. Therefore, I don't see how you can justify the rights of a parent to make a decision about a fetus, and say that the physician, who knows at least what the patient looks like, has no right to decide what is in the patient's best interests.

CAPRON: I am criticizing the substitution of judgment of best interests by one person for another. The person sitting across the table from you is able to make judgments for himself, whereas the fetus is not. Traditionally the role of making substitute judgment for children in our society has been given to the parents. If we were to conclude that the parent is no more able to make an accurate or an informed judgment for a fetus than a doctor is able to make for a patient, then we ought to find someone else to do it.

KILBRANDON: It may be a very serious question for the doctor whether he tells the truth or whether he gives the information which he judges to be most beneficial to his patient. If these two are in conflict, there is no doubt at all which he has to do. He has to give the information which is most beneficial to his patient. This may be a very difficult decision, and I really was quite horrified when Dr. Murray expressed the view that you can't win, because they will get you either way. If that were so, the law would be in a very shocking state. As I understand the law, a suit brought against a doctor raises the question of whether or not he has been negligent, not whether he has offered some treatment which another doctor would not have offered, or he has taken a view of the case which might not appeal to some of his other colleagues.

Whether you offer the truth or some modified part of the truth, or whether you offer beneficial information, is a very tricky question on which there is ample room for bona fide difference of opinion. If the law says that, having come down on one side in good faith, with adequate skill, and perhaps having discussed it with your colleagues, you are liable for damages, then the law ought to be changed.

HAVIGHURST: I pose the possibility that we litigate the matter. I will present some 20 expert witnesses drawn from this audience to indicate that the custom and practice in the profession of genetic counseling is to the effect that some information may be withheld. They would agree that in a particular case, it was professionally appropriate to withhold the information. Now, who would win, if that evidence were presented and not seriously challenged?

What I am asking is a clearer statement of what the law in fact is. I suggest that, in some states at least, the law on informed consent is that the doctor is obligated to inform his patient only to the extent that other practitioners in the area would inform the patient in similar circumstances.

CAPRON: Your premise is one which Lord Kilbrandon has already highlighted in that there is a great deal of "ought" as opposed to "is." Doctors have asked me exactly that question, and my answer has been that the prevailing law in judging the disclosure of information is, indeed, the standard which has always applied in malpractice, which is "the reasonable medical practitioner."

I suggest that some of the informed consent cases, for example, *Salgo v. Stanford University Board of Trustees* (154 Cal. App. 2d 560, 317 P 2d 170 (1957)) have conceived of the doctor's action not so much as a violation of the old standards of negligence, but under another tort standard whereby an intentional withholding of information or a deception would be judged by a reasonable man standard, so that the jury would be asked to decide whether it was reasonable to withhold information, and expert testimony as such would not be pertinent. Experts might persuade a jury that this was a reasonable course, but they would not be bound by that testimony under the instructions of the judge. An example of this approach in a therapeutic setting is *Berkey v. Anderson* (1 Cal. App. 3d 790, 805, 82 Cal. Rptr. 67, 78 (1969)) where the court stated:

> We cannot agree that the matter of informed consent must be determined on the basis of medical testimony . . . a physician's duty to disclose is not governed by the standard practice of the physician's community, but is a duty imposed by law which governs his conduct in the same manner as others in a similar fiduciary relationship. To hold otherwise would permit the medical profession to determine its own responsibilities. . . .

For all the reasons I gave that is the rule that should be adopted in these circumstances because the old idea of the family physician knowing so well his patient and his family and the conditions of the community is no longer an accurate one, particularly vis-à-vis consultants, such as genetic counselors, who see a family only briefly. For the theoretical reasons which prompt my "ought," the rule should be one of reasonableness and not of medical malpractice.

VEATCH: A dilemma arises when the norms of professional ethics conflict with the normative system operating more universally in society. Many medical professionals operate within the context of professional ethics which may be summarized as doing no harm or acting only for the benefit of the patient. However, it is not at all clear that that ethical principle is shared by the general public or by moral philosophers. Thus, a medical professional may be forced by the nature of his occupation to interact with a person who is not operating within the same ethical frame of reference. A very fundamental problem is created once one articulates moral responsibility in terms of a particular ethical system for the professional sphere.

MANGEL: There is a distinction between the information that you give a patient, depending on whether you are in a research situation or whether you are in a therapeutic situation. The test Mr. Capron enunciated is probably applicable to the pure clinical research situation, in which case it is difficult to justify the withholding of any relevant information. This position was held in the recent case of *Halushka* v. *University of Saskatchewan* (53 D. L. R. 2nd 436 (1965). I do not think that the case law in this country has yet taken the position that there must be full disclosure in a therapeutic situation. Courts always deal with the question of whether negligence existed in something done, and I haven't seen any case in which liability was based solely on a failure to disclose information in a therapeutic situation.

RAMSEY: Regardless of the law, the ethics of medical practice has to agree with the principle of full disclosure and must put upon itself the moral burden of justifying the withholding of information. This is not really out of accord with the ordinary man's understanding of truth-telling in his interpersonal relations.

FRIED: I want to remove any excessive sense of assurance that doctors may have about the state of the law, where it has been said that the standard is what do most reasonable practitioners do. There is clearly movement in the law in respect to all experts and special professional groups, not to let their relations to persons outside of their group be determined by the judgments of a majority of their own fraternity. There is a growing realization in the law that what doctors decide is subject ultimately to legal scrutiny. I suspect the only reasons that that movement has not gone further with doctors is that it might, one day, be applied to lawyers.

MacINTYRE: Dr. Lubs mentioned the testicular feminization syndrome. In my judgment, this case is one in which it is not only undesirable but highly dangerous to divulge complete information. Such individuals are genetically males, but externally they develop as females. In our society I can think of no psychological framework which is more emotionally important and sensitive than that associated with one's sexual identification.

Let's assume a situation in which a patient, married for some time and apparently female, comes to you asking why she has never menstruated or been able to become pregnant, and you ascertain that this individual is genetically male and is a case of the testicular feminization syndrome. If you divulge your complete findings and thereby destroy the patient's sexual identification as a female, I don't believe anyone could prevent emotional catastrophe in this patient and in her husband. I see no possible benefit, immediate or potential, to be derived from divulging complete information. I am familiar with two cases in which the total information was given carefully and with understanding and compassion. Nevertheless, the emotional impact was such that both previously happy marriages ended in divorce because of the inability of the members of each couple to look upon each other as they previously had.

CAPRON: However, isn't there a risk of cancer for these patients?

MacINTYRE: It is true that the testes probably should be removed because of the risk of malignant growth, but that does not mean they have to be specifically described as testes. They could be described by the general term *gonads,* and it should be pointed out that there is a risk of their becoming malignant and it is recommended that they be removed. It should be noted also that because of the developmental problem, the gonads would never be functional in a reproductive sense anyway. Counseling in this fashion protects the individual's identification with femininity which is all-important.

The question frequently will arise with respect to notifying the parents of a child with testicular feminization syndrome. Here, too, I think there is a potential danger. I have seen parents become terribly upset by such information to the extent that they are warped in their attitude toward the child thereafter. I believe that parents ought to know that the condition has a hereditary component but they don't have to find out that their "little girl" is really a "little boy."

It may be argued that by careful and lengthy counseling one could eliminate the dangers I have mentioned, but I don't think so. Regardless of how intelligent individuals may be, emotional stress and shock are a tremendous deterrent to clear understanding and full acceptance of a counselor's statements.

LEJEUNE: It is wrong to tell this woman she is a man, because she really is not. You may tell her that in general the chemical reactions which determine the male sex correspond to an XY chromosomal set, but that sometimes, as in her case, a special chemical change of the genes can produce a female with an XY chromosomal set. Thus there is no reason to conceal the truth. Do not tell her she is a male, which she is not, but that she is an exceptional female with an XY chromosome complement.

LUBS: The only long-term answer is education. If students learn more genetics and biology, it is possible that they can handle information such as this. But it is not appropriate right now with every patient.

MOTULSKY: The public is learning more and more about science, medicine, and genetics and often understands intellectually many of the processes involved. Intellectual understanding, however, does not mean that the emotional resources to accept bad news are available. Most people want a medical advisor or genetic counselor who knows science, but who is also a sympathetic human being who can decide what information will be in the best interest of the patient. I, as a patient, want that kind of physician. I would not want the "health technician" or the "genetics technician" who tells me the cold facts in an objective manner and then brings in a psychiatrist to make me feel better.

RECOMBINANT DNA

JOHN J. MADDEN

Our society acknowledges the prominence of certain individuals, or movements, in a variety of ways not the least of which is the awarding of the cover story in a national magazine. Richard Nixon, the Pope, Dolly Parton, and the Silent Majority have all received bountiful attention and display on magazine racks in supermarkets throughout the country. It is therefore significant that the April 18, 1977 cover of *Time* is devoted not to a rock star but rather to the controversy surrounding the biological techniques known collectively as the recombinant DNA method. The article,[1] "Tinkering with Life," indicates that, while still in its infancy, this method clearly has biological implications which rival the potential consequences of atomic technology because it provides the means for transferring genetic information freely between any two cells. Other articles and books have since appeared, with many bringing tales of unknown genetic horrors lurking in laboratories or in the planning stage. The controversy fed on these lurid monster stories and soon it became a media event which was battled everywhere from the Six O'Clock News to the halls of Congress. Time has removed some of the hysteria from the debate, but the consequences of the technology and of the debate itself are still pertinent and fascinating.

Recombinant DNA methodology encompasses a variety of techniques and assays which can be combined to manipulate the genetic background of any organism. For the sake of discussion, we will include under the heading of recombinant DNA methods all means for transferring a small piece of genetic information (DNA) from one cell into a cell with a different genetic background. Cloning, the transfer of all the genetic material from one cell into a cell which has had its DNA removed, will not be discussed here because it raises questions extraneous to the recombinant DNA controversy. Also, despite the claims of successful human cloning in a recent bestseller, the difficulties in extracting intact human DNA from a cell, transferring it into another cell, and controlling its expression are so overwhelming as to make this procedure unlikely for the near future, if not impossible forever.

Recombinant DNA methods are based on two very simple ideas: first, genetic information is organized in a linear fashion along the DNA in a series of discreet messages, or genes; and second, DNA messages are composed of words, three

[1] F. Golden, "Tinkering with Life," *Time*, pp. 32–45 (April 18, 1977).

chemical bases in length, which are in a universal language understood by all cells. Genes can thus be expected to produce the same product regardless of the cell in which they are used. Cells transcribe the DNA message units into another nucleic acid form, RNA, which is then translated into the primary gene product, a protein. It is the proteins which carry out the cell's metabolic functions and which are, in general, the active molecules in controlling the life of the cell (Figure 1A).

In genetic manipulation by recombinant DNA technology,[2] the first step is to extract the DNA from its cell and to split it into its component messages, or genes. This latter step can be accomplished because of the work of Werner Arber, Hamilton Smith, and Daniel Nathaus (Nobel Prize Winners for Medicine in 1978) on the proteins which split DNA specifically—the restriction endonucleases. The DNA pieces are then separated by electrophoresis on agarose, a material not unlike Jello. The DNA is transported into the host cell by attaching it to a carrier DNA molecule, called a plasmid. Plasmids are small, circular pieces of DNA which can often be found in bacterial cells, but whose origin and purpose is obscure. The DNA piece and the plasmid join to form a recombinant DNA molecule in the classic sense, although vehicles other than plasmids are also currently being used and would fall under the ensuing discussions. These recombinant DNA molecules are introduced into receptive bacteria where they are replicated and their genes expressed. Gene expression means that the product of the gene, regardless of the original source of the DNA, is now produced in the bacterial cell (Figure 1B). By this method biochemicals, like human myglobin, a protein from muscle used in oxygen metabolism, could be prepared from bacteria infected with a recombinant DNA molecule containing the gene for myoglobin.

Two problems immediately arise from this method. While myoglobin is synthesized and utilized without further processing, a proteinlike insulin is initially synthesized as a long chain (called proinsulin) which is then metabolized by the human cell to the usable form. Bacterial cells do not have the natural capacity to metabolize proinsulin to insulin, and they would have to be modified by other recombinant DNA molecules to acquire this ability, a difficult procedure. There are many other examples of such preprocessing in higher organisms, which adds an extra degree of complexity to the problem of expressing genes of higher organisms in bacteria. The second problem inherent in this technology is an inability to determine in advance which piece of DNA contains the desired gene so that, when we separate the pieces by electrophoresis, we cannot predict which piece will produce the lady and which the tiger. In Figure 1B, gene 2 represents all the undescribed cellular genes which code for presently unknown chemicals which could potentially cure cancer, alleviate world hunger, promote mental

[2]C. Grobstein, "The Recombinant DNA Debate," *Scientific American 237:* 22–23, 1977.

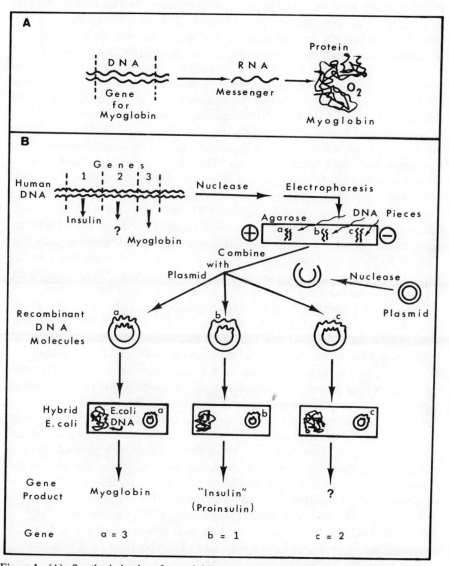

Figure 1. (A): Synthesis *in vivo* of myoglobin, a protein responsible for oxygen transport in human muscle tissue. (B): Production of typical proteins by recombinant DNA methodology.

health, or release a devastating plague. The method of choice for discovering which door we have unlocked is to try all the pieces one at a time ("shotgunning"), and to measure the product(s) formed. If in such an experiment a bacteria infected with the recombinant DNA molecule of a deadly toxin were accidentally released into the environment, the result could be catastrophic.

To head off such a potential ecological disaster, United States scientists proposed in 1975 a series of guidelines for applying safety standards to experiments using recombinant DNA methods. The basic requirements, as formulated by the National Institutes of Health in 1976, specified that experiments be performed in controlled environments, whose degree of isolation would be determined by the estimated risk involved, and that bacterial hosts with reduced potential for surviving outside the laboratory be used. The laboratory isolation conditions are divided into four levels corresponding to varying levels of predicted risk. (It is important to note that all risks discussed here are based on worse-case estimates and not on any danger yet demonstrated.) The least stringent condition of containment requiring only standard microbial safety procedures, P-1, is used for recombinant transfers between bacterial hosts and nonpathogenic prokaryotes, such as bacteria, plasmids, or bacteriophage (bacterial viruses), which would normally exchange genes are part of their natural life cycles. At the next level, P-2, minimal containment procedures, such as the use of a laminar flow hood, are required for transfers from most other prokaryotes and a few lower eukaryotes, such as yeast or cold-blooded animals. The P-3 level requires the use of an isolated laboratory designed exclusively for this research and sterilization of all materials utilized in handling the hybrid bacteria produced. Establishment of a P-3 laboratory is an expensive proposition which requires a serious commitment on the part of the researcher, which should serve as a deterrent to less-experienced researchers without the proper expertise to operate at this level. The final level, P-4, is for experiments with a high potential for risk, such as experiments involving pathogenic or toxin-producing bacteria, viruses implicated in cancer, or experiments involving human DNA. These P-4 laboratories utilize all available modern precautions for completely isolating the products of the experiment from the outside environment, including the use of air filters, high-pressure sterilization of all solutions and glassware used in the experiment, and performance of all experiments in sealed glove boxes. Similar procedures have been successfully utilized for experiments with such infections agents as foot-and-mouth disease, anthrax, and smallpox. These P-4 laboratories will be assembled only at those few institutions with the experience for handling hazardous agents, such as the Center for Disease Control (Atlanta), Fort Detrich (Maryland), and the National Institutes of Health (Bethesda). These laboratories provide an extremely high degree of protection from the escape of a pathogenic recombinant bacteria, but they are not completely fail-safe as was recently demonstrated by the escape of foot-and-mouth virus from a similar facility.[3] Therefore, there is still a remote possibility of a recombinant experiment contaminating the environment even at the highest level of isolation, and so a second set of restrictions was created to prevent an escaped hybrid from surviving in the environment.

Most recombinant DNA experiments are performed in *Escherichia coli*, a bacteria originally isolated from human feces. One of the original concerns of recombinant DNA foes was the fear that an *E. coli* infected with a dangerous recombinant plasmid could infect a laboratory worker and escape laboratory confinement. Once freed from constraint, the hybrid would infest the sewer system, ultimately reinfecting other animals, or, by a process called conjugation, would pass its lethal information on to other bacteria, which would then become the infectious agents. To forestall such a possibility, Dr. Roy Curtiss designed a series of *E. coli* strains which have a reduced ability to survive outside the laboratory, or lack it entirely. Need of one of the crippled strains in an experiment is determined both by the degree of risk estimated and the containment level at which the experiment is to be run.

These safety features form the basis of a series of guidelines established by the National Institutes of Health to be applied to all research funded by NIH grants. The guidelines do not apply to industrial research or research funded by private resources, but scientists from these groups have generally pledged voluntary compliance. Congressional hearings were held for the purpose of broadening application of the guidelines to all recombinant DNA research, but the proposed legislation has been successfully delayed by the argument that the full disclosure of procedures required by the guidelines would jeopardize the justifiable secrecy surrounding industrial experiments. This secrecy is needed to protect the large investments in personnel time and money required in developing patentable processes. On a second front, many scientists have argued that, in view of the proven safety of the methodology, the current guidelines are currently too restrictive. Recent NIH proposals tend to support this contention, and it is expected that new guidelines will soon lower most recombinant experiments into the unrestricted, P-1 or P-2 categories. It thus appears that most of the controversy surrounding recombinant DNA methodology will be ended at the experimental level and reduced to the level of a philosophical barroom debate.

The benefits of the technology are indisputable. At the molecular level, this method has provided invaluable insight into how genes function, and this has important repercussions in such areas as cancer, the study of genetic defects, and cell differentiation, the process which instructs a cell to function as a brain cell or liver cell. The method can also be used to produce scarce but biologically im-

[3] "Cattle Virus Escapes a P4 Lab," *Science 202:*290, 1978.

portant protein molecules like insulin, growth hormone, and the "clotting factor," the proteins required for treatment of diabetes, dwarfism, and hemophilia, respectively. Finally, several suggestions have been made to construct hybrid bacteria with genetic backgrounds useful in various aspects of agricultural and industrial processing.

These benefits are really only the iceberg's tip, for this technology has arrived too quickly for an analysis of its full potential. There is, however, a price to be paid for these benefits, the price of uncertainty, because as with life itself there are no guarantees that we have not unleashed something which we cannot call back. By contrast, nuclear waste can be more or less readily contained because it does not have the potential to generate itself as the hybrid bacteria can. Also it might be many years before the deleterious effects of such a hybrid would make themselves manifest, thus compounding the difficulty of estimating risk potential for any of the proposed experiments. Indeed, one of the major battles concerning safety standards for this technology has revolved around the question of who would establish the guidelines. To date, promulgation of safety measures has been left in the hands of those scientists who have been most active in using the technology and benefiting from it, a clear conflict of interest. The new NIH guidelines, for example, propose giving local safety committees a freer hand in governing the containment procedures to be employed with this technology. On the other side of the issue, the Cambridge, Massachusetts city council, and several other city councils, have proposed that local governmental agencies dictate the safety provisions to be followed. As a practical matter, the recombinant DNA debate has been resolved in favor of those supporting full utilization of the techniques. The burden of proof of potential dangers has been placed on the opposition; and, until someone produces a truly dangerous hybrid capable of environmental catastrophy, the use of the technology will continue to expand at its current phenomenal rate. Hopefully, as the technique is applied to more systems, it will provide answers to some of the most profound questions of modern biology, without generating some calamity that would make the answers moot.

The ending of the recombinant DNA controversy does not, of course, answer the problem of governmental or citizen control of scientific experiments. It does raise questions as to whether science should be under external control, and, if so, whether such control could be effective. This debate may return, for we live in an age in which babies can be conceived in test tubes, then transplanted into their mother's womb, and brought to term. Someday, maybe in this century, maybe the next, it may be possible to use recombinant DNA methods to alter the genetic makeup of the embryo in the test tube, before implantation. At that point, we may well ask ourselves again whether or not we want our scientists tinkering with life. Before that time comes, though, we must be prepared to answer some tough questions as to who should, or can, control science.

THE RECOMBINANT DNA
DEBATE

STEPHEN P. STICH

The debate over recombinant DNA research is a unique event, perhaps a turning point, in the history of science. For the first time in modern history there has been widespread public discussion about whether and how a promising though potentially dangerous line of research shall be pursued. At root the debate is a moral debate and, like most such debates, requires proper assessment of the facts at crucial stages in the argument. A good deal of the controversy over re-combinant DNA research arises because some of the facts simply are not yet known. There are many empirical questions we would like to have answered before coming to a decision—questions about the reliability of proposed con-tainment facilities, about the viability of enfeebled strains of *Escherichia coli*, about the ways in which pathogenic organisms do their unwelcome work, and much more. But all decisions cannot wait until the facts are available; some must be made now. It is to be expected that people with different hunches about what the facts will turn out to be will urge different decisions on how re-combinant DNA research should be regulated. However, differing expectations about the facts have not been the only fuel for controversy. A significant part of the current debate can be traced to differences over moral principles. Also, unfortunately, there has been much unnecessary debate generated by careless moral reasoning and a failure to attend to the logical structure of some of the moral arguments that have been advanced.

In order to help sharpen our perception of the moral issues underlying the controversy over recombinant DNA research, I shall start by clearing away some frivolous arguments that have deflected attention from more serious issues. We may then examine the problems involved in deciding whether the potential benefits of recombinant DNA research justify pursuing it despite the risks that it poses.

Reprinted from *Philosophy & Public Affairs* 7 (3):187–205, copyright 1978 by permission of Princeton University Press.

I. Three Bad Arguments

My focus in this section will be on three untenable arguments, each of which has surfaced with considerable frequency in the public debate over recombinant DNA research.

The first argument on my list concludes that recombinant DNA research should not be controlled or restricted. The central premise of the argument is that scientists should have full and unqualified freedom to pursue whatever inquiries they may choose to pursue. This claim was stated repeatedly in petitions and letters to the editor during the height of the public debate over recombinant DNA research in the University of Michigan community.[1] The general moral principle which is the central premise of the argument plainly does entail that investigators using recombinant DNA technology should be allowed to pursue their research as they see fit. However, we need only consider a few examples to see that the principle invoked in this "freedom of inquiry" argument is utterly indefensible. No matter how sincere a researcher's interest may be in investigating the conjugal behavior of American university professors, few would be willing to grant him the right to pursue his research in my bedroom without my consent. No matter how interested a researcher may be in investigating the effects of massive doses of bomb-grade plutonium on preschool children, it is hard to imagine that anyone thinks he should be allowed to do so. Yet the "free inquiry" principle, if accepted, would allow both of these projects and countless other Dr. Strangelove projects as well. So plainly the simplistic "free inquiry" principle is indefensible. It would, however, be a mistake to conclude that freedom of inquiry ought not to be protected. A better conclusion is that the right of free inquiry is a qualified right and must sometimes yield to conflicting rights and to the demands of conflicting moral principles. Articulating an explicit and properly qualified principle of free inquiry is a task of no small difficulty. We will touch on this topic again toward the end of Section II.

The second argument I want to examine aims at establishing just the op-

---

[1]For example, from a widely circulated petition signed by both faculty and community people: "The most important challenge may be a confrontation with one of our ancient assumptions—that there must be an absolute and unqualified freedom to pursue scientific inquiries. We will soon begin to wonder what meaning this freedom has if it leads to the destruction or demoralization of human beings, the only life forms able to exercise it." And from a letter to the editor written by a Professor of Engineering Humanities: "Is science beyond social and human controls, so that freedom of inquiry implies the absence of usual social restrictions which we all, as citizens, obey, respecting the social contract?"

It is interesting to note that the "freedom of inquiry" argument is rarely proposed by defenders of recombinant DNA research. Rather, it is proposed, then attacked, by those who are opposed to research involving recombinant molecules. Their motivation, it would seem, is to discredit the proponents of recombinant DNA research by attributing a foolish argument to them, then demonstrating that it is indeed a foolish argument.

posite conclusion from the first. The particular moral judgment being defended is that there should be a total ban on recombinant DNA research. The argument begins with the observation that even in so-called low-risk recombinant DNA experiments there is at least a possibility of catastrophic consequences. We are, after all, dealing with a relatively new and unexplored technology. Thus it is at least possible that a bacterial culture whose genetic makeup has been altered in the course of a recombinant DNA experiment may exhibit completely unexpected pathogenic characteristics. Indeed, it is not impossible that we could find ourselves confronted with a killer strain of, say, *E. coli* and, worse, a strain against which humans can marshal no natural defense. Now if this is possible—if we cannot say with assurance that the probability of it happening is zero—then, the argument continues, all recombinant DNA research should be halted. For the negative utility of the imagined catastrophe is so enormous, resulting as it would in the destruction of our society and perhaps even of our species, that no work which could possibly lead to this result would be worth the risk.

The argument just sketched, which might be called the "doomsday scenario" argument, begins with a premise which no informed person would be inclined to deny. It is indeed *possible* that even a low-risk recombinant DNA experiment might lead to totally catastrophic results. No ironclad guarantee can be offered that this will not happen. And while the probability of such an unanticipated catastrophe is surely not large, there is no serious argument that the probability is zero. Still, I think the argument is a sophistry. To go from the undeniable premise that recombinant DNA research might possibly result in unthinkable catastrophe to the conclusion that such research should be banned requires a moral principle stating that *all* endeavors that might possibly result in such a catastrophe should be prohibited. Once the principle has been stated, it is hard to believe that anyone would take it at all seriously. For the principle entails that, along with recombinant DNA research, almost all scientific research and many other commonplace activities having little to do with science should be prohibited. It is, after all, at least logically possible that the next new compound synthesized in an ongoing chemical research program will turn out to be an uncontainable carcinogen many orders of magnitude more dangerous than aerosol plutonium. And, to vary the example, there is a nonzero probability that experiments in artificial pollination will produce a weed that will, a decade from now, ruin the world's food grain harvest.[2]

[2] Unfortunately, the doomsday scenario argument is *not* a straw man conjured only by those who would refute it. Consider, for example, the remarks of Anthony Mazzocchi, spokesman for the Oil, Chemical and Atomic Workers International Union, reported in *Science News*, 19 March 1977, p. 181: "When scientists argue over safe or unsafe, we ought to be very prudent.... If critics are correct and the Andromeda scenario has *even the smallest possibility* of occurring, we must assume it will occur on the basis of our experience" (emphasis added).

I cannot resist noting that the principle invoked in the doomsday scenario argument is not new. Pascal used an entirely parallel argument to show that it is in our own best interests to believe in God. For though the probability of God's existence may be very low, if He nonetheless should happen to exist, the disutility that would accrue to the disbeliever would be catastrophic—an eternity in hell. But, as introductory philosophy students should all know, Pascal's argument only looks persuasive if we take our options to be just two: Christianity or atheism. A third possibility is belief in a jealous non-Christian God who will see to our damnation if and only if we *are* Christians. The probability of such a deity existing is again very small, but nonzero. So Pascal's argument is of no help in deciding whether or not to accept Christianity. For we may be damned if we do and damned if we don't.

I mention Pascal's difficulty because there is a direct parallel in the doomsday scenario argument against recombinant DNA research. Just as there is a nonzero probability that unforeseen consequences of recombinant DNA research will lead to disaster, so there is a nonzero probability that unforeseen consequences of *failing* to pursue the research will lead to disaster. There may, for example, come a time when, because of natural or man-induced climatic change, the capacity to alter quickly the genetic constitution of agricultural plants will be necessary to forestall catastrophic famine. And if we fail to pursue recombinant DNA research now, our lack of knowledge in the future may have consequences as dire as any foreseen in the doomsday scenario argument.

The third argument I want to consider provides a striking illustration of how important it is, in normative thinking, to make clear the moral *principles* being invoked. The argument I have in mind begins with a factual claim about recombinant DNA research and concludes that stringent restrictions, perhaps even a moratorium, should be imposed. However, advocates of the argument are generally silent on the normative principle(s) linking premise and conclusion. The gap thus created can be filled in a variety of ways, resulting in very different arguments. The empirical observation that begins the argument is that recombinant DNA methods enable scientists to move genes back and forth across natural barriers, "particularly the most fundamental such barrier, that which divides prokaryotes from eukaryotes. The results will be essentially new organisms, self-perpetuating and hence permanent."[3] Because of this, it is concluded that severe restrictions are in order. Plainly this argument is an enthymeme; a central premise has been left unstated. What sort of moral principle is being tacitly assumed?

The principle that comes first to mind is simply that natural barriers should not be breached, or perhaps that "essentially new organisms" should not be created. The principle has an almost theological ring to it, and perhaps there

[3] The quotation is from George Wald, "The Case Against Genetic Engineering," *The Sciences*, September/October 1976; reprinted in David A. Jackson and Stephen P. Stich (eds.), *The Recombinant DNA Debate* (Englewood Cliffs, N.J.: Prentice-Hall), forthcoming.

are some people who would be prepared to defend it on theological grounds. But short of a theological argument, it is hard to see why anyone would hold the view that breaching natural barriers or creating new organisms is *intrinsically* wrong. For if a person were to advocate such a principle, he would have to condemn the creation of new bacterial strains capable of, say, synthesizing human clotting factor or insulin, *even if* creating the new organism generated *no unwelcome side effects*.

There is quite a different way of unraveling the "natural barriers" argument which avoids appeal to the dubious principles just discussed. As an alternative, this second reading of the argument ties premise to conclusion with a second factual claim and a quite different normative premise. The added factual claim is that at present our knowledge of the consequences of creating new forms of life is severely limited; thus we cannot know with any assurance that the probability of disastrous consequences is very low. The moral principle needed to mesh with the two factual premises would be something such as the following:

> If we do not know with considerable assurance that the probability of an activity leading to disastrous consequences is very low, then we should not allow the activity to continue.

Now this principle, unlike those marshaled in the first interpretation of the natural barriers argument, is not lightly dismissed. It is, to be sure, a conservative principle, and it has the odd feature of focusing entirely on the dangers an activity poses while ignoring its potential benefits.[4] Still, the principle may have a certain attraction in light of recent history, which has increasingly been marked by catastrophes attributable to technology's unanticipated side effects. I will not attempt a full-scale evaluation of this principle just now. For the principle raises, albeit in a rather extreme way, the question of how risks and benefits are to be weighed against each other. In my opinion, that is the really crucial moral question raised by recombinant DNA research. It is a question which bristles with problems. In Section II I shall take a look at some of these problems and make a few tentative steps toward some solutions. While picking our way through the problems, we will have another opportunity to examine the principle just cited.

II. Risks and Benefits

At first glance it might be thought that the issue of risks and benefits is quite straightforward, at least in principle. What we want to know is whether

[4] It is important to note, however, that the principle is considerably less conservative, and correspondingly more plausible, than the principle invoked in the doomsday scenario argument. That latter principle would have us enjoin an activity if the probability of the activity leading to catastrophe is anything other than zero.

the potential benefits of recombinant DNA research justify the risks involved. To find out we need only determine the probabilities of the various dangers and benefits. And while some of the empirical facts—the probabilities—may require considerable ingenuity and effort to uncover, the assessment poses no particularly difficult normative or conceptual problems. Unfortunately, this sanguine view does not survive much more than a first glance. A closer look at the task of balancing the risks and benefits of recombinant DNA research reveals a quagmire of sticky conceptual problems and simmering moral disputes. In the next few pages I will try to catalogue and comment on some of these moral disputes. I wish I could also promise solutions to all of them, but to do so would be false advertising.

Problems about Probabilities

In trying to assess costs and benefits, a familiar first step is to set down a list of possible actions and possible outcomes. Next, we assign some measure of desirability to each possible outcome, and for each action we estimate the conditional probability of each outcome given that the action is performed. In attempting to apply this decision-making strategy to the case of recombinant DNA research, the assignment of probabilities poses some perplexing problems. Some of the outcomes whose probabilities we want to know can be approached using standard empirical techniques. Thus, for example, we may want to know what the probability is of a specific enfeebled host *E. coli* strain surviving passage through the human intestinal system, should it be accidentally ingested. Or we may want to know what the probability is that a host organism will escape from a P-4 laboratory. In such cases, while there may be technical difficulties to be overcome, we have a reasonably clear idea of the sort of data needed to estimate the required probabilities. But there are other possible outcomes whose probabilities cannot be determined by experiment. It is important, for example, to know what the probability is of recombinant DNA research leading to a method for developing nitrogen-fixing strains of corn and wheat. And it is important to know how likely it is that recombinant DNA research will lead to techniques for effectively treating or preventing various types of cancer. Yet there is no experiment we can perform nor any data we can gather that will enable us to *empirically* estimate these probabilities. Nor are these the most problematic probabilities we may want to know. A possibility that weighs heavily on the minds of many who are worried about recombinant DNA research is that this research may lead to negative consequences for human health or for the environment *which have not yet even been thought of*. The history of technology during the last half-century surely demonstrates that this is not a quixotic concern. Yet here again there would appear to be no data we can gather that would help much in estimating the probability of such potential outcomes.

It should be stressed that the problems just sketched are not to be traced simply to a paucity of data. Rather, they are conceptual problems; it is doubtful whether there is *any clear empirical sense* to be made of objective probability assignments to contingencies such as those we are considering.

Theorists in the Bayesian tradition may be unmoved by the difficulties we have noted. On their view all probability claims are reports of subjective probabilities.[5] And, a Bayesian might quite properly note, there is no special problem about assigning *subjective* probabilities to outcomes such as those that worried us. But even for the radical Bayesian, there remains the problem of *whose* subjective probabilities ought to be employed in making a *social* or *political* decision. The problem is a pressing one since the subjective probabilities assigned to potential dangers and benefits of recombinant DNA research would appear to vary considerably even among reasonably well-informed members of the scientific community.

The difficulties we have been surveying are serious ones. Some might feel they are so serious that they render rational assessment of the risks and benefits of recombinant DNA research all but impossible. I am inclined to be rather more optimistic, however. Almost all the perils posed by recombinant DNA research require the occurrence of a sequence of separate events. For a chimerical bacterial strain created in a recombinant DNA experiment to cause a serious epidemic, for example, at least the following events must occur:

1. A pathogenic bacterium must be synthesized.
2. The chimerical bacteria must escape from the laboratory.
3. The strain must be viable in nature.
4. The strain must compete successfully with other microorganisms which are themselves the product of intense natural selection.[6]

Since *all* these must occur, the probability of the potential epidemic is the product of the probabilities of each individual contingency. And there are at least two items on the list, namely (2) and (3), whose probabilities are amenable to reasonably straightforward empirical assessment. Thus the product of these two individual probabilities places an upper limit on the probability of the epidemic. For the remaining two probabilities, we must rely on subjective probability assessments of informed scientists. No doubt there will be considerable variability. Yet even here the variability will be limited. In the case of

---

[5] For an elaboration of the Bayesian position, see Leonard J. Savage, *The Foundations of Statistics* (New York: Wiley), 1954; also cf. Leonard J. Savage, "The Shifting Foundations of Statistics," in Robert G. Colodny (ed.), *Logic, Laws and Life* (Pittsburgh: University of Pittsburgh Press), 1977.

[6] For an elaboration of this point, see Bernard D. Davis, "Evolution, Epidemiology, and Recombinant DNA," *The Recombinant DNA Debate, op. cit.*

(4), as an example, the available knowledge about microbial natural selection provides no precise way of estimating the probability that a chimerical strain of enfeebled *E. coli* will compete successfully outside the laboratory. But no serious scientist would urge that the probability is *high*. We can then use the highest responsible subjective estimate of the probabilities of (1) and (4) in calculating the "worst case" estimate of the risk of epidemic. If in using this highest "worst case" estimate, our assessment yields the result that benefits outweigh risks, then lower estimates of the same probabilities will, of course, yield the same conclusion. Thus it may well be the case that the problems about probabilities we have reviewed will not pose insuperable obstacles to a rational assessment of risks and benefits.

Weighing Harms and Benefits

A second cluster of problems that confronts us in assessing the risks and benefits of recombinant DNA research turns on the assignment of a measure of desirability to the various possible outcomes. Suppose that we have a list of the various harms and benefits that might possibly result from pursuing recombinant DNA research. The list will include such "benefits" as development of an inexpensive way to synthesize human clotting factor and development of a strain of nitrogen-fixing wheat; and such "harms" as release of a new antibiotic-resistant strain of pathogenic bacteria and release of a strain of *E. coli* carrying tumor viruses capable of causing cancer in man.

Plainly, it is possible that pursuing a given policy will result in more than one benefit and in more than one harm. Now if we are to assess the potential impact of various policies or courses of action, we must assign some index of desirability to the possible *total outcomes* of each policy, outcomes which may well include a mix of benefits and harms. To do this we must confront a tangle of normative problems that are as vexing and difficult as any we are likely to face. We must *compare* the moral desirabilities of various harms and benefits. The task is particularly troublesome when the harms and benefits to be compared are of different kinds. Thus, for example, some of the attractive potential benefits of recombinant DNA research are economic: we may learn to recover small amounts of valuable metals in an economically feasible way, or we may be able to synthesize insulin and other drugs inexpensively. By contrast, many of the risks of recombinant DNA research are risks to human life or health. So if we are to take the idea of cost-benefit analysis seriously, we must at some point decide how human lives are to be weighed against economic benefits.

There are those who contend that the need to make such decisions indicates the moral bankruptcy of attempting to employ risk-benefit analyses when human lives are at stake. On the critics' view, we cannot reckon the possible loss of a human life as just another negative outcome, albeit a grave and heavily weighted one. To do so, it is urged, is morally repugnant and reflects a callous lack of respect for the sacredness of human life.

On my view, this sort of critique of the very idea of using risk-benefit analyses is ultimately untenable. It is simply a fact about the human condition, lamentable as it is inescapable, that in many human activities we run the risk of inadvertently causing the death of a human being. We run such a risk each time we drive a car, allow a dam to be built, or allow a plane to take off. Moreover, in making social and individual decisions, we cannot escape weighing economic consequences against the risk to human life. A building code in the Midwest will typically mandate fewer precautions against earthquakes than a building code in certain parts of California. Yet earthquakes are not impossible in the Midwest. If we elect not to require precautions, then surely a major reason must be that it would simply be too expensive. In this judgment, as in countless others, there is no escaping the need to balance economic costs against possible loss of life. To deny that we must and do balance economic costs against risks to human life is to assume the posture of a moral ostrich.

I have been urging the point that it is not *morally objectionable* to try to balance economic concerns against risks to human life. But if such judgments are unobjectionable, indeed necessary, they also surely are among the most difficult any of us has to face. It is hard to imagine a morally sensitive person not feeling extremely uncomfortable when confronted with the need to put a dollar value on human lives. It might be thought that the moral dilemmas engendered by the need to balance such radically different costs and benefits pose insuperable practical obstacles for a rational resolution of the recombinant DNA debate. But here, as in the case of problems with probabilities, I am more sanguine. For while some of the risks and potential benefits of recombinant DNA research are all but morally incommensurable, the most salient risks and benefits are easier to compare. The major risks, as we have noted, are to human life and health. However, the major potential benefits are *also* to human life and health. The potential economic benefits of recombinant DNA research pale in significance when set against the potential for major breakthroughs in our understanding and ability to treat a broad range of conditions, from birth defects to cancer. Those of us, and I confess I am among them, who despair of deciding how lives and economic benefits are to be compared can nonetheless hope to settle our views about recombinant DNA research by comparing the potential risks to life and health with the potential benefits to life and health. Here we are comparing plainly commensurable outcomes. If the balance turns out to be favorable, then we need not worry about factoring in potential economic benefits.

There is a certain irony in the fact that we may well be able to ignore economic factors entirely in coming to a decision about recombinant DNA research. For I suspect that a good deal of the apprehension about recombinant DNA research on the part of the public at large is rooted in the fear that (once again) economic benefits will be weighed much too heavily and potential damage to health and the environment will be weighed much too lightly. The fear is hardly an irrational one. In case after well-publicized case, we have seen the squalid consequences of decisions in which private or corporate gain took precedence over clear and serious threats to health and to the environment. It is the profit motive that led a giant chemical firm to conceal the deadly consequences of the chemical which now threatens to poison the James River and perhaps all of Chesapeake Bay. For the same reason, the citizens of Duluth drank water laced with a known carcinogen. And the ozone layer that protects us all was eroded while regulatory agencies and legislators fussed over the loss of profits in the spray deodorant industry. Yet while public opinion about recombinant DNA research is colored by a growing awareness of these incidents and dozens of others, the case of recombinant DNA is fundamentally different in a crucial respect. The important projected benefits which must be set against the risks of recombinant DNA research are not economic at all, they are medical and environmental.

Problems about Principles

The third problem I want to consider focuses on the following question. Once we have assessed the potential harms and benefits of recombinant DNA research, how should we use this information in coming to a decision? It might be thought that the answer is trivially obvious. To assess the harms and benefits is, after all, just to compute, for each of the various policies that we are considering, what might be called its *expected utility*. The expected utility of a given policy is found by first multiplying the desirability of each possible total outcome by the probability that the policy in question will lead to that total outcome, and then adding the numbers obtained. As we have seen, finding the needed probabilities and assigning the required desirabilities will not be easy. But once we know the expected utility of each policy, is it not obvious that we should choose the policy with the highest expected utility? The answer, unfortunately, is no, it is not at all obvious.

Let us call the principle that we should adopt the policy with the highest expected utility the *utilitarian principle*. The following example should make it clear that, far from being trivial or tautological, the utilitarian principle is a substantive and controversial moral principle. Suppose that the decision which confronts us is whether or not to adopt policy A. What is more, suppose we know there is a probability close to 1 that 100,000 lives will be saved if we adopt A. However, we also know that there is a probability close to 1 that 1,000 will die as a direct result of our adopting policy A, and these people would survive if we did not adopt A. Finally, suppose that the other possible consequences of adopting A are relatively inconsequential and can be ignored. (For concreteness, we might take A to be the establishment of a mass vaccination program, using a relatively risky vaccine.) Now plainly if we take the moral desirability of saving a life to be exactly offset by the moral undesirability of causing a death, then the utilitarian principle dictates that we adopt policy A. But many people feel uncomfortable with this result, the discomfort increasing with the number of deaths that would result from A. If, to change the example, the choice that confronts us is saving 100,000 lives while causing the deaths of 50,000 others, a significant number of people are inclined to think that the morally right thing to do is to refrain from doing A, and "let nature take its course."

If we reject policy A, the likely reason is that we also reject the utilitarian principle. Perhaps the most plausible reason for rejecting the utilitarian principle is the view that our obligation to *avoid doing harm* is stronger than our obligation to do good. There are many examples, some considerably more compelling than the one we have been discussing, which seem to illustrate that in a broad range of cases we do feel that our obligation to avoid doing harm is greater than our obligation to do good.[7] Suppose, to take but one example, that my neighbor requests my help in paying off his gambling debts. He owes $5,000 to a certain bookmaker with underworld connections. Unless the neighbor pays the debt immediately, he will be shot. Here, I think we are all inclined to say, I have no strong obligation to give my neighbor the money he needs, and if I were to do so it would be a supererogatory gesture. By contrast, suppose a representative of my neighbor's bookmaker approaches me and requests that I shoot my neighbor. If I refuse, he will see to it that my new car, which cost $5,000, will be destroyed by a bomb while it sits unattended at the curb. In this case, surely, I have a strong obligation not to harm my neighbor, although not shooting him will cost me $5,000.

Suppose that this example and others convince us that we cannot adopt the utilitarian principle, at least not in its most general form, where it purports to be applicable to all moral decisions. What are the alternatives? One cluster of alternative principles would urge that in some or all cases we weigh the harm a contemplated action will cause more heavily than we weigh the good it will do. The extreme form of such a principle would dictate that we ignore the benefits entirely and opt for the action or policy that produces the *least* expected harm. (It is this principle, or a close relation, which emerged in the second reading of the "natural barriers" argument discussed in the third part of Section I.) A

[7]For an interesting discussion of these cases, see J. O. Urmson, "Saints and Heros," in A. I. Melden (ed.), *Essays in Moral Philosophy* (Seattle: University of Washington Press), 1958. Also see the discussion of positive and negative duties in Philippa Foot, "The Problem of Abortion and the Doctrine of Double Effect," *Oxford Review 5*, 1967. Reprinted in James Rachels (ed.), *Moral Problems* (New York: Harper & Row), 1971.

more plausible variant would allow us to count both benefits and harms in our deliberations, but would specify how much more heavily harms were to count.

On my view, some moderate version of a "harm-weighted" principle is preferable to the utilitarian principle in a considerable range of cases. *However, the recombinant DNA issue is not one of these cases.* Indeed, when we try to apply a harm-weighted principle to the recombinant DNA case we run head on into a conceptual problem of considerable difficulty. The distinction between doing good and doing harm presupposes a notion of the normal or expectable course of events. Roughly, if my action causes you to be worse off than you would have been in the normal course of events, then I have harmed you; if my action causes you to be better off than in the normal course of events, then I have done you some good; and if my action leaves you just as you would be in the normal course of events, then I have done neither. In many cases, the normal course of events is intuitively quite obvious. Thus in the case of the neighbor and the bookmaker, in the expected course of events I would neither shoot my neighbor nor give him $5,000 to pay off his debts. Thus I am doing good if I give him the money and I am doing harm if I shoot him. But in other cases, including the recombinant DNA case, it is not at all obvious what constitutes the "expected course of events," and thus it is not at all obvious what to count as a harm. To see this, suppose that as a matter of fact many more deaths and illnesses will be prevented as a result of pursuing recombinant DNA research than will be caused by pursuing it. But suppose that there *will* be at least some people who become ill or die as a result of recombinant DNA research being pursued. If these are the facts, then who would be harmed by imposing a ban on recombinant DNA research? That depends on what we take to be the "normal course of events." Presumably, if we do not impose a ban, then the research will continue and the lives will be saved. If this is the normal course of events, then if we impose a ban we have *harmed* those people who would be saved. But it is equally natural to take as the normal course of events the situation in which recombinant DNA research is not pursued. And if *that* is the normal course of events, then those who would have been saved are not harmed by a ban, for they are no worse off than they would be in the normal course of events. However, on this reading of "the normal course of events," if we *fail* to impose a ban, then we have harmed those people who will ultimately become ill or die as a result of recombinant DNA research, since as a result of not imposing a ban they are worse off than they would have been in the normal course of events. I conclude that, in the absence of a theory detailing how we are to recognize the normal course of events, harm-weighted principles have no clear application to the case of recombinant DNA research.

Harm-weighted principles are not the only alternatives to the utilitarian principle. There is another cluster of alternatives that take off in quite a different direction. These principles urge that in deciding which policy to pursue there is a strong presumption in favor of policies that adhere to certain formal moral principles (that is, principles which do not deal with the *consequences* of our policies). Thus, to take the example most directly relevant to the recombinant DNA case, it might be urged that there is a strong presumption in favor of a policy which preserves freedom of scientific inquiry. In its extreme form, this principle would protect freedom of inquiry *no matter what the consequences*; and as we saw in the first part of Section I, this extreme position is exceptionally implausible. A much more plausible principle would urge that freedom of inquiry be protected until the balance of negative over positive consequences reaches a certain specified amount, at which point we would revert to the utilitarian principle. On such a view, if the expected utility of banning recombinant DNA research is a bit higher than the expected utility of allowing it to continue, then we would nonetheless allow it to continue. But if the expected utility of a ban is enormously higher than the expected utility of continuation, banning is the policy to be preferred.[8]

III. Long Term Risks

Thus far in our discussion of risks and benefits, the risks that have occupied us have been what might be termed "short-term" risks, such as the release of a new pathogen. The negative effects of these events, though they might be long-lasting indeed, would be upon us relatively quickly. However, some of those who are concerned about recombinant DNA research think there are longer-term dangers that are at least as worrisome. The dangers they have in mind stem not from the accidental release of harmful substances in the course of recombinant DNA research, but rather from the unwise use of the *knowledge* we will likely gain in pursuing the research. The scenarios most often proposed are nightmarish variations on the theme of human genetic engineering. With the knowledge we acquire, it is conjectured, some future tyrant may have people built to order, perhaps creating a whole class of people who willingly and cheaply do the society's dirty or dangerous work, as in Huxley's *Brave New World*. Though the proposed scenarios clearly are science fiction, they are not to be lightly dismissed. For if the technology they conjure is not demonstrably achievable, neither is it demonstrably impossible. And if only a bit of the science fiction turns to fact, the dangers could be beyond reckoning.

Granting that potential misuse of the knowledge gained in recombinant DNA research is a legitimate topic of concern, how ought we to guard ourselves

[8]Carl Cohen defends this sort of limited protection of the formal free inquiry principle over a straight application of the utilitarian principle in his interesting essay, "When May Research Be Stopped?" *New England Journal of Medicine 296*, 1977. Reprinted in *The Recombinant DNA Debate, op. cit.*

against this misuse? One common proposal is to try to prevent the acquisition of such knowledge by banning or curtailing recombinant DNA research now. Let us cast this proposal in the form of an explicit moral argument. The conclusion is that recombinant DNA research should be curtailed, and the reason given for the conclusion is that such research could possibly produce knowledge which might be misused with disastrous consequences. To complete the argument we need a moral principle, and the one which seems to be needed is something such as this:

> If a line of research can lead to the discovery of knowledge which might be disastrously misused, then that line of research should be curtailed.

Once it has been made explicit, I think relatively few people would be willing to endorse this principle. For recombinant DNA research is hardly alone in potentially leading to knowledge that might be disastrously abused. Indeed, it is hard to think of an area of scientific research that could *not* lead to the discovery of potentially dangerous knowledge. So if the principle is accepted it would entail that almost all scientific research should be curtailed or abandoned.

It might be thought that we could avoid the extreme consequences just cited by retreating to a more moderate moral principle. The moderate principle would urge only that we should curtail those areas of research where the probability of producing dangerous knowledge is comparatively high. Unfortunately, this more moderate principle is of little help in avoiding the unwelcome consequences of the stronger principle. The problem is that the history of science is simply too unpredictable to enable us to say with any assurance which lines of research will produce which sorts of knowledge or technology. There is a convenient illustration of the point in the recent history of molecular genetics. The idea of recombining DNA molecules is one which has been around for some time. However, early efforts proved unsuccessful. As it happened, the crucial step in making recombinant DNA technology possible was provided by research on restriction enzymes, research that was undertaken with no thought of recombinant DNA technology. Indeed, until it was realized that restriction enzymes provided the key to recombining DNA molecules, the research on restriction enzymes was regarded as a rather unexciting (and certainly uncontroversial) scientific backwater.[9] In an entirely analogous way, crucial pieces of information that may one day enable us to manipulate the human genome may come from just about any branch of molecular biology. To guard against the discovery of that knowledge we should have to curtail not only recombinant DNA research but all of molecular biology.

Before concluding, we would do well to note that there is a profound pessimism reflected in the attitude of those who would stop recombinant DNA re-

[9] I am indebted to Prof. Ethel Jackson for both the argument and the illustration.

search because it might lead to knowledge that could be abused. It is, after all, granted on all sides that the knowledge resulting from recombinant DNA research will have both good and evil potential uses. So it would seem the sensible strategy would be to try to prevent the improper uses of this knowledge rather than trying to prevent the knowledge from ever being uncovered. Those who would take the more extreme step of trying to stop the knowledge from being uncovered presumably feel that its improper use is all but inevitable, that our political and social institutions are incapable of preventing morally abhorrent applications of the knowledge while encouraging beneficial applications. On my view, this pessimism is unwarranted; indeed, it is all but inconsistent. The historical record gives us no reason to believe that what is technologically possible will be done, no matter what the moral price. Indeed, in the area of human genetic manipulation, the record points in quite the *opposite* direction. We have long known that the same techniques that work so successfully in animal breeding can be applied to humans as well. Yet there is no evidence of a "technological imperative" impelling our society to breed people as we breed dairy cattle, simply because we know that it can be done. Finally, it is odd that those who express no confidence in the ability of our institutions to forestall such monstrous applications of technology are not equally pessimistic about the ability of the same institutions to impose an effective ban on the uncovering of dangerous knowledge. If our institutions are incapable of restraining the application of technology when those applications would be plainly morally abhorrent, one would think they would be even more impotent in attempting to restrain a line of research which promises major gains in human welfare.[10]

[10] This essay is an abridged and somewhat modified version of my essay, "The Recombinant DNA Debate: Some Philosophical Considerations," which will appear in *The Recombinant DNA Debate* edited by David A. Jackson and Stephen P. Stich, to be published by Prentice-Hall. I am grateful to the editors of *Philosophy & Public Affairs* for their detailed and useful suggestions on modifying the essay to make it appropriate for use in that journal.

THE ETHICS OF
RECOMBINANT DNA
RESEARCH*

JAMES M. HUMBER

Ever since a group of scientists met in April, 1974 to impose a voluntary moritorium on recombinant DNA research, there has been a great deal of discussion concerning the propriety of such experimentation.[1] In 1976 the National Institutes of Health responded to pressure from both the public and the scientific community and issued guidelines governing recombinant DNA research in NIH-funded institutions.[2] These guidelines prohibit some forms of research (for example, experiments attempting to make bacteria or viruses more drug-resistant), and place severe restrictions upon the ways in which others may be performed. Rather than ending the controversy, however, promulgation of the NIH guidelines seems only to have spurred further debate. Some prominent scientists argue that recombinant DNA research should go forward virtually without restriction.[3] On the other hand, a number of researchers of equal stature claim that work in this area is so dangerous that it ought to be pro-

---

[1] The meeting of April 1974 was held at M. I. T. and was followed by a larger gathering at Asilomar, California in February of 1975. For a synopsis of what went on at these meetings, as well as an enlightening description of the procedures involved in recombinant DNA research see, "Tinkering With Life," *Time* (April 18, 1977), pp. 32–45.

[2] "Recombinant DNA Research Guidelines," *Federal Register* (August, 1976), pp. 38426–38483.

[3] Proponents of recombinant DNA experimentation include Bernard Davis of Harvard Medical School (who has offered to drink recombinant DNA), J. D. Watson, Nobel laureate and Director of the Cold Springs Harbor Laboratory, S. Cohen of Stanford University School of Medicine, and Roy Curtiss, University of Alabama Medical Center in Birmingham. For the arguments used in favor of recombinant DNA research see, "Tinkering With Life," *op. cit.*; J. D. Watson, "In Defense of DNA," *The New Republic* (June 25, 1977), pp. 11–14; and Roy Curtiss, "Recombinant DNA Research," paper delivered at a recombinant DNA conference sponsored by the American Association for the Advancement of Science, Athens, Georgia, April 15–16, 1977.

---

*Revised version of a paper originally read at the annual meeting of The Southern Society for Philosophy and Psychology, March, 1978.

hibited, or at least made subject to restrictions far more severe than those imposed by the NIH guidelines.[4] At present, neither the advocates nor the critics of recombinant DNA research can be said to have the upper hand. The debate continues unabated; and neither side seems willing to give an inch.

I do not believe that the debate over recombinant DNA research need remain at a standstill, and in what follows I am going to try to resolve the controversy. In developing my argument I will proceed as follows: First, I will argue that the dispute over recombinant DNA research remains unsettled because the arguments of both the proponents and the critics of such research are misdirected. Next, I will attempt to show that (a) *no* recombinant DNA research ought to be prohibited in the United States, and that (b) the general public ought to have no voice in determining when and how safeguards should be employed in recombinant DNA experimentation. Finally, I will defend my position against the charge that it leaves the public without any means of protecting itself from dangerous recombinant DNA research.

Even a casual observer cannot help but note that there is a bland "sameness" about all the arguments used for and against recombinant DNA research. Invariably, proponents of DNA experimentation stress the benefits of such research, and play down the risks. Just of often, critics emphasize the hazards while minimizing the potential rewards.[5] Both sorts of arguments are possible because no one can predict the outcome of a totally new recombinant DNA experiment. But herein lies the problem: if the results of new recombinant DNA experimentation are unpredictable, it is impossible to say how high the risks or how probable the benefits of such research. And in these circumstances, one has no way of assessing the merits of either the *pro* or *anti* recombinant DNA arguments. If one chooses to stress the potential risks, he may do so. If, on the other hand, one wishes to emphasize the possible benefits, this too is allowed. In the end, then, the recombinant DNA research controversy ends in an inevitable stalemate. This is where we find ourselves; and this is where we shall stay until participants in the recombinant DNA debate find some new grounds for argument.

---

[4] Opponents of recombinant DNA research include Robert Sinsheimer, Chairman of the Biology Department at Caltech, Erwin Chargaff, retired biochemist at Columbia University, and Richard Goldstein, Harvard Medical School. For the arguments used against recombinant DNA research see, "Tinkering With Life," *op. cit.*; R. Sinsheimer, "The Galilean Imperative," paper delivered at a recombinant DNA conference, Athens, Georgia, April 15, 1977; and "Feds See Risk, OK Gene Work," *The Atlanta Journal* (November 18, 1977), p. 12-A.

[5] There is one exception to this generalization. Sometimes critics appear to argue that recombinant DNA research is wrong simply because it interferes with the natural process of evolution (see, for example, Chargaff's argument in "Tinkering With Life," *op. cit.*, p. 33). However, this argument has merit if, and only if, one is willing to assume that the "natural way" is the right way; and this assumption is questionable.

Before any attempt can be made to restructure the recombinant DNA debate, one must first get clear as to the major areas of disagreement within the controversy. So far as I can determine, there are three: (1) Should some or all recombinant DNA experiments be prohibited? (2) If recombinant DNA research is not totally prohibited, should restrictions be placed on the ways in which scientists may conduct some or all of their research? And (3), if safeguards are needed for some (or all) recombinant DNA experimentation, what kinds of safeguards are required? Let us examine each of these questions in turn.

In order to argue for the prohibition of some (or all) recombinant DNA experimentation, it is necessary to assume that proscription of such experimentation will help protect the public from potential harm. But this assumption is questionable. Consider the following facts.

First, it seems clear that no prohibition of recombinant DNA research will be totally effective in the United States. For example, the proscriptions now embodied in the NIH guidelines apply only to NIH-funded institutions; and as a result, any scientist employed by a private drug company may now conduct "prohibited" recombinant DNA research virtually without fear of government reprisal. Furthermore, even if federal laws proscribing certain types of recombinant DNA experimentation were passed, it is likely that these laws would be ineffective. Researchers are ambitious,[6] and drug companies' actions are dictated, in large part, by the profit motive.[7] In all probability, then, legislative proscription of recombinant DNA experiments would do nothing but force prohibited experiments "underground."[8] Finally, even if effective laws pro-

---

[6] Evidence of this ambition is not hard to find. In 1976, for example, researchers at the University of California at San Francisco found themselves competing with scientists at Harvard to isolate the human insulin gene for use in manufacturing insulin protein. There is good reason to believe that researchers at the University of California were in such a hurry to "beat out" their competitors that they broke the National Institutes of Health's guidelines for experimentation. See, "Recombinant DNA: NIH Rules Broken in Insulin Gene Project," *Science* (September 30, 1977), p. 1342.

[7] There is little doubt that recombinant DNA research can be profitable. For example, a company called Genentech took note of the practical implications of the insulin isolation project at the University of California, San Francisco, and reportedly "established a relationship" with Professor Herbert Boyer, one of the pioneers of the project. See *Science*, *op. cit.*, p. 1342.

[8] Ambition and the desire for profit are not the only two forces operating to force prohibited experiments "underground." Many researchers feel that their freedom of inquiry is unjustly curtailed when restrictions are placed upon experimentation. Thus it is reported that approximately one-half of the researchers at the University of California, San Francisco do not attempt to follow the NIH guidelines (see *Science*, *op. cit.*, p. 1343). Furthermore, the National Institutes of Health admits that it "cannot run a policing service," and that its rules are, in effect, unenforceable (*Ibid.*, p. 1343). Now if this is so, what reason is there to believe that laws proscribing recombinant DNA research would be enforceable?

scribing DNA research were enacted in the United States, this could have no influence on the research policies of other nations. And in all likelihood, dangerous recombinant DNA research would continue to be conducted in other countries, regardless of what we did here.[9]   Indeed, this is especially true given the fact that recombinant DNA research has the potential (at least theoretically) for developing new agents for use in biological warfare.[10]

If prohibition of some or all forms of recombinant DNA research would not be effective, it is not clear that proscriptive laws would protect the general public from harm.   But, the proponent of proscription will reply, one can admit that laws prohibiting recombinant DNA research would not be totally effective, and still claim that they could help protect the public.   After all, if dangerous experimentation were prohibited, the total number of hazardous experiments performed in the United States doubtless would decline.   And as the number declined, so too would the danger.   Now it hardly can be denied that the amount of dangerous recombinant DNA research performed in the United States would decrease if such research were banned.   But it does not follow from this that the danger to the general public also would decrease.   There are two reasons why this is so.

First, once it is acknowledged that proscriptive legislation is powerless to halt dangerous recombinant DNA experimentation, proponents of such legislation must admit that (a) the public would be subjected to *some* risk even if dangerous recombinant DNA research were prohibited, and that (b) there is. no way to tell how high this risk would be, because no one can predict how many "prohibited" experiments would be conducted in the United States given proscriptive legislation, and no one can say what sorts of safety precautions (if any) would be utilized when these "prohibited" experiments were performed.   And if this is so—if it is impossible to say how much danger the citizens of this country would face given prohibition of hazardous recombinant DNA research in the United States—then one cannot argue for the proscription of such research by claiming that this action would be helpful in protecting the public from harm.

Second, although it is impossible accurately to gauge the degree of danger that would be placed upon the general public if laws prohibiting recombinant

[9]Consider the following case. In New Zealand, Dr. Kenneth Giles conducted nitrogen-fixing experiments with fungi and pine tree seedlings. In attempting to produce nitrogen-fixing fungi to aid the growth of pine tree, Giles created one altered strain which killed ten pine tree seedlings. Because Giles suspected that the containment facilities available to him were not adequate for studying a possible new pathogen, he destroyed his new fungi strain by autoclaving. Not only are there no signs that Giles will discontinue his experimentation with fungi, he now expresses regret that he killed the altered strain. See, "Genetic Engineering: The Origin of the Long-Distance Rumor," *Science* (October 28, 1977), p. 388.

[10]*The Atlanta Journal, op. cit.*

DNA research were enacted in the United States, there are good reasons to believe that the risk would be greater with proscription than without. For example, if dangerous DNA experiments were forced "underground" by laws prohibiting such experimentation, researchers probably would not have the financial backing necessary to place proper safeguards on their experiments. And in this case, the chances of accident might well increase rather than decrease once hazardous DNA research was proscribed. But this is not the worst of it. If recombinant DNA research were prohibited, scientists could not perform experiments in order to find out how to kill or control new life forms which might accidentally (or purposely) be introduced into the biosphere. And since prohibition could not eliminate all dangerous DNA research, proscription ultimately would allow the citizens of our country to be subjected to a risk of unknown proportions, without letting them develop the means necessary to protect themselves. Surely, this is more dangerous a situation than having scientists assess the risks of recombinant DNA research by performing hazardous experiments under conditions of maximum security.

Thus far I have argued that legislative proscription of recombinant DNA experimentation would not be effective, and that as a result it is safer to permit rather than to prohibit research of this sort. But what if proscriptive laws were effective in the United States? Would this force rejection of my conclusion? I do not think so; for even if prohibition of recombinant DNA research were effective, it only would be so in the United States. Pandora's box has been opened; and even if the United States were to ban hazardous DNA research, there is absolutely no reason to believe that such research would not proceed in foreign countries, especially in Communist bloc nations. And because this is so, advocates of prohibition are faced with a dilemma: If they argue that recombinant DNA experimentation is extremely dangerous (so that a laboratory accident in another country might cause worldwide cancer epidemics, or crop failures on a global scale), then they must admit that there is need to conduct such research in the United States (albeit under conditions of maximum security) in order to learn how to protect ourselves from the effects of a possible accident. On the other hand, if they claim that the deleterious effects of a laboratory accident would be relatively small-scale and localized, then they must acknowledge that the danger is not severe enough to warrant prohibition. Indeed, research of this sort could be conducted with laboratory precautions in sparsely populated areas of our country with little or no risk to the general public.

If my analysis thus far is correct, there is no reason to prohibit any type of recombinant DNA research in the United States. Still, two questions remain. First, if all recombinant DNA research is to be permitted in the United States, should scientists employ safeguards in conducting some or all of their experiments? And second, if precautions need to be taken, what sorts of safeguards are required? Now one view, currently in vogue, is that the public should have

a voice in deciding matters such as these.[11]   I believe that this view is mistaken;
for once it has been determined that no recombinant DNA research should be
prohibited in the United States, there is no place left for public involvement.
That is to say, it clearly seems within the public province to determine the social
goals of experimentation, and hence to determine what kinds of research will be
permitted and prohibited in the United States.   But as we have seen, the public
has no power to halt recombinant DNA experimentation in this country; and
even if the public did have this power, it would be in its own best interest to
allow such experimentation.   Once this is recognized, however, the questions
concerning experimental safeguards must be viewed as technical matters which
need to be resolved by those who have the proper scientific expertise.   How, for
example, could the general public be expected to decide whether or not safeguards were needed for new recombinant DNA experiments if researchers were
unable to reach agreement concerning the degree of risk involved in those experiments?   And even if the public had the ability to make these decisions, how
would it proceed?   Would each new research protocol have to be put to a vote
before experimentation could be conducted?   Furthermore, what if the public
decided that safeguards were needed for some (or all) recombinant DNA experiments?   How could it hope to determine what sorts of precautions would be
sufficient to protect itself from harm?   Faced with this problem, I would not
know where to begin.   And neither, I suspect, would any other nonscientist.
In the end, then, it seems best to leave the resolution of all questions concerning
the safeguarding of recombinant DNA experiments to the experts themselves.[12]

Before closing I would like to defend my position against one possible criticism.   Because I hold that no recombinant DNA research ought to be prohibited
and that the scientific community alone should determine when and how to
safeguard DNA experiments, some might object that I would place the welfare
of all the citizens of this country in the hands of a small body of scientific experts.   Now even if this were true (and I shortly will argue that it is not), I am
not sure that this should be something to be feared.   After all, what is the danger
in this proposal?   One might claim that researchers could make mistakes and so

---

[11] For a defense of the general position that the public should have a say in determining
those research practices which have an effect upon them see, Paul Ramsey, *The Ethics of
Fetal Research* (New Haven: Yale University Press, 1975), pp. 12 ff.   This view was explicitly applied to recombinant DNA research by Professor Richard Robbins in a paper
delivered to the Emory Committee on Biomedical Ethics, November 15, 1977. It also
might be added that the theory was put into practice in Cambridge, Massachusetts, see
Time, op. cit., p. 45.

[12] What sorts of procedures the experts would employ in order to make these decisions is
a matter for further discussion.   My own feeling is that each institution engaging in recombinant DNA research should have a committee to determine when and how safeguards should be employed.

fail properly to safeguard dangerous experiments. But in determining proper laboratory precautions, experts are less likely to err than an uninformed public. Again, one might argue that the scientific community is so driven by ambition and the quest for knowledge that it will be reckless and uncaring in its determination of recombinant DNA policy. But this forgets that scientists, like the rest of us, are human beings dependent upon the environment. They too have a stake in life; and by and large, they will not be prone to make their decisions hastily. In the final analysis, however, I need not quibble over these issues, for it simply is not true that my position leaves the general public without any means for protecting itself from the dangers inherent in recombinant DNA research. To be sure, I would give scientific experts the power to decide when and how to safeguard recombinant DNA experiments. But if the public feels that this power needs to be checked, it may pass laws imposing harsh criminal and/or civil penalties on any laboratory which allows dangerous new life forms to escape into the biosphere. Not only would laws of this sort be enforceable, they also would insure that due care was exercised when researchers estimated the degree of risk posed by their experiments. And unless I am mistaken, this is the best means of protection available to the general public at the present time.

FURTHER READINGS

For lists of further sources see:

Current Literature in Family Planning. Published Monthly by the Library, Planned Parenthood-World Population Information and Education Department, 810 Seventh Avenue, New York, New York 10019.

"Genetic Engineering: Evolution of a Technological Issue." Science Policy Research Division, Congressional Research Service, Library of Congress, Serial W. November, 1972, pp. 109–119.

Richard McCormick, "Genetic Medicine: Notes on the Moral Literature." *Theological Studies* 33 (September 1972): 531–552.

National Institute of Mental Health, National Clearinghouse for Mental Health Information, *Report on the XYZ Chromosome Abnormality.* Public Health Service Publication No. 2103, October, 1970.

National Library of Medicine, Literature search: #70-28 "Amniocentesis," #70-42 "Genetics and Socially Deviant Behavior," and #71-2 "Genetic Counseling." Literature Search Program, National Library of Medicine, Bethesda, Maryland 20014.

James R. Sorenson, *Social and Psychological Aspects of Applied Human Genetics: A Bibliography.* Washington, D.C.: Fogarty International Center DHEW Publication No. NIH 73-412, 1973.

Bibliographies

Sollitto, Sharmon, and Veatch, Robert M., comps. *Bibliography of Society, Ethics and the Life Sciences.* Hastings-on-Hudson, New York: Institute of Society, Ethics and the Life Sciences, 1974–1977.

Sorenson, James R. *Social and Psychological Aspects of Applied Human Genetics: A Bibliography.* Washington, D.C.: U.S. Government Printing Office, 1973.

Walters, LeRoy., ed. *Bibliography of Bioethics.* Vols. 1- . Detroit: Gale Research Co., issued annually.

Books

Bergsma, Daniel, ed. *Medical Genetics Today.* Baltimore: Johns Hopkins University Press, 1974.

——. *Ethical, Social and Legal Dimensions of Screening for Human Genetic Diseases.* Miami: Symposia Specialists Series Vol. 10, No. 6, 1974.

Birch, Charles, and Abrecht, Paul, eds. *Genetics and the Quality of Life.* Elmsford, N.Y.: Pergamon Press, 1975.

Burnet, Sir Macfarlane. *Genes, Dreams and Realities.* Aylesbury, Bucks: Medical and Technical Publishing Company, 1971.

Carter, Bobby G. *Genes and Politics: A Constructive Critique of Paul Ramsey and Leon R. Kass.* Ann Arbor: University Microfilms, 1974.

Cavalli-Sforza, L. L., and Bodmer, W. F. *The Genetics of Human Populations.* San Francisco: Freeman, 1971.

Cooke, Robert. *Improving on Nature.* New York: Quadrangle, 1977.

Crowe, James F., and Kimura, Motoo. *An Introduction to Population Genetics Theory.* New York: Harper & Row, 1970.

Dobzhansky, T. *Genetics and the Evolutionary Process.* New York: Columbia University Press, 1970.

——. *Mankind Evolving.* New Haven: Yale University Press, 1962.

Dorfman, Albert, ed. *Antenatal Diagnosis.* Chicago: University of Chicago Press, 1972.

Ehrman, Lee, Omenn, Gilbert S., and Caspari, Ernest, eds. *Genetics, Environment and Behavior: Implications for Educational Policy.* New York: Academic Press, 1972.

Emery, A. E. H., ed. *Antenatal Diagnosis of Genetic Disease.* Edinburgh: Churchill Livingstone, 1973.

English, Darrel S., comp. *Genetic and Reproductive Engineering.* New York: MSS Information, 1974.

Etzioni, Amitai. *Genetic Fix.* New York: Macmillan, 1973.

Fletcher, Joseph. *The Ethics of Genetic Control: Ending Reproductive Roulette.* Garden City, N.Y.: Anchor Press, 1974.

Francoeur, Robert T. *Utopian Motherhood.* New York: Doubleday, 1970.

Frankel, Mark S. *Genetic Technology: Promises and Problems.* Washington, D.C.: The George Washington University, Program of Policy Studies in Science and Technology, Monograph No. 15, March, 1973.

Goodfield, June. *Playing God: Genetic Engineering and the Manipulation of Life.* New York: Random House, 1977.

Halacy, D. S., Jr. *Genetic Revolution: Shaping Life for Tomorrow.* New York: Harper & Row, 1974.

Hamilton, Michael, ed. *The New Genetics and the Future of Man.* Grand Rapids, Mich.: Eerdmans, 1972.

Haring, Bernard. *The Ethics of Manipulation: Issues in Medicine, Behavior Control and Genetics.* Somers, Conn: Seabury Press (Crossroad Books), 1976.

Harris, Harry, and Hirschhorn, Kurt, eds. *Advances in Human Genetics.* Vols. 1-7. New York: Plenum Press, 1970-1976.

Harris, Maureen, ed. *Early Diagnosis of Human Genetic Defects: Scientific and Ethical Considerations.* Fogarty International Center Proceedings, No. 6, 1972.

Hilton, Bruce, *et al.*, eds. *Ethical Issues in Human Genetics.* New York: Plenum Press, 1973.

Jensen, Arthur R. *Educability and Group Differences.* New York: Harper & Row, 1973.

Lader, Lawrence. *Foolproof Birth Control.* Boston: Beacon Press, 1972.

Leach, Gerald. *The Biocrats.* New York: McGraw-Hill, 1970.

Levitan, Max, and Montagu, Ashley. *Textbook of Human Genetics.* New York: Oxford University Press, 1971.

Lipkin, Mack, and Rowley, Peter T. *Genetic Responsibility: On Choosing Our Children's Genes.* New York: Plenum Press, 1974.

Ludmerer, Kenneth M. *Genetics and American Society.* Baltimore: Johns Hopkins University Press, 1972.

Lynch, H. T. *Dynamic Genetic Counseling for Clinicians.* Springfield, Ill.: Charles C Thomas, 1969.

McKusick, Victor. *Mendelian Inheritance in Man*, third edition. Baltimore: Johns Hopkins University Press, 1971.

Mertens, Thomas R., and Robinson, Sandra, eds. *Human Genetics and Social Problems: A Book of Readings.* New York: MSS Information Corporation, 1973.

Milunsky, Aubrey, ed. *The Prevention of Genetic Disease and Mental Retardation.* Philadelphia. W. B. Saunders, 1975.

Milunsky, Aubrey, and Annas, John, eds. *Genetics and the Law.* New York: Plenum Press, 1976.

Naccarato v. Grob, 162 *Northwestern Reporter* 2nd Series (1968) p. 305.

Nuffield Provincial Hospitals Trust, *Screening in Medical Care.* Oxford: Oxford University Press, 1968.

Planned Parenthood of Southeastern Pennsylvania. *Love, Sex and Birth Control for the Mentally Retarded—A Guide for Parents.* Planned Parenthood of Southeastern Pennsylvania and Family Planning and Population Center of Syracuse University, 1971.

Paoletti, Robert A., ed. *Selected Readings: Genetic Engineering and Bioethics.* New York: MSS Information Corporation, 1972.

Porter, Ian H., and Skalko, Richard G., eds. *Heredity and Society.* New York: Academic Press, 1973.

Ramsey, Paul. *Fabricated Man: The Ethics of Genetic Control.* New Haven: Yale University Press, 1970.

Recombinant Molecules—Impact on Science and Society. Myles International Symposium Series, No. 10. New York: Raven Press, 1977.

Reisman, L. E., and Matheny, A. P., Jr. *Genetics and Counseling in Medical Practice.* St. Louis: C. V. Mosby, 1969.

Restak, Richard M. *Premeditated Man*: *Bioethics and the Control of Human Life*. New York: Viking Press, 1975.

Roberts, J. A. Fraser. *An Introduction to Medical Genetics*, fifth edition. New York: Oxford University Press, 1970.

Robitscher, Jonas, ed. *Eugenic Sterilization*. Springfield, Ill.: Charles C Thomas, 1973.

Rorvik, David. *Brave New Baby*: *Promise and Peril of the Biological Revolution*. New York: Doubleday, 1971.

Rosenfeld, Albert. *The Second Genesis*: *The Coming Control of Life*. Englewood Cliffs, N.J.: Prentice-Hall, 1969.

Smith, David, and Wilson, Ann Asper. *The Child with Down's Syndrome*. Philadelphia: Saunders, 1973.

Taylor, Gordon R. *The Biological Time Bomb*. Cleveland: World, 1968.

Wade, Nicholas. *The Ultimate Experiment*: *Man-Made Evolution*. Chicago: Walker, 1977.

Williams, Preston N., ed. *Ethical Issues in Biology and Medicine*: *Proceedings of a Symposium on the Identity and Dignity of Man*. Cambridge, Mass.: Schenkman, 1973.

Articles

Adams, Margaret. "Social Aspects of Medical Care for the Mentally Retarded." *New Journal of Medicine* 286 (March 23, 1972): 635-638.

Allen, Garland E. "Genetics, Eugenics and Class Struggle." *Genetics* 79, Supplement (June 1975): 29-45.

Annas, George J., and Coyne, Brian. "'Fitness' for Birth and Reproduction: Legal Implications of Genetic Screening." *Family Law Quarterly* 9 (Fall 1975): 463-489.

Aner, Kerstin. "Genetic Manipulation as a Political Issue." In *Genetics and the Quality of Life*, edited by Charles Birch and Paul Abrecht. Elmsford, N.Y.: Pergamon Press, 1975, pp. 62-72.

Ashton, Jean. "Amniocentesis: Safe but Still Ambiguous." *Hastings Center Report* 6 (February 1976): 5-6.

Austin, C. R. "Embryo Transfer and Sensitivity to Teratogenesis." *Nature* 244 (August 10, 1973): 333-334.

Barakat, B. Y., *et al.* "Fetal Quality Control in Pregnancies with High Risk for Genetic Disorders." *Fertility and Sterility* 22 (July, 1971): 409-415.

Bass, Medora S. "Attitudes of Parents of Retarded Children toward Voluntary Sterilization." *Eugenics Quarterly* 14 (March, 1967): 45-53.

———. "Marriage, Parenthood, and the Prevention of Pregnancy for the Mentally Deficient." *American Journal of Mental Deficiency* 55 (1963): 318-333.

Baumiller, Robert C. "Ethical Issues in Genetics." In *Medical Genetics Today*, edited by Daniel Bergsma. Baltimore: John Hopkins University Press, 1974, pp. 297-300.

Becker, Frank. "Law vs. Science: Legal Control of Genetic Research." *Kentucky Law Journal* 65 (1977): 880-894.

Becker, Wayne. "Genetic Engineering: Research That Shouldn't Be Done?" *Wisconsin Academy Review* 21 (Summer 1975): 21-26.

Beckwith, J., and King, J. "The XYZ Syndrome: A Dangerous Myth." *New Scientist* (November, 1974): 474-476.

Benke, Paul J. "Screening Newborn Infants for Disease." *Perspectives in Biology and Medicine* 19 (Autumn 1975): 118-124.

Bennett, Bruce, and Ratmoff, Oscar D. "Detection of the Carrier State for Classic Hemophilia." *New England Journal of Medicine* 288 (February 15, 1973): 342-345.

Bennett, Dorothea, and Boyse, Edward A. "Sex Ratio in Progeny of Mice Inseminated with Sperm Treated with H-Y Antiserum." *Nature* 246 (November 30 1973): 308-309.

Bennett, William, and Gurin, Joel. "Science That Frightens Scientists—The Great Debate over DNA." *Atlantic* (February 1977): 43-62.

Berg, Paul. "Recombinant DNA Research Must and Can Be Done Safely." *Trends in Biochemical Sciences*, Vol. 2 (February 1977): 25-27.

Berg, Paul D., Brenner, Sydney, *et al.* "Asilomar Conference on Recombinant DNA Molecules." *Science* 188 (June 6, 1975): 991-994.

Berg, Paul, *et al.* "Letter to the Editor. Potential Biohazards of Recombinant DNA Molecules." *Science* 185 (July 26, 1974): 303.

Bessman, Samuel P., and Swazey, Judith. "PKU: A Study of Biomedical Legislation." *Human Aspects of Biomedical Innovation*, edited by E. Mendelsohn, J. P. Swazey, and Irene Taviss. Cambridge: Harvard University Press, 1971.

Bergsma, Daniel, ed. "Advances in Human Genetics and Their Impact on Society." *Birth Defects Original Article Series* 8 (July 1972).

Bergsma, Daniel, *et al.* "Contemporary Genetic Counseling." *Birth Defects Original Article Series* 9 (April 1973):

Binney, Cecil. "Legal and Social Implications of Artificial Insemination." *Eugenics Review* 40 (April 1948): 199-204.

Birch, Charles. "Genetics and Moral Responsibility." In *Genetics and the Quality of Life*, edited by Charles Birch and Paul Abrecht. Elmsford, N.Y.: 1975, pp. 6-19.

Blacker, C. P. "Artificial Insemination: The Society's Position." *Eugenics Review* 50 (1958): 51-54.

Bodmer, W. F. "Biomedical Advances: A Mixed Blessing?" In *Problems of Scientific Revolution: Progress and Obstacles to Progress in the Sciences*, edited by Rom Harre. London: Oxford University Press, 1975, pp. 25-41.

Bodmer, Walter and Jones, Alun. "Genetic Screening—The Social Dilemma." *New Scientist* 63 (5 September 1974): 596-597.

Bok, Sissela, and Lappe, Marc. "The Threat of Hemophilia." *Hastings Center Report* 4 (April 1974): 8-10.

Bokser, Ben Z. "Problems of Bio-Medical Ethics: A Jewish Perspective." *Judaism* 24 (Spring 1975): 134-143.

Breyer, Stephen, and Zeckhauser, Richard. "The Regulation of Genetic Engineering." *Man and Medicine: The Journal of Values and Ethics in Health Care* 1 (Autumn 1975): 1-12.

Brimblecombe, F. S. A., and Chamberlain, Jocelyn. "Screening for Cystic Fibrosis." *Lancet* (December 22, 1973): 1428-1431.

British Medical Association, Annual Report of the Council. "Appendix V: Report of Panel on Human Artificial Insemination." *British Medical Journal*, Supplement (April 7, 1973): 3-5.

Buck v. *Bell* 274 U.S. 200 (1927).

Bumpass, Larry L., and Presser, Harriet B. "Contraceptive Sterilization in the United States: 1965 and 1970." *Demography* 9 (November 1972): 531-548.

Callahan, Daniel. "What Obligations Do We Have to Future Generations?" *American Ecclesiastical Review* 164 (April 1971): 265-280.

——. "Human Rights: Biogenetic Frontier and Beyond." *Hospital Progress* 59 (September 1973): 80-84.

——. "The Meaning and Significance of Genetic Disease: Philosophical Perspectives." In *Ethical Issues in Human Genetics: Genetic and Counseling and the Use of Genetic Knowledge*, edited by Bruce Hilton *et al*. New York: Plenum Press, 1973, pp. 83-100.

——. "Recombinant DNA: Science and the Public." *Hastings Center Report* 7 (April 1977): 20-23.

Caplan, Arthur. "Ethics, Evolution and the Milk of Human Kindness." *Hastings Center Report* 6 (April 1976): 20-25.

——. "Review of E. O. Wilson *Sociobiology*." *Philosophy of Science* (June 1976): 305-306.

Capron, Alexander M. "Legal Rights and Moral Rights." In *Ethical Issues in Human Genetics: Genetic Counseling and the Use of Genetic Knowledge*, edited by Bruce Hilton *et al*. New York: Plenum Press, 1973, pp. 221-244.

Carmody, Patrick. "Tay-Sachs Disease: The Use of Tears for the Detection of Heterozygotes." *New England Journal of Medicine* 289 (November 15, 1973): 1072-1074.

Carroll, Charles. "Ethical Issues Raised by Advances in Genetics." In *Heredity and Society*, edited by Ian H. Porter and Richard G. Skalko. New York: Academic Press, 1973, pp. 291-320.

Carter, C. O., *et al*. "Genetic Clinic: A Follow-Up." *Lancet* (February 6, 1971): 281-285.

Cassel, J. Frank. "The Ethics of Genetics." In *The Scientist and Ethical Decision*, edited by Charles Hatfield. Downers Grove, Ill.: Intervarsity Press, 1973, pp. 117-127.

Cedarquist, L. L., and Fuchs, F. "Antenatal Sex Determination: A Historical Review." *Clinical Obstetrics and Gynecology* 13 (1970): 159-177.

Chargaff, Erwin. "A Few Remarks Regarding Research on Recombinant DNA." *Man and Medicine: The Journal of Values and Ethics in Health Care* 2 (1976-1977): 78-82.

Childs, Barton. "Prospects for Genetic Screening." *Journal of Pediatrics* 87 (December 1975): 1125-1132.

Clarke, C. A. "Genetic Counseling." *British Medical Journal* (March 4, 1972): 606-609.

Clow, Carol, *et al.* "Management of Hereditary Metabolic Disease: The Role of Allied Health Personnel." *New England Journal of Medicine* 284 (June 10, 1971): 1292-1298.

Cohen, Carl. "When May Research Be Stopped?" *New England Journal of Medicine* (May 26, 1977): 1203-1210.

Cohen, Stanley N. "Recombinant DNA: Fact and Fiction." *Science* 195 (February 18, 1977): 654-657.

Cohen, Victor. "Products of Genetic Engineering Seen Less than Five Years Away." *Washington Post* (November 11, 1977): A2.

Conley, Ronald, and Milunsky, Aubrey. "The Economics of Prenatal Genetic Diagnosis." In *The Prevention of Genetic Disease and Mental Retardation*, edited by Aubrey Milunsky. Philadelphia: W. B. Saunders, 1975, pp. 442-455.

Cowen, Robert C. "Recombinant DNA: Time to Face the Facts." *Technology Review* (February 1977): 10-11.

Curtiss, Roy III. "Genetic Manipulation of Microorganisms: Potential Benefits and Biohazards." *Annual Review of Microbiology* (1976): 507-533.

Danielli, James F. "Industry, Society, and Genetic Engineering." *Hastings Center Report* 2 (December 1972): 5-7.

Davis, Bernard D. "Prospects for Genetic Intervention in Man." *Science* 170 (1970): 1279-1283.

——. "Genetic Engineering: How Great Is the Danger?" *Science* 186 (25 October 1974): 309.

——. "Threat and Promise in Genetic Engineering." In *Ethical Issues in Biology and Medicine*, edited by Preston N. Williams. Cambridge, Mass.: Schenkman, 1973, pp. 17-32.

Davis, Bernard D., Chargaff, Erwin, and Krimsky, Sheldon. "Recombinant DNA Research—A Debate on the Benefits and Risks." *Chemical and Engineering News* (May 30, 1977): 26-31.

DeGeorge, Richard T. "Freedom, Genetics and the Law: Comment on 'Genetic Equality and Freedom of Reproduction.'" *Journal of Value Inquiry* 11 (Fall 1977): 208-212.

De Nicola, Daniel R. "Genetics, Justice and Respect for Human Life." *Zygon* 11 (June 1976): 115-137.

Dismukes, Key. "Recombinant DNA: A Proposal for Regulation." *Hastings Center Report* 7 (April 1977): 25-30.

Dodson, W. E., *et al.* "Cytogenetic Survey of XYY Males in Two Juvenile Court Populations, with a Case Report." *Journal of Medical Genetics* 9 (September 1972): 287-288.

Dworkin, Gerald, "Autonomy and Behavior Control." *Hastings Center Report* 6 (February 1976): 23-28.

Eckhart, W. "Genetic Manipulation of Cells by Viruses." *BioScience* (February 15, 1971); 171-173.

Editorial, "Genetic Engineering in Man: Ethical Considerations." *Journal of the American Medical Association* 220 (May 1, 1972): 721.

Edwards, R. G. "The Problem of Compensation for Antenatal Injuries." *Nature* (November 9, 1973): 54-55.

———. "The Problems of Artificial Fertilization." *Nature* 233 (1971): 23-25.

———. "Fertilization of Human Eggs *In Vitro*: Morals, Ethics and the Law." *Quarterly Review of Biology* (March 1974): 3-26.

Edwards, R. G., with Fowler, R. E. "Human Embryos in the Laboratory." *Scientific American* 233 (1970): 45-54.

Edwards, R. G., with Sharpe, David J. "Social Values and Research in Human Embryology." *Nature* 231 (May 14, 1971): 87-91.

Eisenberg, Leon. "The Outcome as Cause: Predestination and Human Cloning." *Journal of Medicine and Philosophy* 1 (1976): 318-331.

Emery, A. E. H. "Genetic Counseling." *British Medical Journal* 3 (26 July, 1975): 219-221.

Emery, A. E. H., *et al.* "Social Effects of Genetic Counseling." *British Medical Journal* (March 24, 1973): 724-726.

Emery, A. E. H., *et al.* "The Genetic Register System (RAPID)." *Journal of Medical Genetics* 11 (July 1974): 145ff.

Eptein, C. J., *et al.* "Prenatal Detection of Genetic Disorders," *American Journal of Human Genetics* 24 (March 1972): 214-226.

Ericsson, R. J., *et al.* "Isolation of Fractions Rich in Human Y Sperm." *Nature* 246 (December 14, 1973): 421-424.

Etzioni, Amitai. "Doctors Know More Than They're Telling about Genetic Defects." *Psychology Today* (November 1973): 26ff.

———. "Sex Control, Science and Society." *Science* 161 (September 13, 1968): 1107-1112.

———. "Amniocentesis: A Case Study in the Management of 'Genetic Engineering.'" *Ethics in Science and Medicine* 2 (May 1975): 13-24.

———. "Social Implications of the Use or Non-Use of New Genetic and Medical Techniques." In *Protection of Human Rights in the Light of Scientific and Technological Progress in Biology and Medicine*, edited by Simon Btesh. Geneva: World Health Organization, 1974, pp. 48-90.

———. "Genetic Fix: Should We Dare, Who Will Decide?" *Modern Medicine* 41 (29 October 1973): 480–484.

"Evaluating a Decade of PKU Screening." *Medical World News* (November 19, 1971): 43.

Evans, Philip R. "Hereditary Disease and Its Control." *British Medical Journal* 3 (19 July 1975): 141–144.

Falek, A. "Ethical Issues in Human Behavior Genetics: Civil Rights, Informed Consent and Ethics of Intervention." Position paper #6 presented at Chairman's Workshop on Developmental Human Behavior Genetics, Developmental Behavioral Science Study Section, Division of Research Grants, National Institute of Health, Bethesda, Maryland. April 16–17, 1974.

Farris, E. J., *et al.* "Emotional Impact of Successful Donor Insemination." *Obstetrics and Gynecology* 3 (1954): 19–20.

Farrow, Michael G., and Juberg, Richard C. "Genetics and Laws Prohibiting Marriage in the United States." *Journal of the American Medical Association* 209 (July 28, 1969): 534–538.

Felleenes, George. "Sterilization and the Law." In *New Dimensions in Criminal Justice*, edited by H. K. Becker *et al.* Metuchen, N.J.: Scarecrow Press, 1968.

Fletcher, John C. "Abortion, Euthanasia and Care of Defective Newborns." *New England Journal of Medicine* 292 (9 January, 1975): 75–78.

———. "Parents in Genetic Counseling: The Moral Shape of Decision Making." In *Ethical Issues in Human Genetics: Genetic Counseling and the Use of Genetic Knowledge*, edited by Bruce Hilton *et al.* New York: Plenum Press, 1973, pp. 301–327.

———. "Moral and Ethical Problems of Pre-Natal Diagnosis." *Clinical Genetics* 8 (1975): 251–257.

———. "Genetic Engineering." In *New Catholic Encyclopedia* Vol. 16, Supplement 1967–1974, edited by David Eggenberger. New York: McGraw-Hill, 1974, pp. 188–192.

———. "Applied Genetics: No Ultimate Threat." *Engage/Social Action* 1 (October 1973): 16–27.

———. "Attitudes toward Defective Newborns." *Hastings Center Studies* 2 (January 1974): 21–32.

Fletcher, Joseph. "Ethical Aspects of Genetic Controls." *New England Journal of Medicine* 285 (September 30, 1971): 776–783.

———. "Indicators of Humanhood: A Tentative Profile of Man." *Hastings Center Report* 2 (November 1972): 104.

———. "Sterilization—Our Right to Foreclose Parenthood." *Morals and Medicine*. Boston: Beacon Press, 1960, Chapter 1.

———. "Moral Problems in Genetic Counseling." *Pastoral Psychology* 23 (April 1972): 47–60.

Fong, Melanie, and Johnson, Larry O. "The Eugenics Movement: Some Insight into The Institutionalization of Racism." *Issues in Criminology* 9 (Fall 1974): 89–115.

Fort, A. T. "Counseling the Patient with Sickle Cell Disease about Reproduction: Pregnancy Outcome Does Not Justify the Maternal Risk!" *American Journal of Obstetrics and Gynecology* 111 (1972): 324–327.

Fottesman, I. I., and Erienmeyer-Kimling, L. "Prologue: A Foundation for Informed Eugenics." *Social Biology* 18, Supplement S1-S8 (September 1971).

Frankel, Charles. "Genetics: What Shall the Human Species Make of Itself?" *Washington Post* (21 April, 1974): Section B, p. 1.

——. "The Specter of Eugenics." *Commentary* 57 (March 1974): 22–33.

Fraser, Clarke F. "Genetic Counseling." *Hospital Practice* (January 1971): 49–56.

Fraser, G. R. "The Short-Term Reduction in Birth Incidence of Recessive Diseases as a Result of Genetic Counseling after the Birth of an Affected Child." *Human Heredity* 22 (1972): 1–6.

Friedmann, Theodore. "Prenatal Diagnosis of Genetic Disease." *Scientific American* 225 (November 1971): 34–42.

Frankel, Mark S. "The Public Policy Dimensions of Artificial Insemination and Human Semen Cryobanking." Program of Policy Studies in Science and Technology. George Washington University, Monograph #18 (December 1973).

Freeman, Frank R. "Pretesting for Huntington's Disease." *Hastings Center Report* 3 (September 1973): 13.

Friedman, Jane M. "Legal Implications of Amniocentesis." *University of Pennsylvania Law Review* 123 (November 1974): 92–156.

Friedman, T. and Friedman, Roblin R. "Genetic Therapy for Human Genetic Disease." *Science* 175 (3 March, 1972): 949–955.

Frolov, I. T. "Man-Genetics-Ethics: Social and Ethical Problems of Gene Engineering, Criticism of Neoeugenics." *Dialectical Humanism* 3 (Summer-Autumn 1976): 121–130.

Gastonguay, Paul R. "Human Genetics: A Model of Responsibility." *Ethics in Science and Medicine* 4 (1977): 3–4.

Gaylin, Willard. "Genetic Screening: The Ethics of Knowing." *New England Journal of Medicine* 286 (June 22, 1972): 1361–1362.

——. "We Have the Awful Knowledge to Make Exact Copies of Human Beings." *The New York Times Magazine* (March 6, 1972): 10ff.

Gerbie, Albert, *et al.* "Amniocentesis in Genetic Counseling." *American Journal of Obstetrics and Gynecology* 189 (March 3, 1971): 765–770.

Giannini, Margaret, and Goodman, Lawrence. "Counseling Families during the Crisis Reaction to Mongolism." *American Journal of Mental Deficiency* 67 (1963): 740–747.

Glass, Bentley, "Human Heredity and Ethical Problems." *Perspectives in Biology and Medicine* (Winter 1972): 237–253.

———. "Ethical Problems Raised by Genetics." In *Genetics and the Quality of Life*, edited by Charles Birch and Paul Abrecht. Elmsford, N.Y.: Pergamon Press, 1975, pp. 50–58.

Glowienka, Emerine. "A Brighter Side of the New Genetics." *BioScience* 25 (February 1975): 94–98.

Golding, Martin. "Ethical Issues in Biological Engineering." *U.C.L.A. Law Review* 15 (February 1968): 443–479.

———. "Obligations to Future Generations." *The Monist* 56 (January 1972): 85–99.

Gordon, H. "Genetic Counseling: Considerations for Talking to Parents and Prospective Parents." *Journal of the American Medical Association* 217 (August 30, 1971): 1215–1225.

Graham, Loren R. "Politics and Genetics: The Link between Science and Values." *Hastings Center Report* 7 (October 1977). 30–39.

Green, Harold P., and Capron, Alexander M. "Issues of Law and Public Policy in Genetic Screening." In *Ethical, Social and Legal Dimensions of Screening for Human Genetic Disease*, edited by Daniel Bergsma. Miami: Symposia Specialist, 1974, pp. 57–84.

———. "Genetic Technology: Law and Policy for the Brave New World." *Indiana Law Journal* 48 (Summer 1973): 559–580.

Greenberg, Daniel S. "Lessons of the DNA Controversy." *New England Journal of Medicine* (November 24, 1977): 1187–1188.

Grobstein, Clifford. "The Recombinant-DNA Debate." *Scientific American* (July 1977): 22–23.

———. "Recombinant DNA and the Body Politic." *Hastings Center Report* 7 (October 1977): 47.

Grossman, Edward. "The Obsolescent Mother." *Atlantic Monthly* (May 1971): 39–50.

Gustafson, James M. "Mongolism, Parental Desires, and the Right to Life." *Perspectives in Biology and Medicine* 16 (Summer 1973): 529–557.

———. "Genetic Screening and Human Values: An Analysis." In *Ethical, Social and Legal Dimensions of Screening for Human Genetic Disease*, edited by Daniel Bergsma. Miami: Symposia Specialists, 1974, pp. 201–223.

———. "Genetic Counseling and the Uses of Genetic Knowledge—An Ethical Overview." In *Ethical Issues in Human Genetics: Genetic Counseling and the Use of Genetic Knowledge*, edited by Bruce Hilton *et al*. New York: Plenum Press, 1973; pp. 101–119.

———. "Genetic Engineering and the Normative View of the Human." In *Ethical Issues in Biology and Medicine*, edited by Preston N. Williams. Cambridge, Mass.: Schenkman, 1973, pp. 46–58.

Guthrie, Robert. "Mass Screening for Genetic Disease." *Hospital Practice* 7 (June 1972): 93–100.

Hartung, John, and Ellison, Peter. "A Eugenic Effect of Medical Care." *Social Biology* 24 (Autumn 1977): 192-200.

Hemphill, Michael. "Pretesting for Huntington's Disease." *Hastings Center Report* 3 (June 1973): 12-13.

Heyman, Philip B., and Holtz, Sara. "The Severely Defective Newborn: The Dilemma and the Decision Process." *Public Policy* 23 (Fall 1975): 381-418.

Hilton, Bruce. "Will the Baby Be Normal? . . . and What Is the Cost of Knowing?" *Hastings Center Report* 2 (June 1972): 8-9.

Himsworth, Harold. "The Human Right to Life: It's Nature and Origin." In *Ethical Issues in Human Genetics: Genetic Counseling and the Use of Genetic Knowledge*, edited by Bruce Hilton *et al.* New York: Plenum Press, 1973, pp. 169-172.

Hirschhorn, Kurt. "On Re-Doing Man." *Annals of the New York Academy of Sciences* 184 (June 1971): 103-112.

Holder, A. R. "Voluntary Sterilization." *Journal of the American Medical Association* 225 (September 24, 1973): 1743-1744.

Holtzman, Eric. "Recombinant DNA: Triumph or Trojan Horse?" *Man and Medicine* 2 (1976-1977): 83-102.

Hook, Ernest B. "Behavioral Implications of the Human XYY Genotype." *Science* 179 (January 12, 1973): 139-150.

Hsu, Lillian Y. F., *et al.* "Results in Pitfalls in Prenatal Cytogenetic Diagnosis." *Journal of Medical Genetics* 10 (June 1973): 112-119.

Hudock, George A. "Gene Therapy and Genetic Engineering: Frankenstein is Still a Myth, but It Should Be Re-Read Periodically." *Indiana Law Journal* 48 (Summer 1973): 533-558.

"Human Genetic Engineering." *Medical World News* (May 11, 1973): 45-57.

Huxley, J. "Eugenics in Evolutionary Perspective." *Perspectives in Biology and Medicine* 6 (Winter 1963): 155-187.

Institute of Society, Ethics and the Life Sciences, Research Group on Ethical, Social and Legal Issues in Genetic Counseling and Genetic Engineering, "Ethical and Social Issues in Screening for Genetic Disease." *New England Journal of Medicine* 286 (May 25, 1972): 1129-1132.

Jacobs, Patricia. "Aggressive Behavior, Mental Sub-Normality and the XYY Male." *Nature* (December 25, 1965): 1351-1352.

Jacobs, Patricia, *et al.* "Chromosome Surveys in Penal Institutions and Approved Schools." *Journal of Medical Genetics*, 8 (1971): 49-53.

Jensen, Arthur R., *et al.* "Race, Intelligence and Genetics," *Psychology Today* (December 1973): 80-93.

Jonas, Hans. "Biological Engineering—A Preview." In his *Philosophical Essays: From Ancient Creed to Technological Man*. Englewood Cliffs, N.J.: Prentice-Hall, 1974, pp. 141-167.

Jones, Hardy. "Genetic Endowment and Obligations to Future Generations." *Social Theory and Practice* 4 (Fall 1976): 29-46.

Kaback, Michael M. "Heterozygote Screening: A Social Challenge." *New England Journal of Medicine* 289 (November 15, 1973): 1090-1091.

———. "Perspectives in the Control of Human Genetic Disease." In *Genetics and the Perinatal Patient: A Scientific, Clinical and Ethical Consideration.* Evansville, Ind.: Mead Johnson, 1973, pp. 51-57.

Karefa-Smart, John. "Problems Raised by Eugenics in Africa." In *Genetics and the Quality of Life,* edited by Charles Birch and Paul Abrecht. Elmsford, N.Y.: Pergamon Press, 1975, pp. 59-61.

Kass, Leon R. "Babies by Means of *In Vitro* Fertilization: Unethical Experiments on the Unborn?" *New England Journal of Medicine* 285 (November 18, 1971): 1174-1179.

———. "The New Biology: What Price Relieving Men's Estate?" *Science* 174 (November 19, 1971): 779-788.

———. "Making Babies: The New Biology and the Old Morality." *Public Interest* 26 (Winter 1972): 18-56.

Kellon, Dale B., *et al.* "Physicians' Attitudes about Sickle Cell Disease and Sickle Cell Trait." *Journal of the American Medical Association* 227 (January 7, 1974): 71-72.

Klawans, Harold, *et al.* "Use of L-Dopa in the Detection of Presymptomatic Huntington's Chorea." *New England Journal of Medicine* 286 (June 22, 1972): 1332-1334.

Klein, David. "Genetic Manipulations." *Impact of Science on Society* (January-March 1973): 21-27.

Konotey-Ahula, F. I. D. "Medical Considerations for Legalizing Voluntary Sterilization: Sickel Cell Disease as a Case in Point." *Law and Population Monograph Series* No. 13. Medford, Mass.: Fletcher School of Law, Tufts University, 1973.

Kretzer, D., *et al.* "Transfer of a Human Zygote," *Lancet* (September 29, 1973): 728-729.

Krever, Horace. "Some Legal Implications of Advances in Human Genetics." *Canadian Journal of Genetics and Cytology* 17 (September 1975): 283-296.

Krooth, Robert S. "Genes, Behavior, and What Will Become of Us." *Man and Medicine* 1 (1975-1976): 255-264.

LaChat, Michael R. "Utilitarian Reasoning in Nazi Medical Policy: Some Preliminary Investigations." *Linacre Quarterly* 42 (February 1975): 14-37.

Lackland, Theodore H. "Toward Creating a Philosophy of Fundamental Human Rights," *Columbia Human Rights Law Review* 6 (Fall-Winter 1974-1975): 473-503.

Lappe, Marc. "Allegiances of Human Geneticists: A Preliminary Topology." *Hastings Center Studies* 1 (No. 1, 1973): 63-78.

——. "The Genetic Counselor: Responsible to Who?" *Hastings Center Report* 1 (September 1971): 6-11.

——. "Genetic Knowledge and the Concept of Health." *Hastings Center Report* 3 (September 1973): 1-3.

——. "How Much Do We Want to Know about the Unborn?" *Hastings Center Report* 3 (February 1973): 8-9.

——. "Human Genetics." *Annals of the New York Academy of Sciences* 216 (May 18, 1973): 152-159.

——. "Risk-Taking for the Unborn." *Hastings Center Report* 2 (February 1972): 1-3.

——. "The Danger of Compulsion." Osmundsen, J. A. "We are All Mutants." *Medical Dimensions* (February 1973): 5.

——. "Censoring the Hereditarians." *Commonweal* (26 April 1974): 183-185.

——. "Regulating Recombinant DNA Research: Pulling Back from the Apocalypse." *Man and Medicine* 2 (1976-1977): 103-109.

——. "The Human Uses of Molecular Genetics." *Federation Proceedings* 34 (May 1975): 1425-1427.

——. "Can Eugenic Policy Be Just?" In *The Prevention of Genetic Disease and Mental Retardation*, edited by Aubrey Milunsky. Philadelphia: W. B. Saunders, 1975, pp. 456-475.

——. "Moral Obligations and the Fallacies of Genetic Control." *Theological Studies* 33 (September 1972): 411-427.

Lappe, Marc and Morison, Robert S. "Ethical and Scientific Issues Posed by Human Uses of Molecular Genetics." *Annals of the New York Academy of Science* 265 (23 January, 1976): 1-208.

Lappe, Marc, with Steinfels, Peter. "Choosing the Sex of Our Children." *Hastings Center Report* 4 (February 1974): 1-4.

Lederberg, J. "Experimental Genetics and Human Evolution." *Bulletin of the Atomic Scientists* 23 (October 1966): 4-11.

——. "Options for Genetic Therapy." *Medical Dimensions* (March 1972): 16 ff.

Lederberg, Joshua. "The Genetics of Human Nature." *Social Research* 40 (Autumn 1973): 375-406.

LeJeune, J. "The William Allan Memorial Award Lecture—On the Nature of Man." *American Journal of Human Genetics* 22 (March 1970): 121-128.

Leonard, Claire O., *et al.* "Genetic Counseling: A Consumer's View," *New England Journal of Medicine* 287 (August 31, 1972): 433-439.

Leonard, Martha F., and Schowalter, John E. "Does Research Stigmatize?" *Hastings Center Report* 6 (February 1976): 4-37.

Macintyre, M. Neil. "Genetic Risk, Prenatal Diagnosis, and Selective Abortion." In *Abortion, Society, and the Law*, edited by David F. Walbert and Douglas J. Butler. Cleveland: Case Western Reserve University Press, 1973, pp. 223-239.

Macklin, Ruth. "On the Ethics of Not Doing Scientific Research." *Hastings Center Report* 7 (December 1977): 11-13.

——. "Moral Issues in Human Genetics: Counseling or Control?" *Dialogue* 16 (September 1977): 375-396.

Marshall, John. "Sterilization." In his *The Ethics of Medical Practice*. London: Darton, Longman and Todd, 1960, Chapter 8.

Mayo, D. "On the Effects of Genetic Counseling on Gene Frequencies." *Human Heredity* 20 (1970): 361-370.

McBride, Gail. "Gene-Grafting Experiments Produce Both High Hopes and Grave Worries." *Journal of the American Medical Association* 232 (April 1975): 337-342.

McCormick, Thomas R. "Ethical Issues in Amniocentesis and Abortion." *Texas Reports on Biology and Medicine* 32 (Spring 1974): 299-309.

McFadden, Charles. "Sterilization." In his *Medical Ethics* (Philadelphia: F. A. Davis, 1967). Chapter 13.

Medawar, P. B. "Do Advances in Medicine Lead to Genetic Deterioration?" *Mayo Clinic Proceedings* 40 (1965): 23-33.

Meyers, David W. "Voluntary Sterilization" and "Compulsory Sterilization and Castration." In his *The Human Body and the Law*. Chicago: Aldine Press, 1970, pp. 1-47.

Miller, J. R. "Advances in Medical Genetics." *Canadian Journal of Genetics and Cytology* 17 (September 1975): 305-309.

Milton, Joyce. "The Hazards of Altering Nature." *Nation* Vol. 225(12) (15 October, 1977): 361-365.

Milunsky, Aubrey. "Prenatal Genetic Diagnosis." *New England Journal of Medicine* (December 17, 1970): 1370-1381; (December 24, 1970): 1441-1447; (December 31, 1970: 1498-1504.

Milunsky, Aubrey, and Reilly, P. "The 'New' Genetics: Emerging Medicolegal Issues in the Prenatal Diagnosis of Hereditary Disorders." *American Journal of Law and Medicine* 1 (March 1974): 71-88.

Morison, Robert S. "Implications of Prenatal Diagnosis for the Quality of, and Right to, Human Life: Society as a Standard." In *Ethical Issues in Human Genetics: Genetic Counseling and the Use of Genetic Knowledge*, edited by Bruce Hilton *et al.* New York: Plenum Press, 1973, pp. 201-220.

Motulsky, Arno G. "Human and Medical Genetics: A Scientific Discipline and an Expanding Horizon." *American Journal of Human Genetics* 23 (March 1971): 107-124.

Motulsky, Arno G., *et al.* "Public Health and Long-Term Genetic Implications of Intrauterine Diagnosis and Selective Abortion." *Birth Defects* 7 (1971): 22-32.

Muller, H. J. "The Guidance of Human Evolution." *Perspective in Biology and Medicine* 3 (1959): 1-43.

Murdock, Charles W. "Civil Rights of the Mentally Retarded: Some Critical Issues." *Notre Dame Lawyer* (1972): 133 ff.

Murphy, John R. "Sickle Cell Hemoglobin (Hb AS) in Black Football Players." *Journal of the American Medical Association* 225 (August 20, 1973): 981-982.

Murray, Robert F., Jr. "Problems Behind the Promise: Ethical Issues in Mass Genetic Screening." *Hastings Center Report* 2 (April 1972): 11-13.

——. "The Practitioner's View of the Values Involved in Genetic Screening and Counseling: Individual vs. Societal Imperatives." In *Ethical, Social and Legal Dimensions of Screening for Human Genetic Disease*, edited by Daniel Bergsma. Miami: Symposia Specialists, 1974, pp. 185-199.

——. "Ethical Problems in Genetic Counseling." In *Genetics and the Quality of Life*, edited by Charles Birch and Paul Abrecht. Elmsford, N.Y.: Pergamon Press, 1975, pp. 173-182.

Murray, Robert F., Jr., and Callahan, Daniel. "Genetic Disease and Human Health." *Hastings Center Report* 4 (September 1974): 4-7.

Murphy, Edmond A. "The Normal, Eugenics and Racial Survival." *Johns Hopkins Medical Journal* 136 (February 1975): 98-106.

Murphy, Edmond A., and Chase, Gary A. "Amniocentesis, Prenatal Diagnosis and Selective Abortion." In their *Principles of Genetic Counseling*. Chicago: Year Book Medical Publishers, 1975; pp. 324-342.

Neel, James V. "Thoughts on the Future of Human Genetics." *Medical Clinics of North America* 531 (July 1969): 1001-1011.

——. "Lessons from a 'Primitive' People." *Science* 170 (November 20, 1970): 815-822.

——. "Social and Scientific Priorities in the Use of Genetic Knowledge." In *Ethical Issues in Human Genetics: Genetic Counseling and the Use of Genetic Knowledge*, edited by Bruce Hilton *et al.* New York: Plenum Press, 1973, pp. 353-368.

Nelson, James B. "Genetics and the Control of Human Development." In his *Human Medicine: Ethical Perspectives on New Medical Issues*. Minneapolis: Augsburg, 1973, pp. 97-122.

Nielson, Johannes. "Chromosome Examination of Newborn Children: Purpose and Ethical Aspects." *Humangenetik* 26 (1975): 215-222.

Noonan, John T., Jr. "Sterilizing Operations." In his *Contraception*. Cambridge: Harvard University Press, 1966, pp. 451-460.

Nossal, G. J. V. "Medical Research and the Evolution of Mankind." In his *Medical Science and Human Goals*. London: Edward Arnold, 1975, pp. 143-159.

Olshansky, Simon. "Chronic Sorrow: A Response to Having a Mentally Defective Child." *Social Casework* 43 (1962): 190-193.

Omenn, Gilbert S. "Genetic Engineering: Present and Future." In *To Live and*

To Die: When, Why, and How, edited by Robert H. Williams. New York: Springer-Verlag, 1973, pp. 46-63.

Osborn, Frederick. "The Emergence of a Valid Eugenics." *American Scientist* 61 (July-August 1973): 425-429.

Parry, Renee-Marie C. "The Applications and Limitations of Genetic Engineering—The Ethical Implications." *Futures* 7 (April 1975): 169-173.

Paul, Julius. "Return of Punitive Sterilization Proposals." *Law and Society Review* (August 1968): 77-106.

Pearn, J. H. "Patients' Subjective Interpretation of Risks Offered in Genetic Counseling." *Journal of Medical Genetics* 10 (June 1973): 129-134.

Phillips, Nancy. "The Prevalence of Surgical Sterilization in Suburban Populations." *Demography* 8 (May 1971): 261-270.

Pinkerton, P. "Parental Acceptance of the Handicapped Child." *Developmental Medicine and Child Neurology* 12 (April 1970): 207-212.

Pizzulli, Francis. "Asexual Reproduction and Genetic Engineering: A Constitutional Assessment of Cloning." *Southern California Law Review* 47 (February 1974): 476-584.

Pohlman, Edward, and Callahan, Daniel, commentators. "Case Studies in Bioethics: Good Incentives for Sterilization: Can They Be Just?" *Hasting Center Report* 3 (February 1973): 11-12.

Powledge, Tabitha. "Laws in Question: Confusion over Sickle Cell Testing." *Hastings Center Report* 2 (December 1972): 3-5.

——. "New Trends in Genetic Legislation." *Hastings Center Report* 3 (December 1973): 6-7.

——. "The New Ghetto Hustle." *Saturday Review of the Sciences* (February 1973): 38-47.

——. "Recombinant DNA: The Argument Shifts." *Hastings Center Report* 7 (April 1977): 18-19.

——. "Recombinant DNA: Backing Off on Legislation." *Hastings Center Report* 7 (December 1977): 8-10.

——. "From Experimental Procedure to Accepted Practice." *Hastings Center Report* 6 (February 1976): 6-7.

——. "Prenatal Diagnosis: Now the Problems." *New Scientist* 69 (12 February, 1976): 332-334.

——. "Can Genetic Screening Prevent Occupational Disease?" *New Scientist* 71 (2 September 1976): 486-488.

——. "Genetic Screening as a Political and Social Development." In *Ethical, Social and Legal Dimensions of Screening for Human Genetic Disease*, edited by Daniel Bergsma. Florida: Symposia Specialists for the National Foundation—March of Dimes, 1974.

Powledge, Tabitha, Callahan, D., and Dismukes, K. "Splicing Genes." *Hastings Center Report* 7 (April 1977): 18-30.

Presser, Harriet B., and Bumpass, Larry L. "The Acceptability of Contraceptive Sterilization among U.S. Couples: 1970." *Family Planning Perspectives* 4 (October 1972): 18-26.

Ramm, Bernard. "An Ethical Evaluation of Biogenic Engineering." *Journal of the American Scientific Affiliation* 26 (December 1974): 137-143.

Ramsey, Paul. "Genetic Engineering." *Bulletin of the Atomic Scientists* (December 1972): 14-17.

——. "Parenthood and the Future of Man by Artificial Donor Insemination, et cetera, et cetera." In his *Fabricated Man*. New Haven: Yale University Press, 1970, Chapter 3.

——. "Shall We Clone a Man?" In his *Fabricated Man*. New Haven: Yale University Press, 1970, Chapter 2.

——. "Shall We 'Reproduce'?" *Journal of the American Medical Association* 220 (June 5, 1972): 1346-1350; (June 12, 1972): 1480-1485.

——. "A Theologian's Response." In *The New Genetics and the Future of Man*, edited by Michael Hamilton. Grand Rapids: Eerdmans, 1972, pp. 157-178.

——. "Screening: An Ethicist's View." In *Ethical Issues in Human Genetics*, edited by Bruce Hilton *et al.* New York: Plenum Press, 1973, pp. 147-168.

Reich, Warren T., and Smith, Harmon, commentators. "Case Studies in Bioethics: On the Birth of a Severely Handicapped Infant." *Hastings Center Report* 3 (September 1973): 10-12.

Reilly, Philip. "Sickle Cell Anemia Legislation." *Journal of Legal Medicine* 1 (September-October 1973): 39-48; (November-December 1973): 36-40.

——. "Genetic Counseling and the Law." *Houston Law Review* 12 (March 1975): 640-659.

——. "Genetic Screening Legislation." In *Advances in Human Genetics*, edited by Harry Harris and Kurt Hirschhorn. New York: Plenum Press, 1975, pp. 319-376.

Riga, Peter J. "Genetic Experimentation: The New Ethic." *Hospital Progress* 54 (October 1973): 59-63.

Roblin, Richard. "The Boston XYY Case." *Hastings Center Report* 5 (August 1975): 5-8.

Rosenfeld, Albert. "Procreation without Sex." *Physician's World* (May 1973): 61-63.

Rosoff, Jeannie. "Sterilization: The Montgomery Case." *Hastings Center Report* 3 (September 1973): 6.

Rotenstreich, Nathan. "The Biological Revolution and Ethical Awareness." *Philosophical Forum* 15 (May 1977): 245-260.

Rozorsky, Lorne E. "Legal Aspects of Human and Genetic Engineering." *Manitoba Law Journal* 6 (1975): 291-298.

Russell, Cristine. "Weighing the Hazards of Genetic Research: A Pioneering Case Study." *BioScience* 24 (December 1974): 691-694.

Sabagh, G. and R. B. Edgerton. "Sterilized Mental Defectives Look at Eugenic Sterilization." *Eugenics Quarterly* 9 (1962): 213–222.

Sanford, Barbara H. "Ethical Problems in Foetal Diagnosis and Abortion." In *Genetics and the Quality of Life*, edited by Charles Birch and Paul Abrecht. Elmsford, N.Y.: Pergamon Press, 1975, pp. 86–91.

Schultz, Jack. "Human Values and Human Genetics." *American Naturalist* 107 (September-October 1973): 585–596.

Serra, Angelo. "Ethical Issues in Foetal Diagnosis and Abortion." In *Genetics and the Quality of Life*, edited by Charles Birch and Paul Abrecht. Elmsford, N.Y.: Pergamon Press, 1975, pp. 109–119.

Shaw, Margery W. "Genetic Counseling." *Science* 184 (17 May, 1974): Editorial page.

Shinn, Roger L. "Perilous Progress in Genetics." *Social Research* 41 (Spring 1974): 83–103.

———. "Foetal Diagnosis and Selective Abortion: An Ethical Exploration." In *Genetics and the Quality of Life*, edited by Charles Birch and Paul Abrecht. Elmsford, N.Y.: Pergamon Press, 1975, pp. 74–85.

Sills, Yole G. "Recombinant DNA: Debate Continues." *Hastings Center Report* 6 (August 1976): 9.

Siminovitch, Louis. "Genetic Manipulation: Now Is the Time to Consider Controls." *Science Forum* 6 (June 1973): 7–11.

Simring, Francine R. "Folio for Folly: N.I.H. Guidelines for Recombinant DNA Research." *Man and Medicine* 2 (1976–1977): 110–119.

Singer, Daniel M. "Impact of the Law on Genetic Counseling." In *Contemporary Genetic Counseling*, edited by Daniel Bergsma. White Plains, New York: National Foundation-March of Dimes, 1973, pp. 34–38.

Singer, Maxine F. "The Recombinant DNA Debate." *Science* (8 April 1977): 127.

Sinsheimer, Robert L. "Ambush or Opportunity?" *Hastings Center Report* 2 (September 1972): 407.

Smith, Keith D., and Steinberger, Emil. "Survival of Spermatazoa in a Human Sperm Bank: Effects of Long-Term Storage in Liquid Nitrogen." *Journal of the American Medical Association* 223 (February 12, 1973): 774–777.

Sorenson, James R. "Social Aspects of Applied Human Genetics." New York: The Russell Sage Foundation, 1971.

———. "Biomedical Innovation, Uncertainty, and Doctor–Patient Interaction." *Journal of Health and Social Behavior* (December 1974): 366–374.

Soupart, Pierre, and Morgenstern, Larry L. "Human Sperm Capacitation and *In Vitro* Fertilization." *Fertility and Sterility* 24 (June 1973): 462–478.

Spring, Charles M. "The Ethical and Legal Implications of Genetic Screening, Counseling and Treatment." *Religious Humanism* 8 (Autumn 1974): 177–182.

Stein, Zena, *et al.* "Screening Programme for Prevention of Down's Syndrome." *Lancet* (February 10, 1973): 305–309.

Steinberger, Emil, and Smith, Keith D. "Artificial Insemination with Fresh or Frozen Sperm: A Comparative Study." *Journal of the American Medical Association* 223 (February 12, 1973): 778–783.

Stevas, Norman St. John. "Human Sterilization." In his *Life, Death and the Law.* Bloomington: Indiana University Press, 1961, Chapter 4.

Stenchever, M. "An Abuse of Prenatal Diagnosis." *Journal of the American Medical Association* 221 (July 24, 1972): 408.

Thomas, Lewis. "On Cloning a Human Being." *New England Journal of Medicine* 291 (12 December, 1974): 1296–1297.

———. "The Hazards of Science." *The New England Journal of Medicine* (10 February, 1977): 324–328.

Thorndike, Joseph J. "Genetics and the Future of Man." *Horizon* 15 (Autumn 1973): 56–63.

Tips, Robert L. "Impact of Genetic Counseling upon the Family Milieu." *Journal of the American Medical Association* 184 (April 20, 1963): 183–186.

Tooze, Dr. J. "Genetic Engineering in Europe." *New Scientist* (10 March 1977): 592–594.

Turner, John R. G. "How Does Treating Congenital Diseases Affect the Genetic Load?" *Eugenics Quarterly* 15 (September 1968): 191.

Valenti, Carlo. "Antenatal Detection of Hemoglobinopathies." *American Journal of Obstetrics and Gynecology* 115 (March 15, 1973): 851–853.

Valenti, Carlo, *et al.* "Prenatal Sex Determination." *American Journal of Obstetrics and Gynecology* 112 (April 1, 1972): 890–895.

Veatch, Robert M. "The Unexpected Chromosome . . . A Counselor's Dilemma." *Hastings Center Report* 2 (February 1972): 8–9.

———. "Ethical Issues in Genetics." In *Progress in Medical Genetics*, edited by Arthur G. Steinberg and Alexander G. Bearn. New York: Grune & Stratton, 1974, pp. 223–264.

Viana, Angela M., *et al.* "Searching for XYY Males through Electrocardiograms." *Journal of Medical Genetics* 9 (June 1972): 165–167.

Wade, Nicholas. "Genetic Manipulations: Temporary Embargo Proposed on Research." *Science* 185 (26 July, 1974): 332–334.

———. "Dicing with Nature: Three Narrow Escapes." *Science* (28 January, 1977): 378.

———. "Sociobiology: Troubled Birth for a New Discipline." *Science* (19 March 1976): 1151–1155.

———. "Gene-Splicing: Cambridge Citizens OK Research but Want More Safety." *Science* 95 (21 January, 1977): 268–269.

Wadlington, Walter. "Artificial Insemination: The Dangers of Poorly Kept Secret." *Northwestern University Law Review* 64 (1970): 777–807.

Waltz, Jon R., and Thigpen, Carol R. "Genetic Screening and Counseling: The Legal and Ethical Issues." *Northwestern University Law Review* 68 (1973): 696–768.

Watson, James D. "Moving toward Clonal Man: Is This What We Want?" *Atlantic Monthly* (May 1971): 50–53.

Westin, Alan F. "Medical Records: Should Patients Have Access?" *Hastings Center Report* 7 (December 1977): 23–29.

Westoff, Charles F., and Rindfuss, Ronald R. "Sex Preselection in the U.S.: Some Implications." *Science* 184 (10 May 1974): 633–636.

Westra, John. "Futurity and Permissibility of Genetic Engineering: The Legal Challenges." *Ohio Northern University Law Review* 1 (1974): 499–509.

Weyl, Nathaniel. "Population Control and the Anti-Eugenic Ideology." *Mankind Quarterly* 14 (October-December 1973): 63–82.

Wilson, E. O. "Human Decency Is Animal." *The New York Times Magazine* (12 October, 1975): 38–47.

——. "Academic Vigilantism and the Political Significance of Sociology." *Bio-Science* 26 (March 1976): 186–189.

World Health Organization. "Genetic Counseling: Third Report of the W.H.O. Experiment Committee on Human Genetics." W.H.O. Technical Report Series, No. 416, Geneva, 1969.

Wright, Susan. "Recombinant DNA Research." *Science* (14 January, 1977): 131–132.

Ziff, Edward. "Benefits and Hazards of Manipulating DNA." *New Scientist* 60 (October 25, 1973): 274–275.

Zuk, G. H. "The Religious Factor and the Role of Guilt in Parental Acceptance of the Retarded Child." *American Journal of Mental Deficiency* 64 (July 1959): 139–147.

PART V: DYING

INTRODUCTION

Possessing doctoral degrees in both medicine and law, Jonas Robitscher views the problems encountered in the phenomenon of death from a privileged point. In his essay, "The Problems in Prolongation of Life," Robitscher introduces the reader to almost every issue of importance in this area of concern—the problems involved in defining "death," the distinction between active and passive euthanasia, the difficulties involved in securing legal recognition of "living wills," the distinction between ordinary and extraordinary means of preserving life, etc. The central theme of Robitscher's paper, however, is the right to die. Robitscher contends, albeit with some reservations, that the right is now both legally accepted and socially approved. Thus, the main issue, as he sees it, is whether or not we can devise ways of implementing this right. Robitscher's suggestion in this regard is that we make every effort to find physicians who share our own philosophy of life; for it is only in this way that a person can be asured that his wishes concerning his own death will be observed. But medical personnel are in short supply; and Robitscher acknowledges that his suggestion may not be practicable. If such doctor–patient relationships are not feasible, then, Robitscher says, medicine has taken the wrong path in its search for greater technological proficiency.

One of the issues that Robischer touches upon is active and passive euthanasia, and the issue is further probed by James Rachels in his piece "Active and Passive Euthanasia." Rachel's point is that there is no real logical difference between killing and letting die, and that whatever would justify a policy of passive euthanasia would also justify a policy of active euthanasia. Hence, on Rachels's view, the medical practice of endorsing passive euthanasia and rejecting active euthanasia is inconsistent and inhumane. In "Choosing Not to Prolong Life," Robert Veatch, however, disagrees with Rachels and argues that there is enough of a distinction between killing and letting die to render the policy of active euthanasia immoral for any reason.

In "The Allocation of Exotic Medical Lifesaving Therapy," Nicholas Rescher contends that the problem of allocating scarce medical resources in life-and-death situations is not one that can be solved purely on the basis of medical considerations; and, with this in mind, he seeks to supply us with a set of rational guidelines for making these life-and-death decisions. The selection procedure defended by Rescher is a three-step affair. First, by utilizing general criteria of selection, which he calls general criteria of inclusion, a first phase selection group would be chosen from among all individuals available for treatment. This group would be substantially larger than the number of people capable of being treated by exotic lifesaving techniques; hence, members of this group would be further culled by application of a second set of selection criteria involving individual comparisons and the use of moral criteria. As conceived by Rescher, the resultant second phase selection group would be only slightly larger (e.g., by one-third or one-half) than the number of individuals able to be treated by exotic lifesaving therapy. From this group, then, final selection of patients would take place by random selection. Rescher claims that there is no selection procedure that can lay claim to the title "the best." Still, he defends his system arguing that it is simple enough to be understood by the common man, rationally defensible and, above all, fair. But Robert Almeder takes issue with Rescher's proposal and in his "The Role of Moral Considerations in the Allocation of Exotic Medical Life-saving Therapy" he argues that (a) all things considered, the best conceivable selection system is the one that employs no moral criteria at all, and (b) the ideal selection procedure would consist in the use of a fair lottery in which are placed the names of all and only those patients for whom the therapy would more likely than not succeed.

The next essay in this section is concerned with the definition of "death." Professors Capron and Kass argue that the definition of death is not purely medical in nature and that the public's interest would be best served if the standards for determining human death were set by legislative action. Given this belief, the authors take the following steps: First, they outline in some detail the principles they feel should govern the formulation of any acceptable statutory definition of death. Second, they evaluate the earlier enacted Kansas Death Statute in the light of these principles and find it wanting. And third, they offer an alternative to the Kansas Statute, expressing hope that their proposal will serve as a catalyst for future public debate.

Finally fear of death itself generally has the moral effect of our isolating the dying person and thereby increasing the anxiety and discomfort of the death experience. Accordingly, after viewing M. A. Slote's "Existentialism and the Fear of Dying," we close with excerpts from C. J. Ducasse's *The Belief in a Life after Death*, and also from Raymond Moody's *Life after Life*. Both selections present evidence favoring belief in life after death; and to the extent that such evidence will be found supportive of the thesis of disembodied existence, to that extent it would appear that an attitude of fear toward death should be replaced by an attitude of hope and perhaps even joy.

THE PROBLEMS IN PROLONGATION OF LIFE

JONAS ROBITSCHER

The issue of the right to die was the focus of controversy a few years ago. Could someone who was ill and tired of the struggle elect not to fight for life anymore? Could we allow our fellow travelers in life to give up or were we forced to force them to continue a life that might be pain-ridden and without hope?

This was a new problem on the scene, a problem caused by such advances in medical care as blood transfusions, intravenous feeding, antibiotics, respirators, pacemakers, and other drugs, procedures, and techniques that enabled us to maintain life in the critically ill, the terminally ill, and even in those who met what had been the criteria for the declaration of death—the cessation of heartbeat and respiratory activity.

Before these new advances an occasional moribund or comatose patient had been maintained for years and even for decades, but this was a rarity. Doctors were not concerned about keeping people alive too long, and there had not been a demand for the clarification of criteria for the decision to end life support.

When we discovered that we had a problem on our hands—that life, on one hand, could sometimes be maintained embarrassingly long as one example, that doctors did not know about their liability for harvesting organs from patients who did not meet the traditional criteria for "dead people" as another—we began to work with this problem and we looked to court decisions as one way of determining a doctor's responsibility.

Some of the first court decisions on this subject only served to confuse us. The leading cases all dealt with Jehovah's Witnesses who refused blood transfusions, sometimes to their own detriment, sometimes additionally to the detriment of an unborn child. The legal argument might have been in these cases that everyone who is mature and competent has traditionally had a right to decide what medical treatment he wants and what medical treatment he does not want, and the right to die then could have been established with less confusion. Instead, these cases were argued on a narrower ground, that freedom of religion, guaranteed by the First Amendment to the Constitution, required that we let

---

This paper was originally presented at a Colloquium on Bioethics entitled "Man in Our Image" held at Princeton University, March 1, 1975.

these people refuse treatment. The fact that some people gained the right to die by virtue of their religious convictions left us with the implication that those who did not have the same religious conviction might not have the right to die, and so the law in this area was off on the wrong foot.

Doctors who perhaps needlessly feared criminal indictments if they let patients die a natural death without attempting to extend their lives maintained patients for what we would now see as unconscionably long periods of time; the relatives who had to make the decision which the doctors would follow did not feel society's support for a decision to terminate life maintenance. So further resort to the courts was needed to let us know what we probably should have known all along—that we did indeed have a right to die. This right is not as clearly established as some other of our legal rights. Not all doctors interpret this right as freely as others do, the word has not gotten around to all people involved with these decisions, and some families still fear legal liability or excessive guilt if they order the discontinuance of treatment. We have the great problem of protecting patients who because of their illness are no longer competent to make informed decisions. We have the further problem of close decisions in difficult cases. (A doctor who can clearly recommend that intravenous feeding be discontinued might find it more difficult to order oral feeding to be terminated.) Nevertheless, with a few exceptions and some qualms, we can say that the right to die is both legally accepted and socially approved.*

The cases which have recently given us some assurance that we do indeed have a right to die are not very plentiful, and they are not from courts sufficiently high so that they can be entirely relied on for legal precedent. We do not have anything comparable to *Roe vs. Wade* or *Doe vs. Bolton,* the Supreme Court's famous abortion decisions in 1973, to serve as expressions of judicial authority. But we have had enough cases from courts of inferior jurisdiction, enough physicians have publicly described their withdrawal of life support and

---

*This article was written before the Karen Ann Quinlan case in which a New Jersey judge declared that the decision to prolong the life of an incompetent (comatose) patient in spite of her persistent and apparently irreversible vegetative state was a "medical decision" in which the wishes of next-of-kin had no weight. The judge in this case relied on medical testimony that life prolongation was normal procedure for a patient in this condition, but public discussion of this case since the decision indicates most doctors would not prolong the life of this patient indefinitely; the judge was therefore placing his credence in medical testimony which represented a minority medical view and he was making the doctor responsible for the decision (although traditionally the patient or if the patient is incompetent someone close to him representing his best interest should make the decision after receiving the doctor's advice on medically acceptable alternatives). *In the Matter of Karen Quinlan,* Docket No. C-201-75, Superior Court of New Jersey, Chancery Division, Morris County, November 10, 1975. If other jurisdictions adopt a similar view, so-called Death With Dignity statutes holding the doctor free from harm for terminating prolongation procedures under specified conditions will be pushed in state legislatures.

have not been prosecuted or even condemned for this so that we can be satisfied that the right to die has a fairly firm foundation.

Now that we are reasonably satisfied of this, a whole other series of questions raises itself—who shall exercise this right? How do we satisfy ourselves of the competency of the person who is asserting this right? If the decision maker in this process is not the dying patient but someone who will substitute a judgment for the patient's judgment, how do we know that the substituted judgment approximates the judgment that the patient would have made if he were able to make his own decision?

We ask ourselves these questions, we get involved in these concerns, because we are worried not only about the duration of life but the circumstances of its ending. We wish for all patients what we wish for ourselves—a peaceful death when all possible has been done to restore health and function but before the maintenance of life has become an indignity at the least and possibly a torture. How can we attain this wished-for kind of death in a society where on the one hand an overzealous physician may want to put us out of our misery too soon to make our bed available for a more promising patient, or on the other hand an overzealous physician may want to continue our life beyond a point where that life should be continued in order to satisfy himself personally that he is stronger than death? I have just used the concept of a point beyond which life should or should not be continued, and that would be stricken down by any court as unconstitutionally vague. Still, if we have a right to die that means we can determine to some extent the timing and conditions of our death, and that in turn means that we can strive for a certain *quality of death,* a death with dignity, a death that saves us from a meaningless prolongation of a painful existence or the maintenance of some body processes in the absence of consciousness and the hope of regaining consciousness.

The law, which embodies and creates popular opinion, has always told us that although we do not have to submit to medical treatment we do not want—even though it may save our lives—we do not have a right to take our own lives in a more active way. And the law has often leaned over in the direction of the assumption of mental incompetence when it has seen people trying actively to end their lives or passively allowing their lives to be ended. The law has traditionally been opposed to suicide, although some commentators say that American law, in contrast to English law, is ambivalent on the criminality of suicide. Some states still follow the English Common Law, now repealed in England, that suicide is a crime and—what is more important to the individual bent on self-destruction—that attempted suicide is also a crime. The old English law had the property of the suicide reverting to the Crown, but American law has not been that punitive. Nevertheless, attempted suicide is a crime or a misdemeanor in many jurisdictions and although we do not actually prosecute the attempter we use the police power of the state to prevent the suicide and to take custody of the person. In states where suicide is not an offense, we act on the assumption that the attempter is insane and send him to a psychiatric hospital for evaluation. We are determined not to allow people to kill themselves if they do this in a violent way or if we are not sure they are competent to make decisions in their own best interests.

"So-called 'rational' suicide is a rarity," says Dr. George Murphy, Professor of Psychiatry at Washington University. "The descriptive facts are that most persons who commit suicide are suffering from clinically recognizable psychiatric illnesses often carrying an excellent prognosis; that the majority have sought help from physicians for their symptoms; and that few have received the indicated treatment."[1] He excepts from this description the "few persons who commit suicide" who are suffering from a terminal illness, and he notes that some people—who he says speak on a philosophical rather than a clinical basis—condemn any effort to interfere with an individual's behavior against his wishes. He refers, of course, to Dr. Thomas Szasz and his co-believers in freedom of action circumscribed only by criminal proscriptions, not by mental health control of behavior.

Dr. Szasz represents the minority view and Dr. Murphy the majority; we tend to see—correctly or incorrectly—the would-be suicide as having mental illness and we treat him accordingly.

But other forms of self-destruction less sudden and less capable of being seen as the result of mental derangement are not interfered with in our society.

The law allows anyone who is not seen as incompetent to take extraordinary risks with his life—to jump or attempt to jump the Snake River Canyon, to compete in stock car races, to continue drinking after a diagnosis of cirrhosis of the liver, to smoke after a diagnosis of emphysema—and although such a course of action may be as truly suicidally motivated as an overdose or a self-inflicted gunshot wound, society elects not to interfere.

In previous generations, but not so very long ago, medicine differed from today's practice in important respects. First, doctors did as much harm as they did good, and well educated people—Thomas Jefferson among them—learned as much about medicine as they could to be free of the doctor's strange prescriptions and idiosyncratic kind of care. Avoiding medical treatment was not seen as necessarily pathological. Second, medical treatments caused extreme pain, and the choice of an individual to avoid medical help and to bear his illness or succumb to it without seeking aid was easily understandable. Third, medicine was much more pecuniarily oriented than it is today; there were no third-party payers, prepaid health plans, no Medicare and Medicaid, so a patient's decision not to seek the services of a doctor were seen as not different from a refusal to

---

[1] Murphy, G.: Suicide and the right to die, editorial, *Am. J. Psychiat. 130*:4, April 1973, 472–473.

enter into any other kind of contract which required him to pay. Fourth, there was a doctrine of individual liberty and more recently—very recently—a doctrine of privacy, an area where the state should not enter. The idea that a patient has a right not to be treated has an honorable history; indeed even today a doctor who treats a patient without that patient's consent—short of an emergency situation and a patient unable to give consent to an important procedure—is guilty of a technical battery even where no actual damage has been done to the patient and there is no accusation of negligence. The well-established doctrine of informed consent as a prerequisite for treatment has been additionally emphasized since 1960 when courts began to insist on a broader disclosure to the patient and more patient participation in the decision-making process. The doctor is no longer the captain of a ship with authority over the mutinous crew member. Patients can participate in treatment decisions.

Certainly many people have elected not to take prescribed medical treatment. Christian Scientists and many others who avoided doctors functioned without medical care and exercised their right to refuse treatment without court intervention. They died, or lived, without any issue that brought their refusal to go along with doctors' recommendation into court.

Jehovah's Witnesses were another case. They wanted medical treatment, they did not avoid doctors and hospitals, but they did not want blood transfusions to be a part of that treatment. As hospital patients they represented an ambivalence that was hard to deal with—they wanted surgery but did not give consent to the transfusions without which the surgery might not be safe. Physicians were unwilling to proceed and risk allegations of negligence or malpractice; they sought court rulings on whether the patient had the right to refuse treatment. The issue could have been easily resolved if the patient had given up all claim to treatment—if he had just picked himself up or been picked up and had gone home—but courts did not seem to consider that option. Then Judge and now Chief Justice Warren Burger was one of the few judges who saw to the heart of this issue; in a famous dissent in a case in which a blood transfusion was ordered over the objection of the patient, he said that the right to be let alone included the right to refuse medical treatment even at great risk.

Although the Jehovah's Witnesses cases presented the courts with a strong ground for allowing the refusal of treatment, religious convictions guarded by the First Amendment, the courts refused to allow an absolute right to die. If a mother was pregnant—these cases arose before the abortion decision—the life of the fetus was considered so important and so involved with the mother's life that transfusions were ordered for the mother to save the life of the fetus. Similarly, if a mother or father had minor children, courts said they had the right to die but not to orphan small children. The protection of the fetus might not be seen as valid by today's courts since the abortion decision has given the mother the right to terminate the life of the fetus. Two other bases were found to limit the right to die, and both of these would still stand in any new case. If the patient was a minor it could not be presumed that his wish to die represented an informed opinion, and he would be forcibly transfused or treated so that when he reached his majority he would be in a position to make such life-and-death decisions on his own. Similarly, if a patient was unconscious or otherwise incompetent and the next-of-kin declined to consent for life-saving procedures, the court would not assume that if the patient were conscious and rational he would actually desire to die—even though he may have had a history of dedication to a religious sect that prohibits treatment—and the court would want to err on the side of life rather than to allow death.

It was in such a case that a New Jersey court said a few years ago, I think incorrectly, that, "There is no Constitutional Right to Die." A better expression of the law is to regard the Jehovah's Witnesses cases as clearly setting forth the right to die but somewhat limiting its application and basing it on the narrow ground of religious belief.

When life-saving techniques led doctors to the point where they were concerned with their abilities to keep patients alive for too long, they were not sure whether all their patients, or just their religious patients, had the right to refuse medical treatment. The problem was compounded by laws in some states—Florida is an example—which made doctors fear that if they did not force treatment on a patient and that patient died, they would be an accessory to that death.

The problem had been developing for at least fifty years, and particularly since 1926. That was the year that the intravenous drip technique of feeding was introduced for the maintenance of surgical patients. The new method also made it possible to maintain comatose medical patients more easily and more successfully than the earlier method of tube feeding. This new technique was a natural development from the improved methods of blood transfusion that were used in World War I which had application to surgical patients particularly. Eventually knowledge of electrolytes and the use of plasma during World War II would extend the applicability of intravenous transfusion and nourishment.

The World War II period also saw the introduction of sulfa drugs, and shortly afterwards, antibiotics. Doctors now had a combination of tools to treat debilitated patients and comatose and semicomatose patients; they could supply their nutritional needs and keep them from dying from the infections that had carried off so many seriously ill patients. Pneumonia had been called "the old man's friend" by generations of medical students and doctors; it ushered out those patients with progressive malignancies, with conditions associated with advanced age, and in comas. Now the old man's friend could be barred from the premises.

We have had many more methods of maintaining life—some of them the results of advances in electronic engineering. We have the cardiac pacemaker, electrical cardiac monitoring devices to alter out-of-synchronization heart rhythms. New knowledge of respiratory physiology and advances in oxygen therapy techniques allow patients to be supported through critical periods. Dialysis became available to compensate for kidney failure. Surgery, developing the radical new method of organ transplants, the kidney transplant, if not the heart transplant, allowed doctors to extend the lives of many patients. More recently the membrane lung, outside of the body, can increase the oxygenation of the blood and decrease the carbon dioxide level while lung tissue heals.

Before the introduction of these so-called extraordinary medical measures, doctors could relieve pain and they had some helpful remedies; they were particularly successful in intervening in life-threatening surgical conditions. Still, knowledge of medicine had not given the doctor much power to keep death at bay, and doctors were accustomed to fighting death hard but not fighting death long.

With new methods at their disposal, fending off death became a medical preoccupation. In the earlier period an occasional patient had been kept alive by diligent nursing and tube feeding. Comas of lengthy duration—one record coma of more than thirty years—had been maintained, the result of extremely diligent nursing care. Now methods were available—called "extraordinary" to distinguish them from traditional medical and nursing methods and which in many cases required the cooperation of many specialties and the facilities of large medical centers—by which doctors interested in setting a new record—for the maintenance of a patient in a state of coma longer than any previous case—could aim for inclusion in the *Guinness Book of World Records* with the unwitting assistance of the comatose patients. Some doctors seemed determined to try for this record. Dr. Robert Williams of the Department of Medicine, University of Washington, says that so-called passive euthanasia—the withdrawal of life support—is practiced with less frequency and with much greater delay than is desired by patients, their families, and others, and that although in the last eight years he has witnessed a rapid increase in the number of people with understanding and appreciation of passive euthanasia, "there remains a very strong opposition in the minds of some, especially among those who claim that such approaches constitute usurpation of the role of God." (Letter, *Commentary*, May 1974).

Many physicians, particularly those in modern hospitals with all the new medical hardware available—following the maxim that anything that is invented will find a use—ignored the direction of Arthur Hugh Clough, the Victorian poet, who told doctors more than a century ago:

> Thou shalt not kill; but need not strive
> Officiously to keep alive.

The Jehovah's Witnesses cases were efforts to come to a better legal delineation of the conditions which allowed and did not allow either an intelligent patient or someone acting in the interest of an incompetent patient to refuse potentially life-saving procedures. Although they told us that patients could make this decision for themselves if they were competent, the fact that this right was based on a religious ground raised the question of its application generally. These cases did not give us clear guidelines for incompetent patients who were terminally or irretrievably ill; they dealt with emergency situations where a blood transfusion might make the difference between life and death. They did not tell us whether a substituted consent could be the authority for the discontinuance of treatment in comatose or terminally ill patients. In contrast to the Jehovah's Witnesses cases where doctors urged treatment, some doctors, those not interested in the Guinness book, found themselves on the patient's side of the decision to discontinue treatment but not knowing if this placed them in legal peril. The Jehovah's Witnesses cases were misleading; they contained some hazy implication that if the rationale for allowing Jehovah's Witnesses to refuse treatment was their religious belief, those who did not have any such religious belief perhaps should be subject to coerced treatment. In the discussion that raged about whether there was a right to die, it was not pointed out that the Jehovah's Witnesses cases involved good prognosis patients. Most of the right to die situations, however, concern the very elderly, the fatally ill, the terminally ill.

Legal peril is not the only kind of peril; there is moral peril, too. But the traditional medical codes of ethics and the Nuremberg Code and the Helsinki Convention did not give clear guidance. The Hippocratic Oath states: "The regimen I adopt shall be for the benefit of my patients according to my ability and judgment, and not for their hurt or for any wrong. I will give no deadly drug to any, though it be asked of me, nor will I counsel such. . . ." It very clearly prohibits active euthanasia, but it does not directly deal with the termination of life-maintaining techniques, sometimes called passive euthanasia. The Declaration of Geneva, adopted by the General Assembly of the World Medical Association in 1948, emphasizes respect for life but goes no further: "I will practice my profession with conscience and dignity. The health of my patient will be my first consideration." and: "I will maintain the utmost respect for human life, from the time of conception; even under threat, I will not use my medical knowledge contrary to the laws of humanity."

The "Principles of Medical Ethics" of the American Medical Association which dates back to 1957 gives us even less of a guideline: "Ethical principles are basic and fundamental. Men of good conscience inherently know what is right or wrong, and what is to be done or to be avoided." A brief history of medical ethics accompanying the Principles does refer favorably to the Hippocratic Oath as "a living" and "workable" statement.

In the midst of uncertainty, doctors looked to the courts to confirm that they did not have to "strive officiously to keep alive." A Miami judge ruled that a seventy-two-year-old woman suffering from hemolytic anemia had the right to live or die with dignity and could refuse blood transfusions or surgery that would cause pain. The transfusions were only palliative and not remedial. The patient died the day after the judge's decision. Said the judge: "A person has the right not to suffer pain. A person has the right to live or die in dignity."

In Milwaukee a seventy-seven-year-old woman was allowed, after a bedside hearing in which the judge satisfied himself that she understood the effects of her decision, to refuse to consent to amputation of a leg that was gangrenous from a complication of diabetes. The hospital had insisted that she go through with the treatment. This judge said, "I believe we should leave [the patient] depart in God's own peace."

When the patient was incompetent and a relative believed it was best for him to die, courts were less supporting. A New York State Supreme Court Justice named the director of New York Hospital-Cornell Medical Center as the official guardian with authority to consent to the implantation of a new pacemaker battery for a seventy-nine-year-old patient after his wife had repeatedly refused to authorize the procedure. The patient was considered incompetent, unaware of his condition, incapable of making the decision. The wife had objected to the operation on the ground that he was "turning into a vegetable"; the court was influenced by testimony that the old gentleman, although deteriorated, was not in pain. The wife's reaction is given in a newspaper interview: "What has he got to live for: Nothing. He knows nothing, he has no memory whatsoever, he is turning into a vegetable. Isn't death better?"

When the courts felt that patients were incompetent, they were likely to presume that if they were competent they would want medical treatment. Two recent New Jersey cases ordered treatment—in one instance a hysterectomy, in the other a leg amputation. On the other hand, one recent Massachusetts case allowed a sixty-year-old state mental hospital patient diagnosed as schizophrenic to refuse a breast biopsy. While a patient in the hospital during a period when she was lucid, rational, and understood the possible consequences of her decision, she refused treatment. She continued to refuse treatment, but as time progressed this refusal was more and more based on delusional grounds. She said she feared the surgery because her aunt had died after similar surgery, which was not factual; she said that the surgery would interfere with her genital system and would prohibit a movie career. The court acknowledged this "right to die," which was presented to the court as part of the right of privacy, first recognized by the Supreme Court within recent years in a Connecticut case dealing with contraception and rapidly assuming prominence when it became the rationale for the Court's abortion stand in which the state was not allowed to impinge on an individual's private behavior. It further based the right to die upon the "right of a mature competent adult to refuse to accept medical recommendations that may prolong one's life and which, to a third person at least, appear to be in his best interests." It conceded that sometimes public policy requires treatment—

contagious illness would be an obvious example—and that the presence of minor children might lead to a different result, but it allowed the decision of this incompetent lady to prevail because it had reiterated her stand when competent.[2]

These decisions all come from courts of inferior jurisdiction; and decisions can be cited which go contrary to the Right to Die. Nevertheless, we can assume that we have a great deal of potential authority in the right to determine the length of our lives. If a right to die case ever got to the Supreme Court, we could cite Justice Burger's dissenting decision in a 1964 Jehovah's Witnesses case in which a blood tranfusion was ordered. The majority said a life hung in the balance and there was no time to research the patient's attitudes and to reflect on a judicial decision. Judge Skelly Wright said, "To refuse to act, only to find later that the law required action, was a risk I was unwilling to accept." But Burger's dissent quoted Justice Brandeis on the "right to be let alone—the most comprehensive of rights and the right most valued by civilized man," and it commented: "Nothing in this utterance suggests that Justice Brandeis thought an individual possessed these rights only as to *sensible* beliefs, *valid* thoughts, *reasonable* emotions, or *well-founded* sensations. I suggest that he intended to include a great many . . . ideas which do not conform, such as refusing medical treatment even at great risk." Since 1964 a long string of civil rights decisions in other areas would buttress Burger's minority view.[3]

The development of the kidney transplant operation and the fact that fresh kidneys gave a greater chance of a successful outcome have led to techniques of life support in patients who would otherwise have been allowed to die because they were no longer capable of the integrated functioning of heart, lungs, and brains and this condition was deemed irreversible. We thus have that medical anomaly, a so-called heart-beating cadaver, although the beating heart at one time would have militated against any determination of death. While theoretically not necessary in kidney transplants, a heart-beating cadaver so greatly enhances the likelihood of a successful transplant that, in fact, many programs use them exclusively.[4] Heart-beating cadavers are mandatory for transplantation of the heart and liver. The majority of medically acceptable cadaver donors are young patients who have sustained a head injury and are in an irreversible coma.

Because the wishes of the organ donor were not binding—they were subordinated to the wishes of the next of kin—it became necessary for statutes to

[2] Yetter, Alleged Incompetent, 41 Northamp. 67, 24 Fiduc. Rep. 1; see "Compulsory Medical Treatment and the Free Exercise of Religion," 42 Indiana L.J. 386.

[3] Application of President of Georgetown College, 331 F.2d 1010 (1964), 1016, cert. den. 377 U.S. 978 (1964).

[4] Lynn Banowsky, William Braun, and Magnus Magnusson, The medical and legal determination of death—its effect on cadaveric organ procurement, *The Journal of Legal Medicine,* November/December 1974, 44–48.

enable the potential donor to make the decision while he was competent to donate all or part of his body and have this wish be legally binding and supersede the wishes of the next of kin. The Uniform Anatomical Gift Act or a modified version of it is now law in all 50 states.

Defining when coma is irreversible and setting the time for the organ to be removed and for ordering the respirator to be turned off created legal, ethical, and moral complexities which began to be resolved when the Harvard School of Medicine Ad Hoc Committee's recommendations were made the basis of similar regulations in other medical centers. Although there has been some confusion in the public mind, these standards are to be applied not to the patient who we think deserves "death with dignity," the dying patient whose misery we do not want extended, but to patients who are in irreversible coma, who have had so much brain damage that we feel sure they will never return to consciousness. Because the patient's heart is beating he does not meet the traditional criteria of death, but since there is no discernible activity of the brain he does meet the criteria of brain death and it is assumed that brain death represents the death of the patient. If the patient is totally unaware of external stimuli, even intensely painful stimuli, there is no movement or breathing, over a period of at least one hour, and no elicitable reflexes, neurologists are willing to make a preliminary declaration of brain death. The tests must be repeated at a 24-hour interval before brain death can be finally declared. A flat electroencephalogram, particularly when repeated at an interval of 6, 12, or 24 hours—depending on the policy of the particular medical center—has great confirmatory value. Hypothermia and central nervous system depression caused by such agents as barbiturates must be ruled out before the criteria can be applied.

We have read in the papers of supposed cadavers who twitched or coughed at the point where their organ was about to be harvested—the word "harvested" has both a less personal and a more technicological feel about it than "cut out" or "excised"—and who were then saved from the knife. My neurosurgical friends tell me that in all these cases there had been a breach in the observation of strict criteria and that these patients did not thereafter recover but within the next few days went on to meet the brain death criteria.

There have been a few very interesting legal cases dealing with such patients—a California court held that the death of an auto victim was caused by the stopping of the respirator rather than by the injury which had caused brain death, but a later case in California and a Georgia case indicate that courts are willing to accept medical assurance that brain death is as useful a standard as heart and respiration death. The Georgia case, in which the doctors were held not to be the cause of the death of the patient who was already brain dead when they turned off the respirator, is now on appeal.

One of the problems with the brain death concept has been a misunderstanding on the part of courts, lawyers, journalists, and the general public; they have sometimes felt that brain death was a better standard of death than the conventional heart and respiration standard. Doctors have feared that if brain death is dignified by its use in a statute, such as the 1970 Kansas law which for the first time gave statutory recognition to brain death and subsequent laws passed in Maryland and Virginia, all patients might have to be observed over a period of time, possibly electroencephelogram determinations might have to be made on all patients, before death could be declared. Many doctors and medicine—law experts have advocated that brain death not be mentioned in statutes. The House of Delegates of the American Medical Association voted in 1972 to endorse the recommendation of its Judicial Council that at present a statutory definition of death is neither desirable nor necessary, that death be determined by the clinical judgment of the doctor using available and currently acceptable criteria. The use of generally accepted medical criteria would be relied on to protect the doctor declaring death on this basis. There would not then be the rigidity that is associated with statutory definitions. Doctors have recently also emphasized that EEG tracings are useful for confirmation, but they are not an integral part of the declaration of death determination and should not be considered to be mandated by statute or custom.

A new law in Georgia gets around some of the legal problems of statutory definitions; it states that use of the brain death standard does not supersede any previously accepted methods of determination: "The criteria for determining death authorized [in this statute] shall be cumulative to and shall not prohibit the use of other medically recognized criteria for determining death."

The subjects selected for prolongation of life because their organs are sought represent a much easier problem for us than the subjects who are unconscious or semiconscious who do not meet the criteria for brain death but who are still seen as incapable of recovering, and also the terminally ill patient. If a doctor sees the possibility of a meaningful recovery for this patient he is obligated to use all his skills to preserve the life of the patient. If the patient could see that he had no future he could elect not to have the doctor use further efforts. But "vegetative" patients are not in a position to make their intentions known, the doctors then have no firm guidelines. They turn to next-of-kin and ask them to decide, and although this is legally correct we are not always sure that the wishes of the next-of-kin coincide with those that the patient would express if he could.

This is the situation where we are concerned with quality of life, with which Joseph Fletcher has dealt; Fletcher wishes us to define "humanhood" and to say that when criteria of humanhood can not be found (such a minimal intelligence, self-awareness, self-control, and mentation) the patient is not human. The quality of the patient's life thus becomes the basis for stating whether life should be maintained.

Fletcher's ideas are a rationale for active euthanasia, the use of the physician to promote death, but up to this time the law has only allowed passive euthanasia, the withholding of medical helps, the discontinuance of life maintenance procedures. Sometimes the definition of passive euthanasia is stretched to cover situations where not only no medical help is given a patient but he is denied life support, intravenous nutrition, or even oral feeding. Babies in the neonatal period who have multiple defects are allowed to die over a period of time through starvation, and although this smacks more of active than of passive euthanasia it has not been legally challenged. Recently, however, when Dr. Kenneth Edelin used suffocation as part of an abortion or post-abortion technique—it has been argued that the suffocation occurred after the birth of the baby and therefore was not a part of the abortion—he was successfully prosecuted because some people at least felt he had gone past the passive and into the active area. But there are no important legal challenges to the right of the *adult and competent* patient to dictate his own treatment.

It is agreed then that the law gives a great deal of authority to discontinue life maintenance. The American Hospital Association, the American Medical Association, and some state medical societies have approved the concept that patients can withhold consent for life-saving procedures.[5]

How can that patient authority be exercised? As long as we are competent, there is no problem. Doctors should respect our wishes; if they do not we are free to dismiss them as our doctors. When we are no longer competent, the decision-making is left to next-of-kin. They usually hope to have the doctor make the decision, but although he may tell them what he thinks they should decide, they have the ultimate authority. Some doctors feel it is too guilt-provoking for families to have to decide to terminate life maintenance, but the law says it is the responsibility of patient or next-of-kin, not of the physician. The physician's input is his expression of opinion which is usually determinative. Next-of-kin may and often do have motives for wishing a death hastened, and if a doctor feels that this is against the best interests of the patient he can move to have a disinterested guardian appointed. This problem comes up with the newborn and infants. Recently in Maine parents refused to give consent to possibly life-saving surgery on a baby born with a malformation of his entire left side. The hospital physicians nevertheless obtained a court order and operated. The baby died. The President of the Maine Medical Association said the ruling could have "tremendous and far-reaching implications for any large hospital capable of sustaining life."[6] Some recent reports involve mentally deficient newborns who also have life-threatening congenital anomalies. Without the deficiency, parents invariably consent to the surgery. Should the presence of mental deficiency be a sufficient pretext for parents to refuse consent? When a baby starves to death over several weeks because the neonatal nursery orders are

[5] *Atlanta Journal and Constitution,* January 14, 1973, 3-B.
[6] *American Medical News,* March 11, 1974, 19.

that life support should not be maintained, the distinction between active and passive euthanasia becomes thin, and even those who oppose the assumption by the doctor of a new medical responsibility, the active hastening of death, might want to see a quick termination to this particular life.

We feel much better when we retain control over the manner of our death. This explains the popularity of the Living Will, prepared and distributed by the Euthanasia Educational Fund. But the document does not have legal effect. A will can be changed before the death of the testator; it only becomes final when the testator is dead. The Living Will concerns a living person; it represents a wish of the maker and not necessarily the present wish; it does not have the solemnity of a contract, deed, or testament. One suggestion recently made is that this be put in contract form, with a consideration on the part of both parties, but this would require that it no longer be a generally addressed "To whom it may concern" directive.[7] Another problem is that there is no guarantee that a Living Will's contents will be known to the hospital or doctor providing care. Who shall hold it? Who has the responsibility for making its contents known? The Living Will does have value in giving next-of-kin and physicians some concept of the attitude of the person toward life prolongation. One version reads in part:

> If the time comes when I can no longer take part in decisions for my own future, let this statement stand as the testament of my wishes. If there is no reasonable expectation of my recovery from physical or mental disability, I request to die and not be kept alive by artificial means or heroic measures. Death is as much a reality as birth, growth, maturity and old age—it is the one certainty. I do not fear death as much as I fear the indignity of deterioration, dependence and hopeless pain. I ask that drugs be mercifully administered to me for terminal suffering even if they hasten the moment of death.

I once suggested in an article that the only good way to ensure that our wishes be carried out, that we have the kind of final course that we would most want, is to match our hopes with the philosophical framework of our treating physicians.[8] If we seek out and trust ourselves to a doctor who shares our philosophy of life—whether it is to prolong life to the utmost or to hasten its end by liberal use of pain-killers—then the problem is resolved. An old lady in California sent me a rebuke; the tone implied, "Foolish boy." She said we are lucky to find any doctors at all, let alone a doctor we can get to know well enough to find out what his approach to philosophical questions may be.

Is the lady right? Should we be satisfied to have our dying attended by doctors who do not know our wishes? We have little alternative, but perhaps this is the greatest condemnation of modern medicine we can utter—the belief that medicine has become so depersonalized and the doctor–patient relationship so

---

[7] Smythe, J.: Antidysthanasia contracts: A proposal for legalizing death with dignity, 5 Pacific L.J., 738–763, 1974.

[8] Robitscher, J.: The right to die, *Hastings Center Report, 2*(4):11–14, September, 1972.

superficial that in a time of greatest need we are dependent on strangers and technicians. Now that the courts have given us some assurance that there is indeed a right to die, can we devise ways to implementing this right by making medical practice once again an integral part of a small society, not of a large impersonal society? Perhaps we cannot; my friend in California has insisted that I provide common-sense, not pie-in-the-sky, approaches to the problem of life prolongation. One approach, one that I do not recommend, is described in a recent issue of *Time* magazine—we have a new paramedical professional, the Death Companion who sits with "lonely, dying clients." After an eight-session course on the problems of bringing comfort to a dying stranger, the companions are available to sit for $7.50 an hour. The service is strictly commercial; its president has said, "We believe in free enterprise."[9]

We should be able to do better than that. If we cannot make medicine more personal and bring to doctors and to patients the satisfaction of relating to other humans at time of need, we can at least see this issue as demonstrating the wrong path that medicine has taken in its search for greater technological proficiency.

The differentiation of ordinary and extraordinary medical means has caused ethical and moral problems. At one time it had seemed to be a nice solution to the doctor's dilemma to say that he was obliged to provide the patient with all ordinary means of help—nutrition and routine nursing care—but that he was not obliged to use those extraordinary helps that have resulted from the medical advances that have been described. Monsignor Austin Vaughn has said, "It is permissible to stop the use of extraordinary means of prolonging life. But it is not permissible to intervene and bring about the death of an individual." The Lord Bishop of Exeter has said, "It is in general the Christian view that while there is a moral obligation to maintain life by all ordinary means, there is no obligation to use extraordinary means. Ordinary means are such actions as do not cause grave hardship to the patient and which offer a reasonable hope of success. Extraordinary means are means which involve a great expense, inconvenience, or hardship and which at the same time offer no reasonable expectation either of success or benefit." But one generation's extraordinary means is another's ordinary means, and in practice we define these in relativistic terms. It is ordinary to use dialysis for young people; it is extraordinary for old people. A Pennsylvania man had been in a coma for six years when in 1972 the doctor persuaded his father that the coma was irreversible and that an extraordinary means, of intravenous feeding, should be discontinued. The father gave his authorization, but he could not sleep that night, and the next morning asked that the feeding be resumed. What had been extraordinary had become ordinary.

The Lord Bishop of Exeter includes cost in his differentiating criteria of ordinary and extraordinary. Is cost a valid factor? Father Richard McCormick in

[9] *Time,* February 17, 1975, 68.

an article in the *Journal of the American Medical Association* has suggested that it is not the complexity of the technological advance or its cost that determines its extraordinary quality; he stresses the factor of hardship to the patient. Morally speaking, he says, ordinary means are those whose use does not entail grave hardship to the patient.[10] Dr. Irvine Page has said that if we wanted to keep alive all patients who could be kept alive, we could someday consume the entire national product in this pursuit. He opposes extraordinary means to prolong life unless some positive gain, such as the possibility of a resumption of a level of functional usefulness and some improvement of health, is a possibility.

No precise differentiation of ordinary and extraordinary is possible; the differentiation is to a large extent the responsibility of the individual doctor concerned with the individual patient.

Our decision not to prolong life is usually called passive euthanasia. Euthanasia connotes "mercy killing" to some, but it merely means a "good death." But possibly the use of the term euthanasia for the passive practice helps to break down the opposition to active euthanasia, so those who favor the passive and oppose the active sometimes suggest that we reserve the term euthanasia for induced death and use another term—such as "death with dignity"—for termination of prolongation procedures, for the concept of a good kind of death, a death with quality. Unless we make this distinction, they say, the opinion polls will continue to show increasing acceptance of active euthanasia on the part of both the general public and the physicians.

In 1950 only 36% of Americans said they approved of mercy killing for people with incurable diseases, according to the Gallup Poll. In 1973 this had risen to a majority, 53%, and of those thirty and under, 67% favored mercy killing.[11] One state legislature, Oregon, has had a bill proposed to allow mercy killing; it was later withdrawn. Six states have had passive euthanasia bills proposed to ensure that doctors would not incur any liability through their omitted acts. Most physicians do not favor such bills; they feel that passive euthanasia is now practiced and allowed and any new legal protection might cause notice and problems; in two states the measure have been voted down, and in four others they are bottled up in committees.[12]

Active euthanasia has many adherents in Scandinavia and England and it has won much legislative support there, although not majority support. Walter Alvarez, a physician-author identified with the Mayo Clinic, favors active euthanasia and regrets that in his medical career he was too inhibited and too conscious of the law and of medical tradition to put an end to the pain of some

---

[10] McCormick, R.: To save or let die: The dilemma of modern medicine, *JAMA 229:* 172–176, 1974.

[11] *New York Times,* August 2, 1973, p. 33.

[12] Euthanasia: No present future, *Medical World News,* April 23, 1973, 6.

patients.[13] Lawrence LeShan, a psychologist with the Ayer Foundation who has worked with dying patients, feels that physicians should not fall back on the Hippocratic Oath to justify a refusal to kill, and since he made this statement the Supreme Court has declared that some parts of the Hippocratic Oath are obsolete in terms of the needs of today. In 1973 the Court said that changing times relieved the physician from the necessity of conforming to that part of the Oath which prohibits abortion.[14]

Although active euthanasia continues to be forbidden and is criminal, doctors can come close to it in their efforts to relieve pain. The amount of narcotic needed to relieve severe pain depresses respiration, and this may be the factor that leads most directly to a patient's death. Doctors generally have no problem here as long as they prescribe drugs only in the range that good medical practice dictates; medical ethics has always put the alleviation of suffering on an equal footing with the prolongation of life as a medical goal. Pope Pius, no friend of euthanasia, has said that "the removal of pain and consciousness by means of drugs when medical reasons suggest it is permitted by religion and morality to both doctor and patient; even if the use of drugs will shorten life."

Active euthanasia in its several forms—voluntary, assisted, and involuntary— raises more problems. It has its articulate defenders; it can save pain; but it alters further the role of the doctor in promoting life—already altered by the new policy on abortion—and it prevents the patient from having the assurance that his doctor is his helper, not his executioner. The terrible pain that some patients undergo is the price that is exacted in order for all patients to feel trust in the doctor–patient relationship. The arguments against active euthanasia are equally compelling whether this active euthanasia is to be only at the request of the patient or if it can be imposed involuntarily by the action of a board, whether it involves the doctor's actually administering a lethal dose or only leaving it at the patient's bedside. The latter is what is sometimes called assisted euthanasia. It is legal in Switzerland, but it is seldom employed. Patients find it difficult to ask to be assisted in this way. Alice James, the sister of William and Henry, was dying from cancer when she wrote: "I am being ground slowly on the grim grindstone of physical pain, and on two nights I had almost asked for Katherine's lethal dose, but one steps hestitatingly along such unaccustomed ways, and endures from second to second."

Stewart Alsop, dying of leukemia, wrote that a patient suffering beyond existence should be given the opportunity to end his life, or, if he refused that option, to be allowed as much pain-killing drug, probably heroin, as he requires.[15] "If a human being must die, it is surely better that he die in the

---

[13] Alvarez, W.: Death with dignity, *The Humanist,* Sept.–Oct., 1971, 12–14.
[14] *Roe v. Wade,* 410 US 113, 35 L Ed 2d 147, 93 S Ct 705 (1973).
[15] Alsop, S.: The right to die with dignity, *Good Housekeeping,* August, 1974, p. 69.

illusion of painless pleasure—and heroin is very pleasurable—than in lonely agony."[16]

Most physicians would not support Alsop's first plan, but they would want to help the patient achieve as pain-free a death as he desires.

With a growing consensus that relief of pain and the termination of life-promoting devices are often proper, although killing another human is not, the concept of "death with dignity" has achieved great popularity. It is worth noting that its originator, Paul Ramsey, has written a piece called "The Indignity of 'Death with Dignity.'" In our effort to be mature, to show that we have learned to live with the idea of death, says Ramsey, we trivialize death by saying that death is simply a part of life, that death contributes to evolution.[17] I myself am guilty of such trivilization; I once gave a paper on the right to die and the obligation to die—our additional obligation to leave the earth's resources for use by others. Ramsey says rightly that such an approach is too denying of the grief, the shock, the pain, and the terror of death. There is dignity in our caring for the dying, he says, but death is not dignified and we cannot confer death with dignity on the dying; we can only provide them with some of the necessary but not sufficient conditions for achieving a good death. "If the dying die with a degree of nobility it will be mostly their doing in doing their own dying." We do not achieve a community with the dying by interposing between them and us the bloodless notion of "death with dignity"; we draw closer to them only if our concept includes the final indignity of death itself.[18]

The late Ernest Becker in his Pulitzer-prize-winning book, *The Denial of Death,* writes about the many ways we have to deny the finality, the tragedy, the fearsomeness of death. Becker and Ramsey emphasize the need to face our fears.

This is a timely warning. The movement to deal with death as merely another "fact of life" can make death so banal that we do not fight hard enough against it.

An editorial in *Ca—A Cancer Journal for Clinicians* reminds us that although adjustment and accommodation are acceptable approaches to the inevitable, it is "often difficult to know exactly what is inevitable. Here are but a few examples of what were once considered to be hopelessly irreversible: cardiac arrest, metastatic choriocarcinoma, 'thyroid storm,' acute leukemia in children, the impending rupture of an aortic aneurism and a heart damaged by rheumatic fever." The editorial concludes: "What once inevitably meant death, does no

---

[16] *Time,* June 10, 1974, 65.

[17] One recent addition to the rapidly growing literature on death and dying is called "Death as a Fact of Life." Henden, D.: *Death as a Fact of Life,* New York, W.W. Norton, 1973.

[18] Ramsey, P.: The indignity of "death with dignity," *Hastings Center Studies* 2:47–62, 1974.

longer, and this fact should make physicians pause before too readily accommodating to dying and adjusting to the death of a patient."[19]

So problems still remain even though we have established a right to die. How should death be manipulated so as to allow medicine to remain within its traditional posture of promoting life? How can we live with the ambiguity and the responsibility that comes from a lack of definite guidelines on when to terminate life-saving procedures?

In gaining control over the prolongation of life, we have incurred the responsibility of determining at what point that death is most meaningful.

We will never find the perfect answer. We will not find a point we can define which separates lives terminated prematurely from those that are allowed to continue too long. We will not find the solution productive of only good and no evil. This is a lesson we have learned in other fields in recent years. We have begun to understand the dynamic nature of the forces that bear upon us and the difficulties of our choice. We see this same lesson in ecology, economics, diplomacy, and every other area in which we make choices. We cannot fight inflation without risking unemployment. We cannot employ the internal combustion engine without causing pollution.

These are the same kinds of decisions that medicine has to make. We have awakened from a dream of Social Darwinism, the concept that society is in an onward and upward evolution and that we will work our way to a point where what is unpleasant has been left behind and only the pleasant is in prospect.

Our new view recognizes forces and counterforces which interact with each other and which produce for us victory in defeat and defeat in victory; the view is a tragic view because it forces us to recognize that the solutions to our problems bring to us new and even more exquisite problems. If we are forced to face the fact that life has this tragic element—that dreams of conquering death and disease by replacing organs and prolonging life create new problems in the process of solving old ones—that also has its consoling aspects. We do have the choice to make use of them or not. We continue to have the age-old burden of man, the responsibility of making choices in a universe that has never been without its tragic component.

[19] Holleb, A.: A patient's right to die—the easy way out? Ca—A Cancer Journal for Clinicians, 24(4):256, 1974.

ACTIVE AND PASSIVE EUTHANASIA

JAMES RACHELS

The distinction between active and passive euthanasia is thought to be crucial for medical ethics. The idea is that it is permissible, at least in some cases, to withhold treatment and allow a patient to die, but it is never permissible to take any direct action designed to kill the patient. This doctrine seems to be accepted by most doctors, and is endorsed in a statement adopted by the House of Delegates of the American Medical Association on December 4, 1973:

> The intentional termination of the life of one human being by another—mercy killing—is contrary to that for which the medical profession stands and is contrary to the policy of the American Medical Association.
>
> The cessation of the employment of extraordinary means to prolong the life of the body when there is irrefutable evidence that biological death is imminent is the decision of the patient and/or his immediate family. The advice and judgment of the physician should be freely available to the patient and/or his immediate family.

However, a strong case can be made against this doctrine. In what follows I will set out some of the relevant arguments, and urge doctors to reconsider their views on this matter.

To begin with a familiar type of situation, a patient who is dying of incurable cancer of the throat is in terrible pain, which can no longer be satisfactorily alleviated. He is certain to die within a few days, even if present treatment is continued, but he does not want to go on living for those days since the pain is unbearable. So he asks the doctor for an end to it, and his family joins in the request.

Suppose the doctor agrees to withhold treatment, as the conventional doctrine says he may. The justification for his doing so is that the patient is in terrible agony, and since he is going to die anyway, it would be wrong to prolong his suffering needlessly. But now notice this. If one simply withholds treatment, it may take the patient longer to die, and so he may suffer more than he would if more direct action were taken and a lethal injection given. This fact provides strong reason for thinking that, once the initial decision not to prolong his agony

Reprinted with permission from *The New England Journal of Medicine, 292* (2): 78–80, and with the kind permission of the author.

has been made, active euthanasia is actually preferable to passive euthanasia, rather than the reverse. To say otherwise is to endorse the option that leads to more suffering rather than less and is contrary to the humanitarian impulse that prompts the decision not to prolong his life in the first place.

Part of my point is that the process of being "allowed to die" can be relatively slow and painful, whereas being given a lethal injection is relatively quick and painless. Let me give a different sort of example. In the United States about one in 600 babies is born with Down's syndrome. Most of these babies are other-wise healthy—that is, with only the usual pediatric care, they will proceed to an otherwise normal infancy. Some, however, are born with congenital defects such as intestinal obstructions that require operations if they are to live. Some-times, the parents and the doctor will decide not to operate and let the infant die. Anthony Shaw describes what happens then:

> When surgery is denied [the doctor] must try to keep the infant from suffering while natural forces sap the baby's life away. As a surgeon whose natural inclination is to use the scalpel to fight off death, standing by and watching a salvageable baby die is the most emotionally exhausting experience I know. It is easy at a conference, in a theoretical discussion, to decide that such infants should be allowed to die. It is altogether different to stand by in the nursery and watch as dehydration and in-fection wither a tiny being over hours and days. This is a terrible ordeal for me and the hospital staff—much more so than for the parents who never set foot in the nursery.[1]

I can understand why some people are opposed to all euthanasia and insist that such infants must be allowed to live. I think I can also understand why other people favor destroying these babies quickly and painlessly. But why should anyone favor letting "dehydration and infection wither a tiny being over hours and days?" The doctrine that says that a baby may be allowed to dehydrate and wither, but may not be given an injection that would end its life without suffering, seems so patently cruel as to require no further refutation. The strong language is not intended to offend but only to put the point in the clearest possible way.

My second argument is that the conventional doctrine leads to decisions con-cerning life and death made on irrelevant grounds.

Consider again the case of the infants with Down's syndrome who need operations for congenital defects unrelated to the syndrome to live. Sometimes, there is no operation, and the baby dies, but when there is no such defect, the baby lives on. Now, an operation such as that to remove an intestinal obstruc-tion is not prohibitively difficult. The reason why such operations are not per-formed in these cases is, clearly, that the child has Down's syndrome and the parents and doctor judge that because of that fact it is better for the child to die.

[1] A. Shaw: "Doctor, Do We Have a Choice?" *The New York Times Magazine*, January 30, 1972, p. 54.

But notice that this situation is absurd, no matter what view one takes of the lives and potentials of such babies. If the life of such an infant is worth preserving, what does it matter if it needs a simple operation? Or, if one thinks it better that such a baby should not live on, what difference does it make that it happens to have an unobstructed intestinal tract? In either case, the matter of life and death is being decided on irrelevant grounds. It is the Down's syndrome, and not the intestines, that is the issue. The matter should be decided, if at all, on that basis, and not be allowed to depend on the essentially irrelevant question of whether the intestinal tract is blocked.

What makes this situation possible, of course, is the idea that when there is an intestinal blockage, one can "let the baby die," but when there is no such defect there is nothing that can be done, for one must not "kill" it. The fact that this idea leads to such results as deciding life or death on irrelevant grounds is another good reason why the doctrine should be rejected.

One reason why so many people think that there is an important moral difference between active and passive euthanasia is that they think killing someone is morally worse than letting someone die. But is it? Is killing, in itself, worse than letting die? To investigate this issue, two cases may be considered that are exactly alike except that one involves killing, whereas the other involves letting someone die. Then, it can be asked whether this difference makes any difference to the moral assessments. It is important that the cases be exactly alike, except for this one difference, since otherwise one cannot be confident that it is this difference and not some other that accounts for any variation in the assessments of the two cases. So, let us consider this pair of cases.

In the first, Smith stands to gain a large inheritance if anything should happen to his six-year-old cousin. One evening while the child is taking his bath, Smith sneaks into the bathroom and drowns the child, and then arranges things so that it will look like an accident.

In the second, Jones also stands to gain if anything should happen to his six-year-old cousin. Like Smith, Jones sneaks in planning to drown the child in his bath. However, just as he enters the bathroom Jones sees the child slip and hit his head, and fall face down in the water. Jones is delighted; he stands by, ready to push the child's head back under if it is necessary, but it is not necessary. With only a little thrashing about, the child drowns all by himself, "accidentally," as Jones watches and does nothing.

Now Smith killed the child, whereas Jones "merely" let the child die. That is the only difference between them. Did either man behave better, from a moral point of view? If the difference between killing and letting die were in itself a morally important matter, one should say that Jones's behavior was less reprehensible than Smith's. But does one really want to say that? I think not. In the first place, both men acted from the same motive, personal gain, and both had exactly the same end in view when they acted. It may be inferred from Smith's conduct that he is a bad man, although that judgment may be withdrawn or modified if certain further facts are learned about him—for example, that he is mentally deranged. But would not the very same thing be inferred about Jones from his conduct? And would not the same further considerations also be relevant to any modification of this judgment? Moreover, suppose Jones pleaded, in his own defense, "After all, I didn't do anything except just stand there and watch the child drown. I didn't kill him; I only let him die." Again, if letting die were in itself less bad than killing, this defense should have at least some weight. But it does not. Such a "defense" can only be regarded as a grotesque perversion of moral reasoning. Morally speaking, it is no defense at all.

Now it may be pointed out, quite properly, that the cases of euthanasia with which doctors are concerned are not like this at all. They do not involve personal gain or the destruction of normal healthy children. Doctors are concerned only with cases in which the patient's life is of no further use to him, or in which the patient's life has become or will soon become a terrible burden. However, the point is the same in these cases: the bare difference between killing and letting die does not, in itself, make a moral difference. If a doctor lets a patient die, for humane reasons, he is in the same moral position as if he had given the patient a lethal injection for humane reasons. If his decision was wrong—if, for example, the patient's illness was in fact curable—the decision would be equally regrettable no matter which method was used to carry it out. And if the doctor's decision was the right one, the method used is not in itself important.

The AMA policy statement isolates the crucial issue very well; the crucial issue is "the intentional termination of the life of one human being by another." But after identifying this issue, and forbidding "mercy killing," the statement goes on to deny that the cessation of treatment is the intentional termination of a life. This is where the mistake comes in, for what is the cessation of treatment, in these circumstances, if it is not "the intentional termination of the life of one human being by another?" Of course it is exactly that, and if it were not, there would be no point to it.

Many people will find this judgment hard to accept. One reason, I think, is that it is very easy to conflate the question of whether killing is, in itself, worse than letting die, with the very different question of whether most actual cases of killing are more reprehensible than most actual cases of letting die. Most actual cases of killing are clearly terrible (think, for example, of all the murders reported in the newspapers), and one hears of such cases every day. On the other hand, one hardly ever hears of a case of letting die, except for the actions of doctors who are motivated by humanitarian reasons. So one learns to think of killing in a much worse light than of letting die. But this does not mean that there is something about killing that makes it in itself worse than letting die, for it is not the bare difference between killing and letting die that makes the difference in these cases. Rather, the other factors—the murderer's motive of personal gain, for example, contrasted with the doctor's humanitarian motivation—account for different reactions to the different cases.

I have argued that killing is not in itself any worse than letting die; if my contention is right, it follows that active euthanasia is not any worse than passive euthanasia. What arguments can be given on the other side? The most common, I believe, is the following: "The important difference between active and passive euthanasia is that, in passive euthanasia, the doctor does not do anthing to bring about the patient's death. The doctor does nothing, and the patient dies of whatever ills already afflict him. In active euthanasia, however, the doctor does something to bring about the patient's death: he kills him. The doctor who gives the patient with cancer a lethal injection has himself caused his patient's death; whereas if he merely ceases treatment, the cancer is the cause of the death."

A number of points need to be made here. The first is that it is not exactly correct to say that in passive euthanasia the doctor does nothing, for he does do one thing that is very important: he lets the patient die. "Letting someone die" is certainly different, in some respects, from other types of action—mainly in that it is a kind of action that one may perform by way of not performing certain other actions. For example, one may let a patient die by way of not giving medication, just as one may insult someone by way of not shaking his hand. But for any purpose of moral assessment, it is a type of action nonetheless. The decision to let a patient die is subject to moral appraisal in the same way that a decision to kill him would be subject to moral appraisal: it may be assessed as wise or unwise, compassionate or sadistic, right or wrong. If a doctor deliberately let a patient die who was suffering from a routinely curable illness, the doctor would certainly be to blame for what he had done, just as he would be to blame if he had needlessly killed the patient. Charges against him would then be appropriate. If so, it would be no defense at all for him to insist that he didn't "do anything." He would have done something very serious indeed, for he let his patient die.

Fixing the cause of death may be very important from a legal point of view, for it may determine whether criminal charges are brought against the doctor. But I do not think that this notion can be used to show a moral difference between active and passive euthanasia. The reason why it is considered bad to be the cause of someone's death is that death is regarded as a great evil—and so it is. However, if it has been decided that euthanasia—even passive euthanasia—is desirable in a given case, it has also been decided that in this instance death is no greater an evil than the patient's continued existence. And if this is true, the usual reason for not wanting to be the cause of someone's death simply does not apply.

Finally, doctors may think that all this is only of academic interest—the sort of thing that philosophers may worry about but that has no practical bearing on their own work. After all, doctors must be concerned about the legal consequences of what they do, and active euthanasia is clearly forbidden by the law. But even so, doctors should also be concerned with the fact that the law is forcing upon them a moral doctrine that may well be indefensible, and has a considerable effect on their practices. Of course, most doctors are not now in the position of being coerced in this matter, for they do not regard themselves as merely going along with what the law requires. Rather, in statements such as the AMA policy statement that I have quoted, they are endorsing this doctrine as a central point of medical ethics. In that statement, active euthanasia is condemned not merely as illegal but as "contrary to that for which the medical profession stands," whereas passive euthanasia is approved. However, the preceding considerations suggest that there is really no moral difference between the two, considered in themselves (there may be important moral differences in some cases in their *consequences*, but, as I pointed out, these differences may make active euthanasia, and not passive euthanasia, the morally preferable option). So, whereas doctors may have to discriminate between active and passive euthanasia to satisfy the law, they should not do any more than that. In particular, they should not give the distinction any added authority and weight by writing it into official statements of medical ethics.

CHOOSING NOT TO
PROLONG DYING

ROBERT M. VEATCH

Lucy Morgan is a 94-year-old patient being maintained in a nursing home. Some years ago she suffered a severe cerebral hemorrhage. She is blind, largely deaf, and often in a semiconscious state. Mrs. Morgan is an educated woman, the wife of the former president of Antioch College. About four years ago she wrote an essay, entitled, "On Drinking the Hemlock," in which she pleaded for a dignified and simple way to choose to die. Now she, like thousands of other patients in hospitals, rest homes, and bedrooms throughout the world, is having her dying prolonged. What, before the biological revolution with its technological gadgetry, would have been a short and peaceful exit is now often drawn out for months or years by the unmitigated and sometimes merciless intervention of pencillin, pacemakers, polygraphs, tubes, tetracycline, and transplantation.

Technology's new possibilities have created chaos in the care of the dying. What happens to Mrs. Morgan and others like her depends upon the medical and and nursing staffs of the institutions in which these patients are confined. One patient may be mercilessly probed and primed with infusions so that dying is prolonged endlessly, while another in a similar condition may have heroic treatment stopped so that the process of dying may proceed uninterrupted, whether or not permission for the withdrawal has been given. A third patient may, with or without his consent, have an air embolism injected into a vein.

The Issues at Stake

Before examining some of the policies being proposed, we should get the issues straight. Lawyers and moralists make three distinctions in discussing euthanasia and the choice not to prolong dying. First, there may be legal and moral differences between directly killing the terminal patient, and allowing him to die. In one study, 59% of the physicians in two West Coast hospitals said

Reprinted by permission from *Medical Dimensions*, December, 1972, copyright © 1972, MBA Communications, Inc., and with the kind permission of the author.

that they would practice what was called "negative euthanasia" if it were legal, while 27% said that they would practice positive euthanasia.

Euthanasia has become a terribly confused term in the discussion. In some cases, it is taken literally to mean simply a good death; in others it is limited to the more narrow direct or positive killing of the terminal patient. In light of this confusion, it seems wise to ban the term from the debate entirely.

The legality of directly ending a patient's life is highly questionable, to say the least. Legal cases are very rare. The one decision which is particularly relevant is in the case of Dr. Hermann N. Sander, a New Hampshire physician who entered into the chart of a cancer patient that he had injected air into the patient's blood stream. He admitted that his purpose was to end suffering and pain and the jury returned a verdict for the defendant. But the critical factor in the case was the pathologist's testimony that he could not establish the cause of death with certainty. Thus the jury was not condoning "mercy killing." According to Curran and Shapiro in *Law, Medicine and Forensic Science*, "The general rule in the United States is that one who either kills one suffering from a fatal or incurable disease, even with the consent of that party, or who provides that party with the means of suicide, is guilty of either murder or manslaughter." It is safe to say that no lawyer would advise his medical clients that they would not be prosecuted if they practiced positive euthanasia.

On the other hand, the cessation of treatment may be a different matter morally if not legally. It is well known that a competent patient has the right to refuse even lifesaving treatment. To my knowledge, there are no cases in which a physician has been brought to trial for stopping the treatment of a terminal patient. It seems most unlikely that he would be guilty of either moral or legal offense if a competent patient had ordered the treatment ended. If he had done so without the patient's instructions, however, the charge, presumably, would be abandonment. The legal status of ceasing to treat or omitting treatment is very much in doubt especially when a competent patient has not specifically refused treatment.

At the moral level, some recognize the difference between killing and omitting or ceasing treatment. Others insist that this kind of distinction is mere semantics, because in either case the result is that the patient dies. Yet, if we were given the choice of turning off a respirator to allow a terminal patient to die or actively injecting an embolism, almost all of us would choose the first act, at least barring some extenuating circumstances which changed the moral calculations, such as the presence of extreme intractable pain and suffering.

There are two kinds of cases in which the distinction would make an actual difference. The first is when the prognosis had been in error and merely ceasing certain treatment could result in continued living, while active killing would result in death. The second involves the possibility of actual abuse. In any case, the physician should not be put in a position to dispose of unwanted patients.

It is argued that for practical, if not moral, reasons, we need to separate active killing from cessation and omission of treatment, recognizing that many physicians favor the latter but not the former. It becomes expedient, then, to adopt a policy which would cover virtually all cases, minimize the chances for error, and be acceptable to a broader public.

It is a sad commentary on the tradition of medical ethics that the question of euthanasia is almost always raised in terms of what the medical professional should decide to do for a terminal patient: Should *he* treat; should *he* omit treatment; should *he* stop treatment; should *he* inject the embolism? Yet, there is another perspective: that of the patient. While the legal and moral status of killing and allowing a patient to die may be dubious, the principle of the right to refuse treatment is well recognized. It is morally and legally sound to emphasize the role of the patient as decision-maker when he is legally competent. Of course, this still leaves open cases when the patient is not legally competent, but at least we have a moral and legal foundation from which to form a policy. The next step would be to decide upon an appropriate agent for the legally incompetent patient.

Patient Advocate

First priority should go to an agent whom the patient, while competent, would be permitted to appoint expressly for this purpose. When this has not been done, the next of kin should have both the rights and responsibilities to determine what is in the patient's interest. While the potential for abuse exists, the next of kin is in the best position to know the patient's personal values and beliefs upon which treatment-refusing decisions must be based. There would still be the established possibility of going to court to overturn the judgment of the next of kin in case he was acting maliciously or choosing not to prolong the patient's living rather than his dying. But the choice to refuse some death-prolonging treatment should not, in and of itself, be taken as evidence of immoral or illegal activity. In that rare case where no relatives are available, a court-appointed guardian might provide the best safeguard of the patient's interests.

Ordinary and Extraordinary Means

A second distinction that must be clarified in a policy permitting the choice not to prolong dying is the difference between ordinary and extraordinary means. These terms have three meanings: usual versus unusual treatment, useful versus useless treatment, and simply imperative versus elective treatment. The

Catholic tradition as summarized by Pope Pius XII is: "Normally one is held to use only ordinary means—according to circumstances of persons, places, times and culture—that is to say, means that do not involve any grave burden for oneself or another." Clearly, defining what is ordinary according to the circumstances named will make the distinction a difficult one. We can circumvent this entire quagmire simply by focusing on the moral principle of the right to refuse treatment as a basis for policy. This does not mean that it will always be moral to refuse treatment, but if patient freedom and dignity are to be central to policy decision, we may have to recognize that patients are entitled to make their own decisions and, therefore, to refuse even those treatments which are thought to be usual or useful. This might be the case when, for instance, a patient faces a lifetime hemodialysis regimen for chronic nephritis. Recently, such a patient decided that the thought of being attached by tubes for 16 to 24 hours a week for the rest of his life was an unbearable and dehumanizing possibility. He chose, we think morally and legally, to cease the dialysis treatment.

Allowing to Live and Allowing to Die

Third, it is important to distinguish between the choice not to prolong dying and the choice not to prolong living. Two closely related cases which I have encountered recently reveal the difference. In the first, a baby was born with trisomy-18 and severe respiratory distress as well as gross CNS anomalies. He would not live no matter what heroic procedures were attempted. A second case was that of a Mongoloid infant who had been born with esophageal atresia. The choice of the parents to refuse corrective surgery for the atresia was, in fact, the choice that the quality of life as a Mongoloid would not be satisfactory either for the infant or his parents. On the other hand, the choice to cease respiration for the trisomy-18 baby was made when there was nothing that man could do to save the infant's life.

Any policy which is adopted must come to terms with these distinctions, for it may be morally and legally acceptable to reject an unusually heroic and probably useless procedure but wrong, at least morally, to refuse a simple IV when it would lead relatively painlessly to many years of normal healthy life. It may be wrong to decide that someone else's life is not worth living but acceptable to recognize that even the forces of modern science are not able to cope with some diseases.

What Should Our Policy Be?

Some authorities say that we cannot adopt a systematic policy which would permit the choice not to prolong dying. The physician's duty, they feel, is to preserve life. When some treatment can be offered, even for a patient who is almost certainly going to die, that treatment *must* be offered. Even if this view is correct, it is utopian and one which few clinicians would be able to accept if taken literally as a practical way of dealing with death. We must stop the heroic procedures at some point. If the only course available for a patient in his last days is to fly him and the medical team around the country to try some newly devised experimental surgery, at least some will say that morally we are not required to proceed or, in fact, that it would be wrong to proceed. At some time, the decision must be made that the dying process has been tampered with long enough and that there is nothing more that man can or should do.

Physician Ad Hoc *Decision-Making*

Four policy alternatives are currently being debated. The first is the defense of the status quo: We should have no policy at all. In fact, right now we do have a policy—the individual physician decides, on an *ad hoc* basis at the moment when the patient is in a terminal condition, if and when treatment should be given. This is sometimes done in consultation with other members of the medical team, members of the family, and the clergyman, but, for the most part, the real decision rests in the doctor's hands.

A strong case can be made for the present policy. At least ideally, if not in practice, the physician knows the patient's condition and is committed to his best interest. Every doctor is aware that each medical case is unique, and to develop more systematic decision-making procedures could be very dangerous. Nevertheless, it seems to me that the present policy is the second worst of all possible alternatives. We have already seen that about half of the physicians in one study would exercise the choice not to prolong life if it were clearly made legal. There is also a difference of opinion among patients. A random pairing of patient and physician views would mean that if the physician is making the decision, in many cases the patient who would not want the dying prolonged will have this done against his wishes; another patient who desperately desires the last heroic operation will not receive it.

It may be even worse. There may be systematic differences between the medical professionals and the laymen. Many physicians claim that their special ethical duty is to preserve life. If the physicians have different ethical principles or even if they merely have different ethical judgments about what benefits the patient, it creates a terrible dilemma.

Even if physician and patient would reach the identical conclusion, the patient's freedom and dignity in matters most directly affecting his own living and dying would still be infringed upon. All of these objections have led to the search for other methods of decision-making.

The Professional Committee

In an attempt to take the burden off the shoulders of the individual physician, a growing number of hospitals now use committees of physicians to decide who should receive the last bed in the intensive care unit or the scarce and expensive hemodialysis treatment. The committee eliminates some of the random biases which an individual physician might have either in favor of excessively heroic intervention or inadequate treatment. Yet, is it right that a patient whose position is at one extreme or the other should have his own views moderated? Particularly if there are systematic differences between the professional and lay communities? Even the committee structure would impose upon many patients views which they find unacceptable.

This serious drawback to the committee must be added to the more obvious problem—that with the committee-making structure one loses the primary advantage of decision-making by the individual physician. While, hopefully, he would know some details of the patient's life and values, we cannot hope that this would hold true for the committee. Even more significantly, the committee mechanism perpetuates the view that the medical professional by his training has somehow acquired expertise in making the moral judgment about when it is no longer appropriate to prolong dying. If the committee structure is the alternative, perhaps we should stay with the status quo and let the individual physician make the choice unhindered and unguided.

Personal Letters

Other alternatives are beginning to appear. The Euthanasia Educational Fund has drafted a letter which an individual might address to his family physician, clergyman or lawyer. It directs that "if the time comes when I can no longer take part in decisions for my own future, [and] if there is no reasonable expectation of my recovery from physical or mental disability, I request that I be allowed to die and not be kept alive by artificial means or heroic measures." This "living will" makes no pretense of being legally binding. It merely gives guidance to the physician and others concerned. It also frees the physician from having to guess what the patient's wishes might be.

The instructions are extremely vague, however, and while useful for general guidance, do not go very far in removing the difficulties of earlier proposals. For example, "reasonable expectation" and "artificial means or heroic measures" beg for clarification, and it is the reader of the will who will have to interpret. For this reason, we know of two physicians who have drafted very specific letters as instruction for their own terminal care. One instructs "in the event of cerebral accident other than a subarachnoid hemorrhage, I want no treatment of any kind until it is clear that I will be able to think effectively. . . . In the event of subarachnoid hemorrhage, use your own judgment in the acute state. . . ." The other directs that there be no artificial respiration "to prolong my life if I had lost the ability to breathe for more than two or three (not five or six) minutes," While possibly more specific than the "living will," these instructions may not be of much help to the layman. He simply does not have the technical knowledge to be so precise.

In either case, the idea of a letter preaddressed to one's personal physician assumes that one has a personal physician. This, unfortunately, is not always the case. Also required is that one be dying in the care of the physician to whom the letter is sent. Carrying the letter in a wallet might help, but certainly will not do much to relieve the anxiety of the potentially dying patient. Even if one assumes that a personal physician will be caring for the dying patient, the letter still requires trust and understanding. This can no longer be assumed, but if such a relationship does exist, the need for the letter decreases in proportion.

Legislation to Permit Death With Dignity

All of these problems have instigated legislative proposals which would give clearer procedures for the decision not to prolong dying. In 1969 a bill patterned after the British euthanasia legislative proposal was introduced into the Idaho legislature. It explicitly included both "positive" and "negative" actions and received very little support in this country. Rep. Walter Sackett, himself a physician, has placed several proposals before the Florida legislature. One bill, which was introduced in 1970 but did not pass, would have permitted an individual to execute a document specifying that "his life shall not be prolonged beyond the point of a meaningful existence." If the patient himself cannot execute the document, the bill provided that the person of the next degree of kinship could. While this bill would have eliminated some of the problems of other proposals, the vagueness of the term "meaningful existence" is its critical flaw. The physician on the case presumably would be forced to determine whether or not the patient's life could ever again be meaningful.

A third type of legislation, to be based on the already existing right of the patient to refuse treatment, is worthy of consideration as a public policy. In cases where the patient is not competent, some agent must make the decision on the patient's behalf—that is an unpleasant reality of life. It seems to me that an agent appointed by the patient while competent should have first priority, then the next of kin, and finally, in the rare case where the patient has no relatives, a court-appointed agent.

The physician would thus be protected from having to make a nonmedical, moral judgment about what is right for the patient. At the same time, the patient and his family would be able to fulfill their rights and obligations to look after the patient's welfare. Anything short of this will deprive the patient of life, liberty and probably happiness as well.

These four types of policy proposals will be receiving much more attention in the next few months. None of them is a panacea; each raises serious moral and public policy questions. But the chaos generated by biomedical technology's assault on death demands new policy clarification. That new policy will be forthcoming soon. It must be.

THE ALLOCATION OF EXOTIC MEDICAL LIFESAVING THERAPY

NICHOLAS RESCHER

I. The Problem

Technological progress has in recent years transformed the limits of the possible in medical therapy. However, the elevated state of sophistication of modern medical technology has brought the economists' classic problem of scarcity in its wake as an unfortunate side product. The enormously sophisticated and complex equipment and the highly trained teams of experts requisite for its utilization are scarce resources in relation to potential demand. The administrators of the great medical institutions that preside over these scarce resources thus come to be faced increasingly with the awesome choice: *Whose life to save?*

A (somewhat hypothetical) paradigm example of this problem may be sketched within the following set of definitive assumptions: We suppose that persons in some particular medically morbid condition are "mortally afflicted": It is virtually certain that they will die within a short time period (say ninety days). We assume that some very complex course of treatment (e.g., a heart transplant) represents a substantial probability of life prolongation for persons in this mortally afflicted condition. We assume that the facilities available in terms of human resources, mechanical instrumentalities, and requisite materials (e.g., hearts in the case of a heart transplant) make it possible to give a certain treatment—this "exotic (medical) lifesaving therapy," or ELT for short—to a certain, relatively small number of people. And finally we assume that a substantially greater pool of people in the mortally afflicted condition is at hand. The problem then may be formulated as follows: How is one to select within the pool of afflicted patients the ones to be given the ELT treatment in question; how to select those "whose lives are to be saved"? Faced with many candidates for an ELT process that can be made available to only a few, doctors and medical administrators confront the decision of who is to be given a chance at survival and who is, in effect, to be condemned to die.

This paper originally appeared in *Ethics: An International Journal of Social, Political and Legal Philosophy* (April 1969) and is reprinted with the permission of the author and The University of Chicago Press.

As has already been implied, the "heroic" variety of spare-part surgery can pretty well be assimilated to this paradigm. One can foresee the time when heart transplantation, for example, will have become pretty much a routine medical procedure, albeit on a very limited basis, since a cardiac surgeon with the technical competence to transplant hearts can operate at best a rather small number of times each week and the elaborate facilities for such operations will most probably exist on a modest scale. Moreover, in "spare-part" surgery there is always the problem of availability of the "spare parts" themselves. A report in one British newspaper gives the following picture: "Of the 150,000 who die of heart disease each year [in the U.K.], Mr. Donald Longmore, research surgeon at the National Heart Hospital [in London] estimates that 22,000 might be eligible for heart surgery. Another 30,000 would need heart and lung transplants. But there are probably only between 7,000 and 14,000 potential donors a year."[1] Envisaging this situation in which at the very most something like one in four heart-malfunction victims can be saved, we clearly confront a problem in ELT allocation.

A perhaps even more drastic case in point is afforded by long-term haemodialysis, an ongoing process by which a complex device—an "artificial kidney machine"—is used periodically in cases of chronic renal failure to substitute for a non-functional kidney in "cleaning" potential poisons from the blood. Only a few major institutions have chronic haemodialysis units, whose complex operation is an extremely expensive proposition. For the present and the foreseeable future the situation is that "the number of places available for chronic haemodialysis is hopelessly inadequate."[2]

The traditional medical ethos has insulated the physician against facing the very existence of this problem. When swearing the Hippocratic Oath, he commits

---

[1] Christine Doyle, "Spare-Part Heart Surgeons Worried by Their Success," *Observer,* May 12, 1968.

[2] J. D. N. Nabarro, "Selection of Patients for Haemodialysis," *British Medical Journal* (March 11, 1967), p. 623. Although several thousand patients die in the U.K. each year from renal failure—there are about thirty new cases per million of population—only 10 percent of these can for the foreseeable future be accommodated with chronic haemodialysis. Kidney transplantation—itself a very tricky procedure—cannot make a more than minor contribution here. As this article goes to press, I learn that patients can be maintained in home dialysis at an operating cost about half that of maintaining them in a hospital dialysis unit (roughly an $8,000 minimum). In the United States, around 7,000 patients with terminal uremia who could benefit from haemodialysis evolve yearly. As of mid-1968, some 1,000 of these can be accommodated in existing hospital units. By June 1967, a world-wide total of some 120 patients were in treatment by home dialysis. (Data from a forthcoming paper, "Home Dialysis," by C. M. Conty and H. V. Murdaugh. See also R. A. Baillod *et al.,* "Overnight Haemodialysis in the Home," *Proceedings of the European Dialysis and Transplant Association,* VI [1965], 99 ff.).

himself to work for the benefit of the sick in "whatsover house I enter."[3] In taking this stance, the physician substantially renounces the explicit choice of saving certain lives rather than others. Of course, doctors have always in fact had to face such choices on the battlefield or in times of disaster, but there the issue had to be resolved hurriedly, under pressure, and in circumstances in which the very nature of the case effectively precluded calm deliberation by the decision maker as well as criticism by others. In sharp contrast, however, cases of the type we have postulated in the present discussion arise predictably, and represent choices to be made deliberately and "in cold blood."

It is, to begin with, appropriate to remark that this problem is not fundamentally a medical problem. For when there are sufficiently many afflicted candidates for ELT then—so we may assume—there will also be more than enough for whom the purely medical grounds for ELT allocation are decisively strong in any individual case, and just about equally strong throughout the group. But in this circumstance a selection of some afflicted patients over and against others cannot *ex hypothesi* be made on the basis of purely medical considerations.

The selection problem as we have said, is in substantial measure not a medical one. It is a problem *for* medical men, which must somehow be solved by them, but that does not make it a medical issue—any more than the problem of hospital building is a medical issue. As a problem it belongs to the category of philosophical problems—specifically a problem of moral philosophy or ethics. Structurally, it bears a substantial kinship with those issues in this field that revolve about the notorious whom-to-save-on-the-lifeboat and whom-to-throw-to-the-wolves-pursuing-the-sled questions. But whereas questions of this just-indicated sort are artificial, hypothetical, and far-fetched, the ELT issue poses a *genuine* policy question for the responsible administrators in medical institutions, indeed a question that threatens to become commonplace in the foreseeable future.

Now what the medical administrator needs to have, and what the philosopher is presumably *ex officio* in a position to help in providing, is a body of *rational guidelines* for making choices in these literally life-or-death situations. This is an issue in which many interested parties have a substantial stake, including the responsible decision maker who wants to satisfy his conscience that he is acting in a reasonable way. Moreover, the family and associates of the man who is turned away—to say nothing of the man himself—have the right to an acceptable explanation. And indeed even the general public wants to know that what is being done is fitting and proper. All of these interested parties are

---

[3] For the Hippocratic Oath see *Hippocrates: Works* (Loeb ed.; London, 1959), I, p. 298.

entitled to insist that a reasonable code of operating principles provides a defensible rationale for making the life-and-death choices involved in ELT.

II. The Two Types of Criteria

Two distinguishable types of criteria are bound up in the issue of making ELT choices. We shall call these *Criteria of Inclusion* and *Criteria of Comparison,* respectively. The distinction at issue here requires some explanation. We can think of the selection as being made by a two-stage process: (1) the selection from among all possible candidates (by a suitable screening process) of a group to be taken under serious consideration as candidates for therapy, and then (2) the actual singling out, within this group, of the particular individuals to whom therapy is to be given. Thus the first process narrows down the range of comparative choice by eliminating *en bloc* whole categories of potential candidates. The second process calls for a more refined, case-by-case comparison of those candidates that remain. By means of the first set of criteria one forms a selection group; by means of the second set, an actual selection is made within this group.

Thus what we shall call a "selection system" for the choice of patients to receive therapy of the ELT type will consist of criteria of these two kinds. Such a system will be acceptable only when the reasonableness of its component criteria can be established.

III. Essential Features of an Acceptable ELT Selection System

To qualify as reasonable, an ELT selection must meet two important "regulative" requirements: it must be *simple* enough to be readily intelligible, and it must be *plausible,* that is, patently reasonable in a way that can be apprehended easily and without involving ramified subtleties. Those medical administrators responsible for ELT choices must follow a modus operandi that virtually all the people involved can readily understand to be acceptable (at a reasonable level of generality, at any rate). Appearances are critically important here. It is not enough that the choice be made in a *justifiable* way; it must be possible for people—*plain* people—to "see" (i.e., understand without elaborate teaching or indoctrination) that *it is justified,* insofar as any mode of procedure can be justified in cases of this sort.

One "constitutive" requirement is obviously an essential feature of a reasonable selection system: all of its component criteria—those of inclusion and those of comparison alike—must be reasonable in the sense of being *rationally defensible*. The ramifications of this requirement call for detailed consideration. But one of its aspects should be noted without further ado: it must be *fair*—it must treat relevantly like cases alike, leaving no room for "influence" or favoritism, etc.

IV. The Basic Screening Stage: Criteria of Inclusion (and Exclusion)

Three sorts of considerations are prominent among the plausible criteria of inclusion/exclusion at the basic screening stage: the constituency factor, the progress-of-science factor, and the prospect-of-success factor.

A. The Constituency Factor

It is a "fact of life" that ELT can be available only in the institutional setting of a hospital or medical institute or the like. Such institutions generally have normal clientele boundaries. A veterans' hospital will not concern itself primarily with treating non-veterans, a children's hospital cannot be expected to accommodate the "senior citizen," an army hospital can regard college professors as outside its sphere. Sometimes the boundaries are geographic—a state hospital may admit only residents of a certain state. (There are, of course, indefensible constituency principles—say race or religion, party membership, or ability to pay; and there are cases of borderline legitimacy, e.g., sex.[4]) A medical institution is justified in considering for ELT only persons within its own constituency, provided this constituency is constituted upon a defensible basis. Thus the haemodialysis selection committee in Seattle "agreed to consider only those applications who were residents of the state of Washington. . . . They justified this stand on the grounds that since the basic research . . . had been done at . . . a state-supported institution—the people whose taxes had paid for the research should be its first beneficiaries."[5]

While thus insisting that constituency considerations represent a valid and legitimate factor in ELT selection, I do feel there is much to be said for minimizing their role in life-or-death cases. Indeed a refusal to recognize them at all is a significant part of medical tradition, going back to the very oath of

[4] Another example of borderline legitimacy is posed by an endowment "with strings attached," e.g., "In accepting this legacy the hospital agrees to admit and provide all needed treatment for any direct descendant of myself, its founder."

[5] Shana Alexander, "They Decide Who Lives, Who Dies," *Life*, LIII (November 9, 1962), 102–25 (see p. 107).

Hippocrates. They represent a departure from the ideal arising with the institutionalization of medicine, moving it away from its original status as an art practiced by an individual practitioner.

B. The Progress-of-Science Factor

The needs of medical research can provide a second valid principle of inclusion. The research interests of the medical staff in relation to the specific nature of the cases at issue is a significant consideration. It may be important for the progress of medical science—and thus of potential benefit to many persons in the future—to determine how effective the ELT at issue is with diabetics or persons over sixty or with a negative RH factor. Considerations of this sort represent another type of legitimate factor in ELT selection.

A very definitely *borderline* case under this head would revolve around the question of a patient's willingness to pay, not in monetary terms, but in offering himself as an experimental subject, say by contracting to return at designated times for a series of tests substantially unrelated to his own health, but yielding data of importance to medical knowledge in general.

C. The Prospect-of-Success Factor

It may be that while the ELT at issue is not without *some* effectiveness in general, it has been established to be highly effective only with patients in certain specific categories (e.g., females under forty of a specific blood type). This difference in effectiveness—in the absolute or in the probability of success—is (we assume) so marked as to constitute virtually a difference in kind rather than in degree. In this case, it would be perfectly legitimate to adopt the general rule of making the ELT at issue available only or primarily to persons in this substantial-promise-of-success category. (It is on grounds of this sort that young children and persons over fifty are generally ruled out as candidates for haemodialysis.)

We have maintained that the three factors of constituency, progress of science, and prospect of success represent legitimate criteria of inclusion for ELT selection. But it remains to examine the considerations which legitimate them. The legitimating factors are in the final analysis practical or pragmatic in nature. From the practical angle it is advantageous—indeed to some extent necessary—that the arrangements governing medical institutions should embody certain constituency principles. It makes good pragmatic and utilitarian sense that progress-of-science considerations should be operative here. And, finally, the practical aspect is reinforced by a whole host of other considerations—including moral ones—in supporting the prospect-of-success criterion. The workings of each of these factors are of course conditioned by the ever-present element of

Thus while it is true that the application of particular criteria or tests to determine the death of an individual may call for the expertise of a physician, there are other aspects of formulating a "definition" of death that are not particularly within medical competence. To be sure, in practice, so long as the standards being employed are stable and congruent with community opinion about the phenomenon of death, most people are content to leave the matter in medical hands.[25] But the underlying extra-medical aspects of the "definition" become visible, as they have recently, when medicine departs (or appears to depart) from the common or traditional understanding of the concept of death. The formulation of a concept of death is neither simply a technical matter nor one susceptible of empirical verification. The idea of death is at least partly a philosophical question, related to such ideas as "organism," "human," and "living." Physicians *qua* physicians are not expert on these philosophical questions, nor are they expert on the question of which physiological functions decisively identify a "living, human organism." They, like other scientists, can suggest which "vital signs" have what significance for which human functions. They may, for example, show that a person in an irreversible coma exhibits "total unawareness to externally applied stimuli and inner need and complete unresponsiveness,"[26] and they may predict that when tests for this condition yield the same results over a twenty-four-hour period there is only a very minute chance that the coma will ever be "reversed."[27] Yet the judgment that "total unawareness . . . and complete unresponsiveness" are the salient characteristics of death, or that a certain level of risk of error is acceptable, requires more than technical expertise and goes beyond medical authority, properly understood.

The proposed departure from the traditional standards for determining death not only calls attention to the extra-medical issues involved, but is itself a source of public confusion and concern. The confusion can perhaps be traced to the fact that the traditional signs of life (the beating heart and the expanding chest) are manifestly accessible to the senses of the layman, whereas some of the new criteria require sophisticated intervention to elicit latent signs of life such as

---

Death Act. The court of appeals found that there was sufficient eyewitness testimony by laymen to support the trial court's conclusion that Mrs. Schmidt survived her husband by some minutes, and it found no fault in the use of the *Black's Law Dictionary* "definition of death" despite the argument that it "is an anachronism in view of the recent medical developments relating to heart transplants," since there was no evidence that the deceased were resuscitable. *Id.* at 273, 67 Cal. Rptr. at 854 (dictum).

[25] *See* Arnold, *supra* note 15, at 1950, in which the public's "nearly complete acceptance" of professional practice in this century until cardiac transplantation began is contrasted with the great concern manifested in the 19th century and earlier, before embalming became routine, largely because of the fear of premature burial.

[26] *Irreversible Coma, supra* note 3, at 337.

[27] *See* note 12 *supra.*

brain reflexes. Furthermore, the new criteria may disturb the layman by suggesting that these visible and palpable traditional signs, still useful in most cases, may be deceiving him in cases where supportive machinery is being used. The anxiety may also be attributable to the apparent intention behind the "new definition," which is, at least in part, to facilitate other developments such as the transplantation of cadaver organs. Such confusion and anxiety about the standards for determining death can have far-reaching and distressing consequences for the patient's family, for the physician, for other patients, and for the community at large.[28] If the uncertainties surrounding the question of determining death are to be laid to rest, a clear and acceptable standard is needed. And if the formulation and adoption of this standard are not to be abdicated to the medical fraternity under an expanded view of its competence and authority, then the public and its representatives ought to be involved.[29] Even if the medical profession takes the lead—as indeed it has—in promoting new criteria of death, members of the public should at least have the opportunity to review, and either to affirm or reject the standards by which they are to be pronounced dead.

III. What Manner of Public Involvement?

There are a number of potential means for involving the public in this process of formulation and review, none of them perfect. The least ambitious or comprehensive is simply to encourage discussion of the issues by the lay press, civic groups, and the community at large. This public consideration might be directed or supported through the efforts of national organizations such as the American Medical Association, the National Institutes of Health, or the National

---

[28] *See* Sanders, *supra* note 22, at 407-09; 3 M. Houts & I. H. Haut, Courtroom Medicine § § 1.02(3) (a)-(g) (1971). As long as the legal standard is ambiguous, the possibility exists that the processes of criminal, as well as civil, justice will be impeded. *See, e.g.,* D. Meyers, The Human Body and the Law 116-18 (1970) (discussing an unreported British case, *Regina v. Potter,* in which a manslaughter defendant was convicted of common assault upon proof that surgeons had removed a kidney from the decedent while he was being maintained on a respirator and before he had been found to be "dead"); *Trial to Test M.D.'s Role in Death of Heart Donor,* A.M.A. News, Nov. 11, 1968, at 2 (man charged with manslaughter raised as defense surgeons' removal of victim's heart when he was kept alive by artificial means).

[29] Matte, *Law, Morals, and Medicine: A Method of Approach to Current Problems,* 13 J. For. Sci. 318, 331-32 (1968). *See also* note 19 *supra.*

A theoretical risk of illegal conduct exists in the present state of the law. The law is apparently waiting for a social and theological consensus on this point [of "defining" death]. . . . The theologians, the philosophers and the physicians will have to formulate the judgment of propriety here before it is crystallized into a definite statutory rule.

Discussion of Louisell, *Transplantation: Existing Legal Constraints,* in Medical Progress, *supra* note 1, at 99 (comments of Prof. D. W. Louisell).

Academy of Sciences.[30] A resolution calling for the establishment of an ad hoc body to evaluate public attitudes toward the changes wrought by biomedical advances has been sponsored by Senator Mondale since 1967 and was adopted by the Senate in December 1971.[31] Mondale's proposed National Advisory Commission on Health Science and Society, under the direction of a board of fifteen members of the general public and professionals from "medicine, law, theology, biological science, physical science, social science, philosophy, humanities, health administration, government, and public affairs," would conduct "seminars and public hearings" as part of its two-year study.[32] As important as it is to ventilate the issues, studies and public discussions alone may not be adequate to the task. They cannot by themselves dispel the ambiguities which will continue to trouble decisionmakers and the public in determining whether an artificially-maintained, comatose "patient" is still alive.

A second alternative, reliance upon the judicial system, goes beyond ascertaining popular attitudes and could provide an authoritative opinion that might offer some guidance for decisionmakers. Reliance on judge-made law would, however, neither actively involve the public in the decisionmaking process nor lead to a prompt, clear, and general "definition." The courts, of course, cannot speak in the abstract prospectively, but must await litigation, which can involve considerable delay and expense, to the detriment of both the parties and society. A need to rely on the courts reflects an uncertainty in the law which is unfortunate in an area where private decisionmakers (physicians) must act quickly and irrevocably. An ambiguous legal standard endangers the rights—and in some cases the lives—of the participants. In such circumstances, a person's choice of one course over another may depend more on his willingness to test his views in court than on the relative merits of the courses of action.[33]

---

[30] For example, early in the debate over heart replacement the Board on Medicine of the National Academy issued a "Statement on Cardiac Transplantation," but addressed itself primarily to the need for caution in the spread of the operation to medical centers which were not suited to carrying it out scientifically. 18 News Report of the National Academy of Sciences 1 (Mar. 1968).

[31] S. J. Res. 75, 92d Cong., 1st Sess. (1971), in 117 Cong. Rec. S20,089-93 (daily ed. Dec. 2, 1971). *See also* note 18 *supra.* The joint resolution is now in the House Committee on Interstate Commerce.

[32] S. J. Res. 75, 92d Cong., 1st Sess. (1971), in 117 Cong. Rec. S20,090 (daily ed. Dec. 2, 1971).

[33] For example, suppose that transplant surgeons were willing to employ a neurological definition of death, although most other physicians continued to use the "traditional" definition because of the unsettled nature of the law. If (*ex hypothesis*) those surgeons were less averse to the risks of testing their position in litigation, because of their temperament, training, values and commitments, or desire for success, their "courage" could lead to patients being declared dead prematurely according to the traditional standard.

Once called upon to "redefine" death—for example, in a suit brought by a patient's relatives or, perhaps, by a revived "corpse" against the physician declaring death—the judiciary may be as well qualified to perform the task as any governmental body. If the issue could be resolved solely by a process of reasoning and of taking "judicial notice" of widely known and uncontroverted facts, a court could handle it without difficulty. If, on the other hand, technical expertise is required problems may arise. Courts operate within a limited compass—the facts and contentions of a particular case—and with limited expertise; they have neither the staff nor the authority to investigate or to conduct hearings in order to explore such issues as public opinion or the scientific merits of competing "definitions."[34] Consequently, a judge's decision may be merely a rubberstamping of the opinions expressed by the medical experts who appear before him.[35] Indeed, those who believe that the "definition of death" should be left in the hands of physicians favor the judicial route over the legislative on the assumption that, in the event of a law suit, the courts will approve "the consensus view of the medical profession"[36] in favor of the new standards. Leaving the task of articulating a new set of standards to the courts may prove unsatisfactory, however, if one believes, as suggested previously, that the formulation of such standards, as opposed to their application in particular cases, goes beyond the authority of the medical profession.[37]

Uncertainties in the law are, to be sure, inevitable at times and are often tolerated if they do not involve matters of general applicability or great moment. Yet the question of whether and when a person is dead plainly seems the sort of issue that cannot escape the need for legal clarity on these grounds. Therefore, it is not surprising that although they would be pleased simply to have the courts

---

[34] *See, e.g.,* Repouille v. United States, 165 F.2d 152, 153 (2d Cir. 1947) (L. Hand, J.), 154 (Frank, J., dissenting).

[35] Because of the adversary nature of the judicial process, testimony is usually restricted to the "two sides" of an issue and may not fairly represent the spectrum of opinion held by authorities in the field.

[36] Kennedy, *supra* note 20, at 947. Kennedy's reliance on a medical "consensus" has a number of weaknesses, which he himself seems to acknowledge: (1) there may be "a wide range of opinions" held by doctors, so that "there need not necessarily be only one view" on a subject which is supported by the medical community, in part because (2) the "usual ways" for these matters to be "discussed and debated" are not very clear or rigorous since (3) the "American medical profession is not all that well regulated" unlike its British counterpart and (4) is not organized to give "official approval" to a single position or (5) to give force to its decision, meaning (6) that "the task will be assumed by some other body, most probably the legislature." *Id.*

[37] *Cf.* Blocker v. United States, 288 F.2d 853, 860 (D.C. Cir. 1961) (en banc) (Burger, J., concurring in the result) (criticizing psychiatrists' attempt to alter legal definition of "mental disease").

endorse their views, members of the medical profession are doubtful that the judicial mode of lawmaking offers them adequate protection in this area. [38] There is currently no way to be certain that a doctor would not be liable, criminally or civilly, if he ceased treatment of a person found to be dead according to the Harvard Committee's criteria but not according to the "complete cessation of all vital functions" test presently employed by the courts. Although such "definitions" were adopted in cases involving inheritors' rights and survivorship[39] rather than a doctor's liability for exercising his judgment about when a person has died, physicians have with good reason felt that this affords them little assurance that the courts would not rely upon those cases as precedent.[40] On the contrary, it is reasonable to expect that the courts would seek precedent in these circumstances. Adherence to past decisions is valued because it increases the likelihood that an individual will be treated fairly and impartially; it also removes the need to relitigate every issue in every case. Most importantly, courts are not inclined to depart from existing rules because to do so may upset the societal assumption that one may take actions, and rely upon the actions of others, without fear that the ground rules will be changed retroactively.[41]

Considerations of precedent as well as other problems with relying on the judicial formulation of a new definition were made apparent in *Tucker v. Lower*,[42] the first case to present the question of the "definition of death" in the context of organ transplantation. Above all, this case demonstrates the uncertainty that is inherent in the process of litigation, which "was touch and go

---

[38] *See* note 19 *supra.*

[39] *See* notes 23-24 *supra; cf.* Gray v. Sawyer, 247 S.W.2d 496 (Ky. 1952).

[40] *See* Taylor, *supra* note 5, at 296. *But cf.* Kennedy, *supra* note 20, at 947.

[41] "[R]ules of law on which men rely in their business dealings should not be changed in the middle of the game . . ." Woods v. Lancet, 303 N.Y. 349, 354, 102 N.E.2d 691, 695 (1951). It must be admitted, however, that such principles usually find their most forceful articulation when the court is about to proceed on the counter-principle that when necessary the common law will change with the times to achieve justice. (In *Woods,* for example, the New York Court of Appeals overruled its prior decision in Drobner v. Peters, 232 N.Y. 220, 133 N.E. 567 (1921), in order to permit a child to sue for prenatal injuries.) Although in this country, at least, strict adherence to precedent has been less true on the civil side than on the criminal (where the courts hold closer to the doctrine of *nullum crimen sine lege* than do English courts), it is probably fair to state that judges are more likely to depart from precedent in order to *create* a new cause of action than they are to reject an existing standard and thereby destroy a cause; to adjust the "definition of death" to the perhaps changing views of the medical profession would be to derogate the rights of those litigants injured by declarations of death which departed from previously accepted standards.

[42] Tucker v. Lower, No. 2831 (Richmond, Va., L. & Eq. Ct., May 23, 1972).

for the medical profession"[43] as well as the defendants. *Tucker* involved a $100,000 damage action against Drs. David Hume and Richard Lower and other defendant doctors on the Medical College of Virginia transplant team, brought by William E. Tucker, whose brother's heart was removed on May 25, 1968, in the world's seventeenth human heart transplant. The plaintiff claimed that the heart was taken without approval of the next of kin and that the operation was commenced before his brother had died. On the latter point, William Tucker offered evidence that his brother was admitted to the hospital with severe head injuries sustained in a fall and that after a neurological operation he was placed on a respirator. At the time he was taken to the operating room to have his organs removed "he maintained vital signs of life, that is, . . normal body temperature, normal pulse, normal blood pressure and normal rate of respiration."[44] Based on the neurologist's finding that the brother was dead from a neurological standpoint, the respirator was turned off and he was pronounced dead. The defendants moved to strike the plaintiff's evidence and for summary judgment in their favor, but the trial judge denied the motions.

> The function of This Court is to determine the state of the law on this or any other subject according to legal precedent and principle. The courts which have had occasion to rule upon the nature of death and its timing have all decided that death occurs at a precise time, and that it is defined as the cessation of life; the ceasing to exist; a total stoppage of the circulation of the blood, and a cessation of the animal and vital functions consequent thereto such as respiration and pulsation.[45]

The court adhered to "the legal concept of death" and rejected "the invitation offered by the defendants to employ a medical concept of neurological death in establishing a rule of law."[46] The court ruled that the jury would be allowed to assess damages if it concluded "that the decedent's life was terminated at a time earlier than it would ordinarily have ended had all reasonable medical efforts been continued to prolong his life."[47]

When he sent the case to the jurors, however, the judge permitted them to consider all possible causes of death, including injury to the brain as well as cessation of breathing or heartbeat, and a verdict was returned for the defendants. Unfortunately, the discrepancy between the initial ruling and the subse-

---

[43] 15 Drug Research Rep., June 7, 1972, at 1.

[44] Tucker v. Lower, No. 2831, at 4 (Richmond, Va., L. & Eq. Ct., May 23, 1972).

[45] *Id.* at 8 (citations omitted).

[46] *Id.*

> While it is recognized that none of the cases cited above involved transplants, to employ a different standard in this field would create chaos in other fields of the law and certainly it cannot be successfully argued that there should be one concept of death which applies to one type of litigation while an entirely different standard applies in other areas.

Id. at 8-9.

[47] *Id.* at 11.

quent instructions to the jury did little to resolve the legal uncertainty. The plaintiff has announced that he plans to appeal to the Supreme Court of Virginia,[48] and the creation of a clear and binding rule will depend on the action of that court.[49]

In declining the defendants' suggestion that he adopt a standard based on neurological signs, the judge stated that application for "such a radical change" in the law should be made "not to the courts but to the legislature wherein the basic concepts of our society relating to the preservation and extension of life could be examined and, if necessary, reevaluated."[50] A statutory "definition" of death would have notable advantages as an alternative to a judicial promulgation. Basically, the legislative process permits the public to play a more active role in decisionmaking and allows a wider range of information to enter into the framing the criteria for determining death. Moreover, by providing prospective guidance, statutory standards could dispel public and professional doubt, and could provide needed reassurance for physicians and patients' families, thereby reducing both the fear and the likelihood of litigation for malpractice (or even for homicide).

The legislative alternative also has a number of drawbacks, however. Foremost among these is the danger that a statute "defining" death may be badly drafted. It may be either too general or too specific, or it may be so poorly worded that it will leave physicians or laymen unsure of its intent. There is also the danger that the statutory language might seem to preclude future refinements that expanding medical knowledge would introduce into the tests and procedures for determining death. The problem of bad draftsmanship is compounded by the fact that a statute once enacted may be difficult to revise or repeal, leaving to the slow and uncertain process of litigation the clarification of its intent and meaning.[51] By contrast, although judges usually espouse the doctrine of stare decisis, flexibility over time is a hallmark of the common law. An additional practical problem is the possibility that the statutes enacted may reflect primarily the interests of powerful lobbying groups—for example, state medical societies or transplant surgeons. This possibility—similar to the danger of judicial "rubberstamping" of medical experts' opinions—may be avoided by legislatures' holding open and well-publicized hearings at which sociologists,

[48] N.Y. Times, May 27, 1972, at 15, col. 5; *id.,* June 4, 1972, § 4, at 7, col. 1.

[49] As one medical journal, which favors legislative formulation of a "definition," said of the decision of the Richmond court: "It applies only to cases coming before that court and can be reversed on appeal or overriden by contrary decisions handed down in higher courts." 15 Drug Research Rep., June 7, 1972, at 1.

[50] Tucker v. Lower, No. 2831, at 10 (Richmond, Va., L. & Eq. Ct., May 23, 1972).

[51] The general durability of statutes has the backhanded advantage, however, of emphasizing for the public as well as for legislators the importance of a thorough thrashing out of the issues in hearings and legislative debates.

lawyers, theologians, and representatives of various viewpoints are also called upon to testify.

Professor Ian Kennedy has suggested the further danger that a statutory "definition," rather than protecting the public may leave it vulnerable to physicians who through "liberal interpretation and clever argument" might take actions "just within the letter if not the spirit of the law."[52] Kennedy would rely instead on the medical profession's generalized "consensus view"[53] of the proper "definition of death." It is, however, far from clear why physicians who would violate a statute are unlikely to depart from such an informal "consensus," which may or may not eventually be sanctioned by the courts. Legislation will not remove the need for reasoned interpretation—first by physicians and perhaps then by judges—but it can restrict the compass within which they make their choices to one which has been found acceptable by the public.

Finally, the legislative route may reduce the likelihood that conflicting "definitions" of death will be employed in different jurisdictions in this country. Theoretically, uniformity is also possible in judicial opinions, but it occurs infrequently. If the formulation and reception of the Uniform Anatomical Gift Act provide any precedent, the Commissioners on Uniform State Laws appear to be well situated to provide leadership in achieving an intelligent response to changes in medical procedure.[54]

In sum, then, official action, as opposed to mere discussion of the issues, is needed if the conflict between current medical practice and present law is to be eliminated. A reformulation of the standards for determining death should thus be undertaken by either courts or legislatures. There are strengths and weaknesses in both law-creating mechanisms, but on balance we believe that if legislators approach the issues with a critical and inquiring attitude, a statutory "definition" of death may be the best way to resolve the conflicting needs for definiteness and flexibility, for public involvement and scientific accuracy.[55]

[52] Kennedy, *supra* note 20, at 947.

[53] *Id.*

[54] Completed in July 1968 by the Commissioners on Uniform State Laws and approved by the American Bar Association in August of that year, the Uniform Anatomical Gift Act was adopted with only minor changes in 40 jurisdictions including the District of Columbia in 1969; by the end of 1971, the Act had been adopted in the remaining 11 states. For a detailed discussion of the national acceptance of the Act see Sadler, Sadler & Stason, *Transplantation and the Law: Progress Toward Uniformity,* 282 New Eng. J. Med. 717 (1970). *See also* Brickman, *Medico-Legal Problems with the Question of Death,* 5 Calif. W.L. Rev. 110, 122 (1968) (urging Commissioners to draft uniform act on "the procedures for determining death").

[55] This is, of course, not to say that a judge faced with a case to decide should hold back from engaging in the sort of analysis, or reaching the conclusions about a proper "definition," presented here. As Professor Clarence Morris once observed, the age-old argument that a legislature has a "superior opportunity" to frame general rules should not

Moreover, since pressures for a legislative response to the problem appear to be mounting,[56] careful examination of the proper scope and content of such a statute seems to be called for.

IV. What Can and Should Be Legislated?

Arguments both for and against the desirability of legislation "defining" death often fail to distinguish among the several different subjects that might be touched on by such legislation. As a result, a mistaken impression may exist that a single statutory model is, and must be, the object of debate. An appreciation of the multiple meanings of a "definition of death" may help to refine the deliberations.

Death, in the sense the term is of interest here, can be defined purely formally as the transition, however abrupt or gradual, between the state of being alive and the state of being dead.[57] There are at least four levels of "definitions" that would give substance to this formal notion; in principle, each could be the subject of legislation: (1) the basic concept or idea; (2) general physiological standards; (3) operational criteria; and (4) specific tests or procedures.[58]

---

foreclose judicial reform of the law where the legislature has failed to act. A judge has, after all, "no reliable way of knowing" that legislative action will ever be forthcoming, and if he acts in a way the legislature finds erroneous, his mistake can be set right by statute. Morris, *Liability for Pain and Suffering,* 59 Colum. L. Rev. 476, 482 (1959).

[56] *See* note 8 *supra.* It would certainly be preferable for state legislatures and the Uniform Act Commissioners to begin work on laws now, rather than risking the enactment of "emergency legislation hastily contrived in response to public pressure and emotional reaction to [a] particular medical calamity." Matte, *supra* note 29, at 332; *cf.* Woodside, *Organ Transplantation: The Doctor's Dilemma and the Lawyer's Responsibility* 31 Ohio St. L.J. 66, 96 (1970).

[57] For a debate on the underlying issues see Morison, *Death: Process or Event?,* 173 Science 694 (1970); Kass, *Death as an Event: A Commentary on Robert Morison,* 173 Science 698 (1971).

[58] To our knowledge, this delineation of four levels has not been made elsewhere in the existing literature on this subject. Therefore, the terms "concept," "standard," "criteria," and "tests and procedures" as used here bear no necessary connection to the ways in which others may use these same terms, and in fact we recognize that in some areas of discourse, the term "standards" is more, rather than less, operational and concrete than "criteria"—just the reverse of our ordering. Our terminology was selected so that the category we call "criteria" would correspond to the level of specificity at which the Ad Hoc Harvard Committee framed its proposals, which it called and which are widely referred to as the "new *criteria*" for determining death. We have attempted to be consistent in our use of these terms throughout this Article. Nevertheless, our major purpose here is not to achieve public acceptance of our terms, but to promote awareness of the four different levels of a "definition" of death to which the terms refer.

The *basic concept* of death is fundamentally a philosophical matter. Examples of possible "definitions" of death at this level include "permanent cessation of the integrated functioning of the organism as a whole," "departure of the animating or vital principle," or "irreversible loss of personhood." These abstract definitions offer little concrete help in the practical task of determining whether a person has died but they may very well influence how one goes about devising standards and criteria.

In setting forth the *general physiological standard(s)* for recognizing death, the definition moves to a level which is more medico-technical, but not wholly so. Philosophical issues persist in the choice to define death in terms of organ systems, physiological functions, or recognizable human activities, capacities, and conditions. Examples of possible general standards include "irreversible cessation of spontaneous respiratory and/or circulatory functions," "irreversible loss of spontaneous brain functions," "irreversible loss of the ability to respond or communicate," or some combination of these.

Operational criteria further define what is meant by the general physiological standards. The absence of cardiac contraction and lack of movement of the blood are examples of traditional criteria for "cessation of spontaneous circulatory functions," whereas deep coma, the absence of reflexes, and the lack of spontaneous muscular movements and spontaneous respiration are among criteria proposed for "cessation of spontaneous brain functions" by the Harvard Committee.[59]

Fourth, there are the *specific tests and procedures* to see if the criteria are fulfilled. Pulse, heart beat, blood pressure, electrocardiogram, and examination of blood flow in the retinal vessels are among the specific tests of cardiac contraction and movement of the blood. Reaction to painful stimuli, appearance of the pupils and their responsiveness to light, and observation of movement and breathing over a specified time period are among specific tests of the "brain function" criteria enumerated above.

There appears to be general agreement that legislation should not seek to "define death" at either the most general or the most specific levels (the first and fourth). In the case of the former, differences of opinion would seem hard to resolve, and agreement, if it were possible, would provide little guidance for practice.[60] In the case of the latter, the specific tests and procedures must be kept open to charges in medical knowledge and technology. Thus, arguments concerning the advisability and desirability of a statutory definition of death are usually confined to the two levels we have called "standards" and "criteria," yet often without any apparent awareness of the distinction between them. The need for flexibility in the face of medical advance would appear to be a persuasive argument for not legislating any specific operational criteria. More-

---

[59] *See* notes 3, 10 *supra.*
[60] *Cf.* Robertson, *Criteria of Death,* 175 Science 581 (1972) (letter to the editor).

over, these are almost exclusively technical matters, best left to the judgment of physicians. Thus, the kind of "definition" suitable for legislation would be a definition of the general physiological standard or standards. Such a definition, while not immutable, could be expected to be useful for a long period of time and would therefore not require frequent amendment.

There are other matters that could be comprehended in legislation "defining" death. The statute could specify who (and how many) shall make the determination. In the absence of a compelling reason to change past practices, this may continue to be set at "a physician,"[61] usually the doctor attending a dying patient or the one who happens to be at the scene of an accident. Moreover, the law ought probably to specify the "time of death." The statute may seek to fix the precise time when death may be said to have occurred, or it may merely seek to define a time that is clearly after "the precise moment," that is, a time when it is possible to say "the patient is dead," rather than "the patient has just now died." If the medical procedures used in determining that death has occurred call for verification of the findings after a fixed period of time (for example, the Harvard Committee's recommendation that the tests be repeated after twenty-four hours), the statute could in principle assign the "moment of death" to either the time when the criteria were first met or the time of verification. The former has been the practice with the traditional criteria for determining death.[62]

Finally, legislation could speak to what follows upon the determination. The statute could be permissive or prescriptive in determining various possible subsequent events, including especially the pronouncement and recording of the death, and the use of the body for burial or other purposes.[63] It is our view that these matters are best handled outside of a statute which has as its purpose to "define death."[64]

---

[61] *Cf.* Uniform Anatomical Gift Act § 7(b).

[62] *See* note 99 *infra* & accompanying text.

[63] If . . . sound procedures for stating death are agreed to and carried out, then theologians and moralists and every other thoughtful person should agree with the physicians who hold that it is *then* permissible to maintain circulation of blood and supply of oxygen in the corpse of a donor to preserve an *organ* until it can be used in transplantation. Whether one gives the body over for decent burial, performs an autopsy, gives the cadaver for use in medical education, or uses it as a "vital organ bank" are all alike procedures governed by decent respect for the bodies of deceased men and specific regulations that ensure this. The ventilation and circulation of organs for transplant raises no question not already raised by these standard procedures. None are life-and-death matters.
P. Ramsey, The Patient as Person 72 (1970).

[64] Nevertheless, a statutory "definition" of death would most appropriately be codified with the provisions on the procedures to be followed to certify death, undertake post-mortem examinations, and so forth. For the reasons given below, the statute "defining" death ought not to be appended to the Uniform Anatomical Gift Act or other "special purpose" laws, however. *See* notes 65, 79-80 *infra* & accompanying text.

V. Principles Governing the Formulation of a Statute

In addition to carefully selecting the proper degree of specificity for legislation, there are a number of other principles we believe should guide the drafting of a statute "defining" death. First, the phenomenon of interest to physicians, legislators, and laymen alike is human death. Therefore, the statute should concern the death of a human being, not the death of his cells, tissues or organs, and not the "death" or cessation of his role as a fully functioning member of his family or community. This point merits considerable emphasis. There may be a proper place for a statutory standard for deciding when to turn off a respirator which is ventilating a patient still clearly alive, or, for that matter, to cease giving any other form of therapy.[65] But it is crucial to distinguish this question of "when to allow to die?" from the question with which we are here concerned, namely, "when to declare dead?" Since very different issues and purposes are involved in these questions, confusing the one with the other clouds the analysis of both. The problem of determining when a person is dead is difficult enough without its being tied to the problem of whether physicians, or anyone else, may hasten the death of a terminally-ill patient, with or without his consent or that of his relatives, in order to minimize his suffering or to conserve scarce medical resources.[66] Although the same set of

[65] *See* Potter, *The Paradoxical Preservation of a Principle,* 13 Vill. L. Rev. 784, 791 (1968):
  What type of questions are entailed in the debate concerning when a comatose patient should be declared dead? Medical questions and answers are only one element of the decisionmaking process. Medical skill may be used to establish that a patient has now entered and is likely to remain in a certain condition. But medical personnel along with the other members of the community must then ask: "What are we to do with patients in this condition?" The answer to that question does not flow directly from any medical knowledge. It is a question of social policy which must be decided by the entire community. Implementation of the communal policy may be left in the hands of physicians, but they act as agents of the communal conscience.
  See generally Note, *Death with Dignity: A Recommendation for Statutory Change,* 22 U. Fla. L. Rev. 368 (1970); Fletcher, *Legal Aspects of the Decision Not to Prolong Life,* 203 J.A.M.A. 65 (1968); Sharpe & Hargest, *Lifesaving Treatment for Unwilling Patients,* 36 Fordham L. Rev. 695 (1968); Note, *The Dying Patient: A Qualified Right to Refuse Medical Treatment,* 7 J. Fam. L. 644 (1967); Elkinton, *The Dying Patient, The Doctor and the Law,* 13 Vill. L. Rev. 740 (1968); Biörck, *supra* note 15, at 488-90.
[66] The ease with which the two questions can become confused is demonstrated by the following "general definition of human death" proposed in Halley & Harvey, *Medical vs. Legal Definitions of Death,* 204 J.A.M.A. 423, 425 (1968);
  Death is irreversible cessation of *all* of the following: (1) total cerebral function, (2) spontaneous function of the respiratory system, and (3) spontaneous function of the circulatory system.
  Special circumstances may, however, justify the pronouncement of death when consultation consistent with established professional standards have been obtained and

social and medical conditions may give rise to both problems, they must be kept separate if they are to be clearly understood.

Distinguishing the question "is he dead?" from the question "should he be allowed to die?" also assists in preserving continuity with tradition, a second important principle. By restricting itself to the "is he dead?" issue, a revised "definition" permits practices to move incrementally, not by replacing traditional cardiopulmonary standards for the determination of death but rather by supplementing them. These standards are, after all, still adequate in the majority of cases, and are the ones that both physicians and the public are in the habit of employing and relying on. The supplementary standards are needed primarily for those cases in which artificial means of support of comatose patients render the traditional standards unreliable.

Third, this incremental approach is useful for the additional and perhaps most central reason that any new means for judging death should be seen as just that and nothing more—a change in method dictated by advances in medical practice, but not an alteration of the meaning of "life" and "death." By indicating that the various standards for measuring death relate to a single phenomenon legislation can serve to reduce a primary source of public uneasiness on this subject.[67] Once it has been established that certain consequences—for example, burial, autopsy, transfer of property to the heirs, and so forth—follow from a determination of death, definite problems would arise if there were a number of "definitions" according to which some people could be said to be "more dead" than others.

There are, of course, many instances in which the law has established differing definitions of a term, each framed to serve a particular purpose. One wonders, however, whether it does not appear somewhat foolish for the law to offer a number of arbitrary definitions of a natural phenomenon such as death. Nevertheless, legislators might seek to identify a series of points during the process of dying, each of which might be labelled "death" for certain purposes. Yet so far as we know, no arguments have been presented for special purpose standards except in the area of organ transplantation. Such a separate "defini-

---

when valid consent to withhold or stop resuscitative measures has been given by the appropriate relative or legal guardian.

The authors seem to have realized the mistake in making the state of being dead (rather than the acceptance of imminent death) depend on the "consent" of a relative or guardian, and this aspect of the "definition of death" is absent from their subsequent writings. See, e.g., Halley & Harvey, Law-Medicine Comment: The Definitional Dilemma of Death, 37 J. Kan. B. Ass'n 179, 185 (1968); cf. D. Meyers, supra note 28, at 135-36 (criticizing Halley and Harvey's second definition for its internal inconsistency).

[67] See notes 15, 16 supra. The way in which cardiopulmonary and brain functions relate to each other and to the phenomenon of death is explored in note 89 infra.

tion of death," aimed at increasing the supply of viable organs, would permit physicians to declare a patient dead before his condition met the generally applicable standards for determining death if his organs are of potential use in transplantation. The adoption of a special standard risks abuse and confusion, however. The status of prospective organ donor is an arbitrary one to which a person can be assigned by relatives[68] or physicians and is unrelated to anything about the extent to which his body's functioning has deteriorated. A special "definition" of death for transplantation purposes would thus need to be surrounded by a set of procedural safeguards that would govern not only the method by which a person is to be declared dead but also those by which he is to be classified as an organ donor.[69] Even more troublesome is the confusion over the meaning of death that would probably be engendered by multiple "definitions."[70] Consequently, it would be highly desirable if a statute on death could avoid the problems with a special "definition." Should the statute happen to facilitate organ transplantation, either by making more organs available or by making prospective donors and transplant surgeons more secure in knowing what the law would permit, so much the better.[71]

If, however, more organs are needed for transplantation than can be legally obtained, the question whether the benefits conferred by transplantation justify the risks associated with a broader "definition" of death should be addressed directly[72] rather than by attempting to subsume it under the question "what is

---

[68] Uniform Anatomical Gift Act § 2(c). For example, if a special standard were adopted for determining death in potential organ donors, relatives of a dying patient with limited financial means might feel substantial pressure to give permission for his organs to be removed in order to bring to a speedier end the care given the patient.

[69] The Uniform Anatomical Gift Act, which establishes procedures for the donation of organs by an individual or his relatives, appears to operate on the premise that "death" will be determined by standards which are generally accepted and applied in the ordinary course of events; it does not undertake to "define" death. *But cf.* note 100 *infra*.

[70] For instance, suppose that Mr. Smith, a dying patient in University Hospital, is found to be immunologically well matched with Mr. Jones, a University Hospital patient awaiting a heart transplant. Under the special transplantation "definition" Smith is then declared dead, but just as the surgeons are about to remove Smith's heart, Jones suddenly dies. The doctors then decide that Smith is no longer needed as an organ donor. His condition does not meet the standards for declaring death in nondonors. Is Smith "dead" or "alive"?

[71] This would be the case if the generally applicable standards for determining death permit organs to be removed at a time when they are still useable for transplantation purposes. The "definition" suggested by the Article meets this objective, we believe.

[72] Much of the public's fear of premature excision arises from the failure to distinguish the general practitioner's and the transplant surgeon's meaning of the term 'death'. It would be desirable to distinguish the two formally, and use different terms.
Hillman & Aldridge, *Towards a Legal Definition of Death,* 116 Sol. J. 323, 324 (1972) [hereinafter cited as Hillman]. These British medical-legal commentators suggest that

death?" Such a direct confrontation with the issue could lead to a discussion about the standards and procedures under which organs might be taken from persons near death, or even those still quite alive, at their own option[73] or that of relatives, physicians, or representatives of the state. The major advantage of keeping the issues separate is not, of course, that this will facilitate transplantation, but that it will remove a present source of concern: it is unsettling to contemplate that as you lie slowly dying physicians are free to use a more "lenient" standard to declare you dead if they want to remove your organs for transplantation into other patients.

Fourth, the standards for determining death ought not only to relate to a single phenomenon but should also be applied uniformly to all persons. A person's wealth or his "social utility" as an organ donor should not affect the way in which the moment of his death is determined.

Finally, while there is a need for uniformity of application at any one time, the fact that changes in medical technology brought about the present need for "redefinition" argues that the new formulation should be flexible. As suggested in the previous section, such flexibility is most easily accomplished if the new "definition" confines itself to the general standards by which death is to be determined and leaves to the continuing exercise of judgment by physicians the establishment and application of appropriate criteria and specific tests for determining that the standards have been met.

"irreversible brain damage," which would include patients with no higher brain activity but continued spontaneous respiration, be recognized as a ground for removal of organs prior to ordinary death. They contemplate that certain "essential safeguards" be incorporated into a statute on "irreversible brain damage" to avoid abuse of this category. *Id.* 325.

Prior to the first heart transplant in France, a special "definition" was enacted to remove any uncertainty about the permissibility of removing a beating heart from a "dead" donor. In April 1968 the government decreed a "definition of clinical death" for use with organ donors, based on a flat electroencephalogram of ten minutes duration which was taken to show that an artificially maintained patient lacks "function in the higher nervous centers." D. Meyers, *supra* note 28, at 113. Meyers seems to question this approach; he believes that the public must be shown

not just that the brain has been irreparably damaged, but also that the extent of this damage is absolutely inconsistent with continued maintenance of independent life in the individual. If electro-enphalograph testing can in fact show this, then it is a valuable definitional tool in ascertaining clinical death; but the medical profession as yet appears somewhat divided on its reliability. In such circumstances, the public cannot be expected to accept the evidence of an electro-encephalographic reading as part of a legislative definition of death.

Id. 135.

[73] *See, e.g.,* Blachly, *Can Organ Transplantation Provide an Altruistic-Expiatory Alternative to Suicide?,* 1 Life-Threatening Behavior 6 (1971); Scribner, *Ethical Problems of Using*

VI. The Kansas Statute

The first attempt at a legislative resolution of the problems discussed here was made in 1970 when the State of Kansas adopted "An Act relating to and defining death."[74] The Kansas statute has received a good deal of attention; similar legislation was enacted in the spring of 1972 in Maryland and is presently under consideration in a number of other jurisdictions.[75] The Kansas legislation, which was drafted in response to developments in organ transplantation and medical support of dying patients, provides "alternative definitions of death," [76] set forth in two paragraphs. Under the first, a person is considered "medically and legally dead" if a physician determines "there is the absence of spontaneous respiratory and cardiac function and . . . attempts at resuscitation are considered hopeless."[77] In the second "definition," death turns on the absence of spon-

---

Artificial Organs to Sustain Human Life, 10 Trans. Am. Soc. Artif. Internal Organs 209, 211 (1964) (advocating legal guidelines to permit voluntary euthanasia for purpose of donating organs for transplantation).

[74] Law of Mar. 17, 1970, ch. 378, [1970] Kan. Laws 994 (codified at Kan. Stat. Ann. § 77-202 (Supp. 1971)). It provides in full:

A person will be considered medically and legally dead if, in the opinion of a physician, based on ordinary standards of medical practice, there is the absence of spontaneous respiratory and cardiac function and, because of the disease or condition which caused, directly or indirectly, these functions to cease, or because of the passage of time since these functions ceased, attempts at resuscitation are considered hopeless; and, in this event, death will have occurred at the time these functions ceased; or

A person will be considered medically and legally dead if, in the opinion of a physician, based on ordinary standards of medical practice, there is the absence of spontaneous brain function; and if based on ordinary standards of medical practice, during reasonable attempts to either maintain or restore spontaneous circulatory or respiratory function in the absence of aforesaid brain function, it appears that further attempts at resuscitation or supportive maintenance will not succeed, death will have occurred at the time when these conditions first coincide. Death is to be pronounced before artificial means of supporting respiratory and circulatory function are terminated and before any vital organ is removed for purposes of transplantation.

These alternative definitions of death are to be utilized for all purposes in this state, including the trials of civil and criminal cases, any laws to the contrary notwithstanding.

[75] *See* note 4 *supra.* In the Maryland law, which is nearly identical to its Kansas progenitor, the phrase "in the opinion of a physician" was deleted from the first paragraph, and the phrase "and because of a known disease or condition" was added to the second paragraph following "ordinary standards of medical practice." Maryland Sessions Laws ch. 693 (1972). Interestingly, Kansas and Maryland were also among the first states to adopt the Uniform Anatomical Gift Act in 1968, even prior to its official revision and approval by the National Conference of Commissioners on Uniform State Laws.

[76] Note 74 *supra.*

[77] *Id.* In using the term "hopeless," the Kansas legislature apparently intended to indicate that the "absence of spontaneous respiratory and cardiac function" must be irreversible

taneous brain function if during "reasonable attempts" either to "maintain or restore spontaneous circulatory or respiratory function," it appears that "further attempts at resuscitation or supportive maintenance will not succeed."[78] The purpose of the latter "definition" is made clear by the final sentence of the second paragraph:

> Death is to be pronounced before artificial means of supporting respiratory and circulatory function are terminated and *before any vital organ is removed for the purpose of transplantation.*[79]

The primary fault with this legislation is that it appears to be based on, or at least gives voice to, the misconception that there are two separate phenomena of death. This dichotomy is particularly unfortunate because it seems to have been inspired by a desire to establish a special definition for organ transplantation, a definition which physicians would not, however, have to apply, in the drafts-man's words, "to prove the irrelevant deaths of most persons."[80] Although there is nothing in the Act itself to indicate that physicians will be less concerned with safeguarding the health of potential organ donors, the purposes for which the Act was passed are not hard to decipher, and they do little to inspire the average patient with confidence that his welfare (including his not being prematurely declared dead) is of as great concern to medicine and the State of Kansas as is the facilitation of organ transplantation.[81] As Professor Kennedy cogently observes, "public disquiet [over transplantation] is in no way allayed by the existence in legislative form of what appear to be alternative definitions of death."[82] One hopes that the form the statute takes does not reflect a conclusion on the part of the Kansas legislature that death occurs at two distinct points during the process of dying.[83] Yet this inference can be derived from the Act, leaving open the prospect "that X at a certain stage in the

---

before death is pronounced. In addition to being rather roundabout, this formulation is also confusing in that it might be taken to address the "when to allow to die?" question as well as the "is he dead?" question. *See* note 85 *infra* & accompanying text.

[78] Note 74 *supra.*

[79] *Id.* (emphasis added).

[80] Taylor, *supra* note 5, at 296.

[81] *Cf.* Kass, *A Caveat on Transplants,* The Washington Post, Jan. 14, 1968, § B, at 1, col. 1; *Discussion* of Murray, *Organ Transplantation: The Practical Possibilities,* in Medical Progress, *supra* note 1, at 67 (comments of Dr. T. E. Starzl): "[T]he new risk is introduced [by the use of cadaver organs] that the terminal care of such potential donors may be adversely influenced by the events which are expected to follow after death, which might conceivably remove whatever small chance there might have been for survival."

[82] Kennedy, *supra* note 20, at 947.

[83] General use of the term "resuscitation" might suggest the existence of a common notion that a person can die once, be revived (given life again), and then die again at a later

process of dying can be pronounced dead, whereas Y, having arrived at the same point, is not said to be dead."[84]

The Kansas statute appears also to have attempted more than the "definition" of death, or rather, to have tried to resolve related questions by erroneously treating them as matters of "definition." One supporter of the statute praises it, we think mistakenly, for this reason: "Intentionally, the statute extends to these questions: When can a physician avoid attempting resuscitation? When can he terminate resuscitative efforts? When can he discontinue artificial maintenance?"[85] To be sure, "when the patient is dead" is one obvious answer to these questions, but by no means the only one. As indicated above, we believe that the question "when is the patient dead?" needs to be distinguished and treated separately from the questions "when may the doctor turn off the respirator?" or "when may a patient—dying yet still alive—be allowed to die?"

VII. A Statutory Proposal

As an alternative to the Kansas statute we propose the following:

> A person will be considered dead if in the announced opinion of a physician, based on ordinary standards of medical practice, he has experienced an irreversible cessation of spontaneous respiratory and circulatory functions. In the event that artificial means of support preclude a determination that these functions have ceased, a person will be considered dead if in the announced opinion of a physician, based on ordinary standards of medical practice, he has experienced an irreversible cessation of spontaneous brain functions. Death will have occurred at the time when the relevant functions ceased.

This proposed statute provides a "definition" of death confined to the level of *general physiological standards,* and it has been drafted in accord with the five

---

time—in other words, that death can occur at two or more distinct points in time. But resuscitation only restores life "from *apparent* death or unconsciousness." Webster's Third New International Dictionary 1937 (1966) (emphasis added). The proposed statute, text accompanying note 88 *infra,* takes account of the possibility of resuscitation by providing that death occurs only when there has been an *irreversible* cessation of the relevant vital bodily functions. *Cf.* 3 M. Houts & I. H. Haut, Courtroom Medicine § 1.01 (3) (d) (1971):

> The ability to resuscitate patients after apparent death, coupled with observations that in many cases the restoration was not to a state of consciousness, understanding and intellectual functioning, but merely to a decerebrate, vegetative existence, and with advances in neurology that have brought greater, though far from complete, understanding of the functions of the nervous system, has drawn attention to the role of the nervous system in maintaining life.

[84] Kennedy, *supra* note 20, at 948.
[85] Mills, *The Kansas Death Statute: Bold and Innovative,* 285 New Eng. J. Med. 968 (1971).

principles set forth above in section V. First, the proposal speaks in terms of the *death of a person.* The determination that a person has died is to be based on an evaluation of certain vital bodily functions, the permanent absence of which indicates that he is no longer a living human being. By concentrating on the death of a human being as a whole, the statute rightly disregards the fact that some cells or organs may continue to "live" after this point,[86] just as others may have ceased functioning long before the determination of death. This statute would leave for resolution by other means the question of when the absence or deterioration of certain capacities, such as the ability to communicate, or functions, such as the cerebral, indicates that a person may or should be allowed to die without further medical intervention.

Second, the proposed legislation is predicated upon the single phenomenon of death. Moreover, it applies uniformly to all persons,[87] by specifying the circumstances under which each of the standards is to be used rather than leaving this to the unguided discretion of physicians. Unlike the Kansas law, the model statute does not leave to arbitrary decision a choice between two apparently equal yet different "alternative definitions of death."[88] Rather, its second standard is applicable only when "artificial means of support preclude" use of the first. It does not establish a separate kind of death, called "brain death." In other words, the proposed law would provide two standards gauged by different functions, for measuring different manifestations of the same phenomenon. If cardiac and pulmonary functions have ceased, brain functions cannot continue; if there is no brain activity and respiration has to be maintained artificially, the same state (*i.e.,* death) exists.[89] Some people might prefer a single standard, one based either on cardiopulmonary or brain functions. This

---

[86] *Cf.* F. Moore, Transplant 27-36 (1972).

[87] Differences in the exact mode of diagnosing death will naturally occur as a result of differing circumstances under which the physician's examination is made. Thus, the techniques employed with an automobile accident victim lying on the roadside at night may be less sophisticated than those used with a patient who has been receiving treatment in a well-equipped hospital.

[88] Kan. Stat. Ann. § 77-202 (Supp. 1971).

[89] [L]ife is supported by the smooth and integrated function of three principal systems: circulatory, respiratory and nervous. . . . So long as the integrated function of these three systems continues, the individual lives. If any one of them ceases to function, failure of the other two will shortly follow, and the organism dies. In any case it is *anoxia,* or deprivation of oxygen, that is the ultimate cause of death of cells: in central nervous system failure, because the impulses which maintain respiration cease; in cardiac failure, because oxygenated blood is not moved to the cells; and in respiratory failure, because the blood, although circulating, is not releasing carbon dioxide nor replenishing oxygen in the lungs. Although other organs, such as the liver and kidneys, perform functions essential to life, their failure does not *per se* result in immediate death; it results, rather, in the

would have the advantage of removing the last trace of the "two deaths" image, which any reference to alternative standards may still leave. Respiratory and circulatory indicators, once the only touchstone, are no longer adequate in some situations. It would be possible, however, to adopt the alternative, namely that death is *always* to be established by assessing spontaneous brain functions. Reliance only on brain activity, however, would represent a sharp and unnecessary break with tradition. Departing from continuity with tradition is not only theoretically unfortunate in that it violates another principle of good legislation suggested previously, but also practically very difficult, since most physicians customarily employ cardiopulmonary tests for death and would be slow to change, especially when the old tests are easier to perform,[90] more accessible

---

eventual failure of one of the three systems described, and is thus only in indirect cause of death.

3 M. Houts & I. H. Haut, Courtroom Medicine § 1.01(2)(a) (1971).

It has long been known that, even when a patient loses consciousness and becomes areflexive, he may recover if heartbeat and breathing continue, but if they do not there is no hope of recovery. Thus, death came to be equated with the absence of these two "vital signs," although what was being detected was really the permanent cessation of the integrated functioning of the circulatory, respiratory, and nervous systems. In recent years, the traditional concept of death has been departed from, or at least severely strained, in the case of persons who were dead according to the rationale underlying the traditional standards in that they had experienced a period of anoxia long enough to destroy their brain functions, but in whom respiration and circulation were artifically re-created. By recognizng that such artificial means of support may preclude reliance on the traditional standards of circulation and respiration, the statute proposed here merely permits the logic behind the long-existing understanding (*i.e.*, integrated trisystemic functioning) to be served; it does not create any "new" type of death. Practically, of course, it accomplishes this end by articulating the "new" standard of "irreversible cessation of spontaneous brain functions," as another means of measuring the existing understanding. Dr. Jean Hamburger has observed, "After the guillotine has cut off a criminal's head, it is possible now to keep the heart and lungs going for days. Do you think that such a person is dead or alive?" *Discussion* of Louisell, *Transplantation: Existing Legal Constraints,* in Medical Progress, *supra* note 1, at 100. The purpose of the "new" standard is to make it clear that the answer to Hamburger's question is unequivocably that the person is dead. *Cf.* Gray v. Sawyer, 247 S.W.2d 496 (Ky. 1952) (newly discovered evidence that blood was gushing from decedent's decapitated body is significant proof that she was still alive following an accident); Biörck, *supra* note 15, at 485; Note, *supra* note 1, at 206.

[90] The clinical signs of irreversible loss of brain functions are probably not a great deal more difficult to elicit than the traditional signs of death are to detect, although the former are less accessible since they require active intervention to be educed and are not susceptible of mere observation. Aside from the taking of an electroencephalogram, the tests involved (such as tickling the cornea, irrigating the ear with ice water, and tapping the tendons with a reflex hammer) are fairly simple, but unlike the customary tests (such as listening for heartbeat with a stethoscope, seeing if a mirror held by the nose and mouth is clouded by breathing, and measuring pulse), they require equipment which a physician may be less likely to have at hand.

and acceptable to the lay public, and perfectly adequate for determining death in most instances.

Finally, by adopting standards for death in terms of the cessation of certain vital bodily functions but not in terms of the specific criteria or tests by which these functions are to be measured, the statute does not prevent physicians from adapting their procedures to changes in medical technology.[91]

A basic substantive issue remains: what are the merits of the proposed standards? For ordinary situations, the appropriateness of the traditional standard, "an irreversible cessation of spontaneous respiratory and circulatory functions,"[92] does not require elaboration. Indeed, examination by a physician may be more a formal than a real requirement in determining that most people have died. In addition to any obvious injuries, elementary signs of death such as absence of heartbeat and breathing, cold skin, fixed pupils, and so forth, are usually sufficient to indicate even to a layman that the accident victim, the elderly person who passes away quietly in the night, or the patient stricken with a sudden infarct has died.[93] The difficulties arise when modern medicine

[91] For example, it remains to be determined whether an electroencephalographic reading is necessary for an accurate diagnosis, as many now hold, or whether it should be regarded as having only "confirmatory value," as urged by the Harvard Committee. *See* note 11 *supra*.

[92] This language, taken from the proposed statute, is intended as a succinct summary of the standard now employed in ordinary circumstances. Of course, the requirement that the cessation of these functions be *irreversible* cannot be emphasized too strongly. A physician may be needed to make this determination in some cases—and to apply the means necessary to reverse a temporary cessation caused by a heart attack or the like. But laymen are also aware of the significance of the requirement as is indicated by the common practice of giving "first aid," in the form of artificial respiration, to restore breathing in victims of mishaps, particularly drowning, electric shock, and poisoning.

Two British commentators suggest that legislation "defining" death also prescribe the resuscitative efforts required to be made before death may be declared. Hillman, *supra* note 72, at 325. We believe it is enough to demand "irreversibility," as a consequence of which whatever attempts at resuscitation are established by current standards of good medical practice would be compelled.

[93] The statute provides that the determination of death depends on "the announced opinion of a physician." This raises two distinct sorts of questions. First, which physician's opinion is decisive? As previously observed, text accompanying note 64 *supra*, under "ordinary standards of medical practice" the physician declaring death would be the patient's own attending physician; this is particularly true of a patient who is receiving cardiopulmonary support in a hospital. Since, however, circumstances such as an automobile accident may arise in which death will have to be determined by a physician who had not previously attended the decedent, it was thought best to cast the language in terms of "a physician."

Second, questions may arise concerning the determination of death by nonphysicians. In an emergency, laymen may sometimes have to decide whether death has occurred, and to act on that determination, as in deciding whether to attempt to rescue someone who may or may not have already died. The proposed statute does nothing to change that

intervenes to sustain a patient's respiration and circulation. As we noted in discussing the Harvard Committee's conclusions, the indicators of brain damage appear reliable, in that studies have shown that patients who fit the Harvard criteria have suffered such extensive damage that they do not recover.[94] Of course, the task of the neurosurgeon or physician is simplified in the common case where an accident victim has suffered such gross, apparent injuries to the head that it is not necessary to apply the Harvard criteria in order to establish cessation of brain functioning.

The statutory standard, "irreversible cessation of spontaneous brain functions," is intended to encompass both higher brain activities and those of the brainstem. There must, of course, also be no spontaneous respiration; the second standard is applied only when breathing is being artificially maintained. The major emphasis placed on brain functioning, although generally consistent with the common view of what makes man distinctive as a living creature, brings to the fore a basic issue: What aspects of brain function should be decisive? The question has been reframed by some clinicians in light of their experience with patients who have undergone what they term "neocortical death" (that is, complete destruction of higher brain capacity, demonstrated by a flat E.E.G.). "Once neocortical death has been unequivocally established and the possibility of any recovery of consciousness and intellectual activity [is] thereby excluded, . . . although [the] patient breathes spontaneously, is he or she alive?"[95] While patients with irreversible brain damage from cardiac arrest seldom survive more than a few days, cases have recently been reported of survival for up to two and one-quarter years.[96] Nevertheless, though existence in this state falls far short of a full human life, the very fact of spontaneous respiration, as well as

---

practice or to alter any liability that might result under such circumstances, but merely specifies that an official determination must rest on "the opinion of a physician." This is consistent with existing state laws on the procedures by which death is "certified." These provisions, as well as ordinary medical practices, make it unnecessary to spell out in the model statute the exact manner in which the physician's opinion should be recorded or certified in the medical files or official documents.

[94] See note 12 supra & accompanying text.

[95] Brierley, Adams, Graham & Simpsom, Neocortical Death After Cardiac Arrest, 2 Lancet 560, 565 (1971) [hereinafter cited as Brierley]. In addition to a flat (isoelectric) electroencephalogram, a "neuropathological examination of a biopsy specimen . . . from the posterior half of a cerebral hemisphere" provides further confirmation. Id. The editors of a leading medical journal question "whether a state of cortical death can be diagnosed clinically." Editorial, Death of a Human Being, 2 Lancet 590 (1971). Cf. note 14 supra.

[96] Brierley and his colleagues report two cases of their own in which the patients each survived in a comatose condition for five months after suffering cardiac arrest before dying of pulmonary complications. They also mention two unreported cases of a Doctor Lewis, in one of which the patient survived for 2¼ years. Brierley, supra note 95, at 565.

coordinated movements and reflex activities at the brainstem and spinal cord levels, would exclude these patients from the scope of the statutory standards. [97] The condition of "neocortical death" may well be a proper justification for interrupting all forms of treatment and allowing these patients to die, but this moral and legal problem cannot and should not be settled by "defining" these people "dead."

The legislation suggested here departs from the Kansas statute in its basic approach to the problem of "defining" death: the proposed statute does not set about to establish a special category of "brain death" to be used by transplanters. Further, there are a number of particular points of difference between them. For example, the proposed statute does not speak of persons being "medically and legally dead," thus avoiding redundancy and, more importantly, the mistaken implication that the "medical" and "legal" definitions could differ.[98] Also, the proposed legislation does not include the provision that "death is to be pronounced before" the machine is turned off or any organs removed. Such a *modus operandi,* which was incorporated by Kansas from the Harvard Committee's report, may be advisable for physicians on public relations grounds, but it has no place in a statute "defining" death. The proposed statute already provides that "Death will have occurred at the time when the relevant functions ceased."[99] If supportive aids, or organs, are withdrawn after this time,

[97] The exclusion of patients without neocortical function from the category of death may appear somewhat arbitrary in light of our disinclination to engage in a philosophical discussion of the basic concepts of human "life" and "death." *See* text accompanying notes 57-60 *supra*. Were the "definition" contained in the proposed statute a departure from what has traditionally been meant by "death," such a conceptual discussion would clearly be in order. But, as this Article has tried to demonstrate, our intention has been more modest: to provide a clear restatement of the traditional understanding in terms which are useful in light of modern medical capabilities and practices. *See* note 89 *supra*.

A philosophical examination of the essential attributes of being "human" might lead one to conclude that persons who, for example, lack the mental capacity to communicate in any meaningful way, should be regarded as "not human" or "dead." It would nevertheless probably be necessary and prudent to treat the determination of that kind of "death" under special procedures until such time as medicine is able routinely to diagnose the extent and irreversibility of the loss of the "central human capacities" (however defined) with the same degree of assurance now possible in determining that death has occurred. Consequently, even at the conceptual level, we are inclined to think that it is best to distinguish the question "is he dead?" from such questions as "should he be allowed to die?" and "should his death be actively promoted?"

[98] The use of the word "legally" (as in "a person will be considered legally dead") in a law defining death is redundant. Besides, if there were a distinction between a "medical" and a "legal" standard of death, a statute could only legislate the legal standard. Consequently, the adjectives "medical" and "legal" are unnecessary as well as potentially misleading. *Cf.* Halley & Harvey, *Medical vs. Legal Definition of Death,* 204 J.A.M.A. 423 (1968).

[99] It is necessary to state a standard for judging *when* death occurred for disputes, typically concerning inheritance or rights of survivorship, in which the exact time of death is a

such acts cannot be implicated as having caused death. The manner in which, or exact time at which, the physician should articulate his finding is a matter best left to the exigencies of the situation, to local medical customs or hospital rules, or to statutes on the procedures for certifying death or on transplantation if the latter is the procedure which raises the greatest concern of medical impropriety. The real safeguard against doctors killing patients is not to be found in a statute "defining" death. Rather, it inheres in physicians' ethical and religious beliefs, which are also embodied in the fundamental professional ethic of *primum non nocere* and are reinforced by homicide and "wrongful death" laws and the rules governing medical negligence applicable in license revocation proceedings or in private actions for damages.

The proposed statute shares with the Kansas legislation two features of which Professor Kennedy is critical. First, it does not require that two physicians participate in determining death, as recommended by most groups which set forth suggestions about transplantation. The reasons for the absence of such a provision should be obvious. Since the statute deals with death in general and not with death in relation to transplantation, there is no reason for it to establish a general rule which is required only in that unusual situation. If particular dangers lurk in the transplantation setting, they should be dealt with in legislation on that subject, such as the Uniform Anatomical Gift Act.[100] If all current means of determining "irreversible cessation of spontaneous brain functions" are inherently so questionable that they should be double-checked by a second (or

---

decisive factor. The proposed statute, in accordance with existing practice, *see* text accompanying note 62 *supra,* fixes the time of death as the point at which the person actually dies, not the point at which the diagnosis is confirmed. This approach conforms to the commonsense understanding that both a man who dies in a coal mine and cannot be found for 24 hours and one who dies in a hospital where the practice is to require confirmation of the diagnosis by repeating the tests after 24 hours have been dead for a day before their deaths can be pronounced with certainty. The statutory phrase "relevant functions" refers to whichever functions are being measured: cardiopulmonary functions in the usual case, or brain functions where the others are obscured by the artificial means being employed.

[100] In fact, § 7(b) of the Uniform Anatomical Gift Act calls only for one physician: "The time of death [of a donor] shall be determined by a physician who attends the donor at his death, or, if none, the physician who certifies the death."

In *Tucker v. Lower* (*see* notes 42-50 *supra* & accompanying text) the defendants argued that this provision amounted to a "definition" of death (death is when a physician says you're dead), although Virginia had not adopted the Act until 1970, two years after the transplantation of the plaintiff's brother's heart. The court rejected this argument since "neither the decedent nor anyone acting on his behalf had made a gift of any part of his body" and the Act was therefore inapplicable. The reasons for rejecting the defendant's suggestion seem to us to go deeper; they have been presented throughout this Article and are summarized in the concluding section.

third, fourth, etc.) physician to be trustworthy, or if a certain means of measuring brain function requires as a technical matter the cooperation of two, or twenty, physicians, then the participation of the requisite number of experts would be part of the "ordinary standards of medical practice" that circumscribe the proper, non-negligent use of such procedures. It would be unfortunate, however, to introduce such a requirement into legislation which sets forth the general standards for determining who is dead, especially when it is done in such a way as to differentiate between one standard and another.

Kennedy's second objection, that a death statute ought to provide "for the separation and insulation of the physician (or physicians) attending the patient donor and certifying death, from the recipient of any organ that may be salvaged from the cadaver," is likewise unnecessary.[101] As was noted previously, language that relates only to transplantation has no place in a statute on the determination of death.

VIII. Conclusion

Changes in medical knowledge and procedures have created an apparent need for a clear and acceptable revision of the standards for determining that a person has died. Some commentators have argued that the formulation of such standards should be left to physicians. The reasons for rejecting this argument seem compelling: the "definition of death" is not merely a matter for technical expertise, the uncertainty of the present law is unhealthy for society and physicians alike, there is a great potential for mischief and harm through the possibility of conflict between the standards applied by some physicians and those assumed to be applicable by the community at large and its legal system, and patients and their relatives are made uneasy by physicians apparently being free to shift around the meaning of death without any societal guidance. Accordingly, we conclude the public has a legitimate role to play in the formulation and adoption of such standards. This article has proposed a model statute which bases a determination of death primarily on the traditional standard of final respiratory and circulatory cessation; where the artificial maintenance of these functions precludes the use of such a standard, the statute authorizes that death be determined on the basis of irreversible cessation of spontaneous brain functions. We believe the legislation proposed would dispel public confusion and concern and protect physicians and patients, while avoiding the creation of "two types of death," for which the statute on this subject

---

[101] Kennedy, *supra* note 20, at 949. Again, § 7(b) of the Uniform Anatomical Gift Act covers this point adequately: "The physician [who declares death] shall not participate in the procedures for removing or transplanting a part."

first adopted in Kansas has been justly criticized. The proposal is offered not as the ultimate solution to the problem, but as a catalyst for what we hope will be a robust and well-informed public debate over a new "definition." Finally, the proposed statute leaves for future resolution the even more difficult problems concerning the conditions and procedures under which a decision may be reached to cease treating a terminal patient who does not meet the standards set forth in the statutory "definition of death."

EXISTENTIALISM AND
THE FEAR OF DYING

MICHAEL A. SLOTE

In this paper I shall present a fairly systematic "existentialist" view of human anxiety about death and human responses to that anxiety, based on the work of Pascal, Kierkegaard, Heidegger, and Sartre. My main purpose is constructive, rather than exegetical. What seems to me most distinctive and important about the work of these existentialist authors is their approach to the fear of dying— or at least the relevance of what they say to that subject, for sometimes, when they deal with other topics, what they say can (I shall attempt to show) be used to illuminate the nature of human responses to the fear of death. But I think that much of what these authors say about the fear of dying is inchoate, confusing, or incomplete, and requires supplementation, clarification, and systematization of the kind I shall be attempting to provide here.[1]

I

Perhaps the central locus of discussion, by an existentialist, of human attitudes toward and responses to death is the section of Kierkegaard's *Concluding Unscientific Postscript* called "The Task of Becoming Subjective." According to Kierkegaard, becoming subjective is "the most difficult of all tasks in fact, precisely because every human being has a strong natural bent and passion to become something more and different."[2] But what is it to be subjective or to be objective, and why is the former so difficult and the latter so tempting? Part of Kierkegaard's explanation involves him in a contrast between the subjective and objective acceptance of Christianity. But Kierkegaard also applies the subjective/objective distinction to attitudes toward life and death generally.

---

[1] I shall by no means, however, be discussing all the things these authors say on the topic of death.

[2] *Concluding Unscientific Postscript* (Princeton, 1960), p. 116.

Reprinted from *American Philosophical Quarterly*, *12*(1): 17–28, January 1975, with the kind permission of the author and editor.

And what unites Kierkegaard in the "Becoming Subjective" section of the *Postscript* with such nonreligious existentialists as Heidegger and Sartre is the fact that he has something to say about human attitudes toward life and death that presupposes no particular form of religiosity and that has not, I think, been said by anyone outside the existentialist tradition. And it is this aspect of Kierkegaard's work that I shall be examining.

According to Kierkegaard, to have an objective attitude toward one's life is to have the kind of attitude toward one's life encouraged by an Hegelian view of the world. On such a view, one is part of a larger "world-historical" process of the self-realization of Reason or Spirit, and one's life takes on significance if one plays a role, however minor, in that world-historical process. One does not have to be an Hegelian to think in this kind of way. One can be thinking in a similar way if, as a scientist or philosopher, e.g., one devotes oneself to one's field in the belief or hope that one's life gains significance through one's contribution to something "bigger."

Kierkegaard says that people with such an attitude have an objective attitude toward their lives; and he wants each of us to dare to become subjective and renounce this "loftily pretentious and yet delusive intercourse" with the world historical.[3] Those who live objectively are, according to Kierkegaard, under a delusion of illusion, and if so, then surely he has a real argument in favor of being subjective. For Kierkegaard, at least part of the illusion is, I think, the belief that by living objectively, one's dividend, what (good) one gets from life, is greater.[4] In the first place, even if a certain world-historical process of development is a great good, it is a good that is divided up among those participating in that development into many parts, none of which, presumably, is large in relation to the whole, and so perhaps the good to be derived from participating in that development will be less than the good to be gained by living subjectively. But Kierkegaard then seems to question whether indeed there is *any* good to be gained from living for some world-historical process, since one who does so may not be around when it comes to fruition. But it is not clear that the good of such a process of development must all come at the end of that development, so I think Kierkegaard has still not given us any very strong reason for believing that one who lives objectively is under some kind of illusion that his life is better.

However, in the *Postscript* Kierkegaard attempts to tie up his discussion of living objectively, i.e., of living for the world historical, with certain illusory "objective" attitudes toward death. One who lives world-historically will sometimes say: "What does it matter whether I die or not; the work is what is important, and others will be able to carry it forward." But this is to think

[3]*Ibid.*, p. 133.
[4]*Ibid.*, p. 130ff.

of one's death as nothing special, as just one death among others, as a "something in general." And Kierkegaard seems to believe that one who thinks this way is under an illusion, the illusion that his own death has no more significance *for him* than the death of (random) others, or, to put it slightly differently, that he *should be* no more concerned about his own death than about that of others. However, various Stoic philosophers would, I think, tend to argue that it is Kierkegaard's belief that one should be especially concerned about one's own death that is an illusion, an illusion born of irrational self-centeredness. So it is not obvious that Kierkegaard is correct about the illusory nature of objective living, or about the advisability of living subjectively. In any case, the attitude of people who live for the world historical toward their own deaths is of some interest: they are, at least at some level, not as afraid of dying as they might be or as some people are. And I think there are interesting implications to be drawn from this fact that have some of the spirit of what Kierkegaard says in the *Postscript*.

II

Those who live world-historically for some enterprise like science or philosophy seem not to be very anxious about dying. And I would like to suggest, what Kierkegaard never actually says, that we may be able to *explain* the tendency to life for the world-historical as resulting from our characteristically human fear of dying. For no one wants to live in fear, and since one who lives objectively, for the world historical, does not feel the fear of dying that some of us do, there is reason and motive for people who have experienced anxiety or fear at the prospect of dying to (try to) adopt an objective existence, including an objective attitude toward their own deaths. But what are the psychological mechanisms by which living world-historically assuages someone's fear of death. Here I can only suggest, not establish, an answer, and what I shall say is intended as exploratory and somewhat speculative.

Consider the claim that people who live for the world historical sometimes make that they will *be or become immortal through their works*, or that they will *live on through their works*. Why do people ever say such things; if what they are saying is just metaphorical, why do they use *that* metaphor and why do they seem to take the metaphor seriously?[5] It seems to me that such claims of immortality or living on are not (if there is no afterlife along traditional religious lines) literally true. It is not even literally true to say that part of one lives on in one's works, for books, e.g., are not literally parts of those who write them.

---

[5]Horace in the *Odes* (3, XXX) seems to be an example of someone who takes the metaphor seriously.

Moreover, even if there is a traditional religious type of afterlife, one presumably does not live on *through one's works.*[6]

When we say that we shall live on or be immortal through our writings, e.g., I think we sometimes make that claim in a serious spirit. We are not just joking or deliberately speaking loosely. But when someone points out that what we are saying is not literally true, I think that most of us are willing to admit that what we have said is not literally true. How is this possible? It is my conjecture that someone who says he will live on, at least unconsciously believes that what he has said is (literally) true. Part of the evidence for the *unconsciousness* of the belief, if it exists, is the fact that when someone brings it to our attention that it cannot literally be true, we are ready, at least on a conscious level, to admit that this is so. What (further) supports the idea that the belief exists on some unconscious level is the fact that we at first express it in a serious vein and are not fully conscious that what we are saying is not literally true. We have to be reminded that what we have said is not literally true, and in this respect are not like someone who says that a certain person has a heart of gold. In the latter case, one is quite clear in one's mind *ab initio* that what one is saying is not the literal truth. One is, I think, often less clear, and in some sense more confused, about the literal falsehood of what one says when one says that one will live on in one's works. And this unclarity or confusion, as compared with the "heart of gold" case, is some evidence that one who speaks of living on in his works unconsciously believes that he will do so, inasmuch as the existence of such an unconscious belief is one very obvious possible explanation of that unclarity or confusion.[7] But what lends the greatest support to the view that such an unconscious belief exists in those who live world-historically and say they will live on in their works is the generally accepted fact that human beings naturally tend to fear dying. It is to be expected that men will try to avoid that fear and repress it, if possible. One way of doing this would be to convince oneself that one was immortal through one's works, so that death was not really or fully the end of one's existence. It would be hard to convince oneself of such a claim on a conscious level, just because of its literal falseness. But such belief in one's immortality could perhaps survive on an unconscious level where it would be less subject to rational scrutiny, and perhaps be capable of counteracting one's fear of death. The unconscious delusion of one's immortality (or living

---

[6]I think that people who talk of gaining immortality through their children also say what is literally false, and their psychology is, I think, significantly similar to the psychology of those who talk of living through their books.

[7]Kierkegaard hints at the idea that world-historical people believe they live on through their works when he implies (*Postscript*, p. 140) that such people need to be reminded that "in the world-historical process the dead are not recalled to life."

on) through one's works can, if we adopt Freudian terminology, be thought of as an unconscious defense mechanism of the ego that protects us from conscious fear about death by repressing that fear and counterbalancing it in such a way that it for the most part remains unconscious.[8] And this would explain why people who live for the world historical are not consciously afraid of dying much of the time, and, in effect, why people so often live for the world historical.[9]

Let me carry my speculation further. At one point in the *Postscript* (p. 274) Kierkegaard says that to live for the world historical is to forget that one exists. This curious claim is, I think, more plausible or forceful than it may seem at first. Consider a person who lives objectively and unconsciously believes that he will live on through his books. Such a belief is not just false, but necessarily false, since it involves both the idea that one is alive and the idea that the existence of certain works like books is sufficient for one's continued existence; and nothing whose continued existence is entailed by the existence of such works can be *alive*. Moreover, the belief that one's books' existence is sufficient for one's continued existence seems to involve the idea that one has roughly the same kind of being as a book or series of books. So I think there is something to the idea that one who lives objectively somehow thinks of himself as not existing as a person, and as not being alive. But he presumably does not think this on a conscious level, for much the same reason that one does not on a conscious level think that one is going to live on through one's works. On the other hand, the *unconscious* delusion that one is not alive (or is of the same kind as a series of books) would seem capable of counteracting and allaying anxiety about dying just as easily as the unconscious belief that one is immortal through one's works does so. If one is going to live on in books, one is not going to lose one's life and there is nothing to fear from death, so that fears about dying may be prevented from becoming conscious by being allayed on an unconscious level. Similarly, if one is not really alive, or is of the same "stuff" as

---

[8]For examples of reasoning similar to that just used that appear in the psychoanalytic literature, see, e.g., S. Freud's "Splitting of the Ego in the Defensive Process" (in his *Collected Papers* [London, 1956], vol. 5, pp. 372–375) and Otto Fenichel's *The Psychoanalytic Theory of Neurosis* (New York, 1945, pp. 479–484). For another *philosophical* use of an argument like mine above, see M. Lazerowitz' *The Structure of Metaphysics* (London, 1955, p. 69ff.) and *Studies in Metaphilosophy* (London, 1964, pp. 225ff., 251). I am indebted to Lazerowitz' account for some of the structure of my own analysis.

[9]J. P. Sartre (in *Being and Nothingness* [New York, 1956], p. 543) says that "to be dead is to be a prey for the living." And Thomas Nagel (in "Death," *Noûs*, vol. 4 [1970], p. 78) has tentatively claimed that a man can be harmed or unfortunate as a result of things that happen after his death, e.g., if his reputation suffers posthumously. I wonder whether these views are not, perhaps, indicative of some sort of unconscious belief that people live on in their works.

books, then one also has nothing to fear from dying; and one's ceasing to be, if it occurs, will be no more tragic than the ceasing to be of a book.[10] So if one believes this kind of thing on an unconscious level, it is again not hard to see how one's fear of death may be allayed and kept unconscious.[11] Thus it would seem that people so often live for the world historical because such living involves unconscious beliefs (delusions) that help them, more or less successfully, to avoid conscious fears about dying.[12]

According to Kierkegaard, however, not only does one who lives for the world historical forget that he exists, but such a person, at least to some extent, ceases to exist as a person, ceases to live.[13] For if we use our lives as a means to the existence of certain works and/or to be mentioned in some paragraph or footnote of some authoritative history of our field of endeavor, then we are valuing our lives no more than we value the existence of certain works or our being mentioned in paragraphs or footnotes. And when we unconsciously think of ourselves as immortal through our works, we are in effect thinking that what we lose when we die cannot be that important or valuable. And to do and think in this way is to put a low value on one's living. But if one places a low value on actual living, one will not take full advantage of one's life (living) and that is a bit like already being dead, or not alive. So I think there really is something to Kierkegaard's claim that to live world-historically is to some extent

[10]The unconscious belief that one is going to live on and the unconscious belief that one is not alive seem to counteract the unconscious belief or fear that one is going to die in contradictory ways, the former with the "message" that we are not really going to lose what we have, the latter with the "message" that we really have nothing to lose. But we have already seen that the unconscious belief that one lives on in books is itself contradictory or necessarily false, so it should not, perhaps, be so surprising that the unconscious uses mutually contradictory means to repress death-fears. On this see Freud's *The Interpretation of Dreams*, Chapter 2. For similar use of the (metaphorical?) notion of unconscious "messages," see Otto Fenichel's *Outline of Clinical Psychoanalysis* (New York, 1934), esp. pp. 13, 30, 33, 52, 250, 260, 275f.

[11]In "A Lecture on Ethics," *The Philosophical Review*, vol. 74 (1965), pp. 8ff., Ludwig Wittgenstein speaks of the feeling people sometimes have of being safe whatever happens. He claims that such a feeling or belief is nonsensical; but perhaps this occasional feeling is better thought of as the expression of a meaningful, but necessarily or clearly false, unconscious belief that we are safe whatever happens, a belief that counteracts the fear of dying and that is roughly equivalent to the unconscious belief that one is not alive. For one is absolutely safe (from death) if and only if one is not alive.

[12]I do not want to claim that everyone dedicated to some "cause," to something "bigger" than himself, is living world-historically. Such dedication may result from altruism or "conviction" and may not involve the world-historical psychology if it is not accompanied by delusions of immortality through one's works or actions, or the view that one's own death is unimportant.

[13]*Ibid.*, pp. 118, 175, 271, 273.

STANDARDS FOR DETERMINING HUMAN DEATH 581

to cease to exist as a person, to cease to be alive. The claim constitutes not literal truth, but a forceful and penetrating metaphor.

It is well known that the fear of dying is a prime source of much of human religiosity. Belief in an afterlife of the traditional religious sort is one way that men can assuage their anxiety about dying. What is perhaps not so well known is how the fear of dying can give rise to (and explain) certain attitudes and activities of people who are not in any ordinary way religious and perhaps also certain attitudes and activities of religious people that are not generally associated with religion. What I have tried to show here is that there are in Kierkegaard's *Concluding Unscientific Postscript* insights about our attitudes toward life and death that can be used to help us understand how certain nonreligious aspects of human life result from the fear of dying.

In doing so, I have assumed that people who live objectively and say that they are not terribly anxious about dying are nonetheless afraid of dying at some level. And this may seem high-handed. However, I am inclined to think that in general people living world-historically (who do not believe in some traditional religious type of life after death) continue to be subject to a certain welling-up of death anxiety that can overtake them in the midst of their daily lives.[14] Despite my own tendencies toward the world historical, I have often experienced this sudden welling-up of death anxiety, and I think that the fact that this phenomenon is widespread among nonreligious world-historical people (and indeed among people in general) is evidence that fear of dying never entirely ceases to exist in (such) people, but always continues to exist at least on an unconscious plane. For it is easier to imagine such a sudden welling-up of fear as the "return of the repressed" and as indicating a certain inefficiency of one's repressive mechanisms than to think of it as resulting from the sudden regeneration of death fears within one. What could plausibly explain such a sudden rebirth of death anxiety *in medias res?* Moreover, the earlier-mentioned fact that world-historical people (people who live for the world historical) sometimes seriously say that they will be immortal through their works, without being clear in their own minds that this is just a metaphor, is, as I have already argued, evidence that such people unconsciously believe that they are immortal through their works (or that they are not alive). But why should they have such unconscious beliefs, except as part of a mechanism to relieve and keep repressed their fear of dying? So even such seemingly innocuous locutions as that we shall be immortal through our works indicate the existence of death fears even on the part of people who live for the world historical and claim not to be afraid of dying. Let us now turn to Pascal's *Pensées* to see how the fear of dying affects other aspects of human life.

[14] See Heidegger's *Being and Time* (New York, 1962), p. 233f.

III

There is a famous long passage in the *Pensées* in which Pascal talks about diversion, its role in human life, and its sources. Men "cannot stay quietly in their own chamber" alone and meditating, for any length of time.[15] We need or think we need diversion and activity and cannot be happy without diverting ourselves from ourselves because of the "natural poverty of our feeble and mortal condition, so miserable that nothing can comfort us when we think of it closely."[16] Now Pascal does not go on to decry the vanity of human diversion and claim that life would be less vain if we thought more about ourselves and our mortality. He is not arguing for the vanity of worldly human concerns in the time-worn manner of *Ecclesiastes*. He has an entirely new perspective on where the vanity of human life really lies. The vanity of our lives consists, for Pascal, in the fact that when we divert ourselves (from ourselves), we typically deceive ourselves about our motives for behaving as we do.[17] For example, a man who gambles often convinces himself that obtaining the money he is gambling for would make him happy (at least for a while). He focuses on the getting of the money and forgets that his real or main purpose is to divert himself. Thus, if he were offered the money on condition that he does not gamble, he would be (at least temporarily) unhappy, because he seeks diversion. On the other hand, if he were offered the diversion, say, of playing cards without being able to gamble for money, he would also be unhappy. For it is not just diversion he seeks; he must also have some imagined goal that he focuses on in such a way that he does not see that diversion is his real or main goal. Pascal does not, however, explain why men cannot simply seek diversion without fooling themselves about their goal. But an explanation can be given along lines that Pascal might have approved. Imagine that we divert ourselves in order not to have to think of ourselves and also realize that this is so. Shall we not *ipso facto* be thrust back into that very awareness of self that we sought to avoid through diversion? To realize that one wants not to think of oneself because it is unpleasant to dwell on one's feeble and mortal condition is *ipso facto* to be thinking of oneself and opening oneself up to the very unpleasantness one wishes to avoid. And if those who want to avoid thinking of themselves must remain ignorant of that fact if they are to succeed in not thinking of themselves, how better to accomplish this than by focusing on something outside themselves and thinking of it as their goal?

This explanation of human striving and activity applies not just to gambling,

[15] *Pensées* (New York, 1958), p. 39.
[16] *Ibid.*
[17] *Ibid.*, p. 40.

but, as Pascal says to the waging of campaigns in love or in war and to many other human activities. Many of us fool ourselves about our motives much of the time when engaged in such activities. One objection to this analysis, however, would be that to explain so much human activity in terms of the fear of, or desire not to be, thinking of oneself is to offer a gratuitous explanation of our behavior. Why not just say that as animals we have an instinctive desire for certain activities that typically involve a lack of self-consciousness and that are called "diversions"? But the instinct theory of the origin of our diversions has, as it stands, no obvious way of explaining the self-deception Pascal points out. If we simply have an instinct for certain activities, activities that in fact tend to divert us from ourselves, why do some of us much of the time and many of us some of the time deceive ourselves into thinking that it is winning a certain victory or honor or woman that is our main goal, when it is the diverting activity leading up to that winning that is our main goal. On the theory that we do not like thinking about ourselves, however, the fact of self-deception can be explained along the above lines; so the assumption of a desire not to think of oneself is not gratuitous.

Furthermore, there is good independent evidence that people do not like to think about themselves. There is, for example, an experience that I have sometimes had, and that I think the reader will probably also have had; in the middle of thinking about something else I have all of a sudden thought to myself: "All this is being done by *me* and all these people are talking about *me*." I hope this description will suffice to convey the kind of experience I have in mind. What is interesting, but also perplexing and distressing to me, are the following facts. When I have this experience of myself, there seems to me to be something precious about it; and I think: "This is the moment when I am most alive; it is very good to have this experience." (There is, after all, a long tradition in which self-consciousness is a great, or the greatest, good.) I usually also think that though I am at the moment too busy to prolong the self-consciousness, I shall definitely set aside a good deal of time in the future to take full advantage of this kind of experience of self-awareness. But somehow that never happens. And when I am again momentarily self-conscious in the way I have been describing, I again put off a long bout of such self-consciousness to the future, despite my typical accompanying conviction that the experience of being self-conscious is a wonderful one that I really should and shall take greater advantage of. All this needs explaining, and the obvious explanation, I think, is that I really do not like the experience of self-consciousness, as Pascal suggests.

But why, in the end, should we not want to think about ourselves? Pascal suggests that the reason is that thinking about ourselves makes us think of our feeble and mortal condition. He also says about man: "to be happy, he would have to make himself immortal; but, not being able to do so, it has occurred to him to prevent himself from thinking of death."[18] Presumably, then, Pascal thinks there is a connection between thinking about oneself and thinking unpleasant thoughts about one's death; and this seems to me to be quite plausible. For at least while we are absorbed in things outside us, we do not think of ourselves, or thus, it would seem, of our death; whereas if and when one does think about oneself, one might very easily think about one's death. It would seem, then, that the explanation of our diverting ourselves from (thinking about) ourselves is that this at least to some degree enables us to avoid thinking anxiously about our mortality. And so we have now clarified two general areas or aspects of human life in terms of the fear of dying. Let us turn next to Heidegger.

IV

Men's attitudes toward death are a major theme in Heidegger's *Being and Time*.[19] For Heidegger, in everyday life we exist in a mode that Heidegger calls the "they" (German: "das Man"). Heidegger characterizes this mode of existence as inauthentic, at least in part because in it, one is forgetful of the fact that death is one's ownmost possibility and cannot be outstripped. By this he means something close to the Kierkegaardian idea that one's own death has greater significance for one than does the death of others. Heidegger says that such a mode of existence is tempting because it tranquilizes one's anxiety in the face of death.[20] So it would seem that Heidegger can be thought of as providing a psychological explanation of certain aspects of human life, which he calls collectively "(being lost in) the 'they',", and thus that Heidegger is doing something similar to what we have seen Kierkegaard doing in the *Postscript* and Pascal doing in the *Pensées*.[21]

---

[18] *Ibid.*, p. 49.

[19] Our discussion here will be based on Sections 27, 35–42, and 47–53 of *Being and Time*, *op. cit.*

[20] Heidegger uses "fear" only with respect to things in the world. For death "anxiety" is reserved; but this is not necessarily dictated by ordinary usage.

[21] Of course, some philosophers will say that by treating Heidegger as an explanatory psychologist, I am treating him as if he were operating on the "ontic" level, whereas Heidegger thinks of himself as operating on an "ontological" level deeper than the "ontic" level on which science, psychology, and most pre-Heideggerian philosophy typically function. However, despite many efforts, I myself have never been able to make satisfactory sense of the ontic/ontological distinction. If the distinction is viable, Heidegger may have a good deal more to say than I shall be giving him credit for; but we can at least credit him with insights on a level with those of a Pascal or a Kierkegaard.

According to Heidegger, one important aspect of our average everyday lostness in the "they" is its typical modes of discourse, chatter, and idle talk, and the busy-body curiosity that characterizes such discourse. Heidegger points out that when people are idly and curiously talking about whether John and Mary will get divorced, the actual event, the divorce, if it occurs, actually disappoints the idle talkers; for then they are no longer able to conjecture about and be in on the thing in advance. The curiosity of everyday idle talk is concerned with the very latest thing(s), with novelty; and what interests in anticipation may be "old hat" or out of date when it occurs. Horse races and even pennant races in baseball seem to me to be good examples of this tendency. We have the keenest interest in who will win, but it is hard to maintain much interest in such races once we know their outcome; there is even a certain disappointment or "let-down" sometimes when the results of such things finally do become known.[22] Heidegger's discussion here seems to have a good deal in common with what Pascal says about diversion, for one way of diverting ourselves from ourselves would be to be constantly curious about the latest things. But why not be interested in things that are not new and be diverted by them? The answer here—though it is not one that Heidegger actually gives—seems to me to lie precisely in the desire not to think of oneself that Pascal lays such emphasis on. What is newer is less well known, and the more there is to learn about something, the less likely one is to get bored with it or to cease being absorbed in it, and so be thrust back into thoughts about oneself. Furthermore, our earlier discussion of Pascal can help us explain why we are sometimes let down when a certain event we have (only) conjectured about occurs, even though in advance we thought that "nothing would make us happier" than to know exactly when and how the event would occur. For if our goal is distraction from ourselves through conjecturing, we cannot very well admit this to ourselves without (running a grave risk of) defeating that goal; so we somehow fool ourselves into thinking that what we want is to know for sure about the character of the event we are conjecturing about, as a means to our real goal of diverting ourselves through conjecturing about something or someone outside ourselves; and when we cannot conjecture any more, then, of course, we are let down.

There may be a further reason why the desire for novelty is so pervasive in human life—though what I shall now be saying is perhaps more speculative than anything else I have to say here. As Heidegger says (p. 217), when one has the desire for novelty, it is as if one's motive were to have known (seen) rather than to know (see); for as soon as one has known (seen) something, one no longer

---

[22]Of course, some people constantly dwell on past (sporting) events (and their part in them), but I do not think this is imcompatible with the general tendency I am describing.

wants to know (see) it. And there seems to be a certain vanity in such a way of dealing with things. Now consider what is implicitly involved in wanting, say, to have seen Rome, but not to see (keep seeing) Rome. There are tours whose advertising has the feeling: "Come to Europe with us and you will see 8—count'em—8 countries in 8 days"; and such advertising and such tours appeal to many people who want to (say they) have been, e.g., in Rome, but who do not much want to *be* in Rome. When one makes such a tour, one often even wishes the tour were already over so that one (could say that one) had already been to Rome in Italy (and to the other seven countries). The actual touring, with its "inconveniences," is often not desired or enjoyed. But to want the eight days and the trip to be already over with is in a certain sense to want a part of one's life over with in exchange for a being able to say one has been. This desire is in many cases unconscious. Sometimes some of us say, with an air of seriousness, that we wish that a certain trip or period of time were already over. But when confronted with the implications of what we have said, we almost inevitably recoil from what we have said and say that, of course, we do not *really* want a certain part of our life to be already over, perhaps adding that we were only speaking loosely or jokingly in making our original remark. In that case our desire to have a certain part of our life over with exists, if at all, only on an unconscious level. Evidence that there *is* such an unconscious desire comes from the fact of our original seriousness in saying that we wished a certain trip over with and from the fact that we are by no means clear in our own minds that we do not mean our statement literally, the way a hungry man is, for example, when he says that he could eat a mountain of flapjacks. I think this initial unclarity is best explained by (and thus evidence for) the existence of an unconscious desire to have a certain part of our life over with.[23] And perhaps for the very purpose of keeping this desire out of consciousness, we convince ourselves at least temporarily that we really want to *be* in Rome, or *feel* its living antiquity, etc. But then, after we have spent the tour rushing about, impatient with tarrying in one place too long, we *may*, upon reflection, recognize that we wanted the having seen more than the seeing of the places like Rome, that we visited.

The logical extension of the wish to have a certain portion of one's life already over with is the wish to have one's whole life over with, and I would like now very tentatively to argue that at some deep level many of us have this latter wish, and so want not to be alive. Part of the reason for thinking so consists in the way we deceive ourselves about the extent of our desires to have portions of our lives over with. We sometimes think: if only it were a week from now so that I knew whether p, everything would be all right. But then

---

[23] Compare here our earlier argument for the existence, in world-historical people, of an unconscious belief in their immortality through their works.

when the time comes at which everything is supposed to be going to be all right, we soon find another reason for thinking things are not all right and for wishing other parts of our lives over with. I think that the initially implausible assumption that some people unconsciously wish their whole lives over with, wish not to be alive, provides the best explanation of this whole perplexing phenomenon. For if one has the unconscious desire to have one's whole life over with, there will be mechanisms in force to prevent it from becoming conscious. If one were conscious that one wanted *many different parts* of one's life over with *seriatim*, one would be dangerously close to being conscious that one wanted one's *whole life* over with. So it might reasonably be expected that someone with the unconscious wish or desire that his whole life was over with would be (made to be) unaware of the extent to which he wanted particular portions of his life over with before they were lived. Thus I think there is reason to believe that people who deceive themselves in this way unconsciously wish not to be alive.[24]

It will perhaps seem more plausible to hold that such a wish exists if I can show how it is explained by our fear of dying. One way of allaying fear of the loss of something is a kind of denial that one might call the technique of "sour grapes in advance." We can convince ourselves that the thing we may lose is not worth having or that we do not really want it. (This recalls the studies psychologists have done on the resolution of "cognitive dissonance.") An unconscious desire not to be alive might, then, help us counterbalance or keep repressed our fear of dying. The existence of such a desire can thus be supported in various ways and fits well into the kind of theory about our attitudes toward death so far proposed. But there is no time to speculate further in its favor.[25]

We argued earlier that if someone thinks of himself as not alive, he will not

[24] Our earlier argument that we do not like thinking about ourselves can be strengthened along the lines of our present argument for the existence of an unconscious wish not to be alive. Similar self-deception occurs in the two cases.

[25] I have posited the wish not to be alive as an unconscious defense mechanism of the ego that responds to (prior) fear of dying. Freud, on the other hand, late in his career posited a basic (id-based) death instinct to account for various phenomena. See *Beyond the Pleasure Principle* (New York, 1950). The two sorts of views are incompatible, and so the explanation given just now in the text may be mistaken. However, there is some reason to prefer it. Our ego-theory of the death wish fits in better with our earlier-discussed theories about the ego's unconscious handling of the fear of dying. Moreover, other things being equal, it is better to treat a phenomenon as a derived phenomenon, within a theory, than to treat it as basic, within that theory. In addition, there is the sheer unintuitiveness of supposing that we have death wished *ab initio*, rather than acquiring such (irrational) wishes in the *neurotic* process of repression. Finally, it is by no means clear that a basic death instinct is needed to account for clinical phenomena. On this see Otto Fenichel's "A Critique of the Death Instinct" in *The Collected Papers of Otto Fenichel*, first series (New York, 1953), pp. 363–372.

take full advantage of his life and it will be as if he is not (fully) alive. The same can be said for someone who wants not to be alive. We saw earlier the force of the metaphor that some of us are dead. Since it is as if some of us are dead because of what we have, unconsciously, done to ourselves, there is also force to the metaphor that some of us have killed ourselves. To live for the having seen and known of things is, metaphorically speaking, not to be alive, and to have killed oneself.[26] And one can also say this about those who live for the world historical. I have a tendency to put myself entirely into my work and to live for something "bigger," philosophy. But sometimes I recoil from such an existence and from myself, and I feel that I have really just thrown my life away, have been personally emptied, through world-historical living. At such a time the metaphor of killing oneself seems particularly compelling.

We have thus far characterized those who live world-historically as assuaging the fear of dying via the *beliefs* that they are immortal and/or that they are not alive. But I think such people also sometimes unconsciously wish not to be alive in the manner of those who divert themselves with novelties.[27] (Of course, those who live world-historically can be diverting themselves as well, e.g., with busy research or advocacy of causes.) For one thing, as we have already seen, people who live world-historically unconsciously think that they are not alive. And they want to think this, at least unconsciously, as a means to less fear or anxiety. But presumably if one wants to think one is not alive, that is because one wants not to be alive. This kind of inference from what one wants to think to what one wants is surely *usually* in order. Secondly, there is evidence that world-historical people tend to want parts of their lives over with in much the same way that seekers after novelty do. Someone writing a book that is intended to advance some field in the long run will often wish that the next six months of his life were already over so that he could see the book in finished form and have the writing of it over with. If only this were possible, everything would start being all right, he thinks, and he would be ready really to live his life again. Such a person, however, will, in many cases, be fooling himself about the extent to which he wants to "put off living" by missing parts of his life. As

---

[26] I think we have some inkling of this metaphorical killing when we speak of "killing time" at moments when we want to have something over with, want a certain (perhaps boring) part of our lives over with. Use of that phrase may be a disguised conscious expression of the unconscious desire not to be alive.

[27] Kierkegaard's claim in the *Postscript* (p. 137) that one whose eye is on world-historical things has perhaps found "a highly significant way of . . . killing time" seems to indicate some awareness on his part that world-historical people want not to be alive and have, metaphorically speaking, killed themselves. Whose time, after all, does one kill except one's own? And one's time is one's life. Incidentally, it is natural to say that world-historical people "bury themselves in their work," and this metaphor seems to suggest the very same things that our use of the metaphor of killing time does.

soon as there is another book to write, or academic appointment in the offing, he may very well once again want some part of his life already over with. Saying that such a man really wants to live, but only wants to avoid certain tense or burdensome parts of his life, does not really allow us to understand why he so often on such slight pretexts (is writing a book really so unpleasant and tense, considering the rest of the things that can be going on in one's life at the same time?) thinks up reasons for wanting to postpone living by omitting some part of his life. Just as a man who is always *just about* to take a vacation and really live (it up) for a change, but who never does, can be plausibly suspected of preferring his work to a vacation or to "life" despite his protestations to the contrary, the perplexing behavior of one who lives world-historically and keeps wanting parts of his life over with while remaining unconscious or unaware of the extent to which this is so can, I think, only be made sense of in terms of an unconscious desire not to be alive.[28] Such a desire is strange and perplexing, perhaps, but no more so than the behavior it is supposed to explain.

Heidegger says many more interesting things about the "they." Idle talk and curiosity seem to be interested in anything and everything, though in fact, unbeknown to us, limits have been set on what we are to be interested in. For example, one is not, in the midst of curious talk, supposed to bring up the tragedy of life or the inevitability of death. Anyone who brings up such things is told not to be "morbid." Heidegger suggests that idle talk and curiosity function as a way of keeping us from thinking of our own death. For one thing—if I may borrow again from our discussion of Pascal to supplement what Heidegger is saying here—the illusion of interest in everything is an excellent means for blocking off thought about dying and its consequent anxiety, since if we believed, while we were engaged in idle talk, that we were not supposed to be deeply talking about death, we might very easily be thrust back into the very anxiety that idle talk was supposed to avoid. Moreover, the very self-assurance and harshness with which someone who brings up death in the midst of idle talk is branded as morbid tends to encourage and rationalize our avoidance of the topic of death.

Another device by which everyday living in the "they" keeps us from fears of death is by branding such fears as cowardly. Heidegger, however, thinks that it is more cowardly *not* to face death anxiously. Now there certainly seems to be room for disagreement on this issue. Some of the Stoics seem to have thought that it was irrational, rather than courageous, to be anxious about one's own death because death was a matter of indifference. And this latter philosophy of death may be correct; but it might be interesting at this point to make some educated guesses about the psychology of those who have advocated the "Stoic"

---

[28]Cf. Emerson's remark in his *Journals* (13 April, 1834) that "we are always getting ready to live, but never living."

view of death. For to my mind there is something strange and suspicious about (holding) the view that one's own death is not an evil. I have already discussed the fact that despite our best repressive mechanisms, the fear of dying sometimes comes upon (some of) us suddenly in the midst of life. When others tell us that it is morbid or cowardly to worry about death, we are given an excuse or motive not to worry about death, and such advice may well help us to get rid of the conscious fear of death at least temporarily. The philosophical view that it is irrational to worry about death because death is a matter of indifference may have a similar function to play in the psychic lives of those who propound it. Philosophers pride themselves on being rational, and by branding the fear of dying as "irrational," they may give themselves a motive for ceasing consciously to worry about death and actually help themselves get rid of the conscious fear of dying. I am inclined to think, then, that the view that it is irrational, and not courageous, to fear death, because death is no evil, may well be motivated, in many of those who propound it, by the fear of death itself, a fear that they are consequently able to repress, but not to get rid of. If so, then those who are helped to repress their fear of dying by holding a "Stoic" view of death are under an illusion when they claim as rational philosophers to be totally indifferent to death. But it might be better to live under such an illusion without consciously worrying about death than to know that one was not indifferent to death because one *was* consciously afraid of death. In the light of these complexities, it would seem hard to decide between Heidegger, on the one hand, and the Stoics and the "they," on the other, as to whether it is courageous to be (consciously) anxious in the face of dying.

Heidegger suggests yet further ways in which existence in the "they" tranquilizes our anxiety about dying. In the "they" there is an emphasis on keeping busy doing things, as the means to, or sign of, a full and good life. When someone suggests that one might do better to be more reflective and less busy, the response of the "they" is that by keeping busy, one is living "concretely" and avoiding self-defeating and morbid self-consciousness; this encourages the person who hears this to keep busy and not reflect on himself, and thus functions as a means to keeping us from the conscious fear of dying. (Consider, in particular, how the old, who are especially subject to fears of death, are told to keep busy and active.)

Heidegger points out that someone lost in the "they" will *admit* that death is certain and that one (everyone) dies in the end. According to Heidegger, in speaking of what happens to "everyone" or to "one" eventually, we "depersonalize" and "intellectualize" death. In thus depersonalizing death, it is as if the person were saying that death has nothing to do with *him right now*, and this enables him to talk about death without focusing on himself or having that particularly intimate experience of self-awareness described earlier or, thus, having fearful thoughts about death. Also talk about the inevitability or certainty of death, etc., may be part of a process of "isolation of affect" in which one intellectualizes (about) a certain phenomenon to keep away from (consciousness of) certain related feelings.[29]   Heidegger also points out that social scientists often seek to create "typologies" and systematic theories about humanity in the belief that they are thereby penetrating to the deepest level on which one can understand humanity and oneself, but that such intellectual "hustle and bustle" may entirely ignore the question of the significance for men of their own death and death anxiety; such intellectualization, he suggests, may serve to keep one from anxious thoughts about death by convincing one that one has reflected as deeply as it is possible to do.   And the very stuffiness and detachment with which some sociologists, psychologists, etc., sometimes declare their desire to plumb the depths of the human spirit is, I would think, some evidence that they have a deeper need to avoid the *feeling* of their own mortality.

An important further point that is due to Kierkegaard rather than to Heidegger is that one can even overintellectualize one's response to a work, like that of Kierkegaard or Heidegger, that attempts to reveal in an "existential" manner the importance of our attitudes toward dying.[30] Spinoza has said that "passive" feelings like fear tend to dissipate when we scrutinize them, and this may well mean that it is difficult at one and the same time both intellectually to focus on and learn the significance of death anxiety and to *feel* that significance. And so there seems to be a real danger that someone who reads the writings of Existentialists will only intellectually understand and agree with what they say, and thus fail to derive all the benefit one could or should get from reading them.   Of course, Spinoza's dictum also implies that it is difficult to think intellectually about death anxiety while feeling such anxiety.   And one reason why I and others may be so interested in thinking and writing about death anxiety is that such thinking and writing may, in effect, involve an isolation of affect about death.[31]

In discussing Heidegger, we have brought in Kierkegaard and Pascal to help "deepen" his analysis of how death anxiety affects large portions of human life. I would like now to make use of certain ideas of Sartre's (in ways that Sartre undoubtedly would not approve) to point out yet another aspect of human life that can be explained in terms of the fear of dying. (However, I

---

[29]Cf. O. Fenichel's *Outline of Clinical Psychoanalysis, op. cit.*, p. 190f., for ideas about "isolation of affect" that are related to some of the things we have said here and earlier in the paper.

[30]*Postscript*, p. 166f.

[31]Heidegger also points out that the force of living in the "they" is such as to make people lost in the "they" scoff at his analysis of such lostness.   Once one is aware of one's tendencies to cover up certain anxieties, it may be harder to use the mechanisms one has previously used in doing so; so one who wishes at some level to keep covering up his anxiety has a motive to reject Heidegger's analysis and, indeed, our analysis here.

shall not discuss Sartre's own views on death, which, in fact, run counter to much of what we have to say on that subject.)

V

Being and Nothingness is perhaps most famous for its discussion of what Sartre calls "bad faith," which consists in being or putting oneself under the illusion that one is not free and cannot do other than what one in fact does.[32] For Sartre, one is in bad faith when one says: I have to get up and get to work; I can't stay in bed, I have a family to feed. Bad faith is involved because one does not *have* to get up and go to work.

Some people will immediately object to what Sartre is saying on the grounds that if determinism about human behavior is true and a certain person, in fact, will not stay in bed, then he is under no illusion when he says that he cannot stay in bed. Since, despite anything Sartre says, it is by no means obvious to me that such determinism is not (approximately) true or that human beings possess free will, I would like now to (re)interpret Sartre's "bad faith" in such a way as to avoid assuming either human indeterminism or human free will.

Someone who says he has to go to work in the morning will sometimes say: "I have no choice in the matter." But I think that he does have a choice, even if a determined and unfree one, and that if he cannot stay at home, that is in part *because* of his (perhaps determined and unfree) choice. Moreover, I think that someone who is reminded of these facts will typically be willing to take back his original claim to have no choice in some matter, will grant that he had been speaking loosely or metaphorically. But it seems to me that such a person will typically not have been clear in his own mind about all this at the time when he originally claimed to have "no choice." And for reasons we have already gone into at length, I think this indicates that the person making such a claim unconsciously believes that he has no choice in a certain matter, even though he really does have a (possibly determined and unfree) choice in that matter and can be brought to conscious awareness of that fact. Such a person is under an illusion about the part he (and his choosing or deciding) plays in certain events or situations, and it is *this kind* of illusion that *I* shall call "bad faith."

Bad faith in this new sense is clearly related to bad faith in Sartre's sense. And, assuming that the new kind of bad faith does exist, it would be good if we could give some sort of explanation of it. Sartre's explanation of bad faith in the old sense will not be of much help to us here, since it assumes not only that human behavior is undetermined but also (implausibly enough) that human

---

[32] See *Being and Nothingness, op. cit.*, Pt. I.

beings basically realize (believe) that this is so. My suggestion is that we explain bad faith in my new sense in much the same way that we have been explaining various other phenomena, namely, in terms of the fear of dying. (Indeed, Heiaegger hints at this idea in *Being and Time*, p. 239.) I think that we can explain bad faith in terms of the fear of dying, if we suppose that the illusion of bad faith helps to repress such fear and if we borrow one further idea of Sartre's. According to Sartre, someone in bad faith (in his sense) who denies his own freedom is, in effect, thinking of himself as a thing or object, since things and objects are unfree, etc. I would like tentatively to claim that people who unconsciously believe that they have no choice, say, about getting up in the morning are, in effect, thinking of themselves as things or objects,[33] since things and objects really do lack choice. If we make this assumption, we can explain how bad faith in my sense enables one to relieve or repress death fears. For objects cannot die, and so unconsciously thinking of oneself as an object is unconsciously to think that one has nothing to fear from death.[34] (And if one passes away but is a mere object, then that is no more tragic than the passing away of a rock.)

Bad faith in the new sense seems to have much in common with living for the world historical. In the latter case, one thinks of oneself as not alive; in the former, one thinks of oneself as a mere thing; and one might wonder whether there is much difference here either in the content of these unconscious beliefs or in the way they act on the fear of dying. Furthermore, just as one who lives for the world historical can aptly be described metaphorically as not alive[35] and as having killed himself, one who lives in bad faith is, metaphorically speaking, a mere thing and not alive, and since he has (unconsciously) done this to himself, he has, metaphorically speaking, turned himself into a thing. And given the fact that the only way a person really can turn himself into a corpse, it is perhaps metaphorically appropriate to describe someone who is (constantly) in bad faith as having killed himself. Sartre holds that someone who thinks of himself as a mere thing wants (among other things) to *be* a mere thing. And I think we could argue that people in bad faith in my sense sometimes unconsciously want to be things in something like the way we earlier argued that people living for the world historical want not to be alive. Furthermore, the unconscious desire to be an object would seem capable of countering the fear

---

[33] I hope I shall be forgiven for ignoring plants.

[34] This recalls the Simon and Garfunkel song that goes: "I am a rock, I am an island; and a rock feels no pain, and an island never cries." The idea that we sometimes want to think of ourselves as things to avoid the pain of life or of facing death is not new or silly. Moreover, even if people in bad faith only think of themselves, unconsciously, as *similar to* mere things, that thought may itself be capable of relieving the fear of death.

[35] Kierkegaard says that such a person is also a "walking stick," which suggests the similarity of such a person to someone in bad faith who exists as a mere object.

of dying in much the same way that the unconscious desire not to be alive does so, and so there is this further similarity between living in bad faith and living for the world historical.

VI

If what has been said here is on the right tract, then it would seem that Pascal, Kierkegaard, Heidegger, and Sartre all describe phenomena that pervade our lives and that are best explained in terms of their efficacy in relieving or repressing the fear of dying. Our explanation has made use of a Freudian type of view of repression and of the unconscious. This will certainly make our arguments here suspect in the eyes of some people. I have, in effect, been "practicing" a kind of "existential psychoanalysis," and though this term is one that was originally used by Sartre in *Being and Nothingness* to describe some of his own procedures, it may well apply more accurately to the kinds of things I have been doing here. For Sartre does not posit an unconscious, but I have followed Freud in doing just that.[36] In any case, I hope that this paper may bring to light an area, or areas, where existentialism and psychoanalysis can be mutually enlightening.

Of course, in addition to using psychoanalytic ideas, I have also frequently appealed to my own experience and intuitions, to how things strike me and to the "feel" of certain ideas. Although some things, I trust, will strike readers the way they have struck me, this will no doubt not always be the case; and when it is not, my appeals to how things feel to me, etc., are bound to seem like special pleading. Perhaps I *am* guilty of this, but I do not know how to avoid it in a paper like this in which personal experience may be more relevant to seeing certain points than abstract arguments. And perhaps some of the ideas or intuitions I have relied on will seem more palatable to the reader if he "lives with them" and takes the time to see whether they do not, perhaps, make sense in and of his experience of himself and the world. For it is in something like this way that many of the ideas and intuitions of this paper have become acceptable to me.

In this paper, I have pieced together various ideas from Pascal, Heidegger, Sartre, and Kierkegaard as well as extrapolated beyond what any of them has said, to provide a fairly general picture of how the fear of dying accounts for many aspects of human life. The explanatory "theory" we have presented links together phenomena that the various existentialists discussed separately, and as such should, given any standard account of scientific method, be more

---

[36] Sartre rejects the unconscious for reasons that seem to me to be interesting, but ultimately unacceptable.

plausible than the accounts of the various existentialists taken separately. So I hope I have helped to support and fill out the basically existentialist notion that the quality of a (nonreligious) man's life greatly depends on his attitude toward his own death. And even if this idea is not particularly prevalent in Sartre, we can use things Sartre says to substantiate it.

Some people will complain that I have only been doing psychology, not philosophy. But it may not be important whether this accusation is true. And I also think that when psychology is general enough and speaks directly to the human condition, it can also count as philosophy. If, as we have argued, the main motive for world-historical (busily self-distractive) participation in certain enterprises comes from (desire to avoid) the fear of dying, then a good many intellectuals, scientists, and others may be less pure in motive, less selfless, than they are often thought to be.[37] And this fact, if it is one, is surely very relevant to our understanding of the human condition, and so counts in favor of calling what we have been doing philosophy.[38]

---

[37]This is not to say that such people should stop doing science, etc., with their present motives. They may be happier than they are otherwise likely to be and may be contributing to the intellectual or practical good of other people. See also footnote 12.

[38]I am indebted to G. Boolos, E. Erwin, B. Jacobs, D. Levin, S. Ogilvy, and M. Wilson for helpful comments on earlier drafts of this paper.

THE BELIEF IN A LIFE AFTER DEATH

1. Apparitions and Hauntings

The *prima facie* evidence of survival provided by an apparition is greatest when it supplies information that was unknown to the percipient. Among a number of well-attested reports of just this, two, which are so clear-cut that they have become classics in this field, may be cited briefly.

One is of the case of a traveling salesman, whose sister had died in 1867, and who in 1876 was in his hotel room at noon in St. Joseph, Missouri, smoking a cigar and writing up the orders he had obtained: "I suddenly became conscious that someone was sitting on my left, with one arm resting on the table. Quick as a flash I turned and distinctly saw the form of my dead sister, and for a brief second or so looked her squarely in the face; and so sure was I that it was she, that I sprang forward in delight calling her by name, and, as I did so, the apparition instantly vanished. . . . I was near enough to touch her . . . and noted her features, expression, and details of dress, etc. She appeared as alive."

He was so moved by the experience that he cut his trip short and returned to his home in St. Louis, where he related the occurrence to his parents, mentioning among other details of the apparition that, on the right side of the girl's nose, he had noticed a bright, red scratch about three fourths of an inch long. "When I mentioned this," he states, "my mother rose trembling to her feet and nearly fainted away, and . . . with tears streaming down her face, she exclaimed that I had indeed seen my sister, as no living mortal but herself was aware of that scratch, which she had accidentally made while doing some little act of kindness after my sister's death. She said she well remembered how pained she was to think she should have, unintentionally, marred the features of her dead daughter, and that unknown to all, she had carefully obliterated all

---

*This selection is from C. J. Ducasse, *The Belief in a Life after Death* (Springfield, Ill.: Charles C Thomas, 1961, pp. 156–174), and is reprinted here with the kind permission of the publisher.

traces of the slight scratch with the aid of powder, etc., and that she had never mentioned it to a human being from that day to this."[1]

The other famous case—the Chaffin will case—concerns not a similarly waking vision, but one occurring as either a vivid dream, or in a state between waking and dreaming. The essential facts are as follows: On November 16, 1905, James L. Chaffin, a North Carolina farmer, made a will attested by two witnesses, in which he left his farm to his son Marshall, the third of his four sons; and nothing to the other three or to his wife. On January 16, 1919, however, he made a new will, not witnessed but legally valid because wholly in his own handwriting. In it, he stated first that it was being made after his reading of the 27th chapter of Genesis; and then that he wanted his property divided equally between his four children, and that they must take care of their mother. He then placed this holograph will at the 27th chapter of Genesis in a Bible that had belonged to his father, folding over the pages to enclose the will.

He died on September 7, 1921, without, so far as ascertainable, ever having mentioned to anybody the existence of the second will. The first will was not contested and was probated on the 24th of the same month by its beneficiary, Marshall Chaffin.

Some four years later, in June, 1925, the second son, James Pinkney Chaffin, began to have very vivid dreams that his father appeared to him at his bedside without speaking. Later that month, however, the father again appeared at the bedside, wearing a familiar black overcoat, and then spoke, saying, "You will find my will in my overcoat pocket." In the morning, James looked for the overcoat, but was told by his mother that it had been given to his brother John, who lived twenty miles away. Some days later, James went to his brother's house, found the coat, and examined it. The inside lining of the inside pocket had been stitched together. On cutting the stitches, he found a little role of paper on which, in his father's handwriting, were written only the words: "Read the 27th chapter of Genesis in my Daddie's old Bible." He then returned to his mother's house, accompanied by his daughter, by a neighbor, and by the neighbor's daughter. They had some trouble finding the old Bible, but when they finally did, and the neighbor opened it at the 27th chapter of Genesis, they found the second will. The testator's wife and James P. Chaffin's wife were also present at the time. The second will was admitted to probate in December of the same year.[2]

Hauntings are apparitions that recur and that seem to be connected with a place rather than intended for a particular witness. A famous, well-attested case is that of the Morton ghost. It is described by Miss R. C. Morton (pseudonym),

---

[1] A full account of the case appears in Vol. 6:17-20, *S.P.R. Proceedings*, 1889–90. It is reproduced in F. W. H. Myer's *Human Personality and its Survival of Bodily Death*, Vol. 2:27-30.

[2] *S.P.R. Proceedings*, Vol. 36:517-24, 1927.

in Vol. VIII, 1892, of the *S.P.R. Proceedings*, pp. 311–332, who at that time was a medical student and apparently viewed the occurrences without fear or nervousness but only with scientific curiosity. The case dates back to 1882.

Miss Morton states that, having one evening gone up to her room, she heard someone at the door, opened it, and saw in the passage the figure of a tall lady, dressed in black, whose face was hidden by a handkerchief held in her right hand. She descended the stairs, and Miss Morton followed; but the small piece of candle she carried went out, and she returned to her room. The figure was seen again half a dozen times during the next two years by Miss Morton, once by her sister Mrs. K, once by the housemaid, and once by Miss Morton's brother and by a boy. After the first apparition, Miss Morton made it a practice to follow the figure downstairs into the drawing room. She spoke to the apparition but never got any reply; she cornered it several times in order to touch it, but it then simply disappeared. Its footsteps were audible and characteristic and were heard by Miss Morton's three sisters and by the cook. Miss Morton stretched some threads across the stairs, but the figure passed right through them without detaching them. The figure was seen in the orchard by a neighbor as well as in the house by Miss Morton's sisters, E. and M., by the cook, by the charwoman, and by a parlormaid, and by the gardener. But Miss Morton's father could not see it even when he was shown where it stood. The apparition was seen during the day as well as at night. In all, about twenty people saw it, some of them many times; and some of them not having previously heard of the apparition or of the sounds. The figure was described in the same way by all. The apparitions continued to occur until 1889. The figure wore widow's cuffs and corresponded to the description of a former tenant of the house, Mrs. S., whose life there had been unhappy.

The weight of apparitions as evidence of survival is decreased by the fact that there are numerous cases on record of apparitions of the living. Many of them are cited in Gurney, Myers, and Podmore's *Phantasms of the Living*.[3] Like apparitions in general, they are most impressive when more than one of the percipient's senses is affected—for instance, touch and hearing, or touch and sight. Several such cases are described on pp. 446 ff. of the book just cited. One is that of a girl, reading at night in her room, who suddenly "felt" (heard?) someone come into the room but, looking, could see no one. Then, she writes, "I felt a *kiss* on my forehead—a lingering, loving pressure. I looked up without the least sensation of fear, and saw my lover standing behind my chair, stooping as if to kiss me again. His face was very white and inexpressibly sad. As I rose from my chair in great surprise, before I could speak, he had gone, how I do not know; I only know that, one moment I saw him, saw distinctly every feature of

---

[3] In two vols. 1886. Abridged edition in one volume prepared by Mrs. Henry Sidgwick. (London: Kegan Paul, Trench, Trubner & Co.; New York: E. P. Dutton & Co.), 1918.

his face, saw the tall figure and broad shoulders as clearly as I ever saw them in my life, and the next moment there was no sign of him" (p. 447). A few days later, she heard that her lover had at the time been riding a vicious horse which, in order to unseat him, reared perfectly straight and pressed its back against a wall, with him between, making him lose consciousness—his last thought having been that he was dying and that he wanted to see his fiancée again before he died. It turned out, however, that only his hand had been severely injured, so that, for some days, he could not write to tell her what had occurred.

Such cases of apparitions of the living, veridical in the sense stated earlier, are most plausibly accounted for as telepathically caused hallucinations since they cannot really be apparitions of the dead. If, however, they are considered together with the cases of "out-of-the-body" experience—so-called projection of the double—of which instances are cited in Section 2 of the present chapter, then what suggests itself is that what is seen in cases of apparitions—whether of the living or of the dead—is the "projected," i.e., externalized, "double" assumed to be possessed by man but to be normally collocated with the body. It is con-jectured that at death the dislocation of it from the body is complete and permanent, whereas in apparitions of the living, the dislocation is temporary and incomplete in that a connection—the reported "silver thread"—remains between the externalized "double" and the body. If this should actually be the state of affairs, then apparitions would not really be visual hallucinations, but rather *sights*, fleeting but genuine, of something very tenuous though objectively present at the place where it is perceived.

In the way of this supposition, however, stands a fact to which we shall have occasion to return; namely that, since apparitions are seldom if ever naked, then their clothes too would have to be supposed to have an externalizable "double."

But even when telepathy is admitted to be a fact and is invoked, apparitions, veridical in the sense stated, remain very difficult to explain plausibly. How difficult will be appreciated by readers who may be interested to look up the seemingly far-fetched explanations to which able thinkers have found themselves forced to have recourse when they have insisted on taking scrupulously into consideration *all* the facts on record.[4]

---

[4]*Apparitions*, by G. N. M. Tyrrell, with a preface by H. H. Price; Gerald Duckworth and Co., Ltd., revised edition, 1953; "A Theory of Apparitions," by W. F. Barrett, E. Gurney, and F. Podmore, *S.P.R. Proceedings*, Vol. 2:109-36; 1884. "Six Theories about Apparitions," by Hornell Hart, *S.P.R. Proceedings*, 1955-56, pp. 153-239. For additional references on the subject of apparitions, see G. Zorab's *Bibliography of Parapsychology*, Parapsychology Foundation, Inc., New York 1957, pp. 27-28. Concerning Haunting, see H. H. Price's presidential address to the S.P.R.; *S.P.R. Proceedings*, Vol. 45:307-343, 1938-39.

2. "Out-of-the-Body" Experiences

Let us turn next to the "out-of-the-body," experiences alluded to in the latter part of the preceding section, of which many cases have been reported. Those who have undergone the experience generally consider it impressive evidence that the human consciousness is separable in space from the human body and, it would therefore seem, can exist independently of the latter. That experience has variously been termed projection of "the double," "ESP projection," "projection of the astral body," "out-of-the-body" experience, and "bilocation." In the most striking form of it, the person concerned, having gone to sleep or being under anaesthesia, wakens to see his body inert on the bed and is able to observe it from the same variety of angles as he could the body of another. He is also able to observe the various objects in the room, and, in some cases, he perceives and is later able to describe persons who came into the room and went out before his body awoke. The thus temporarily excarnate observer may or may not find himself able to travel away from the vicinity of his sleeping body. In some of the cases when he does so and visits a distant place, he is reported to have been seen at that place at the time. These are the cases of "bilocation." A famous one is that of Alfonso de Liguori who in 1774 was at Arezzo, in prison, fasting. On awakening one morning, he stated that he had been at the bedside of the then dying Pope, Clement XIV; where, it turned out, he had been seen by those present.

For the sake of concreteness, a few of the many reports of out-of-the-body experience will now be cited.

Dr. E. Osty, in the May–June issue of the *Revue Métapsychique* for 1930, quotes a letter addressed by a gentleman named L. L. Hymans to Charles Richet, dated June 7, 1928, in which the former relates two such experiences: "The first time it was while in a dentist's chair. Under anaesthesia, I had the sensation of awaking and of finding myself floating in the upper part of the room, from where, with great astonishment, I watched the dentist working on my body, and the anaesthetist at his side. I saw my inanimate body as distinctly as any other object in the room. . . . The second time I was in a hotel in London. I awoke in the morning feeling unwell (I have a weak heart) and shortly thereafter I fainted. Greatly to my astonishment, I found myself in the upper part of the room, from where, with fear, I beheld my body inanimate in the bed with its eyes closed. I tried without success to reenter my body and concluded that I had died. . . . Certainly I had not lost either memory or self-consciousness. I could see my inanimate body like a separate object: I was able to look at my face. I was, however, unable to leave the room: I felt myself as it were chained, immobilized in the corner where I was. After an hour or two I heard a knock on the locked door several times, without being able to answer. Soon after, the hotel porter appeared on the fire escape. I saw him get into the room, look anxiously at my face, and open the door. The hotel manager and others then entered. A physician came in. I saw him shake his head after listening to my heart, and then insert a spoon between my lips. I then lost consciousness and awoke in the bed." In the same article, Dr. Osty cites the similar experiences of two other persons.

Dr. Ernesto Bozzano cites the case of a friend of his, the engineer Giuseppe Costa who, while asleep, so disturbed the kerosene lamp on his bedside table that it filled the room with dense, choking smoke. Signor Costa writes: "I had the clear and precise sensation of finding myself with only my thinking personality, in the middle of the room, *completely separated from my body*, which continued to lie on the bed. . . . I was seized with an inexpressible anguish from which I felt intuitively that I could only free myself by freeing my material body from that oppressive situation. I wanted therefore to pick up the lamp and open the window, but it was a material act that I could not accomplish. . . . Then I thought of my mother, who was sleeping in the next room. . . . It seemed to me that no effort of any kind was needed to cause her to approach my body. I saw her get hurriedly out of bed, run to her window and open it . . . then leave her room, walk along the corridor, enter my room and approach my body gropingly and with staring eyes." He then awoke. He writes further: "My mother, questioned by me soon after the event, confirmed the fact that she had first opened her window as if she felt herself suffocating, before coming to my aid. Now the fact of my *having seen this act of hers through the wall*, while lying *inanimate on the bed*, entirely excludes the hypothesis of hallucination and nightmare. . . . I thus had the most evident proof that *my soul had detached itself from my body during its material existence*. I had, in fact, received proof of the existence of the soul and also of its immortality, since it was true that it had freed itself . . . from the material envelope of the body, acting and thinking outside it."[5] In order to explain this case, however, telepathy plus clairvoyance would be enough.

In some persons, out-of-the-body experience becomes voluntary. The best-known account of the process involved is that of the late Sylvan Muldoon,[6] whose description of his own experiences brought him numerous communications from strangers who had themselves had out-of-the-body experiences. Many of these are quoted by him in a later book,[7] including one which, some years

---

[5]Quoted in Bozzano's *Discarnate Influence in Human Life*, pp. 112–115, from Giuseppe Costa's *Di la della Vita*, p. 18.

[6]*The Projection of the Astral Body*, David McKay Co., Philadelphia, 1929.

[7]*The Phenomena of Astral Projection*, by Sylvan Muldoon and Hereward Carrington, Rider and Co., London, 1951.

before that book appeared, was related to the present writer by the person concerned, Miss Mary Ellen Frallic. Her "projection" experience occurred not during sleep or under anaesthesia, but while walking on the street. She gradually became conscious of rising higher and higher, up to the height of the second floor of the surrounding buildings, and then felt an urge to look back; whereupon she saw her body walking about one block behind. That body was apparently able to see "her" for she noticed the look of bewilderment on its face. Her consciousness of location then shifted a few times from that of the "double" to that of the body, and back, each being able to perceive the other. She then felt afraid and immediately reentered her body.[8]

Besides Muldoon's account of voluntary "projections," one of the most interesting is by a Frenchman who, under the pseudonym, Yram, wrote, in 1926, a book entitled *The Physician of the Soul*, which has since been translated under the title *Practical Astral Projection*. In it he describes twelve years of his own experimentation in conscious out-of-the-body experience. Another writer, Oliver Fox, in a book entitled *Astral Projection*, related his own experiences.[9]

In a number of cases, the projected "double" is reported to remain connected with the sleeping body by a "silver cord" which is extensible in various degrees. Persons who have had the out-of-the-body experience have usually assumed, as did the engineer Giuseppe Costa quoted above, that the spatial separation in it of the observing and thinking consciousness from the body on the bed means that the former is capable of existing and of functioning independently of the latter not only thus temporarily during "projection," but enduringly at death, which is then simply permanent, definitive projection when the "silver cord" snaps.

This conclusion, however, does not necessarily follow, for it tacitly assumes that the conscious "double" is what animates the body—normally in being collocated with it, but also, when dislocated from it, through connection with it by the "silver cord." The fact, however, could equally be that the animation is in the converse direction, i.e., that death of the body entails death of the conscious "double" whether the latter be, at the time, dislocated from or collocated with the former.

Hence, out-of-the-body experience, however impressive to those who have it, and however it may tempt them to conclude that they then know that consciousness is not dependent on the living material body, does not really warrant this conclusion; but only the more modest one, which, of course, is arresting

---

[8]Cf. *op. cit.*, pp. 189–190.
[9]Rider and Co., London (no date). A number of interesting cases are quoted in some detail on pp. 220–229 of Dr. Raynor C. Johnson's *The Imprisoned Splendour*, Harper and Bros., New York, 1953. A bibliography of the subject is furnished on pp. 221–222 of Muldoon and Carrington's *The Phenomena of Astral Projection*.

enough, that correct visual perception of physical events and objects, including perception of one's own body from a point distant in space from it, can occur, exceptionally, at times when the eyes are shut and the body asleep—this fact, of course, not being at all explained by labeling the occurrences of it "heautoscopic hallucinations" since, as pointed out earlier, what is paranormal, instead of merely abnormal, in certain hallucinations is that they are *veridical* in the same sense in which perceptions are so, even if not through the same mechanism.

3. Materializations and Other Paranormal Physical Phenomena

Among paranormal phenomena, certain physical ones—especially materializations and the so-called "direct voice"—are easily accepted by persons who witness them as evidence of survival. There are numerous reports, some of them circumstantial and made by careful and experienced observers, of the materialization of portions of human bodies—of hands, for example, which move and grasp and carry things; or of faces or even of entire bodies which act, speak, and breathe like ordinary living human bodies; and after a while dematerialize, suddenly or slowly.

Sir William Crookes, for instance, in an article he published in the Quarterly Journal of Science[10] writes: "A beautifully formed small hand rose up from an opening in a dining table and gave me a flower; it appeared and then disappeared three times at intervals, affording me ample opportunity of satisfying myself that it was as real in appearance as my own. This occurred in the light in my own room, whilst I was holding the medium's hands and feet. On another occasion a small hand and arm, like a baby's, appeared playing about a lady who was sitting next to me. It then passed to me and patted my arm and pulled my coat several times. At another time a finger and thumb were seen to pick the petals from a flower in Mr. Home's button-hole and lay them in front of several persons who were sitting near him. . . . I have more than once seen, first an object move, then a luminous cloud appear to form about it, and lastly, the cloud condense into shape and become a perfectly-formed hand. . . . At the wrist, or arm, it becomes hazy, and fades off into a luminous cloud. To the touch the hand sometimes appears icy cold and dead, at other times warm and life-like, grasping my own with the firm pressure of an old friend. I have retained one of these hands in my own, firmly resolved not to let it escape. There was no struggle or effort made to get loose, but it gradually seemed to resolve itself into vapour and faded in that manner from my grasp."

Among the materializations of entire bodies that have been reported, those

---

[10] "Notes of an Enquiry into the Phenomena Called Spiritual during the Years 1870–73." Reprinted with other articles by Crookes under the tital *Researches in the Phenomena of Spiritualism*, Two Worlds Publishing Co., 1926. The quotation is from pp. 102–103.

of "Katie King," repeatedly observed by Sir William Crookes under his own conditions as well as by others, and measured, auscultated, tested and photographed by him—Florence Cook being the medium—are probably the most famous and most carefully described.[11]

The apparent materialization, in whole or in part, of human bodies and of their clothing and accoutrements, is supposed to depend on and to consist at least, in part, of a mysterious substance that emanates from the medium's body, and to which the name of "ectoplasm" has therefore been given. It seems able to exert or to conduct force. It is said to have various consistencies—sometimes vaporous, sometimes filmy like a veil, sometimes gelatinous, sometimes pasty like thick dough.

The latter was its consistency on the one occasion when in the house of a friend of mine I personally had an opportunity to see in good red light, to touch, and take ten flash-light photographs of a substance emanating from the mouth of an entranced nonprofessional medium; which substance, whether or not it was "ectoplasm," did not behave, feel, or look as any other substance known to me could, I think, have done under the conditions that existed. It was coldish, about like steel. This made it seem moist, but it was dry and slightly rough like dough the surface of which had dried. Its consistency and weight were also doughlike. It was a string, of about pencil thickness, varying in length from some six to twelve feet. On other photographs, not taken by me, of the same medium, it has veillike and ropelike forms.

Professor Charles Richet, who had many occasions to observe what appeared to be materializations, discusses at one point in his *Thirty Years of Psychical Research*[12] the possibilities of fraud in purported materializations and the precautions necessary to preclude it; and he concludes that, in the case of the best of the available reports of the phenomenon—a number of which he mentions—neither fraud nor illusion is a possible explanation: "When I recall the precautions that all of us have taken, not once, but twenty, a hundred, or even a thousand times, it is inconceivable that we should have been deceived on all these occasions."

Concerning occurrences he personally observed under especially favorable conditions, he writes: "Sometimes these ectoplasms can be seen in process of organization; I have seen an almost rectilinear prolongation emerge from Eusapia's body, its termination acting like a living hand.... I have ... been able to see the first lineaments of materializations as they were formed. A kind of liquid or pasty jelly emerges from the mouth or the breast of Marthe which organizes itself by degrees, acquiring the shape of a face or a limb. Under very good conditions of visibility, I have seen this paste spread on my knee, and

[11] *Loc. cit.*, pp. 115–128.
[12] Collins and Sons, London, 1923, p. 460. English translation by Stanley De Brath, p. 467.

slowly take form so as to show the rudiment of the radius, the cubitus, or metacarpal bone whose increasing pressure I could feel on my knee.[13]

The *prima facie* most impressive evidence there could be of the survival of a deceased friend or relative would be to see and touch his materialized, recognizable bodily form, which then speaks in his or her characteristic manner. This is what appeared to occur in my presence on an occasion three or four years ago when, during some two hours and in very good red light throughout, some eighteen fully material forms—some male, some female, some tall and some short, and sometimes two together—came out of and returned to the curtained cabinet I had inspected beforehand, in which a medium sat, and to which I had found no avenue of surreptitious access.

These material forms were apparently recognized as those of a deceased father, mother, or other relative by one or another of the fourteen or fifteen persons present; and some touching scenes occurred, in which the form of the deceased spoke with and caressed the living.

One of those forms called my name and, when I went up to her and asked who she was, she answered "Mother." She did not, however, speak, act, or in the least resemble my mother. This was no disappointment to me since I had gone there for purposes not of consolation but of observation. I would have felt fully rewarded if the conditions of observation had been such that I could have been quite sure that the material form I saw, that spoke to me and patted me on the head, was genuinely a materialization, no matter of whom or of what. Indeed, materialization of half a human body would, for my purpose, have been even more significant than materialization of an entire one.

I should add, however, that the friend who had taken me to that circle, who is a careful and critical observer, and who had been there a number of times before, told me that on the occasions when a material form that purported to be a materialization of his mother had come out of the cabinet and spoken to him, the form was sometimes recognizably like her, and sometimes not.

Apparitions and genuine materializations (if any) are alike in being visible, and usually in reproducing the appearance of a human body or of parts of one; and, in cases where at least the face is reproduced, sometimes in being recognizably like that of one particular person known to someone present. On the other hand, materializations are tangible whereas apparitions are not so.

The question then arises whether apparitions are incomplete materializations (a mist or haze is visible but not tangible, and yet is material), or whether materializations are "complete" hallucinations, i.e., hallucinations not only of sight and of sound of voice or of footsteps, but also of the sense of touch and the others. As regards the second alternative, I can say only that if the form I saw, which said it was my mother and which patted me on the head, was a hallucination—a hallucination "complete" in the sense just stated—then no dif-

[13] *Thirty Years of Psychical Research*, Collins and Sons, London, 1923, p. 469.

ference remains between a complete hallucination, on the one hand, and, on the other, ordinary veridical perception of a physical object; for every further test of the physicality of the form seen and touched could then be alleged to be itself hallucinatory, and the allegation of complete hallucination then automatically becomes completely vacuous.

On the other hand, cases are on record of apparitions of the living but, so far as I know, no good cases have been reported of materializations of the living in the sense that a living person was not merely seen and perhaps heard but also *tangibly* present at a place distant from that of his body. In such cases of "bi-location" as that of Alphonse of Liguori, who, while in prison at Arezzo, was seen among the persons in attendance at the bedside of the then dying Pope Clement XIV in Rome, the testimony does not, I believe, include any statement that he was *touched*, while there, as well as seen.

But no matter whether we say that apparitions are incomplete materializations, or that materializations are complete hallucinations, a fact remains concerning both that has bearing on the question whether they constitute evidence of survival after death. It is that both apparitions and materializations wear clothing of some sort; so that, as someone has put the point, "if ghosts have clothes, then clothes have ghosts." That is, if one says that the apparition or materialization is the deceased's surviving "spirit," temporarily become perceptible, then does not consistency require one to say that the familiar dress or coat or other accoutrement it wears had a spirit too that has also survived? On the other hand, if one assumes that the clothing the apparition or materialization wears is materialization only of a memory image of the deceased's clothing, then would not consistency dictate the conclusion that the now temporarily perceptible parts of the deceased's body are materializations likewise only of a memory image of his appearance and behavior?

If one is fortunate enough to witness an apparition, or even better, a materialization where the materialized form duplicates the appearance of a deceased friend or relative, speaks and behaves as the latter did, and mentions facts of an intimate nature which few if any but the deceased and oneself knew, then the temptation may well be psychologically irresistible to believe that the deceased himself is with us again in temporarily materialized form, and therefore that he does indeed survive the death of the body that was his. The remarks made above, however, show that this interpretation of the experience, no matter how hard psychologically it then is to resist, is not the only one of which the experience admits, and is not necessarily the one most probably true.

On this point, some words of Richet—who as we have seen became certain that materializations do really occur—are worth quoting. Comparing the evidence for survival from mediumistic communications with that which materializations are thought to furnish, he writes: "The case of George Pelham [one of Mrs. Piper's best communicators], though there was no materialization, is vastly more evidential for survival than all the materializations yet known . . .

materializations, however perfect, cannot prove survival; the evidence that they sometimes seem to give is much less striking than that given by subjective metaphysics," i.e., chiefly, by mediumistic communications (p. 490). It is worth bearing in mind in this connection that in the star case of "Katie King," who claimed to have in life been Annie Owen Morgan, daughter of the buccaneer Sir Henry Owen Morgan, no evidence exists that such a woman did actually live. But unless she actually did, and died, the question whether "her" spirit survived death, and materialized as Katie King, becomes vacuous.

As regards the evidence for survival supposedly constituted by physical paranormal phenomena such as "poltergeist" occurrences, telekinesis, raps, levitation, "direct" voice, etc., H. F. Saltmarsh writes that "in order that events of this kind should have any value as evidence of survival they must possess some characteristic which will connect them with some deceased person. The bare fact that a material object is moved in a way we cannot account for by normal means does not afford any clue to the identity of the agent. All we could say in the most favourable circumstances would be that some unknown agency is involved and that that agency exhibits intelligence; we could not argue that it was, or even had been, human, still less that it was connected with some one particular person. Thus when any special characteristics which might connect them with a deceased person are absent, we can rule out physical phenomena as completely unevidential of survival. Where, however, the phenomena show some special characteristics which connect with some definite deceased person, any evidential value for survival rests entirely on those characteristics."[14]

4. "Possessions"

Another sort of paranormal occurrence, some cases of which invite interpretation as evidence of survival, is that popularly known as "possession," i.e., prima facie possession of a person's body by a personality—whether devilish, divine, or merely human—radically different from his or her own. The most probably correct interpretation of the great majority of such cases is that the "possessing" personality is only a dissociated, normally repressed portion or aspect of the total personality of the individual concerned.

The case of the Rev. Ansel Bourne, of Greene, R.I.[15] the still more famous cases of the alternating personalities of Miss Beauchamp, reported by Dr. Morton

[14] "Is Proof of Survival Possible?" S.P.R. Proceedings, Vol. 40:106–107, Jan. 1932.
[15] Proceedings of the Society for Psychical Research, Vol. 7, 1891–1892: "A Case of Double Consciousness," by Richard Hodgson, M.D., pp. 221–257. It is commented upon by William James in Chapter 10 of his Principles of Psychology, 1905, pp. 390–393, who also cites a number of others.

Prince, and the Doris Fischer case described by Dr. Walter F. Prince,[16] would be examples of such temporary "possession." The survival interpretation has little or no plausibility as regards most such cases, but is less easy to dismiss in a few others, different from these in that the intruding personality gives more or less clear and abundant evidence of being that of one particular individual who had died some time before.

About as impressive a case of this as any on record is that of the so-called Watseka Wonder. An account of it was first published in 1879 in the *Religio-Philosophical Journal*, and, in 1887, republished as a pamphlet, *The Watseka Wonder*, by the Religio-Philosophical Publishing House, Chicago. The subtitle is "A Narrative of Startling Phenomena Occurring in the Case of Mary Lurancy Vennum." The author of the narrative was a medical man, Dr. E. Winchester Stevens (1822–1885), who had been consulted at the time in the case.

Two girls were concerned. One, Mary Roff, had died on July 5, 1865 at the age of 18. From an early age, she had had frequent "fits" becoming more violent with the years; she had complained of a "lump of pain in the head" (p. 10), to relieve which she had repeatedly bled herself; and she is stated to have been able, while "heavily blindfolded by critical intelligent, investigating gentlemen" to read readily books even when closed and letters even in envelopes, and to do other tasks normally requiring the use of the eyes (p. 11).

The other girl, Lurancy Vennum, was born on April 16, 1864 and was therefore a little over one year old at the time Mary Roff died. At the age of 13 in July 1877, Lurancy, who until then "had never been sick, save a light run of measles" (p. 3), complained of feeling queer, went into a fit including a cataleptic state lasting five hours. On subsequent similar occasions, while in trance, she conversed and described "angels" or "spirits" of persons who had died. She was believed insane and was examined by two local physicians. On January 31, 1878, Mr. Roff, who had heard of Lurancy's case and become interested in it, was allowed by her father to bring Dr. E. W. Stevens to observe her. On that occasion, she became apparently "possessed" by two alien personalities in turn— one a sullen, crabbed, old hag, and the second a young man who said he had run away from home, got into trouble, and lost his life (pp. 5, 6). Dr. Stevens then "magnetized" her and "was soon in full and free communication with the sane and happy mind of Lurancy Vennum herself" (p. 7). She described the "angels" about her and said that one of them wanted to come to her instead of the evil spirits mentioned above." On being asked if she knew who it was, she said: "Her name is Mary Roff" (p. 7). The next day, "Mr. Vennum called at the office of Mr. Roff and informed him that the girl claimed to be Mary Roff and wanted

[16] Morton Prince: *The Dissociation of a Personality*, London, Longmans Green, 1906; W. F. Prince: "The Doris Case of Multiple Personality," *Proceedings of the A.S.P.R.* Vols. 9 and 10, 1915, 1916; and in Vol. 11, discussed by J. H. Hyslop.

to go home. . . . 'She seems like a child real homesick, wanting to see her pa and ma and her brothers'" (p. 9).

Some days later, she was allowed to go and live with the Roffs. There, she "seemed perfectly happy and content, knowing every person and everything that Mary knew in her original body, twelve to twenty-five years ago, recognizing and calling by name those who were friends and neighbors of the family from 1852 to 1865, [i.e., during the 12 years preceding Lurancy's birth], calling attention to scores, yes, hundreds of incidents that transpired during [Mary's] natural life" (p. 14). She recognized a headdress Mary used to wear; pointed to a collar, saying she had tatted it; remembered details of the journey of the family to Texas in 1857 [i.e., 7 years before Lurancy's birth). On the other hand, she did not recognize any of the Vennum family nor their friends and neighbors, nor knew anything that had until then been known by Lurancy.

Lurancy's new life as Mary Roff lasted 3 months and 10 days. Then Lurancy's own personality returned to her body, and she went back to the Vennums, who reported her well in mind and body from then on. She eventually married and had children. Occasionally then, when Lurancy was visiting the Roffs, the Mary personality would come back for some little time.

What distinguishes this case from the more common ones of alternating personalities is, of course, that the personality that displaced Lurancy's was, by every test that could be applied, not a dissociated part of her own, but the personality and all the memories that had belonged to a particular 18 year old girl who had died at a time when Lurancy was but 14 months old; and that no way, consistent with Dr. Stevens' record of the facts, has been suggested in which Lurancy, during the 13 years of her life before her sojourn with the Roffs, could have obtained the extensive and detailed knowledge Mary had possessed, which Lurancy manifested during the sojourn. For the Vennums were away from Wateska for the first 7 years of Lurancy's life; and when they returned to Watseka, their acquaintance with the Roffs consisted only of one brief call of a few minutes by Mrs. Roff on Mrs. Vennum, and of a formal speaking acquaintance between the two men, until the time when Mr. Roff brought Dr. Stevens to the Vennums on account of Lurancy's insane behavior.

In commenting on various cases of seeming "possession" of a person's organism by a personality altogether different, William James notes that "many persons have found evidence conclusive to their minds that in some cases the control is really the departed spirit whom it pretends to be," but that "the phenomena shade off so gradually into cases where this is obviously absurd, that the presumption (quite apart from a priori 'scientific' prejudice) is great against its being true,"[17] He then turns to the Watseka case just described, introducing

[17]*Principles of Psychology*, New York, Henry Holt and Co., 1905, p. 396.

it by the statement that it is "perhaps as extreme a case of 'possession' of the modern sort as one can find," but he makes no attempt to explain it.

The only way that suggests itself, to avoid the conclusion that the Mary Roff personality which for fourteen weeks "possessed" Lurancy's organism was "really the departed spirit whom it pretended to be," is to have recourse to the method of orthodoxy, whose maxim is: "When you cannot explain all the facts according to accepted principles, then explain those you can and ignore the rest; or else deny them, distort them, or invent some that would help."

This procrustean method, of course, has a measure of validity, since errors of observation or of reporting do occur. Yet some facts turn out to be too stubborn to be disposed of plausibly by that method; and the present one would appear to be one of them, . . . that no impossibility either theoretical or empirical attaches to the supposition of survival of a human personality after death.

5. Memories, Seemingly of Earlier Lives

Brief mention may be made at this point of another kind of occurrence, of which only a few cases at all impressive have been reported, but which, like those of the other kinds considered in the preceding sections, constitute *prima facie* evidence of survival. I refer to the cases where a person has definite apparent memories relating to a life he lived on earth before his present one, and where the facts and events he believes he remembers turn out to be capable of verification. If these should indeed be memories in the same literal sense as that in which each of us has memories of places he visited years before, of persons he met there, of incidents of his school days, and so on, then this would constitute proof not strictly that he *will* survive the death of his body but that he *has* survived that of the different body he remembers having had in an earlier life.

THE EXPERIENCE OF DYING

RAYMOND MOODY*

Despite the wide variation in the circumstances surrounding close calls with death and in the types of persons undergoing them, it remains true that there is a striking similarity among the accounts of the experiences themselves. In fact, the similarities among various reports are so great that one can easily pick out about fifteen separate elements which recur again and again in the mass of narratives that I have collected. On the basis of these points of likeness, let me now construct a brief, theoretically "ideal" or "complete" experience which embodies all of the common elements, in the order in which it is typical for them to occur:

A man is dying and, as he reaches the point of greatest physical distress, he hears himself pronounced dead by his doctor. He begins to hear an uncomfortable noise, a loud ringing or buzzing, and at the same time feels himself moving very rapidly through a long dark tunnel. After this, he suddenly finds himself outside of his own physical body, but still in the immediate physical environment, and he sees his own body from a distance, as though he is a spectator. He watches the resuscitation attempt from this unusual vantage point and is in a state of emotional upheaval.

After a while, he collects himself and becomes more accustomed to his odd condition. He notices that he still has a "body," but one of a very different nature and with very different powers from the physical body he has left behind. Soon other things begin to happen. Others come to meet and to help him. He glimpses the spirits of relatives and friends who have already died, and a loving, warm spirit of a kind he has never encountered before—a being of light—appears before him. This being asks him a question, nonverbally, to make him evaluate his life and helps him along by showing him a panoramic, instantaneous playback of the major events of his life. At some point he finds himself approaching

---

*This selection is from Raymond Moody *Life After Life* (New York: Bantam Books, 1975, pp. 21–25, 34–43, and 98–101), and is reprinted here with the kind permission of the author and publisher.

some sort of barrier or border, apparently representing the limit between earthly life and the next life. Yet, he finds that he must go back to the earth, that the time for his death has not yet come. At this point he resists, for by now he is taken up with his experiences in the afterlife and does not want to return. He is overwhelmed by intense feelings of joy, love, and peace. Despite his attitude, though, he somehow reunites with his physical body and lives.

Later he tries to tell others, but he has trouble doing so. In the first place, he can find no human words adequate to describe these unearthly episodes. He also finds that others scoff, so he stops telling other people. Still, the experience affects his life profoundly, especially his views about death and its relationship to life.

It is important to bear in mind that the above narrative is not meant to be a representation of any one person's experience. Rather, it is a "model," a composite of the common elements found in very many stories. I introduce it here only to give a preliminary, general idea of what a person who is dying may experience. Since it is an abstraction rather than an actual account, in the present chapter I will discuss in detail each common element, giving many examples.

Before doing that, however, a few facts need to be set out in order to put the remainder of my exposition of the experience of dying into the proper framework.

1. Despite the striking similarities among various accounts, no two of them are precisely identical (though a few come remarkably close to it).
2. I have found no one person who reports every single component of the experience. Very many have reported most of them (that is, eight or more of the fifteen or so) and a few have reported up to twelve.
3. There is no one element of the composite experience which every single person has reported to me, which crops up in every narrative. Nonetheless, a few of these elements come fairly close to being universal.
4. There is not one component of my abstract model which has appeared in only one account. Each element has shown up in many separate stories.
5. The order in which a dying person goes through the various stages briefly delineated above many vary from that given in my "theoretical model." To give one example, various persons have reported seeing the "being of light" before, or at the same time, they left their physical bodies, and not as in the "model," some time afterward. However, the order in which the stages occur in the model is a very typical order, and wide variations are unusual.
6. How far into the hypothetical complete experience a dying person gets seems to depend on whether or not the person actually underwent an apparent clinical death, and if so, on how long he was in this state. In

general, persons who were "dead" seem to report more florid, complete experiences than those who only came close to death, and those who were "dead" for a longer period go deeper than those who were "dead" for a shorter time.

7. I have talked to a few people who were pronounced dead, resuscitated, and came back reporting none of these common elements. Indeed, they say that they don't remember anything at all about their "deaths." Interestingly enough, I have talked with several persons who were actually adjudged clinically dead on separate occasions years apart, and reported experiencing nothing on one of the occasions, but having had quite involved experiences on the other.

8. It must be emphasized that I am writing primarily about reports, accounts, or narratives, which other persons have given to me verbally during interviews. Thus, when I remark that a given element of the abstract, "complete" experience does not occur in a given account, I do not mean necessarily to imply that it did not happen to the person involved. I only mean that this person did not tell me that it did occur, or that it does not definitely come out in his account that he experienced it. Within this framework, then, let us look at some of the common stages and events of the experiences of dying . . . .

Out of the Body

It is a truism that most of us, most of the time, identify ourselves with our physical bodies. We grant, of course, that we have "minds," too. But to most people our "minds" seem much more ephemeral than our bodies. The "mind," after all might be no more than the effect of the electrical and chemical activity which takes place in the brain, which is a part of the physical body. For many people it is an impossible task even to conceive of what it would be like to exist in any other way than in the physical body to which they are accustomed.

Prior to their experiences, the persons I have interviewed were not, as a group, any different from the average person with respect to this attitude. That is why, after his rapid passage through the dark tunnel, a dying person often has such an overwhelming surprise. For, at this point, he may find himself looking upon his own physical body from a point outside of it, as though he were "a spectator" or "a third person in the room" or watching figures and events "onstage in a play" or "in a movie." Let us look now at portions of some accounts in which these uncanny out-of-the-body episodes are described:

> I was seventeen years old and my brother and I were working at an amusement park. One afternoon, we decided to go swimming, and there were quite a few of the other young people who went in with us. Someone said, "Let's swim across the lake."

I had done that on numerous occasions, but that day for some reason, I went down, almost in the middle of the lake . . . . I kept bobbling up and down, and all of a sudden, it felt as though I were away from my body, away from everybody, in space by myself. Although I was stable, staying at the same level, I saw my body in the water about three or four feet away, bobbling up and down. I viewed my body from the back and slightly to the right side. I still felt as though I had an entire body form, even while I was outside my body. I had an airy feeling that's almost indescribable. I felt like a feather.

A woman recalls:

About a year ago, I was admitted to the hospital with heart trouble, and the next morning, lying in the hospital bed, I began to have a very severe pain in my chest. I pushed the button beside the bed to call for the nurses, and they came in and started working on me. I was quite uncomfortable lying on my back so I turned over, and as I did I quit breathing and my heart stopped beating. Just then, I heard the nurses shout, "Code pink! Code pink!" As they were saying this, I could feel myself moving out of my body and sliding down between the mattress and the rail on the side of the bed—actually it seemed as if I went *through* the rail—on down to the floor. Then, I started rising upward, slowly. On my way up, I saw more nurses come running into the room-there must have been a dozen of them. My doctor happened to be making his rounds in the hospital so they called him and I saw him come in, too. I thought, "I wonder what he's doing here." I drifted on up past the light fixture—I saw it from the side and very distinctly—and then I stopped, floating right below the ceiling, looking down. I felt almost as though I were a piece of paper that someone had blown up to the ceiling.

I watched them reviving me from up there! My body was lying down there stretched out on the bed, in plain view, and they were all standing around it. I heard one nurse say, "Oh, my God! She's gone!", while another one leaned down to give me mouth-to-mouth resuscitation. I was looking at the *back* of her head while she did this. I'll never forget the way her hair looked; it was cut kind of short. Just then, I saw them roll this machine in there, and they put the shocks on my chest. When they did, I saw my whole body just jump right up off the bed, and I heard every bone in my body crack and pop. It was the most awful thing!

As I saw them below beating on my chest and rubbing my arms and legs, I thought. "Why are they going to so much trouble? I'm just fine now."

A young informant states:

It was about two years ago, and I had just turned nineteen. I was driving a friend of mine home in my car, and as I got to this particular intersection downtown, I stopped and looked both ways, but I didn't see a thing coming. I pulled on out into the intersection and as I did I heard my friend yell at the top of his voice. When I looked I saw a blinding light, the headlights of a car that was speeding towards us. I heard this awful sound—the side of the car being crushed in—and there was just an instant during which I seemed to be going through a darkness, an enclosed space. It was very quick. Then, I was sort of floating about five feet above the street, about five yards away from the car, I'd say, and I heard the echo of the crash dying away. I saw people come running up and crowding around the car, and I saw my friend get out of the car, obviously in shock. I could see my own body in the wreckage among all those people, and could see them trying to get it out. My legs were all twisted and there was blood all over the place.

As one might well imagine, some unparalleled thoughts and feelings run through the minds of persons who find themselves in this predicament. Many people find the notion of being out of their bodies so unthinkable that, even as they are experiencing it, they feel conceptually quite confused about the whole thing and do not link it with death for a considerable time. They wonder what is happening to them; why can they suddenly see themselves from a distance, as though a spectator?

Emotional responses to this strange state vary widely. Most people report, at first, a desperate desire to get back into their bodies but they do not have the faintest idea about how to proceed. Others recall that they were very afraid, almost panicky. Some, however, report more positive reactions to their plight, as in this account:

> I became very seriously ill, and the doctor put me in the hospital. This one morning a solid gray mist gathered around me, and I left my body. I had a floating sensation as I felt myself get out of my body, and I looked back and I could see myself on the bed below and there was no fear. It was quiet—very peaceful and serene. I was not in the least bit upset or frightened. It was just a tranquil feeling, and it was something which I didn't dread. I felt that maybe I was dying, and I felt that if I did not get back to my body, I would be dead, gone.

Just as strikingly variable are the attitudes which different persons take to the bodies which they have left behind. It is common for a person to report feelings of concern for his body. One young woman, who was a nursing student at the time of her experience, expresses an understandable fear:

> This is sort of funny, I know, but in nursing school they had tried to drill it into us that we ought to donate our bodies to science. Well, all through this, as I watched them trying to start my breathing again, I kept thinking, "I don't want them to use that body as a cadaver."

I have heard two other persons express exactly this same concern when they found themselves out of their bodies. Interestingly enough, both of them were also in the medical profession—one a physician, the other a nurse.

In another case, this concern took the form of regret. A man's heart stopped beating following a fall in which his body was badly mangled, and he recalls:

> At one time—now, I know I was lying on the bed there—but I could actually see the bed and the doctor working on me. I couldn't understand it, but I looked at my own body lying there on the bed. And I felt real bad when I looked at my body and saw how badly it was messed up.

Several persons have told me of having feelings of unfamiliarity toward their bodies, as in this rather striking passage:

> Boy, I sure didn't realize that I looked like that! You know, I'm only used to seeing myself in pictures or from the front in a mirror, and both of those look *flat*. But all of a sudden there I—or my body—was and I could see it. I could definitely

see it, full view, from about five feet away. It took me a few moments to recognize myself.

In one account, this feeling of unfamiliarity took a rather extreme and humorous form. One man, a physician, tells how during his clinical "death" he was beside the bed looking at his own cadaver, which by then had turned the ash gray color assumed by bodies after death. Desperate and confused, he was trying to decide what to do. He tentatively decided just to go away, as he was feeling very uneasy. As a youngster he had been told ghost stories by his grandfather and, paradoxically, he "didn't like being around this thing that looked like a dead body—even if it was me!"

At the other extreme, some have told me that they had no particular feelings at all toward their bodies. One woman, for example, had a heart attack and felt certain she was dying. She felt herself being pulled through darkness out of her body and moving rapidly away. She says:

> I didn't look back at my body at all. Oh, I knew it was there, all right, and I could've seen it had I looked. But I didn't want to look, not in the least, because I knew that I had done my best in my life, and I was turning my attention now to this other realm of things. I felt that to look back at my body would be to look back at the past, and I was determined not to do that.

Similarly, a girl whose out-of-body experience took place after a wreck in which she sustained severe injuries says:

> I could see my own body all tangled up in the car amongst all the people who had gathered around, but, you know, I had no feelings for it whatsoever. It was like it was a completely different human, or maybe even just an object . . . I knew it was my body but I had no feelings for it.

Despite the eeriness of the disembodied state, the situation has been thrust upon the dying person so suddenly that it may take some time before the significance of what he is experiencing dawns upon him. He may be out of his body for some time, desperately trying to sort out all the things that are happening to him and that are racing through his mind, before he realizes that he is dying, or even dead.

When this realization comes, it may arrive with powerful emotional force, and provoke startling thoughts. One woman remembers thinking, "Oh, I'm dead! How lovely!"

A man states that the thought came to him, "This must be what they call 'death'." Even when this realization comes, it may be accompanied by bafflement and even a certain refusal to accept one's state. One man, for example, remembers reflecting upon the Biblical promise of "three score and ten" years, and protesting that he had had "just barely one score." A young woman gave a very impressive account of such feelings when she told me that,

> I thought I was dead, and I wasn't sorry that I was dead, but I just couldn't figure out where I was supposed to go. My thought and my consciousness were just

like they are in life, but I just couldn't figure all this out. I kept thinking, "Where am I going to go? What am I going to do?" and "My God, I'm dead! I can't believe it!" Because you never really believe, I don't think, fully that you're going to die. It's always something that's going to happen to the other person, and although you know it you really never believe it deep down . . . And so I decided I was just going to wait until all the excitement died down and they carried my body away, and try to see if I could figure out where to go from there.

In one or two cases I have studied, dying persons who souls, minds, consciousnesses (or whatever you want to label them) were released from their bodies say that they didn't feel that, after release, they were in any kind of "body" at all. They felt as though they were "pure" consciousness. One man relates that during his experience he felt as though he were "able to see everything around me—including my whole body as it lay on the bed—without occupying any space," that is, as if he were a point of consciousness. A few others say that they can't really remember whether or not they were in any kind of "body" after getting out of their physical one, because they were so taken up with the events around them.

Far and away the majority of my subjects, however, report that they did find themselves in another body upon release from the physical one. Immediately, though, we are into an area with which it is extremely difficult to deal. This "new body" is one of the two or three aspects of death experiences in which the inadequacy of human language presents the greatest obstacles. Almost everyone who has told me of this "body" has at some point become frustrated and said, "I can't describe it," or made some remark to the same effect . . .

Corroboration

The question naturally arises whether any evidence of the reality of near-death experiences might be acquired independently of the descriptions of the experiences themselves. Many persons report being out of their bodies for extended periods and witnessing many events in the physical world during the interlude. Can any of these reports be checked out with other witnesses who were known to be present, or with later confirming events, and thus be corroborated?

In quite a few instances, the somewhat surprising answer to this question is, "yes." Furthermore, the description of events witnessed while out of the body tend to check out fairly well. Several doctors have told me, for example, that they are utterly baffled about how patients with no medical knowledge could describe in such detail and so correctly the procedure used in resuscitation attempts, even though these events took place while the doctors knew the patients involved to be "dead."

In several cases, persons have related to me how they amazed their doctors or others with reports of events they had witnessed while out of the body. While she was dying, for example, one girl went out of her body and into another room in the hospital where she found her older sister crying and saying, "Oh, Kathy, please don't die, please don't die." The older sister was quite baffled when, later, Kathy told her exactly where she had been and what she had been saying, during this time. In the two passages which follow, similar events are described:

> 1. After it was all over, the doctor told me that I had a really bad time, and I said, "Yeah, I know." He said, "Well, how do you know?" and I said, "I can tell you everything that happened." He didn't believe me, so I told him the whole story, from the time I stopped breathing until the time I was kind of coming around. He was really shocked to know that I knew everything that had happened. He didn't know quite what to say, but he came in several times to ask me different things about it.
>
> 2. When I woke up after the accident, my father was there, and I didn't even want to know what sort of shape I was in, or how I was, or how the doctors thought I would be. All I wanted to talk about was the experience I had been through. I told my father who had dragged my body out of the building, and even what color clothes that person had on, and how they got me out, and even about all the conversation that had been going on in the area. And my father said, "Well, yes, these things were true." Yet, my body was physically out this whole time, and there was no way I could have seen or heard these things without being outside of my body.

Finally, in a few cases, I have been able to get the independent testimony of others about corroborating events. In assessing the evidential value of such independent reports, however, several complicating factors arise. First, in most of the cases the corroborating event itself is attested to only by the dying person himself and by, at most, a couple of close friends and acquaintances. Second, even in the exceptionally dramatic, well-attested instances I have collected, I have promised not to reveal actual names. Even if I could, though, I do not think that such corroborating stories collected after the fact would constitute *proof*, for reasons which I shall explain in the final chapter . . .

FURTHER READINGS

Bibliographies

Kutscher, Martin L., *et al.*, eds. *A Comprehensive Bibliography of the Thanatology Literature*. New York: MSS Information, 1975.

Sollitto, Sharmon, and Veatch, Robert M., comps. *Bibliography of Society, Ethics and the Life Sciences*. Hastings-on-Hudson, N.Y.: Institute of Society, Ethics and the Life Sciences.

Walters, LeRoy, ed. *Bibliography of Bioethics*. Vols. 1-. Detroit: Gale Research Co., issued annually.

For lists of further sources see:

Clouser, Danner K., with Zucker, Arthur. *Abortion and Euthanasia: An Annotated Bibliography*. Philadelphia: Society for Health and Human Values, 1974.

Euthanasia Educational Fund. "Euthanasia—An Annotated Bibliography." Euthanasia Educational Fund, 250 W. 57th Street, New York, N.Y. 10019, May, 1970.

Kalish, Richard A. "Death and Dying: A Briefly Annotated Bibliography." In *The Dying Patient*, edited by Orville G. Brim, Jr. *et al*. New York: The Russell Sage Foundation, 1970, pp. 323-380.

Books

Alvarez, A. *The Savage God: A Study of Suicide*. New York: Random House, 1972.

Beauchamp, Tom L, and Perlin, Seymour *Ethical Issues in Death and Dying*. Englewood Cliffs, N.J.: Prentice-Hall, 1978.

Becker, Ernest. *The Denial of Death*. New York: Free Press, 1973.

Bender, David L., ed. *Problems of Death: Opposing Viewpoints*. Anoka, Minn: Greenhaven Press, 1974.

Behnke, John A., and Bok, Sissela, eds. *The Dilemmas of Euthanasia*. New York: Anchor Books, 1975.

Brim, O. G. *The Dying Patient*. New York: Russell Sage Foundation, 1970.

California Medical Association. Committee on Evolving Trends in Society Affecting Life. *Death and Dying: Determining and Defining Death—A Compilation of Definitions, Selected Readings and Bibliography*. San Francisco: Sutter, 1975.

Cartwright, Ann, *et al. Life before Death*. London: Routledge and Kegan Paul, 1973.

Choron, Jacques. *Death and Western Thought*. New York: Collier Books, 1973.
——. *Suicide*. New York: Scribners, 1972.

Conference on Euthanasia. London: Royal Society of Health, 1973.

Crane, Diana. *The Social Aspects of Prolongation of Life, Social Sciences Frontiers*. New York: The Russell Sage Foundation, 1969.

Cutler, Donald, ed. *Updating Life and Death*. Boston: Beacon Press, 1969.

Dempsey, David. *The Way We Die: An Investigation of Death and Dying in America Today*. New York: Macmillan, 1975.

Douglas, J. D. *The Social Meaning of Suicide*. Princeton: Princeton University Press, 1967.

Downing, A. B. *Euthanasia and the Right to Die*. New York: Humanities Press, 1970.

Durkheim, E. *Suicide*. Glencoe: Free Press, 1951.

Farberow, N. L., and Shneidman, E. S., eds. *The Cry for Help*. New York: McGraw-Hill, 1961.

Feifel, Herman. *The Meaning of Death*. New York: McGraw-Hill, 1965.

Fletcher, Joseph. *Morals and Medicine*. Boston: Beacon Press, 1954.

Fuchs, Victor. *Who Shall Live?* New York: Basic Books, 1974.

Gatch, Milton McC. *Death: Meaning and Mortality in Christian Thought and Contemporary Culture*. New York: Seabury Press, 1969.

Glaser, B. G., and Strauss, A. C. *Awareness of Dying*. Chicago: Aldine, 1975.
——. *Time for Dying*. Chicago: Aldine, 1975.

Goldberg, Ivan K., *et al.*, eds. *Psychopharmacologic Agents for the Terminally Ill and Bereaved*. New York: Columbia University Press, 1973.

Gorer, Geoffrey. *Death, Grief and Mourning*. New York: Doubleday, 1965.

Gould, Jonathan, and Craigmyle, Lord, eds. *Your Death Warrant? The Implications of Euthanasia*. New York: Arlington House, 1973.

Greicher, Norbert, and Muller, Alois, eds. *The Experience of Dying*. New York: Herder & Herder, 1974.

Heifetz, Milton D., and Mangel, Charles *The Right to Die: A Neurosurgeon Speaks of Death with Candor*. New York: G. P. Putnam's Sons, 1975.

Hendin, David. *Death as a Fact of Life*. New York: Norton, 1973.

Katz, Jay, and Capron, Alexander M. *Catastrophic Diseases: Who Decides What? A Psychological and Legal Analysis*. New York: Russell Sage Foundation, 1975.

Kluge, Eike-Henner W. *The Practice of Death*. New Haven: Yale University Press, 1975.

Kohl, Marvin, ed. *Beneficient Euthanasia*. Buffalo: Prometheus Books, 1975.

——. *The Morality of Killing: Sanctity of Life, Abortion and Euthanasia*. New York: Humanities Press, 1974.

Krant, Melvin J. *Dying and Dignity: The Meaning and Control of a Personal Death*. Springfield, Ill.: Charles C Thomas, 1974.

Kübler-Ross, Elisabeth. *On Death and Dying*. New York: Macmillan, 1969.

——. *Questions and Answers on Death and Dying*. New York: Macmillan, 1974.

Kutscher, Austin H., and Goldberg, Michael R. *Caring for the Dying Patient and His Family: A Model for Medical Education—Medical Center Conferences*. New York: Health Sciences Publishing Corp., 1973.

Lamerton, Richard. *Care of the Dying*. London: Priory Press, 1973.

Mack, Arien, ed. *Death in the American Experience*. New York: Schocken, 1973.

Maguire, Daniel C. *Death by Choice*. New York: Doubleday, 1974.

Neale, Robert E. *The Art of Dying*. New York: Harper & Row, 1973.

Pearson, Leonard, ed. *Death and Dying: Current Issues in the Treatment of the Dying Person*. Cleveland: Case Western Reserve University Press, 1969.

Perkins, Thomas C. *Medical Termination of the Irreversibly Comatose: A Moral Analysis from a Christian Perspective*. Ann Arbor: University Microfilms, 1975.

Ramsey, Paul. *The Patient as Person*. New Haven: Yale University Press, 1970.

Rescher, Nicholas. *Distributive Justice*. Indianapolis: Bobbs-Merrill, 1966.

Resnick, H. L. P., ed. *Suicidal Behaviors*. Boston: Little, Brown, 1968.

Russell, O. Ruth. *Freedom to Die: Moral and Legal Aspects of Euthanasia*. New York: Human Sciences Press, 1975.

Shibles, Warren. *Death: An Interdisciplinary Analysis*. Whitewater, Wis.: Language Press, 1974.

Shneidman, Edwin S. *Deaths of Man*. New York: Quadrangle Books, 1973.

——. ed. *Essays in Self-Destruction*. New York: Science House, 1967.

——. ed. *On the Nature of Suicide*. San Francisco: Jossey-Bass, 1969.

Shneidman, Edwin S., and Farberow, Norman L. *Clues to Suicide*. New York: McGraw-Hill, 1959.

Shneidman, Edwin S., Farberow, Norman L., and Litman, Robert E. *The Psychology of Suicide*. New York: Science House, 1970.

Sophocles. *Antigone*, translated by Michael Townsend. New York: Harper & Row, 1962.

Steinfels, Peter, and Veatch, Robert M., eds. *Death Inside Out: The Hastings Center Report*. New York: Harper & Row, 1975.

Sudnow, David. *Passing On: The Social Organization of Dying*. Englewood Cliffs, N.J.: Prentice-Hall, 1960.

Tolstoy, Leo. *Death of Ivan Illyich*. New York: Signet Books, New American Library, 1960.

Toynbee, Arnold, *et al*. *Man's Concern with Death*. New York: McGraw-Hill, 1968.

Trowell, Hugh. *The Unfinished Debate on Euthanasia.* London: SCM Press, 1973.

Trubo, Richard. *An Act of Mercy: Euthanasia Today.* Los Angeles: Nash, 1973.

Vaux, K., ed. *Who Shall Live?* Philadelphia: Westminster Press, 1970.

Veatch, Robert M. *Death, Dying and the Biological Revolution.* New Haven: Yale University Press, 1976.

Williams, Robert H., ed. *To Live and to Die: When, Why and How.* New York: Springer-Verlag, 1973.

Wilson, Jerry B. *Death by Decision: The Medical, Moral and Legal Dilemmas of Euthanasia.* Philadelphia: Westminster Press, 1975.

Winter, Arthur, ed. *The Moment of Death: A Symposium.* Springfield, Ill.: Charles C Thomas, 1965.

Worcester, Alfred. *The Care of the Aging, The Dying and the Dead,* second ed. Springfield, Ill.: Charles C Thomas, 1961.

Articles

Abramson, Ronald. "A Dying Patient: The Question of Euthanasia." *International Journal of Psychiatry in Medicine* 6 (1975): 431-454.

Agate, John. "Care of the Dying in Geriatric Departments." *Lancet* (February 17, 1973): 364-366.

Alderete, J. F., *et al.* "Irreversible Coma: A Clinical, Electroencephalographic, and Neuropathological Study." *Transactions of the American Neurologic Association* 93 (1968): 16-20.

Annas, George. "Law and Life Sciences: *In Re* Quinlan: The Legal Comfort for Doctors." *Hastings Center Report* 6 (June 1976): 29-31.

——. "Judges at the Bedside: The Case of Joseph Saikewicz." *Medicolegal News* 6 (Spring 1978): 10-13.

——. "The Incompetent's Right to Die: The Case of Joseph Saikewicz." *Hastings Center Report* 8 (February 1978): 21-23.

Arnet, William F. "The Criteria for Determining Death in Vital Organs Transplants—A Medical-Legal Dilemma." *Missouri Law Review* 38 (Spring 1973): 220-234.

Arnold, J. D., *et al.* "Public Attitudes and the Diagnosis of Death." *Journal of the American Medical Association* 206 (November 25, 1968): 1949-1954.

Avery, Gordon B. "The Right to Life: Can We Decide?" *Clinical Proceedings, Children's Hospital Medical Center* 29 (December, 1973): 265-286.

Ayd, F. J., Jr. "The Hopeless Case: Medical and Moral Considerations." *Journal of the American Medical Association* 181 (1962): 1099-1102.

Bard, B., and Fletcher, J. "The Right to Die." *Atlantic* (April 1968): 59-64.

Barkin, Elizabeth, and Macdonald, Sally B. "The Option of Death! Euthanasia:

An Issue for the Seventies." *University of San Fernando Valley Law Review* 4 (Fall 1975): 301-316.

Barrington, Mary R. "The Voluntary Euthanasia Bill 1963: An Appraisal." In *Conference on Euthanasia*. London: Royal Society of Health, 1973, pp. 11-14.

Barton, David. "Death and Dying: A Psychiatrist's Perspective." *Soundings* 55 (Winter, 1972): 459-471.

Baughman, William H. "Euthanasia: Criminal Tort, Constitutional and Legislative Questions." *Notre Dame Lawyer* 48 (1973): 1202-1260.

Beauchamp, Joyce M. "Euthanasia and the Nurse Practitioner." *Nursing Forum* 14 (1975): 56-73.

Becker, D. P., *et al*. "An Evaluation of the Definition of Cerebral Death." *Neurology* 20 (1970): 459-462.

Becker, Lawrence C. "Human Being: The Boundaries of the Concept." *Philosophy and Public Affairs* 4 (Summer 1975): 334-359.

Becker, Douglas W., Fleming, Robert W., and Overstreet, Rebecca M. "The Legal Aspects of the Right to Die: Before and after the Quinlan Decision." *Kentucky Law Journal* 65 (1977): 823-879.

Beecher, Henry K. "After the 'Definition of Irreversible Coma.'" *New England Journal of Medicine* 281 (November 6, 1969): 1070-1071.

——. "Definitions of Life and Death for Medical Science and Practice." *Annals of the New York Academy of Sciences* 169 (January 21, 1970): 471-474.

——. "Ethical Problems Created by the Hopelessly Unconscious Patient." *New England Journal of Medicine* 278 (1968): 1425-1430.

——. "Procedures for the Appropriate Management of Patients Who May Have Supportive Measures Withdrawn." *Journal of the American Medical Association* 209 (1969): 405.

——. "Definitions of 'Life' and 'Death' for Medical Sciences and Practices." *Annals of the New York Academy of Sciences* 169 (1970): 471-474.

Benjamin, Martin, "Death, Where is Thy Cause?" *Hastings Center Report* 6 (June 1976): 15-16.

Black, Peter. "Three Definitions of Death." *Monist* 60 (January, 1977): 136-146.

——. "Criteria of Brain Death: Review and Comparison." *Postgraduate Medicine* 57 (February 1975): 69-74.

Bleich, J. David. "Establishing Criteria of Death." *Tradition: A Journal of Orthodox Thought* 13 (Winter 1973): 90-113.

Bok, Sissela. "Personal Directions for Care at the End of Life." *New England Journal of Medicine* 295 (12 August, 1976): 367-369.

Bok, Sissela, *et al*. "The Dilemmas of Euthanasia." *BioScience* 23 (August 1973): 461-478.

Biorck, G. "On the Definitions of Death." *World Medical Journal* 14 (September/ October 1967): 137-139.

Boshes, Benjamin. "A Definition of Cerebral Death." In *Annual Review of Medicine Selected Topics in the Clinical Sciences*, edited by William P. Creger. Palo Alto, Cal.: Annual Review, 1975, pp. 465-470.

Boyd, Kenneth. "Attitudes to Death: Some Historical Notes." *Journal of Medical Ethics* 3 (September 1977): 124-218.

Braustein, P., *et al.* "A Simple Bedside Evaluation for Cerebral Blood Flow in the Study of Cerebral Death: A Prospective Study on 34 Deeply Comatose Patients." *Journal of Roentgenology, Radium Therapy and Nuclear Medicine* 118 (August 1973): 757-767.

Brierley, J. B., *et al.* "Neocortical Death after Cardiac Arrest." *Lancet* (September 11, 1971): 560-565.

Brill, Howard W. "Death with Dignity: A Recommendation for Statutory Change." *University of Florida Law Review* 12 (Winter 1970): 368-383.

Brown, Norman, *et al.* "The Preservation of Life." *Journal of the American Medical Association* 221 (January 5, 1970): 76-82.

Brown, Stuart M., Jr. "'Natural Death'; Clarifying the Definition." *Hastings Center Report* 7 (December 1977): 39.

Boyle, Joseph M., Jr. "On Killing and Letting Die." *New Scholasticism* 51 (Fall 1977): 433-452.

Brauson, Roy, Casebeer, Kenneth, Levine, Melvin D., Oden, Thomas C., Ramsey, Paul, and Capron, Alexander Morgan. "The Quinlan Decision: Five Commentaries." *Hastings Center Report* 6 (February 1976): 8-19.

Cable, Karen Ruth. "The Tell-Tale Heart." *Baylor Law Review* 27 (Winter 1975): 157-168.

Calabresi, Guido. "Birth, Death and the Law." *Pharos* 37 (April 1974): 39-41.

California Medical Association. "Euthanasia—An Overview for Our Time." *California Medicine* 118 (March 1973): 55-58.

Callahan, Daniel. "Health and Society: Some Ethical Imperatives." *Daedalus* (Winter 1977): 23-33.

———. "Doing Well by Doing Good: Garrett Hardin's 'Lifeboat Ethic.'" *Hastings Center Report* 4 (December 1974): 1-4.

———. "On Defining a 'Natural Death.'" *Hastings Center Report* 7 (June 1977): 32-37.

Cantor, Norman L. "A Patient's Decision to Decline Life-Saving Medical Treatment: Bodily Integrity versus the Preservation of Life." *Rutgers Law Review* 26 (Winter 1972): 228-264.

Capron, Alexander Morgan. "Shifting the Burden of Decision Making." *Hastings Center Report* 6 (February 1976): 17-19.

———. "The Purpose of Death: A Reply to Professor Dworkin." *Indiana Law Journal* 48 (Summer 1973): 640-646.

——. "Determing Death: Do We Need a Statute?" *Hastings Center Report* 3 (February 1973): 6-7.

Capron, Alexander Morgan, and Kass, Leon R. "A Statutory Definition of the Standard for Determining Human Death: An Appraisal and a Proposal." *University of Pennsylvania Law Review* 121 (November 1972): 87-118.

Cassell, Eric J. "Death and the Physician." *Commentary* (June 1969): 73-79.

——. "Permission to Die." *BioScience* 23 (August 1973): 475-478.

——. "Dying in a Technological Society." *Hastings Center Studies* 2 (May 1974): 31-36.

——. "Learning to Die." *Bulletin of the New York Academy of Medicine* 49 (December 1973): 1110-1118.

Cassem, Ned H. "Confronting the Decision to Let Death Come." *Critical Care Medicine* 2 (May-June 1974): 113-117.

——. "Controversies Surrounding the Hopelessly Ill Patient." *Linacre Quarterly* 42 (May 1975): 89-98.

Cassem, Ned H., and Stewart, Rege S. "Management and Care of the Dying Patient." *International Journal of Psychiatry in Medicine* 6 (1975): 293-304.

Cheng, Charles L. Y. "Natural Death: Clarifying the Definition." *Hastings Center Report* 7 (December 1977): 40.

Childress, James F. "Who Shall Live When Not All Can Live?" *Soundings* 53 (Winter 1970): 339-362.

Clouser, K. Danner. "The Sanctity of Life: An Analysis of a Concept." *Annals of Internal Medicine* 78 (January 1973): 119-125.

Coene, Roger E. "Dialysis or Transplant: One Patient's Choice." *Hastings Center Report* 7 (December 1977): 5-7.

Cole, Sheila S., and Shea, Marta S. "Voluntary Euthanasia: A Proposed Remedy." *Albany Law Review* 39 (1975): 826-856.

Collins, V. U. "Limits of Medical Responsibility in Prolonging Life: Guides to Decisions." *Journal of the American Medical Association* 206 (1968): 389-392.

Collins, Vincent J. "Considerations in Prolonging Life—A Dying and Recovery Score." *Illinois Medical Journal* 147 (June 1975): 543-547.

——. "Considerations in Prolonging Life—A Dying and Recovery Score: Part II." *Illinois Medical Journal* 148 (July 1975): 42-46.

——. "The Right to Die: Limits of Medical Responsibility in Prolonging Life." *Journal of American Nurse Anethetists* 41 (February 1973): 27-36.

Condrau, G. "The Dying Patient—A Challenge for the Doctor." *Hexagon (Roche)* 3: 15-24.

Converse, Ronald. "But *When* Did He Die? *Tucker* v. *Lower* and the Brain-Death Concept." *San Diego Law Review* 12 (March 1975): 424-435.

Conway, Daniel J. "Medical and Legal Views of Death: Confrontation and Reconciliation." *St. Louis University Law Journal* 19 (Winter 1-74): 172–188.

Cooper, Robert M. "Euthanasia and the Notion of 'Death with Dignity.'" *Christian Century* 90 (21 February, 1973): 225–227.

Curran, W. J. "Legal and Medical Death: Kansas Takes the First Step." *New England Journal of Medicine* 284 (1971): 260–261.

Curran, William J. "Law-Medicine Notes: The Saikewicz Decision." *New England Journal of Medicine* 298 (2 March, 1978): 499–500.

Dagi, Teodoro F. "The Paradox of Euthanasia." *Judaism* 24 (Spring 1975): 157–167.

Delgado, Richard. "Euthanasia Reconsidered—The Choice of Death as an Aspect of the Right of Privacy." *Arizona Law Review* 17 (1975): 474–494.

Delmonico, Francis L., and Randolph, Judson G. "Death: A Concept in Transition." *Pediatrics* 51 (February 1973): 234–239.

Duff, Raymond S., and Campbell, A. G. M. "Moral and Ethical Dilemmas in the Special-Care Nursery." *New England Journal of Medicine* 289 (October 25, 1973): 890–894.

Dyck, Arthur J. "Beneficient Euthanasia and Benemortasia: Alternative Views of Mercy." In *Beneficient Euthanasia*, edited by Marvin Kohl. Buffalo: Prometheus Books, 1975, pp. 117–129.

——. "The Good Samaritan Ideal and Beneficent Euthanasia: Conflicting Views of Mercy." *Linacre Quarterly* 42 (August 1975): 176–188.

——. "An Alternative to the Ethics of Euthanasia." In *To Live and To Die: When, Why and How*, edited by Robert H. Williams. New York: Springer-Verlag, 1973, pp. 113–122.

Elliott, Neil. "Prolonging Life or Prolonging Dying?" In his *The Gods of Life*. New York: Macmillan, 1974, pp. 83–146.

Engelhardt, H. Tristram. "The Patient as Person: An Empty Phrase?" *Texas Medicine* 71 (September 1975): 57–63.

——. "Defining Death: A Philosophical Problem for Medicine and Law." *American Review of Respiratory Disease* 112 (November 1975): 587–590.

Epp, Ronald H. "Philosophical Speculation and Biomedical Innovation." *Southern Journal of Philosophy* 11 (Spring-Summer 1973): 91–97.

Epstein, Franklin H. "No, It's Our Duty to Keep Patients Alive." *Medical Economics* 50 (2 April, 1973): 97–98.

Etzioni, Amitai. "Life, Dying, Death, Ethics and Open Decisions." *Science News* 106 (17 August, 1976): 109.

"Extension of Life: Panel Discussion." In *Ethical Issues in Biology and Medicine*, edited by Preston N. Williams. Cambridge, Mass.: Schenkman, 1973, pp. 128–143.

Fager, W. A. P. "Do We Need a Legal Definition of Death?" *New Zealand Law Journal* (6 May, 1975): 171–174.

Farley, Marilyn. "Determining Death." *Respiratory Therapy* 5 (July–August 1975): 31–37.

Feifel, Herman, *et al.* "Physicians Consider Death." *Proceedings American Psychological Association Convention* (1967): 201–202.

Feinberg, Joel. "Voluntary Euthanasia and the Inalienable Right to Life." *Philosophy and Public Affairs* 7 (Winter 1978): 93–123.

Ferber, Stanley. "When to Withhold Life-Prolonging Treatment." *Medical Economics* 50 (6 August, 1973): 29.

Fishbein, Morris. "When Life Is No Longer Life." *Medical World News* 15 (15 March, 1974): 84.

Fletcher, George. "Legal Aspects of the Decision Not to Prolong Life." *Journal of the American Medical Association* 203 (January 1, 1968): 65–68.

———. "Prolonging Life." *Washington Law Review* 42 (1967): 999–1016.

Fletcher, John. "Attitudes towards Defective Newborns." *Hastings Center Studies* 2 (January 1974): 21–32.

Fletcher, John C. "Abortion, Euthanasia, and the Care of Defective Newborns." *New England Journal of Medicine* 292 (9 January, 1975): 75–78.

Fletcher, Joseph. "Ethics and Euthanasia." In *To Live and to Die: When, Why and How*, edited by Robert H. Williams. New York: Springer-Verlag, 1973, pp. 113–122.

———. "The 'Right' to Live and the 'Right' to Die: A Protestant View of Euthanasia." *Humanist* 34 (July–August 1974): 12–15.

Freeman, John, and Cooke, Robert E. "Is There a Right to Die—Quickly?" *Journal of Pediatrics* 80 (Spring 1972): 904–908.

Fried, Charles. "Equality and Rights in Medical Care." *Hastings Center Report* 6 (February 1976): 29–34.

Foot, Philippa. "Euthanasia." *Philosophy and Public Affairs* 6 (Winter 1977): 68–112.

Foreman, Percy. "The Physician's Criminal Liability for the Practice of Euthanasia." *Baylor Law Review* 27 (Winter 1975): 54–61.

Forkosch, Morris D. "Privacy, Human Dignity, Euthanasia—Are These Independent Constitutional Rights?" *University of San Fernando Valley Law Review* 3 (1974): 1–25.

Fox, Renée. "A Sociological Commentary on the Interest in Death and Dying in Modern Society." In *Protection of Human Rights in the Light of Scientific and Technological Progress in Biology and Medicine*, edited by Simon Btesh. Geneva: World Health Organization, 1974, pp. 125–142.

Freireich, Emil J. "The Best Medical Care for the 'Hopeless' Patient." *Medical Opinion* (February 1972): 51–55.

Friloux, C. Anthony. "Death, When Does It Occur?" *Baylor Law Review* 27 (Winter 1975): 10–21.

Garland, Michael. "Politics, Legislation and Natural Death." *Hastings Center Report* 6 (October 1976): 5–6.

Gerber, Alex. "Let's *Forget* about Equality of Care." *PRISM* 3:9 (October 1975): 20 ff.

Glaser, Robert J. "A Time to Live and a Time to Die: The Implications of Negative Euthanasia." In *The Dilemmas of Euthanasia*, edited by John A. Behnke and Sissela Bok. New York: Anchor Books, 1975, pp. 133-150.

Ginzberg, Eli. "Health Services, Power Centers, and Decision-Making Mechanisms." *Daedelus* (Winter 1977): 203-213.

Goldreich, Gloria. "What Is Death? The Answers in Children's Books." *Hastings Center Report* 7 (June 1977): 18-20.

Goodwin, Robert. "How to Determine Who Should Get What?" *Ethics* 85 (July 1975): 310-321.

Gruman, Gerald J. "An Historical Introduction to Ideas about Voluntary Euthanasia: With a Bibliographic Survey and Guides for Interdisciplinary Studies." *Omega* 4 (Summer 1973): 87-138.

Guentert, Kenneth and Warren T. Reich. "Should We Let That Child Die?" *U. S. Catholic* 40 (October 1975): 6-13.

Gurney, Edward J. "Is There a Right to Die? A Study of the Law of Euthanasia." *Cumberland Sanford Law Review* 3 (Summer 1972): 235-261.

Gustafson, James M. "Mongolism, Parental Desires, and the Right to Life." *Perspectives in Biology and Medicine* 16 (Summer 1973): 529-557.

Habgood, J. S. "Euthanasia—A Christian View." In *Conference on Euthanasia*. London: Royal Society of Health, 1973, pp. 23-25.

Halley, M. M., and Harvey, W. F. "Medical vs. Legal Definitions of Death." *Journal of the American Medical Association* 204 (March 6, 1968): 423-425.

——. "Law-Medicine Comment: The Definitional Dilemma of Death." *Journal of the Bar Association of the State of Kansas* 37 (Fall 1968): 179.

—— et al. "Definition of Death." *New England Journal of Medicine* 279 (1968): 834.

Hammer, Marian B. "Turn Off the Machines! A Plea for Death with Dignity." *Marriage* 59 (January 1973): 28-35.

Hancock, Sheila, et al. "Care of the Dying." *British Medical Journal* (January 6, 1973): 29-41.

Hardin, Garrett. "Living on a Lifeboat." *BioScience* 24 (October 1974): 561-568.

Hare, R. M. "Euthanasia—A Christian View." *Philosophic Exchange* 2 (Summer 1975): 43-52.

Harp, James R. "Criteria for the Determination of Death." *Anestesiology* 40 (April 1974): 391-397.

Harrison, Colin P. "Euthanasia, Medicine and the Law." *Canadian Medical Association Journal* 113 (8 November, 1975): 833-834.

Hauerwas, Stanley. "The Ethics of Death: Letting Die or Putting to Death?" In his *Vision and Virtue: Essays in Christian Ethical Reflection.* Notre Dame, Indiana: Fides, 1974, pp. 166-186.

Hausman, David B. "On Abandoning Life Support: An Alternative Proposal." *Man and Medicine: The Journal of Values and Ethics in Health Care* 2 (1976-1977): 169-177.

Harvard Medical School, Ad Hoc Committee of the Harvard Medical School to Examine the Definition of Brain Death. "A Definition of Irreversible Coma." *Journal of the American Medical Association* 205 (1968): 337-340.

Hertzberg, Leonard J. "Cancer and the Dying Patient." *American Journal of Psychiatry* 128 (January 1972): 806-810.

High, Dallas M. "Death: Its Conceptual Elusiveness." *Soundings* 55 (Winter 1972): 438-458.

Hirsh, Harold L. "Brain Death: Medico-Legal Fact or Fiction?" *Northern Kentucky State Law Forum* 3 (1975): 16-41.

———. "Death: A Medical Status or Legal Definition." *Case and Comment* 79 (September-October 1974): 27-30.

———. "Death as a Legal Entity." *Journal of Forensic Sciences* 20 (January 1975): 159-168.

———. "Brain Death." *Medical Trial Technique Quarterly* 21 (Spring 1975): 377-405.

Humphrey, David C. "Dissection and Discrimination: The Social Origins of Cadavers in America: 1760-1915." *Bulletin of the New York Academy of Medicine* 49 (September 1973): 819-827.

Illich, Ivan. "The Political Uses of Natural Death." *Hastings Center Studies* 2 (January 1974): 3-20.

Ingelfinger, Franz J. "Bedside Ethics for the Hopeless Case." *New England Journal of Medicine* 289 (October 1973): 914-915.

Institute of Society, Ethics and the Life Sciences, Task Force on Death and Dying. "Refinements on Criteria for the Determination of Death." *Journal of the American Medical Association* 221 (July 3, 1972): 48-53.

Isaacs, Leonard. "Death, Where Is Thy Distinguishing?" *Hastings Center Report* 8 (February, 1978): 5-9.

Jonas, Hans. "Against the Stream." In his *Philosophical Essays.* Englewood Cliffs, N.J.: Prentice-Hall, 1974.

Jonsen, Albert R. "The Totally Implantable Artificial Heart." *Hastings Center Report* 3 (November 1973): 1-4.

Jordan, Thomas D. "Euthanasia." *Medico-Legal Bulletin* 22 (August 1973): 1-6.

Kahana, B., and Kahana, E. "Attitudes of Young Men and Women toward Awareness of Death." *Omega* 3 (February 1972): 37-44.

Kamisar, Yale. "Euthanasia Legislation: Some Non-Religious Objections." In *Ethical Issues in Death and Dying*, edited by Tom L. Beauchamp and Seymour Perlin. Englewood Cliffs, N.J.: Prentice-Hall, 1978.

Kanoti, George. "Doctors, Death and Dying." *Linacre Quarterly* 42 (November 1975): 262-267.

Kaufer, Christoph. "A Medical View of the Process of Death." In *The Experience of Dying*, edited by Norbert Greinacher and Alois Muller. New York: Herder & Herder, 1974, pp. 33-42.

Kelly, Gerald. "The Duty of Using Artificial Means of Perserving Life." *Theological Studies* 11 (June 1950): 203-220.

———. "The Duty to Preserve Life." *Theological Studies* 12 (December 1951): 550-556.

Kennedy, Ian M. "A Legal Perspective on Determining Death." *Month 8* (February 1975): 46-51.

———. "The Legal Definition of Death." *Medico-Legal Journal* 41 (1973): 36-41.

———. "The Definition of Death." *Journal of Medical Ethics* 3 (March 1977): 3, 5-6.

Kennedy, Ian McColl. "The Kansas Statute on Death—An Appraisal." *New England Journal of Medicine* 285 (1971): 946-950.

Kielanowski, Tadeusz. "Medical and Moral Problems of Death and Dying." *Dialectical Humanism* 4 (Summer 1977): 113-118.

Kimura, J., et al. "The Isoelectric Electroencephalogram: Significance in Establishing Death in Patients Maintained on Mechanical Respirators." *Archives of Internal Medicine* 121 (1968): 511-517.

Koenig, Ronald. "Dying vs. Well-Being." *Omega* 4 (Fall 1973): 181-194.

Kohl, Marvin. "Voluntary Beneficent Euthanasia." In *Beneficent Euthanasia*, edited by Marvin Kohl. Buffalo: Prometheus Books, 1975, pp. 130-141.

———. "Understanding the Case for Beneficent Euthanasia." *Science, Medicine and Man* 1 (December 1973): 111-121.

———. "Beneficent Euthanasia." *Humanist* 34 (July-August 1974): 9-11.

Korein, J., et al. "On the Diagnosis of Cerebral Death: A Prospective Study." *Electronencephalography and Clinical Neurophysiology* 27 (1969): 700.

Korein, Julius. "On Cerebral, Brain and Systemic Death." *Current Concepts of Cerebrovascular Disease: Stroke* 8 (May-June 1973): 9-14.

Kosnik, Anthony R. "Theological Reflections on Criteria for Defining the Moment of Death." *Hospital Progress* 54 (December 1973): 64-69.

Krant, Melvin J. "Does a Person Have a Right to Die?" *Journal: Forum for Contemporary History* (5 October, 1973): 6-8.

Kübler-Ross, Elisabeth. "Life and Death: Lessons from the Dying." In *To Live and to Die: When, Why and How*, edited by Robert H. Williams. New York: Springer-Verlag, 1973, pp. 150-159.

Lamerton, Richard. "Why Not Euthanasia?" *Contemporary Review* 227 (August 1975): 92-95.

———. "The Case against Euthanasia." In *Conference on Euthanasia*. London: . Royal Society of Health, 1973, pp. 19-21.

Lebacqz, Karen. "On Natural Death." *Hastings Center Report* 7 (1977): 14.

Lescoe, Richard J. "Legislative Proposals for Death with Dignity." *Journal of Legal Medicine* 3 (September 1975): 34-35.

Lester, David. "Attitudes toward Death Today and Thirty-Five Years Ago." *Omega* 2 (August 1971): 168.

Levine, Melvin D. "Disconnection: The Clinician's View." *Hastings Center Report* 6 (February 1976): 11-12.

Levine, Carol. "Dialysis or Transplant: Values and Choices, the Dilemmas of Half-Way Technology." *Hastings Center Report* 8 (April 1978): 8-10.

Maguire, Daniel. "The Freedom to Die." *Commonweal* 96 (August 11, 1972): 423-427.

Maguire, Daniel C. "Death, Legal and Illegal." *Atlantic Monthly* 233 (February 1974): 72-85.

———. "A Catholic View of Mercy-Killing." *Humanist* 34 (July-August 1974): 16-18.

———. "Ethical Method and the Problem of Death." *Anglican Theological Review* 56 (July 1974): 258-279.

Maguire, Daniel C. "A 'Fine Distinction' on Killing." *Hastings Center Report* 7 (June 1977): 4.

Mahoney, John. "Ethical Aspects of Donor Consent in Transplantation." *Journal of Medical Ethics* 1 (July 1975): 67-70.

Malone, Robert J. "Is There a Right to a Natural Death?" *New England Law Review* 9 (Winter 1974): 293-310.

Mansson, Helge H. "Justifying the Final Solution." *Omega* 3 (May 1972): 79-87.

Margolis, Joseph, and Margolis, Clorinda. "On Being Allowed to Die." *Humanist* 36 (January-February 1976): 13-19.

Margolis, Joseph. "Death." and "Suicide." In his *Negativities: The Limits of Life*. Columbus, Ohio: Charles E. Merrill, 1975, pp. 9-22, 23-36.

Marsh, Michael. "Beyond Death: The Rebirth of Immortality." *Hastings Center Report* 7 (October 1977): 40-42.

Masland, Richard L. "When is a Person Dead?" *Resident and Staff Physician* 21 (April 1975): 48-52.

May, William. "Attitudes toward the Newly Dead." *Hastings Center Studies* 1 (No. 1, 1973): 3-13.

———. "The Sacral Power of Death in Contemporary Experience." *Social Research* 20 (Autumn 1972): 463-488.

McCormick, Richard A. "To Save or Let Die: The Dilemma of Modern Medicine." *Journal of the American Medical Association* 229 (July 8, 1974): 172–176.

——. "The New Medicine and Morality." Theology Digest 21 (Winter 1973): 308–321.

——. "The Quality of Life, the Sanctity of Life." *Hastings Center Report* 8 (February 1978): 3.

McCormick, Richard A. "A Proposal for 'Quality of Life' Criteria for Sustaining Life." *Hospital Progress* 56 (September 1975): 76–79.

——. "Life-Saving and Life-Taking: A Comment." *Linacre Quarterly* 42 (May 1975): 110–115.

Meyers, David W. "The Legal Aspect of Medical Euthanasia." *BioScience* 23 (August 1973): 467–470.

Michael, Donald N. "Who Decides Who Decides?" *Hastings Center Report* 7 (April 1977): 23.

Middleton, Carl L. "Principles of Life–Death Decision-Making." *Linacre Quarterly* 42 (November 1975): 268–278.

Mills, Don Harper. "The Kansas Death Statute—Bold and Innovative." *The New England Journal of Medicine* 285 (November 21, 1971): 968–969.

Moellering, Ralph L. "Mercy Killing or the Right to Die with Dignity." *Currents in Theology and Mission* 1 (December 1974): 98–101.

Montange, Charles H. "Informed Consent and the Dying Patient." *Yale Law Journal* 83 (July 1974): 1632–1664.

Moore, Marvin M. "The Case for Voluntary Euthanasia." *UMKC Law Review* 2 (Spring 1974): 327–340.

Moraczewski, Albert S. "Euthanasia in the Light of a Contemporary Theology of Death." *Catholic Hospital* 2 (November–December 1974): 211–218.

Morison, Robert. "Death: Process or Event?" Kass, Leon R. "Death as an Event: A Commentary on Robert Morison." *Science* 173 (20 August, 1971), pp. 694–702.

Morison, Robert S. "Dying." *Scientific American* 229 (September 1973): 55–62.

McKegney, F. P., and Lange, P. "The Decision to No Longer Live on Chronic Hemodialysis." *American Journal of Psychiatry* 128 (September 1971): 267–274.

Moore, F. D. "Medical Responsibility for the Prolongation of Life." *Journal of the American Medical Association* 206 (1968): 384–386.

Morgan, Lucy Griscom. "On Drinking the Hemlock." *Hastings Center Report* 1 (December 1971): 4–5.

Neale, Robert E. "Between the Nipple and the Everlasting Arms." *Archives of the Foundation of Thanatology* 3 (Spring 1971): 21–30.

Nell, Onora. "Lifeboat Earth." *Philosophy and Public Affairs* 4 (Spring 1975): 273–292.

Nelson, James B. "Humanizing the Dying Process." In his *Human Medicine: Ethical Perspectives on New Medical Issues.* Minneapolis, Minn.: Augsburg, 1973, pp. 123-147.

Nelson, Lawrence J. "Death, Who Is Thy 'Cause'?" *Hastings Center Report* 6 (October 1976): 6.

New York Academy of Medicine. "Statement on Measures Employed to Prolong Life in Terminal Illness." *New York Academy of Medicine* 49 (April 1973): 349-351.

Nicholson, Richard. "Should the Patient Be Allowed to Die?" *Journal of Medical Ethics* 1 (March 1975): 5-9.

Noyes, Russell, and Travis, Terry A. "The Care of Terminally Ill Patients." *Archives of Internal Medicine* 132 (October 1973): 607-611.

Nuttgens, Bridget. "The Ethics of Living and Dying Today." *New Blackfriars* 56 (February 1975): 78-81.

Olinger, Sheff D. "Medical Death." *Baylor Law Review* 27 (Winter 1975): 22-26.

Opp, Marcia. "Pulling the Plug." *Medical World News* 19 (29 May, 1978): 50-57.

Parsons, Talcott, and Fox, Renée C., and Lisz, Victor M. "The 'Gift of Life' and Its Reciprocation." *Social Research* 39 (1972): 367-415.

Paulson, George W. "Who Shall Live?" *Geriatrics* 28 (March 1973): 132-136.

Peretz, David, *et al.* "Survey of Physicians' Attitudes toward Death and Bereavement: Comparison of Psychiatrists and Non-Psychiatrists." *Journal of Thanatology* 1 (March 1971): 91.

Pius XII. "The Pope Speaks, Prolongation of Life." *Osservatore Romano* 4 (1957): 393-398.

Platt, Michael. "On Asking to Die." *Hastings Center Report* 5 (December 1975): 9-12.

Potter, Ralph B. "The Paradoxical Preservation of a Principle." *Villanova Law Review* 13 (1968): 784-792.

Powledge, Tabitha M. "The Ethics of Kidney Transplants: Physicians in Controversy—Who Shall Mete Our Life?" *Physician's World* (April 1974): 357.

Pretzel, P. W. "Philosophical and Ethical Considerations of Suicide Prevention." *Bulletin of Suicidology* (July 1968): 30-38.

Proceedings of the Royal Society of Medicine, report of a meeting, "Euthanasia," 63 (July 1970): 659-670.

Rabkin, Mitchell T., Gillerman, Gerald, and Rice, Nancy R. "Orders Not to Resuscitate." *New England Journal of Medicine* 295 (12 August, 1976): 364-369.

Rachels, James. "Active and Passive Euthanasia." *New England Journal of Medicine* 292 (9 January, 1975): 78-80.

Ramsey, Paul. "The Indignity of 'Death With Dignity.'" *Hastings Center Studies* 2 (May 1974): 47-62.

Reeves, Robert B. "When Is It Time to Die? Prologomenon to Voluntary Euthanasia." *New England Law Review* 8 (Spring 1973): 183-196.

Reich, Walter. "The Physician's 'Duty' to Preserve Life." *Hastings Center Report* 5 (April 1975): 14-15.

Reich, Warren T., and Smith, Harmon, commentators. "Case Studies in Bioethics: On the Birth of a Severely Handicapped Infant." *Hastings Center Report* (September 1973): 10-12.

Reid, Robert. "Spina Fida: The Fate of the Untreated." *Hastings Center Report* 7 (August 1977): 16-19.

Reiser, Stanley J. "The Dilemma of Euthanasia in Modern Medical History: The English and American Experience." In *The Dilemmas of Euthanasia*, edited by John A. Behnke and Sissela Bok. New York: Anchor Books, 1975, pp. 27-49.

Relman, Arnold. "The Saikewicz Decision: Judges as Physicians." *New England Journal of Medicine* 298 (2 March, 1978): 508-509.

Reynolds, Frank. "The Lizard, the Chamelon and the Future Buddha." *Hastings Center Report* 7 (June 1977): 38.

Rhodes, Philip, Ogg, Chisholm, and Irvine, Donald. "Priorities in Medicine." *British Medical Journal* 2 (16 June, 1973): 648-653.

Rizzo, Robert F., and Yonder, Joseph M. "Definition and Criteria of Clinical Death." *Linacre Quarterly* 40 (November 1973): 223-233.

Robertson, John A., and Fost, Norman "Passive Euthanasia of Defective Newborn Infants: Legal Considerations." *Journal of Pediatrics* 88 (May 1976): 883-889.

Robitscher, Jonas. "The Right to Die." *Hastings Center Report* 2 (September 1972): 11-14.

———. "Living and Dying: A Delicate Balance." *Engage/Social Action* 1 (October 1973): 38-53.

Rockwell, Don A., and O'Brien, William "Physicians' Knowledge and Attitudes about Suicide." *Journal of the American Medical Association* 225 (September 10, 1973): 1347-1349.

Rosoff, S. D., *et al.* "The EEG in Establishing Brain Death: A 10-Year Report with Criteria and Legal Safeguards in the 50 States." *Electroencephalography and Clinical Neurophysiology* 24 (1968): 283-284.

Roth, Richard G. "Legislation: The Need for a Current and Effective Statutory Definition of Death." *Oklahoma Law Review* 27 (Fall 1974): 729-735.

Roupas, T. G. "The Value of Life." *Philosophy and Public Affairs* 7 (Winter 1978): 154-183.

Rudikoff, Sonya. "The Problem of Euthanasia." *Commentary* 57 (February 1974): 62-68.

Sackett, Walter W. "Death with Dignity." *Medical Opinion and Review* 5 (June 1969): 25-31.

———. "Euthanasia: Why No Legislation." *Baylor Law Review* 27 (Winter 1975): 3-5.

———. "Death with Dignity: A Legislative Necessity." *Journal of the Florida Medical Association* 61 (May 1974): 366-367.

Saunders, Cicely. "Living with Dying." *Man and Medicine: The Journal of Values and Ethics in Health Care* 1 (1975-1976): 227-242.

Saunders, Michael G. "Determining the Presence of Death—A Medical, Legal and Ethical Problem." *Manitoba Law Journal* 6 (1975): 327-332.

Sarda, Francois. "A French Lawyer's View of Life and Death." *Hastings Center Report* 6 (April 1976): 8-9.

Schiffer, R. B., and Freedman, Benjamin "The Last Bed in the ICU." *Hastings Center Report* 7 (December 1977): 21-22.

Schwiddle, Jess T. "On Death and Dying." *Rocky Mountain Medical Journal* 70 (November 1973): 23-26.

Scott, Byron T. "Physicians' Attitude Survey: Doctors and Dying—Is Euthanasia Now Becoming Accepted?" *Medical Opinion* 3 (May 1974): 31-34.

Shapiro, Michael H. "Who Merits Merit? Problems in Distributive Justice and Utility Posed by the New Biology." *Southern California Law Review* 48 (November 1974): 318-370.

Shaw, Anthony. "Dilemmas of 'Informed Consent' in Children." *New England Journal of Medicine* 289 (October 25, 1973): 885-890.

———. "Defining the Quality of Life." *Hastings Center Report* 7 (October 1977): 11.

Sharp, Thomas H., and Crofts, Thomas H. "Death with Dignity: The Physicians's Civil Liability." *Baylor Law Review* 27 (Winter 1975): 86-108.

Sherwin, Byron L. "Jewish Views on Euthanasia." *Humanist* 34 (July–August, 1974): 19-21.

Sidel, Victor W. "The Allocation of Expensive Medical Resources: Who Should Decide?" *New Physician* 22 (April 1973): 229.

Silverman, D., *et al.* "Irreversible Coma Associated with Electrocerebral Silence." *Neurology* 20 (1970): 525-533.

Silving, Helen. "Euthanasia: A Study in Comparative Criminal Law." *University of Pennsylvania Law Review* 103 (1954): 350-389.

Skegg, P. D. G. "Case for a Statutory 'Definition of Death.'" *Journal of Medical Ethics* 2 (December 1976): 190-192.

———. "Irreversibly Comatose Individuals: 'Alive' or 'Dead'?" *Cambridge Law Journal* 33 (April 1974): 130-144.

Slaby, Andrew E., and Tancredi, Laurence R. "Suicide and the Right to Die." In their *Collusion for Conformity*. New York: Jason Arsonson, 1975, pp. 154-176.

Slater, Eliot. "Assisted Suicide: Some Ethical Considerations." In *Conference on Euthanasia.* London: Royal Society of Health, 1973, pp. 15-18.

Smith, David H. "On Letting Some Babies Die." *Hastings Center Studies* 2 (May 1974): 37-46.

———. "Fatal Choices: Recent Discussions of Dying." *Hastings Center Report* 7 (April 1977): 7-10.

Smith, G., and Smith, E. D. "Selection for Treatment on Spina Bifida Cystica." *British Medical Journal* (October 27, 1973): 189-204.

Sparer, Edward. "The Legal Right to Health Care: Public Policy and Equal Access." *Hastings Center Report* 6 (October 1976): 39-47.

Stason, William, and Weinstein, Milton C. "Allocating Resources: The Case of Hypertension." *Hastings Center Report* 7 (October 1977): 24-29.

Stewart, Stephen M. "The Problem of Prolonged Death: Who Should Decide?" *Baylor Law Review* 27 (Winter 1975): 169-173.

Strauss, Anselm, and Glaser, Barney, and Quint, Jeanne "The Nonaccountability of Terminal Care." *Hospitals* 38 (January 1964): 73-87.

Suckiel, Ellen Kappy. "Death and Benefit in the Permanently Unconcious Patient: A Justification of Euthanasia." *Journal of Medicine and Philosophy* 3 (March 1978): 38-52.

Sullivan, Michael T. "The Dying Person—His Plight and His Right." *New England Law Review* 8 (Spring 1973): 197-216.

Szasz, Thomas S. "The Ethics of Suicide." *The Antioch Review* 31 (Spring 1971): 7-17.

Thomas, Lewis. "A Meliorist View of Disease and Dying." *Journal of Medicine and Philosophy* 1 (September 1976): 212-221.

———. "Biological Aspects of Death." *Pharos* 37 (July 1974): 83-89.

Thompson, Judith. "Rights and Deaths." *Philosophy and Public Affairs*, Vol. 2, No. 2 (Winter 1973): 146-160.

Trammell, Richard. "Euthanasia and the Law." *Journal of Social Philosophy* (January 1978): 14-18.

Travis, Terry A., Brightwell, Russell and Brightwell, Dennis R. "The Attitudes of Physicians toward Prolonging Life." *International Journal of Psychiatry in Medicine* 5 (Winter 1974): 17-26.

Tupin, Joe P. "Some Psychiatric Issues of Euthanasia." In *Beneficent Euthanasia*, edited by Marvin Kohl. Buffalo: Prometheus Books, 1975, pp. 193-203.

Tuycross, R. G. "A Plea for 'Euthanatos.'" *World Medical Journal* 21 (July-August, 1974): 66-69.

Uniform Anatomical Gift Act: Final Draft, July 30, 1968, prepared by National Conference of Commissioners on Uniform State Laws. In *The Moment of Death: A Symposium*, edited by A. Winter. Springfield, Ill.: Charles C Thomas, 1969.

Van Till-d'Aulnis de Bourouill, Adrienne. "How Dead Can You Be? *Medicine, Science, and the Law* 15 (1975): 133-147.

Veatch, Robert M. "Brain Death: Welcome Definition—or Dangerous Judgment?" *Hastings Center Report* 2 (November 1972): 10-13.

——. "Death and Dying." *U. S. Catholic* (April 1972): 6-13.

——. "Death and Dying: The Legislative Options." *Hastings Center Report* 7 (October 1977): 5-8.

——. "Death and Dying: The Legislative Options." *Hastings Center Report* 8 (April 1978): 18-19.

——. "The Whole-Brain-Oriented Concept of Death: An Outmoded Philosphical Formulation." *Journal of Thanatology* 3 (1975): 13-30.

——. "What Is a 'Just' Health Care Delivery?" In *Ethics and Health Policy*, edited by Robert M. Veatch and Roy Branson. Cambridge, Mass.: Ballinger, 1976, pp. 127-153.

——. "Choosing Not to Prolong Dying." *Medical Dimensions* (December 1972): 9-10.

Veith, Frank J., *et al.* "Brain Death: Part 1, 'A Status Report of Medical and Ethical Considerations,' and Part II, 'A Status Report of Legal Considerations.'" *Journal of the American Medical Association* 238 (October 10 and 17, 1977): 1651-1655, 1744-1748.

Vodiga, Bruce. "Euthanasia and the Right to Die—Moral, Ethical and Legal Perspectives." *Chicago-Kent Law Review* 51 (Summer 1974): 1-40.

Walker, A. Earl. "Cerebral Death." In *The Nervous System.* Volume 2: *The Clinical Neurosciences*, edited by Thomas N. Chase. New York: Raven Press, 1975, pp. 75-87.

Wasmuth, Carl E., Jr. "The Concept of Death." *Ohio Law Journal* 30 (1969): 32-60.

Wassmer, Thomas A. "Between Life and Death: Ethical and Moral Issues Involved in Recent Medical Advances." *Villanova Law Review* 13 (1968): 759-783.

Weber, Leonard J. "Human Death as Neocortical Death: The Ethical Context." *Linacre Quarterly* 41 (May 1974): 106-113.

Weigel, Charles J. "The Dying Patient's Rights—Do They Exist?" *South Texas Law Journal* 16 (1975): 153-172.

White, David. "Death Control." *New Society* 22 (November 30, 1972): 502-505.

White, Laurens P., ed. "Care of Patients with Fatal Illness." *Annals of the New York Academy of Sciences* 164 (December 1969): 635-896.

White, Robert B., and Tristram, Engelhardt H. "A Demand to Die." *Hastings Center Report* 5 (June 1975): 9-10.

Williams, Glanville. "Mercy-Killing Legislation: A Rejoinder." (answering to

Kamser's article). In *Ethical Issues in Death and Dying*, edited by Tom L. Beauchamp and Seymour Perlin. Englewood Cliffs, N.J.: Prentice-Hall, 1978.

———. "Euthanasia." *Medico-Legal Journal* 41 (1973): 14-34.

Williams, Robert H. "Our Role in the Generation, Modification and Termination of Life." *Journal of the American Medical Association* 209 (August 11, 1969): 914-917.

Wilshaw, Charles. "The Right to Die: A Rational Approach to Voluntary Euthanasia." London: *British Humanist Association*, 1974, 22 pages.

"World Famine and Lifeboat Ethics." *Soundings* 59 (Spring 1976): 1-137.

Young, Robert. "Some Criteria for Making Decisions Concerning the Distribution of Scarce Medical Resources." *Theory and Decision* 6 (November, 1975): 439-455.

———. "Voluntary and Non-Voluntary Euthanasia." *Monist* 59 (April 1976): 264-283.

Ziembinski, Zygmunt. "Legal and Moral Problems Associated with Death and Dying." *Dialectical Humanism* 4 (Summer 1977): 119-125.

Zimring, Joseph G. "The Right to Die with Dignity." *New York State Journal of Medicine* 73 (July 1973): 1815-1817.

INDEX